Auteurs and Authorship

To Norty, a special uncle for whom this should have come sooner

Auteurs and Authorship

A Film Reader

Edited by Barry Keith Grant

BLACKWELL PUBLISHING
350 Main Street, Malden, MA 02148-5020, USA
9600 Garsington Road, Oxford OX4 2DQ, UK
550 Swanston Street, Carlton, Victoria 3053, Australia

First published 2008 by Blackwell Publishing Ltd

1 2008

Library of Congress Cataloging-in-Publication Data is available for this book.

ISBN: 978-1-4051-5333-1 (hardback)
ISBN: 978-1-4051-5334-8 (paperback)

A catalogue record for this title is available from the British Library.

Set in 10 on 12 pt Bembo
by SNP Best-set Typesetter Ltd., Hong Kong

The publisher's policy is to use permanent paper from mills that operate a sustainable forestry policy, and which has been manufactured from pulp processed using acid-free and elementary chlorine-free practices. Furthermore, the publisher ensures that the text paper and cover board used have met acceptable environmental accreditation standards.

For further information on
Blackwell Publishing, visit our website at
www.blackwellpublishing.com

Contents

Illustrations

Preface: How to Use This Book

Today critics, while acknowledging the collaborative nature of the filmmaking process, still discuss directors – and occasionally producers, screenwriters, cinematographers, and actors – as auteurs, although such discussions are more grounded in historical, industrial, and ideological contexts than in the past. Despite the common view that its emphasis on individual creative genius is an outdated concept, auteurism and questions of authorship remain central to much published film scholarship as well as popular writing. Books and articles on individual filmmakers and actors continue to be published with undiminished enthusiasm.

Similarly, in academic film studies, auteurism remains a standard approach. First year survey courses often contain a unit on auteur theory and criticism, and more advanced undergraduate (as well as graduate level) courses are taught under a variety of auteurist rubrics. Film studies programs (or other programs featuring some film courses) typically offer such courses as "Authorship in the Cinema," "The Auteur Director," "Film Authors," "Directors," "Major Auteurs," "Great Film Directors," and "The Film Art of . . .".

This reader is designed to offer students in such courses a comprehensive view of auteurism and authorship in the cinema by addressing both the aesthetic and historical debates that these concepts have generated, as well as by providing examples of auteur criticism and analysis in practice. Some of the selections have been chosen for their historical significance, for the influence they have had; others provide accessible overviews or critiques of developments in auteurism; and still others (primarily those in the third section) present a series of case studies of individual directors that discuss them from a range of critical and theoretical perspectives. A short preface for each reading contextualizes it within the evolving debate about authorship in the cinema. A select bibliography at the end of each section provides further references for those readers who wish to pursue the topics taken up in the sections they conclude.

Part I, "Classic Auteur Theory," covers the beginnings of auteurism in France and its extension to Britain and the US as well as the theoretical debates that quickly ensued. Foundational polemical pieces by Truffaut, Bazin, Sarris, and Kael set the terms of the debate, while the others essays in the section place the rise of classic auteurism within wider historical and critical contexts. The essays in Part II, "The Contexts of Authorship," consider the limitations of regarding the director as auteur given the collaborative practicalities of the film making process, as well as the creative role of others involved in film production. Scriptwriters, producers, cinematographers, actors, and studios are discussed in relation to auteurism. Part III, "Close Readings," addresses a range of theoretical contexts involving authorship in the cinema such as genre, the studio system, ideology, and issues of gender, sexuality, and race. Together, these selections offer a number of model readings by treating the work of mainstream directors (John Ford, Alfred Hitchcock, Howard Hawks, Douglas Sirk, Frank Capra, Kathryn Bigelow) whose films are likely to be screened in a course on auteurism and authorship in the cinema.

Each of the readings collected in this book engages with others, whether to question or endorse, elaborate or move beyond ideas they offer. Together, then, they gather more meaning, providing readers with a more complete understanding of the complexities of the idea of authorship in the cinema than in any of them alone. In other words, collectively these essays become more than merely the sum of them individually. While this should be true of any good reader, it is particularly appropriate for this one because the most important lesson of auteurism has been to show us how to understand individual films within the larger context of a body of work.

Acknowledgments

First and foremost I wish to extend my deep gratitude to Jayne Fargnoli, Executive Editor at Blackwell Publishing, for her unwavering support of and enthusiasm for this book from the outset. I am also indebted to Ken Provencher, Senior Development Editor at Blackwell, my point man for everything practical. His calm demeanor and professional advice was indispensable throughout the production process. Louise Spencely was outstanding as project manager, as was copy-editor Mervyn Thomas.

My graduate student research assistant, Curtis Maloley, did much of the preparatory legwork for the manuscript even as he was loaded with students as a teaching assistant.

I also owe thanks to the anonymous readers who offered very helpful suggestions for improving the reader as I originally proposed it. I'm sure they will see some of their comments reflected in its final form.

The editor and publisher gratefully acknowledge the permission granted to reproduce the copyright material in this book:

1 François Truffaut, "A Certain Tendency of the French Cinema," from *Cahiers du Cinéma* in English 1. Originally published in French in *Cahiers du Cinéma* 31 (1954). © 1954. Reprinted by permission of *Cahiers du Cinéma.*
2 André Bazin, "*De la politique des auteurs*," pp. 137–55 from Peter Graham (ed.), *The New Wave* (London: BFI/New York: Doubleday, 1968). © 1968 by Peter Graham. Reprinted by permission of BFI Publishing.
3 Ian Cameron, "Films, Directors and Critics," pp. 4–7 from *Movie* 2 (1962). © 1962.
4 Andrew Sarris, "Notes on the Auteur Theory in 1962," pp. 1–8 from *Film Culture* 29 (Winter 1962/1963). © 1962 by Andrew Sarris. Reprinted by permission of the author.
5 Pauline Kael, "Circles and Squares," pp. 12–26 from *Film Quarterly* 16, no. 3 (Spring, 1963).
6 Peter Wollen, "The Auteur Theory" (excerpt), pp. 74–105 from *Signs and Meaning in the Cinema*, 3rd ed. (Bloomington: Indiana University Press, 1972). © 1969, 1972 by Peter Wollen. Reprinted by permission of BFI Publishing.
7 V. F. Perkins, "Directions and Authorship" (excerpt), pp. 167–86 from *Film as Film: Understanding and Judging Movies* (Harmondsworth, Baltimore, MD: Penguin, 1972). © V. F. Perkins, 1972. Reprinted by permission of Penguin Books Ltd.
8 Edward Buscombe, "Ideas of Authorship," pp. 75–85 from *Screen* 14, no. 3 (Autumn 1973). © 1973 by Edward Buscombe. Reprinted by permission of the author and *Screen.*
9 Robin Wood, "Ideology, Genre, Auteur," pp. 1, 16, 18 from *Film Comment* 13, no. 1 (January–February 1977). © 1977 by The Film Society of Lincoln Center. All rights reserved. Reprinted by permission of the Film Society of Lincoln Center.
10 Roland Barthes, "The Death of the Author," pp. 142–8 from *Image/Music/Text*, ed. and trans. Stephen Heath (New York: Hill and Wang, 1977). Originally published in French (1968). Copyright © 1977 by Stephen Heath. Reprinted by permission of Hill and Wang, a division of Farrar, Straus and Giroux, LLC and Editions du Seuil.

11 Charles W. Eckert, "The English Cine-Structuralists," pp. 46–51 from *Film Comment* 9, no. 3 (May–June 1973). © 1973 by Film Comment Publishing Corporation. Reprinted by permission of the Film Society of Lincoln Center.

12 Graham Petrie, "Alternatives to Auteurs," pp. 27–35 from *Film Quarterly* 26, no. 3 (Spring 1973). © 1973. Reprinted by permission of The Copyright Clearance Center, on behalf of *Film Quarterly*.

13 Claire Johnston, "Women's Cinema as Counter-Cinema," from *Notes on Women's Cinema* (London: Society for Education in Film and Television, 1973). © 1973.

14 Angela Martin, "Refocusing Authorship in Women's Cinema," pp. 29–37 from Jacqueline Levitin, Judith Plessis, and Valerie Raoul (eds.), *Women Filmmakers: Refocusing* (Vancouver: University of British Columbia Press, 2003). © 2003 by University of British Columbia Press. All rights reserved by the publisher. Reprinted by permission of UBC Press.

15 Richard Koszarski, "The Men with the Movie Cameras," pp. 27–9 from *Film Comment* 8, no. 2 (Summer 1972). © 1972 by Film Comment Publishing Corporation. Reprinted by permission of the Film Society of Lincoln Center.

16 Richard Corliss, "Notes on a Screenwriter's Theory, 1973," pp. xvii–xxviii from *Talking Pictures: Screenwriters in the American Cinema 1927–1973* (Woodstock, NY: Overlook Press, 1974). © 1974 by Richard Corliss. Reprinted by permission of The Overlook Press.

17 Gore Vidal, "Who Makes the Movies?" pp. 35–9 from *New York Review of Books* (November 25, 1976). © 1976 by Gore Vidal. Reprinted by permission of the author.

18 Peter Lehman, "Script/Performance/Text: Performance Theory and Auteur Theory," pp. 197–206 from *Film Reader* 3 (Northwestern University). © 1978 by Peter Lehman. Reprinted by permission of the author.

19 Jerome Christensen, "Studio Authorship." Adapted from "Studio Authorship, Warner Bros and *The Fountainhead*," pp. 17–21 from *The Velvet Light Trap* 57 (Spring 2006). © 2007 by Jerome Christensen. Used by permission of the author.

20 Matthew Bernstein, "The Producer as Auteur." New contribution.

21 Bruce Kawin, "Authorship, Design and Execution," pp. 291–301 from *How Movies Work* (The University of California Press 1992). Copyright © 1992 by The Regents of The University of California. Reprinted by permission of The Copyright Clearance Center, on behalf of The University of California Press.

22 Maurice Yacowar, "Hitchcock's Imagery and Art," pp. 256–69 from *Hitchcock's British Films* (Hamden, CT: Archon Books [Shoestring Press], 1977). © 1977 by Maurice Yacowar. Reprinted by permission of the author.

23 Editors of *Cahiers du Cinéma*, "John Ford's *Young Mr Lincoln*" (excerpt), from *Cahiers du Cinéma* 223 (1970). Reprinted in *Screen* 13, no. 3 (1972). © 1970. Reprinted by permission of *Cahiers du Cinéma*.

24 Paul Willemen, "Towards an Analysis of the Sirkian System," pp. 128–34 from *Screen* 13, no. 4 (Winter 1972/1973). © 1972 by Paul Willemen. Reprinted by permission of the author and *Screen*.

25 Paul Kerr, "My Name is Joseph H. Lewis," pp. 48–67 from *Screen* 24, nos. 4–5 (July/October 1983). © 1983 by Paul Kerr. Reprinted by permission of the author and *Screen*.

26 Michael Budd, "Authorship as a Commodity: The Art Cinema and *The Cabinet of Dr Caligari*," pp. 12–19 from *Wide Angle* 6, no. 1 (1984). © 1984 by Michael Budd. Reprinted by permission of the author.

27 Pam Cook and Claire Johnston, "The Place of Woman in the Cinema of Raoul Walsh," pp. 93–109 from Phil Hardy (ed.), *Raoul Walsh* (Edinburgh: Edinburgh Film Festival, 1974). © 1974 by Pam Cook and Claire Johnston. Reprinted by permission of Pam Cook.

28 Judith Mayne, "Female Authorship Reconsidered (The Case of Dorothy Arzner)," pp. 89–105, 110–15 from ch. 5 of *The Woman at the Keyhole: Feminism and Women's Cinema* (Bloomington and Indianapolis: Indiana University Press, 1990). © 1990 by Judith Mayne. Reprinted by permission of the author and Indiana University Press.

29 Barry Keith Grant, "Man's Favorite Sport?: The Action Films of Kathryn Bigelow," pp. 371–84 from Yvonne Tasker (ed.), *Action and Adventure Cinema* (London and New York: Routledge, 2004). © 2004 by Barry Keith Grant. Reprinted by permission of the author.

30 Michael DeAngelis, "Authorship and New Queer Cinema: The Case of Todd Haynes." Revised version of "The Characteristics of New Queer Filmmaking: Case Study – Todd Haynes," pp. 42–51 from Michele Aaron (ed.), *New Queer Cinema: A Critical Reader* (New Brunswick, NJ: Rutgers University Press, 2004). © 2004 by Michael DeAngelis. Used by permission of the author.

31 J. Ronald Green, "Twoness and the Film Style of Oscar Micheaux." Chapter 3 from *Sraight hick: The Cinema of Oscar Micheaux* (Bloomington and London: Indiana University Press, 2007. © 2000 by J. Ronald Green. Reprinted by permission of the author and publisher.

32 S. Craig Watkins, "Spike's Joint" (excerpt), pp. 159–66 from ch. 5 of *Representing Hip Hop Culture and the Production of Black Cinema* (Chicago and London: University of Chicago Press, 1998). © 1998 by S. Craig Watkins. Reprinted by permission of the author and The University of Chicago Press.

Introduction

Robin Wood began his 1965 landmark auteurist book *Hitchcock's Films* by pointedly asking "Why should we take Hitchcock seriously?" Although no one needs to ask this question today, with Hitchcock's critical reputation well established, it was crucial at the time, when auteurism was just beginning to take root in America. Noting that if the cinema was regarded as an art like the other arts, then the question would be unnecessary, Wood proceeded in his book to answer it by offering an extended and convincing analogy between the films of this popular Hollywood director and the Elizabethan plays of William Shakespeare, and proposing a consistent theme in the films whereby spectators are forced to confront their own unacknowledged darker impulses and thus come to terms with them (Wood, 1965: 9 ff.). The proposition that a popular filmmaker, an entertainer, might express a personal vision, explore ethical and metaphysical issues as the best artists in the traditional arts do, was at the time almost heretical in the context of traditional aesthetics. Such views were reserved for canonical writers like Shakespeare or Wordsworth or George Eliot, but certainly not appropriate for popular movies and their makers. Hollywood cinema was generally thought of not as art but as mass entertainment produced by an industry that anthropologist Hortense Powdermaker famously called "the dream factory."

Yet despite the seismic changes in critical fashion during the past half century, auteurism – at its most basic, the idea that there is an author to a film – has been central to the historical development of both popular film culture and serious film criticism and theory. Aspects of auteurism have overlapped with virtually every subsequent critical theory and paradigm. Considered radical when it was first introduced, the claim that some directors may express an individual vision, a worldview, over a series of films with stylistic and thematic consistency is now simply common wisdom in everyone's understanding not only of cinema, but also of other forms of popular culture, from music to sports to comic books. The concept of authorship has been seized upon by the culture industry ("from the producer who brought you xxx") as a marketing tool. Seeping into common consciousness and discourse as a way of understanding popular art, auteurism has had enormous influence on culture as well as criticism.

While it may be difficult for readers today to imagine, the debate generated by what Penelope Houston, editor of the venerable British film magazine *Sight and Sound*, in the heat of the fray called "the rather repellent title" of the auteur theory (Houston, 1963: 159) was once intense and passionate. Critical barbs went back and forth in the pages of film journals, cultural periodicals, and the popular press. As Charles Eckert writes in his overview of the later debate involving auteur-structuralism, reprinted in this collection: "There is so much oversimplification, obtuseness, and downright unfairness running through the whole debate that one must resist the temptation to leap in." Several public feuds ensued, the most celebrated of which was the ongoing war of words between Andrew Sarris and Pauline Kael, two influential critics who developed wide, devoted readerships largely through their columns in New York's *Village Voice* and *New Yorker* magazine, respectively. Arthur Knight, film reviewer for *Saturday Review*, put it rather delicately when he said that auteurism was "currently stirring in the teacups of our more recondite film critics" (Knight, 1963). It surely was more than a tempest in a teapot when Dwight Macdonald, a well-known cultural voice of the day and author of an important critical attack on the debasing nature of popular culture, parted ways with *Film Quarterly* because he refused to be associated with a magazine that included a critic (Sarris) who could be of the opinion that Hitchcock in *The Birds* (1962) was "at the summit of his artistic powers" (Magid, 1964: 70).

It all began with Francois Truffaut's manifesto, "A Certain Tendency of the French Cinema," which appeared in the January 1954 issue (no. 31) of *Cahiers du Cinéma*, a major French film journal founded in 1951, and also reprinted here. In the article Truffaut attacked French cinema's "Tradition of Quality," a cycle of literate films that were considered among the nation's best cinema, and called for an alternative "*cinéma des auteurs*" of more personal directors who also write their own scripts. The idea began to characterize the writings and reviews of the magazine through the 1950s and developed into a critical practice for such critics and soon-to-be New Wave directors as Truffaut, Jean-Luc Godard, Jacques Rivette, Eric Rohmer, and Claude Chabrol, who discussed movies as an expression of the director. In French culture, cinema had been taken seriously as an art form almost from its inception, and even before Truffaut, in 1948, Alexandre Astruc published an essay entitled "The Birth of the Avant Garde: Le Caméra Stylo," in which he imagined cinema developing as an art to the point that the camera would function like a pen for a writer and the image would "become a means of writing just as flexible and subtle as written language" (Astruc, 1968: 18). So Truffaut's use of the French term "auteur" to mean "author" in regard to film was perhaps less provocative than applying it in the Hollywood context, where, as studio mogul Samuel Goldwyn was reputed to have said, if you have to send a message use Western Union. The *Cahiers* critics had a more immediate pragmatic goal informing their aesthetic, as they were looking to break into the film industry by creating the conditions that were more hospitable to the production of less expensive, more personal films. The banner of auteurism contributed significantly to that aim in large part by providing a distinct identity for the magazine and its contributors. But its legacy has had considerably wider impact.

Many were shocked by these critics' serious embrace of Hollywood films, and the mention of names like Frank Tashlin, Vincente Minnelli, and Samuel Fuller alongside such sacrosanct figures as D.W. Griffith, Carl Dreyer, and Sergei Eisenstein. After all, during the studio era directors were contract employees, like actors, electricians, and editors, assigned to projects by the head office. Even those few directors who wielded some degree of clout ("the name above the title") in Hollywood, like Hitchcock or Frank Capra, had to work within the parameters of the producing studio's dominant style or genre. Rarely did they have the right to final cut. But the young critics of *Cahiers*, taken with the kinetic, robust appeal of the Hollywood genre movies they discovered after World War 2, doggedly proceeded to look for film authors in this least likely of places. If they could find an author, an artist, even in movies from Hollywood, which was based on a Fordist, assembly line model, then surely cinema was an art and filmmakers were artists.

Cahiers' embrace of Hollywood cinema was shared by the British film journal *Movie*, which began publication in 1962. As its name implies, the magazine championed popular film, devoting much of its content to auteurist discussions of and interviews with such directors as Hitchcock and Howard Hawks, and such important postwar Hollywood directors as Nicholas Ray and Otto Preminger. In the magazine's first issue that Spring, its writers deliberately set out to provoke established critical orthodoxy by including a chart ranking major directors of the day. In the top category of "Great" there were only two names – Hawks and Hitchcock (John Ford only made it to the third level, "Very Talented") – while most of the British filmmakers were lumped into the bottom two categories, "Competent or Ambitious" and the ignominious "The Rest." The magazine's contributors, such as V.F. Perkins, Charles Barr, and, most importantly, Robin Wood, elicited the ire of established British critics such as Houston, who regarded auteurism as abandoning traditional humanist values. But the writing of these critics often tempered the more excessive claims and abstractions of the *Cahiers* group with textual evidence, that is, discussion of specific shots and camera movements. Wood published a series of book-length auteur studies, including *Hitchcock's Films* (1965), mentioned above, and *Howard Hawks* (1972), that were exemplary (and for that reason widely influential) in providing close textual analysis with elegantly reasoned arguments about the director's vision and the moral value to which it speaks.

In the US Andrew Sarris opened the floodgates of critical scorn in 1962 by calling the approach "the auteur theory." In that classic essay, also reprinted here, Sarris offers a questionable but nonetheless influential theoretical framework, conceived as three concentric circles with the innermost, "interior meaning," achieved only by the few true auteurs, somewhat anti-climactically concluding with the admission that the best he could do was merely to point to interior meaning when he saw it. Sarris seems in the end to wind up no further ahead than Jacques Rivette a decade earlier who, in reviewing Hawks' *Monkey Business* (1952), had mystically declared that "The evidence on the screen is proof of Hawks's genius: you only have to watch *Monkey Business* to know that it is a brilliant film. Some people refuse to admit this, however; they refuse to be satisfied by proof. There can't be any other reason why they don't recognize it" (Rivette, 1962: 19). Such a tautological statement seems fundamentally opposed to the very idea of criticism, which is to present an aesthetic argument about a work. Sarris' description of the distinguishing quality of the auteur as an "élan of the soul" (a term he borrowed from Astruc) was both mystical, as he himself explicitly feared, and mystifying.

Sarris continued the trend established by both *Cahiers* and *Movie* of ranking directors in auteurist terms by presenting his "pantheon" of great auteurs and then, in his major and groundbreaking work, *The American Cinema,* published in 1968, ranking every important director in the history of Hollywood. Subsequently every aspiring auteurist had his or her own pantheon, whether orthodox or quirky. In his book on American screenwriters, which explicitly acknowledges its indebtedness to Sarris' work, Richard Corliss even included with his introduction, also reprinted here, an Acropolis chart in which he ranked the 40 screenwriters he goes on to discuss. Sarris repeatedly argued that the least satisfying film of an auteur is better than the most interesting work by a director who isn't, a view that seemed for some to foster the very cult of personality about which French critic and editor of *Cahiers* in its peak auteurist days, André Bazin, warned in his own discussion of the auteur theory, reprinted here as well. As Sam Rhodie opined: "The best, the select, sit in state, enthroned on Mt. Olympus, a theological, near transcendent classical pantheon of creators" (Rhodie, 1971: 10).

If such rankings rankled, so did the auteurists' grand claims regarding the relationship between the auteur and his material. In *Cahiers*, writing on Nicholas Ray's *Party Girl* (1958), Fereydoun Hoveyda admitted that the film's subject is "idiotic," but nevertheless followed with the challenge "So what?" (Hoveyda, 1981: 42). Hoveyda's rhetorical question assumes that content is only minimally related to style, and that the true meaning of an auteur's film lies below the surface content. Chabrol went so far as to offer the outrageous proposition in *Cahiers* that the more trivial the narrative (surface level) of a film, the more room there is for the director to express his vision through style (Chabrol, 1968: 77). Such a concept was opposite to the traditional values of unity in art, where ideally artists use all the elements of their medium harmoniously for an expressive purpose. Once auteurism caught on, there was a rush to erect new auteurs out of previously unacknowledged Hollywood stalwarts like Raoul Walsh, Frank Tashlin, Don Siegel, and Edgar G. Ulmer and interesting postwar directors like Delmer Daves. For a time, it seemed enough to find a "personality" in a given director's films, regardless of the actual qualities of that personality. As Truffaut later remarked, while he and the Cahiers group had discovered auteurs, his successors invented them.

But as criticism and cultural theory grew more aware of and concerned with issues of ideology in the 1970s, the concept of the author changed from the comparatively naïve and impressionistic romanticism of classic auteurism, in which the director's world view was inscribed into the film by force of his (rarely her) personality, to a more rigorous, even "scientific" consideration of the film text. Embracing the new methodologies of semiotics and structuralism, critics became more concerned with how films signified their meaning than with what they signified. In 1958 Godard had boasted of auteurism's romantic basis, declaring in a piece on Swedish director Ingmar Bergman that "The cinema is not a craft. It is an art. It does not mean teamwork. One is always alone; on the set as before the blank page," adding that "Nothing could be more classically romantic" (Godard, 1972: 77). For this reason auteurs such as Fritz Lang, Orson

Welles, and Erich von Stroheim gained additional status, their compromised careers casting them as visionaries victimized by the system. Yet now Roland Barthes and others were claiming that the author no longer carried authority over the meaning of the text, and that auteurs were defined apart from their cultural contexts. As Sam Rhodie put it, "Auteurs are out of time. The theory which makes them sacred makes no inroad on vulgar history, has no concepts for the social or the collective, or the national" (Rhodie, 1971: 10).

Influenced by Barthes and British theorist Stuart Hall, the newly emerging approach of reception studies suggested that textual meaning was not inherent in the text and could be appropriated by readers. Thus the author, in John Caughie's words, moved from "standing behind the text as a source [to become] a term in the process of reading and spectating" (Caughie, 1981: 200). In 1972, Peter Wollen made a crucial distinction between Howard Hawks, an actual biological person and an authorial source, and "Howard Hawks," a critical concept that serves as one of many codes that organize the discourse of the films which bear his name. Thus the director was no longer an artist but a conceptual construct that linked a series of film texts, no longer an individual genius but a reading strategy. Ironically, Robin Wood, once criticized for writing so seriously about Hitchcock and Hawks, now was singled out for attack as an "unreconstructed humanist." Influenced by structuralism, film theorist Geoffrey Nowell-Smith argued that the aim of the auteur approach was to uncover behind "the superficial contrasts of subject and treatment a structural hard core of basic and often recondite motifs" (Nowell-Smith, 1968: 10), although politically oriented critical theory now saw the auteur's personality as itself shaped by the ideology his films embodied. In France, in the wake of the events of May 1968, a new editorial board for *Cahiers du Cinéma* grew more political and theoretical. Taking a position opposed to classic auteurism, they published a collectively written article on John Ford's *Young Mr Lincoln* (1939), excerpted in this volume, that offered an exhaustively detailed analysis of the film showing how it was affected by studio politics, the Depression, and cultural codes of representation, all of which are seen as influencing the film as much as the director's personal artistry.

Hitchcock and his films became "the Hitchcock text" and Lang and his movies "the Lang text." Writing specifically on Lang, Stephen Jenkins struggled to resolve the new theoretical paradigms with already old-fashioned auteurism: writing a book on Lang's films, he offers as justification the fact that " 'Lang' here is a space where a multiplicity of discourses intersect, an unstable, shifting configuration of discourses produced by the interaction of a specific group of films (Lang's filmography) with particular, historically and socially locatable ways of reading/viewing those films" (Jenkins, 1981: 7). As one critic now defined the concept of the author, pushing it to the point that it seems to disappear entirely within a chorus of discourses, he:

> is a juncture of multiple codes (representational, narrative, iconographic, cinematic, cultural) and multiple practices (production, promotion, reading, critical reading, theoretical analysis). The collective voice, generated by this nexus of codes and practices and manifested as the author-function, is ultimately a cultural voice imbued with a culturally defined world view that invades every aspect of the film's representation. (Saxton, 1986: 29)

Ultimately, however, the death of the author, like that of Mark Twain, was greatly exaggerated. Already in 1988 film scholars were noticing "a renewed auteur interest" and opining that the "poststructuralist period of 'the death of the author' " was waning (Telotte, 1988: 42). For despite the most excessive claims of its adherents, auteurism in fact never entirely ignored the historical contexts in which directors worked. It is for this reason that Wollen famously concludes that Ford is a better director than Hawks, because whereas Hawks was remarkably consistent throughout his career, it is the "richness of the shifting relations between antinomies in Ford's work that makes him a great artist." By the 1980s most adherents of auteurism would agree with Raymond Durgnat's sensible observation that "*Kiss Me Deadly* isn't important because it tells us anything about an individual called Robert Aldrich. Aldrich is important because *Kiss Me Deadly* reveals something about America, and about us all" (Durgnat, 1967: 76).

Sarris vaguely defined interior meaning as "extrapolated from the tension between a director's personality and his material," and although he fails to explain what this means, it may be understood, at least within the context of classic Hollywood cinema, as the way a director mobilizes, inflects, or deploys the elements of genre he was obliged to use. Genre provides a frame within which auteurs can animate conventions and iconography to their own purpose. While of course some directors floundered against the pressures of the studio system, many in fact flourished, using the rules of genre as convenience rather than constraint, as guidelines from which to deviate rather than blueprints to follow. As Robin Wood explains in his comparison of films by Hitchcock and Capra in this collection, the received framework of Hollywood's genre system gave filmmakers a flexible tradition within which to work. Clearly, some directors developed their vision within particular genres, such as Ford with the western, Fuller with the war film, and Douglas Sirk with melodrama. In short, the auteur approach provides a way of looking at directors' style foregrounded against the background of genre. As Lawrence Alloway notes, "the personal contribution of many directors can only be seen fully after typical iconographical elements have been identified" (Alloway, 1971: 41). And genres, of course, are intimately connected to social and historical forces.

Beginning with *Cahiers*' practice of assigning reviews to writers who already admired the work of that director, a film was implicitly if not forthrightly regarded as good if one could find something of the director in it. And, of course, if the director was an auteur, one always could. As a result, auteurism lost its ability to function as an evaluative tool. But there is no doubt that auteurism's great legacy is that it encouraged a more serious examination of the movies beyond mere "entertainment" and helped move the nascent field of film studies beyond its literary beginnings to a consideration of film's visual qualities. While structuralism and semiotics ultimately seem limited in film analysis, in part because they tend to emphasize narrative over the visual aspects of texts, auteurism was in fact responsible for shifting critical focus from story to style, from content to form, and for showing how form was crucial in shaping content. Already in 1960 Richard Roud, in his attack on auteurism, was forced to concede that the main thing we might gain from the auteurists is to accept that "form is at least *as* important as content" (Roud, 1960: 171). To appreciate the extent to which auteurism has filtered through popular culture, we need only note how John Ford's reputation has been reversed, so that now his major works are seen to be such westerns as *Stagecoach* (1939), *The Searchers* (1956), and *The Man Who Shot Liberty Valance* (1962) rather than the overtly socially conscious prestige pictures such as *The Informer* (1935) and *The Grapes of Wrath* (1940), once touted as his most important works. Auteurism's reassessment of American film history, which Sarris claimed was its most important function, has had profound impact on cultural taste.

Because of its usefulness in understanding and appreciating the role and function of artistic expression in contemporary mass media, the auteur approach has also been applied convincingly to artists in other forms of popular culture such as television and popular music, and it has become one of the paradigms for how consumers think about works of popular culture in all media. Auteurism has become common discourse in popular culture, and, indeed, a vital part of popular culture as an institution. As Sarris observed in 1993, thirty years after he announced that henceforth *la politique des auteurs* (an argument for auteurs) would be called the auteur theory, its "ultimate vindication" is that MTV was including the director's name at the beginning and end of every music video (Grimes, 1993: 9).

References

Alloway, Lawrence. *Violent America: The Movies, 1946–1964*. New York: Museum of Modern Art, 1971.

Astruc, Alexandre. "The Birth of a New Avant-Garde: La Caméra-Stylo." In *The New Wave*, ed. Peter Graham. Garden City, NY: Doubleday, 1968: 17–23.

Caughie, John, ed. *Theories of Authorship*. London and Boston: Routledge & Kegan Paul/British Film Institute, 1981.

Chabrol, Claude. "Little Themes." In *The New Wave*, ed. Peter Graham. Garden City, NY: Doubleday, 1968: 73–9.

Durgnat, Raymond. *Films and Feelings*. Cambridge, MA: MIT Press/London: Faber and Faber, 1967.

Godard, Jean-Luc. "Bergmanorama." In *Godard on Godard*, ed. and trans. Tom Milne. New York: Viking, 1972.

Grimes, William. "The Auteur Theory of Film: Holy or Just Full of Holes?" *New York Times* (20 February 1993): C9, C15.

Houston, Penelope. "The Figure in the Carpet." *Sight and Sound* 32, no. 4 (Autumn 1963): 159–64.

Hoveyda, Fereydoun. "La réponse de Nicholas Ray." In *Theories of Authorship*, ed. John Caughie. London and Boston: Routledge & Kegan Paul/British Film Institute, 1981: 42–3.

Jenkins, Stephen, ed. *Fritz Lang: The Image and the Look*. London: British Film Institute, 1981.

Macdonald, Dwight. "A Theory of Mass Culture." In *Mass Culture: The Popular Arts in America*, ed. Bernard Rosenberg and David Manning White. New York: Free Press/London: Collier Macmillan, 1964: 59–73.

Magid, Marion. "Auteur! Auteur!" *Commentary* 37, no. 3 (March 1964): 70–4.

Knight, Arthur. "The Auteur Theory." *Saturday Review* (May 4 1963): 22.

Nowell-Smith, Geoffrey. *Visconti*. Garden City, NY: Doubleday/London: British Film Institute, 1968.

Rhodie, Sam. "Education and Criticism: Notes on Work to Be Done." *Screen* 12, no. 1 (Spring 1971): 9–13.

Rivette, Jacques. "The Genius of Howard Hawks." *Movie* 5 (December 1962): 19–20. The article originally appeared in *Cahiers du Cinéma* 23 (May 1953).

Roud, Richard. "The French Line." *Sight and Sound* 29, no. 4 (Autumn 1960): 166–71.

Sarris, Andrew. *The American Cinema: Directors and Directions, 1929–1968*. New York: Dutton, 1968.

Saxton, Christine. "The Collective Voice as Cultural Voice." *Cinema Journal* 26, no. 1 (Fall 1986): 19–30.

Telotte, J.P. "Introduction" to Annual Bibliography of Film Studies, *Post Script* 7: 3 (Summer 1988): 42.

Wood, Robin. *Hitchcock's Films*. London: Zwemmer/New York: A.S. Barnes, 1965.

Wood, Robin. *Hitchcock's Films Revisited*, revised ed. New York: Columbia University Press, 2002

Part I

Classic Auteur Theory

1

A Certain Tendency of the French Cinema

François Truffaut

Francois Truffaut began his career as a film critic writing for *Cahiers du Cinéma* beginning in 1953. He went on to become one of the most celebrated and popular directors of the French New Wave, beginning with his first feature film, *Les Quatre cents coup* (*The Four Hundred Blows*, 1959). Other notable films written and directed by Truffaut include *Jules et Jim* (1962), *The Story of Adele H.* (1975), and *L'Argent de Poche* (*Small Change*, 1976). He also acted in some of his own films, including *L'Enfant Sauvage* (*The Wild Child*, 1970) and *La Nuit Américain* (*Day for Night*, 1973). He appeared as the scientist Lacombe in Steven Spielberg's *Close Encounters of the Third Kind* (1977). Truffaut's controversial essay, originally published in *Cahiers du Cinéma* in January 1954, helped launch the development of the magazine's auteurist practice by rejecting the literary films of the "Tradition of Quality" in favor of a *cinéma des auteurs* in which filmmakers like Jean Renoir and Jean Cocteau express a more personal vision. Truffaut claims to see no "peaceful co-existence between this 'Tradition of Quality' and an 'auteur's cinema.'" Although its tone is provocative, perhaps even sarcastic, the article served as a touchstone for *Cahiers*, giving the magazine's various writers a collective identity as championing certain filmmakers and dismissing others.

These notes have no other object than to attempt to define a certain tendency of the French cinema – a tendency called "psychological realism" – and to sketch its limits.

Ten or Twelve Films

If the French cinema exists by means of about a hundred films a year, it is well understood that only ten or twelve merit the attention of critics and ciné-philes, the attention, therefore of *Cahiers*.

These ten or twelve films constitute what has been prettily named the "Tradition of Quality"; they force, by their ambitiousness, the admiration of the foreign press, defend the French flag twice a year at Cannes and at Venice where, since 1946, they regularly carry off medals, golden lions and *grands prix*.

With the advent of "talkies," the French cinema was a frank plagiarism of the American cinema. Under the influence of *Scarface*, we made the amusing *Pépé Le Moko*. Then the French scenario is most clearly obliged to Prévert for its evolution: *Quai Des Brumes (Port Of Shadows)* remains the masterpiece of *poetic realism*.

François Truffaut, "A Certain Tendency of the French Cinema," from *Cahiers du Cinéma* in English 1. Originally published in French in *Cahiers du Cinéma* 31 (1954).

Figure 1.1 *Quai des Brumes (Port of Shadows)* (Ciné-Alliance, 1938): A masterpiece of the Tradition of Quality, directed by Marcel Carné and written by Jacques Prévert. Produced by Gregor Rabinovitch

The war and the post-war period renewed our cinema. It evolved under the effect of an internal pressure and for *poetic realism* – about which one might say that it died closing *Les Portes De La Nuit* behind it – was substituted *psychological realism*, illustrated by Claude Autant-Lara, Jean Delannoy, René Clement, Yves Allégret and Marcel Pagliero.

Scenarists' Films

If one is willing to remember that not so long ago Delannoy filmed *Le Bossu* and *La Part De L'Ombre*, Claude Autant-Lara *Le Plombier Amoureux* and *Lettres D'Amour*, Yves Allégret *La Boîte Aux Rêves* and *Les Démons De L'Aube*, that all these films are justly recognized as strictly commercial enterprises, one will admit that, the successes or failures of these cinéastes being a function of the scenarios they chose, *La Symphonie Pastorale*, *Le Diable Au Corps (Devil In The Flesh)*, *Jeux Interdits (Forbidden Games)*, *Manèges*, *Un Homme Marche Dans La Ville* are essentially *scenarists' films*.

Today No One is Ignorant Any Longer . . .

After having sounded out directing by making two forgotten shorts, Jean Aurenche became a specialist in adaptation. In 1936, he was credited, with Anouilh, with the dialogue for *Vous N'Avez Rien A Déclarer* and *Les Dégourdis De La 11e*.

At the same time Pierre Bost was publishing excellent little novels at the N.R.F.

Aurenche and Bost worked together for the first time while adapting and writing dialogue for *Douce*, directed by Claude Autant-Lara.

Today, no one is ignorant any longer of the fact that Aurenche and Bost rehabilitated adaptation by upsetting old preconceptions of being faithful to the letter and substituting for it the contrary idea of being faithful to the spirit – to the point that this audacious aphorism has been written: "An honest adaptation is a betrayal" (Carlo Rim, "Traveling and Sex-Appeal").

In adaptation there exists filmable scenes and unfilmable scenes, and that instead of omitting the latter (as was done not long ago) it is necessary to invent *equivalent* scenes, that is to say, scenes as the novel's author would have written them for the cinema.

"Invention without betrayal" is the watchword Aurenche and Bost like to cite, forgetting that one can also betray by omission.

The system of Aurenche and Bost is so seductive, even in the enunciation of its principles, that nobody even dreamed of verifying its functioning close-at-hand. I propose to do a little of this here.

The entire reputation of Aurenche and Bost is built on two precise points: 1. *Faithfulness* to the spirit of the works they adapt: 2. The talent they use.

That Famous Faithfulness . . .

Since 1943 Aurenche and Bost have adapted and written dialogue for: *Douce* by Michel Davet, *La Symphonie Pastorale* by Gide, *Le Diable Au Corps* by Radiguet, *Un Recteur A L'Ile De Sein (Dieu A Besoin Des Hommes – God Needs Men)* by Queffelec, *Les Jeux Inconnus (Jeux Interdits)* by François Boyer, *Le Blé En Herbe* by Colette.

In addition, they wrote an adaptation of *Journal D'Un Curé De Campagne* that was never filmed, a scenario on *Jeanne D'Arc* of which only one part has been made (by Jean Delannoy) and, lastly, scenario and dialogue for *L'Auberge Rouge (The Red Inn)* (directed by Claude Autant-Lara).

You will have noticed the profound diversity of inspiration of the works and authors adapted. In order to accomplish this tour de force which consists of remaining faithful to the spirit of Michel Davet, Gide, Radiguet, Queffelec, François Boyer, Colette and Bernanos, one must oneself possess, I imagine, a suppleness of spirit, a habitually geared-down personality as well as singular eclecticism.

You must also consider that Aurenche and Bost are led to collaborate with the most diverse directors: Jean Delannoy, for example, sees himself as a mystical moralist. But the petty meanness of *Garçon Sauvage (Savage Triangle)*, the shabbiness of *La Minute De Vérité*, the insignificance of *La Route Napoléon* show rather clearly the intermittent character of that vocation.

Claude Autant-Lara, on the contrary, is well known for his non-conformity, his "advanced" ideas, his wild anti-clericalism; let us recognize in this cinéaste the virtue of always remaining, in his films, honest with himself.

Pierre Bost being the technician in tandem, the spiritual element in this communal work seems to come from Jean Aurenche.

Educated by the Jesuits, Jean Aurenche has held on to nostalgia and rebellion, both at the same time. His flirtation with surrealism seemed to be out of sympathy for the anarchists of the thirties. This tells how strong his personality is, also how apparently incompatible it was with the personalities of Gide, Bernanos, Queffelec, Radiguet. But an examination of the works will doubtless give us more information.

Abbot Amdée Ayffre knew very well how to analyse *La Symphonie Pastorale* and how to define the relationship between the written work and the filmed work:

"Reduction of Faith to religious psychology in the hands of Gide, now becomes a reduction to psychology, plain and simple . . . with this qualitative abasement we will now have, according to a law well-known to aestheticians, a corresponding quantitative augmentation. New characters are added: Piette and Casteran, charged with representing certain sentiments. Tragedy becomes drama, melodrama" (*Dieu Au Cinéma*, p. 131).

What Annoys Me . . .

What annoys me about this famous process of equivalence is that I'm not at all certain that a novel contains unfilmable scenes, and even less certain that these scenes, decreed unfilmable, would be so for everyone.

Praising Robert Bresson for his faithfulness to Bernanos, André Bazin ended his excellent article "La Stylistique de Robert Bresson" with these words. "After *The Diary Of A Country Priest*, Aurenche and Bost are no longer anything but the Viollet-Leduc of adaptation."

All those who admire and know Bresson's film well will remember the admirable scene in the confessional when Chantal's face "began to appear little by little, by degrees" (Bernanos).

When, several years before Bresson, Jean Aurenche wrote an adaptation of *Diary*, refused by Bernanos, he judged this scene to be unfilmable and substituted for it the one we reproduce here.

"Do you want me to listen to you here?" He indicates the confessional.

"I never confess."

"Nevertheless, you must have confessed yesterday, since you took communion this morning?"

"I didn't take communion."

He looks at her, very surprised.

"Pardon me, I gave you communion."

Chantal turns rapidly towards the pri-Dieu she had occupied that morning.

"Come see."

The curé follows her. Chantal indicates the missal she had left there.

"Look in this book, Sir. Me, I no longer, perhaps, have the right to touch it."

The curé, very intrigued, opens the book and discovers, between two pages, the host that Chantal had spit out. His face is stupified and confused.

"I spit out the host," says Chantal.

"I see," says the curé, with a neutral voice.

"You've never seen anything like that, right?" says Chantal, harsh almost triumphant.

"No, never," says the curé, very calmly.

"Do you know what must be done?"

The curé closes his eyes for a brief instant. He is thinking or praying, he says, "It is very simple to repair, Miss. But it's very horrible to commit."

He heads for the altar, carrying the open book. Chantal follows him.

"No, it's not horrible. What is horrible is to receive the host in a state of sin."

"You were, then, in a state of sin?"

"Less than the others, but then – it's all the same to them."

"Do not judge."

"I do not judge, I condemn," says Chantal with violence.

"Silence in front of the body of Christ!"

He kneels before the altar, takes the host from the book and swallows it.

In the middle of the book, the curé and an obtuse atheist named Arsène are opposed in a discussion on Faith. This discussion ends with this line by Arsène, "When one is dead, everything is dead." In the adaptation, this discussion takes place on the very tomb of the curé, between Arsène and another curé, and *terminates the film*. This line, "When one is dead, everything is dead," carries, perhaps the only one retained by the public. Bernanos did not say, for conclusion, "When one is dead, everything is dead," but "What does it matter, all is grace."

"Invention without betrayal," you say – it seems to me that it's a question here of little enough invention for a great deal of betrayal. One or two more details. Aurenche and Bost were unable to make *The Diary Of A Country Priest* because Bernanos was alive. Bresson declared that were Bernanos alive he would have taken more liberties. Thus, Aurenche and Bost are annoyed because someone is alive, but Bresson is annoyed because he is dead.

Unmask

From a simple reading of that extract, there stands out:

1. A constant and deliberate care to be *unfaithful* to the spirit as well as the letter;
2. A very marked taste for profanation and blasphemy.

This unfaithfulness to the spirit also degrades *Le Diable Au Corps* – a love story that becomes an anti-militaristic, anti-bourgeois film, *La Symphonie Pastorale* – a love story about an amorous pastor – turns Gide into a Béatrix Beck, *Un Recteur à l'île de Sein* whose title is swapped for the equivocal one of *Dieu A Besoin Des Hommes* in which the islanders are shown like the famous "cretins" in Buñuel's *Land Without Bread.*

As for the taste for blasphemy, it is constantly manifested in a more or less insidious manner, depending on the subject, the *metteur-en-scène* nay, even the star.

I recall from memory the confessional scene from *Douce,* Marthe's funeral in *Le Diable*, the profaned hosts in that adaptation of *Diary* (scene carries over to *Dieu A Besoin Des Hommes*), the whole scenario and the character played by Fernandel in *L'Auberge Rouge*, the scenario *in toto* of *Jeux Interdits* (joking in the cemetery).

Thus, everything indicates that Aurenche and Bost are the authors of *frankly* anti-clerical films, but, since films about the cloth are fashionable, our authors have allowed themselves to fall in with that style. But as it suits them – they think – not to betray their convictions, the theme of profanation and blasphemy, dialogues with double meanings, turn up here and there to prove to the guys that they know the art of "cheating the producer," all the while giving him satisfaction, as well as that of cheating the "great public," which is equally satisfied.

This process well deserves the name of "alibi-ism"; it is excusable and its use is necessary during a time when one must ceaselessly feign stupidity in order to work intelligently, but if it's all in the game to "cheat the producer," isn't it a bit scandalous to re-write Gide, Bernanos and Radiguet?

In truth, Aurenche and Bost work like all the scenarists in the world, like pre-war Spaak and Natanson.

To their way of thinking, every story includes characters A, B, C, and D. In the interior of that equation, everything is organized in function of criteria known to them alone. The sun rises and sets like clockwork, characters disappear, others are invented, the script deviates little by little from the original and becomes a whole, formless but brilliant: a new film, step by step makes its solemn entrance into the "Tradition of Quality."

So Be It, They Will Tell Me . . .

They will tell me, "Let us admit that Aurenche and Bost are unfaithful, but do you also deny the existence of their talent . . . ?" Talent, to be sure, is not a function of fidelity, but I consider an adaptation of value only when written by a *man of the cinema*. Aurenche and Bost are essentially literary men and I reproach them here for being contemptuous of the cinema by underestimating it. They behave, *vis-à-vis* the scenario, as if they thought to reeducate a delinquent by finding him a job; they always believe they've "done the maximum" for it by embellishing it with subtleties, out of that science of nuances that make up the slender merit of modern novels. It is, moreover, only the smallest caprice on the part of the exegetists of our art that they believe to honor the cinema by using literary jargon. (Haven't Sartre and Camus been talked about for Pagliero's work, and phenomenology for Allégret's?)

The truth is, Aurenche and Bost have made the works they adapt insipid, for *equivalence* is always with us, whether in the form of treason or timidity. Here is a brief example: in *Le Diable Au Corps*, as Radiguet wrote it, François meets Marthe on a train platform with Marthe jumping from the train while it is still moving; in the film, they meet in the school which has been transformed into a hospital. What is the point of this *equivalence*? It's a decoy for the anti-militarist elements added to the work, in concert with Claude Autant-Lara.

Well, it is evident that Radiguet's idea was one of *mise-en-scène*, whereas the scene invented by Aurenche and Bost is *literary*. One could, believe me, multiply these examples infinitely.

One of These Days . . .

Secrets are only kept for a time, formulas are divulged, new scientific knowledge is the object of communications to the Academy of Sciences and since, if we will believe Aurenche and Bost, adaptation is an exact science, one of these days they really could apprise us in the name of what criterion, by virtue of what system, by what mysterious and internal geometry of the work, they abridge, add, multiply, devise and "rectify" these masterpieces.

Now that this idea is uttered, the idea that these equivalences are only timid astuteness to the end of getting around the difficulty, of resolving on the soundtrack problems that concern the image, plundering in order to no longer obtain anything on the screen but scholarly framing, complicated lighting-effects, "polished" photography, the whole keeping the "Tradition of Quality" quite alive – it is time to come to an examination of the ensemble of these films adapted, with dialogue, by Aurenche and Bost, and to research the permanent nature of certain themes that will explain, without justifying, the constant *unfaithfulness* of two scenarists to works taken by them as "pretext" and "occasion."

In a two line résumé, here is the way scenarios treated by Aurenche and Bost appear:

La Symphonie Pastorale: He is a pastor, he is married. He loves and has no right to.

Le Diable Au Corps: They make the gestures of love and have no right to.

Dieu A Besoin Des Hommes: He officiates, gives benedictions, gives extreme unction and has no right to.

Jeux Interdits: They bury the dead and have no right to.

Le Blé En Herbe: They love each other and have no right to.

You will say to me that the book also tells the same story, which I do not deny. Only, I notice that Gide also wrote *La Porte Etroite*, Radiguet *La Bal Du Comte d'Orgel*, Colette *La Vagabonde* and that each one of these novels did not tempt Delannoy or Autant-Lara.

Let us notice also that these scenarios, about which I don't believe it useful to speak here, fit into the sense of my thesis: *Au-Delà Des Grilles, Le Château De Verre, L'Auberge Rouge. . . .*

One sees how competent the promoters of the "Tradition of Quality" are in choosing only subjects that favor the misunderstandings on which the whole system rests.

Under the cover of literature – and, of course, of quality – they give the public its habitual dose of smut, non-conformity and facile audacity.

The Influence of Aurenche and Bost is Immense . . .

The writers who have come to do film dialogue have observed the same imperatives; Anouilh, between the dialogues for *Dégourdis de la 11e* and *Un Caprice De Caroline Chérie*, introduced into more ambitious films his universe with its affection of the bizarre with a background of nordic mists transposed to Brittany (*Pattes Blanches*). Another writer, Jean Ferry, made sacrifices for fashion; he too, and the dialogue for *Manon* could just as well have been signed by Aurenche and Bost: "He believed me a virgin and, in private life, he is a professor of psychology!" Nothing better to hope for from the young scenarists. They simply work their shift, taking good care not to break any taboos.

Jacques Sigurd, one of the last to come to "scenario and dialogue," teamed up with Yves Allégret. Together, they bequeathed the French cinema some of its blackest masterpieces: *Dêdée D'Anvers, Manèges, Une Si Jolie Petite Plage, Les Miracles N'Ont Lieu Qu'une Fois, La Jeune Folle.* Jacques Sigurd very quickly assimilated the recipe; he must be endowed with an admirable spirit of synthesis, for his scenarios oscillate ingeniously between Aurenche and Bost, Prêvert and Clouzot, the whole lightly modernized. Religion is never involved, but blasphemy always makes its timid entrance thanks to several daughters of Mary or several good sisters who make their way across the field of vision at the moment when their presence would be least expected (*Manèges, Une Si Jolie Petite Plage*).

The cruelty by which they aspire to "rouse the trembling of the bourgeois" finds its place in well-expressed lines like: "he was old, he could drop dead" (*Manèges*). In *Une Si Jolie Petite Plage*, Jane Marken envies Berck's prosperity because of the tubercular cases found there: *Their family comes to see them and that makes business good!* (One dreams of the prayer of the rector of Sein Island).

Roland Laudenbach, who would seem to be more endowed than most of his colleagues, has collaborated on films that are most typical of that spirit: *La Minute De Vérité, Le Bon Dieu Sans Confession, La Maison Du Silence.*

Robert Scipion is a talented man of letters. He has only written one book; a book of pastiches. Singular badges: the daily frequenting of the Saint-Germain-des-Prés cafés, the friendship of Marcel Pagliero who is called the Sartre of the cinema, probably because his films resemble the articles in "Temps Modernes." Here are several lines from *Amants De Brasmort,* a populist film in which sailors are "heroes," like the dockers were in *Un Homme Marche Dans La Ville*:

"The wives of friends are made to sleep with."

"You do what agrees with you; as for that, you'd mount anybody, you might well say."

In one single reel of the film, towards the end, you can hear in less than ten minutes such words as: *prostitute, whore, slut* and *bitchiness.* Is this realism?

Prévert is to be Regretted . . .

Considering the uniformity and equal filthiness of today's scenarios, one takes to regretting Prévert's scenarios. He believed in the Devil, thus in God, and if, for the most part, his characters were by his whim alone charged with all the sins in creation, there was always a couple, the new Adam and Eve, who could end the film, so that the story could begin again.

Psychological Realism, Neither Real Nor Psychological . . .

There are scarcely more than seven or eight scenarists working regularly for the French cinema. Each one of these scenarists has but one story to tell, and, since each only aspires to the success of the "two greats," it is not exaggerating to say that the hundred-odd French films made each year tell the same story: it's always a question of a victim, generally a cuckold. (The cuckold would be the only sympathetic character in the film if he weren't always infinitely grotesque: Blier-Vilbert, etc. . . .) The knavery of his kin and the hatred among the members of his family lead the "hero" to his doom; the injustice of life, and for local color, the wickedness of the world (the curés, the concierges, the neighbors, the passers-by, the rich, the poor, the soldiers, etc. . . .)

For distraction, during the long winter nights, look for titles of French films that do not fit into this framework and, while you're at it, find among these films those in which this line or its equivalent does not figure, spoken by the most abject couple in the film: "It's always they that have the money (or the luck, or love, or happiness). It's too unjust, in the end."

This school which aspires to realism destroys it at the moment of finally grabbing it, so careful is the school to lock these beings in a closed world, barricaded by formulas, plays on words, maxims, instead of letting us see them for ourselves, with our own eyes. The artist cannot always dominate his work. He must be, sometimes, God and, sometimes, his creature. You know that modern play in which the principal character, normally constituted when the curtain rises on him, finds himself crippled at the end of the play, the loss of each of his members punctuating the changes of acts. Curious epoch when the least flash-in-the-pan performer uses Kafkaesque words to qualify his domestic avatars. This form of cinema comes straight from modern literature – half-Kafka, half Bovary!

A film is no longer made in France that the authors do not believe they are re-making Madame Bovary.

For the first time in French literature, an author adopted a distant, exterior attitude in relation to his subject, the subject becoming like an insect under the entomologist's microscope. But if, when starting this enterprise, Flaubert could have said, "I will roll them all in the same mud – and be right" (which today's authors would voluntarily make their exergue), he could declare afterwards "I am Madame Bovary" and I doubt that the same authors could take up that line and be sincere!

Mise-en-Scène, Metteur-en-Scène, Texts

The object of these notes is limited to an examination of a certain form of cinema, from the point of view of the scenarios and scenarists only. But it is appropriate, I think, to make it clear that the *metteurs-en-scène* are and wish to be responsible for the scenarios and dialogues they illustrate.

Scenarists' films, I wrote above, and certainly it isn't Aurenche and Bost who will contradict me. When they hand in their scenario, the film is done; the *metteur-en-scène*, in their eyes, is the gentleman who adds the pictures to it and it's true, alas! I spoke of the mania for adding funerals everywhere. And, for all that, death is always juggled away. Let us remember Nana's admirable death, or that of Emma Bovary, presented by Renoir; in *La Pastorale*, death is only a make-up job and an exercise for the camera man: compare the close-ups of Michèle Morgan in *La Pastorale*, Dominique Blanchar in *Le Secret De Mayerling* and Madeleine Sologne in *L'Eternel Retour*: it's the same face! Everything happens *after* death.

Let us cite, lastly, that declaration by Delannoy that we dedicate, with perfidy, to the French scenarists: "When it happens that authors of talent, whether in the spirit of gain or out of weakness, one day let themselves go to "write for the cinema," they do it with the feeling of lowering themselves. They deliver themselves rather to a curious temptation towards mediocrity, so careful are they to not compromise their talent and certain that, to write for the cinema, one must make oneself understood by the lowliest. ("*La Symphonie Pastorale* ou L'Amour Du Métier," review Verger, November 1947).

I must, without further ado, denounce a sophism that will not fail to be thrown at me in the guise of argument: "This dialogue is spoken by abject people and it is in order to better point out their nastiness that we give them this hard language. It is our way of being moralists."

To which I answer: it is inexact to say that these lines are spoken by the most abject characters. To be sure, in the films of "psychological realism" there are nothing but vile beings, but so inordinate is the authors' desire to be superior to their characters that those who, perchance, are not infamous are, at best, infinitely grotesque.

Well, as for these abject characters, who deliver these abject lines – I know a handful of men in France who would be INCAPABLE of conceiving them, several cinéastes whose world-view is at least as valuable as that of Aurenche and Bost, Sigurd and Jeanson. I mean Jean Renoir, Robert Bresson, Jean Cocteau, Jacques Becker, Abel Gance, Max Ophuls, Jacques Tati, Roger Leenhardt; these are, nevertheless, French cinéastes and it happens – curious coincidence – that they are *auteurs* who often write their dialogue and some of them themselves invent the stories they direct.

They Will Still Say To Me . . .

"But why," they will say to me, "why couldn't one have the same admiration for all those cinéastes who strive to work in the bosom of this 'Tradition of Quality' that you make sport of so lightly? Why not admire Yves Allégret as much as Becker, Jean Delannoy as much as Bresson, Claude Autant-Lara as much as Renoir?" ("Taste is made of a thousand distastes" – Paul Valéry).

Well – I do not believe in the peaceful co-existence of the "Tradition of Quality" and an *"auteur's* cinema."

Basically, Yves Allégret and Delannoy are only caricatures of Clouzot, of Bresson.

It is not the desire to create a scandal that leads me to depreciate a cinema so praised elsewhere. I rest convinced that the exaggeratedly prolonged existence of *psychological realism* is the cause of the lack of public comprehension when faced with such new works as *Le Carrosse D'Or (The Golden Coach), Casque D'or*, not to mention *Les Dames Du Bois De Boulogne* and *Orphée.*

Long live audacity, to be sure, still it must be revealed as it is. In terms of this year, 1953, if I had to draw up a balance-sheet of the French cinema's audacities, there would be no place in it for either the vomiting in *Les Orgueilleux (The Proud And The Beautiful)* or Claude Laydu's refusal to be sprinkled with holy water in *Le Bon Dieu Sans Confession* or the homosexual relationships of the characters in *Le Salaire De La Peur (The Wages Of Fear)*, but rather the gait *of Hulot*, the maid's soliloquies in *La Rue De L'Estrapade*, the *mise-en-scène* of *La Carrosse D'Or*, the direction of the actors in *Madame de (The Earrings Of Madame De)*, and also Abel Gance's studies in Polyvision. You will have understood that these audacities are those of *men of the cinema* and no longer of scenarists, directors and littérateurs.

For example, I take it as significant that the most brilliant scenarists and *metteurs-en-scène* of the "Tradition of Quality" have met with failure when they approach comedy: Ferry-Clouzot *Miguette Et Sa Mère*, Sigurd-Boyer *Tous Les Chemins Mènent A Rome*, Scipion-Pagliero *La Rose Rouge*, Laudenbach-Delannoy *La Route Napoléon*, Auranche-Bost-Autant-Lara *L'Auberge Rouge* or, if you like, *Occupe-toi d'Amélie.*

Whoever has tried, one day, to write a scenario wouldn't be able to deny that comedy is by far the most difficult genre, the one that demands the most work, the most talent, also the most humility.

All Bourgeois . . .

The dominant trait of psychological realism is its anti-bourgeois will. But what are Aurenche and Bost, Sigurd, Jeanson, Autant-Lara, Allégret, if not bourgeois, and what are the fifty thousand new readers, who do not fail to see each film from a novel, if not bourgeois?

What then is the value of an anti-bourgeois cinema made by the bourgeois for the bourgeois? Workers, you know very well, do not appreciate this form of cinema at all even when it aims at relating to them. They refused to recognize themselves in the dockers of *Un Homme Marche Dans La Ville*, or in the sailors of *Les Amants De Brasmort.* Perhaps it is necessary to send the children out on the stairway landing in order to make love, but their parents don't like to hear it said, above all at the cinema, even with "benevolence." If the public likes to mix with low company under the alibi of literature, it also likes to do it under the alibi of society. It is instructive to consider the programming of films in Paris, by neighborhoods. One comes to realize that the public-at-large perhaps prefers little naive foreign films that show it men "as they should be" and not in the way that Aurenche and Bost believe them to be.

Like Giving Oneself a Good Address . . .

It is always good to conclude, that gives everyone pleasure. It is remarkable that the "great" *metteurs-en-scène* and the "great" scenarists have, for a long time, all made minor films, and the talent they have put into them hasn't been sufficient to enable one to distinguish them from others (those who don't put in talent). It is also remarkable that they all came to "Quality" at the same time, as if they were giving themselves a good address. And then, a producer – even a director – earns more money making *Le Blé En Herbe* than by making *Le Plombier Amoureux*. The "courageous" films are revealed to be very profitable. The proof: someone like Ralph Habib abruptly renounces demi-pornography, makes *Les Compagnes De La Nuit* and refers to Cayatte. Well, what's keeping the André Tabets, Companeer, the Jean Guittons, the Pierre Vérys, the Jean Lavirons, the Ciampis, the Grangiers, from making, from one day to the next, intellectual films, from adapting masterpieces (there are still a few left) and, of course, adding funerals, here, there and everywhere?

Well, on that day we will be in the "Tradition of Quality" up to the neck and the French cinema, with rivalry among "psychological realism," "violence," "strictness," "ambiguity," will no longer be anything but one vast funeral that will be able to leave the studio in Billancourt and enter the cemetery directly – it seems to have been placed next door expressly, in order to get more quickly from the producer to the grave-digger.

Only, by dint of repeating to the public that it identified with the "heroes" of the films, it might well end by believing it, and on the day that it understands that this fine big cuckold whose misadventures it is solicited to sympathize with (a little) and to laugh at (a lot), is not, as had been thought, a cousin or neighbor down the hall but ITSELF, that abject family ITS family, that scoffed-at religion ITS religion – well, on that day it may show itself to be ungrateful to a cinema that will have labored so hard to show it life as one sees it on the fourth floor in Saint-Germandes Prés.

To be sure, I must recognize it, a great deal of emotion and taking-sides are the controlling factors in the deliberately pessimistic examination I have undertaken of a certain tendency of the French cinema. I am assured that this famous "school of psychological realism" had to exist in order that, in turn, *The Diary Of a Country Priest, La Carrosse D'Or, Orpheus, Casque D'Or, Mr. Hulot's Holiday* might exist.

But our authors who wanted to educate the public should understand that perhaps they have strayed from the primary paths in order to become involved with the more subtle paths of psychology; they have passed on to that sixth grade so dear to Jouhandeau, but it isn't necessary to repeat a grade indefinitely!

Notes

(When translated in *Cahiers du Cinema in English* no. 1, there were no indications of where in the text these notes should be placed.)

1 *La Symphonie Pastorale*. Characters added to the film: Piette, Jacques' fiancée; Casteran, Piette's father. Characters omitted: the Pastor's three children. In the film, no mention is made of what happens to Jacques after Gertrude's death. In the book, Jacques enters an order.

Operation *Symphonie Pastorale*: a. Gide himself writes an adaptation of his book; b. This adaptation is judged "unfilmable"; c. Jean Aurenche and Jean Delannoy, in turn, write an adaptation; d. Gide refuses it; e. Pierre Bost's entry on the scene conciliates everyone.

2 *Le Diable Au Corps*. On the radio, in the course of a program by André Parinaud devoted to Radiguet, Claude Autant-Lara declared in substance, "*What led me to make a film out of Le Diable Au Corps was that I saw it as an anti-war novel.*"

On the same program, Francois Poulenc, a friend of Radiguet's, said he had found nothing of the book on seeing the film.

3 To the proposed producer of *The Diary Of A Country Priest* who was astonished to see the character of Doctor Delbende disappear in the adaptation, Jean Aurenche (who had signed the

script) answered, "*Perhaps, in ten years, a scenarist will be able to retain a character who dies midway through the film but, as for me, I don't feel capable of it.*" Three years later, Robert Bresson retained Doctor Delbende and allowed him to die in the middle of the film.

4 Aurenche and Bost never said they were "faithful." This was the critics.

5 *La Blé En Herbe.* There was an adaptation of Colette's novel as early as 1946. Claude Autant-Lara accused Roger Leenhardt of having plagiarized Colette's *Le Blé En Herbe* with his *Les Dernières Vacances.* The arbitration of Maurice Garcon went against Claude Autant-Lara. With Aurenche and Bost the intrigue imagined by Colette was enriched by a new character, that of Dick, a lesbian who lived with the "White Lady." This character was suppressed, several weeks before the film was shot, by Madame Ghislaine Auboin, who "reviewed" the adaptation with Claude Autant-Lara.

6 The characters of Aurenche and Bost speak, at will, in maxims. Several examples: *La Symphonie Pastorale*: "Ah! It would be better if children like that were never born." "Not everyone has the luck to be blind." "A cripple is someone who pretends to be like everyone else."

Le Diable Au Corps (a soldier has lost a leg): "He is perhaps the last of the wounded." "That makes a fine leg for him."

Jeux Interdits: François: "What does this mean – 'to put the cart before the horse?'" Berthe: "Oh, it's what we're doing." (They are making love.) François: "I didn't know that's what it was called."

7 Jean Aurenche was on the crew of *Les Dames Du Bois De Boulogne*, but he had to leave Bresson because of incompatibility of inspiration.

8 An extract from the dialogue Aurenche and Bost wrote for *Jeanne D'Arc* was published in *La Revue Du Cinéma*, #8, page 9.

9 In fact, "psychological realism" was created parallel to "poetic realism," which had the tandem Spaak-Feyder. It really will be necessary, one day, to start an ultimate quarrel with Feyder, before he has dropped definitively into oblivion.

2

De la Politique des Auteurs

André Bazin

André Bazin was one of the founding editors of *Cahiers du Cinéma* along with Jacques Doniol-Valcroze and Lo Duca. He was an influential voice in French film culture and a major film theorist, approaching realism from the perspective of style in relation to space and time rather than in mimetic terms. As such, he became a champion of Italian neorealism. After his death in 1958, a four-volume collection of his writings was published entitled *Qu'est-ce que le cinéma?* (*What is Cinema?*). Two of these volumes were translated into English and have been required reading in film studies courses since their publication more than 30 years ago. In this essay, originally published in 1957 when he was editor of *Cahiers*, Bazin addressed "la politique des auteurs", the auteurist polemic, of his "young firebrands." Bringing his typical acumen to weigh the pros and cons of auteurism, Bazin seeks to rein in the excessive claims of his junior colleagues by pointing out that individuals transcend society, but society is also internalized within each of us, so that any auteurist analysis must necessarily take into account relevant social forces and technical circumstances. As well, Bazin cautions against ignoring the context of genre and studio production ("the genius of the system") in considering Hollywood directors as auteurs.

Goethe? Shakespeare? Everything they put their name to is supposed to be good, and people rack their brains to find beauty in the silliest little thing they bungled. All great talents, like Goethe, Shakespeare, Beethoven, Michelangelo, created not only beautiful works, but things that were less than mediocre, quite simply awful.

(*Tolstoy*, Diary 1895–99)

I realize my task is fraught with difficulties. *Cahiers du Cinéma* is thought to practise the *politique des auteurs*. This opinion may perhaps not be justified by the entire output of articles, but it has been true of the majority, especially for the last two years. It would be useless and hypocritical to point to a few scraps of evidence to the contrary, and claim that our magazine is a harmless collection of wishywashy reviews.

Nevertheless, our readers must have noticed that this critical standpoint – whether implicit or explicit – has not been adopted with equal enthusiasm by all the regular contributors to *Cahiers*, and that there might exist serious differences in our admiration, or rather in the degree of our admiration. And yet the truth is that the most enthusiastic among us nearly always win the day. Eric Rohmer put his finger on the reason in his reply to a reader in *Cahiers* 63: when

André Bazin, "*De la politique des auteurs*," pp. 137–55 from Peter Graham (ed.), *The New Wave* (London: BFI/New York: Doubleday, 1968). © 1968 by Peter Graham. Reprinted by permission of BFI Publishing.

opinions differ on an important film, we generally prefer to let the person who likes it most write about it.[1] It follows that the strictest adherents of the *politique des auteurs* get the best of it in the end, for, rightly or wrongly, they always see in their favourite directors the manifestation of the same specific qualities. So it is that Hitchcock, Renoir, Rossellini, Lang, Hawks, or Nicholas Ray, to judge from the pages of *Cahiers*, appear as almost infallible directors who could never make a bad film.

I would like to avoid a misunderstanding from the start. I beg to differ with those of my colleagues who are the most firmly convinced that the *politique des auteurs* is well founded, but this in no way compromises the general policy of the magazine. Whatever our differences of opinion about films or directors, our common likes and dislikes are numerous enough and strong enough to bind us together; and although I do not see the role of the *auteur* in the cinema in the same way as François Truffaut or Eric Rohmer for example, it does not stop me believing to a certain extent in the concept of the *auteur* and very often sharing their opinions, although not always their passionate loves. I fall in with them more reluctantly in the case of their hostile reactions; often they are very harsh with films I find defensible – and I do so precisely because I find that the work transcends the director (they dispute this phenomenon, which they consider to be a critical contradiction). In other words, almost our only difference concerns the relationship between the work and its creator. I have never been sorry that one of my colleagues has stuck up for such and such director, although I have not always agreed about the qualities of the film under examination. Finally, I would like to add that although it seems to me that the *politique des auteurs* has led its supporters to make a number of mistakes, its total results have been fertile enough to justify them in the face of their critics. It is very rare that the arguments drawn upon to attack them do not make me rush to their defence.

So it is within these limits, which, if you like, are those of a family quarrel, that I would like to tackle what seems to me to represent not so much a critical mistranslation as a critical 'false nuance of meaning'. My point of departure is an article by my friend Jean Domarchi on Vincente Minnelli's *Lust for Life*,[2] which tells the story of Van Gogh. His praise was very intelligent and sober, but it struck me that such an article should not have been published in a review which, only one month previously, had allowed Eric Rohmer to demolish John Huston.[3] The relentless harshness of the latter, and the indulgent admiration of the former, can only be explained by the fact that Minnelli is one of Domarchi's favourites and that Huston is not a *Cahiers auteur*. This partiality is a good thing, up to a certain point, as it leads us to stick up for a film that illustrates certain facets of American culture just as much as the personal talent of Vincente Minnelli. I could get Domarchi caught up in a contradiction, by pointing out to him that he ought to have sacrificed Minnelli in favour of Renoir, since it was the shooting of *Lust for Life* that forced the director of *French Cancan* to give up his own project on Van Gogh. Can Domarchi claim that a *Van Gogh* by Renoir would not have brought more prestige to the *politique des auteurs* than a film by Minnelli? What was needed was a painter's son, and what we got was a director of filmed ballets!

But whatever the case, this example is only a pretext. Many a time I have felt uneasy at the subtlety of an argument, which was completely unable to camouflage the naïveté of the assumption whereby, for example, the intentions and the coherence of a deliberate and well thought out film are read into some little 'B' feature.

And of course as soon as you state that the filmmaker and his films are one, there can be no minor films, as the worst of them will always be in the image of their creator. But let's see what the facts of the matter are. In order to do so, we must go right back to the beginning.

Of course, the *politique des auteurs* is the application to the cinema of a notion that is widely accepted in the individual arts. François Truffaut likes to quote Giraudoux's remark: 'There are no works, there are only *auteurs*' – a polemical sally which seems to me of limited significance. The opposite statement could just as well be set as an exam question. The two formulae, like the maxims of La Rochefoucauld and Chamfort, would simply reverse their proportion of truth and error. As for Eric Rohmer, he states (or rather asserts) that in art it is the *auteurs*, and not the works, that remain; and the programmes of film societies would seem to support this critical truth.

But one should note that Rohmer's argument does not go nearly as far as Giraudoux's aphorism, for, if

Figure 2.1 *Lust for Life* (MGM, 1956), by Vincente Minnelli, "a director of filmed ballets." Produced by John Houseman

auteurs remain, it is not necessarily because of their production as a whole. There is no lack of examples to prove that the contrary is true. Maybe Voltaire's name is more important than his bibliography, but now that he has been put in perspective it is not so much his *Dictionnaire philosophique* that counts nowadays as his Voltairean wit, a certain *style* of thinking and writing. But today where are we to find the principle and the example? In his abundant and atrocious writings for the theatre? Or in the slim volume of short stories? And what about Beaumarchais? Are we to go looking in *La Mère coupable*?

In any case, the authors of that period were apparently themselves aware of the relativity of their worth, since they willingly disowned their works, and sometimes did not mind even being the subject of lampoons whose quality they took as a compliment. For them, almost the only thing that mattered was the work itself, whether their own or another's, and it was only at the end of the eighteenth century, with Beaumarchais in fact, that the concept of the *auteur* finally crystallized legally, with his royalties, duties and responsibilities. Of course I am making allowances for historical and social contingencies; political and moral censorship has made anonymity sometimes inevitable and always excusable. But surely the anonymity of the writings of the French Resistance in no way lessened the dignity or responsibility of the writer. It was only in the nineteenth century that copying or plagiarism really began to be considered a professional breach that disqualified its perpetrator.

The same is true of painting. Although nowadays any old splash of paint can be valued according to its measurements and the celebrity of the signature, the objective quality of the work itself was formerly held in much higher esteem. Proof of this is to be found in the difficulty there is in authenticating a lot of old pictures. What emerged from a studio might simply be the work of a pupil, and we are now unable to *prove* anything one way or the other. If one goes back even further, one has to take into consideration the anonymous works that have come down to us as the products not of an artist, but of an art, not of a man, but of a society.

I can see how I will be rebutted. We should not objectify our ignorance or let it crystallize into a reality. All these works of art, the Venus de Milo as well as the Negro mask, did in fact have an *auteur*; and the whole of modern historical science is tending to fill in the gaps and give names to these works of art. But did one really have to wait for such erudite addenda before being able to admire and enjoy them? Biographical criticism is but one of many possible critical dimensions – people are still arguing about the identity of Shakespeare or Molière.

But that's just the point! People *are* arguing. So their identity is not a matter of complete indifference. The evolution of Western art towards greater personalization should definitely be considered as a step forward, as a refinement of culture, but only as long as this individualization remains only a final perfection and does not claim to *define* culture. At this point, we should remember that irrefutable commonplace we learnt at school: the individual transcends society, but society is also and above all *within* him. So there can be no definitive criticism of genius or talent which does not first take into consideration the social determinism, the historical combination of circumstances, and the technical background which to a large extent determine it. That is why the anonymity of a work of art is a handicap that impinges only very slightly on our understanding of it. In any case, much depends on the particular branch of art in question, the style adopted, and the sociological context. Negro art does not suffer by remaining anonymous – although of course it is unfortunate that we know so little about the societies that gave birth to it.

But *The Man Who Knew Too Much*, *Europa 51*, and *Bigger Than Life* are contemporary with the paintings of Picasso, Matisse, and Singier! Does it follow that one should see in them the same degree of individualization? I for one do not think so.

If you will excuse yet another commonplace, the cinema is an art which is both popular and industrial. These conditions, which are necessary to its existence, in no way constitute a collection of hindrances – no more than in architecture – they rather represent a group of positive and negative circumstances which have to be reckoned with. And this is especially true of the American cinema, which the theoreticians of the *politique des auteurs* admire so much. What makes Hollywood so much better than anything else in the world is not only the quality of certain directors, but also the vitality and, in a certain sense, the excellence of a tradition. Hollywood's superiority is only incidentally technical; it lies much more in what one might call the American cinematic genius, something which should be analysed, then defined, by a sociological approach to its production. The American cinema has been able, in an extraordinarily competent way, to show American society just as it wanted to see itself; but not at all passively, as a simple act of satisfaction and escape, but dynamically, i.e. by participating with the means at its disposal in the building of this society. What is so admirable in the American cinema is that it cannot help being spontaneous. Although the fruit of free enterprise and capitalism – and harbouring their active or still only virtual defects – it is in a way the truest and most realistic cinema of all because it does not shrink from depicting even the contradictions of that society. Domarchi himself, who has demonstrated the point very clearly in a penetrating and well-documented analysis,[4] exempts me from developing this argument.

But it follows that every director is swept along by this powerful surge; naturally his artistic course has to be plotted according to the currents – it is not as if he were sailing as his fancy took him on the calm waters of a lake.

In fact it is not even true of the most individual artistic disciplines that genius is free and always self-dependent. And what is genius anyway if not a certain combination of unquestionably personal talents, a gift from the fairies, and a moment in history? Genius is an H-bomb. The fission of uranium triggers off the fusion of hydrogen pulp. But a sun cannot be born from the disintegration of an individual alone unless this disintegration has repercussions on the art that surrounds it. Whence the paradox of Rimbaud's life. His poetic flash in the pan suddenly died out and a Rimbaud the adventurer became more and more distant like a star, still glowing but heading towards extinction. Probably Rimbaud did not change at all. There was simply nothing left to feed the flames that had reduced the whole of literature to ashes. Generally, the rhythm of this combustion in the cycles of great art is usually greater than the lifespan of a man. Literature's step is measured in centuries. It will be said that genius foreshadows that which comes after it. This is true, but only dialectically. For one could also say that every age has the geniuses it needs in order to define, repudiate and transcend itself. Consequently, Voltaire was a horrible playwright when he thought he was Racine's successor and a story-teller of genius when he made the parable a vehicle for the ideas which were going to shatter the eighteenth century.

And even without having to use as examples the utter failures which had their causes almost entirely in the sociology of art, creative psychology alone could easily account for a lot of patchiness even in the best authors. *Notre-Dame-de-Paris* is pretty slight compared with *La Légende des siècles, Salammbô* does not come up to *Madame Bovary,* or *Corydon* to *Le Journal des faux-monnayeurs.* There is no point in quibbling about these examples, there will always be others to suit everyone's taste. Surely one can accept the permanence of talent without confusing it with some kind of artistic infallibility or immunity against making mistakes, which could only be divine attributes. But God, as Sartre has already pointed out, is not an artist! Were one to attribute to creative man, in the face of all psychological probability, an unflagging richness of inspiration, one would have to admit that this inspiration always comes up against a whole complex of particular circumstances which make the result, in the cinema, a thousand times more chancy than in painting or in literature.

Inversely, there is no reason why there should not exist – and sometimes there do – flashes in the pan in the work of otherwise mediocre film-makers. Results of a fortunate combination of circumstances in which there is a precarious moment of balance between talent and milieu, these fleeting brilliancies do not prove all that much about personal creative qualities; they are not, however, intrinsically inferior to others – and probably would not seem so if the critics had not begun by reading the signature at the bottom of the painting.

Well, what is true of literature is even truer of the cinema, to the extent that this art, the last to come on to the scene, accelerates and multiplies the evolutionary factors that are common to all the others. In fifty years the cinema, which started with the crudest forms of spectacle (primitive but not inferior), has had to cover the same ground as the play or the novel and is often on the same level as they are. Within this same period, its technical development has been of a kind that cannot compare with that of any traditional art within a comparable period (except perhaps architecture, another industrial art). Under such conditions, it is hardly surprising that the genius will burn himself out ten times as fast, and that a director who suffers no loss of ability may cease to be swept along by the wave. This was the case with Stroheim, Abel Gance and Orson Welles. We are now beginning to see things in enough perspective to notice a curious phenomenon: a film-maker can, within his own lifetime, be refloated by the following wave. This is true of Abel Gance or Stroheim, whose modernity is all the more apparent nowadays. I am fully aware that this only goes to prove their quality of *auteur,* but their eclipse still cannot be entirely explained away by the contradictions of capitalism or the stupidity of producers. If one keeps a sense of proportion, one sees that the same thing has happened to men of genius in the cinema as would have happened to a 120-year-old Racine writing Racinian plays in the middle of the eighteenth century. Would his tragedies have been better than Voltaire's? The answer is by no means clear-cut; but I bet they would not have been.

One can justifiably point to Chaplin, Renoir or Clair. But each of them was endowed with further gifts that have little to do with genius and which were precisely the ones that enabled them to adapt themselves to the predicament of film production. Of course, the case of Chaplin was unique since, as both *auteur* and producer, he has been able to be both the cinema and its evolution.

It follows, then, according to the most basic laws of the psychology of creation, that, as the objective factors of genius are much more likely to modify themselves in the cinema than in any other art, a rapid maladjustment between the film-maker and the cinema can occur, and this can abruptly affect the quality of his films as a result. Of course I admire *Confidential Report*, and I can see the same qualities in it as I see in *Citizen Kane.* But *Citizen Kane* opened up a new era of American cinema, and *Confidential Report* is a film of only secondary importance.

Figure 2.2 Deep focus cinematography by Gregg Toland in *Citizen Kane* (RKO, 1941). Produced, directed, and co-written by Orson Welles

But let's pause a moment on this assertion – it may, I feel, allow us to get to the heart of the matter. I think that not only would the supporters of the *politique des auteurs* refuse to agree that *Confidential Report* is an inferior film to *Citizen Kane*;[5] they would be more eager to claim the contrary, and I can well see how they would go about it. As *Confidential Report* is Welles's sixth film, one can assume that a certain amount of progress has already been made. Not only did the Welles of 1953 have more experience of himself and of his art than in 1941, but however great was the freedom he was able to obtain in Hollywood *Citizen Kane* cannot help remaining to a certain extent an RKO product. The film would never have seen the light of day without the co-operation of some superb technicians and their just as admirable technical apparatus. Gregg Toland, to mention only one, was more than a little responsible for the final result. On the other hand, *Confidential Report* is completely the work of Welles. Until it can be proved to the contrary, it will be considered *a priori* a superior film because it is more personal and because Welles's personality can only have matured as he grew older.

As far as this question is concerned, I can only agree with my young firebrands when they state that age as such cannot diminish the talent of a film-maker, and react violently to that critical prejudice which consists in always finding the works of a young or mature film-maker superior to the films of an old man. It has been said that *Monsieur Verdoux* was not up to *The Gold Rush*; people have criticized *The River* and *Carrosse d'or*, saying they miss the good old days of *La Règle du jeu*. Eric Rohmer has found an excellent answer to this: 'The history of art offers no example, as far as I know, of an authentic genius who has gone through a period of true decline at the end of his career; this should encourage us rather to detect, beneath what seems to be clumsy or bald, the traces of that desire for simplicity that characterizes the "last manner" of painters such as Titian, Rembrandt, Matisse or Bonnard, composers such as Beethoven and Stravinsky . . .' (*Cahiers* 8, 'Renoir Américain'). What kind of absurd discrimination has decided that film-makers alone are victims of a senility that other artists are protected from? There do remain the exceptional cases of dotage, but they are much rarer than is sometimes supposed. When Baudelaire was paralysed and unable to utter anything other than his 'cré nom', was he any less Baudelairean? Robert Mallet tells us how Valéry Larbaud, Joyce's translator into French, struggling against paralysis after twenty years of immobility and silence, had managed to build up for himself a vocabulary of twenty simple words. With these, he was still able to bring out some extraordinarily shrewd literary judgments. In fact, the few exceptions one could mention only go to prove the rule. A great talent matures but does not grow old. There is no reason why this law of artistic psychology should not also be valid for the cinema. Criticism that is based implicitly on the hypothesis of senility cannot hold water. It is rather the opposite postulate that ought to be stated: we should say that when we think we can discern a decline it is our own critical sense that is at fault, since an impoverishment of inspiration is a very unlikely phenomenon. From this point of view, the bias of the *politique des auteurs* is very fruitful, and I will stick up for them against the naïveté, the foolishness even, of the prejudices they are fighting.

But, always remembering this, one has nevertheless to accept that certain indisputable 'greats' have suffered an eclipse or a loss of their powers. I think what I have already said in this article may point to the reason for this. The drama does not reside in the growing old of men but in that of the cinema: those who do not know how to grow old *with* it will be overtaken by its evolution. This is why it has been possible for there to have been a series of failures leading to complete catastrophe without it being necessary to suppose that the genius of yesterday has become an imbecile. Once again, it is simply a question of the appearance of a clash between the subjective inspiration of the creator and the objective situation of the cinema, and this is what the *politique des auteurs* refuses to see. To its supporters *Confidential Report* is a more important film than *Citizen Kane* because they justifiably see more of Orson Welles in it. In other words, all they want to retain in the equation *auteur* plus *subject* = *work* is the *auteur*, while the subject is reduced to zero. Some of them will pretend to grant me that, all things being equal as far as the *auteur* is concerned, a good subject is naturally better than a bad one, but the more outspoken and foolhardy among them will admit that it very much looks as if they prefer small 'B' films, where the banality of the scenario leaves more room for the personal contribution of the author.

Of course I will be challenged on the very concept of *auteur*. I admit that the equation I just used was artificial, just as much so, in fact, as the distinction one learnt at school between form and content. To benefit from the *politique des auteurs* one first has to be worthy of it, and as it happens this school of criticism claims to distinguish between true *auteurs* and directors, even talented ones: Nicholas Ray is an *auteur*, Huston is supposed to be only a director; Bresson and Rossellini are *auteurs*, Clément is only a great director, and so on. So this conception of the author is not compatible with the *auteur*/subject distinction, because it is of greater importance to find out if a director is worthy of entering the select group of *auteurs* than it is to judge how well he has used his material. To a certain extent at least, the *auteur* is a subject to himself; whatever the scenario, he always tells the same story, or, in case the word 'story' is confusing, let's say he has the same attitude and passes the same moral judgments on the action and on the characters. Jacques Rivette has said that an *auteur* is someone who speaks in the first person. It's a good definition; let's adopt it.

The *politique des auteurs* consists, in short, of choosing the personal factor in artistic creation as a standard of reference, and then assuming that it continues and even progresses from one film to the next. It is recognized that there do exist certain important films of quality that escape this test, but these will systematically be considered inferior to those in which the personal stamp of the *auteur*, however run-of-the-mill the scenario, can be perceived even minutely.

It is far from being my intention to deny the positive attitude and methodological qualities of this bias. First of all, it has the great merit of treating the cinema as an adult art and of reacting against the impressionistic relativism that still reigns over the majority of film reviews. I admit that the explicit or admitted pretension of a critic to reconsider the production of a film-maker with every new film in the light of his judgment has something presumptuous about it that recalls Ubu. I am also quite willing to admit that if one is human one cannot help doing this, and, short of giving up the whole idea of actually criticizing, one might as well take as a starting point the feelings, pleasant or unpleasant, one feels personally when in contact with a film. Okay, but only on condition that these first impressions are kept in their proper place. We have to take them into consideration, but we should not use them as a basis. In other words, every critical act should consist of referring the film in question to a scale of values, but this reference is not merely a matter of intelligence; the sureness of one's judgment arises also, or perhaps even first of all (in the chronological sense of the word), from a general impression experienced during a film. I feel there are two symmetrical heresies, which are (*a*) objectively applying to a film a critical all-purpose yardstick, and (*b*) considering it sufficient simply to state one's pleasure or disgust. The first denies the role of taste, the second presupposes the superiority of the critic's taste over that of the author. Coldness . . . or presumption!

What I like about the *politique des auteurs* is that it reacts against the impressionist approach while retaining the best of it. In fact the scale of values it proposes is not ideological. Its starting-point is an appreciation largely composed of taste and sensibility: it has to discern the contribution of the artist as such, quite apart from the qualities of the subject or the technique: i.e. the man behind the style. But once one has made this distinction, this kind of criticism is doomed to beg the question, for it assumes at the start of its analysis that the film is automatically good as it has been made by an *auteur*. And so the yardstick applied to the film is the aesthetic portrait of the film-maker deduced from his previous films. This is all right so long as there has been no mistake about promoting this film-maker to the status of *auteur*. For it is objectively speaking safer to trust in the genius of the artist than in one's own critical intelligence. And this is where the *politique des auteurs* falls in line with the system of 'criticism by beauty'; in other words, when one is dealing with a genius, it is always a good method to presuppose that a supposed weakness in a work of art is nothing other than a beauty that one has not yet managed to understand. But as I have shown, this method had its limitations even in traditionally individualistic arts such as literature, and all the more so in the cinema where the sociological and historical cross-currents are countless. By giving such importance to 'B' films, the *politique des auteurs* recognizes and confirms this dependence *a contrario*.

Another point is that as the criteria of the *politique des auteurs* are very difficult to formulate the whole thing becomes highly hazardous. It is significant that our finest writers on *Cahiers* have been practising it for three or four years now and have yet to produce the main corpus of its theory. Nor is one particularly likely to forget how Rivette suggested we should admire Hawks: 'The evidence on the screen is proof of Hawks's genius: you only have to watch *Monkey Business* to know that it is a brilliant film. Some people refuse to admit this, however; they refuse to be satisfied by proof. There can't be any other reason why they don't recognize it . . .'[6] You can see the danger: an aesthetic personality cult.

But that is not the main point, at least to the extent that the *politique des auteurs* is practised by people of taste who know how to watch their step. It is its negative side that seems the most serious to me. It is unfortunate to praise a film that in no way deserves it, but the dangers are less far-reaching than when a worthwhile film is rejected because its director has made nothing good up to that point. I am not denying that the champions of the *politique des auteurs* discover or encourage a budding talent when they get the chance. But they do systematically look down on anything in a film that comes from a common fund and which can sometimes be entirely admirable, just as it can be utterly detestable. Thus, a certain kind of popular American culture lies at the basis of Minnelli's *Lust for Life*, but another more spontaneous kind of culture is also the principle of American comedy, the Western, and the gangster film. And its influence here is beneficial, for it is this that gives these cinematic genres their vigour and richness, resulting as they do from an artistic evolution that has always been in wonderfully close harmony with its public. And so one can read a review in *Cahiers* of a Western by Anthony Mann (and God knows I like Anthony Mann's Westerns!)[7] as if it were not above all a Western, i.e. a whole collection of conventions in the script, the acting, and the direction. I know very well that in a film magazine one may be permitted to skip such mundane details; but they should at least be implied, whereas what in fact happens is that their existence is glossed over rather sheepishly, as though they were a rather ridiculous necessity that it would be incongru-

Figure 2.3 Howard Hawks's *Monkey Business* (Twentieth Century Fox, 1952): Authorship as self-evident genius. Produced by Sol C. Siegel

ous to mention. In any case, they will look down on, or treat condescendingly, any Western by a director who is not yet approved, even if it is as round and smooth as an egg. Well, what is *Stagecoach* if not an ultra-classical Western in which the art of Ford consists simply of raising characters and situations to an absolute degree of perfection;[8] and while sitting on the Censorship Committee I have seen some admirable Westerns, more or less anonymous and off the beaten track, but displaying a wonderful knowledge of the conventions of the genre and respecting the style from beginning to end.

Paradoxically, the supporters of the *politique des auteurs* admire the American cinema, where the restrictions of production are heavier than anywhere else. It is also true that it is the country where the greatest technical possibilities are offered to the director. But the one does not cancel out the other. I do however admit that freedom is greater in Hollywood than it is said to be, as long as one knows how to detect its manifestations, and I will go so far as to say that the tradition of genres is a base of operations for creative freedom. The American cinema is a classical art, but why not then admire in it what is most admirable, i.e. not only the talent of this or that film-maker, but the genius of the system, the richness of its ever-vigorous tradition, and its fertility when it comes into contact with new elements – as has been proved, if proof there need be, in such films as *An American in Paris, The Seven Year Itch* and *Bus Stop*. True, Logan is lucky enough to be considered an *auteur,* or at least a budding *auteur.* But then when *Picnic* or *Bus Stop* get good reviews the praise does not go to what seems to me to be the essential point, i.e. the social truth, which of course is not offered as a goal that suffices in itself but is integrated into a style of cinematic narration just as pre-war America was integrated into American comedy.

To conclude: the *politique des auteurs* seems to me to hold and defend an essential critical truth that the cinema needs more than the other arts, precisely because an act of true artistic creation is more uncertain and vulnerable in the cinema than elsewhere. But its exclusive practice leads to another danger: the negation of the film to the benefit of praise of its *auteur*. I have tried to show why mediocre *auteurs* can, by accident, make admirable films, and how, conversely, a genius can fall victim to an equally accidental sterility. I feel that this useful and fruitful approach, quite apart from its polemical value, should be complemented by other approaches to the cinematic phenomenon which will restore to a film its quality as a work of art. This does not mean one has to deny the role of the *auteur*, but simply give him back the preposition without which the noun *auteur* remains but a halting concept. *Auteur*, yes, but what *of*?

Translated by Peter Graham

Notes

1 Eric Rohmer, 'Les Lecteurs des *Cahiers* et la politique des auteurs', *Cahiers* 63, October 1956, pp. 54–8.

2 Jean Domarchi, 'Monsieur Vincent', *Cahiers* 68, February 1957, pp. 44–6.

3 Eric Rohmer, 'Leçon d'un échec: à propos de *Moby Dick*', *Cahiers* 67, January 1957, pp. 23–8.

4 Jean Domarchi, 'Le Fer dans la plaie', *Cahiers* 63, October 1956, pp. 18–28.

5 Cf. Eric Rohmer, 'Une Fable du XXe siècle' (on *Confidential Report*), *Cahiers* 61, July 1956, pp. 37–40; cf. *Cahiers'* 'All-Time Best Films', in Appendix 1 in Jim Hillier (ed.), *Cahiers du Cinema: The 1950s – Neo-Realism, Hollywood, New Wave* (London: Routledge, 1985).

6 Jacques Rivette, 'Génie de Howard Hawks', *Cahiers* 23, May 1953, pp. 16–23.

7 Cf. André Bazin, 'Beauté d'un western' (on Mann's *The Man from Laramie*), *Cahiers* 55, January 1956, pp. 33–6.

8 Cf. André Bazin, 'Evolution du Western', *Cahiers* 54, Christmas 1955, pp. 22–6, translated as 'Evolution of the Western' in André Bazin, *What is Cinema? Vol. 2*, reprinted in Bill Nichols (ed.), *Movies and Methods* (Berkeley: University of California Press, 1976–85).

3

Films, Directors and Critics

Ian Cameron

Ian Cameron was the founding editor of *Movie*, the brash British film journal that brought auteurism to England beginning in 1962. Cameron also co-authored several books on the cinema, including *Dames*, *The Heavies*, and *Antonioni* with Robin Wood. In this piece, published in *Movie*'s second issue, Cameron provides a spirited defense of auteurism and articulates clearly the critical assumptions underlying the magazine. He considers the question of the intentional fallacy in the context of auteur criticism, and in relation to Hollywood distinguishes *Movie*'s embrace of auteurism from the established views of *Sight and Sound*.

Why does the camera go up now? Because he's watching the sky.

This question and answer, printed in an interview with Vincente Minnelli from the first *Movie*, have excited more comment than anything else in the magazine. Derek Hill in *The Financial Times* found them so absurd that he used them to dismiss the whole of *Movie* as an expensive joke. I suspect that there were a number of causes behind Mr. Hill's mirth: the idea of asking such questions on minute detail to a director would have seemed pointless to him, particularly when the answer was so simple that he probably took it at once to explode the grandiose theories which the foolish young critics were doubtless hatching about the director's intentions and to stamp him as ambitionless or simple.

Had we found Minnelli's answers stupid, we would obviously not have printed them in *Movie*. And if they were in flat contradiction to our theories about his work, we would certainly have hesitated to use them without comment. Where we differ from Mr. Hill, then, is in our attitude to directors. Apparently our assumptions are still sufficiently strange to need explanation. In aiming to fill that need here, I do not want to say anything particularly new or to provide a defence of our views. Our only defence is that our approach seems to work when actually applied to films. Before starting to recapitulate our assumptions, though, I would like to say a little more about the Minnelli business.

In *The Four Horsemen of the Apocalypse*, the shot in question occurs just after the death of Lee J. Cobb. Shattered by the discovery that one of his grandsons is a Nazi, he has rushed out into the garden, haunted by the destructive vision of the Four Horsemen. As he collapses to the ground and dies of a heart attack, another grandson (Glenn Ford) rushes out to him, kneels down on the ground and cradles the body in his arms. As he looks up at the sky, sobbing, and sees the vision of the horsemen, the camera cranes up and moves in. Our question and its answer may look a little less rudimentary if one bothers to think of other reasons why the camera might have craned up. Thus: (1) Emotional: the camera moves up to leave him cowering

Ian Cameron, "Films, Directors and Critics," pp. 4–7 from *Movie* 2 (1962). © 1962.

Figure 3.1 Mise-en-scène in Vincente Minnelli's *The Four Horsemen of the Apocalypse* (MGM, 1962). Produced by Julian Blaustein

before the vision. (2) Symbolic: the camera looks down on him in judgment because he feels himself (or the director feels him) responsible in some way for the old man's death. (3) As a way of linking the shot to its successor, which shows the Horsemen in the sky. (4) As orchestration, taking up the bravura of the camera movements which have preceded it. That Minnelli cranes up simply because of the movement of his actor is indicative of his whole method (and confirms what was said elsewhere in the magazine). The camera moves so that we can see Ford's face as clearly as possible. The reason is neither inevitable nor foolish.

The motive for interviewing directors at all is to see how far their ideas of their aims square with the critics' rationalisations from the films. When the director disagrees with the critics this does not mean that the critics are wrong, for, after all, the value of a film depends on the film itself, and not on the director's intentions, which may not be apparent from the finished work.

For talking about one small section of a film in great detail, whether in an interview or in an article, we have been accused of fascination with technical *trouvailles* at the expense of meaning. The alternative which we find elsewhere is a *gestalt* approach which tries to present an overall picture of the film without going into "unnecessary" detail, and usually results in giving almost no impression of what the film was actually like for the spectator.

The film critic's raw materials – apart from his own intelligence – are his observations in the cinema: what he sees, hears and feels. By building up our theses about films from these observations, we are going through the same processes as the audience although, of course, our reactions are conscious whereas those induced in the cinema, particularly at the first viewing of a film, tend to be reached unconsciously. We believe that our method is likely to produce criticism which is closer, not just to objective description of the film itself but to the spectator's experience of the film.

The assumption which underlies all the writing in *Movie* is that the director is the author of a film, the person who gives it any distinctive quality it may have. There are quite large exceptions, with which I shall deal later. On the whole we accept this cinema of directors, although without going to the farthest-out extremes of *la politique des auteurs* which makes it difficult to think of a bad director making a good film and almost impossible to think of a good director making a bad one. One's aesthetic must be sufficiently flexible to cope with the fact that Joseph Pevney, having made dozens of stinkers, can suddenly come up with an admirable western in *The Plunderers*, or that Minnelli, after years of doing wonders often with unpromising material, could produce anything as flat-footed as *The Bells Are Ringing*.

Everyone accepts the cinema of directors for France, Italy, Japan, India, Argentina, Sweden and Poland – everywhere, in fact, that the Art is easily identifiable. Critics will talk happily about a Bergman film, or a Mizoguchi film, or even a Carol Reed film. It is only over American movies that the trouble starts, and reviews are likely to end with a desultory "George Cukor directed efficiently." The reasons are easy enough to find. Hollywood pictures are not so much custom-built as manufactured. The responsibility for them is shared, and the final quality is no more the fault of the director than of such parties as the producer, the set designer, the cameraman or the hairdresser. Only by a happy accident can anything good escape from this industrial complex. The good American film comes to be regarded as the cinematic equivalent of a mutant.

Now there are qualities superimposed on most big studio films (these days there are very few of them indeed) that depend not on the director but on the studio: the look of colour films is particularly prone to this sort of control. An extreme example is Fox films in the late forties and early fifties which are almost immediately identifiable by their photography and music, particularly if these are by the leading exponents – photographers Joseph la Shelle and Joe MacDonald and composers Leigh Harline and David Raksin. However, these qualities are rather peripheral, and one common accusation of this sort, that Gregg Toland effectively directed the films he photographed so remarkably, has been disposed of by Andrew Sarris in *Film Culture*: "Subtract Gregg Toland from Welles and you still have a mountain; subtract Toland from Wyler and you have a molehill."

The closer one looks at Hollywood films, the less they seem to be accidents. There is a correlation between the quality of the films and the names of their directors. When one notices that such masterpieces as *Scarface*, *Bringing Up Baby* and *Gentlemen Prefer Blondes* were all directed by the same man, one begins to wonder whether the merits of these otherwise dissimilar films might not be explained by this man's talent. On a slightly closer look, one finds that he was also responsible for such generally admired movies as *Twentieth Century*, *Sergeant York*, *Red River* and *Monkey Business*, not to mention *Rio Bravo*, a film which gained little attention on its release and is now accepted as a masterpiece, even by *Sight and Sound*, which greeted its appearance with a singular lack of enthusiasm.

Hawks is just beginning to be accepted in Britain and the US. Raoul Walsh, on the other hand, is virtually unknown. Yet if one looks at Walsh's films (or some of them – he has made 200 since he started directing in 1913), one can identify the same talent and highly sympathetic personality behind a British cheapie of 1937, *Jump for Glory*, a 1945 racecourse movie, *Salty O'Rourke*, and more recent works like *Blackbeard the Pirate* (1952), *The Lawless Breed* (1952), *Battle Cry* (1955), *Esther and the King* (1960) and *Marines, Let's Go* (1961). The similarity of these movies made in three different countries over a period of 25 years by a director whose name does not spell prestige, who will thus not have an exceptional degree of freedom, should leave no doubt that, provided he has any talent, it is the director, rather than anyone else, who determines what finally appears on the screen.

Part of the neglect of American directors comes from the simple fact that it is easier to accept foreign films as Art: a status word to indicate that the film is worth the critic's serious attention. In foreign language movies, one of the biggest obstacles has been limited: the dialogue. Even if they are bad, subtitles provide a shock-absorber between the dialogue and the audience. Everyone knows that laughable subtitles do not necessarily indicate defects in the original language. But two lines of ill-written dialogue in an American picture will put the critics on their guard. Almost invariably it is duff dialogue that alienates them, not unconvincing motivation, or false movements of actors or pointless camerawork. A recent victim is *The Four Horsemen*, which did have rather more than a couple of bad lines.

When a *Sight and Sound* critic does manage to work up some enthusiasm for an American film, it is usually self-limiting: "very good . . . of its kind." So we are treated to dimly remembered sections of John Russell Taylor's childhood erotic fantasies about Maria Montez and Veronica Lake as a picture of the Forties. Reviews of American films tend to link them together in remarkably ill-assorted pairs. One would be amazed at the current review of *The Man Who Shot Liberty Valance* and *Guns in the Afternoon* (both "so consciously old-fashioned and nostalgic that, appearing in 1962, they seem almost esoteric") if one had not already been treated to such unlikely joint reviews as *Exodus* plus *The Guns of Navarone* and *Psycho* plus *The Apartment.* If the writers of these pieces were literary critics, which, barring a certain illiteracy, they very nearly are, one imagines that they would happily review *Tender Is the Night, Miss Lonelihearts* and *Manhattan Transfer* together entirely in terms of American *mal-de-siècle* in the twenties. Any other qualities would be written off in a well-chosen sentence: "Mr. Dos Passos's narrative technique of intertwining a number of almost unconnected stories does not make for easy comprehension." *Sight and Sound* has just produced the most accurate piece of unconscious self-criticism in its most recent and most desperate attempt to be hip: a column in which the glad hand of John Russell Taylor is hidden behind the name of Arkadin. "Why," he opens brightly, "don't we take horror films more seriously? Well, not seriously seriously . . ."

The worst sufferer from restricted admiration has been Hitchcock. *Psycho* was passed over as one big laugh. As a joke it could not possibly be anything else. *Psycho*'s joke-content is very large, but that doesn't mean it is only joke. Example: the scene of Janet Leigh and Anthony Perkins getting acquainted is both an ingeniously extended *double entendre* on stuffing birds and a very real and touching picture of two people, isolated from others by their actions, voluntary or otherwise, trying to talk to each other.

The great weakness of *la politique des auteurs* is its rigidity: its adherents tend to be, as they say, totally committed to a cinema of directors. There are, however, quite a few films whose authors are not their directors. The various film versions of Paddy Chayefsky's works are all primarily Chayefsky movies rather than Delbert Mann, or John Cromwell or even Richard Brooks movies. Given a weak director the effective author of a film can be its photographer (Lucien Ballard, *Al Capone*), composer (Jerome Moross, *The Big Country*), producer (Arthur Freed, *Light in the Piazza*) or star (John Wayne, *The Comancheros*). None of those films was more than moderately good. Occasionally, though, something really remarkable can come from an efficient director with magnificent collaborators. Such a film was Michael Curtiz's *Casablanca*, which contained Humphrey Bogart, Ingrid Bergman, Paul Henreid, Claude Rains, Sidney Greenstreet, Conrad Veidt, Peter Lorre and Marcel Dalio, and was somehow missed from John Russell Taylor's knee-high panorama of the forties. More recently we have had *The Sins of Rachel Cade*, which, although directed by the excellent Gordon Douglas, was above all an Angie Dickinson movie, being entirely shaped by her personality and deriving all its power, which was considerable, from her performance.

Many films have also an iconographical interest, which is something quite apart from any aesthetic merits they may have. This interest comes from their relationship either to conditions external to their making (things as diverse as the discovery of the H bomb or current trends in automobile design, which influenced the design of the submarine in *Voyage to the Bottom of the Sea*) or to other films. Joseph Newman's *Spin of a Coin* (*The George Raft Story*) is fascinating because of its similarity to other period gangster movies: the sequences are built in the same way towards a climax of slaughter – only in this case the burst of gunfire is replaced by equally staccato laughter, for instance, as Al Capone (played by Neville Brand, who was Capone in Karlson's *The Scarface Mob*) tells Georgie (Ray Danton, whose performance is an extension of his previous *Legs Diamond* in Boetticher's film) how much he liked his performance as Capone in *Scarface*, the climatic scene of which has been reconstructed for us. This sort of kick is also available even more lavishly in Vincente Minnelli's amazing new *Two Weeks In Another Town*, where faded movie star Kirk Douglas sits in a viewing theatre watching a film he has previously made with the director for whom he is now working in the dubbing room. The film is *The Bad and the Beautiful*, which Minnelli made ten years ago with Douglas, as well as the same writer, producer and composer (Charles Schnee, John

Houseman and David Raksin). In another Joseph Newman movie, *The Big Bankroll* (*Arnold Rothstein, King of the Roaring Twenties*), it is assumed that the audience has seen the earlier movies which found it necessary to explain how bootlegging and protection worked. *The Big Bankroll* (in spite of 26 missing minutes in the British version one of the very best of its kind) builds on the knowledge it assumes to tell the story of Arnold Rothstein, who turned the mechanics of corruption to his own ends.

A few films are interesting for a related reason: the picture of their audience which they provide. The best example is Delmer Daves, who makes movies for stenographers and provides them with just what they wish to see. His pictures may be trivial, dishonest; immoral – Daves' movies have every fault in the book except bad production values – but they do provide a picture of the girl Daves is aiming his films at (very successfully, it seems). However irritating one may find Suzanne Pleshette in *Lovers Must Learn* (*Rome Adventure*), one has to admit that her performance is brilliantly pitched at just the right level of gush.

While one can appreciate films for their iconographical significance or as a critique of their audience, any merit they may have still comes from the director, much more than from any other source. Although finally our belief in the cinema of directors can only be justified though continuous application of our ideas in *Movie*, I want to conclude this article with an extended example of the part played by the director, based on three films, two of them well-liked, more or less, British offerings, J. Lee Thompson's *The Guns of Navarone* and David Lean's *Bridge on the River Kwai*, the third a much less respected American film, Don Siegel's *Hell Is for Heroes*.

All three contain the simple moral that war is futile and degrading; all three use one of the basic war film stories: the strategic action of considerable importance which devolves on a very few men. *Navarone* sets out with the obvious intention of telling a rattling good yarn about the way our chaps heroically battled against almost impossible obstacles to knock out the Jerry guns. Even this it almost fails to do by disastrously overplaying its suspense potential in a lengthy sequence of spurious thrills as the team crawl up a crumbling cardboard cliff so early in the movie that everyone will need to survive to justify their billing on the credits. However, its worst sin is stopping off at least twice in the course of the narrative for dialogue meditations on the nastiness of war, which the audience is meant to accept and which would in themselves be perfectly sympathetic, if slightly superfluous, in a film that refused to present war as enjoyable. But here their effect is completely vitiated by the rest of the action, and in context they seem almost hypocritical. I have a feeling that the failure is not inherent in the script but comes from the lack of any firm control in the direction. Even the one moment which could hardly help having some force, the shooting of Gia Scala as a collaborator, in the film has none. Here admittedly the script does side-step by letting Irene Papas, who is Greek and only a secondary character, forestall Peck and Niven in shooting her, when they are both more directly affected by the responsibility for her death. But even allowing for this, the lack of conviction is total.

Hell Is for Heroes is based on a story by Robert Pirosh which could easily have been turned into the sort of plug for the gallantry of the American fighting man which William Wellman made 13 years ago from a Pirosh story in *Battleground* (recently re-released with Anthony Mann's remarkable ex-3D western *The Naked Spur*). I am not concerned here with the central theme in the film which is embodied in the Steve McQueen character, the psychopath who makes an ideal soldier but goes to pieces outside the field of combat. Two sequences are particularly relevant to my purpose here as they could easily have degenerated to the same level as *Kwai* and *Navarone*. In the first, three soldiers set out at night on a manoeuvre to trick the enemy into thinking that they are sending out large patrols and therefore have the front well-manned. The idea is to take empty ammunition tins out into no-man's land, fill them with stones and rattle them by remote control from their position by means of lengths of telephone wire. The noise of these would be picked up by the enemy's ground microphones and all hell would be let loose to greet the ghost patrol. Siegel does not tell us what they are doing until their mission is almost completed. We take the episode seriously, which is right because it is serious and no less dangerous than a real patrol. If he had shown us beforehand exactly what they were doing, the episode would have been invested for us in the safety of our cinema seats with a feeling of fun, of fooling the enemy. Never once in the film do we get this feeling.

Figure 3.2 Steve McQueen in Don Siegel's *Hell Is for Heroes* (Paramount, 1962). Produced by Henry Blanke

The last sequence for once does sum up the whole film by its picture of the contribution an individual can make to the action. In serious trouble after leading an abortive attack on the crucial pillbox, which has resulted in the death of his two companions, McQueen takes it upon himself to put the pillbox out of action. He manages by a suicidal charge to get close enough to lob a satchel charge into the mouth of the box. Inevitably he is shot. Seeing the charge thrown out of the pillbox, he staggers forward, grabs it and rolls into the mouth of the box with it as it explodes. A flame-thrower is played on the mouth of the pillbox to make sure it is out of action. The last shot of the film is a longshot of a general advance beginning along the section of the front around the pillbox. The advance is obviously going to be very costly. The camera zooms into the mouth of the pillbox and the end title is superimposed. The zoom in from the general view to the detail emphasises the smallness of the gain from McQueen's death. One pillbox has been put out of action, and as the advance continues that pillbox ceases to have any significance. It is left behind a dead, almost abstract object. Unlike *Navarone*, there is no conflict between the intended content and the form which expresses it.

Contrast with the last shot of *Hell Is for Heroes* the end of *Bridge on the River Kwai*. James Donald stands surveying the wreckage after the destruction of the bridge. "Madness, madness," he says, and the camera soars back away from him in a mood of triumph which is taken up by the martial music on the soundtrack. In the contradiction between the sentiments expressed by the dialogue and the meaning contained in the treatment, critics have noticed only the former. *Bridge on the River Kwai*'s anti-war content is widely accepted to be impeccable. But *Hell Is for Heroes*, where the ideas are expressed by the whole form of the film, can pass nearly unnoticed and even be described as equivocal in its attitude to war. The lack of perception which results in this sort of fuzzy thinking is the best argument for a detailed criticism.

4

Notes on the Auteur Theory in 1962

Andrew Sarris

Writing for New York's *Village Voice*, a counter-cultural newspaper with a national profile, Andrew Sarris attained national prominence reviewing films from an auteurist perspective. He was the first and most eloquent of auteurists in the US, beginning in his early days writing for Jonas Mekas' *Film Culture*, a small journal devoted primarily to experimental and avant-garde cinema that began publication in 1955. Sarris' groundbreaking book, *The American Cinema*, published in 1968, was the first attempt to offer a systematic map of important directors throughout the history of Hollywood. This essay, which originally appeared in *Film Culture*, introduced auteurism to North American readers and was the first attempt to give auteurism a theoretical framework ("Henceforth, I will abbreviate *la politique des auteurs* as the auteur theory to avoid confusion"). Sarris' proposed theoretical framework has been the subject of much comment and attack, particularly from Pauline Kael.

I call these sketches Shadowgraphs, partly by the designation to remind you at once that they derive from the darker side of life, partly because, like other shadowgraphs, they are not directly visible. When I take a shadowgraph in my hand, it makes no impression on me, and gives me no clear conception of it. Only when I hold it up opposite the wall, and now look not directly at it, but at that which appears on the wall, am I able to see it. So also with the picture I wish to show here, an inward picture that does not become perceptible until I see it through the external. This external is perhaps not quite unobtrusive, but, not until I look through it, do I discover that inner picture that I desire to show you, and inner picture too delicately drawn to be outwardly visible, woven as it is of the tenderest moods of the soul.

Søren Kierkegaard, in *Either/Or*

An exhibitor once asked me if an old film I had recommended was *really* good or good only according to the *auteur* theory. I appreciate the distinction. Like the alchemists of old, *auteur* critics are notorious for rationalizing leaden clinkers into golden nuggets. Their judgments are seldom vindicated, because few spectators are conditioned to perceive in individual works the organic unity of a director's career. On a given evening, a film by John Ford must take its chances as if it were a film by Henry King. Am I implying that the weakest Ford is superior to the strongest King? Yes! This kind of unqualified affirmation seems to reduce the *auteur* theory to a game of aesthetic solitaire with all the cards turned face up. By *auteur* rules, the Fords will come up aces as invariably as the Kings will come up deuces. Presumably, we can all go home as soon as the directorial signature is flashed on the screen. To those who linger, *The Gunfighter* (King 1950) may appear worthier than *Flesh* (Ford 1932).

Andrew Sarris, "Notes on the Auteur Theory in 1962," pp. 1–8 from *Film Culture* 29 (Winter 1962/1963). © 1962 by Andrew Sarris. Reprinted by permission of the author.

(And how deeply one must burrow to undermine Ford!) No matter. The *auteur* theory is unyielding. If, by definition, Ford is invariably superior to King, any evidence to the contrary is merely an optical illusion. Now what could be sillier than this inflexible attitude? Let us abandon the absurdities of the *auteur* theory so that we may return to the chaos of common sense.

My labored performance as devil's advocate notwithstanding, I intend to praise the *auteur* theory, not to bury it. At the very least, I would like to grant the condemned system a hearing before its execution. The trial has dragged on for years, I know, and everyone is now bored by the abstract reasoning involved. I have little in the way of new evidence or new arguments, but I would like to change some of my previous testimony. What follows is, consequently, less a manifesto than a credo, a somewhat disorganized credo, to be sure, expressed in formless notes rather than in formal brief.

I. Aimez-Vous Brahms?

> Goethe? Shakespeare? Everything signed with their names is considered good, and one wracks one's brains to find beauty in their stupidities and failures, thus distorting the general taste. All these great talents, the Goethes, the Shakespeares, the Beethovens, the Michelangelos, created, side by side with their masterpieces, works not merely mediocre, but quite simply frightful.
>
> Leo Tolstoy, *Journal*, 1895–9

The preceding quotation prefaces the late André Bazin's famous critique of "*la politique des auteurs,*" which appeared in the *Cahiers du Cinéma* of April, 1957. Because no comparably lucid statement opposing the *politique* has appeared since that time, I would like to discuss some of Bazin's arguments with reference to the current situation. (I except, of course, Richard Roud's penetrating article "The French Line," which dealt mainly with the post-*Nouvelle Vague* situation when the *politique* had degenerated into McMahonism.)

As Tolstoy's observation indicates, *la politique des auteurs* ante-dates the cinema. For centuries, the Elizabethan *politique* has decreed the reading of every Shakespearean play before any encounter with the Jonsonian repertory. At some point between *Timon of Athens* and *Volpone*, this procedure is patently unfair to Jonson's reputation. But not really. On the most superficial level of artistic reputations, the *auteur* theory is merely a figure of speech. If the man in the street could not invoke Shakespeare's name as an identifiable cultural reference, he would probably have less contact with all things artistic. The Shakespearean scholar, by contrast, will always be driven to explore the surrounding terrain, with the result that all the Elizabethan dramatists gain more rather than less recognition through the pre-eminence of one of their number. Therefore, on balance, the *politique*, as a figure of speech, does more good than harm.

Occasionally, some iconoclast will attempt to demonstrate the fallacy of this figure of speech. We will be solemnly informed that *The Gambler* was a potboiler for Dostoyevsky in the most literal sense of the word. In Jacques Rivette's *Paris Nous Appartient*, Jean-Claude Brialy asks Betty Schneider if she would still admire *Pericles* if it were not signed by Shakespeare. Zealous musicologists have played *Wellington's Victory* so often as an example of inferior Beethoven that I have grown fond of the piece, atrocious as it is. The trouble with such iconoclasm is that it presupposes an encyclopedic awareness of the *auteur* in question. If one is familiar with every Beethoven composition, *Wellington's Victory*, in itself, will hardly tip the scale toward Mozart, Bach, or Schubert. Yet that is the issue raised by the *auteur* theory. If not Beethoven, who? And why? Let us say that the *politique* for composers went Mozart, Beethoven, Bach, and Schubert. Each composer would represent a task force of compositions, arrayed by type and quality with the mighty battleships and aircraft carries flanked by flotillas of cruisers, destroyers, and mine sweepers. When the Mozart task force collides with the Beethoven task force, symphonies roar against symphonies, quartets maneuver against quartets, and it is simply no contest with the operas. As a single force, Beethoven's nine symphonies, outgun any nine of Mozart's forty-one symphonies, both sets of quartets are most on a par with Schubert's, but *The Magic Flute, The Marriage of Figaro,* and *Don Giovanni* will blow poor *Fidelio* out of the water. Then, of course, there is Bach with an entirely different deployment of composition and instrumentation. The Haydn and Handel cultists are moored in their inlets ready to join the fray, and the moderns with their nuclear noises are still mobilizing their forces.

It can be argued that any exact ranking of artists is arbitrary and pointless. Arbitrary up to a point, perhaps, but pointless, no. Even Bazin concedes the polemical value of the *politique*. Many film critics would rather not commit themselves to specific rankings ostensibly because every film should be judged on its own merits. In many instances, this reticence masks the critic's condescension to the medium. Because it has not been firmly established that the cinema is an art at all, it requires cultural audacity to establish a pantheon for film directors. Without such audacity, I see little point in being a film critic. Anyway, is it possible to honor a work of art without honoring the artist involved? I think not. Of course, any idiot can erect a pantheon out of hearsay and gossip. Without specifying any work, the Saganesque seducer will ask quite cynically, "Aimez-vous Brahms?" The fact that Brahms is included in the pantheon of high-brow pickups does not invalidate the industrious criticism that justifies the composer as a figure of speech.

Unfortunately, some critics have embraced the *auteur* theory as a short-cut to film scholarship. With a "you-see-it-or-you-don't" attitude toward the reader, the particularly lazy *auteur* critic can save himself the drudgery of communication and explanation. Indeed, at their worst, *auteur* critiques are less meaningful than the straight-forward plot reviews that pass for criticism in America. Without the necessary research and analysis, the *auteur* theory can degenerate into the kind of snobbish racket that is associated with the merchandising of paintings.

It was largely against the inadequate theoretical formulation of *la politique des auteurs* that Bazin was reacting in his friendly critique. (Henceforth, I will abbreviate *la politique des auteurs* as the *auteur* theory to avoid confusion.) Bazin introduces his arguments within the context of a family quarrel over the editorial policies of *Cahiers*. He fears that, by assigning reviews to admirers of given directors, notably Alfred Hitchcock, Jean Renoir, Roberto Rossellini, Fritz Lang, Howard Hawks, and Nicholas Ray, every work, major and minor, of these exalted figures is made to radiate the same beauties of style and meaning. Specifically, Bazin notes a distortion when the kindly indulgence accorded the imperfect work of a Minnelli is coldly withheld from the imperfect work of Huston. The inherent bias of the *auteur* theory magnifies the gap between the two films.

I would make two points here. First, Bazin's greatness as a critic, (and I believe strongly that he was the greatest film critic who ever lived) rested in his disinterested conception of the cinema as a universal entity. It follows that he would react against a theory that cultivated what he felt were inaccurate judgments for the sake of dramatic paradoxes. He was, if anything, generous to a fault, seeking in every film some vestige of the cinematic art. That he would seek justice for Huston vis-à-vis Minnelli on even the secondary levels of creation indicates the scrupulousness of his critical personality.

However, my second point would seem to contradict my first. Bazin was wrong in this instance, insofar as any critic can be said to be wrong in retrospect. We are dealing here with Minnelli in his *Lust for Life* period and Huston in his *Moby Dick* period. Both films can be considered failures on almost any level. The miscasting alone is disastrous. The snarling force of Kirk Douglas as the tormented Van Gogh, the brutish insensibility of Anthony Quinn as Gauguin, and the nervously scraping tension between these two absurdly limited actors, deface Minnelli's meticulously objective decor, itself inappropriate for the mood of its subject. The director's presentation of the paintings themselves is singularly unperceptive in the repeated failure to maintain the proper optical distance from canvases that arouse the spectator less by their detailed draughtsmanship than by the shock of a *gestalt* wholeness. As for *Moby Dick*, Gregory Peck's Ahab deliberates long enough to let all the demons flee the Pequod, taking Melville's Lear-like fantasies with them. Huston's epic technique with its casually shifting camera viewpoint then drifts on an intellectually becalmed sea toward a fitting rendezvous with a rubber whale. These two films are neither the best nor the worst of their time. The question is: Which deserves the harder review? And there's the rub. At the time, Huston's stock in America was higher than Minnelli's. Most critics expected Huston to do "big" things, and, if they thought about it at all, expected Minnelli to stick to "small" things like musicals. Although neither film was a critical failure, audiences stayed away in large enough numbers to make the cultural respectability of the projects suspect. On the whole, *Lust for Life* was more successful with the audiences it did reach than was *Moby Dick*.

In retrospect, *Moby Dick* represents the turning downward of Huston as a director to be taken seriously. By contrast, *Lust for Life* is simply an isolated

Figure 4.1 Gregory Peck as Ahab in *Moby Dick* (Warner Bros, 1956). Produced and directed by John Huston

episode in the erratic career of an interesting stylist. The exact size of Minnelli's talent may inspire controversy, but he does represent something in the cinema today. Huston is virtually a forgotten man with a few actors' classics behind him surviving as the ruins of a once-promising career. Both Eric Rohmer, who denigrated Huston in 1957, and Jean Domarchi, who was kind to Minnelli that same year, somehow saw the future more clearly on an *auteur* level than did Bazin. As Santayana has remarked: "It is a great advantage for a system of philosophy to be substantially true." If the *auteur* critics of the 1950s had not scored so many coups of clairvoyance, the *auteur* theory would not be worth discussing in the 1960s. I must add that, at the time, I would have agreed with Bazin on this and every other objection to the *auteur* theory, but subsequent history, that history about which Bazin was always so mystical, has substantially confirmed most of the principles of the *auteur* theory. Ironically, most of the original supporters of the *auteur* theory have now abandoned it. Some have discovered more useful *politiques* as directors and would-be directors. Others have succumbed to a European-oriented pragmatism where intention is now more nearly equal to talent in critical relevance. Luc Moullet's belated discovery that Samuel Fuller was, in fact, fifty years old, signaled a reorientation of *Cahiers* away from the American cinema. (The handwriting was already on the wall when Truffaut remarked recently that, whereas he and his colleagues had "discovered" *auteurs*, his successors have "invented" them.)

Bazin then explores the implications of Giraudoux's epigram: "There are no works; there are only authors." Truffaut has seized upon this paradox as the battle cry of *la politique des auteurs*. Bazin casually demonstrates how the contrary can be argued with equal probability of truth or error. He subsequently dredges up the equivalents of *Wellington's Victory* for Voltaire, Beaumarchais, Flaubert, and Gide to document his point. Bazin then yields some ground to Rohmer's argument that the history of art does not confirm the decline with age of authentic geniuses like Titian, Rembrandt, Beethoven, or nearer to us, Bonnard, Matisse, and Stravinsky. Bazin agrees with Rohmer that it is inconsistent to attribute senility only to aging film directors while, at the same time, honoring the gnarled austerity of Rembrandt's later style. This is one of the crucial propositions of the *auteur* theory, because it refutes the popular theory of decline for aging giants like Renoir and Chaplin and asserts, instead, that, as a director grows older, he is likely to become more profoundly personal than most audiences and critics can appreciate. However, Bazin immediately retrieves his lost ground by arguing that, whereas the senility of directors is no longer at issue, the evolution of an art form is. Where directors fail and fall is in the realm not of psychology but of history. If a director fails to keep pace with the development of his medium, his work will become obsolescent. What seems like senility is, in reality, a disharmony between the subjective inspiration of the director and the objective evolution of the medium. By making this distinction between the subjective capability of an *auteur* and the objective value of a work in film history, Bazin reinforces the popular impression that the Griffith of *Birth of a Nation* is superior to the Griffith of *Abraham Lincoln* in the perspective of timing, which similarly distinguishes the Eisenstein of *Potemkin* from the Eisenstein of *Ivan the Terrible*, the Renoir of *La Grande Illusion* from the Renoir of *Picnic in the Grass*, and the Welles of *Citizen Kane* from the Welles of *Mr. Arkadin*.

I have embroidered Bazin's actual examples for the sake of greater contact with the American scene. In fact, Bazin implicitly denies a decline in the later works of Chaplin and Renoir and never mentions Griffith. He suggests circuitously that Hawks's *Scarface* is clearly superior to Hawks's *Gentlemen Prefer Blondes*, although the *auteur* critics would argue the contrary. Bazin is particularly critical of Rivette's circular reasoning on *Monkey Business* as the proof of Hawks's genius. "One sees the danger," Bazin warns, "which is an aesthetic cult of personality."

Bazin's taste, it should be noted, was far more discriminating than that of American historians. Films Bazin cites as unquestionable classics are still quite debatable here in America. After all, *Citizen Kane* was originally panned by James Agee, Richard Griffith, and Bosley Crowther, and *Scarface* has never been regarded as one of the landmarks of the American cinema by native critics. I would say that the American public has been ahead of its critics on both *Kane* and *Scarface*. Thus, to argue against the *auteur* theory in America is to assume that we have anyone of Bazin's sensibility and dedication to provide an alternative, and we simply don't.

Bazin, finally, concentrates on the American cinema, which invariably serves as the decisive battleground of the *auteur* theory, whether over *Monkey Business* or *Party Girl*. Unlike most "serious" American critics, Bazin likes Hollywood films, but not solely because of the talent of this or that director. For Bazin, the distinctively American comedy, western, and gangster genres have their own mystiques apart from the personalities of the directors concerned. How can one review an Anthony Mann western, Bazin asks, as if it were not an expression of the genre's conventions. Not that Bazin dislikes Anthony Mann's westerns. He is more concerned with otherwise admirable westerns that the *auteur* theory rejects because their directors happen to be unfashionable. Again, Bazin's critical generosity comes to the fore against the negative aspects of the *auteur* theory.

Some of Bazin's arguments tend to overlap each other as if to counter rebuttals from any direction. He argues, in turn, that the cinema is less individualistic an art than painting or literature, that Hollywood is less individualistic than other cinemas, and that, even so, the *auteur* theory never really applies anywhere. In upholding historical determinism, Bazin goes so far as to speculate that, if Racine had lived in Voltaire's century, it is unlikely that Racine's tragedies would have been any more inspired than Voltaire's. Presumably, the Age of Reason would have stifled Racine's neoclassical impulses. Perhaps. Perhaps not. Bazin's hypothesis can hardly be argued to a verifiable conclusion, but I suspect somewhat greater reciprocity between an artist and his *zeitgeist* than Bazin would allow. He mentions, more than once and in other contexts, capitalism's influence on the cinema. Without denying this influence, I still find it impossible to attribute X directors and Y films to any particular system or culture. Why should the Italian cinema be superior to the German cinema after one war, when the reverse was true after the previous one? As for artists conforming to the spirit of their age, that spirit is often expressed in contradictions, whether between Stravinsky and Sibelius, Fielding and Richardson, Picasso and Matisse, Chateaubriand and Stendhal. Even if the artist does not spring from the idealized head of Zeus, free of the embryonic stains of history, history itself is profoundly affected by his arrival. If we cannot imagine Griffith's *October* or Eisenstein's *Birth of a Nation* because we find it difficult to transpose one artist's unifying conceptions of Lee and Lincoln to the other's dialectical conceptions of Lenin and Kerensky, we are, nevertheless, compelled to recognize other differences in the personalities of these two pioneers beyond their respective cultural complexes. It is with these latter differences that the *auteur* theory is most deeply concerned. If directors and other artists cannot be wrenched from their historical environments, aesthetics is reduced to a subordinate branch of ethnography.

I have not done full justice to the subtlety of Bazin's reasoning and to the civilized skepticism with which he propounds his own arguments as slight probabilities rather than absolute certainties. Contemporary opponents of the *auteur* theory may feel that Bazin himself is suspect as a member of the *Cahiers* family. After all, Bazin does express qualified approval of the *auteur* theory as a relatively objective method of evaluating films apart from the subjective perils of impressionistic and ideological criticism. Better to analyze the director's personality than the critic's nerve centers or politics. Nevertheless, Bazin makes his stand clear by concluding: "This is not to deny the role of the author, but to restore to him the preposition without which the noun is only a limp concept. 'Author,' undoubtedly, but of what?"

Bazin's syntactical flourish raises an interesting problem in English usage. The French preposition "de" serves many functions, but among others, those of possession and authorship. In English, the preposition "by" once created a scandal in the American film industry when Otto Preminger had the temerity to advertise *The Man With the Golden Arm* as a film "by Otto Preminger." Novelist Nelson Algren and The Screenwriters' Guild raised such an outcry that the offending preposition was deleted. Even the noun "author" (which I cunningly mask as "*auteur*") has a literary connotation in English. In general conversation, an "author" is invariably taken to be a writer. Since "by" is a preposition of authorship and not of ownership like the ambiguous "de," the fact that Preminger both produced and directed *The Man with the Golden Arm* did not entitle him in America to the preposition "by." No one would have objected to the possessive form: "Otto Preminger's *The Man with the Golden Arm*." But, even in this case, a novelist of sufficient reputation is usually honored with the possessive designation. Now, this is hardly the case in France, where *The Red and the Black* is advertised as "un film de Claude Autant-Lara." In America, "directed by" is all the director can claim, when he is not also a well-known producer like Alfred Hitchcock or Cecil B. de Mille.

Since most American film critics are oriented toward literature or journalism, rather than toward future film-making, most American film criticism is directed toward the script instead of toward the screen. The writer-hero in *Sunset Boulevard* complains that people don't realize that someone "writes a picture; they think the actors make it up as they go along." It would never occur to this writer or most of his colleagues that people are even less aware of the director's function.

Of course, the much-abused man in the street has a good excuse not to be aware of the *auteur* theory even as a figure of speech. Even on the so-called classic level, he is not encouraged to ask "Aimez-vous Griffith?" or "Aimez-vous Eisenstein?" Instead, it is which Griffith or which Eisenstein? As for less acclaimed directors, he is lucky to find their names in the fourth paragraph of the typical review. I doubt that most American film critics really believe that an indifferently directed film is comparable to an indifferently written book. However, there is little point in

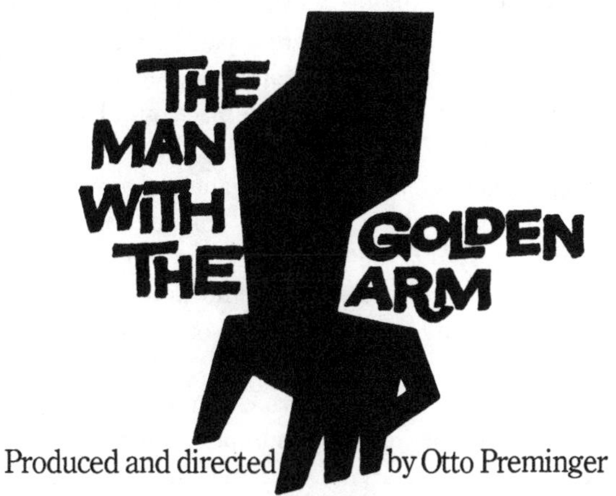

THE MAN WITH THE GOLDEN ARM

Figure 4.2 Saul Bass designed the advertising for *The Man with the Golden Arm* (United Artists, 1955). Produced and directed by Otto Preminger

wailing at the Philistines on this issue, particularly when some progress is being made in telling one director from another, at least when the film comes from abroad. The Fellini, Bergman, Kurosawa, and Antonioni promotions have helped push more directors up to the first paragraph of a review, even ahead of the plot synopsis. So, we mustn't complain.

Where I wish to redirect the argument is toward the relative position of the American cinema as opposed to the foreign cinema. Some critics have advised me that the *auteur* theory only applies to a small number of artists who make personal films, not to the run-of-the-mill Hollywood director who takes whatever assignment is available. Like most Americans who take films seriously, I have always felt a cultural inferiority complex about Hollywood. Just a few years ago, I would have thought it unthinkable to speak in the same breath of a "commercial" director like Hitchcock and a "pure" director like Bresson. Even today, *Sight and Sound* uses different type sizes for Bresson and Hitchcock films. After years of tortured revaluation, I am now prepared to stake my critical reputation, such as it is, on the proposition that Alfred Hitchcock is artistically superior to Robert Bresson by every criterion of excellence and, further, that, film for film, director for director, the American cinema has been consistently superior to that of the rest of the world from 1915 through 1962. Consequently, I now regard the *auteur* theory primarily as a critical device for recording the history of the American cinema, the only cinema in the world worth exploring in depth beneath the frosting of a few great directors at the top.

These propositions remain to be proven and, I hope, debated. The proof will be difficult because direction in the cinema is a nebulous force in literary terms. In addition to its own jargon, the director's craft often pulls in the related jargon of music, painting, sculpture, dance, literature, theatre, architecture, all in a generally futile attempt to describe the indescribable. What is it the old jazz man says of his art? If you gotta ask what it is, it ain't?. Well, the cinema is like that. Criticism can only attempt an approximation, a reasonable preponderance of accuracy over inaccuracy. I know the exceptions to the *auteur* theory as well as anyone. I can feel the human attraction of an audience going one way when I am going the other. The temptations of cynicism, common sense, and facile culture-mongering are always very strong, but, somehow, I feel that the *auteur* theory is the only hope for extending the appreciation of personal qualities in the cinema. By grouping and evaluating films according to directors, the critic can rescue individual achievements from an unjustifiable anonymity. If medieval architects and African sculptors are anonymous today, it is not because they deserved to be. When Ingmar Bergman bemoans the alienation of the modern artist from the collective spirit that rebuilt the cathedral at Chartres, he is only dramatizing his own individuality for an age that has rewarded him handsomely for the travail of his alienation. There is no justification for penalizing Hollywood directors for the sake of collective mythology. So, invective aside, "Aimez-vous Cukor?"

II. What Is the *Auteur* Theory?

As far as I know, there is no definition of the *auteur* theory in the English language, that is, by any American or British critic. Truffaut has recently gone to great pains to emphasize that the *auteur* theory was merely a polemical weapon for a given time and a given place, and I am willing to take him at his word. But, lest I be accused of misappropriating a theory no one wants anymore, I will give the *Cahiers* critics full credit for the original formulation of an idea that reshaped my thinking on the cinema. First of all, how does the *auteur* theory differ from a straightforward theory of directors. Ian Cameron's article "Films, Directors, and Critics," in *Movie* of September, 1962, makes an interesting comment on the issue: "The assumption that underlies all the writing in *Movie* is that the director is the author of a film, the person who gives it any distinctive quality. There are quite large exceptions, with which I shall deal later." So far, so good, at least for the *auteur* theory, which even allows for exceptions. However, Cameron continues: "On the whole, we accept the cinema of directors, although without going to the farthest-out extremes of *la politique des auteurs*, which makes it difficult to think of a bad director making a good film and almost impossible to think of a good director making a bad one." We are back to Bazin again, although Cameron naturally uses different examples. That three otherwise divergent critics like Bazin, Roud, and Cameron make essentially the same point about the *auteur* theory suggests a common fear of its abuses. I believe there is a misunderstanding here about what the *auteur* theory actually claims, particularly since the theory itself is so vague at the present time.

First of all, the *auteur* theory, at least as I understand it and now intend to express it, claims neither the gift of prophecy nor the option of extracinematic perception. Directors, even *auteurs*, do not always run true to form, and the critic can never assume that a bad director will always make a bad film. No, not always, but almost always, and that is the point. What is a bad director, but a director who has made many bad films? What is the problem then? Simply this: The badness of director is not necessarily considered the badness of a film. If Joseph Pevney directed Garbo, Cherkassov, Oliver, Belmondo, and Harriet Andersson in *The Cherry Orchard*, the resulting spectacle might not be entirely devoid of merit with so many subsidiary *auteurs* to cover up for Joe. In fact, with this cast and this literary property, a Lumet might be safer than a Welles. The realities of casting apply to directors as well as to actors, but the *auteur* theory would demand the gamble with Welles, if he were willing.

Marlon Brando has shown us that a film can be made without a director. Indeed, *One-Eyed Jacks* is more entertaining than many films with directors. A director-conscious critic would find it difficult to say anything good or bad about direction that is nonexistent. One can talk here about photography, editing, acting, but not direction. The film even has personality, but, like *The Longest Day* and *Mutiny on the Bounty*, it is a cipher directorially. Obviously, the *auteur* theory cannot possibly cover every vagrant charm of the cinema. Nevertheless, the first premise of the *auteur* theory is the technical competence of a director as a criterion of value. A badly directed or an undirected film has no importance in a critical scale of values, but one can make interesting conversation about the subject, the script, the acting, the color, the photography, the editing, the music, the costumes, the decor, and so forth. That is the nature of the medium. You always get more for your money than mere art. Now, by the *auteur* theory, if a director has no technical competence, no elementary flair for the cinema, he is automatically cast out from the pantheon of directors. A great director has to be at least a good director. This is true in any art. What constitutes directorial talent is more difficult to define abstractly. There is less disagreement, however, on this first level of the *auteur* theory than there will be later.

The second premise of the *auteur* theory is the distinguishable personality of the director as a criterion of value. Over a group of films, a director must exhibit certain recurring characteristics of style, which serve as his signature. The way a film looks and moves should have some relationship to the way a director thinks and feels. This is an area where American directors are generally superior to foreign directors. Because so much of the American cinema is commissioned, a director is forced to express his personality through the visual treatment of material rather than through the literary content of the material. A Cukor, who works with all sorts of projects, has a more developed abstract style than a Bergman, who is free to develop his own scripts. Not that Bergman lacks personality, but his work has declined with the depletion of his ideas largely because his technique never equaled his sensibility. Joseph L. Mankiewicz and Billy Wilder are other examples of writer-directors without adequate technical mastery. By contrast, Douglas Sirk and Otto Preminger have moved up the scale because their miscellaneous projects reveal a stylistic consistency.

The third and ultimate premise of the *auteur* theory is concerned with interior meaning, the ultimate glory of the cinema as an art. Interior meaning is extrapolated from the tension between a director's personality and his material. This conception of interior meaning comes close to what Astruc defines as *mise en scène*, but not quite. It is not quite the version of the world a director projects nor quite his attitude toward life. It is ambiguous, in any literary sense, because part of it is imbedded in the stuff of the cinema and cannot be rendered in noncinematic terms. Truffaut has called it the temperature of the director on the set, and that is a close approximation of its professional aspect. Dare I come out and say what I think it to be is an *élan* of the soul?

Lest I seem unduly mystical, let me hasten to add that all I mean by "soul" is that intangible difference between one personality and another, all other things being equal. Sometimes, this difference is expressed by no more than a beat's hesitation in the rhythm of a film. In one sequence of *La Règle du Jeu*, Renoir gallops up the stairs, turns to his right with a lurching movement, stops in hop-like uncertainty when his name is called by a coquettish maid, and, then, with marvelous postreflex continuity, resumes his bearishly shambling journey to the heroine's boudoir. If I could describe the musical grace note of that momentary suspension, and I can't, I might be able to provide a more precise definition of the *auteur* theory. As it is, all I can do is point at the specific beauties of interior meaning on the screen and, later, catalogue the moments of recognition.

The three premises of the *auteur* theory may be visualized as three concentric circles: the outer circle as technique; the middle circle, personal style; and the inner circle, interior meaning. The corresponding roles of the director may be designated as those of a technician, a stylist, and an *auteur*. There is no prescribed course by which a director passes through the three circles. Godard once remarked that Visconti had evolved from a *metteur en scène* to an *auteur*, whereas Rossellini had evolved from an *auteur* to a *metteur en scène*. From opposite directions, they emerged with comparable status. Minnelli began and remained in the second circle as a stylist; Buñuel was an *auteur* even before he had assembled the technique of the first circle. Technique is simply the ability to put a film together with some clarity and coherence. Nowadays, it is possible to become a director without knowing too much about the technical side, even the crucial functions of photography and editing. An expert production crew could probably cover up for a chimpanzee in the director's chair. How do you tell the genuine director from the quasichimpanzee? After a given number of films, a pattern is established.

In fact, the *auteur* theory itself is a pattern theory in constant flux. I would never endorse a Ptolemaic constellation of directors in a fixed orbit. At the moment, my list of *auteurs* runs something like this through the first twenty: Ophuls, Renoir, Mizoguchi, Hitchcock, Chaplin, Ford, Welles, Dreyer, Rossellini, Murnau, Griffith, Sternberg, Eisenstein, von Stroheim, Buñuel, Bresson, Hawks, Lang, Flaherty, Vigo. This list is somewhat weighted toward seniority and established reputations. In time, some of these *auteurs* will rise, some will fall, and some will be displaced either by new directors or rediscovered ancients. Again, the exact order is less important than the specific definitions of these and as many as two hundred other potential *auteurs*. I would hardly expect any other critic in the world fully to endorse this list, especially on faith. Only after thousands of films have been revaluated, will any personal pantheon have a reasonably objective validity. The task of validating the *auteur* theory is an enormous one, and the end will never be in sight. Meanwhile, the *auteur* habit of collecting random films in directorial bundles will serve posterity with at least a tentative classification.

Although the *auteur* theory emphasizes the body of a director's work rather than isolated masterpieces, it is expected of great directors that they make great films every so often. The only possible exception to this rule I can think of is Abel Gance, whose greatness is largely a function of his aspiration. Even with Gance,

Figure 4.3 *High Sierra* (Warner Bros, 1941) reveals a "crucial link" to Raoul Walsh's other films. Produced by Mark Hellinger

La Roue is as close to being a great film as any single work of Flaherty's. Not that single works matter that much. As Renoir has observed, a director spends his life on variations of the same film.

Two recent films – *Boccaccio '70* and *The Seven Capital Sins* – unwittingly reinforced the *auteur* theory by confirming the relative standing of the many directors involved. If I had not seen either film, I would have anticipated that the order of merit in *Boccaccio '70* would be Visconti, Fellini, and De Sica, and in *The Seven Capital Sins* Godard, Chabrol, Demy, Vadim, De Broca, Molinaro. (Dhomme, Ionesco's stage director and an unknown quantity in advance, turned out to be the worst of the lot.) There might be some argument about the relative badness of De Broca and Molinaro, but, otherwise, the directors ran true to form by almost any objective criterion of value. However, the main point here is that even in these frothy, ultracommercial servings of entertainment, the contribution of each director had less in common stylistically with the work of other directors on the project than with his own previous work.

Sometimes, a great deal of corn must be husked to yield a few kernels of internal meaning. I recently saw *Every Night at Eight*, one of the many maddeningly routine films Raoul Walsh has directed in his long career. This 1935 effort featured George Raft, Alice Faye, Frances Langford, and Patsy Kelly in one of those familiar plots about radio shows of the period. The film keeps moving along in the pleasantly unpretentious manner one would expect of Walsh until one incongruously intense scene with George Raft thrashing about in his sleep, revealing his inner fears in mumbling dream-talk. The girl he loves comes into the room in the midst of his unconscious avowals of feeling and listens sympathetically. This unusual scene was later amplified in *High Sierra* with Humphrey Bogart and Ida Lupino. The point is that one of the screen's most virile directors employed an essentially feminine narrative device to dramatize the emotional vulnerability of his heroes. If I had not been aware of Walsh in *Every Night at Eight*, the crucial link to *High Sierra* would have passed unnoticed. Such are the joys of the *auteur* theory.

5

Circles and Squares

Pauline Kael

As the film critic for *New Yorker* magazine from 1967 to 1991, where she had virtually free rein, Pauline Kael became perhaps the most influential US film critic of the time. Her reviews were said to be able to make or break a film's chances of success at the box-office. She responded to Sarris' auteurism with a savage attack on his claims to have established an auteur *theory*, and thus began a celebrated war of words between the two critics for years. Kael's antipathy to auteurism is perhaps best seen in her book *The Citizen Kane Book* (1971), which includes the shooting script for Orson Welles' classic film and a lengthy analysis, "Raising Cain," in which Kael argues against Welles as its primary auteur by demonstrating through a combination of historical research and textual analysis the contributions of others such as co-screenwriter Herman Mankiewicz and cinematographer Gregg Toland. In this essay, which appeared originally in the journal *Film Quarterly* in 1963, her critique of Sarris' auteur theory was at once the most reasoned and the most accessible of the many that appeared in print.

Joys and Sarris

> . . . the first premise of the *auteur* theory is the technical competence of a director as a criterion of value . . . The second premise of the *auteur* theory is the distinguishable personality of the director as a criterion of value. . . . The third and ultimate premise of the *auteur* theory is concerned with interior meaning, the ultimate glory of the cinema as an art. Interior meaning is extrapolated from the tension between a director's personality and his material. . . .
>
> Sometimes a great deal of corn must be husked to yield a few kernels of internal meaning. I recently saw *Every Night at Eight*, one of the many maddeningly routine films Raoul Walsh has directed in his long career. This 1935 effort featured George Raft, Alice Faye, Frances Langford and Patsy Kelly in one of those familiar plots about radio shows of the period. The film keeps moving along in the pleasantly unpretentious manner one would expect of Walsh until one incongruously intense scene with George Raft thrashing about in his sleep, revealing his inner fears in mumbling dream talk. The girl he loves comes into the room in the midst of his unconscious avowals of feeling, and listens sympathetically. This unusual scene was later amplified in *High Sierra* with Humphrey Bogart and Ida Lupino. The point is that one of the screen's most virile directors employed an essentially feminine narrative device to dramatize the emotional vulnerability of his heroes. If I had not been aware of Walsh in *Every Night at Eight*, the crucial link to *High Sierra* would have passed unnoticed. Such are the joys of the *auteur* theory.
>
> Andrew Sarris, "Notes on the Auteur Theory in 1962," *Film Culture*, Winter 1962–3

Perhaps a little more corn should be husked; perhaps, for example, we can husk away the word "internal" (is "internal meaning" any different from "meaning"?).

Pauline Kael, "Circles and Squares," pp. 12–26 from *Film Quarterly* 16, no. 3 (Spring, 1963).

We might ask why the link is "crucial"? Is it because the device was "incongruously intense" in *Every Night at Eight* and so demonstrated a try for something *deeper* on Walsh's part? But if his merit is his "pleasantly unpretentious manner" (which is to say, I suppose, that, recognizing the limitations of the script, he wasn't trying to do much) then the incongruous device was probably a misconceived attempt that disturbed the manner – like a bad playwright interrupting a comedy scene because he cannot resist the opportunity to tug at your heartstrings. We might also ask why this narrative device is "essentially feminine": is it more feminine than masculine to be asleep, or to talk in one's sleep, or to reveal feelings? Or, possibly, does Sarris regard the device as feminine because the listening woman becomes a sympathetic figure and emotional understanding is, in this "virile" context, assumed to be essentially feminine? Perhaps only if one accepts the narrow notions of virility so common in our action films can this sequence be seen as "essentially feminine," and it is amusing that a critic can both support these clichés of the male world and be so happy when they are violated.

This is how we might quibble with a different *kind* of critic but we would never get anywhere with Sarris if we tried to examine what he is saying sentence by sentence.

So let us ask, what is the meaning of the passage? Sarris has noticed that in *High Sierra* (not a very good movie) Raoul Walsh repeated an uninteresting and obvious device that he had earlier used in a worse movie. And for some inexplicable reason, Sarris concludes that he would not have had this joy of discovery without the *auteur* theory.

But in every art form, critics traditionally notice and point out the way the artists borrow from themselves (as well as from others) and how the same devices, techniques, and themes reappear in their work. This is obvious in listening to music, seeing plays, reading novels, watching actors; we take it for granted that this is how we perceive the development or the decline of an artist (and it may be necessary to point out to *auteur* critics that repetition without development is decline). When you see Hitchcock's *Saboteur* there is no doubt that he drew heavily and clumsily from *The 39 Steps*, and when you see *North by Northwest* you can see that he is once again toying with the ingredients of *The 39 Steps* – and apparently having a good time with them. Would Sarris not notice the repetition in the Walsh films without the *auteur* theory? Or shall we take the more cynical view that without some commitment to Walsh as an *auteur*, he probably wouldn't be spending his time looking at these movies?

If we may be permitted a literary analogy, we can visualize Sarris researching in the archives of the *Saturday Evening Post*, tracing the development of Clarence Budington Kelland, who, by the application of something like the *auteur* theory, would emerge as a much more important writer than Dostoyevsky; for in Kelland's case Sarris's three circles, the three premises of the *auteur* theory, have been consistently congruent. Kelland is technically competent (even "pleasantly unpretentious"), no writer has a more "distinguishable personality," and if "interior meaning" is what can be extrapolated from, say, *Hatari!* or *Advise and Consent* or *What Ever Happened to Baby Jane?* then surely Kelland's stories with their attempts to force a bit of character and humor into the familiar plot outlines are loaded with it. Poor misguided Dostoyevsky, too full of what he has to say to bother with "technical competence," tackling important themes in each work (surely the worst crime in the *auteur* book) and with his almost incredible unity of personality and material leaving you nothing to extrapolate from, he'll never make it. If the editors of *Movie* ranked authors the way they do directors, Dostoyevsky would probably be in that almost untouchable category of the "ambitious."

It should be pointed out that Sarris's defense of the *auteur* theory is based not only on aesthetics but on a rather odd pragmatic statement: "Thus to argue against the *auteur* theory in America is to assume that we have anyone of Bazin's sensibility and dedication to provide an alternative, and we simply don't." Which I take to mean that the *auteur* theory is necessary in the absence of a critic who wouldn't need it. This is a new approach to aesthetics, and I hope Sarris's humility does not camouflage his double-edged argument. If his aesthetics is based on expediency, then it may be expedient to point out that it takes extraordinary intelligence and discrimination and taste to *use* any theory in the arts, and that without those qualities, a theory becomes a rigid formula (which is indeed what is happening among *auteur* critics). The greatness of critics like Bazin in France and Agee in America may have something to do with their using their full range of intelligence and intuition, rather than relying on

Figure 5.1 "Interior meaning" in *What Ever Happened to Baby Jane?* (Warner Bros/ Seven Arts, 1962). Produced and directed by Robert Aldrich

formulas. Criticism is an art, not a science, and a critic who follows rules will fail in one of his most important functions: perceiving what is original and important in *new* work and helping others to see.

The Outer Circle

> . . . the first premise of the auteur theory is the technical competence of a director as a criterion of value.

This seems less the premise of a theory than a commonplace of judgment, as Sarris himself indicates when he paraphrases it as, "A great director has to be at least a good director." But this commonplace, though it *sounds* reasonable and basic, is a shaky premise: sometimes the greatest artists in a medium bypass or violate the simple technical competence that is so necessary for hacks. For example, it is doubtful if Antonioni could handle a routine directorial assignment of the type at which John Struges is so proficient (*Escape from Fort Bravo* or *Bad Day at Black Rock*), but surely Antonioni's *L'Avventura* is the work of a great director. And the greatness of a director like Cocteau has nothing to do with mere technical competence: his greatness is in being able to achieve his own personal expression and style. And just as there were writers like Melville or Dreiser who triumphed over various kinds of technical incompetence, and who were, as artists, incomparably greater than the facile technicians of their day, a new great film director may appear whose very greatness is in his struggling toward grandeur or in massive accumulation of detail. An artist who is not a good technician can indeed create new standards, because standards of technical competence are based on comparisons with work already done.

Just as new work in other arts is often attacked because it violates the accepted standards and thus seems crude and ugly and incoherent, great new directors are very likely to be condemned precisely on the grounds that they're not even good directors, that they don't know their "business." Which, in some cases, is true, but does it matter when that "business" has little to do with what they want to express in films? It may even be a hindrance, leading them to banal slickness, instead of discovery of their own methods. For some, at least, Cocteau may be right: "The only technique worth having is the technique you invent for yourself." The director must be judged on the basis of what he produces – his films – and if he can make great films without knowing the standard methods, without the usual craftsmanship of the "good director," then that is the way he works. I would amend Sarris's premise to, "In works of a lesser rank, technical competence can help to redeem the weaknesses of the material." In fact it seems to be precisely this category that the *auteur* critics are most interested in – the routine material that a good craftsman can make into a fast and enjoyable movie. What, however, makes the *auteur* critics so incomprehensible is not their *preference* for works of this category (in this they merely follow the lead of children who also prefer simple action films and westerns and horror films to works that make demands on their understanding) but their truly astonishing inability to exercise taste and judgment *within* their area of preference. Moviegoing kids are, I think, much more reliable guides to this kind of movie than the *auteur* critics: every kid I've talked to knows that Henry Hathaway's *North to Alaska* was a surprisingly funny, entertaining movie and *Hatari!* (classified as a "masterpiece" by half the *Cahiers* Conseil des Dix, Peter Bogdanovich, and others) was a terrible bore.

The Middle Circle

> . . . the second premise of the auteur theory is the distinguishable personality of the director as a criterion of value.

Up to this point there has really been no theory, and now, when Sarris begins to work on his foundation, the entire edifice of civilized standards of taste collapses while he's tacking down his floorboards. Traditionally, in any art, the personalities of all those involved in a production have been a factor in judgment, but that the *distinguishability* of personality should in itself be a criterion of value completely confuses *normal* judgment. The smell of a skunk is more distinguishable than the perfume of a rose; does that make it better? Hitchcock's personality is certainly more distinguishable in *Dial M for Murder*, *Rear Window*, *Vertigo*, than Carol Reed's in *The Stars Look Down*, *Odd Man Out*, *The Fallen Idol*, *The Third Man*, *An Outcast of the Islands*, if for no other reason than because Hitchcock repeats while Reed tackles new subject matter. But how does this distinguishable personality function as a criterion for judging the works? We recognize the hands of Carné and Prévert in *Le Jour se Lève*, but that is not what makes it a beautiful film; we can just as easily recognize their hands in *Quai des Brumes* – which is not such a good film. We can recognize that *Le Plaisir* and *The Earrings of Madame de . . .* are both the work of Ophuls, but *Le Plaisir* is not a great film, and *Madame de . . .* is.

Often the works in which we are most aware of the personality of the director are his worst films – when he falls back on the devices he has already done to death. When a famous director makes a good movie, we look at the movie, we don't think about the director's personality; when he makes a stinker we notice his familiar touches because there's not much else to watch. When Preminger makes an expert, entertaining whodunit like *Laura*, we don't look for his personality (it has become part of the texture of the film); when he makes an atrocity like *Whirlpool*, there's plenty of time to look for his "personality" – if that's your idea of a good time.

It could even be argued, I think, that Hitchcock's uniformity, his mastery of tricks, and his cleverness at getting audiences to respond according to his calculations – the feedback he wants and gets from them – reveal not so much a personal style as a personal theory of audience psychology, that his methods and approach are not those of an artist but a prestidigitator. The *auteur* critics respond just as Hitchcock expects the gullible to respond. This is not so surprising – often the works *auteur* critics call masterpieces are ones that seem to reveal the contempt of the director for the audience.

It's hard to believe that Sarris seriously attempts to apply "the distinguishable personality of the director as a criterion of value" because when this premise becomes troublesome, he just tries to brazen his way out of difficulties. For example, now that John Huston's work has gone flat[1] Sarris casually dismisses him with: "Huston is virtually a forgotten man with a few actors' classics behind him . . ." If *The Maltese Falcon*, perhaps the most high-style thriller ever made in America, a film Huston both wrote and directed, is not a director's film, what is? And if the distinguishable personality of the director is a criterion of value, then how can Sarris dismiss the Huston who comes through so unmistakably in *The Treasure of Sierra Madre*, *The African Queen*, or *Beat the Devil*, or even in a muddled Huston film like *Key Largo*? If these are actors' movies, then what on earth is a director's movie?

Isn't the *auteur* theory a hindrance to clear judgment of Huston's movies and of his career? Disregarding the theory, we see some fine film achievements and we perceive a remarkably distinctive directorial talent; we also see intervals of weak, half-hearted assignments like *Across the Pacific* and *In This Our Life*. Then, after *Moulin Rouge*, except for the blessing of *Beat the Devil*, we see a career that splutters out in ambitious failures like *Moby Dick* and confused projects like *The Roots of Heaven* and *The Misfits*, and strictly commercial projects like *Heaven Knows, Mr Allison*. And this kind of career seems more characteristic of film history, especially in the United States, than the ripening development and final mastery envisaged by the *auteur* theory – a theory that makes it almost de rigeur to regard Hitchcock's American films as superior to his early English films. Is Huston' s career so different, say, from Fritz Lang's? How is it that Huston's early good – almost great – work, must be rejected along with his mediocre recent work, but Fritz Lang, being sanctified as an *auteur*, has his bad recent work praised along with his good? Employing more usual norms, if you respect the Fritz Lang who made *M* and *You Only Live Once*, if you enjoy the excesses of style and the magnificent absurdities of a film like *Metropolis*, then it is only good sense to reject the ugly stupidity of *Journey to the Lost City*. It is an insult to an artist to praise his bad work along with his good; it indicates that you are incapable of judging either.

A few years ago, a friend who reviewed Jean Renoir's University of California production of his play *Carola* hailed it as "a work of genius." When I asked my friend how he could so describe this very unfortunate play, he said, "Why, of course, it's a work of genius. Renoir's a genius, so anything he does is a work of genius." This could almost be a capsule version of the *auteur* theory (just substitute *Hatari*! for *Carola*) and in this reductio ad absurdum, viewing a work is superfluous, as the judgment is a priori. It's like buying clothes by the label: this is Dior, so it's good. (This is not so far from the way the *auteur* critics work, either.)

Sarris doesn't even play his own game with any decent attention to the rules: it is as absurd to praise Lang's recent bad work as to dismiss Huston's early good work; surely it would be more consistent if he also tried to make a case for Huston's bad pictures? That would be more consistent than devising a category called "actors' classics" to explain his good pictures away. If *The Maltese Falcon* and *The Treasure of Sierra Madre* are actors' classics, then what makes Hawks's *To Have and Have Not* and *The Big Sleep* (which were obviously tailored to the personalities of Bogart and Bacall) the work of an *auteur*?

Sarris believes that what makes an *auteur* is "an élan of the soul." (This critical language is barbarous. Where else should élan come from? It's like saying "a digestion of the stomach." A film critic need not be a theoretician, but it is necessary that he know how to use words. This might, indeed, be a first premise for a theory.) Those who have this élan presumably have it forever and their films reveal the "organic unity" of the directors' careers; and those who don't have it – well, they can only make "actors' classics." It's ironic that a critic trying to establish simple "objective" rules as a guide for critics who he thinks aren't gifted enough to use taste and intelligence, ends up – where, actually, he began – with a theory based on mystical insight. This might really make demands on the *auteur* critics if they did not simply take the easy way out by arbitrary decisions of who's got "it" and who hasn't.

Their decisions are not merely not based on their theory; their decisions are *beyond* criticism. It's like a woman's telling us that she feels a certain dress *does* something for her: her feeling has about as much to do with critical judgment as the *auteur* critics' feeling that Minnelli *has* "it," but Huston never had "it."

Even if a girl had plenty of "it," she wasn't expected to keep it forever. But this "élan" is not supposed to be affected by the vicissitudes of fortune, the industrial conditions of moviemaking, the turmoil of a country, or the health of a director. Indeed, Sarris says, "If directors and other artists cannot be wrenched from their historical environments, aesthetics is reduced to a subordinate branch of ethnography." May I suggest that if, in order to judge movies, the *auteur* critics must wrench the directors from their historical environments (which is, to put it mildly, impossible) so that they can concentrate on the detection of that "élan," they are reducing aesthetics to a form of idiocy. Élan as the permanent attribute Sarris posits can only be explained in terms of a cult of personality. May I suggest that a more meaningful description of élan is what a man feels when he is working at the height of his powers – and what we respond to in works of art with the excited cry of "This time, he's really done it" or "This shows what he could do when he got the chance" or "He's found his style" or "I never realized he had it in him to do anything so good," a response to his joy in creativity.

Sarris experiences "joy" when he recognizes a pathetic little link between two Raoul Walsh pictures (he never does explain whether the discovery makes him think the pictures are any better) but he wants to see artists in a pristine state – their essences, perhaps? – separated from all the life that has formed them and to which they try to give expression.

The Inner Circle

> The third and ultimate premise of the auteur theory is concerned with interior meaning, the ultimate glory of the cinema as an art. Interior meaning is extrapolated from the tension between a director's personality and his material.

This is a remarkable formulation: it is the opposite of what we have always taken for granted in the arts, that the artist expresses himself in the unity of form and content. What Sarris believes to be "the ultimate glory of the cinema as an art" is what has generally been considered the frustrations of a man working against the given material. Fantastic as this formulation is, it does something that the first two premises didn't do: it clarifies the interests of the *auteur* critics. If we have been puzzled because the *auteur* critics seemed so deeply involved, even dedicated, in becoming connoisseurs of trash, now we can see by this theoretical formulation that trash is indeed their chosen province of film.

Their ideal *auteur* is the man who signs a long-term contract, directs any script that's handed to him, and expresses himself by shoving bits of style up the crevasses of the plots. If his "style" is in conflict with the story line or subject matter, so much the better – more chance for tension. Now we can see why there has been so much use of the term "personality" in this aesthetics (the term which seems so inadequate when discussing the art of Griffith or Renoir or Murnau or Dreyer) – a routine, commercial movie can sure use a little "personality."

Now that we have reached the inner circle (the bull's eye turns out to be an empty socket) we can see why the shoddiest films are often praised the most. Subject matter is irrelevant (so long as it isn't treated sensitively – which is bad) and will quickly be disposed of by *auteur* critics who know that the smart director isn't responsible for that anyway; they'll get on to the important subject – his *mise-en-scène*: The director who fights to do something he cares about is a square. Now we can at least begin to understand why there was such contempt toward Huston for what was, in its way, a rather extraordinary effort – the *Moby Dick* that failed; why *Movie* considers Roger Corman a better director than Fred Zinnemann and ranks Joseph Losey next to God, why Bogdanovich, Mekas, and Sarris give their highest critical ratings to *What Ever Happened to Baby Jane?* (mighty big crevasses there). If Carol Reed had made only movies like *The Man Between* – in which he obviously worked to try to make something out of a ragbag of worn-out bits of material – he might be considered "brilliant" too. (But this is doubtful: although even the worst Reed is superior to Aldrich's *Baby Jane*, Reed would probably be detected, and rejected, as a man interested in substance rather than sensationalism.)

Figure 5.2 Ingmar Bergman's "abstract" technique in *The Seventh Seal* (Svensk Filmindustri, 1957). Produced by Allan Ekelund

I am angry, but am I unjust? Here's Sarris:

> A Cukor who works with all sorts of projects has a more developed abstract style than a Bergman who is free to develop his own scripts. Not that Bergman lacks personality, but his work has declined with the depletion of his ideas largely because his technique never equaled his sensibility. Joseph L. Mankiewicz and Billy Wilder are other examples of writer-directors without adequate technical mastery. By contrast, Douglas Sirk and Otto Preminger have moved up the scale because their miscellaneous projects reveal a stylistic consistency.

How neat it all is – Bergman's "work has declined with the depletion of his ideas largely because his technique never equaled his sensibility." But what on earth does that mean? How did Sarris perceive Bergman's sensibility except through his technique? Is Sarris saying what he seems to be saying, that if Bergman had developed more "technique," his work wouldn't be dependent on his ideas? I'm afraid this *is* what he means, and that when he refers to Cukor's "more developed abstract style" he means by "abstract" something unrelated to ideas, a technique not dependent on the content of the films. This is curiously reminiscent of a view common enough in the business world, that it's better not to get too involved, too personally interested in business problems, or they take over your life; and besides, you don't function as well when you've lost your objectivity. But this is the *opposite* of how an artist works. His technique, his *style*, is determined by his range of involvements, and his preference for certain themes. Cukor's style is no more *abstract*(!) than Bergman's: Cukor has a range of subject matter that he can handle and when he gets a good script within his range (like *The Philadelphia Story* or *Pat and Mike*) he does a good job; but he is at an immense *artistic* disadvantage, compared with Bergman, because he is dependent on the ideas of so many (and often bad) scriptwriters and on material which is often alien to his talents. It's amusing (and/or depressing) to see the way *auteur* critics tend to downgrade writer-directors – who are in the *best* position to use the film medium for personal expression.

Sarris does some pretty fast shuffling with Huston and Bergman; why doesn't he just come out and admit that writer-directors are disqualified by his third premise? They can't arrive at that "interior meaning, the ultimate glory of the cinema" because a writer-director has no tension between his personality and his material, so there's nothing for the *auteur* critic to extrapolate from.

What is all this nonsense about extrapolating "interior" meaning from the tension between a director's personality and his material? A competent commercial director generally does the best he can with what he's got to work with. Where is the "tension"? And if you can locate some, what kind of meaning could you draw out of it except that the director's having a bad time with lousy material or material he doesn't like? Or maybe he's trying to speed up the damned production so he can do something else that he has some *hopes* for? Are these critics honestly (and futilely) looking for "interior meanings" or is this just some form of intellectual diddling that helps to sustain their pride while they're viewing silly movies? Where is the tension in Howard Hawks's films? When he has good material, he's capable of better than good direction, as he demonstrates in films like *Twentieth Century*, *Bringing Up Baby*, *His Girl Friday*; and in *To Have and Have Not* and *The Big Sleep* he demonstrates that with help from the actors, he can jazz up ridiculous scripts. But what "interior meaning" can be extrapolated from an enjoyable, harmless, piece of kitsch like *Only Angels Have Wings*; what can the *auteur* critics see in it beyond the sex and glamor and fantasies of the high-school boys' universe – exactly what the mass audience liked it for? And when Hawks's material and/or cast is dull and when his heart isn't in the production – when by the *auteur* theory he should show his "personality," the result is something soggy like *The Big Sky*.

George Cukor's modest statement, "Give me a good script and I'll be a hundred times better as a director"[2] provides some notion of how a director may experience the problem of the given material. What can Cukor do with a script like *The Chapman Report* but try to kid it, to dress it up a bit, to show off the talents of Jane Fonda and Claire Bloom and Glynis Johns, and to give the total production a little flair and craftsmanship. At best, he can make an entertaining bad movie. A director with something like magical gifts *can* make a silk purse out of a sow's ear. But if he has it in him to do more in life than make silk purses, the triumph is minor – even if the purse is lined with gold. Only by the use of the *auteur* theory does this little victory become "ultimate glory." For some unexplained reason those traveling in *auteur* circles believe that making that purse out of a sow's ear is an infinitely greater accomplishment than making a solid carrying case out of a good piece of leather (as, for example, a Zinnemann does with *From Here to Eternity* or *The Nun's Story*).

I suppose we should be happy for Sirk and Preminger elevated up the glory "scale," but I suspect that the "stylistic consistency" of say, Preminger, could be a matter of his *limitations*, and that the only way you could tell he made some of his movies was that he used the same players so often (Linda Darnell, Jeanne Cram, Gene Tierney, Dana Andrews, et al., gave his movies the Preminger look). But the argument is ludicrous anyway, because if Preminger shows stylistic consistency with subject matter as varied as *Carmen Jones*, *Anatomy of a Murder*, and *Advise and Consent*, then by any rational standards he should be attacked rather than elevated. I don't think these films are stylistically consistent, nor do I think Preminger is a great director – for the very simple reason that his films are consistently superficial and facile. (*Advise and Consent*, an *auteur* "masterpiece" – Ian Cameron, Paul Mayersberg, and Mark Shivas of *Movie* and Jean Douchet of *Cahiers du Cinéma* rate it first on their ten best lists of 1962 and Sarris gives it his top rating – seems not so much Preminger-directed as other-directed. That is to say, it seems calculated to provide what as many different groups as possible want to see: there's something for the liberals, something for the conservatives, something for the homosexuals, something for the family.) An editorial in *Movie* states: "In order to enjoy Preminger's films the spectator must apply an unprejudiced intelligence; he is constantly required to examine the quality not only of the characters' decisions but also of his own reactions," and "He presupposes an intelligence active enough to allow the spectator to make connections, comparisons and judgments." May I suggest that this spectator would have better things to do than the editors of *Movie* who put out Preminger issues? They may have, of course, the joys of discovering links between *Centennial Summer*, *Forever Amber*, *That Lady in Ermine*, and *The Thirteenth Letter*, but I refuse to believe in these ever-so-intellectual protestations. The *auteur* critics aren't a very *convincing* group.

I assume that Sarris's theory is not based on his premises (the necessary causal relationships are absent), but rather that the premises were devised in a clumsy attempt to prop up the "theory." (It's a good thing he stopped at three: a few more circles and we'd really be in hell, which might turn out to be the last refinement of film tastes – Abbott and Costello comedies, perhaps?) These critics work embarrassingly hard trying to give some semblance of intellectual respectability to a preoccupation with mindless, repetitious commercial products – the kind of action movies that the restless, rootless men who wander on Forty-Second Street and in the Tenderloin of all our big cities have always preferred just because they could respond to them without thought. These movies soak up your time. I would suggest that they don't serve a very different function for Sarris or Bogdanovich or the young men of *Movie* – even though they devise elaborate theories to justify soaking up their time. An educated man must have to work pretty hard to set his intellectual horizons at the level of *I Was a Male War Bride* (which, incidentally, wasn't even a good *commercial* movie).

"Interior meaning" seems to be what those in the know know. It's a mystique – and a mistake. The *auteur* critics never tell us by what divining rods they have discovered the élan of a Minnelli or a Nicholas Ray or a Leo McCarey. They're not critics; they're inside dopesters. There must be another circle that Sarris forgot to get to – the one where the secrets are kept. . . .

Notes

1 And, by the way, the turning point came, I think, not with *Moby Dick*, as Sarris indicates, but much earlier, with *Moulin Rouge*. This may not be so apparent to *auteur* critics concerned primarily with style and individual touches, because what was shocking about *Moulin Rouge* was that the content was sentimental mush. But critics who accept even the worst of Minnelli probably wouldn't have been bothered by the fact that *Moulin Rouge* was soft in the center, it had so many fancy touches at the edges.

2 In another sense, it is perhaps immodest. I would say, give Cukor a clever script with light, witty dialogue, and he will know what to do with it. But I wouldn't expect more than glossy entertainment. (It seems almost too obvious to mention it, but can Sarris really discern the "distinguishable personality" of George Cukor and his "abstract" style in films like *Bhowani Junction, Les Girls, The Actress, A Life of Her Own, The Model and the Marriage Broker, Edward, My Son, A Woman's Face, Romeo and Juliet, A Double Life*? I wish I could put him to the test. I can only *suspect* that many *auteur* critics would have a hard time seeing those telltale traces of the beloved in their works.)

6

The Auteur Theory

Peter Wollen

A British film critic, filmmaker, and teacher, Peter Wollen's films include *Penthesilea* (1974), *Riddles of the Sphinx* (1977) and *Crystal Gazing* (1982), all co-directed with feminist film theorist Laura Mulvey. Wollen's most important critical work was the book *Signs and Meaning in the Cinema*, first published in 1969 and revised in 1972. The book's three parts were devoted to analyses of Eisenstein and montage theory, semiology, and the auteur theory, from which this reading is excerpted. Here Wollen offers his influential comparison between Howard Hawks and John Ford in the process of combining the insights of both auteurism and structuralism. In his reading of Hawks' movies Wollen offers a model of how auteurism allows one to read individual films by an auteur in relation to the auteur's entire *oeuvre*.

The *politique des auteurs* – the *auteur* theory, as Andrew Sarris calls it – was developed by the loosely knit group of critics who wrote for *Cahiers du Cinéma* and made it the leading film magazine in the world. It sprang from the conviction that the American cinema was worth studying in depth, that masterpieces were made not only by a small upper crust of directors, the cultured gilt on the commercial gingerbread, but by a whole range of authors, whose work had previously been dismissed and consigned to oblivion. There were special conditions in Paris which made this conviction possible. Firstly, there was the fact that American films were banned from France under the Vichy government and the German Occupation. Consequently, when they reappeared after the Liberation they came with a force – and an emotional impact – which was necessarily missing in the Anglo-Saxon countries themselves. And, secondly, there was a thriving ciné-club movement, due in part to the close connections there had always been in France between the cinema and the intelligentsia: witness the example of Jean Cocteau or André Malraux. Connected with this ciné-club movement was the magnificent Paris *Cinémathèque*, the work of Henri Langlois, a great *auteur*, as Jean-Luc Godard described him. The policy of the *Cinémathèque* was to show the maximum number of films, to plough back the production of the past in order to produce the culture in which the cinema of the future could thrive. It gave French *cinéphiles* an unmatched perception of the historical dimensions of Hollywood and the careers of individual directors.

The *auteur* theory grew up rather haphazardly; it was never elaborated in programmatic terms, in a manifesto or collective statement. As a result, it could be interpreted and applied on rather broad lines; different critics developed somewhat different methods within a loose framework of common attitudes. This looseness and diffuseness of the theory has allowed flagrant misunderstandings to take root, particularly among critics in Britain and the United States. Ignorance has been

Peter Wollen, "The Auteur Theory" (excerpt), pp. 74–105 from *Signs and Meaning in the Cinema*, 3rd ed. (Bloomington: Indiana University Press, 1972).

compounded by a vein of hostility to foreign ideas and a taste for travesty and caricature. However, the fruitfulness of the *auteur* approach has been such that it has made headway even on the most unfavourable terrain. For instance, a recent straw poll of British critics, conducted in conjunction with a Don Siegel Retrospective at the National Film Theatre, revealed that, among American directors most admired, a group consisting of Budd Boetticher, Samuel Fuller and Howard Hawks ran immediately behind Ford, Hitchcock and Welles, who topped the poll, but ahead of Billy Wilder, Josef Von Sternberg and Preston Sturges.

Of course, some individual directors has always been recognised as outstanding: Charles Chaplin, John Ford, Orson Welles. The *auteur* theory does not limit itself to acclaiming the director as the main author of a film. It implies an operation of decipherment; it reveals authors where none had been seen before. For years, the model of an author in the cinema was that of the European director, with open artistic aspirations and full control over his films. This model still lingers on; it lies behind the existential distinction between art films and popular films. Directors who built their reputations in Europe were dismissed after they crossed the Atlantic, reduced to anonymity. American Hitchcock was contrasted unfavourably with English Hitchcock, American Renoir with French Renoir, American Fritz Lang with German Fritz Lang. The *auteur* theory has led to the revaluation of the second, Hollywood careers of these and other European directors; without it, masterpieces such as *Scarlet Street* or *Vertigo* would never have been perceived. Conversely, the *auteur* theory has been sceptical when offered an American director whose salvation has been exile to Europe. It is difficult now to argue that *Brute Force* has ever been excelled by Jules Dassin or that Joseph Losey's recent work is markedly superior to, say, *The Prowler*.

In time, owing to the diffuseness of the original theory, two main schools of *auteur* critics grew up: those who insisted on revealing a core of meanings, of thematic motifs, and those who stressed style and *mise en scène*. There is an important distinction here, which I shall return to later. The work of the *auteur* has a semantic dimension, it is not purely formal; the work of the *metteur en scène*, on the other hand, does not go beyond the realm of performance, of transposing into the special complex of cinematic codes and channels a pre-existing text: a scenario, a book or a play. As we shall see, the meaning of the films of an *auteur* is constructed *a posteriori*; the meaning – semantic, rather than stylistic or expressive – of the films of a *metteur en scène* exists *a priori*. In concrete cases, of course, this distinction is not always clear-cut. There is controversy over whether some directors should be seen as *auteurs* or *metteurs en scène*. For example, though it is possible to make intuitive ascriptions, there have been no really persuasive accounts as yet of Raoul Walsh or William Wyler as *auteurs*, to take two very different directors. Opinions might differ about Don Siegel or George Cukor. Because of the difficulty of fixing the distinction in these concrete cases, it has often become blurred; indeed, some French critics have tended to value the *metteur en scène* above the *auteur*. MacMahonism sprang up, with its cult of Walsh, Lang, Losey and Preminger, its fascination with violence and its notorious text: 'Charlton Heston is an axiom of the cinema.' What André Bazin called 'aesthetic cults of personality' began to be formed. Minor directors were acclaimed before they had, in any real sense, been identified and defined.

Yet the *auteur* theory has survived despite all the hallucinating critical extravaganzas which it has fathered. It has survived because it is indispensable. Geoffrey Nowell-Smith has summed up the *auteur* theory as it is normally presented today:

> One essential corollary of the theory as it has been developed is the discovery that the defining characteristics of an author's work are not necessarily those which are most readily apparent. The purpose of criticism thus becomes to uncover behind the superficial contrasts of subject and treatment a hard core of basic and often recondite motifs. The pattern formed by these motifs . . . is what gives an author's work its particular structure, both defining it internally and distinguishing one body of work from another.

It is this 'structural approach', as Nowell-Smith calls it, which is indispensable for the critic.

The test case for the *auteur* theory is provided by the work of Howard Hawks. Why Hawks, rather than, say, Frank Borzage or King Vidor? Firstly, Hawks is a director who has worked for years within the Hollywood system. His first film, *Road to Glory*, was made in 1926. Yet throughout his long career he has only once received general critical acclaim, for his wartime film, *Sergeant York*, which closer inspection reveals to be eccentric and atypical of the main *corpus* of Hawks's films. Secondly, Hawks has worked in almost every genre. He has made westerns (*Rio Bravo*), gangsters (*Scarface*), war films (*Air Force*), thrillers (*The Big Sleep*), science fiction (*The Thing from Another World*), musicals (*Gentlemen Prefer Blondes*), comedies (*Bringing up Baby*), even a Biblical epic (*Land of the Pharaohs*). Yet all of these films (except perhaps *Land of the Pharaohs*, which he himself was not happy about) exhibit the same thematic preoccupations, the same recurring motifs and incidents, the same visual style and tempo. In the same way that Roland Barthes constructed a species of *homo racinianus*, the critic can construct a *homo hawksianus*, the protagonist of Hawksian values in the problematic Hawksian world.

Hawks achieved this by reducing the genres to two basic types: the adventure drama and the crazy comedy. These two types express inverse views of the world, the positive and negative poles of the Hawksian vision. Hawks stands opposed, on the one hand, to John Ford and, on the other hand, to Budd Boetticher. All these directors are concerned with the problem of heroism. For the hero, as an individual, death is an absolute limit which cannot be transcended: it renders the life which preceded it meaningless, absurd. How then can there be any meaningful individual action during life? How can individual action have any value – be heroic – if it cannot have transcendent value, because of the absolutely devaluing limit of death? John Ford finds the answer to this question by placing and situating the individual within society and within history, specifically within American history. Ford finds transcendent values in the historic vocation of America as a nation, to bring civilisation to a savage land, the garden to the wilderness. At the same time, Ford also sees these values themselves as problematic; he begins to question the movement of American history itself. Boetticher, on the contrary, insists on a radical individualism. 'I am not interested in making films about mass feelings. I am for the individual.' He looks for values in the encounter with death itself: the underlying metaphor is always that of the bull-fighter in the arena. The hero enters a group of companions, but there is no possibility of group solidarity. Boetticher's hero acts by dissolving groups and collectivities of any kind into their constituent individuals, so that he confronts each person face-to-face; the films develop, in Andrew Sarris's words, into 'floating poker games, where every character takes turns at bluffing about his hand until the final showdown'. Hawks, unlike Boetticher, seeks transcendent values beyond the individual, in solidarity with others. But, unlike Ford, he does not give his heroes any historical dimension, any destiny in time.

For Hawks the highest human emotion is the camaraderie of the exclusive, self-sufficient, all-male group. Hawks's heroes are cattlemen, marlin-fishermen, racing-drivers, pilots, big-game hunters, habituated to danger and living apart from society, actually cut off from it physically by dense forest, sea, snow or desert. Their aerodromes are fog-bound; the radio has cracked up; the next mail-coach or packet-boat does not leave for a week. The *élite* group strictly preserves its exclusivity. It is necessary to pass a test of ability and courage to win admittance. The group's only internal tensions come when one member lets the others down (the drunk deputy in *Rio Bravo*, the panicky pilot in *Only Angels Have Wings*) and must redeem himself by some act of exceptional bravery, or occasionally when too much 'individualism' threatens to disrupt the close-knit circle (the rivalry between drivers in *Red Line 7000*, the fighter pilot among the bomber crew in *Air Force*). The group's security is the first commandment: 'You get a stunt team in acrobatics in the air – if one of them is no good, then they're all in trouble. If someone loses his nerve catching animals, then the whole bunch can be in trouble.' The group members are bound together by rituals (in *Hatari!* blood is exchanged by transfusion) and express themselves univocally in communal sing-songs. There is a famous example of this in *Rio Bravo*. In *Dawn Patrol* the camaraderie of the pilots stretches even across the enemy lines: a captured German ace is immediately drafted into the group and joins in the sing-song; in *Hatari!* hunters of different nationality and in different places join together in a song over an intercom radio system.

Hawks's heroes pride themselves on their professionalism. They ask: 'How good is he? He'd better be good.' They expect no praise for doing their job well. Indeed, none is given except: 'The boys did all right.' When they die, they leave behind them only the most meagre personal belongings, perhaps a handful of medals. Hawks himself has summed up this desolate and barren view of life:

Figure 6.1 Group camaraderie and the problem of heroism in *Only Angels Have Wings* (Columbia, 1939). Produced and directed by Howard Hawks

> It's just a calm acceptance of a fact. In *Only Angels Have Wings*, after Joe dies, Cary Grant says: 'He just wasn't good enough.' Well, that's the only thing that keeps people going. They just have to say: 'Joe wasn't good enough, and I'm better than Joe, so I go ahead and do it.' And they find out they're not any better than Joe, but then it's too late, you see.

In Ford films, death is celebrated by funeral services, an impromptu prayer, a few staves of 'Shall we gather at the river?' – it is inserted into an ongoing system of ritual institutions, along with the wedding, the dance, the parade. But for Hawks it is enough that the routine of the group's life goes on, a routine whose only relieving features are 'danger' (*Hatari!*) and 'fun'. Danger gives existence pungency: 'Every time you get real action, then you have danger. And the question, "Are you living or not living?" is probably the biggest drama we have.' This nihilism, in which 'living' means no more than being in danger of losing your life – a danger entered into quite gratuitously – is augmented by the Hawksian concept of having 'fun'. The word 'fun' crops up constantly in Hawks's interviews and scripts. It masks his despair.

When one of Hawks's *élite* is asked, usually by a woman, why he risks his life, he replies: 'No reason I can think of makes any sense. I guess we're just crazy.' Or Feathers, sardonically, to Colorado in *Rio Bravo*: 'You haven't even the excuse I have. We're all fools.' By 'crazy' Hawks does not mean psychopathic: none of his characters are like Turkey in Peckinpah's *The Deadly Companions* or Billy the Kid in Penn's *The Left-Handed Gun*. Nor is there the sense of the absurdity of life which we sometimes find in Boetticher's films: death, as we have seen, is for Hawks simply a routine occurrence, not a *grotesquerie*, as in *The Tall T* ('Pretty soon that well's going to be chock-a-block') or *The Rise and Fall of Legs Diamond*. For Hawks 'craziness' implies difference, a sense of apartness from the ordinary, everyday, social world. At the same time,

Hawks sees the ordinary world as being 'crazy' in a much more fundamental sense, because devoid of any meaning or values. 'I mean crazy reactions – I don't think they're crazy, I think they're normal – but according to bad habits we've fallen into they seemed crazy.' Which is the normal, which the abnormal? Hawks recognises, inchoately, that to most people his heroes, far from embodying rational values, are only a dwindling band of eccentrics. Hawks's 'kind of men' have no place in the world.

The Hawksian heroes, who exclude others from their own *élite* group, are themselves excluded from society, exiled to the African bush or to the Arctic. Outsiders, other people in general, are perceived by the group as an undifferentiated crowd. Their role is to gape at the deeds of the heroes whom, at the same time, they hate. The crowd assembles to watch the showdown in *Rio Bravo*, to see the cars spin off the track in *The Crowd Roars*. The gulf between the outsider and the heroes transcends enmities among the *élite*: witness *Dawn Patrol* or Nelse in *El Dorado*. Most dehumanised of all is the crowd in *Land of the Pharaohs*, employed in building the Pyramids. Originally the film was to have been about Chinese labourers building a 'magnificent airfield' for the American army, but the victory of the Chinese Revolution forced Hawks to change his plans. ('Then I thought of the building of the Pyramids; I thought it was the same kind of story.') But the presence of the crowd, of external society, is a constant covert threat to the Hawksian *élite*, who retaliate by having 'fun'. In the crazy comedies ordinary citizens are turned into comic butts, lampooned and tormented: the most obvious target is the insurance salesman in *His Girl Friday*. Often Hawks's revenge becomes grim and macabre. In *Sergeant York* it is 'fun' to shoot Germans 'like turkeys'; in *Air Force* it is 'fun' to blow up the Japanese fleet. In *Rio Bravo* the geligniting of the bad men 'was very funny'. It is at these moments that the *élite* turns against the world outside and takes the opportunity to be brutal and destructive.

Besides the covert pressure of the crowd outside, there is also an overt force which threatens: woman. Man is woman's 'prey'. Women are admitted to the male group only after much disquiet and a long ritual courtship, phased round the offering, lighting and exchange of cigarettes, during which they prove themselves worthy of entry. Often they perform minor feats of valour. Even then though they are never really full members. A typical dialogue sums up their position:

> *Woman*: You love him, don't you?
> *Man* (embarrassed): Yes . . . I guess so. . . .
> *Woman*: How can I love him like you?
> *Man*: Just stick around.

The undercurrent of homosexuality in Hawks's films is never crystallised, though in *The Big Sky*, for example, it runs very close to the surface. And he himself described *A Girl in Every Port* as 'really a love story between two men'. For Hawks men are equals, within the group at least, whereas there is a clear identification between women and the animal world, most explicit in *Bringing Up Baby, Gentlemen Prefer Blondes* and *Hatari!* Man must strive to maintain his mastery. It is also worth noting that, in Hawks's adventure dramas and even in many of his comedies, there is no married life. Often the heroes were married or at least intimately committed, to a woman at some time in the distant past but have suffered an unspecified trauma, with the result that they have been suspicious of women ever since. Their attitude is 'Once bitten, twice shy.' This is in contrast to the films of Ford, which almost always include domestic scenes. Woman is not a threat to Ford's heroes; she falls into her allotted social place as wife and mother, bringing up the children, cooking, sewing, a life of service, drudgery and subordination. She is repaid for this by being sentimentalised. Boetticher, on the other hand, has no obvious place for women at all; they are phantoms, who provoke action, are pretexts for male modes of conduct, but have no authentic significance in themselves. 'In herself, the woman has not the slightest importance.'

Hawks sees the all-male community as an ultimate; obviously it is very retrograde. His Spartan heroes are, in fact, cruelly stunted. Hawks would be a lesser director if he was unaffected by this, if his adventure dramas were the sum total of his work. His real claim as an author lies in the presence, together with the dramas, of their inverse, the crazy comedies. They are the agonised exposure of the underlying tensions of the heroic dramas. There are two principal themes, zones of tension. The first is the theme of regression:

of regression to childhood, infantilism, as in *Monkey Business*, or regression to savagery: witness the repeated scene of the adult about to be scalped by painted children, in *Monkey Business* and in *The Ransom of Red Chief*. With brilliant insight, Robin Wood has shown how *Scarface* should be categorised among the comedies rather than the dramas: Camonte is perceived as savage, child-like, subhuman. The second principal comedy theme is that of sex-reversal and role-reversal. *I Was A Male War Bride* is the most extreme example. Many of Hawks's comedies are centred round domineering women and timid, pliable men: *Bringing Up Baby* and *Man's Favourite Sport*, for example. There are often scenes of male sexual humiliation, such as the trousers being pulled off the hapless private eye in *Gentlemen Prefer Blondes*. In the same film, the Olympic Team of athletes are reduced to passive objects in an extraordinary Jane Russell song number; big-game hunting is lampooned, like fishing in *Man's Favourite Sport*; the theme of infantilism crops up again: 'The child was the most mature one on board the ship, and I think he was a lot of fun.'

Whereas the dramas show the mastery of man over nature, over woman, over the animal and childish; the comedies show his humiliation, his regression. The heroes become victims; society, instead of being excluded and despised, breaks in with irruptions of monstrous farce. It could well be argued that Hawks's outlook, the alternative world which he constructs in the cinema, the Hawksian heterocosm, is not one imbued with particular intellectual subtlety or sophistication. This does not detract from its force. Hawks first attracted attention because he was regarded naïvely as an action director. Later, the thematic content which I have outlined was detected and revealed. Beyond the stylemes, semantemes were found to exist; the films were anchored in an objective stratum of meaning, a plerematic stratum, as the Danish linguist Hjelmslev would put it. Thus the stylistic expressiveness of Hawks's films was shown to be not purely contingent, but grounded in significance.

Something further needs to be said about the theoretical basis of the kind of schematic exposition of Hawks's work which I have outlined. The 'structural approach' which underlies it, the definition of a core of repeated motifs, has evident affinities with methods which have been developed for the study of folklore and mythology. In the work of Olrik and others, it was noted that in different folk-tales the same motifs reappeared time and time again. It became possible to build up a lexicon of these motifs. Eventually Propp showed how a whole cycle of Russian fairy-tales could be analysed into variations of a very limited set of basic motifs (or moves, as he called them). Underlying the different, individual tales was an archi-tale, of which they were all variants. One important point needs to be made about this type of structural analysis. There is a danger, as Lévi-Strauss has pointed out, that by simply noting and mapping resemblances, all the texts which are studied (whether Russian fairy-tales or American movies) will be reduced to one, abstract and impoverished. There must be a moment of synthesis as well as a moment of analysis: otherwise, the method is formalist, rather than truly structuralist. Structuralist criticism cannot rest at the perception of resemblances or repetitions (redundancies, in fact), but must also comprehend a system of differences and oppositions. In this way, texts can be studied not only in their universality (what they all have in common) but also in their singularity (what differentiates them from each other). This means of course that the test of a structural analysis lies not in the orthodox canon of a director's work, where resemblances are clustered, but in films which at first sight may seem eccentricities.

In the films of Howard Hawks a systematic series of oppositions can be seen very near the surface, in the contrast between the adventure dramas and the crazy comedies. If we take the adventure dramas alone it would seem that Hawks's work is flaccid, lacking in dynamism; it is only when we consider the crazy comedies that it becomes rich, begins to ferment: alongside every dramatic hero we are aware of a phantom, stripped of mastery, humiliated, inverted. With other directors, the system of oppositions is much more complex: instead of there being two broad strata of films there are a whole series of shifting variations. In these cases, we need to analyse the roles of the protagonists themselves, rather than simply the worlds in which they operate. The protagonists of fairy-tales or myths, as Lévi-Strauss has pointed out, can be dissolved into bundles of differential elements, pairs of opposites. Thus the difference between the prince and the goose-girl can be reduced to two antinomic pairs: one natural, male versus female, and the other cultural, high versus low. We can proceed with the same kind of operation in the study of films, though, as we shall see, we shall find them more complex than fairy-tales.

It is instructive, for example, to consider three films of John Ford and compare their heroes: Wyatt Earp in *My Darling Clementine,* Ethan Edwards in *The Searchers* and Tom Doniphon in *The Man Who Shot Liberty Valance.* They all act within the recognisable Ford world, governed by a set of oppositions, but their *loci* within that world are very different. The relevant pairs of opposites overlap; different pairs are foregrounded in different movies. The most relevant are garden versus wilderness, ploughshare versus sabre, settler versus nomad, European versus Indian, civilised versus savage, book versus gun, married versus unmarried, East versus West. These antinomies can often be broken down further. The East, for instance, can be defined either as Boston or Washington and, in *The Last Hurrah*, Boston itself is broken down into the antipodes of Irish immigrants versus Plymouth Club, themselves bundles of such differential elements as Celtic versus Anglo-Saxon, poor versus rich, Catholic versus Protestant, Democrat versus Republican, and so on. At first sight, it might seem that the oppositions listed above overlap to the extent that they become practically synonymous, but this is by no means the case. As we shall see, part of the development of Ford's career has been the shift from an identity between civilised versus savage and European versus Indian to their separation and final reversal, so that in *Cheyenne Autumn* it is the Europeans who are savage, the victims who are heroes.

The master antinomy in Ford's films is that between the wilderness and the garden. As Henry Nash Smith has demonstrated, in his magisterial book *Virgin Land*, the contrast between the image of America as a desert and as a garden is one which has dominated American thought and literature, recurring in countless novels, tracts, political speeches and magazine stories. In Ford's films it is crystallised in a number of striking images. *The Man Who Shot Liberty Valance*, for instance, contains the image of the cactus rose, which encapsulates the antinomy between desert and garden which pervades the whole film. Compare with this the famous scene in *My Darling Clementine*, after Wyatt Earp has gone to the barber (who civilises the unkempt), where the scent of honeysuckle is twice remarked upon: an artificial perfume, cultural rather than natural. This moment marks the turning-point in Wyatt Earp's transition from wandering cowboy, nomadic, savage, bent on personal revenge, unmarried, to married man, settled, civilised, the sheriff who administers the law.

Earp, in *My Darling Clementine*, is structurally the most simple of the three protagonists I have mentioned: his progress is an uncomplicated passage from nature to culture, from the wilderness left in the past to the garden anticipated in the future. Ethan Edwards, in *The Searchers*, is more complex. He must be defined not in terms of past versus future or wilderness versus garden compounded in himself, but in relation to two other protagonists: Scar, the Indian chief, and the family of homesteaders. Ethan Edwards, unlike Earp, remains a nomad throughout the film. At the start, he rides in from the desert to enter the log-house; at the end, with perfect symmetry, he leaves the house again to return to the desert, to vagrancy. In many respects, he is similar to Scar; he is a wanderer, a savage, outside the law: he scalps his enemy. But, like the homesteaders, of course, he is a European, the mortal foe of the Indian. Thus Edwards is ambiguous; the antinomies invade the personality of the protagonist himself. The oppositions tear Edwards in two; he is a tragic hero. His companion, Martin Pawley, however, is able to resolve the duality; for him, the period of nomadism is only an episode, which has meaning as the restitution of the family, a necessary link between his old home and his new home.

Ethan Edwards's wandering is, like that of many other Ford protagonists, a quest, a search. A number of Ford films are built round the theme of the quest for the Promised Land, an American re-enactment of the Biblical exodus, the journey through the desert to the land of milk and honey, the New Jerusalem. This theme is built on the combination of the two pairs: wilderness versus garden and nomad versus settler; the first pair precedes the second in time. Thus, in *Wagonmaster*, the Mormons cross the desert in search of their future home; in *How Green Was My Valley* and *The Informer*, the protagonists want to cross the Atlantic to a future home in the United States. But, during Ford's career, the situation of home is reversed in time. In *Cheyenne Autumn* the Indians journey in search of the home they once had in the past; in *The Quiet Man*, the American Sean Thornton returns to his ancestral home in Ireland. Ethan Edwards's journey is a kind of parody of this theme: his object is not

Figure 6.2 Wyatt Earp (Henry Fonda) progresses from nature to culture in John Ford's *My Darling Clementine* (Twentieth Century Fox, 1946). Produced by Samuel G. Engel

constructive; to found a home, but destructive, to find and scalp Scar. Nevertheless, the weight of the film remains orientated to the future: Scar has burned down the home of the settlers, but it is replaced and we are confident that the homesteader's wife, Mrs Jorgensen, is right when she says: 'Some day this country's going to be a fine place to live.' The wilderness will, in the end, be turned into a garden.

The Man Who Shot Liberty Valance has many similarities with *The Searchers*. We may note three: the wilderness becomes a garden – this is made quite explicit, for Senator Stoddart has wrung from Washington the funds necessary to build a dam which will irrigate the desert and bring real roses, not cactus roses; Tom Doniphon shoots Liberty Valance as Ethan Edwards scalped Scar; a log-home is burned to the ground. But the differences are equally clear: the log-home is burned after the death of Liberty Valance; it is destroyed by Doniphon himself; it is his own home. The burning marks the realisation that he will never enter the Promised Land, that to him it means nothing; that he has doomed himself to be a creature of the past, insignificant in the world of the future. By shooting Liberty Valance he has destroyed the only world in which he himself can exist, the world of the gun rather than the book; it is as though Ethan Edwards had perceived that by scalping Scar, he was in reality committing suicide. It might be mentioned too that, in *The Man Who Shot Liberty Valance*, the woman who loves Doniphon marries Senator Stoddart. Doniphon when he destroys his log-house (his last words before doing so are 'Home, sweet home!') also destroys the possibility of marriage.

The themes of *The Man Who Shot Liberty Valance* can be expressed in another way. Ransom Stoddart represents rational-legal authority, Tom Doniphon represents charismatic authority. Doniphon abandons his charisma and cedes it, under what amount to false pretences, to Stoddart. In this way charismatic and rational-legal authority are combined in the person of Stoddart and stability thus assured. In *The Searchers* this transfer does not take place; the two kinds of authority remain separated. In *My Darling Clementine* they are combined naturally in Wyatt Earp, without any transfer being necessary. In many of Ford's late films – *The Quiet Man, Cheyenne Autumn, Donovan's Reef* – the accent is placed on traditional authority. The island of Ailakaowa, in *Donovan's Reef*, a kind of Valhalla for the homeless heroes of *The Man Who Shot Liberty Valance*, is actually a monarchy, though complete with the Boston girl, wooden church and saloon, made familiar by *My Darling Clementine*. In fact, the character of Chihuahua, Doc Holliday's girl in *My Darling Clementine*, is split into two: Miss Lafleur and Lelani, the native princess. One represents the saloon entertainer, the other the non-American in opposition to the respectable Bostonians, Amelia Sarah Dedham and Clementine Carter. In a broad sense, this is a part of a general movement which can be detected in Ford's work to equate the Irish, Indians and Polynesians as traditional communities, set in the past, counterposed to the march forward to the American future, as it has turned out in reality, but assimilating the values of the American future as it was once dreamed.

It would be possible, I have no doubt, to elaborate on Ford's career, as defined by pairs of contrasts and similarities, in very great detail, though – as always with film criticism – the impossibility of quotation is a severe handicap. My own view is that Ford's work is much richer than that of Hawks and that this is revealed by a structural analysis; it is the richness of the shifting relations between antinomies in Ford's work that makes him a great artist, beyond being simply an undoubted *auteur*. Moreover, the *auteur* theory enables us to reveal a whole complex of meaning in films such as *Donovan's Reef*, which a recent filmography sums up as just 'a couple of Navy men who have retired to a South Sea island now spend most of their time raising hell'. Similarly, it throws a completely new light on a film like *Wings of Eagles*, which revolves, like *The Searchers*, round the vagrancy versus home antinomy, with the difference that when the hero does come home, after flying round the world, he trips over a child's toy, falls down the stairs and is completely paralysed so that he cannot move at all, not even his toes. This is the macabre *reductio ad absurdum* of the settled.

Perhaps it would be true to say that it is the lesser *auteurs* who can be defined, as Nowell-Smith put it, by a core of basic motifs which remain constant, without variation. The great directors must be defined in terms of shifting relations, in their singularity as well as their uniformity. Renoir once remarked that a director spends his whole life making one film; this film, which it is the task of the critic to construct, consists not only of the typical features of its variants, which are merely its redundancies, but of the principle of variation which governs it, that is its esoteric structure, which can only manifest itself or 'seep to the surface', in Lévi-Strauss's phrase, 'through the repetition process'. Thus Renoir's 'film' is in reality a 'kind of permutation group, the two variants placed at the far ends being in a symmetrical, though inverted, relationship to each other'. In practice, we will not find perfect symmetry, though as we have seen, in the case of Ford, some antinomies are completely reversed. Instead, there will be a kind of torsion within the permutation group, within the matrix, a kind of exploration of certain possibilities, in which some antinomies are foregrounded, discarded or even inverted, whereas others remain stable and constant. The important thing to stress, however, is that it is only the analysis of the whole *corpus* which permits the moment of synthesis when the critic returns to the individual film.

Of course, the director does not have full control over his work; this explains why the *auteur* theory involves a kind of decipherment, decryptment. A great many features of films analysed have to be dismissed as indecipherable because of 'noise' from the producer, the cameraman or even the actors. This concept of 'noise' needs further elaboration. It is often said that a film is the result of a multiplicity of factors, the sum total of a number of different contributions. The contribution of the director – the 'directorial factor', as it were – is only one of these, though perhaps the one which carries the most weight. I do not need to emphasise that this view is quite the contrary of the *auteur* theory and has nothing in common with it at all. What the *auteur* theory does is to take a group of films – the work of one director – and analyse their structure. Everything irrelevant to this, everything non-pertinent, is considered logically secondary, contingent, to be discarded. Of course, it is possible to approach films by studying some other feature; by an effort of critical ascesis we could see films, as Von Sternberg sometimes urged, as abstract light-show or as histrionic feasts. Sometimes these separate texts – those of the cameraman or the actors – may force themselves into prominence so that the film becomes an indecipherable palimpsest. This does not mean, of course, that it ceases to exist or to sway us or please us or intrigue us; it simply means that it is inaccessible to criticism. We can merely record our momentary and subjective impressions.

Myths, as Lévi-Strauss has pointed out, exist independently of style, the syntax of the sentence or musical sound, euphony or cacophony. The myth functions 'on an especially high level where meaning succeeds practically in "taking off" from the linguistic ground on which it keeps rolling'. *Mutatis mutandis,* the same is true of the *auteur* film. 'When a mythical schema is transmitted from one population to another, and there exist differences of language, social organisation or way of life which make the myth difficult to communicate, it begins to become impoverished and confused.' The same kind of impoverishment and confusion takes place in the film studio, where difficulties of communication abound. But none the less the film can usually be discerned, even if it was a quickie made in a fortnight without the actors or the crews that the director might have liked, with an intrusive producer and even, perhaps, a censor's scissors cutting away vital sequences. It is as though a film is a musical composition rather than a musical performance, although, whereas a musical composition exists *a priori* (like a scenario), an *auteur* film is constructed *a posteriori.* Imagine the situation if the critic had to construct a musical composition from a number of fragmentary, distorted versions of it, all with improvised passages or passages missing. [. . .]

7

Direction and Authorship

V.F. Perkins

V.F. Perkins was one of the group of young critics to contribute to the British magazine *Movie*, which introduced auteurism to English readers. Perkins led off the very first issue of *Movie* in June 1962 with a polemical call, "on behalf of the editorial board," for a more personal cinema instead of the British equivalent of the "Tradition of Quality." His book *Film as Film: Understanding and Judging Movies*, first published in 1972, coalesced the discerning auteurist aesthetic that was characteristic of his writing for *Movie*: it opens with the stated aim of presenting "criteria for our judgements of movies" and "is written in the belief that film criticism becomes rational" when it presents clear evidence and reflects on its own methodology. In this reading, excerpted from his chapter on authorship, Perkins was one of the first to explore some of the assumptions of auteurism by considering several aspects of the production context in which directors work as well as the inevitably collaborative nature of the filmmaking process.

[. . .]

The greater the investment in a movie, the greater become the pressures to avoid any form of risk, and the more likely the director becomes to fall victim to executive panic, intrigue or inefficiency. Books have been written about the chaos in which *Cleopatra* was created, a chaos which resulted, not so much from some well-publicized displays of temperament and ill-health, as from a lack of coordination between, and management within, the various departments of the 20th-Century-Fox organization. One's surprise when *Cleopatra* finally emerged was not that the film was in many ways unsatisfactory and incoherent. The amazing thing was that there was actually a movie to show, and that so much of it was intelligent, witty and genuinely glamorous. The rule that managerial feet freeze as budgets ascend has claimed such other notable victims as George Cukor's *A Star Is Born*, Luchino Visconti's *The Leopard*, John Ford's *Cheyenne Autumn*, Sam Peckinpah's *Major Dundee*, and Nicholas Ray's *King of Kings*.

This last can serve as an example of what, one hopes, is the worst that may be inflicted on a picture and its creators. Among the insanities which it suffered were: the insertion of a new character into the script several weeks after filming had begun; the later elimination of that character, in the cutting, together with a key sequence into which he had been introduced; re-recording of the sound-track so as to change the dialogue and bring its delivery into line with M-G-M's concept of 'the traditional religious quietness of Christ'; censorship in relation to the character of Salome which robbed her actions of coherent motivation. *King of Kings*, said Ray, 'was in my opinion atrociously edited.

V. F. Perkins, "Directions and Authorship" (excerpt), pp. 167–86 from *Film as Film: Understanding and Judging Movies* (Harmondsworth, Baltimore, MD: Penguin, 1972).

Figure 7.1 Vincente Minnelli's *King of Kings* (MGM, 1961): A victim of executive interference. Produced by Samuel Bronston

This has nothing to do with the technicians, only with those who do not know that "There is no formula for success, but there *is* a formula for failure and that is to try to please everybody." '[1]

Probably the director's bitterest subjection is not to the taste of his public nor to the occasional ineptitudes of his employers, but to the industrial system, the mechanism of movie finance, production and distribution.

In 1959, Robert Aldrich found himself obliged to start filming *The Angry Hills* with a 'loose, wandering' script because the studio's commitments did not leave time for the necessary overhaul. 'You get locked into these situations,' said Aldrich, 'and it's difficult to know what to do about them.'[2]

The defects of the system, the necessity for *a* system and the unavoidable expense of movie production put the director at a great disadvantage when compared with, say, the novelist. He is continually making irreversible decisions, passing points of no return, which the writer does not encounter until his work has been corrected, revised, polished and sent to the printer. The director cannot abandon a work when it is failing to fulfil his expectations: even his least satisfactory work has to go on display. He is not allowed the privilege of failure. He cannot go back to revise his work and eliminate faults of structure, characterization or style. He cannot allow his mood to dictate his hours of work; he has to meet a schedule which is perfectly indifferent to depression, sickness or creative exhaustion. Imagination, perception and intelligence are not enough; he must also be a diplomat, able as occasion demands to persuade, reconcile, dominate, scare and inspire his co-workers. We shall never know how many films have turned out badly not through any fault in their conception but through personal incompatibilities within the production team; or through the need to rush the work in order to meet a commitment; or through financial troubles necessitating drastic changes in production plans; or through simple bad luck with locations, the weather, ill-health, censorship and so on.

As long as we concentrate on the director's working conditions and measure them against some ideal notion of how and why good work is created, so long will it seem impossible for good work to emerge from the 'commercial machine'. Thus Rotha reflected on the alleged imbecility of the American cinema (not of specific American films).

> Perhaps it was impossible to produce, let alone conceive any work of real aesthetic value when surrounded by the Hollywood atmosphere of dollars and opportunism, where culture and sincerity seem to be unknown qualities. . . . Sincerity of purpose and surroundings bring out good work. Transfer the painter from his disordered studio into a luxurious apartment with every new-fangled contrivance to hand and he is at a loss.[3]

This nostalgia for a garret-and-absinthe system of production makes righteous, perhaps envious, indignation a substitute for judgement or understanding. Ultimately it frees the critic from the bother of seeing or thinking about the foredoomed failures.

A knowledge of the film industry's mechanics and structure helps us to understand many things. It explains why many promising projects remain unrealized, why directors are often employed on subjects in which they have little interest, why they must often work in collaboration with people for whose talents they have little respect. In brief, it explains why direction is an activity surrounded by compromise and frustration.

'I've been making films for thirty years,' said Mizoguchi.

> If I look back on all I've done in that time I see nothing but a series of compromises with the capitalists, whom we nowadays call producers, in order to make a film in which I could take pleasure. My only real desire has been to be able to make a film according to my own taste. But I have often been forced to accept a job knowing in advance that it couldn't offer the least chance of success and would mean nothing for me but an absolute failure.[4]

Yet Mizoguchi's best films display a continuity of style in which the highly individual compound of sensuality, elegance, bitterness and vigour is very marked. Through a series of assignments, he was able to create a consistent world, a place of brief pleasures and enduring sadness where moments of tenderness and repose break the action with a suddenness that is itself close to violence.

'The system' can account for some of the director's failures and frustrations. But it does not help us to understand or appreciate his success. The accepted image of 'Hollywood', graveyard of artistic integrity and creative ambition, is the product of some notable martyrdoms: Von Stroheim, Sternberg, Eisenstein, Welles. . . . But it does not take account of the large number of directors who functioned superbly within the commercial framework when it was at its most restricting: Ford, Vidor, Hitchcock, Preminger, Hawks, Boetticher, Fuller . . .

I have offered a frightening picture of what *may* happen to films and directors through their involvement with a huge commercial enterprise. But this needs to be balanced by a recognition that the commercial system can, often does, work in the director's favour. If he has the good fortune to want to make pictures on subjects and in styles which the mass public wants to see, the director need never be aware of restriction or compromise. Minnelli made most of his pictures for M-G-M, by reputation the most repressive of the big companies and the one most insistent on its own 'studio style'. His *Two Weeks in Another Town* suffered, as we have seen, at the company's hands; but thirty pictures were produced in fruitful collaboration to offset that one disaster. Not all the movies were successful, of course, but the list includes such fine pictures as *Meet Me in St Louis, Under the Clock, The Pirate, An American in Paris, Lust for Life, Designing Woman, Gigi, Some Came Running* and *The Courtship of Eddie's Father.* About his working conditions Minnelli said:

> Nearly always I have the opportunity of working with the writer more or less from the beginning. In cases where the script has not been completed, I generally work with the writer for at least five or six weeks. In some cases I haven't had that time for giving directions; in that case it's been done as we go along. The director usually works with the writer in preparing the script. I found it that way in all cases. . . . Cutting has never been a problem because I've always worked on it in harmony with the producer and the studio. There are compromises, of course, but I've always been quite satisfied with the cutting in the end. *Two Weeks* was just an arbitrary cutting which was completely wrong. That happens to everyone, I find.[5]

Any system claims its own victims. The cinema's industrial setup promotes certain sorts of subject and treatment at the expense of others; it involves a waste of much that is potentially valuable. Judged by their fruits, other systems are not noticeably better. John Huston said: 'Some of the worst pictures I've made, I've made since I've had complete freedom.'[6] Creative freedom does not guarantee, nor does industrial production rule out, a good result. In the cinema we are involved with a product, not a system of production. We can reach a judgement without knowing how a film was made.

The movies offer a constant challenge of connoisseurship. The credits supplied at the beginning of a picture are notoriously unreliable. Even when they are accurate they suggest a clearer demarcation of responsibility than exists among most film-makers during most productions. They may lead us to credit the writer with dialogue or action improvised by the director or the performers. Conversely, they may result in our attributing to the director visual effects devised by the designer, photographer or colour consultant. Unless one has watched the planning and making of a picture, it is impossible to know precisely who contributed each idea or effect to the finished movie. We cannot, for example, tell to what extent the editing was foreseen by the director during filming, supervised by him in the cutting rooms, or left to the ingenuity of the man named as editor.

Only external information call tell us whether, and for what reason, the subject of a film was chosen by the men who made it; whether the finished product represents what they *wanted* to do or what they were allowed (perhaps obliged) to do. Intentions and creative processes are invisible. At best we guess them or are given external, often suspect, information about them. We cannot do what Ernest Lindgren asks us to do in forming our judgements: 'Look to the operations of the mind which precede conscious creation'[7] – because there is no single mind to which we can look.

Lindgren gives as an example of total creative control the director Vittorio de Sica and his two films *Bicycle Thieves* and *Umberto D.* Both films were written by Cesare Zavattini, a scenarist who exerted considerable influence over the post-war Italian cinema. They are certainly the best de Sica has directed. But they are *not* what Lindgren demands of the finest film, an 'expression of the experience and vision of a single man'.[8] As much of their impact comes from the situations devised by the writer and from the construction of their scripts as from the director's realization of their scenarios. At the very least Zavattini must be granted his share in the responsibility for these pictures. The fact that Lindgren can illustrate his argument in favour of undivided authorship with two films whose authorship *was* divided is sufficient to undermine his theory.

We can sustain the belief that a good film is necessarily an expression of one man's vision, a communication from the director to his audience, only if we can demonstrate a difference in kind and effect between the personal film and the factory movie. The 'stamp of one predominating creative mind' must be visibly distinct from the stamp of several collaborating creative minds. Provided that a film has its own unity, it seems unimportant whether the unity was evolved through cooperation and compromise within the production team or conceived by one man and imposed on his collaborators.

If the relationships established in a film are significant, it makes no difference to the spectator how they came, or were brought about, or to what extent their significance was intended. A movie has a meaning for the spectator when he is able to interpret its pattern of actions and images. Provided that its relationships are coherently shaped, the film embodies – and can be shown to embody – a consistent meaning which may or may not have been sought, or sincerely felt, by the director.

Jacques Tourneur's *The Night of the Demon* is a striking illustration of this. It presents a story of the occult, drawn from M. R. James's *The Casting of the Runes,* in which a modern scientist is gradually persuaded that his life is endangered by the demonic powers of a black magician. The film employs a whole arsenal of devices – shock effects, grotesque comedy, camera and cutting tricks, ambiguities of character and image. Particularly clever is its exploitation of the spectator's inability to distinguish between truth and convincing lies; we are continually aware that some of the characters within the film story may be 'acting' but we have no means of confirming or rejecting the suspicion. The film's devices are justified in relation to its effect, or purpose, since they have a consistent tendency. They involve the spectator in the

Figure 7.2 The undermining of rationality in Jacques Tourneur's *Night of the Demon* (Columbia/Sabre Film Productions, 1957). Produced by Frank Bevis

process undergone by the hero, steady undermining of rational scepticism and final reduction to a state of panic in which the reality of occult power is recognized.

We can translate the meaning of the movie in two ways, on the basis of its form and on the basis of our experience. In so far as it succeeds in terrorizing the spectator the movie acts as a demonstration. If the film had been unable to call on reserves of superstitious belief in the powers of darkness it would have been unable to convince and so to scare us. To enter into the experience of the film is to share, however temporarily or playfully, its assumptions.

Even if we watch Tourneur's movie with complete emotional detachment it remains, in its dramatic structure, an assertion of the inadequacy of rational scepticism. We may challenge this argument. There is no denying that it is contained (that is consistently provoked) by the picture. But we cannot know from seeing the film how far its 'message' was intended or how far it was an accidental by-product of other intentions. It may be that *Night of the Demon* was made by men who genuinely believe in the power of Satanism. It may have been designed in agnostic fashion to test the hypothesis that we all, secretly and irrationally, harbour such a belief. Or it may have been created simply to provide its audience with ninety minutes of enjoyable terror, and its metaphysical content used, without sincerity, as a means to this end.

We may regard the last as the most likely explanation. But likelihood is a long way from certainty. The question of intended meaning, of sincerity, is left open by the film. Its effective meaning is all that we can be sure of. And it is all that we need to know. If as connoisseurs we wished to place the picture in the context of Tourneur's work and beliefs it would be important to find out how far *Night of the Demon* embodies a sincere attitude to the occult. But so long as we are concerned, as critics, with the meaning and quality of this particular movie such information remains irrelevant.

The fact that movie production is a collaborative enterprise makes the cinema accident-prone. The interaction between the various personalities and talents engaged in making a film cannot be foreseen. Tbe composition of a film unit, like that of a jazz group, determines the personality of the end product.

This is not a matter simply of 'correct' casting among the various artists and technicians who make a definable contribution to a movie. Two talented designers may produce décors of equal excellence, equally appropriate to the job in hand, yet quite distinct in the sorts of emphasis and suggestion which they evoke. Selecting the production team is like a chemical or culinary experiment. The separate elements/ingredients are known but their impact upon each other is a subject for hopeful speculation rather than certainty.

Out of the confusion of temperaments, ambitions and talents, good things often, and extraordinary things sometimes, come. The meal has frequently proved more satisfying than the recipe would suggest or the chef could expect. Some notable examples: *Pillow Talk*, *Forbidden Planet*, *Gypsy*, *The Manchurian Candidate*, *North to Alaska*, *Them!*, *House of Wax*, *Foreign Intrigue*, *The Wonderful Country*, *Sweet Smell of Success*. It would be hard to establish that any of these shows us 'an artist working at the height of his powers', etc. For the most part, the various functions are performed with intelligence rather than inspiration. These pictures are cleverly written, effectively acted and skilfully filmed. But with the possible exceptions of *North to Alaska* and *Foreign Intrigue* (which are perhaps mainly John Wayne and Robert Mitchum movies) their individuality does not seem to derive from one contribution rather than another.

It is not possible for me to trace the precise 'flavour' of these films in other work by the same writers or directors or actors. Their personalities seem the result of particular combinations of talents. Films are 'accidental' to the extent that they evolve unpredictably under the impact of different, often opposed, personalities. They are also impersonal in so far as their styles and meanings are not derived from one man's conceptions. Individual creative responsibility and artistic control are limited wherever film-making is a group activity; that is, almost always. In expressing and exploring group concerns rather than the private interests of a solitary artist, popular films tap one source of coherence that is independent of 'artistic' self-expression.

There are others, notably the story itself. If the director is successful in his attempt to examine subject through story, theme through action, then significance becomes so deeply embedded in the movie that it seems a by-product of the narrative. Conversely, the intention to make a statement becomes unmistakeable when the message is detached from the dynamic of the movie, tacked on to its structure rather than built into it. In John Schlesinger's *Darling*, for example, there is a scene where the heroine wanders into the library of a posh gaming club. There she reads aloud John of Gaunt's speech in praise of England from *Richard II*. We know that the scene is intended to work as ironic comment simply because it has no other function in the film. It does not advance the plot. It tells us nothing about the characters. The speech could as well have been read by a passing charlady as by the movie's heroine; the effect would have been much the same. We notice the meaning because the scene gives us nothing else to notice. Conversely, by following the logic of a story, setting out to solve its problems and realize its possibilities, making it credible and effective, the director may not create a meaning; but he may allow it to emerge. It seems probable that such good movies as *Them!*, *Panic in the Year Zero*, *House of Wax* and *The Scarface Mob* were films of this sort.

The opening sequence of Don Sharp's otherwise uninteresting *Kiss of the Vampire* provides a very striking example of the way in which a strong situation can generate meanings of its own. We are watching the last moments of a burial service. A small group is gathered in respectful mourning around an open grave. The priest intones the ritual of committal with mechanical fervour. Isolated at some distance from the mumbling mourners, a shabby figure drunkenly observes the scene. As the priest finishes his recital the man approaches the scandalized group, pushes his way through to the graveside, claims the gravedigger's spade and, we suppose, the right to be first in casting earth upon the coffin. Instead, he drives the shaft of the spade through the coffin-lid. From inside the box there comes a scream, and the blood of a 'living' person gathers round the break in the wood. A vampire has been exterminated.

The feebleness of what follows suggests that this sequence was devised as nothing more than a suitably shocking hors-d'oeuvre to yet another saga of the undead. But, efficiently filmed, the scene is so dominated by its basic concept that it becomes something altogether more provocative: consecration versus exorcism, a conflict of rituals holy and unholy, the Christian one recognized, complacent and comforting, the other furtive, demonic, violent but effective. The flatness of the filming itself adds to the effect by putting both rites on the same level. We can accept both as necessary or dismiss both as superstitious, but they are so linked that we cannot endorse one while rejecting the other. The significance of the scene is contained in the tension it poses between 'faith' and 'superstition'. All the spectator needs is an adequate grounding in vampire lore. Without that the sequence would not make sense. It would seem that the coffin had contained a live body and that the scream had come from one of the onlookers. Film reviewers have made us familiar with the notion that a director can transcend the limitations of a genre; here, as quite often in the movies, we see genre transcending the limitations of the director.

This can happen whenever the genre contains within its own evolving 'rules' the possibility of coherent meaning. One example, notable in both number and quality, was the series of Western and adventure films produced in the fifties where the shifting settings of a journey paralleled the moral and psychological development of the characters: *Red River*, *The Big Sky*, *River of No Return*, *The African Queen*, *The Far Country*, *The Naked Spur*, *Legend of the Lost*, and many more. Similarly, any credible gangster film, from *Scarface* and *Public Enemy* to *Pay or Die* and *Underworld U.S.A.*, touches on questions of political philosophy. When it shows the mechanics of gang rule the gangster movie is dealing with the concept of Law, and with the relationship between power and fear. A convincing reconstruction demands a coherent attitude to motives and pressures. Theme and meaning are, in a sense, ready-made.

But a director can also exploit consciously the ambiguities of his medium and the possibilities of his genre. Thus we are unable to tell from the film itself whether the variations on a political theme which emerge from Samuel Fuller's *Underworld U.S.A.* are a by-product of the story or the reason for which the story was created. The moral pattern in *River of No Return* seems too fully developed to have been accidental; yet Preminger talks of the film as an assignment undertaken for strictly contractual reasons. In Preminger's film, and in Fuller's, effect and meaning are quite clear. The source alone is at issue and that can be traced mainly by reference to their other works. Again, *The Servant* is a movie with a rhythm, style and texture of its own. Anyone who had read *The Birthday Party* or *The Caretaker* would recognize it as the work of Harold Pinter. Equally, those familiar with *The Criminal* or *Time Without Pity* would soon detect the hand of Joseph Losey. The signatures of both writer and director are quite evident. In various contexts it may be convenient to treat *The Servant* as a Pinter film directed by Losey, or as a Losey picture written by Pinter. But neither the writing nor the direction is submerged or absorbed in the manner required by the 'solitary man' theories of film. *The Servant* is dominated by the tension between two creative minds, two styles, two personalities and two attitudes. But it is *Losey's* version of the Pinter script; and if we are concerned with film as film it is the realization that must claim our interest and judgement.

Any claims made for direction are of course claims about its possibilities, not rules governing its exercise. However wide or narrow the theoretical limits that we place on the director's function, the actual extent to which his authority is established within those limits must vary with each director's ability and involvement.

The director may be little more than an adviser or a catalyst. Certainly it is one of his most important jobs to stand in the place of the future spectator, to embody in himself the absent audience and so to inspire actors and technicians that they give the clearest and most convincing realization of each character and event. His task as the audience's representative is largely a critical one; but his criticism has to be constructive. He must decide on our behalf what we need to see and how and when we need to see it. He is required not only to say when a particular point is obscure or overstated but also to suggest how it may be made more clearly, more subtly or more effectively. His advisory function already begins to be a creative one.

His other most vital responsibility is that of coordination. Directors are needed precisely because film-making involves so many and such varied kinds of creative decision. If a movie is to have even the most elementary form of unity – that is, one in which the various elements at least do not jar – it is essential that actors, designers and technicians work coherently towards an agreed end. The most obvious method of achieving this result is to put one man in charge of the entire operation. The director is there to ensure that the details of performance and recording are related to the total design. It is through his control over detail that the director may become chiefly responsible for the effect and quality of the completed movie.

His task of organization is, in part, a matter of technique and craftsmanship. As interpreter of the screenwriter's work he is employed to ensure that the actors respect the dynamics of the scenario in the rhythms and tempo with which they play each scene. Through his supervision of the camera team he must achieve a sufficient variety in the images to interest the spectator's eye. At the same time he has to secure images that the editor will be able to assemble into flowing and coherent sequence. As a craftsman he must keep a balance that avoids both monotony and disintegration.

Here again, the work of the interpreting craftsman shades off very quickly into the work of the creator. There can be no clear distinction between supervising the cameraman and creating the images, or between advising the actors and moulding the performances. But unless we consider acting and photography to be the whole process of film-making, the director is still a long way from the total authorship that is often claimed for him.

It is clear that, in outline at least, the shape of a picture is controlled by the construction of its script. Over this the director may have no influence at all. Certainly, the word 'direction' implies no such control. By the time the work of direction begins, plot and dialogue are already established; more or less detailed decisions have been taken on character, casting, motivation and setting. The shape of the film has already been sketched and, with that, some part of its meaning has been determined.

Some producers insist that the director's work should begin and end on the studio floor; that he should have no influence over design, cutting, music or any other process that is independent of the shooting. More usually, a director would expect to work in close contact with the writer, to have a voice in the casting, to be allowed dialogue changes at his own discretion, and to guide the work of the editor and the composer. The most powerful directors are virtually their own screenwriters; it is pure formality (plus union demarcation) that prevents, for example, Hitchcock, Preminger and Hawks from receiving credit as co-authors of their screenplays. A more accurate arrangement would often be the French one whereby the director shares the scenario credit and the writer is named separately as author of the dialogue. Direction's most significant fields of control are also those which make up the smallest area of responsibility that a director can be given: at the very least direction determines how a film is performed and how it is recorded.

Control over performance is control over what happens in the film. This control is clearly incomplete. It is exercised within the limits imposed by the scenario and the cast. The scenario dictates a certain minimum of action essential to the plot mechanism. The director's first task is to make that action convincing, interesting and effective. If the plot demands that hero and heroine meet at a party, there is nothing direction can do about that, however much greater the significance that might be derived from having them meet in an elevator or at a gathering of the local parent-teacher association. The director works within the prescribed situation. But given that he works with enthusiasm, and of course talent, the way that he works is necessarily personal.

It is a commonplace that each of us has his own image of a scene described in a novel; in other words that we each direct the scene differently in our minds. How much more must this apply when the director has to complete the vague images of the mind, the sketched action of a scenario, and to produce the concrete, detailed action of a film image. Even when the director himself thinks that he is merely 'doing the script', his choices of gesture, rhythm and emphasis will reflect his own experience, sympathies and convictions.

In order to make a scene convincing for us, the director has first to convince himself. But what, within the given context, is convincing? Whether the characters move or stand still, look at or away from one another, are close together or widely spaced, speak confidently or with hesitation – these and a host of other detailed decisions are required at every moment. These sorts of detail are to a very small extent controlled by the writing. They are part of the business of direction and, in sum, they are largely responsible for the spectator's attitude to the characters and their actions and so for the mood and effect of the scene. The director begins to be the author of the film from the moment when he finds *his* way to make the details significant as well as credible.

Of course, it is open to the writer to state, in some detail, how he wants the scene played; and the director may well believe that his writer knows best. Similarly, the actors may arrive at their own way of playing it, leaving the director simply to accept or reject their decisions.

At the same time it is important to recognize that the director controls the film as much by what he allows as by what he invents. He has to decide whether to accept the suggestions and demands of his colleagues. That decision is itself positive and creative. The resulting action 'belongs' to the director as much as do the details that he himself suggests. Preminger, by reputation the most autocratic of directors, has said:

> I never want to have an actor feel that he is directed. . . . If there are two possibilities and the one that the actor suggests is, in my opinion, a little less effective than the one I could suggest, I let him do it his way because I feel I will get something in exchange. It comes easier; it's more right for him, even if it could be improved. It's like a suit which you've worn for a long time; it's more comfortable, it fits better than a new suit.[9]

With actors, as with scripts, the director is given material which can be used and organized but not transformed at will. The star performers influence what the audience expects and therefore how it reacts. The familiar styles and personalities of such skilled performers as Grant, Mitchum, Wayne, Hepburn and Newman necessarily contribute to the total style of any film in which they appear.

The director who is also a producer can allow for this fact when casting his picture. Among Hitchcock movies distinctions of tone, style and meaning can be drawn between those starring Cary Grant and those with James Stewart in the lead. Hitchcock profits from the different sorts of impact that the two personalities make. Another director, Leo MacCarey, remarked that any film with Cary Grant tends to turn towards comedy because the actor automatically seeks out the humour in a dramatic situation. Hitchcock recognizes this in casting Grant for films (*To Catch a Thief, North by Northwest*) whose tones are predominantly light and in which Grant's presence acts as our guarantee that all will turn out well. At the same time, he centres his meaning on the moral weakness of the hero's disengaged attitude. In the Stewart films (*Rope, Rear Window, Vertigo*) the tone is much darker, reflecting the disturbing ambiguities of the central personality. Stewart's bemused detachment is seen as a mask which thinly disguises a deep and dangerous involvement.

Hitchcock is able to absorb the strong personalities of Grant and Stewart into the textures and meanings of his movies. But Hitchcock has the advantage of control over casting: *Vertigo* would have been a very different film if its obsessed hero had been played by Cary Grant. Where the director joins the production after its casting is complete, the personalities of the actors become part of the given material, like the script, which cannot be altered. A Wayne movie is a Wayne movie. How good a picture it is will depend largely upon the extent to which the 'Big John' image can be made to coexist with, or intensify, the significance of the action.

Here again, the director's job is to exploit and organize imaginatively as often as it is to invent. I do not know of a James Stewart performance which is less than accomplished. But the best Stewart pictures are those in which the direction has managed to integrate the tensions of his (screen) personality, to make them contribute to the total pattern: the

Hitchcock pictures, Mann's *The Far Country,* Ford's *Two Rode Together* and Preminger's *Anatomy of a Murder* are some of the most notable examples.

Tackling the same problem from the opposite angle, we can observe the continuity of response that a forceful director can achieve with distinctive personalities in a series of different pictures. Nicholas Ray, for example, has drawn unexpected performances from actors whose names have usually suggested toughness and self-sufficiency. Under Ray's direction, Bogart (*In a Lonely Place*), Mitchum (*The Lusty Men*), Cagney (*Run for Cover*) and Heston (*55 Days at Peking*) revealed surprising dimensions of uncertainty, tenderness and vulnerability. In these respects Cagney's performance in *Run for Cover* was more consistent with Mitchum's in *The Lusty Men*, and with Ray's work generally, than with the established Cagney image. That is not to say that he ceased to be recognizable as James Cagney. The matter is one of emphasis, not of transformation. The personalities of the real stars are complex enough to reward examination from many viewpoints. We should expect different directors to explore and stress different qualities in the same actor. The task for both director and star is to find an effective way of matching the familiar personality of the actor with the special demands of the role.

The director is the only member of the production team who can see (whose job it is to see) the whole film rather than particular aspects, the interrelationship of the parts rather than the parts as separate tasks. As Max Ophuls expressed it: 'There are as many creators to a film as there are people who work on it. My job as director consists of making out of this choir of people a creator of films.'[10] The director takes charge at the point where the components of the film have been assembled and they await their organization into synthesis. From this point those components are going willy-nilly to enter into relationship. Their interaction can be mutually enriching, controlled and coherent. Since it will exist, it is best that it exist to positive effect. Correlation occurs within the image, between images, and across the film's complete time-span. Change must take place. But organized, significant change is development. Actors, designers, writers, photographers contribute major components of this development; the director is best placed to design the development itself. Being in charge of relationships, of synthesis, he is in charge of what makes a film a *film*.

Direction can determine which objects and actions are to be seen as foreground and which as background. By controlling the balance between the elements, by creating a coherence of emphasis, it can control the priorities of significance and so shape the movie's theme. The more closely it is adjusted, the more intimately personal the balance is likely to become. Density of interrelationship between parts is both the source of contained significance and the touchstone of style. Style and meaning are twin products of synthesis; they do not result from a simple accumulation of independent statements by actors and technicians.

A film may assemble a number of such 'statements' and they may well be interesting in themselves. To this extent it can usefully be seen as a group work. But if the film's form embodies a viewpoint, explored in depth and with complexity, it is almost certain to be the director's. He is in control throughout the period in which virtually all the significant relationships are defined. He has possession of the means through which all other contributions acquire meaning *within* the film.

The director's authority is a matter not of total creation but of sufficient control. The inadequacies of an actor, an editor or a composer may inflict more or less brutal damage on work which ought to have yielded a fine picture. Or, skilled cutters and musicians can do much to make bad work less noticeably bad. But they cannot put on to film the close correspondence between character and design, gesture and image, movement and motive, which a director has failed to create.

That is part of the reason for resisting the claim that the screen-writer is normally the major source of meaning and quality in good movies. So far from creating a finished work, he offers an outline open to an infinite variety of treatments. It may be so rambling, inconsistent and self-contradictory as to defy redemption. However rich its possibilities may seem, it cannot determine the significance or excellence of the realization. There is no such thing as the movie which 'simply films the script'. Too much is added in the transfer from paper to celluloid. If all that is added yields little of extra significance or complexity, why make or watch the movie?

CONTROL vs. CREATION

The case is overstated if we fail to consider the possibility of the screenplay's being so tightly constructed and coherently designed towards particular ends that the director needs only to achieve and coordinate the prescribed effects in order to let the *writer's* meanings come through. Here the writer's creative authority could hardly be denied. But there is no reason to wish to deny it. If we observe the frequency with which precision of style and complexity of meaning are chiefly attributable to the director, we do not thereby claim that direction must always and everywhere be the sole source of any meaning we find in a film and any pleasure it gives us.

Nor do we deny that a lively interaction between members of the film-making team *may* create a composite personality for the movie. I have named some films which attain a rewarding level of quality and significance without betraying a dominant 'signature'. The fluke masterpiece – where the various contributions fall into an intricate reciprocity of meaning without the director's causing them to do so – must remain a possibility. But I do not know of such a film. The 'team-movies' which I cited still seem very worthwhile, yet they fall rather short of the best the cinema has offered. The argument is circular, since I recognized them as team products by their common deficiency: a looseness of organization, of relationship between parts, that resulted in a provocative combination of ingredients rather than an indissoluble synthesis.

The most telling argument for a critical belief in the 'director's cinema' is that it has provided the richest base for useful analyses of the styles and meanings of particular films. Yet on theoretical grounds alone, when a movie offers a complex and meaningful interrelation of event, image, idea and feeling, it surely makes sense to think the most likely source a gifted director's full involvement with his materials. At this level of involvement decisions which critics may analyse in relation to total style and meaning may be taken by the director simply because they 'feel right' – they *fit*.

The connoisseurship implicit in a view of the director as author does not demand that we see a great director's failures as master-pieces, although it may make them more interesting than a feebler artist's successes. By seeing the connections between a director's films we can become more sensitive to the pattern within each of them. 'Director's cinema' offers us most clues to the understanding which must precede judgement.

Notes

1 Nicholas Ray, *Movie*, no. 9, May 1963 p. 23.
2 Robert Aldrich, *Movie*, no. 8, April 1963 p. 10.
3 Paul Rotha, *The Film Till Now* (London: Vision Press, 1949), p. 78.
4 Kenji Mizoguchi, *Cahiers du Cinéma*, vol. 20, no. 116, February 1961, p. 15.
5 Minnelli, *Movie*, no. 10, June 1963 pp. 23–4.
6 John Huston, quoted in James Goode, *The Story of The Misfits*, (Bobbs-Merrill, New York, 1963), p. 46.
7 Ernest Lindgren, *The Art of the Film* (London: Allen and Unwin, 1963), p. 202.
8 Ibid., p. 192.
9 Preminger, *Movie*, no. 4, November 1962, p. 20.
10 Max Ophuls, *Cahiers du Cinéma,* no. 81, March 1958, p. 4.

8

Ideas of Authorship

Edward Buscombe

Edward Buscombe has taught at a number of universities and served as general editor in the Publishing Department of the British Film Institute. His work has focused largely on the western genre, with important monographs on John Ford's *Stagecoach* and *The Searchers* and Clint Eastwood's *Unforgiven* as well as editing the authoritative *BFI Companion to the Western*. In this essay, first published in 1973 in *Screen*, a journal that was more concerned with ideology and theory than *Movie*, Buscombe connects earlier auteurism with the more recent developments of "auteur-structuralism." Critiquing *Cahiers* and Andrew Sarris and building on Peter Wollen's distinction between Howard Hawks and "Howard Hawks," he contrasts auteurism's Romantic conception of the artist as an isolated, unified individual at odds with society with structuralism's concern with repeated structural patterns that reveal cultural values and beliefs.

The *auteur* theory was never, in itself, a theory of the cinema, though its originators did not claim that it was. The writers of *Cahiers du Cinéma* always spoke of '*la politique des auteurs*'. The translation of this into 'the *auteur* theory' appears to be the responsibility of Andrew Sarris. In an essay entitled 'Notes on the Auteur Theory in 1962' he remarked, 'Henceforth, I will abbreviate "*la politique des auteurs*" as the *auteur* theory to avoid confusion.'[1] Confusion was exactly what followed when the newly christened 'theory' was regarded by many of its supporters and opponents alike as a total explanation of the cinema.

Not only was the original *politique* of *Cahiers* somewhat less than a theory; it was itself only loosely based upon a theoretical approach to the cinema which was never to be made fully explicit. The *politique*, as the choice of term indicates, was polemical in intent and was meant to define an attitude to the cinema and a course of action. In the pursuit of this course *Cahiers* did inevitably reveal some of the theory on which the *politique* was based; but usually this appeared incidentally, and at times incoherently.

One thing is clear, however. From the beginning *Cahiers*, and its predecessor *La Revue du Cinéma*, were committed to the line that the cinema was an art of personal expression. (In the second issue of *La Revue* an article appeared entitled: 'La création doit être l'ouvrage d'un seul'). At the period (the late 1940s) it was inevitable that part of the project of a new film magazine would be to raise the cultural status of the cinema. The way to do this, it seemed, was to advance the claim of the cinema to be an art form like painting or poetry, offering the individual the freedom of personal expression. The main difference at that time between *Cahiers* and other film magazines was that *Cahiers* did not feel that opportunities of this kind

Edward Buscombe, "Ideas of Authorship," pp. 75–85 from *Screen* 14, no. 3 (Autumn 1973). © 1973 by Edward Buscombe. Reprinted by permission of the author and *Screen*.

Figure 8.1 John Huston's *The Red Badge of Courage* (MGM, 1951): An example of adaptation rather than creative transformation. Produced by Gottfreid Reinhardt

were to be found exclusively in the European 'art' cinema. Right from the very earliest issues there are discussions of Hollywood directors such as Welles, Ford and Lang. *Cahiers* was concerned to raise not only the status of the cinema in general, but of American cinema in particular, by elevating its directors to the ranks of the artists.

The *politique* in the sense of a line that will be rigorously pursued and provocatively expressed, really dates from an article in issue no. 31 by François Truffaut entitled 'Une certaine tendance du cinéma français'. Truffaut attacks what he calls the tradition of quality in the French cinema, by which he means the films of directors such as Delannoy, Allégret and Autant-Lara, and especially the adaptations by Aurenche and Bost of well-known novels. They are attacked for being literary, not truly cinematic, and are also found guilty of 'psychological realism'. Truffaut defines a true film *auteur* as one who brings something genuinely personal to his subject instead of merely producing a tasteful, accurate but lifeless rendering of the original material. Examples of true *auteurs* are Bresson and Renoir. Instead of merely transferring someone else's work faithfully and self-effacingly, the *auteur* transforms the material into an expression of his own personality.

So successful was Truffaut's call to arms, and so many were the *auteurs* subsequently discovered, that in all the later articles in *Cahiers* in which the '*politique*' was explicitly discussed, a great deal of space had to be devoted to dissociating the journal from the excesses committed in its name. (See, for example, issues nos 63, 70, 126, 172). Truffaut had referred only to French directors, but *Cahiers* began to give more and more space to the American cinema. In its special issue nos 150–1 on the American cinema no fewer than 120 *cinéastes* (i.e. *auteurs*) were identified.

Yet even by this late date (1964) the questions of what an *auteur* is and why the cinema should be discussed largely in terms of individual artists are ones that are only answered by implication. Clear articulations of a theory behind the practice are rare and sketchy. But a review by André Bazin of *the Red Badge of Courage* (no. 27, pp. 49f.) gives a clue. Bazin distinguishes between Hitchcock, a true *auteur*, and

Huston, who is only a *metteur en scène*, who has 'no truly personal style'. Huston merely adapts, though often very skilfully, the material given him, instead of transforming it into something genuinely his own. A similar point is made by Jacques Rivette in a later issue (no. 126), in the course of a discussion on criticism. Rivette declares that Minnelli is not a true *auteur*, merely a talented director at the mercy of his script. With a bad script he makes a bad and uninteresting film. Fritz Lang, on the other hand, can somehow transform even indifferent material into something personal to him (and this, Rivette assumes, makes it interesting).

Such discussions, however, do not advance much beyond Truffaut's original position, though they serve to confirm *Cahiers'* stance on the issue of personal expression. Some attempt to modify this was made by Eric Rohmer. Rejecting the lunatic fringe who took the issue of personality to extremes, Rohmer writes, 'Le film est pour lui [the *auteur*] une architecture dont les pierres ne sont pas – ne doivent pas être – filles de sa propre chair.'[2] The comparison with architecture, another industrial art, would seem to lead in a different direction from comparisons with literature, the best known of which is, of course, Alexandre Astruc's article 'The Birth of a New Avant Garde: *La Caméra-Stylo*'.[3] But it was Astruc's article which was to prove more influential over the critics of *Cahiers*. The more romantic conception of the director as the 'only begetter' of a film was the one that dominated the journal.

One expression of this which seems particularly indebted to Romantic artistic theory is that of Rivette in issue no. 126: 'Un cinéaste, qui a fait dans le passé de très grands films, peut faire des erreurs, mais les erreurs qu'il fera ont toutes chances, a priori,[4] d'être plus passionantes que les réussites d'un confectionneur.'[5] What seems to lie behind such a statement is the notion of the 'divine spark' which separates off the artist from ordinary mortals, which divides the genius from the journeyman. All the articles by Truffaut, Bazin and Rivette from which I have quoted share this belief in the absolute distinction between *auteur* and *metteur en scène*, between *cinéaste* and '*confectionneur*', and characterise it in terms of the difference between the *auteur*'s ability to make a film truly his own, i.e. a kind of original, and the *metteur en scène*'s inability to disguise the fact that the origin of his film lies somewhere else.

When this is compared with a statement from early Romantic literary theory, it is easy enough to see the derivation of this distinction.

> An Original may be said to be of *vegetable* nature; it rises spontaneously from the vital root of genius; it grows, it is not made; Imitations are often a sort of *manufacture*, wrought up by those *mechanics*, *art* and *labour*, out of pre-existent materials not their own.[6]

It's not surprising, therefore, to find the *auteur* critics draw others of their assumptions from Romantic theorists. For example, Coleridge makes a distinction between two kinds of literature which makes use of the metaphor of organic unity contained in the above passage: 'The plays of Beaumont and Fletcher are mere aggregations without unity; in the Shakespearean drama there is a vitality which grows and evolves itself from within – a keynote which guides and controls the harmonies throughout.'[7] This notion of the unity produced by the personality of the *auteur* is central to the *Cahiers'* position; but it is made even more explicit by their American apologist, Andrew Sarris: 'The *auteur* critic is obsessed with the wholeness of art and the artist. He looks at a film as a whole, a director as a whole. The parts, however entertaining individually, must cohere meaningfully.'[8] The work of a *metteur en scène* will never be more than the sum of its parts, and probably less. The *auteur's* personality, on the other hand, endows his work with organic unity. The belief that all directors must be either *auteurs* or *metteurs en scène* led inevitably to a kind of apartheid, according to which, as Rivette says, the failures of the *auteurs* will be more interesting than the successes of the rest. Another formulation of what is essentially the same distinction occurs in *Cahiers* no. 172:

> l'être doué du moindre talent esthétique, si sa personalité 'éclate' dans l'oeuvre, l'emportera sur le technicien le plus avisé. Nous découvrons qu'il n'y pas de règles. L'intuition, la sensibilité, triomphent de toutes théories.[9]

Whether this zeal to divide directors into the company of the elect on the right and a company of the damned on the left owes anything to the Catholic influence in *Cahiers* is hard to say at this distance; but what can be identified, yet again, is the presence of Romantic artistic theory in the opposition of intuition and rules, sensibility and theory.

This tendency in *Cahiers* to make a totem of the personality of the *auteur* went to such extremes that every now and again the editors felt the need to redress the balance. André Bazin, writing in issue no. 70, introduces a different perspective:

> The evolution of Western art towards greater personalisation should definitely be considered as a step forward, but only so long as this individualisation remains only a final perfection and does not claim to *define* culture. At this point, we should remember that irrefutable commonplace we learnt at school: the individual transcends society, but society is also and above all *within* him. So there can be no definitive criticism of genius or talent which does not first take into consideration the social determinism, the historical combination of circumstances, and the technical background which to a large extent determines it.[10]

Bazin, as Rohmer had done before, takes up the analogy of architecture:

> If you will excuse yet another commonplace, the cinema is an art which is both popular and industrial. These conditions, which are necessary to its existence, in no way constitute a collection of hindrances – no more than in architecture – they rather represent a group of positive and negative circumstances which have to be reckoned with.[11]

To be fair, *Cahiers* never entirely forgot these commonplaces, and quite frequently ran articles on the organisation of the film industry, on film genres (such as Bazin's own 'The Evolution of the Western' in December 1955) and on the technology of the cinema. The development of '*la politique des auteurs*' into a cult of personality gathers strength with the emergence of Andrew Sarris, for it is Sarris who pushes to extremes arguments which in *Cahiers* were often only implicit.

Sarris, for example, rejects Bazin's attempt to combine the *auteur* approach with an acknowledgement of the forces conditioning the individual artist. Arguing strongly against any kind of historical determinism, Sarris states:

> Even if the artist does not spring from the idealised head of Zeus, free of the embryonic stains of history, history itself is profoundly affected by his arrival. If we cannot imagine Griffith's *October* or Eisenstein's *Birth of a Nation* because we find it difficult to transpose one artist's unifying conceptions of Lee and Lincoln to the other's dialectical conceptions of Lenin and Kerensky, we are nevertheless compelled to recognise other differences in the personalities of these two pioneers beyond their respective cultural complexes. It is with these latter differences that the *auteur* theory is most deeply concerned. If directors and other artists cannot be wrenched from their historical environments, aesthetics is reduced to a subordinate branch of ethnography.[12]

(Pauline Kael is for once correct to write of this: 'And when is Sarris going to discover that aesthetics is indeed a branch of ethnography; what does he think it is – a sphere of its own, separate from the study of man and his environment?'[13] But her own confusion re-emerges later in the same essay when she remarks, 'Criticism is an art, not a science . . .'[14] Is ethnography, then, not a science?)

If Sarris is not saying that genius is independent of time and place, then he comes dangerously close to it. The critic's task as he sees it is to scan the cinema for signs of 'personality', and having found them to mine the film so as to bring as much as possible of it to the surface. It is not his job to explain how it got there. He is canny enough to remain aware that his position is partly determined by the need to maintain a polemic, both against those who are contemptuous of the American cinema and against the crudities of 'mass media critics'. ('*Auteur* criticism is a reaction against sociological criticism that enthroned the *what* against the *how*.'[15]) But this awareness does not save him from being driven further and further into an untenable position. That position is reached, I think, when he writes in his essay of 1962: 'The second premise of the *auteur* theory is the distinguishable personality of the director as a criterion of value. Over a group of films a director must exhibit certain recurring characteristics of style which serve as his signature.'[16] Here, surely, is a fatal flaw in Sarris's argument, and the sleight of hand he uses to cover it cannot disguise its vulnerability. He is attempting to make the *auteur* theory perform two functions at the same time. On the one hand, it is a method of classification. Sarris talks elsewhere about the value of the theory as a way of ordering film history, or a tool for producing a map of the cinema, and no one could deny that in this sense the theory has, whatever its faults, been extremely productive, as a map should be, in opening up unexplored territory. But at the same time Sarris also requires the theory to act as a means of measuring value. Films, he is saying, become valuable in so far as they reveal directorial personality. He therefore does precisely what Bazin said should not be done: he uses individuality as a test of cultural value. It's worth noting that Sarris is not consistent in practising what he preaches, for several directors whose work undoubtedly exhibits a high degree of personality do not rank very far up the league tables of *The American Cinema*. Kazan, Wilder, Dassin, even Brian Forbes, all produce films easily recognizable as 'theirs' which are not rated by Sarris.

As one means, among others, of classifying films, the *auteur* theory has proved its usefulness. But to assert that personality is *the* criterion of value seems altogether more open to question. The assumption that individuality and originality are valuable in themselves is, as Bazin points out in 'La Politique des Auteurs', derived from Romantic artistic theory. Sarris goes further; 'the *auteur* theory values the personality of the director precisely because of the barriers to its expression.'[17] In *Culture and Society* Raymond Williams describes the way in which aesthetic theory came in the Romantic period to see the artist as essentially opposed to society, achieving personal expression in the face of a hostile environment and valuing it all the more for this.[18] Sarris is directly in this tradition.

Sarris, like *Cahiers* before him, then uses this criterion of value as a means of raising the status of American cinema. He admits that in Hollywood there are pressures which might work against individual expression. But so there are elsewhere:

> All directors, and not just in Hollywood, are imprisoned by the conditions of their craft and their culture. The reason foreign directors are almost invariably given more credit for creativity is that the local critic is never aware of all the influences operating in a foreign environment. The late Robert Warshow treated Carl Dreyer as a solitary artist and Leo McCarey as a social agent, but we know now that there were cultural influences in Denmark operating on Dreyer. *Day of Wrath* is superior by any standard to *My Son John*, but Dreyer is not that much freer an artist than McCarey. Dreyer's chains are merely less visible from our vantage point across the Atlantic.[19]

Taken at face value this is unexceptionable; of course no director has total freedom, and there is no reason *a priori* why American cinema should not be as good as any other. And in fact, says Sarris, it is better:

> After years of tortured revaluation, I am now prepared to stake my critical reputation, such as it is, on the proposition that Alfred Hitchcock is artistically superior to Robert Bresson by every criterion of excellence, and further that, film for film, the American cinema has been consistently superior to that of the rest of the world from 1915 through 1962. Consequently, I now regard the *auteur* theory primarily as a critical device for recording the history of the American cinema, the only cinema in the world worth exploring in depth beneath the frosting of a few great directors on top.[20]

Again, this in itself is fair enough; the problem is that, having obtained our easy assent to the proposition that all film-makers are subject to conditions, he appears, by a sleight of hand, to proceed on the assumption that therefore conditions are unimportant. America can produce film artists in just the same way as Europe, but more of them, and of a higher standard. Film history is for Sarris the history of *auteurs*. The acknowledgement of 'conditions' turns out to be mere lip service. And it is not, I think, difficult to see why: if personality is the criterion of value, and can be achieved in the face of 'conditions', then it is not the critic's job to be much concerned with them.

One obvious objection to employing individuality as a test of value is that a director could well be highly individual, but a bad director. In the first edition of *Signs and Meaning in the Cinema* Peter Wollen does not seem wholly to avoid this trap. In the chapter on the *auteur* theory he writes:

> My own view is that Ford's work is much richer[21] than that of Hawks and that this is revealed by a structural analysis; it is the richness of the shifting relations between antinomies in Ford's work that makes him a great artist, beyond being simply an undoubted *auteur*. Moreover, the *auteur* theory enables us to reveal a whole complex of meaning in films such as *Donovan's Reef*, which a recent filmography sums up as just 'a couple of Navy men who have retired to a South Sea island now spend most of their time raising hell.'[22]

There is no doubt that films such as *Donovan's Reef*, *Wings of Eagles* and especially *The Sun Shines Bright* (almost indecipherable to those unacquainted with

Ford's work) do reveal a great deal of meaning when seen in the context of Ford's work as a whole. But does this make them 'good' films as well as interesting ones? The question is worth asking, because it seems to be just this smuggling in of one thing under the guise of another that is most responsible for the reputation in some quarters of the *auteur* theory as merely the secret password of an exclusive and fanatical sect.

Possibly people such as Pauline Kael, who are roused to fury by Sarris's version of the *auteur* theory, should simply be left to stew in their own juice. And perhaps those who won't accept that *Wings of Eagles* is a good film have a very narrow concept of what is good and are unreasonable in demanding that all films should have formal perfection, should be 'intelligent', 'adult', etc. But the *auteur* theory becomes more tenable if in fact it is not required to carry in its baggage the burden of being an evaluative criterion. And Wollen, in the third edition of his book, dumps it along with much else.[23]

> At this point, it is necessary to say something about the *auteur* theory since this has often been seen as a way of introducing the idea of the creative personality into the Hollywood cinema. Indeed, it is true that many protagonists of the *auteur* theory do argue this way. However, I do not hold this view and I think it is important to detach the *auteur* theory from any suspicion that it simply represents a 'cult of personality' or apotheosis of the director. To my mind the *auteur* theory actually represents a radical break with the idea of an 'art' cinema, not the transplant of traditional ideas about art into Hollywood. The 'art' cinema is rooted in the idea of creativity and the film as the expression of an individual vision. What the *auteur* theory argues is that any film, certainly a Hollywood film, is a network of different statements, crossing and contradicting each other, elaborated into a final 'coherent' version. Like a dream, the film the spectator sees is, so to speak, the 'film façade', the end product of 'secondary revision', which hides and masks the process which remains latent in the film's 'unconscious'; by a process of comparison with other films, it is possible to decipher, not a coherent message or world-view, but a structure which underlies the film and shapes it, gives it a certain pattern of energy cathexis. It is this structure which *auteur* analysis disengages from the film.
>
> The structure is associated with a single director, an individual, not because he has played the role of artist, expressing himself or his own vision in the film, but because it is through the force of his preoccupations that an unconscious, unintended meaning can be decoded in the film, usually to the surprise of the individual concerned. . . . It is wrong, in the name of a denial of the traditional idea of creative subjectivity, to deny any status to individuals at all. But Fuller or Hawks or Hitchcock, the directors, are quite separate from 'Fuller' or 'Hawks' or 'Hitchcock', the structures named after them, and should not be methodologically confused.[24]

Wollen does not claim that this is a total theory of the cinema:

> *Auteur* theory cannot simply be applied indiscriminately. Nor does an *auteur* analysis exhaust what can be said about any single film. It does no more than provide one way of decoding a film, by specifying what its mechanics are at one level. There are other kinds of code that could be proposed, and whether they are of any value or not will have to be settled by reference to the text, to the films in question.[25]

There is much in this position that is attractive. It satisfies our sense that on the one hand the American cinema is the richest field for study, and on the other hand that the more one knows about its habitual methods of working the less it becomes possible to conceive of Hollywood as populated by autonomous geniuses. And certainly *a priori* evidence suggests that the themes of transferred guilt in Hitchcock, of home, and the desert/garden antithesis in Ford, for example, are almost entirely unconscious, making it inappropriate to speak, as so much *auteur* criticism does, about a director's world-view (and especially about the moral worth of that world-view). And the avoidance of the problem of evaluation is surely justified until we have an adequate description of what we should evaluate.

Structural analysis of *auteurs* has produced important results, not least in Wollen's own book. Yet there are surely problems in using techniques which were developed for the analysis of forms of communications which are entirely unconscious such as dreams, myths and language itself. For what is the exact relation between the structure called 'Hitchcock' and the film director called Hitchcock, who actually makes decisions about the story, the acting, the sets, the camera placing? It is possible to reveal structures in Hitchcock's work which are by no means entirely unconscious, such as the use of certain camera angles

Figure 8.2 Themes of subjectivity and guilt inform *The Wrong Man* (Warner Bros, 1956). Produced and directed by Alfred Hitchcock

to involve and implicate the audience in the action. Hitchcock remarks about *The Wrong Man*:

> The whole approach is subjective. For instance, they've slipped on a pair of handcuffs to link him to another prisoner. During the journey between the station house and the prison, there are different men guarding him, but since he's ashamed, he keeps his head down, staring at his shoes, so we never show the guards.[26]

This kind of thing occurs in almost all Hitchcock's films, and so could be said to identify him as an *auteur* in the traditional sense. But it also connects to his obsessional and no doubt largely unconscious (till he read about it) concern with guilt and voyeurism, which have been revealed in structural analysis.

Earlier versions of the *auteur* theory made the assumption that because there was meaning in a work someone must have deliberately put it there, and that someone must be the *auteur*. Wollen rightly resists that. But this doesn't mean that one can only talk about unconscious structures (admittedly Wollen does say it is wrong to deny any status to individuals at all, but is there not something a little disingenuous in this concession?). The conscious will and talent of the artist (for want of a better word) may still be allowed some part, surely. But of course, that conscious will and talent are also in turn the product of those forces that act upon the artist, and it is here that traditional *auteur* theory most seriously breaks down. As Sam Rohdie says:

> *Auteurs* are out of time. The theory which makes them sacred makes no inroad on vulgar history, has no concepts for the social or the collective, or the national.
>
> The primary act of *auteur* criticism is one of dissociation – the *auteur* out of time and history and society is also freed from any productive process, be it in Los Angeles or Paris.[27]

The test of a theory is whether it produces new knowledge. The *auteur* theory produced much, but of a very partial kind, and much it left totally unknown. What is needed now is a theory of the cinema that locates directors in a total situation, rather than one which assumes that their development has only an internal dynamic. This means that we should jettison such loaded terms as 'organic', which inevitably suggest that a director's work derives its impetus from within. All such terms reveal often unformulated and always unwarranted assumptions about the cinema; a film is not a living creature, but a product brought into existence by the operation of a complex of forces upon a body of matter. Unfortunately, criticism which deals with only one aspect of the artistic object is easier to practise than that which seeks to encompass the totality. Three approaches seem possible, and each of them must inevitably squeeze out the *auteur* from his position of prominence, and transform the notion of him which remains. First, there is the examination of the effects of the cinema on society (research into the sociology of mass media, and so on). Second is the effect of society on the cinema; in other words, the operation of ideology, economics, technology, etc. Lastly, and this is in a sense only a sub-section of the preceding category, the effects of films on other films; this would especially involve questions of genre, which only means that some films have a *very* close relation to other films. But all films are affected by the previous history of the cinema. This is only one more thing that traditional *auteur* theory could not cope with. It identified the code of the *auteur*; but was silent on those codes intrinsic to the cinema, as well as to those originating outside it.

Notes

1 *Film Culture*, no. 27 (Winter 1962–3); reprinted in *Perspectives on the Study of Film*, ed. John Stuart Katz, Boston, Little, Brown, 1971 (p. 129). Sarris later conceded, 'Ultimately, the *auteur* theory is not so much a theory as an attitude, a table of values that converts film history into directorial biography.' *The American Cinema,* New York, Dutton, 1968, p. 30.

2 'For the *auteur,* the film is a piece of architecture whose bricks are not – must not be – the children of his own body.' *Cahiers du Cinéma*, no. 63, October 1956, p. 55.

3 Alexandre Astruc, 'The Birth of a New Avant-Garde: "*La Caméra-Stylo*" ', reprinted in *The New Wave*, ed. Peter Graham, London, Secker & Warburg, 1968.

4 It's hard to see how this can be so *a priori* in any case; only according to the balance of probabilities.

5 'A *cinéaste* who has made great films in the past may make mistakes, but his mistakes will have every chance of being, *a priori*, more impressive than the successes of a "manufacturer" '. *Cahiers,* no. 126, p. 17. The same idea is to be found in Sarris, in *The American Cinema*, p. 17: 'the worst film of a great director may be more interesting than the best film of a fair to middling director.'

6 Quoted in Raymond Williams, *Culture and Society 1780–1950*, Harmondsworth, Penguin, 1961, p. 54.

7 S. T. Coleridge, *Lectures and notes on Shakespeare and other English poets* (1818), London, Dent, 1951.

8 Sarris, *American Cinema*, p. 30.

9 *Cahiers*, no. 172, November 1965, p. 3: 'a man endowed with the least aesthetic talent, if his personality "shines out" in the work, will be more successful than the cleverest technician. We discover that there are no rules. Intuition and sensibility triumph over all theories.'

10 André Bazin, 'La Politique des Auteurs', trans. in *The New Wave*, p. 142.

11 Ibid.

12 Sarris, in Katz, op. cit., pp. 132–3.

13 Pauline Kael, 'Circles and Squares: Joys and Sarris', in Katz, op. cit., p. 154.

14 Ibid., p. 142.

15 Sarris, *American Cinema*, p. 36.

16 Sarris, in Katz, op. cit., p. 137.

17 Sarris, *American Cinema*, p. 31.

18 See Williams, op. cit., pp. 48–64 and *passim*.

19 Sarris, *American Cinema*, p. 36.

20 Sarris in Katz, op. cit., p. 134.

21 Possibly by 'richer' Wollen does not imply 'has greater aesthetic value'; but if that is the case his terminology is a little confusing.

22 Peter Wollen, *Signs and Meaning in the Cinema*, 3rd edn, London, Secker & Warburg, 1972, p. 102.

23 The virtual obsession with aesthetic – even moral – evaluation which has characterised so much British criticism undoubtedly gave the *auteur* theory much of its appeal. (It's hard to ascribe moral value to, say, the studio system.)

24 Ibid., pp. 167–8.

25 Ibid., p. 168.

26 François Truffaut, *Hitchcock*, London, Panther edn 1969, p. 296.

27 Sam Rohdie, 'Education and Criticism', *Screen*, vol. 12, no. 1, p. 10.

9

Ideology, Genre, Auteur

Robin Wood

Robin Wood is one of the most influential film critics in English. An early proponent of classic auteurism in such volumes as *Ingmar Bergman* and *Howard Hawks*, his *Hitchcock's Films* (first published in 1965) combined close textual analysis with incisive prose and demonstrated auteurism as a viable critical methodology. Profoundly affected by feminist and ideological criticism and theory in the 1970s, Wood later re-examined his earlier work on Hitchcock and Hawks while tackling new questions of gender and ideology rather than focusing on universal human values. Wood's view of Hawks has remained fundamentally unchanged 30 years later, Hawks for him continuing to be regarded as a great communal director concerned with fundamental human issues of self-respect, emotional maturity, and personal relationships; by contrast, Wood has revised or revisited his critical views of Hitchcock's films in several revisions, the most recent of which was published in 2002, wherein he takes into account other developments in film studies, most notably feminism. In this essay, Wood's project is similar in that he is seeking a satisfying synthesis of critical methodologies. Here he considers the place of the auteur in relation to genre and ideology through a comparison of Frank Capra's *It's a Wonderful Life* (1946) and Alfred Hitchcock's *Shadows of a Doubt* (1943) in terms of how each director's personal vision negotiates the inevitable presence of dominant ideology in Hollywood cinema.

The truth lies not in one dream but in many.
– Arabian Nights (Pier Paolo Pasolini, 1974)

Each theory of film so far has insisted on its own particular polarization. Montage theory enthrones editing as the essential creative act at the expense of other aspects of film; Bazin's realist theory, seeking to right the balance, merely substitutes its own imbalance, downgrading montage and artifice; the revolutionary theory centered in Britain in *Screen* (but today very widespread) rejects – or at any rate seeks to "deconstruct" – realist art in favor of the so-called open text. Auteur theory, in its heyday, concentrated attention exclusively on the fingerprints, thematic or stylistic, of the individual artist; recent attempts to discuss the complete "filmic text" have tended to throw out ideas of personal authorship altogether. Each theory has, given its underlying position, its own validity – the validity being dependent upon and restricted by the position. Each can offer insights into different areas of cinema and different aspects of a single film.

I have suggested elsewhere[1] the desirability for critics – whose aim should always be to see the work a wholly as possible, as it is – to be able to draw on the discoveries and particular perceptions of each

Robin Wood, "Ideology, Genre, Auteur," pp. 1, 16, 18 from *Film Comment* 13, no. 1 (January–February 1977).

theory, each position, without committing themselves exclusively to any one. The ideal will not be easy to attain, and even the attempt raises all kinds of problems, the chief of which is the validity of evaluative criteria that are not supported by a particular system. For what, then, *do* they receive support? No critic, obviously, can be free from a structure of values, nor can he or she afford to withdraw from the struggles and tensions of living to some position of "aesthetic" contemplation. Every critic who is worth reading has been, on the contrary, very much caught up in the effort to define values beyond purely aesthetic ones (if indeed such things exist). Yet to "live historically" need not entail commitment to a system or a cause; rather, it can involve being alive to the opposing pulls, the tensions, of one's world.

The past two decades have seen a number of advances in terms of the opening up of critical possibilities, of areas of relevance, especially with regard to Hollywood: the elaboration of auteur theory in its various manifestations; the interest in genre; the interest in ideology. I want here tentatively to explore some of the ways in which these disparate approaches to Hollywood movies might interpenetrate, producing the kind of synthetic criticism I have suggested might now be practicable.

In order to create a context within which to discuss *It's a Wonderful Life* (Frank Capra, 1946) and *Shadow of a Doubt* (Alfred Hitchcock, 1943), I want to attempt (at risk of obviousness) a definition of what we mean by American capitalist ideology – or, more specifically, the values and assumptions so insistently embodied in and reinforced by the classical Hollywood cinema. The following list of components is not intended to be exhaustive or profound, but simply to make conscious, prior to a discussion of the films, concepts with which we are all perfectly familiar:

1. Capitalism, the right of ownership, private enterprise, personal initiative; the settling of the land.
2. The work ethic: the notion that "honest toil" is in itself and for itself morally admirable, this and concept 1 both validating and reinforcing each other. The moral excellence of work is also bound up with the necessary subjugation or sublimation of the libido: "the Devil finds work for idle hands." The relationship is beautifully epitomized in the zoo-cleaner's song in *Cat People* (Jacques Tourneur, 1942):

   Nothing else to do,
   Nothing else to do,
   I strayed, went a-courting
   'cause I'd nothing else to do.

3. Marriage (legalized heterosexual monogamy) and family – at once the further validation of concepts 1 and 2 (the homestead is built for the woman, whose function is to embody civilized values and guarantee their continuance through her children) and an extension of the ownership principle to personal relationships ("*My* house, *my* wife, *my* children") in a male-dominated society.

4a. Nature as agrarianism; the virgin land as Garden of Eden. A concept into which, in the western, concept 3 tends to become curiously assimilated (ideology's function being to "naturalize" cultural assumptions): e.g., the treatment of the family in *Drums Along the Mohawk* (John Ford, 1939).

4b. Nature as the wilderness, the Indians, on whose subjugation civilization is built; hence by extension the libido, of which in many westerns the Indians seem an extension or embodiment, as in *The Searchers* (Ford, 1956).

5. Progress, technology, the city ("New York, New York, it's a wonderful town").
6. Success and wealth – a value of which Hollywood ideology is also deeply ashamed, so that, while hundreds of films play on its allure, very few can allow themselves openly to extol it. Thus its ideological "shadow" is produced.
7. The Rosebud syndrome. Money isn't everything; money corrupts; the poor are happier. A very convenient assumption for capitalist ideology; the more oppressed you are, the happier you are, as exemplified by the singing "darkies" of *A Day at the Races* (Sam Wood, 1937).
8. America as the land where everyone is or can be happy; hence the land where all problems are solvable within the existing system (which may need a bit of reform here and there but no *radical* change). Subversive systems are assimilated wherever possible to serve the dominant ideology. Andrew Britton, in a characteristically brilliant

article on Hitchcock's *Spellbound* (1945), argues that there even Freudian psychoanalysis becomes an instrument of ideological repression.[2] Above all, this assumption gives us that most striking and persistent of all classical Hollywood phenomena, the happy ending: often a mere "emergency exit" (Sirk's phrase)[3] for the spectator, a barely plausible pretense that the problems the film has raised are now resolved. *Hilda Crane* (Philip Dunne, 1956) offers a suitably blatant example among the hundreds possible.

Out of this list logically emerge two ideal figures:

9. The ideal male: the virile adventurer, the potent, untrammelled man of action.
10. The ideal female: wife and mother, perfect companion, the endlessly dependable mainstay of hearth and home.

Since these combine into an ideal couple of quite staggering incompatibility, each has his or her shadow:

11. The settled husband/father, dependable but dull.
12. The erotic woman (adventuress, gambling lady, saloon "entertainer"), fascinating but dangerous, liable to betray the hero or turn into a black panther.

The most striking fact about this list is that it presents an ideology that, far from being monolithic, is *inherently* riddled with hopeless contradictions and unresolvable tensions. The work that has been done so far on genre has tended to take the various genres as "given" and discrete, defining them in terms of motifs, iconography, conventions, and themes. What we need to ask, if genre theory is ever to be productive, is less *what* than *why*. We are so used to the genres that the peculiarity of the phenomenon itself has been too little noted. The idea I wish to put forward is that the development of the genres is rooted in the sort of ideological contradictions my list of concepts suggests. One impulse may be the attempt to deny such contradiction by eliminating one of the opposed terms, or at least by a process of simplification.

Robert Warshow's seminal essays on the gangster hero and the westerner (still fruitfully suggestive, despite the obvious objection that he took too little into account) might be adduced here. The opposition of gangster film and western is only one of many possibilities. *All* the genres can be profitably examined in terms of ideological oppositions, forming a complex interlocking pattern: small-town family comedy/sophisticated city comedy; city comedy/film noir; film noir/small-town comedy, and so on. It is probable that a genre is ideologically "pure" (i.e., safe) only in its simplest, most archetypal, most aesthetically deprived and intellectually contemptible form – such as the Hopalong Cassidy films or Andy Hardy comedies.

The Hopalong Cassidy films (in which Indians, always a potentially disruptive force in ideological as well as dramatic terms, are, in general, significantly absent), for example, seem to depend on two strategies for their perfect ideological security: the strict division of characters into good and evil, with no "grays"; and Hoppy's sexlessness (he never becomes emotionally entangled). Hence the possibility of evading all the wandering/settling tensions on which aesthetically interesting westerns are generally structured. (An intriguing alternative: the ideal American family of Roy Rogers/Dale Evans/Trigger.) *Shane* (George Stevens, 1953) is especially interesting in this connection. A deliberate attempt to create an "archetypal" western, it also represents an effort to resolve the major ideological tensions harmoniously.

One of the greatest obstacles to any fruitful theory of genre has been the tendency to treat the genres as discrete. An ideological approach might suggest why they can't be, however hard they may appear to try: at best, they represent different strategies for dealing with the same ideological tensions. For example, the small-town movie with a contemporary setting should never be divorced from its historical correlative, the western. In the classical Hollywood cinema motifs cross repeatedly from genre to genre, as can be made clear by a few examples. The home/wandering opposition that Peter Wollen rightly sees as central to Ford[4] is not central only to Ford or even to the western; it structures a remarkably large number of American films covering all genres, from *Out of the Past* (Tourneur, 1947) to *There's No Business Like Show Business* (Walter Lang, 1954), The explicit comparison of women to cats connects screwball comedy (*Bringing Up Baby*, Howard Hawks, 1938), horror film (*Cat People*, Tourneur, 1942), melodrama (*Rampage*, Phil Karlson,

1963), and psychological thriller (*Marnie*, Hitchcock, 1964). Another example brings us to this essay's specific topic: notice the way in which the potent male adventurer, when he enters the family circle, immediately displaces his "shadow," the settled husband/father, in both *The Searchers* and *Shadow of a Doubt*.

Before we attempt to apply these ideas to specific films, however, one more point needs to be especially emphasized: the presence of ideological tensions in a movie, though it may give it an interest beyond Hopalong Cassidy, is not in itself a reliable evaluative criterion. It seems probable that artistic value has always been dependent on the presence – somewhere, at some stage – of an individual artist, whatever the function of art in the particular society and even when (as with the Chartres cathedral) one no longer knows who the individual artists were. It is only through the medium of the individual that ideological tensions come into particular focus, hence become of aesthetic as well as sociological interest. It can perhaps be argued that works are of especial interest when the defined particularities of an auteur interact with specific ideological tensions and when the film is fed from more than one generic source.

The same basic ideological tensions operate in both *It's a Wonderful Life* and *Shadow of a Doubt*. They furnish further reminders that the home/wandering antinomy is by no means the exclusive preserve of the western. Bedford Falls and Santa Rosa can be seen as the frontier town seventy or so years on; they embody the development of the civilization whose establishment was celebrated around the same time by Ford in *My Darling Clementine* (1946). With this relationship to the western in the background (but in Capra's film made succinctly explicit), the central tension in both films can be described in terms of genre: the disturbing influx or film noir into the world of small-town domestic comedy. (It is a tension clearly present in *Clementine* as well: the opposition between the daytime and nighttime Tombstones.)

The strong contrast presented by the two films testifies to the decisive effect of the intervention of a clearly defined artistic personality in an ideological-generic structure. Both films have as a central ideological project the reaffirmation of family and small-town values that the action has called into question. In Capra's film this reaffirmation is magnificently convincing (but with full acknowledgment of the suppressions on which it depends and, consequently, of its precariousness); in Hitchcock's it is completely hollow. The very different emotional effects of the films – the satisfying catharsis and emotional fullness of Capra's, the "bitter taste" (on which so many have commented) of Hitchcock's – are very deeply rooted not only in our response to two opposed directorial personalities but in our own ideological structuring.

One of the main ideological and thematic tensions of *It's a Wonderful Life* is beautifully encapsulated in the scene in which George Bailey (James Stewart) and Mary (Donna Reed) smash windows in a derelict house as a preface to making wishes. George's wish is to get the money to leave Bedford Falls, which he sees as humdrum and constricting, and travel about the world; Mary's wish (not expressed in words, but in its subsequent fulfillment – confirming her belief that wishes don't come true if you speak them) is that she and George will marry, settle down, and raise a family in the same derelict house, a ruined shell that marriage-and-family restores to life.

This tension is developed through the extended sequence in which George is manipulated into marrying Mary. His brother's return home with a wife and a new job traps George into staying in Bedford Falls to take over the family business. With the homecoming celebrations continuing inside the house in the background, George sits disconsolately on the front porch; we hear an off-screen train whistle, to which he reacts. His mother (the indispensable Beulah Bondi) comes out and begins "suggesting" that he visit Mary; he appears to go off in her direction, physically pointed that way by his mother, then reappears and walks away past the mother – in the opposite direction.

This leads him, with perfect ideological/generic logic, to Violet (Gloria Grahame). The Violet/Mary opposition is an archetypally clear rendering of that central Hollywood female opposition that crosses all generic boundaries – as with Susan (Katharine Hepburn) and Alice (Virginia Walker) in *Bringing Up Baby*, Irena (Simone Simon) and Alice (Jane Randolph) in *Cat People*, Chihuahua (Linda Darnell) and Clementine (Cathy Downs) in *My Darling Clementine*, Debby (Gloria Grahame) and Katie (Jocelyn Brando) in *The Big Heat* (Fritz Lang, 1953). But Violet (in front of an amused audience) rejects his poetic invitation to a barefoot ramble over the hills in the moonlight; the good-time gal offers no more solution to the hero's wanderlust than the wife-mother figure.

So back to Mary, whom he brings to the window by beating a stick aggressively against the fence of the neat, enclosed front garden – a beautifully precise expression of his ambivalent state of mind: desire to attract Mary's attention warring with bitter resentment of his growing entrapment in domesticity. Mary is expecting him; his mother has phoned her, knowing that George would end up at her house. Two ideological premises combine here: the notion that the "good" mother always knows, precisely and with absolute certitude, the workings of her son's mind; and the notion that the female principle is central to the continuity of civilization, that the "weaker sex" is compensated with a sacred rightness.

Indoors, Mary shows George a cartoon she has drawn of George, in cowboy denims, lassoing the moon. The moment is rich in contradictory connotations. It explicitly evokes the western and the figure of the adventurer-hero to which George aspires. Earlier, it was for Mary that George wanted to "lasso the moon," the adventurer's exploits motivated by a desire to make happy the woman who will finally entrap him in domesticity. From Mary's point of view, the picture is at once affectionate (acknowledging the hero's aspirations), mocking (reducing them to caricature), and possessive (reducing George to an image she creates and holds within her hands).

The most overtly presented of the film's structural oppositions is that between the two faces of capitalism, benign and malignant. On the one hand, there are the Baileys (father and son) and their building and loan company, its business practice based on a sense of human needs and a belief in human goodness; on the other, there is Potter (Lionel Barrymore), described explicitly as a spider, motivated by greed, egotism, and miserliness, with no faith in human nature. Potter belongs to a very deeply rooted tradition. He derives most obviously from Dickens's Scrooge (the film is set at Christmas) – a Scrooge disturbingly unrepentant and irredeemable – but his more distant antecedents are in the ogres of fairy tales.

The opposition gives us not only two attitudes to money and property but two father images (Bailey, Sr., and Potter), each of whom gives his name to the land (Bailey Park, in small-town Bedford Falls, and Pottersville, the town's dark alternative). Most interestingly, the two figures (representing American choices, American tendencies) find their vivid ideological extensions in Hollywood genres: the happy, sunny world of small-town comedy (Bedford Falls is seen mostly in the daytime) and the world of film noir, the dark underside of Hollywood ideology.

Pottersville – the vision of the town as it would have been if George had never existed, shown him by his guardian angel (Henry Travers) – is just as "real" as (or no more stylized than) Bedford Falls. The iconography of small-town comedy is exchanged, unmistakably, for that of film noir, with police sirens, shooting in the streets, darkness, vicious dives, alcoholism, burlesque shows, strip clubs, and the glitter and shadows of noir lighting. George's mother, embittered and malevolent, runs a seedy boarding-house; the good-time gal/wife-mother opposition, translated into noir terms, becomes an opposition of prostitute and repressed spinster-librarian. The towns emerge as equally valid images of America – validated by their generic familiarity.

Beside *Shadow of a Doubt*, *It's a Wonderful Life* manages a convincing and moving affirmation of the values (and value) of bourgeois family life. Yet what is revealed, when disaster releases George's suppressed tensions, is the intensity of his resentment of the family and desire to destroy it – and with it, in significant relationship, his work (his culminating action is furiously to overthrow the drawing board with his plans for more small-town houses). The film recognizes explicitly that behind every Bedford Falls lurks a Pottersville, and implicitly that within every George Bailey lurks an Ethan Edwards of *The Searchers*. Potter, tempting George, is given the devil's insights into his suppressed desires. His remark, "You once called me a warped, frustrated old man – now you're a warped, frustrated *young* man," is amply supported by the evidence the film supplies. What is finally striking about the film's affirmation is the extreme precariousness of its basis; and Potter survives without remorse, his crime unexposed and unpunished. It may well be Capra's masterpiece, but it is more than that. Like all the greatest American films – fed by a complex generic tradition and, beyond that, by the fears and aspirations of a whole culture – it at once transcends its director and would be inconceivable without him.

Shadow of a Doubt has always been among the most popular of Hitchcock's middle-period films, with

Figure 9.1 *It's a Wonderful Life* (RKO, 1946) affirms the values of bourgeois family life. Produced and directed by Frank Capra

critics and public alike, but it has been perceived in very different, almost diametrically opposed ways. On its appearance it was greeted by British critics as the film marking Hitchcock's coming to terms with America; his British films were praised for their humor and "social criticism" as much as for their suspense, and the early American films, notably *Rebecca* (1940) and *Suspicion* (1941), seemed like attempts artificially to reconstruct England in Hollywood. In *Shadow of a Doubt* Hitchcock (with the aid of Thornton Wilder and Sally Benson) at last brought to American middle-class society the shrewd, satirical, affectionate gaze previously bestowed on the British. A later generation of French critics (notably Rohmer and Chabrol in their Hitchcock book) praised the film for very different reasons, establishing its strict formalism (Truffaut's "un film fondé sur le chiffre 2") and seeing it as one of the keys to a consistent Catholic interpretation of Hitchcock, a rigorous working out of themes of original sin, the loss of innocence, the fallen world, the exchange (or interchangeability) of guilt.[5] The French noted the family comedy beloved of British critics, if at all, as a mildly annoying distraction.

That both these views correspond to important elements in the film and throw light on certain aspects of it is beyond doubt; both, however, now appear false and partial, dependent upon the abstracting of elements from the whole. If the film is, in a sense, completely dominated by Hitchcock (nothing in it is unmarked by his artistic personality), a complete reading would need to see the small-town-family elements and the Catholic elements as threads weaving through a complex fabric in which, again, ideological and generic determinants are crucial.

The kind of "synthetic" analysis I have suggested (going beyond an interest in the individual auteur) reveals *It's a Wonderful Life* as a far more potentially subversive film than has been generally recognized, but its subversive elements are, in the end, successfully contained. In *Shadow of a Doubt* the Hollywood ideology I have sketched is shattered beyond convincing recuperation. One can, however, trace through the film its attempts to impose itself and render things "safe." What is in jeopardy is above all the family – but, given the family's central ideological significance, once that is in jeopardy, everything is. The small town (still rooted in the agrarian dream, in ideals of the virgin land as a garden of innocence) and the united happy family are regarded as the real sound heart of American civilization; the ideological project is to acknowledge the existence of sickness and evil but preserve the family from their contamination.

A number of strategies can be discerned here: the attempt to insist on a separation of Uncle Charlie from Santa Rosa; his death at the end of the film as the definitive purging of evil; the production of the young detective (the healthy, wholesome, small-town male) as a marriage partner for Young Charlie so that the family may be perpetuated; above all, the attribution of Uncle Charlie's sexual pathology to a childhood accident as a means of exonerating the family of the charge of producing a monster, a possibility the American popular cinema, with the contemporary overturning of traditional values, can now envisage – e.g., *It's Alive* (Larry Cohen, 1974).

The famous opening, with its parallel introductions of Uncle Charlie and Young Charlie, insists on the city and the small town as *opposed*, sickness and evil being of the city. As with Bedford Falls/Pottersville, the film draws lavishly on the iconography of usually discrete genres. Six shots (with all movement and direction – the bridges, the panning, the editing – consistently rightward) leading up to the first interior of Uncle Charlie's room give us urban technology, wreckage both human (the down-and-outs) and material (the dumped cars by the sign "No Dumping Allowed"), children playing in the street, the number 13 on the lodging-house door. Six shots (movement and direction consistently left) leading to the first interior of Young Charlie's room give us sunny streets with no street games (Santa Rosa evidently has parks), an orderly town with a smiling, paternal policeman presiding over traffic and pedestrians.

In Catholic terms, this is the fallen world against a world of apparent prelapsarian innocence; but it is just as valid to interpret the images, as in *It's a Wonderful Life*, in terms of the two faces of American capitalism. Uncle Charlie has money (the fruits of his crimes and his aberrant sexuality) littered in disorder over table and floor; the Santa Rosa policeman has behind him the Bank of America. The detailed paralleling of uncle and niece can of course be read as comparison as much as contrast, and the opposition that of two sides of the same coin. The point is clearest in that crucial, profoundly disturbing scene where film noir erupts into Santa Rosa itself: the visit to the Til Two bar, where Young Charlie is confronted with her alter ego Louise the waitress, her former classmate. The scene equally invites Catholic and Marxist commentaries; its force arises from the revelation of the fallen world/capitalist-corruption-and-deprivation at the heart of the American small town. The close juxtaposition of genres has implications that reach throughout the whole generic structure of the classical Hollywood cinema.

The subversion of ideology within the film is everywhere traceable to Hitchcock's presence, to the skepticism and nihilism that lurk just behind the jocular facade of his public image. His Catholicism is in reality the lingering on in his work of the darker aspects of Catholic mythology: hell without heaven. The traces are clear enough. Young Charlie wants a "miracle"; she thinks of her uncle as "the one who can save us" (and her mother immediately asks, "What do you mean, *save* us?"); when she finds his telegram, in the very act of sending hers, her reaction is an ecstatic "He heard me, he heard me!" Hitchcock cuts at once to a low-angle shot of Uncle Charlie's train rushing toward Santa Rosa, underlining the effect with an ominous crashing chord on the sound track.

Uncle Charlie is one of the supreme embodiments of the key Hitchcock figure: ambiguously devil and lost soul. When he reaches Santa Rosa, the image is blackened by its smoke. From his first appearance, Charlie is associated consistently with a cigar (its phallic connotations evident from the outset, in the scene with the landlady) and repeatedly shown with a wreath of smoke curling around his head (no one else in the film smokes except Joe, the displaced father, who has a paternal pipe, usually unlit). Several incidents (the escape from the policemen at the beginning, the garage door slammed as by remote control) invest him with a quasi-supernatural power. Rather than restrict the film to a Catholic reading, it seems logical to connect these marks with others; the thread of superstition that runs through the film (the number 13; the hat on the bed; "Sing at table and you'll marry a crazy husband"; the irrational dread of the utterance,

Figure 9.2 Alfred Hitchcock's *Shadow of a Doubt* (Universal, 1943) reveals the oppression of dominant ideology. Produced by Jack H. Skirball

however innocent, of the forbidden words "Merry Widow") and the telepathy motif (the telegrams, the tune "jumping from head to head") – the whole Hitchcockian sense of life at the mercy of terrible, unpredictable forces that have to be kept down.

The Hitchcockian dread of repressed forces is characteristically accompanied by a sense of the emptiness of the surface world that represses them, and this crucially affects the presentation of the American small-town family in *Shadow of a Doubt.* The warmth and togetherness, the mutual responsiveness and affection that Capra so beautifully creates in the Bailey families, senior and junior, of *It's a Wonderful Life* are here almost entirely lacking – and this despite the fact, in itself of great ideological interest, that the treatment of the family in *Shadow of a Doubt* has generally been perceived (even, one guesses, by Hitchcock himself) as affectionate.

The most striking characteristic of the Spencers is the separateness of each member; the recurring point of the celebrated overlapping dialogue is that no one ever listens to what anyone else is saying. Each is locked in a separate fantasy world: Emmy in the past, Joe in crime, Anne in books that are read apparently less for pleasure than as a means of amassing knowledge with which she has little emotional contact (though she also believes that everything she reads is "true"). The parents are trapped in a petty materialism (both respond to Young Charlie's dissatisfaction with the assumption that she's talking about money) and reliance on "honest toil" as the means of using up energies. In *Shadow of a Doubt* the ideological image of the small-town happy family becomes the flimsiest facade. That so many are nonetheless deceived by it testifies only to the strength of the ideology – one of whose functions is of course to inhibit the imagining of radical alternatives.

I have argued elsewhere that the key to Hitchcock's films is less suspense than sexuality (or, alternatively, that his "suspense" always carries a sexual charge in ways sometimes obvious, sometimes esoteric); and that sexual relationships in his work are inevitably based on power, the obsession with power and dread of impotence being as central to his method as to his thematic. In *Shadow of a Doubt* it is above all sexuality that cracks apart the family facade. As far as the Hays Code permitted, a double incest theme runs through the film: Uncle Charlie and Emmy, Uncle Charlie and Young Charlie. Necessarily, this is expressed through images and motifs, never becoming verbally explicit; certain of the images depend on a suppressed verbal play for their significance.

For the reunion of brother and sister, Hitchcock gives us an image (Emmy poised left of screen, arrested in mid-movement, Charlie right, under trees and sunshine) that iconographically evokes the reunion of lovers (Charlie wants to see Emmy again as she was when she was "the prettiest girl on the block"). And Emmy's breakdown, in front of her embarrassed friends and neighbors, at the news of Charlie's imminent departure is eloquent. As for uncle and niece, they are introduced symmetrically lying on beds, Uncle Charlie fondling his phallic cigar, Young Charlie, prone, hands behind head. When Uncle Charlie gets off the train he is bent over a stick, pretending to be ill; as soon as he sees Young Charlie, he "comes erect," flourishing the stick. One of his first actions on taking over her bedroom is to pluck a rose for his buttonhole ("deflowering"). More obviously, there is the business with the ring, which, as a symbolic token of engagement, not only links Charlie sexually with her uncle, but also links her, through its previous ownership, to his succession of merry widows. The film shows sexual pathology at the heart of the American family, the necessary product of its repressions and sublimations.

As for the "accident" – that old critical stumbling block – it presents no problem at all, provided one is ready to acknowledge the validity of a psychoanalytical reading of movies. Indeed, it provides a rather beautiful example of the way in which ideology, in seeking to impose itself, succeeds merely in confirming its own subversion. The "accident" (Charlie was "riding a bicycle" for the first time, which resulted in a "collision") can be read as an elementary Freudian metaphor for the trauma of premature sexual awakening (after which Charlie was "never the same again"). The smothering sexual/possessive devotion of a doting older sister may be felt to provide a clue to the sexual motivation behind the merry-widow murders; Charlie isn't interested in money. Indeed, Emmy is connected to the merry widows by an associative chain in which important links are her own practical widowhood (her ineffectual husband is largely ignored), her ladies' club, and its leading light, Mrs. Potter, Uncle Charlie's potential next-in-line.

A fuller analysis would need to dwell on the limitations of Hitchcock's vision, nearer the nihilistic than the tragic; on his inability to conceive of repressed energies as other than evil and the surface world that represses them as other than shallow and unfulfilling. This explains why there can be no heaven corresponding to Hitchcock's hell, for every vision of heaven that is not merely negative is rooted in a concept of the liberation of the instincts, the resurrection of the body, which Hitchcock must always deny. But my final stress is less on the evaluation of a particular film or director than on the implications for a criticism of the Hollywood cinema of the notions of interaction and multiple determinacy I have been employing. Its roots in the Hollywood genres, and in the very ideological structure it so disturbingly subverts, make *Shadow of a Doubt* so much more suggestive and significant a work than Hitchcock the bourgeois entertainer could ever have guessed.

Notes

1 Robin Wood, "Old Wine, New Bottles: Structuralism or Humanism?" *Film Comment* 12, no. 6 (November–December 1976): 22–5.

2 Andrew Britton, "Hitchcock's *Spellbound:* Text and Counter-Text," *Cine-Action!* no. 3/4 (January 1986): 72–83.

3 See *Sirk on Sirk*, edited by Jon Halliday (London: Secker & Warburg/British Film Institute, 1971).

4 Peter Wollen, *Signs and Meaning in the Cinema*, 3d. edn. (Bloomington and London: Indiana University Press, 1972), pp. 94–101.

5 See Eric Rohmer and Claude Chabrol, *Hitchcock: The First Forty-Four Films*, translated by Stanley Hochman (New York: Ungar, 1979), p. 72.

Further Reading

Braudy, Leo and Dickstein, Morris (eds.). *Great Film Directors: A Critical Anthology*. New York: Oxford University Press, 1978.

Cameron, Ian (ed.). *Movie Reader*. New York and Washington: Praeger/London: November Books, 1972.

Coursodon, Pierre, with Pierre Sauvage. *American Directors*, 2 vols. New York: McGraw-Hill, 1983.

Graham, Peter (ed.). *The New Wave*. London: Secker & Warburg, 1968.

Hess, John. "La Politique des Auteurs," *Jump Cut*, no. 1 (May-June 1974), pp. 19–22, and no. 2 (July-August 1974), pp. 20–2.

Hillier, Jim (ed.). *Cahiers du Cinéma: The 1950s: Neo-Realism, Hollywood, New Wave*. Cambridge, MA: Harvard University Press, 1985.

Hillier, Jim (ed.). *Cahiers du Cinéma: The 1960s: New Wave, New Cinema, Reevaluating Hollywood*. Cambridge, MA: Harvard University Press, 1986.

Kael, Pauline. *The Citizen Kane Book*. New York: Little Brown, 1971.

Kitses, Jim. *Horizons West*. Bloomington/London: Secker & Warburg, 1969. Revised edn., London: British Film Institute, 2004.

Lapsey, Robert and Westlake, Michael. *Film Theory: An Introduction*. Manchester, UK: Manchester University Press, 1988.

Sarris, Andrew. *The American Cinema, Directors and Directions, 1929–1968*. New York: Dutton, 1968. Reprinted Chicago: University of Chicago Press, 1985.

Sarris, Andrew (ed.). *Interviews with Film Directors*. New York: Bobbs-Merrill, 1967.

Stam, Robert. *Film Theory: An Introduction*. New York and Oxford: Blackwell, 2000.

Wood, Robin. *Hitchcock's Films*. London: A. Zwemmer/New York: A.S. Barnes, 1965.

Wood, Robin. *Howard Hawks*. London: Secker & Warburg/British Film Institute. Revised edn., Detroit: Wayne State University Press, 2006.

Part II

The Contexts of Authorship

10

The Death of the Author

Roland Barthes

Roland Barthes was a major figure in ideological analysis and deconstruction. His publications include *Writing Degree Zero* (1953), *S/Z* (1977), and *Image-Music-Text* (1977). His early book *Mythologies*, first published in France in 1957 but not translated and published in English until 1972, was a pioneering work in the field of cultural studies, offering brief semiological analyses of selected artifacts and events of popular culture. *S/Z*, a detailed discussion of a novella by French writer Honoré de Balzac, presents a model of semiological analysis, introducing a system of cultural "codes" that work to produce textual meaning. Although he seldom wrote about cinema, Barthes' broad semiological approach to cultural texts ranging from the traditional arts to popular rituals and advertising as systems of signs was highly influential in film studies because it offered the possibility of a more objective, scientific analysis of films. In this piece on "The Death of the Author," first published in 1968 and translated for inclusion in *Image-Music-Text*, Barthes argues that a work of art contains no fixed meaning but is rather a field of potential meanings that may be taken up by readers, thus dethroning the auteur of any privileged status in interpretation.

In his story *Sarrasine* Balzac, describing a castrato disguised as a woman, writes the following sentence: '*This was woman herself, with her sudden fears, her irrational whims, her instinctive worries, her impetuous boldness, her fussings, and her delicious sensibility.*' Who is speaking thus? Is it the hero of the story bent on remaining ignorant of the castrato hidden beneath the woman? Is it Balzac the individual, furnished by his personal experience with a philosophy of Woman? Is it Balzac the author professing 'literary' ideas on femininity? Is it universal wisdom? Romantic psychology? We shall never know, for the good reason that writing is the destruction of every voice, of every point of origin. Writing is that neutral, composite, oblique space where our subject slips away, the negative where all identity is lost, starting with the very identity of the body writing.

No doubt it has always been that way. As soon as a fact is *narrated* no longer with a view to acting directly on reality but intransitively, that is to say, finally outside of any function other than that of the very practice of the symbol itself, this disconnection occurs, the voice loses its origin, the author enters into his own death, writing begins. The sense of this phenomenon, however, has varied; in ethnographic societies the responsibility for a narrative is never assumed by a person but by a mediator, shaman or relator whose 'performance' – the mastery of the narrative code – may possibly be admired but never his 'genius'. The author is a modern figure, a product of

Roland Barthes, "The Death of the Author," pp. 142–8 from *Image/Music/Text*, ed. and trans. Stephen Heath (New York: Hill and Wang, 1977). Originally published in French (1968).

our society insofar as, emerging from the Middle Ages with English empiricism, French rationalism and the personal faith of the Reformation, it discovered the prestige of the individual, of, as it is more nobly put, the 'human person'. It is thus logical that in literature it should be this positivism, the epitome and culmination of capitalist ideology, which has attached the greatest importance to the 'person' of the author. The *author* still reigns in histories of literature, biographies of writers, interviews, magazines, as in the very consciousness of men of letters anxious to unite their person and their work through diaries and memoirs. The image of literature to be found in ordinary culture is tyrannically centred on the author, his person, his life, his tastes, his passions, while criticism still consists for the most part in saying that Baudelaire's work is the failure of Baudelaire the man, Van Gogh's his madness, Tchaikovsky's his vice. The *explanation* of a work is always sought in the man or woman who produced it, as if it were always in the end, through the more or less transparent allegory of the fiction, the voice of a single person, the *author* 'confiding' in us.

Though the sway of the Author remains powerful (the new criticism has often done no more than consolidate it), it goes without saying that certain writers have long since attempted to loosen it. In France, Mallarmé was doubtless the first to see and to foresee in its full extent the necessity to substitute language itself for the person who until then had been supposed to be its owner. For him, for us too, it is language which speaks, not the author; to write is, through a prerequisite impersonality (not at all to be confused with the castrating objectivity of the realist novelist), to reach that point where only language acts, 'performs', and not 'me'. Mallarmé's entire poetics consists in suppressing the author in the interests of writing (which is, as will be seen, to restore the place of the reader). Valéry, encumbered by a psychology of the Ego, considerably diluted Mallarmé's theory but, his taste for classicism leading him to turn to the lessons of rhetoric, he never stopped calling into question and deriding the Author; he stressed the linguistic and, as it were, 'hazardous' nature of his activity, and throughout his prose works he militated in favour of the essentially verbal condition of literature, in the face of which all recourse to the writer's interiority seemed to him pure superstition. Proust himself, despite the apparently psychological character of what are called his *analyses*, was visibly concerned with the task of inexorably blurring, by an extreme subtilization, the relation between the writer and his characters; by making of the narrator not he who has seen and felt nor even he who is writing, but he who *is going to write* (the young man in the novel – but, in fact, how old is he and who is he? – wants to write but cannot; the novel ends when writing at last becomes possible), Proust gave modern writing its epic. By a radical reversal, instead of putting his life into his novel, as is so often maintained, he made of his very life a work for which his own book was the model; so that it is clear to us that Charlus does not imitate Montesquiou but that Montesquiou – in his anecdotal, historical reality – is no more than a secondary fragment, derived from Charlus. Lastly, to go no further than this prehistory of modernity, Surrealism, though unable to accord language a supreme place (language being system and the aim of the movement being, romantically, a direct subversion of codes – itself moreover illusory: a code cannot be destroyed, only 'played off'), contributed to the desacrilization of the image of the Author by ceaselessly recommending the abrupt disappointment of expectations of meaning (the famous surrealist 'jolt'), by entrusting the hand with the task of writing as quickly us possible what the head itself is unaware of (automatic writing), by accepting the principle and the experience of several people writing together. Leaving aside literature itself (such distinctions really becoming invalid), linguistics has recently provided the destruction of the Author with a valuable analytical tool by showing that the whole of the enunciation is an empty process, functioning perfectly without there being any need for it to be filled with the person of the interlocutors. Linguistically, the author is never more than the instance writing, just as *I* is nothing other than the instance saying *I*: language knows a 'subject', not a 'person', and this subject, empty outside of the very enunciation which defines it, suffices to make language 'hold together', suffices, that is to say, to exhaust it.

The removal of the Author (one could talk here with Brecht of a veritable 'distancing', the Author diminishing like a figurine at the far end of the literary stage) is not merely an historical fact or an act of writing; it utterly transforms the modern text (or – which is the same thing – the text is henceforth made and read in such a way that at all its levels the author is absent). The temporality is different. The Author, when believed in, is always conceived of as the past of his own book: book and author stand automatically on a single line divided into a *before* and an *after*. The Author is thought to *nourish* the book, which is to say that he exists before it, thinks, suffers, lives for it, is in the same relation of antecedence to his work as a father to his child. In complete contrast, the modern scriptor is born simultaneously with the text, is in no way equipped with a being preceding or exceeding the writing, is not the subject with the book as predicate; there is no other time than that of the enunciation and every text is eternally written *here and now*. The fact is (or, it follows) that *writing* can no longer designate an operation of recording, notation, representation, 'depiction' (as the Classics would say); rather, it designates exactly what linguists, referring to Oxford philosophy, call a performative, a rare verbal form (exclusively given in the first person and in the present tense) in which the enunciation has no other content (contains no other proposition) than the act by which it is uttered – something like the *I declare* of kings or the *I sing* of very ancient poets. Having buried the Author, the modern scriptor can thus no longer believe, as according to the pathetic view of his predecessors, that this hand is too slow for his thought or passion and that consequently, making a law of necessity, he must emphasize this delay and indefinitely 'polish' his form. For him, on the contrary, the hand, cut off from any voice, borne by a pure gesture of inscription (and not of expression), traces a field without origin – or which, at least, has no other origin than language itself, language which ceaselessly calls into question all origins.

We know now that a text is not a line of words releasing a single 'theological' meaning (the 'message' of the Author-God) but a multi-dimensional space in which a variety of writings, none of them original, blend and clash. The text is a tissue of quotations drawn from the innumerable centres of culture. Similar to Bouvard and Pécuchet, those eternal copyists, at once sublime and comic and whose profound ridiculousness indicates precisely the truth of writing, the writer can only imitate a gesture that is always anterior, never original. His only power is to mix writings, to counter the ones with the others, in such a way as never to rest on any one of them. Did he wish to *express himself*, he ought at least to know that the inner 'thing' he thinks to 'translate' is itself only a ready-formed dictionary, its words only explainable through other words, and so on indefinitely; something experienced in exemplary fashion by the young Thomas de Quincey, he who was so good at Greek that in order to translate absolutely modern ideas and images into that dead language, he had, so Baudelaire tells us (in *Paradis Artificiels*), 'created for himself an unfailing dictionary, vastly more extensive and complex than those resulting from the ordinary patience of purely literary themes'.

Succeeding the Author, the scriptor no longer bears within him passions, humours, feelings, impressions, but rather this immense dictionary from which he draws a writing that can know no halt: life never does more than imitate the book, and the book itself is only a tissue of signs, an imitation that is lost, infinitely deferred.

Once the Author is removed, the claim to decipher a text becomes quite futile. To give a text an Author is to impose a limit on that text, to furnish it with a final signified, to close the writing. Such a conception suits criticism very well, the latter then allotting itself the important task of discovering the Author (or its hypostases: society, history, psyché, liberty) beneath the work: when the Author has been found, the text is 'explained' – victory to the critic. Hence there is no surprise in the fact that, historically, the reign of the Author has also been that of the Critic, nor again in the fact that criticism (be it new) is today undermined along with the Author. In the multiplicity of writing, everything is to be *disentangled*, nothing *deciphered*; the structure can be followed, 'run' (like the thread of a stocking) at every point and at every level, but there is nothing beneath: the space of writing is to be ranged over, not pierced; writing ceaselessly posits meaning ceaselessly to evaporate it, carrying out a systematic exemption of meaning. In precisely this way literature (it would be better from now on to say *writing*), by refusing to assign a 'secret', an ultimate meaning, to the text (and to the world as text), liberates what may be called an anti-theological activity, an activity that is truly revolutionary since to refuse to fix meaning is, in the end, to refuse God and his hypostases – reason, science, law.

Let us come back to the Balzac sentence. No one, no 'person', says it: its source, its voice, is not the true place of the writing, which is reading. Another – very precise – example will help to make this clear: recent research (J.-P. Vernant[1]) has demonstrated the constitutively ambiguous nature of Greek tragedy, its texts being woven from words with double meanings that each character understands unilaterally (this perpetual misunderstanding is exactly the 'tragic'); there is, however, someone who understands each word in its duplicity and who, in addition, hears the very deafness of the characters speaking in front of him – this someone being precisely the reader (or here, the listener). Thus is revealed the total existence of writing: a text is made of multiple writings, drawn from many cultures and entering into mutual relations of dialogue, parody, contestation, but there is one place where this multiplicity is focused and that place is the reader, not, as was hitherto said, the author. The reader is the space on which all the quotations that make up a writing are inscribed without any of them being lost; a text's unity lies not in its origin but in its destination. Yet this destination cannot any longer be personal: the reader is without history, biography, psychology; he is simply that *someone* who holds together in a single field all the traces by which the written text is constituted. Which is why it is derisory to condemn the new writing in the name of a humanism hypocritically turned champion of the reader's rights. Classic criticism has never paid any attention to the reader; for it, the writer is the only person in literature. We are now beginning to let ourselves be fooled no longer by the arrogant antiphrastical recriminations of good society in favour of the very thing it sets aside, ignores, smothers, or destroys; we know that to give writing its future, it is necessary to overthrow the myth: the birth of the reader must be at the cost of the death of the Author.

Note

1 [Cf. Jean-Pierre Vernant (with Pierre Vidal-Naquet), *Mythe et tragédie en Grèce ancienne*, Paris 1972, esp. pp. 19–40, 99–131.]

11

The English Cine-Structuralists

Charles W. Eckert

Charles W. Eckert taught in the English Department at Indiana University, where his research was on Shakespeare and film and Hollywood cinema of the 1930s. His published work includes the collection *Focus on Shakespearean Films*, and articles on the ideology of stars such as Shirley Temple ("a kind of artifact thrown up by a unique concatenation of social and economic forces") and Bette Davis in the Warner Bros. gangster film *Marked Woman* (1937). In this essay, which originally appeared in the New York-based magazine *Film Comment* in 1973, as the author himself explains in a followup essay, he was looking at the work of a group of English critics "faulting some of them for what I considered an improper and unproductive application of the structural method of Lévi-Strauss to the study of directors." Eckert's critique, in which he considers how auteur-structuralism seems to slide from a descriptive method to an evaluative tool, elicited attacks in turn from others, including Geoffrey Nowell-Smith, who acknowledged the distortions of Lévi-Strauss for the purposes of film analysis.

In the late 1960s, just when the *politique des auteurs* began to look shopworn and foxed at the edges, a group of English critics gave it a hard inspection, stripped it to its framework, and refurbished it with a bright new critical material called structuralism. In its new habit, and viewed from a distance, auteurism might pass as the creation of Claude Lévi-Strauss, or Roland Barthes, or Christian Metz – or even such un-structuralists as Freud and Jung – though certainly it bears little resemblance to Truffaut and Sarris. But seen close up it quickly proves to have few distinctive features, to pertain, in fact, to all its fathers – or to none of them – like a ragamuffin promiscuously conceived in the streets and dropped on the nearest doorstep.

The English critics in question are Geoffrey Nowell-Smith, Peter Wollen, Jim Kitses, Alan Lovell, and Ben Brewster. An assessment of their work would seem in order before discussing the future of the method they have developed. But before assessing it, we must define the major forms of criticism which are today called structuralist and with which their work is easily confused. Although structural insights have always underpinned conceptual thinking in philosophy and the sciences (Aristotle, Hegel, Marx, Jung), their wide modern vogue derives from the structural linguists. The basic insights of de Saussure, Jacobson, and others have been ramified into three forms of structural criticism of special interest to film critics: the study of linguistic structures in narrative, mainly by Todorov and Barthes; the semiological study of the 'language' of cinema by Metz, Pasolini, Eco and others (really an attempt to determine how cinema signifies and whether it can be analyzed like a language); and Lévi-Strauss's study of the underlying structures of

Charles W. Eckert, "The English Cine-Structuralists," pp. 46–51 from *Film Comment* 9, no. 3 (May–June 1973).

thought and of the codes employed in the dialectical systems which operate in mythic thought.

The last form of structural study most closely approximates that used by the English critics, and is the one I shall concentrate upon. The study of narrative structure in film employing purely linguistic analogues does not look promising; in fact, Barthes has said as much and, more importantly, has professed to find little that is intellectually interesting in the cinema (certainly a comment on his method rather than the cinema). Metz, the most thorough of the semiologists, seems satisfied that the study of film as a language is limited in scope and in the applicability of the insights it achieves. But we have not as yet seen any *thorough* attempt to apply Lévi-Strauss's study of mythic thought and codes to film. I emphasize the word *thorough* because Lévi-Strauss's name and his method are frequently alluded to by the English auteur-structuralists.

Perhaps the best way to elaborate these complex matters is, first, to assess the work of this group of critics and to compare their methods with those formulated by Lévi-Strauss, and then to define both the achievements and the promise of auteur-structuralism, and of structuralism in general. From this point on, any reference I make to structuralism should be considered a reference to Lévi-Strauss's method. (For those interested in the recent *Cahiers* disparagement of structural study as opposed to a Marxist-ideological analysis I have appended a brief note.[1]) The first influential work – indeed, the generative locus for the auteur-structuralist criticism we are considering – was Geoffrey Nowell-Smith's *Luchino Visconti* (1967). This work influenced Peter Wollen, whose *Signs and Meaning in the Cinema* (1969) in turn gave rise to a series of articles concerned with structuralism in *Screen*. Nowell-Smith moved from the assertions that authorship is a necessary dimension for the study of films, and that 'the defining characteristics of an author's work are not those that are most readily apparent,' to his main thesis: 'the purpose of criticism becomes therefore to uncover behind the superficial contrasts of subject and treatment a structural hard core of basic and often recondite motifs.'[2] The principal drawbacks to this approach, he found, were a radical narrowing of the field of inquiry, the 'possibility of an author's work changing over time and of the structures being variable and not constant', and the temptation to neglect the myriad aspects of a film's production and aesthetic effect that a study of motifs does not impinge upon. In Visconti's films Nowell-Smith did not find a 'single and comprehensive structure,' largely because Visconti has developed with the years and has adopted many styles of filmmaking.

As a structuralist approach this is tentative and qualified indeed. And Nowell-Smith's entire study of Visconti brings under analysis many aspects of production, history, and stylistic influence that have no bearing upon structure, yet are considered indispensable for understanding the films. Yet the dominant impression one receives from this thoughtful, independent analysis is that structured themes are indeed at the heart of Visconti's enterprise and Nowell-Smith's critical interest. In the later discussion of Lévi-Strauss I will attempt to position and to assess Nowell-Smith's method. For the moment let us consider Peter Wollen's use of his conceptions.

Signs and Meaning in the Cinema must be, after *Film Form* and *What is Cinema?*, the most widely read work on film theory among present-day film students. Its faults are many, but they have proven to be seminal faults, spawning as many ideas and thoughtful reactions as the Bazin–Eisenstein controversies. The centrality of this work makes its views on auteur-structuralism especially important. Wollen begins with quotations from Nowell-Smith's study, then chooses the films of Howard Hawks as a test case for the 'structural approach.' He first dichotomizes Hawks's films into two categories: the adventure drama and the crazy comedy (he here follows Robin Wood, who also has structuralist affinities). These types 'express inverse views of the world, the positive and negative poles of the Hawksian vision.'[3] An awareness of 'differences and oppositions,' he continues, must be cultivated along with the awareness of 'resemblances and repetitions' usually found in thematic or motif-seeking criticism. He then cites main sets of antinomies in Hawks's work and notes how they break down into lesser sets – any of which may overlap or be 'foregrounded in different movies.'

But Wollen's most intensive criticism is saved for John Ford, in whose work he finds the 'master antinomy' of wilderness and garden (the terms are derived by Wollen from Henry Nash Smith's *The Virgin Land*). The entire analysis of Ford reaches its principal conclusion in this statement: 'Ford's work is much richer than that of Hawks and . . . this is revealed by a structural analysis; it is the richness of the shifting relations between antinomies in Ford's work that makes him a great artist, beyond being simply an undoubted auteur.' This statement captures the essence of Wollen's species of structuralism, just as the search for a 'hard core of basic and often recondite motifs' defines Nowell-Smith's.

Both of these definitions were harmonious with the intentions of a work appearing in the same year as Wollen's – Jim Kitses's *Horizons West*. Kitses began, 'But I should make clear what I mean by auteur theory. In my view the term describes a basic principle and a method: the idea of personal authorship in the cinema and – of key importance – the concomitant responsibility to honour all of a director's works by a systematic examination in order to trace characteristic themes, structures and formal qualities.'[4] Kitses also draws upon Smith's *The Virgin Land* for the insight that the image of the West has a dialectical form: 'Thus central to the form we have a philosophical dialectic, an ambiguous cluster of meanings and attitudes that provide the traditional thematic structure of the genre.' Kitses provides a chart listing the principal antinomies, and notes that polar terms may be transposed in the course of an auteur's development. His study of individual auteurs is very subtle, yet, as I will show later, not as close in spirit to Lévi-Strauss as Wollen's.

The works of Nowell-Smith, Wollen and Kitses, all produced in the late Sixties, might have represented a mere eddy in the current of auteur criticism had their methods and their cause not been taken up by other English critics. In the March/April 1969 issue of *Screen* Alan Lovell published a strongly dissenting criticism of the work of Robin Wood, finding it deficient in analytic method and concerned with gaining assent rather than giving proof as it measured films and directors against an established system of beliefs and values. As an antidote, Lovell proposed an auteur-structuralist method strongly resembling those already discussed: 'any director creates his films on the basis of a central structure and . . . all of his films can be seen as variations or developments of it.'[5] To illustrate his method he analyzed a pattern found in Arthur Penn's work consisting of a polarity between social groups and heroes, and a father-figure who mediates between the two (both the groups and heroes are prone to violence; the fathers mediate the violent camps much as the Prince does in *Romeo and Juliet*). Lovell's article began a chain-reaction of response including an attack on Lovell's structuralism by Robin Wood, a reply by Lovell, an independent defense of Wood by John C. Murray, and a well-informed discussion of the structural contributions of Barthes, Metz and others by Ben Brewster.[6]

Although much of the discussion is contentious, when one pares away the *ad hominem* forensics and the quite pointless debates over the 'value' of totally divergent critical methods, one finds both the intentions and the limitations of auteur-structuralist criticism clarified. Both Wood and Murray note that Kitses, Wollen, and Lovell are making judgments of the worth of directors on such bases as the clarity of the antinomic structures or the complexity of their interrelations (Wollen on Ford; Lovell on Penn). Structuralism, Wood and Murray contend, is not used as a mere analytic tool, but as a measure of a director's maturity or artistic stature. And they find its discoveries – the pairs of opposites, the patterns of interchange – banal, of no great significance, mere critical jargon that cannot help us distinguish between a great film and a highly polarized and structured cartoon by Tex Avery or Chuck Jones (Murray).

There is so much oversimplification, obtuseness, and downright unfairness running through the whole debate that one must resist the temptation to leap in. But what one principally feels is the need for a re-truing of terms, for a fresh look at the notion of structuralism, and at the suitability of a structural study of a director's body of work – or of films in general. We must begin with the writings of the doyen of structuralism, Claude Lévi-Strauss. There are two indispensable essays, both of them attempts to formulate and delimit the uses of structuralism. 'The Structural Study of Myth' (1958),[7] and the 'Overture' to *The Raw and the Cooked* (1964).[8] The essays are so broad-ranging, especially the latter, that we would do best to define our interests before aproaching them. We might express these interests as a series of questions directly bearing upon film: Has a truly Lévi-Straussian study of a director been made? In what would it consist? Should structural study be limited to directors, or has it promise for genres of film, the output of individual studios, or more specialized aspects of films such as visuals and sound tracks? Or is film too syncretic and complex an art form to yield anything of value to such an approach?

We should begin with a definition of Lévi-Strauss's object (myth) and the analytic method he devised to comprehend it. Lévi-Strauss's object is relatively simple and uniform: a body of myth (usually short narratives) collected by ethnographers and anthropologists in a given region of the world. It is immaterial whether one has all the available versions of a myth or is able to assess the 'reliability' of one's sources: myths are interminable and have no definitive or 'ur' form. All versions of a given myth constitute the myth; and one can begin the task of analysis with any of the versions. The myths are analyzed sequentially, each 'gross unit' of the analysis consisting of a term and a relation which are one half of an antinomic pair: Oedipus kills his father – the Sphinx's death gives life to Thebes. A given term may enter into many relations; the sun, for instance, may figure in the first relation in the pairs. It gives light – darkens; burns – freezes; causes growth – causes death. Or it may be ambivalent and represent both relations: causes drought – gives new life. Its value at any moment in a myth must, therefore, be determined through careful assessment of its function in (usually) a number of polarized relations. It is the next analytic step, however, that is most unique in Lévi-Strauss's method: 'The true constituent units of a myth are not the isolated relations but *bundles of such relations*, and it is only as bundles that these relations can be put to use and combined so as to produce a meaning.'[9] Lévi-Strauss's brilliance resides in his ability to discern central 'bundles' of relations in myths and to suggest *why* they are meaningful – a task that requires more intelligence and discernment than analytic rigor. One cannot, without extended quotation from Lévi-Strauss's work, show how the analysis proceeds. I can only refer the reader to specific passages and to commentaries on the method by interpreters.[10] The entire task is additionally complicated by the possibilities for permutation among the relations one is analyzing: 'two opposite terms with no intermediary always tend to be replaced by two equivalent terms which admit of a third one as mediator; then one of the polar terms and the mediator becomes replaced by a new triad, and so on.'[11] These 'transformations' of the myth usually express the same opposition(s) by working through a variety of similarly structured taxonomies – in primitive societies, taxonomies of plants, animals, stones, heavenly bodies, and so forth. The opposition sun–moon may carry the same meaning as the opposition eagle–bear, even though the terms are drawn from separate taxonomies.

Again and again, Lévi-Strauss emphasizes the importance of *polarized* thought ('myth works from an awareness of oppositions to their progressive mediation') and the *dynamic, fluctuating nature* of this thought. Polarization is basic to all processes of thought and language, as a form of clarification and ordering of the world about us; dynamism reflects both the ongoing process of thought and – this is *most* crucial – the essential nature of myth: an obsessive repetitive conceptualizing of a dilemma or contradiction, the meaning of which is hidden from the narrator who rather compulsively tells and retells versions of the myth.

Structural study consists, then, in breaking down many versions of a myth into significant elements, arranging these in the polarized patterns natural to myth, and noting clusters of relations. One discovers the core of the myth only upon an examination of all of the individual analyses. What the myth is 'about' usually proves to be something quite different from its surface meaning. If its content were not hidden from the narrators, they would have no reason to obsessively reshape it, retell it, and accord it such significance in their lives. Once a myth has been penetrated and understood, it dies; it no longer functions as an expression of a dilemma or contradiction. The nonliving mythologies of the world are fossilized dynamic thought which has been discarded because it was resolved, outgrown, or made irrelevant by events or cultural evolution. The analyst begins his task on the same footing with the creator of myth – in a condition of ignorance. If he is assiduous he can read the riddle at the center of the myth and see how all of its versions are related.

This is all general and abstruse and can only be clarified through specific applications to film. I will take up the most provocative of Lévi-Strauss's insights in the general order of their importance and breadth of application. We will then be in a position to assess the achievements of current auteur-structural studies and to suggest further uses that might be made of the structural approach.

Before films can be equated with myths they must fulfil one fundamental condition: they must originate in a community possessed of a 'common conception of the world.' Only in such a community can the sort of dialectical system typical of myth be coherent. Given this criterion, myth may be 'any manifestation of the mental or social activities of the communities under consideration.'[12] Let us measure film against this primary criterion. Film history is usually written as an analysis of communal blocks of art, defined as national schools or styles (German expressionism, Italian neo-realism), as international movements (Surrealism, the New Wave) or as studio-centered styles (Biograph, Ufa, Warner Brothers). Such tidy bins always do violence to the dynamic, creative interplay of art history, but they are probably no less arbitrary than the 'communities' that Lévi-Strauss defines for study. And they do reflect the fact that films are generally produced as communal efforts. Hollywood at its zenith resembled a complex social structure not unlike the family-clan-village structures that Lévi-Strauss works with. Within the larger community called Hollywood there existed the distinctive cultures of Warners, MGM, Paramount, Republic, and others, and within these, units made up of given production teams or devoted to creating certain genres of film (topical, comedy, epic, serial).

Whether Warner Brothers or Ufa or the Russian experimentalists were possessed of 'a common conception of the world' is a matter for research and study, not for arbitrary pronouncement. But if one can draw upon the kind of intuitive judgment built up from seeing films, this criterion seems likely to be met. One would have to allow for the syncretic forces that affect all communities in the modern world (Lang travels to Hollywood, Kubrick to England), but the gestalt ambiance of a community is more frequently reflected in films than not. Before leaving this topic it is worth underlining Lévi-Strauss's statement that a myth may be 'any manifestation' of the social or mental activities of a community. By this token, the publicity and life-style of a film community (say Hollywood in the Twenties) would qualify as versions of its myth or myths.

A second major criterion that films would have to answer in order to qualify as bona fide myths is that they must arise out of a 'dialectical system of contrasts and correlations' that is logical, consistent, and demonstrably typical of the community under study. Such systems in the myths Lévi-Strauss analyzes are usually zoological, botanical, or made up of tangible qualities (the raw and the cooked). Lévi-Strauss's major contribution to myth may be the insight that abstract ideas can be conveyed through the manipulation of such 'empirical categories.' Modern societies no longer employ taxonomic schemes made up of plants and animals, but we do employ comparable schemes of many sorts. Films are especially rich in schemes constructed of physical objects (clothing, parts of the body, furnishings, topography) or of qualities (beauty–ugliness, darkness–light). These systems function in myths as codes: one must discover, frequently through interview or research, the meaning or significance accorded a land tortoise by a primitive community before one can 'read' a myth in which it appears; similarly one must discover the significance accorded a monocle in Hollywood in the late Twenties or a black shirt in the early Thirties to 'read' the appropriate character traits of Von Stroheim or Tim McCoy. Certainly films, with their almost compulsive and fetishistic attachment to physical objects, reveal many codified schemes upon even casual analysis. And such schemes can, with discernment, be found in lighting, camera, editing, and acting styles, as well as musical scores (the codification of music begins early with the Kinotheks).

Whether these codes are part of a careful, logical system can only be established through research. My own preliminary attempts at analysis suggest that they are – but that they are affected by many more contingencies than appear in Lévi-Strauss's myths. With myths one must contend with the abilities of narrators, lapses of memory, all sorts of disruptive cultural forces (although Lévi-Strauss virtually negates all of these by treating individual myths as 'found objects'); whereas with films one must consider physical as well as artistic and cultural forces – that is, accidents that affect the achievement of the screen image (casting, change of script, censorship, loss of a shot, and so forth) and of the conceptual schemes of the writer and/or director. Perhaps these problems are no more inhibiting for structuralism than for any form of film criticism; but we cannot treat films as found objects, because we know too much about how they are made.

The study of codes central to periods of film, studios, genres, even individual directors could also illuminate the logical systems of directors who react against traditional codified systems or work subversively within them (Truffaut, Godard, Buñuel, Sirk). I am not implying something as simple as a study of how Hollywood thugs wear hats in order to footnote

Figure 11.1 The Hollywood image of the hired killer in François Truffaut's *Tirez sur le pianiste (Shoot the Piano Player)* (Cocinor, 1960). Produced by Pierre Braunberger

the image of the hired killers in *Shoot the Piano Player* (we don't need analysis of what is already an implicit analysis), but rather a study that would help us comprehend the ambiguous tensions Truffaut maintains between traditional and novel images, gestures, or musical effects – those details of the film which may lead us to the central myth that Truffaut expresses. If the meaning of a myth is hidden from its creator, Truffaut's film is neither an homage to nor a satire on Hollywood (even if – or especially if – these definitions satisfy Truffaut). The myth it embodies will be discovered through analysis of the 'bundle of relations' that constitute the entire film, and comparison with analyses of other French New Wave films.

Before leaving the subject of the codes that constitute the 'dialectical system of contrasts and correlations' in films, we should note one important distinction between films and the narratives that Lévi-Strauss analyzes. To put the distinction aphoristically: anyone in a community can tell a myth, but only MGM can make a movie. The codes found in films are closely linked to the creative processes behind the film: they are narrative, visual, and aural codes of great variety originating often in individual minds, often evolved as part of a studio or production team style, or even derived from the larger community that surrounds the filmmakers (documentary, locale shooting, exposé). Even when evolved within a film community, they are related to the codes of the larger community of filmgoers – or else audiences would find the films incomprehensible. The most accessible film codes, I would suggest, are those intrinsic in the script, in the visuals, and in the music, especially when it is through-composed or thoroughly cut to the film (as were the best Kinothek scores for silent films). Films seem to meet the criteria discussed so far, although the analyst's task is undeniably complex.

The next requirement, that the meaning of a myth be hidden from its narrator, seems less problematical. Perhaps no other major art form is so characteristically opaque to its creators and consumers as is the cinema. The dominant metaphor for the film experience from Méliès to Fellini has been a 'dream,' and like dreams, films perform magical psychic functions. They are also endlessly repetitive and compulsively consumed ('they're showing four Clint Eastwoods at the Drive-In'). This dreamlike repetitiveness points unerringly to their mythic character. In Lévi-Strauss's terms, a myth is the embodiment of a dilemma or contradiction; and its repetitiveness, which grows out of its compulsive nature, functions to make its structure apparent. Or to make the same point in applied terms, the hero who is central to the detective action film is an embodied dilemma: if this dilemma were resolved by filmmakers and viewers the hero would cease to attract them. That is, I believe, an extremely seminal insight. It can be applied to individual character types, to entire plots, to genres of film, to series or 'runs' (Andy Hardy, motorcycle films) and so forth. The dioscuric union of filmmakers and their audience produces a strange Janus of art – myths made by mythmakers that are only certified as true or untrue after they have been created. Perhaps the best index to authentically mythic films, then, is the yearly box-office ratings.

Two more of Lévi-Strauss's stipulations deserve brief consideration. The first is that every myth is only a limited application of the pattern that emerges as the analysis of a body of myths proceeds. This means, quite simply, that many films must be analyzed before a valid structure can be discerned. Presumably, one must analyze a substantial quantity of De Mille epics of Republic Westerns before substantive discoveries will be made. Or if one is focusing upon a given studio or era, one would have to consider films of many genres.

The second stipulation brings us to the end of this discussion and can serve as a bridge back to the subject of auteur-structuralism. It is that figures in myths have meanings only in relation to other figures. They cannot be assigned set meanings, as is typically done in an archetypal or Freudian analysis, nor should they be expected to maintain the same meaning in so dynamic a thought-form as myth. Again we can illustrate the argument better than we can paraphrase it. Jane Darwell is Jung's archetype of the 'Good Mother' as certainly as Joan Collins is an 'Evil Anima.' The Jungian system also allows for mixed archetypes, but one way or another the meaning tends to get fixed. For a structuralist, Jane Darwell's 'meaning' in, say, *The Grapes of Wrath* would be expressed as a series of relations – to other characters, to ideas if she functions allegorically, or expressed in terms of contrasting camera treatments, musical leit motifs, or mimetic styles. The search is not for what she resembles or for what she symbolizes, but rather for the meaning of the myth in which she is one figure entering into many relations.

The issue of how figures are to be interpreted takes us to the heart of the whole enterprise I have characterized as auteur-structuralism. Each of the authors mentioned earlier employs a unique critical method, although each is nominally a structuralist. Which of them most closely approximates the method elaborated by Lévi-Strauss? Nowell-Smith makes a careful analysis of relationships in individual films, and is especially attentive to the shifting nature of these relationships and to dialectical progressions. But his initial premise is that Visconti developed too much as an artist to make a comparative study of his films possible. He prefers to 'consider the film singly, attempting in the analysis of each to bring out its relationship, hidden or overt, to the rest of Visconti's work.' The absence of a thoroughly comparative method not only qualifies his structuralism, it raises the profound issue of whether or not the body of films produced by an individual director over a period of years can qualify as a 'set' of myths. Let us return to this question at the end of the discussion.

Kitses does analyze the canon of a director's works as a single body of myth, but his individual figures are defined in archetypal and iconic terms; their meanings are traditional rather than dependent upon relationships within each film. Only his emphasis upon the dynamic interaction of the figures and their tendency to form antinomic pairs resembles Lévi-Strauss's analysis. Lovell's method is extremely close to Kitses, employing a mixture of archetypal and structural insights.

Of all the critics, Peter Wollen shows the closest familiarity with Lévi-Strauss's writings. His analysis of Hawks and Ford, though only intended to be exploratory and suggestive, is less attuned to archetypes, is thoroughly directed at 'bundles of relations' and is founded on the premise that 'it is only the analysis of the whole *corpus* which permits the moment of synthesis when the critic returns to the individual film'.

Figure 11.2 Jane Darwell (l.) as Ma Joad with Henry Fonda and Russell Simpson in John Ford's *The Grapes of Wrath* (Twentieth Century-Fox, 1940). Produced by Darryl F. Zanuck and Nunnally Johnson

It would seem, then, that there are two *bêtes noires* roaming the domain of the current auteur-structuralists: the questions of how figures are to be interpreted, and of the degree to which an auteur's works possess the same unity to a communal body of myth. The laying of the first beast was Lévi-Strauss's primary task in 'The Structural Study of Myth': 'If there is a meaning to be found in mythology, it cannot reside in the isolated elements which enter into the composition of a myth, but only in the way those elements are combined,' So much, it appears, for father-figures, traditional icons, and Henry Nash Smith's wilderness and garden. The acceptance of such set meanings may not only blind us to important shifts of relationship, it may also commit us to the surface meaning of the myth – to the narrator's rationalized account of what his story is about, or the critic's overlay of fossilized myth upon a living structure. Of course, traditional meanings may well emerge from the process of analysis; but the point is that they will be *discovered* rather than established *a priori*.

The question of the degree of unity in an auteur's work is less easily resolved, although two reflections come to mind: Renoir's opinion that a director spends his life making one film; and Elizabeth Sewell's contention that every artist creates the myth by which he is to be interpreted. Both buttress the main premise that is implicit in the auteur theory: that a director's body of work possesses unity. The alternative notion, that an artist evolves through disparate stages of thought and technique, is a more nineteenth-century conception, attuned to the belief in purposive evolution. The modern study of myth has attacked or militated against evolutionary schemes and has substituted synchronic studies of motifs, types, and forms, The reaction has undoubtedly been extreme. We must use judgment in deciding to what degree a director conforms to Renoir's definition and invites a mythic analysis; and we must anticipate that an apparent evolution in style and theme may only mask what is recurrent in a body of work.

The structuralist method, considered in all of its potential applications, will probably be productive in proportion to the discretion and intelligence with which it is applied. Its promise, however, is undeniable: the cinema, after sensationalist and arty beginnings, took over the communal myth-making functions of a variety of dramatic, literary and oral forms – and all but supplanted them. And it came to serve as a vehicle for more private mythologies like those of Cocteau, Buñuel, and Bergman. What is more problematical is the pursuing of studies that depend upon long-term access to or possession of large numbers of films. My own experience is that only third, fourth and fifth viewings of films bring the intimate familiarity required for structural analysis. But for those who can surmount this obstacle, there remains much to be done beyond what current auteur-structuralism has suggested.

Notes

1 *Screen* has recently published a translation of *Cahiers'* very important collective analysis of Ford's *Young Mr Lincoln*. In the introductory remarks *Cahiers* characterizes structural analysis as the 'dissection of an object conceived of as a closed structure, the cataloguing of progressively smaller and more "discreet" units,' ignoring their use by filmmaker and 'the dynamic of the inscription' (*Screen*, 13, no. 3, p. 6). This reflects early attitudes of Althusser, *Cahiers'* principal mentor, toward all forms of intellectual effort conceived within bourgeois ideologies which show little or no consciousness of their own premises and restrictions, But in his 1968 essay, 'Lenin and Philosophy,' Althusser acknowledged that philosophy in the future has a true object – 'pure thought,' and then added: 'what else is Lévi-Strauss up to today, on his own admission, and by appeal to Engels' authority? He, too, is studying the laws, let us say the structures of *thought*' (*Lenin and Philosophy and Other Essays*, trans. Ben Brewster, London, New Left Books, 1971, p. 59). I interpret this as a validation of Lévi-Strauss's objectives and his method: a Marxist reading of myth must also comprehend the structures that the mind creates and imposes upon all art; it will simply see more and different structures (see Althusser's reading of the temporal structures of Bertolazzi and Brecht in *For Marx*).

2 Geoffrey Nowell-Smith, *Luchino Visconti* (1967), New York, Doubleday, 1968, p. 10.

3 Peter Wollen, *Signs and Meaning in the Cinema*, Indiana University Press, 1969, p. 81.

4 Jim Kitses, *Horizons West* (1969), Indiana University Press, 1970, p. 7.

5 Alan Lovell, 'Robin Wood – a dissenting view,' *Screen*, 10, no, 2, March/April 1969, pp. 47–8.

6 Robin Wood, 'Ghostly paradigm and H.C.F.: an answer to Alan Lovell,' *Screen*, 10, no. 3, May/June 1969, pp. 35–47; Alan Lovell, 'The common pursuit of true judgement,' *Screen*, 11, no. 4/5, August/September, 1970, pp. 76–88; John C. Murray, 'Robin Wood and the structural critics,' *Screen* 12, no. 3, Summer 1971, pp. 101–10; Ben Brewster, 'Structuralism in film criticism,' *Screen*, 12, no. 1, Spring, 1971, pp. 49–58.

7 'The structural study of myth', in *Structural Anthropology*, trans. Claire Jacobson and Brook Schoepf (1958), New York, Doubleday, 1963.

8 'Overture' to *The Raw and the Cooked*, trans. John and Doreen Weightman (1964), New York, Harper and Row, 1970, pp. 1–32.

9 'Structural study,' p. 207.

10 See Lévi-Strauss's analysis of the Oedipus and 'Zuni emergence' myths in 'Structural study,' and his article 'Le Triangle culinaire,' *L'Arc*, no. 26, Aix-en-Provence, 1965, pp. 19–29. The latter serves as an introduction to the analysis employed throughout the three published volumes of *Mythologiques*. The best interpretation is that of Edmund Leach, *Claude Lévi-Strauss*, New York, Viking Press, 1970.

11 'Structural study,' p. 221.

12 'Overture,' p. 8.

12

Alternatives to Auteurs

Graham Petrie

A Canadian scholar of European cinema, Graham Petrie's numerous publications includes one of the first books on Truffaut, *The Cinema of François Truffaut*, published in 1970, and *Hollywood Destinies*, about the careers of several European film directors after coming to Hollywood. In this article, which originally appeared in the Spring, 1973 issue of *Film Quarterly*, Petrie questioned auteurism's neglect of production realities and contexts and began to ask logical questions about the question of control of a film production. Petrie also raises questions about the potential distortions of film history when it is based on a series of auteurs, in opposition to Sarris, who had claimed that auteurism was a way of conceptually organizing the history of cinema. Petrie concludes by offering his own variation of the pantheon, in which only a few filmmakers who had virtually complete control of their films emerge as auteurs, although other categories are more inclusive of those in other roles (actors, producers, cinematographers, scriptwriters) than the pantheon of Sarris and other auteurists.

"No one ever really has final cut, even when you're the producer. Somebody else always owns the picture, and there's always always someone ready to take it away from you and screw it up."

John Huston[1]

GEIST: *I don't know if you have final cut . . .*
SCHAFFNER: *I don't. I don't think anybody in the U.S. of A., who makes a film for a major distributor, has final cut.*[2]

The *auteur* theory was essentially an attempt to by-pass the issue of who, ultimately, has control over a film – an issue that Huston and Schaffner disclose with brutal frankness. By distilling something called "personal vision" from a film, and marketing this as the "essence" of its success, it was hoped to evade all the sordid and tedious details of power conflicts and financial interests that are an integral part of any major movie project. "Personal vision" made it unnecessary to pay much attention to such minor matters as: Who instigated the project, and for what motives? Who actually wrote the script, and how much of it survived? Who cast the film, and for what reasons? Who edited the final product, and under whose directives? All these could gratefully be swept aside, and attention concentrated on what was really of significance: the discovery of recurring themes, characters, and situations in film after film of one's chosen hero.

The contempt for fact displayed by *auteurists* at their peak sometimes achieved breathtaking proportions. Time and again they would confess ingenuously that they hadn't the faintest idea whether Hawks or Ford or Fuller or Aldrich had really *wanted* to make a particular film, had contributed anything to the script

Graham Petrie, "Alternatives to Auteurs," pp. 27–35 from *Film Quarterly* 26, no. 3 (Spring 1973). © 1973. Reprinted by permission of The Copyright Clearance Center, on behalf of *Film Quarterly*.

or casting, or had even directed several of the key sequences. All this, they confided was of little importance when set against their own intuition that the film *obviously* bore the director's personal stamp from beginning to end. This habit of arguing from preconceptions has so thoroughly permeated contemporary film criticism that a recent article on "Welles's Use of Sound" can use the railway station scene in *The Magnificent Ambersons* as one of its key illustrations without mentioning – or even showing awareness of – the fact that this scene was not directed by Welles himself.[3]

After this kind of thing it is something of a relief to read Garson Kanin's malicious comments on the Warner Brothers assembly line and to discover that Michael Curtiz (a recent candidate for hagiography) "sometimes started shooting a script without reading it" and that "frequently a director at Warner's wouldn't even see his assembled stuff."[4] To a hard-core *auteurist*, of course, this would merely provide further confirmation of his belief that a director's personal vision can somehow transcend otherwise insurmountable obstacles, but the recent massive accumulation of evidence of this kind must surely give the rest of us pause.

As books on cameramen and scriptwriters begin to pour off the presses, and interviews with them begin to fill the pages of the magazines,[5] it becomes evident that some radical rethinking will have to be done, and that most of the lazy and comfortable assumptions that have become habitual even to many who would indignantly deny that they were *auteurists* will have to be abandoned. It is no longer going to be enough to assume that the director's contribution is automatically of major significance; equally, it will be necessary to avoid the dangers of replacing one culture hero by another and launching into "The Cameraman as Superstar" and solemn studies of the personal vision of Sol Polito or James Wong Howe.

There are two directions that this reassessment might fruitfully take. One could be a thorough consideration of the cinema as a cooperative art and of the ways in which it thereby differs from fiction, poetry, painting, and even music and drama. (The two last require collaborators before they can fully exist and they can be performed badly or well, but *King Lear* is still a great play and Beethoven's Ninth a great symphony despite all the inadequate or horrendous incarnations they have achieved: one is dissatisfied with a particular interpretation and not with the original work itself. One has only one version of a film to judge, however, and it is *that* which becomes either bad or good.)[6] And a second might be a serious attempt to analyze the status of the director in Europe (and perhaps America in the silent period and the last five years) as opposed to the Hollywood of 1927–1967 – the heyday of the big studios and producers.

It is ironic that, at the very moment when *auteur* critics have begun to get over their obsession with themes and are making daring forays into the territory of visual style, the whole question of the responsibility for the way a film "looks" should be thrown into doubt by cameramen who tell us that X "knew nothing about lighting" or Y "left all the lighting to me." But this in turn may produce unexpected benefits, for it forces critics, perhaps for the first time, to ask what it is that constitutes a "visual style." To what extent is it the arrangement of the lights and the choice of lenses, filters, and gauzes (almost invariably the prerogative of the director of photography), and to what extent is it framing and composition, the use of a static or moving camera, the type of location and setting, the establishment of a particular color scheme, the choice of costumes and make-up, and the creation of a basic editing rhythm (all of which *may* be the responsibility of the director)? The complexities of this type of approach are evident when one considers that it is perfectly possible that in a given film the balance of light and shadow, the visual effect of the close-ups, and the movement of the camera may be totally the work of the director of photography; the pattern, order, and type of shot may have been laid down in the script; the costumes and sets may have been chosen by the studio; and the editor and producer may create the final shape of the film between them without even consulting the director. In these circumstances what sense does it make to talk confidently of so-and-so's "visual style" and how can we ever be sure that we are attributing credit where it really belongs? Yet these are questions that have to be answered if we are ever to go beyond the bland assumption that "everything" (or at least "everything that matters") in a film can be credited to its director.

It is also worthy of note that, once the young French critics who had inaugurated and polemicized the *auteur* theory actually came to the stage of making films of their own, their enthusiasm for their earlier ideas began rapidly to fade. Truffaut has recently been expressing much more interest in the nature of a film's *script* than its direction, while Rohmer has abandoned the whole process of film criticism completely. It is possible that their own experience of the complexities of getting a film into production has led them to see how over-simplified their previous assumptions had been – at a time when, paradoxically, their own films have given the term "personal cinema" a coherent and justifiable meaning. The theory can then be seen as a kind of wish-fulfillment, a convincing of themselves that it was possible for *them* to make films, their own films and on their own terms; once they had succeeded in doing this, the theory had served its purpose and could be left behind. The staunchest defenders of *auteurism* now are probably to be found in America, where it serves to bolster the self-respect and boost the egos of American directors, as well as providing a convenient way of organizing a film course or getting a book into print. Its connections with the realities of film-making, however, remain as tenuous as they ever were.

The flaw in the *auteur* theory is not so much its assumption that the director's role is of primary importance as its naive and often arrogant corollary that it is *only* the director who matters and that even the most minor work by *auteur* X is automatically more interesting than the best film of non-*auteur* Y. What good does it do Kazan's reputation, for instance, to insist on including in a retrospective of his films the unwatchable *Sea of Grass*, a work that Kazan himself has disowned as a purely commissioned piece, and that the program notes to the showing at the BFI glumly admitted is worthless? And why continue to inflict on Fritz Lang "credit" for *Der Tiger von Eschnapur/Das Indische Grabmal* and bewail the "slaughter" performed on them by English and American distributors, when Lang spent most of his time on the set lamenting the depths to which he had sunk in being obliged to make these films, and concerned himself chiefly with adjusting the folds of Valery Inkijinoff's costume and saying that what he *really* wanted to do was to film Camus?[7] One of the *auteurist*'s main defenses is that his methods allow him to rescue neglected films – but there are some films that probably deserve to remain neglected.

By focusing attention so exclusively on a limited number of figures the *auteurist* also runs the opposite risk of overlooking eminently worthwhile films that cannot conveniently be slotted into any of his favorable categories. Films like *Dark Victory* and *Now, Voyager* are left in limbo because Edmund Goulding and Irving Rapper are not considered worthy of *auteur* status; yet both films are still thoroughly watchable and transcend magnificently the stupidity of their plots. It is not, however, through the "personal vision" or "personal style" of the director that the films achieve this, and it would be impossible to take five minutes at random from either *Dark Victory* or *Now, Voyager* and attribute them with any confidence to either Goulding or Rapper on the basis of visual style or thematic material alone. In most respects the two films are interchangeable: they are the product of a particular *genre* and a particular studio, and in theme, structure, moral tone, sets, costumes, lighting, and camera style they meet the requirements laid down by these rather than expressing anything deeply felt on the part of director or cameraman.

The films, however, are not totally anonymous: they are studio products, put together by craftsmen who were also minor artists, but what gives them their lasting quality is the artistry of Bette Davis, who wielded much more power at Warner's at that time than most directors (and even read her scripts right through before committing herself to filming them). She is not in any sense the "author" or "creator" of these films, she did not write or photograph or direct them, but in a very real sense they were conceived for and around her, and she probably had as decisive an effect on their shaping as any of her collaborators. They are *her* films, and when people go to see them today it is Bette Davis they go to see them for.

The situation becomes more complex if we try to apply a similar approach to a film that is almost universally considered to "belong" to its director: *Ninotchka*. Certainly this film is full of Lubitsch "touches": it displays the elegance, the wit, the cynicism, the total lack of respect for conventional moral susceptibilities that we associate with his work (and which even pre-*auteurist* critics of the thirties had managed to isolate and identify). In moral tone and social milieu, in characters and situations, it forms part of a world that Lubitsch had been creating as recognizably his own for the previous 15 years. And yet, from today's standpoint, the film belongs as much to Garbo as it does to Lubitsch. It forms an integral stage of her own career – a career that displays a degree of continuity and artistic coherence comparable to that of most Hollywood directors. It was a film that Garbo wanted, and needed, to make at least as much as Lubitsch did: it gave her a chance to display a neglected facet of her talent and to show her potential as a comedienne. She had more say in the choice of technicians than Lubitsch and insisted, as usual, that William Daniels act as director of photography. The film was made by Garbo's MGM rather than Lubitsch's Paramount, and though the differences between Paramount glamor (in terms of sets, costumes, and lighting) and MGM glamor may be slight, there is no doubt that they exist. And although Lubitsch supervised and contributed to the script, it is certainly possible to see Billy Wilder and Charles Brackett's writing as having as much connection with Wilder's later *One, Two, Three* and *Some Like it Hot* as with Lubitsch's earlier films.

An understanding of the basic intersecting forces that went together to make up films like *Ninotchka* and *Now, Voyager* can only help to enrich our appreciation of the films, and is surely preferable to distorting *Ninotchka* by trying to see it as "all" Lubitsch, or neglecting *Now, Voyager* because there is no convenient category in which to slot Irving Rapper. Indeed we might begin to develop a degree of sophistication that allows us to enjoy a film for something more than the "personal vision" of its director – for its photography, its costumes, its music and even (like the humble and much-despised fans of Hollywood's past) for its stars.

There is no need, of course, to neglect or degrade the director and it is worth remembering that many European and even American directors had been identified (and written about) as artists with something personal to convey many decades before the *auteur* theory appeared. A partial list of these figures would include: Eisenstein, Griffith, Hitchcock, Murnau, Pudovkin, Chaplin, Von Stroheim, Ford, Lubitsch, Capra, Mamoulian, and Preston Sturges. The *auteur* theory had the effect of shaking up and often reversing conventional evaluations, and its most lasting contribution has probably been the discovery and rehabilitation of the neglected figures of the formerly despised "action" genres, together with the American films of Lang and Renoir; yet here too it should be pointed out that Manny Farber has been praising the "masculine" values of Walsh, Fuller, and Siegel for many years and for reasons that have little to do with *auteurism*. What we can usefully do now, is to start sorting out and re-examining some of the *auteurist* preconceptions that have become petrified into meaningless dogma.

Granted that the cinema *can* be a "personal art," how do we set about defining this? It is certainly possible to identify recurring themes, characters, and situations that reappear throughout the work of many directors, but to rely on these alone, as *auteurists* tend to do, is to court disaster. The continuity may be the result of working within a certain genre, or for a particular studio, or in habitual collaboration with a favorite scriptwriter or actor, just as much as it may spring from a deeply felt need of the director's temperament (and even here the recurrence of a particular theme may indicate a shallow or obsessive vision rather than a fruitful one). To try to isolate a "personal style" based on visual qualities is even more dangerous: there are not more than a handful of American directors to whom one can safely attribute a distinctive visual (or aural, or editing) style that persists no matter with whom they are collaborating or for whom they are making the film. My own list would include Griffith, Welles, Keaton, Chaplin, Von Sternberg (in the films with Dietrich), Ford (in the Westerns at least), Nicholas Ray (for the consistently bizarre quality of his images), and Kubrick.

Even if these difficulties have been overcome, and we have succeeded in agreeing on something – in theme, characters, visual composition, editing, settings, use of music, or what have you – that sets one director apart from his fellows and can reliably be traced as persisting in at least a significant number of his films, there are other problems to be taken into account. Do we insist on pursuing this personal factor into the deepest recesses of the hack and commissioned work that the director may have been forced to churn out, or do we settle on some kind of dividing line that marks off work that is worth considering from that which is not? How do we cope with actors, cameramen, composers, set designers, and scriptwriters who may also have evolved a "personal style" over a series of films (bearing in mind that here too we have difficulties in establishing degrees of freedom and of choice, many cameramen having confessed that they changed their lighting style according to the studio they worked for; while the precarious and often humiliating status of the writer in Hollywood needs little further documentation)?

All these questions lead ultimately back to the issue of control raised in the quotes from Huston and Schaffner. One can take the *auteurist* position that "personality" is some kind of mystic quality that exists in a vacuum, and can be examined in total isolation from such mundane factors as whether the director had anything very much to do with initiating, writing, casting, photographing, scoring, designing, producing, or editing the film for which we are giving him sole credit. It is at least consistent with this standpoint that those few Hollywood figures of the thirties and forties who *did* manage to secure something of this kind of control, being able to choose, write or produce their own projects – men like Stevens, Wyler, Huston, Capra, Sturges, and Mamoulian – have been steadfastly belittled by *auteurists* and insulted for displaying no "personality." Or one can try to work towards a viewpoint based on some kind of knowledge of who actually did what in a particular film, and why; and only then begin to apply criteria of artistic evaluation. As far as the status of the director as an artist is concerned, a useful starting point (though it would have to be used with modesty and flexibility) might be this quotation from Eisenstein:

> Unity makes any form of creative cooperation possible – not only between a director and an actor, but between a director and a composer and, particularly between a cameraman and a director. This applies primarily to the cinema, where all these problems acquire particular significance and acuteness. Cooperation exists in every collective where there is unity of style.
>
> When, then, is a "conflict" justified? When can the director behave like a "tyrant"? First, when a member of the collective does not fully perceive the importance of stylistic requirements. Useless to cry dictatorship; it is the director who is responsible for the organic unity of style of the film. That is his function, and in this sense he is a unifier.[8]

It may very well be true, as Andrew Sarris has argued, that English-language critics and audiences have overestimated the freedom of the European director and that he has often had to put up with restrictions at least as confining as those of his American counterpart. The fact remains, however, that Hollywood between the coming of sound and the end of the fifties had no exact equivalent anywhere else in the world. Films were shaped to suit the talents and the tastes of the producers and the stars, or to fit the requirements of an established film *genre*, or to exploit a mood or a theme that was fashionable (or thought to be fashionable) at that time; they were rarely made because a director desperately wanted to make them. Once filming began, the director had to adapt himself to the whims of his producer, the accepted "look" and moral tone of his studio, the requirements of a script that, in most cases, someone else had written, the limitations imposed by the talents or the screen image of his actors, a tightly organized budget and production schedule, and the knowledge that, once he was finished, the film would be taken away and edited by someone else, often in accordance with imperatives that had nothing whatever to do with what he may have been trying to express. All this is familiar enough, but it bears repeating in the light of some of the more starry-eyed versions of the Hollywood director that we have been given in the past few years. The European director encountered some or all of the same limitations, but rarely in so massive and uncompromising a form, and there has always been a greater opportunity in Europe for the director to *inaugurate* his own film and not merely do the best he can with material allotted to him.

In the groupings which follow, therefore, I have placed together figures from the American, European, and Oriental film-making traditions, *not* on the basis of some elusive and idiosyncratically applied "personality," but according to the degree of creative freedom they can reasonably be assumed to have enjoyed during the most important periods of their careers. A reformulation of this kind might provide a valuable antidote to the almost maniacal "Pantheon-building" that has dominated much of the discussion of film during the last decade (in *Cahiers du Cinéma* and *Movie* as much as by Andrew Sarris). My aim is to restore some sense of practicality to an activity that has become increasingly divorced from reality, and my groupings are not intended to imply value judgments as between one category and its fellow. The fact that one man had more creative freedom than another does not automatically make him a better artist (and many film-makers have wasted or abused the freedom granted to them); but a knowledge of the degree and type of freedom enjoyed will allow us to replace fantasy by common sense when talking about their work.

The listings also make no pretense at being exhaustive and are intended simply to suggest the considerations that should be taken into account and to offer a few representative names of each type.

Creators

Those who, in all or most of their completed films, were able to do all or most of the following: write, choose, or collaborate closely on the script; have a decisive voice in the choice of actors and technicians; direct; produce, or work closely with a sympathetic producer; edit or supervise the editing of the version that was released for public viewing.

Strictly speaking, only *Chaplin* truly belongs in this category: he is the only figure in the history of the cinema to have been able to make *all* his feature-length works exactly as he wanted to make them and to release them without interference or alteration to the finished product.

However, some others come close to this level:

Eisenstein: if we leave aside films like *Que Viva Mexico!* and *Bezhin Meadow*, that were never completed, Eisenstein was given total artistic freedom in the preparing and shooting of all his films. Only *October* was altered after completion, and even *Ivan the Terrible, Part II* was finally released exactly as he had made it.

Griffith: from about 1914 to 1925 had complete artistic and usually financial control of his work, writing his own scripts and editing the films himself. Any assessment of his work, however, should take into account his collaboration with Billy Bitzer, Lillian Gish, and others, and should note the decline of his career after 1925.

Keaton: enjoyed a freedom similar to that of Chaplin between 1920 and 1928. *The Cameraman* and *Spite Marriage* after that period are still recognizably, and

Figure 12.1 Charlie Chaplin (with Paulette Goddard) wrote, produced, directed, scored and starred in *Modern Times* (United Artists, 1936)

beautifully, Keaton, despite the pressures that were to destroy his career soon afterwards.

Von Sternberg: seems to have possessed a good deal of freedom even before the collaboration with Dietrich. For her, he wrote, designed, and often photographed the films, and was left in peace by Paramount to do so, as long as box-office receipts held up.

Lubitsch: was his own producer at Paramount for most of his career in sound films and was able to control scripts and casting to a very large extent.

Capra: enjoyed almost total freedom at Columbia during the thirties, his work being both financially and artistically profitable.

Hitchcock: both in Britain in the thirties and in Hollywood after that obtained a position of respect and authority. Some of his early Hollywood work is largely routine, but over his career as a whole he has generally made only the films he wanted to make, and on his own terms. He is far from being a one-man show, however, and his writers, cameramen (especially Robert Burks), composers (Bernard Herrmann), and actors (James Stewart, Grace Kelly, etc.) deserve a good deal of credit for the success of his films.

Bergman: since 1950 has exerted total control over all his films. But he works with collaborators of genius: Gunnar Fischer, Sven Nykvist, Max von Sydow, Eva Dahlbeck, Bibi Andersson, Liv Ullman, etc.

Fellini: since *The White Sheik* has made films on his own terms, to the extent that his name is now routinely attached to their titles.

Truffaut: all his films have been his own projects, scripted or co-scripted by himself. Only *The Mississippi Mermaid* has suffered from external interference, and there only in the version shown in North America.

Kubrick: the most totally independent of major contemporary American film-makers. But he "voluntarily" cut *2001* and has just done the same on *A Clockwork Orange*. The scale of his projects requires a good deal of assistance on the level of special effects, but, on the other hand, script and photography are often handled by Kubrick himself, uncredited.

Misfits, Rebels, Unfortunates, and Professionals

Those who had this kind of control often enough for it to make sense to talk about *some at least* of their films as displaying artistic coherence and continuity. At significant stages of their career, however, they did work that was purely routine and to which it is probably unnecessary to devote much attention (whereas with the first group almost every film is one which the director *chose* to make and all should therefore be taken into account when evaluating his achievement). Or, in some cases, several key films have been so mutilated before release that critics spend more time lamenting the "lost" film than studying what remains.

Von Stroheim: the archetypal representative of this group.

Welles: had complete control over *Citizen Kane*. But to what extent *in The Magnificent Ambersons* and *Touch of Evil* are we seeing the film that Welles intended us to see?

Ford: the thorough professional, who makes three films he has little interest in, in order to make the fourth that he really cares about. Some 25% of his work, then, was made with a large degree of creative freedom. But which is that 25%? Ford, for one, won't tell us, and his British admirers think that it was *Seven Women*.

Buñuel: since *Viridiana* (1961) has obtained the freedom that he possessed only sporadically in Mexico in the fifties.

Lang: the German films were made by a man with a pretty free hand (though he was heavily indebted to the scripts of Thea von Harbou). The American films were mostly assignments, though he did a good job on many of them.

Renoir: a few beautiful, uniquely personal films, and many that suffered from the demands and compromises effected by studios. *Madame Bovary, Toni, Elena et les Hommes* and *La Règle du Jeu* (until its restoration in 1965) were among those that suffered from cuts by producers and distributors. Most of the films of the twenties and some in the thirties were done purely on commission.

Losey: his career has been a running battle with producers and distributors. Only the films with Pinter perhaps emerge as "pure."

Pudovkin: had something of the freedom of Eisenstein in the twenties and up to *Deserter* (1933). His work after that serves the Russian state more than himself.

Kurosawa: The Seven Samurai and *The Idiot* were butchered by his studio. Others were only lightly massacred. A few have survived intact.

Chabrol: a period of total self-indulgence in the late fifties and early sixties (originally financed from his own funds) was followed by the routine thrillers of the mid-sixties. The films since *Les Biches* have been very much a team effort, with Stéphane Audran, Michel Bouquet, Paul Gégauff, and Jean Rabier contributing perhaps as much as Chabrol himself.

Mann: the Westerns of the fifties (and *El Cid*) form a coherent group of films on which Mann suffered little outside interference or pressure and worked with sympathetic producers and scriptwriters.

Scene-Stealers and Harmonizers

This is not limited solely to directors and includes any major collaborator on a film whose influence seems to have been decisive in creating its quality or lasting impact. It could be the star round whom the script was written and for whom the technicians were chosen; the scriptwriter whose work was so powerfully visualized that it needed little alteration in the filming; the director of photography who created images that transcended a banal script and poor acting; a creative or domineering producer in whose hands the director was little more than a puppet; or an erratic or routine director who rose to the challenge of particularly congenial material or circumstances.

This category includes several figures mentioned already as collaborators in the first category. It also overlaps with the second, to the extent that these people rarely had *total* artistic control over their films and that their influence is evident only in a *proportion* of the films on which they worked. There is value, however, in studying aspects of their careers as a whole and in trying to establish patterns of continuity.

Among film stars, for example, *Greta Garbo* and *Bette Davis* were, at the peak of their careers, almost invariably the factor around which discussion of a film would start. Director, cameraman, and supporting actors were chosen to suit *them*, and they possessed powers of veto or noncooperation which ensured that any debate was usually settled to their satisfaction. Each developed a consistent artistic personality on the screen, around which the script, sets, and lighting were shaped: there is a fine line to be drawn between this and mere type-casting, of which Garbo was more nearly the victim than Davis. James Stewart might come into this category too, so many films of quality – from *Mr Smith Goes to Washington*, through *Vertigo* and *The Man from Laramie* to *The Man Who Shot Liberty Valance* – having centered round his varied *personae* as the slow-burning, passive, almost victimized spectator who finally rouses himself to action.

Val Lewton is perhaps the classic example of a producer whose films display a homogeneity of theme and atmosphere, no matter who happened to direct them.

Boris Kaufman, Gregg Toland, and *Raoul Coutard* are cameramen whose work is recognizable no matter which director they are filming for. Normally they have worked with men of great distinction, but we will have to learn to talk of the visual style of Godard *and* Coutard, of Vigo *and* Kaufman, of Wyler *and* Toland.

Scriptwriters would include *Dudley Nichols* (taking into account his collaboration with Ford in particular), *Jacques Prévert* (who imposes his own patterns on Renoir as well as on Carné) and *Thea von Harbou* and *Carl Mayer*, whose impact on German Expressionist film is all-pervasive.

There are many directors who were identified with a particular kind of film and could be trusted to carry that through efficiently, but have displayed little noticeable talent outside their chosen area. Some of these would be: *James Whale* (horror films), *Vittorio de Sica* (neo-realism), *Raoul Walsh* (gangster and war), *Michael Curtiz* (melodrama and costume dramas), *Roger Corman* (horror) and *Budd Boetticher* (Western). All these enjoyed a considerable degree of freedom in making films of this type (partly because so many of them were low-budget) and all are quite heavily dependent on the quality of their collaborators.[9]

It would be possible to continue, inventing other categories and drawing more and more refined and tenuous distinctions, but I prefer to stop here. I am concerned simply with suggesting that there are other ways of thinking about the personal factor in film-making than those propagated by *auteurism* and the common assumption that one must start with the director when trying to determine the quality or value of any particular film. In many cases, of course, the director *is* the decisive influence – in one or two or a group of films, or, more rarely, over his entire career – but this is far from being always, or even normally, the case, at least as far as Hollywood is concerned; and too much injustice and distortion has been performed in recent film criticism for the sake of providing a neat and tidy solution to the extremely complex question of artistic freedom and creativity in the movies. Good and even great films have been produced in circumstances where directional control has been negligible, or where other contributors have played an equally significant role; a major concern of film criticism should now be to discover how and why this should be so.

Notes

1 *New York Times* (Sunday, December 10, 1972).

2 *Film Comment*, vol. 8, no. 3 (September–October 1972), p. 36.

3 Phyllis Goldfarb. "Orson Welles's Use of Sound," *Take One*, vol. 3, no. 6 (1972), p. 11.

4 *Sight and Sound*, vol. 41, no. 3 (Summer 1972), p. 136. Kanin also claims that, to the best of his knowledge, *no* Hollywood director of this period (the late thirties and early forties) had the right to final cut.

5 Spreading, in an interesting reversal of the usual trend, West–East across the Atlantic: see *Cinéma 72*, no. 168 for one of the rare French articles on cinematographers.

6 This is true even of a remake, which – unless it was originally taken from a stage play – is never *exactly* the same material merely performed in a different manner. Which also accounts for the fact that a script that was never made into a film – even one by Eisenstein – has a curiosity rather than an artistic value.

7 "Souvenirs de Valery Inkijinoff (II)," *Cinéma 72*, no. 168, pp. 82–3.

8 *Notes of a Film Director* (Dover, New York, 1970), p. 113.

9 I am not intending to slight these men by calling attention to their limitations. Bergman would probably make a mess of directing a Western. The point is that he has not tried – or been forced – to do so.

13

Women's Cinema as Counter-Cinema

Claire Johnston

Claire Johnston was an important early voice in British feminist film criticism. She is the editor of *Notes on Women's Cinema* (1973) and *The Work of Dorothy Arzner – Towards a Feminist Cinema* (1975) for the British Film Institute. Johnston was one of the first critics to challenge the almost exclusively masculine orientation of orthodox auteurism. In this essay, which originally appeared in *Notes on Women's Cinema*, she rejects "sociological" analysis of film and its false issues of realism for the representation of women, and instead approaches the depictions of women in the male-dominated world of movies as signs of masculinist ideology. From this perspective she reconsiders the by-then standard comparison of Ford and Hawks, as well as opening up auteurism to the consideration of women directors such as Ida Lupino, Dorothy Arzner, and Agnès Varda.

Myths of Women in the Cinema

. . . there arose, identifiable by standard appearance, behaviour and attributes, the well-remembered types of the Vamp and the Straight Girl (perhaps the most convincing modern equivalents of the medieval personifications of the Vices and Virtues), the Family Man and the Villain, the latter marked by a black moustache and walking stick. Nocturnal scenes were printed on blue or green film. A checkered table-cloth meant, once for all, a 'poor but honest' milieu; a happy marriage, soon to be endangered by the shadows from the past symbolised by the young wife's pouring of the breakfast coffee for her husband; the first kiss was invariably announced by the lady's gently playing with her partner's necktie and was invariably accompanied by her kicking out with her left foot. The conduct of the characters was predetermined accordingly.

(Erwin Panofsky in "Style and Medium in the Motion Pictures," 1934 and in "Film: An Anthology," D. Talbot, ed., New York, 1959)

Panofsky's detection of the primitive stereotyping which characterised the early cinema could prove useful for discerning the way myths of women have operated in the cinema: why the image of man underwent rapid differentiation, while the primitive stereotyping of women remained with some modifications. Much writing on the stereotyping of women in the cinema takes as its starting point a monolithic view of the media as repressive and manipulative: in this way, Hollywood has been viewed as a dream factory producing an oppressive cultural product. This over-politicised view bears little relation to the ideas on art expressed either by Marx or Lenin, who both pointed to there being no direct connection between the development of art and the material basis of society. The idea of the intentionality of art which this view implies is extremely misleading and retrograde, and short-circuits the possibility of a critique

Claire Johnston, "Women's Cinema as Counter-Cinema," from *Notes on Women's Cinema* (London: Society for Education in Film and Television, 1973).

which could prove useful for developing a strategy for women's cinema. If we accept that the developing of female stereotypes was not a conscious strategy of the Hollywood dream machine, what are we left with? Panofsky locates the origins of iconography and stereotype in the cinema in terms of practical necessity; he suggests that in the early cinema the audience had much difficulty deciphering what appeared on the screen. Fixed iconography, then, was introduced to aid understanding and provide the audience with basic facts with which to comprehend the narrative. Iconography as a specific kind of sign or cluster of signs based on certain conventions within the Hollywood genres has been partly responsible for the stereotyping of women within the commercial cinema in general, but the fact that there is a far greater differentiation of men's roles than of women's roles in the history of the cinema relates to sexist ideology itself, and the basic opposition which places man inside history, and woman as ahistoric and eternal. As the cinema developed, the stereotyping of man was increasingly interpreted as contravening the realisation of the notion of 'character'; in the case of woman, this was not the case; the dominant ideology presented her as eternal and unchanging, except for modifications in terms of fashion etc. In general the myths governing the cinema are no different from those governing other cultural products: they relate to a standard value system informing all cultural systems in a given society. Myth uses icons, but the icon is its weakest point. Furthermore, it is possible to use icons (i.e. conventional configurations) in the face of and against the mythology usually associated with them. In his magisterial work on myth (*Mythologies*, Jonathan Cape, London 1971), the critic Roland Barthes examines how myth, as the signifier of an ideology, operates, by analysing a whole range of items: a national dish, a society wedding, a photograph from *Paris Match*. In his book he analyses how a sign can be emptied of its original denotative meaning and a new connotative meaning superimposed on it. What was a complete sign, consisting of a signifier plus a signified, becomes merely the signifier of a new signified, which subtly usurps the place of the original denotation. In this way, the new connotation is mistaken for the natural, obvious and evident denotation: this is what makes it the signifier of the ideology of the society in which it is used.

Myth then, as a form of speech or discourse, represents the major means in which women have been used in the cinema: myth transmits and transforms the ideology of sexism and renders it invisible – when it is made visible it evaporates – and therefore natural. This process puts the question of the stereotyping of women in a somewhat different light. In the first place, such a view of the way cinema operates challenges the notion that the commercial cinema is more manipulative of the image of woman than the art cinema. It could be argued that precisely because of the iconography of Hollywood, the system offers some resistance to the unconscious workings of myth. Sexist ideology is no less present in the European art cinema because stereotyping appears less obvious; it is in the nature of myth to drain the sign (the image of woman/the function of woman in the narrative) of its meaning and superimpose another which thus appears natural: in fact, a strong argument could be made for the art film inviting a greater invasion from myth. This point assumes considerable importance when considering the emerging women's cinema. The conventional view about women working in Hollywood (Arzner, Weber, Lupino etc.) is that they had little opportunity for real expression within the dominant sexist ideology; they were token women and little more. In fact, because iconography offers in some ways a greater resistance to the realist characterisations, the mythic qualities of certain stereotypes become far more easily detachable and can be used as a short-hand for referring to an ideological tradition in order to provide a critique of it. It is possible to disengage the icons from the myth and thus bring about reverberations within the sexist ideology in which the film is made. Dorothy Arzner certainly made use of such techniques and the work of Nelly Kaplan is particularly important in this respect. As a European director she understands the dangers of myth invading the sign in the art film, and deliberately makes use of Hollywood iconography to counteract this. The use of crazy comedy by some women directors (e.g. Stephanie Rothman) also derives from this insight.

In rejecting a sociological analysis of woman in the cinema we reject any view in terms of realism, for this would involve an acceptance of the apparent natural denotation of the sign and would involve a denial of the reality of myth in operation. Within a sexist ideology and a male-dominated cinema, woman

Figure 13.1 Marlene Dietrich's masculine clothing in Josef von Sternberg's *Morocco* (Paramount, 1930). Produced by Hector Turnbull

is presented as what she represents for man. Laura Mulvey in her most useful essay on the pop artist Allen Jones ('You Don't Know What You're Doing Do You, Mr. Jones?', Laura Mulvey in *Spare Rib*, February 1973) points out that woman as woman is totally absent in Jones' work. The fetishistic image portrayed relates only to male narcissism: woman represents not herself, but by a process of displacement, the male phallus. It is probably true to say that despite the enormous emphasis placed on woman as spectacle in the cinema, woman as woman is largely absent. A sociological analysis based on the empirical study of recurring roles and motifs would lead to a critique in terms of an enumeration of the notion of career/home/motherhood/sexuality, an examination of women as the central figures in the narrative, etc. If we view the image of woman as sign within the sexist ideology, we see that the portrayal of woman is merely one item subject to the law of verisimilitude, a law which directors worked with or reacted against. The law of verisimilitude (that which determines the impression of realism) in the cinema is precisely responsible for the repression of the image of woman as woman and the celebration of her nonexistence.

This point becomes clearer when we look at a film which revolves around a woman entirely and the idea of the female star. In their analysis of Sternberg's *Morocco*, the critics of *Cahiers du Cinema* delineate the system which is in operation: in order that the man remain within the centre of the universe in a text which focuses on the image of woman, the auteur is forced to repress the idea of woman as a social and sexual being (her Otherness) and to deny the opposition man/woman altogether. The woman as sign, then, becomes the pseudo-centre of the filmic discourse. The real opposition posed by the sign is male/non-male, which Sternberg establishes by his use of masculine clothing enveloping the image of Dietrich. This masquerade indicates the absence of man, an absence which is simultaneously negated and recuperated by man. The image of the woman becomes merely the trace of the exclusion and repression of Woman. All fetishism, as Freud has observed, is a phallic replacement, a projection of male narcissistic fantasy. The star system as a whole depended on the fetishization of woman. Much of the work done on the star system concentrates on the star as the focus for false and alienating dreams. This empirical approach is essentially concerned with the effects of the star system and audience reaction. What the fetishisation of the star does indicate is the collective fantasy of phallocentrism. This is particularly interesting when we look at the persona of Mae West. Many women have read into her parody of the star system and her verbal aggression an attempt at the subversion of male domination in the cinema. If we look more closely there are many traces of phallic replacement in her persona which suggest quite the opposite. The voice itself is strongly masculine, suggesting the absence of the male, and establishes a male/non-male dichotomy. The characteristic phallic dress possesses elements of the fetish. The female element which is introduced, the mother image, expresses male oedipal fantasy. In other words, at the unconscious level, the persona of Mae West is entirely consistent with sexist ideology; it in no way subverts existing myths, but reinforces them.

In their first editorial, the editors of *Women and Film* attack the notion of auteur theory, describing it as 'an oppressive theory making the director a superstar as if film-making were a one-man show.' This is to miss the point. Quite clearly, some developments of the auteur theory have led to a tendency to deify the personality of the (male) director, and Andrew Sarris (the major target for attack in the editorial) is one of the worst offenders in this respect. His derogatory treatment of women directors in *The American Cinema* gives a clear indication of his sexism. Nevertheless, the development of the auteur theory marked an important intervention in film criticism: its polemics challenged the entrenched view of Hollywood as monolithic, and stripped of its normative aspects the classification of films by director has proved an extremely productive way of ordering our experience of the cinema. In demonstrating that Hollywood was at least as interesting as the art cinema, it marked an important step forward. The test of any theory should be the degree to which it produces new knowledge: the auteur theory has certainly achieved this. Further elaborations of the auteur theory (cf Peter Wollen, *Signs and Meanings in the Cinema*, Secker & Warburg, Cinema One Series, London 1972) have stressed the use of the theory to delineate the unconscious structure of the film. As Peter Wollen says, 'the structure is associated with a single director, an individual, not because he has played the role of artist, expressing himself or his vision in the film, but it is through the force of his preoccupations that an unconscious, unintended meaning can be decoded in the film, usually to the surprise of the individual concerned.' In this way Wollen disengages both from the notion of creativity which dominates the notion of 'art', and from the idea of intentionality.

In briefly examining the myths of woman which underlie the work of two Hollywood directors, Ford and Hawks, making use of findings and insights derived from auteur analysis, it is possible to see that the image of woman assumes very different meanings within the different texts of each author's work. An analysis in terms of the presence or absence of 'positive' heroine figures within the same directors' *oeuvre* would produce a very different view. What Peter Wollen refers to as the 'force of the author's preoccupations' (including the obsessions about women) is generated by the psychoanalytic history of the author. This organised network of obsessions is outside the scope of the author's choice.

Hawks vs. Ford

Hawks' films celebrate the solidarity and validity of the exclusive all-male group, dedicated to the life of action and adventure, and a rigid professional ethic. When women intrude into their world, they represent a threat to the very existence of the group. However, women appear to possess 'positive' qualities in Hawks' films: they are often career women and show signs of independence and aggression in the face of the male, particularly in his crazy comedies. Robin Wood has pointed out quite correctly that the crazy comedies portray an inverted version of Hawks' universe. The male is often humiliated or depicted as infantile or regressed. Such films as *Bringing Up Baby*, *His Girl Friday* and *Gentlemen Prefer Blondes* combine, as Robin Wood has said, 'farce and horror'; they are 'disturbing'.

Figure 13.2 Cary Grant and Rosalind Russell as the "traumatic presence" in *His Girl Friday* (Columbia, 1940). Produced and directed by Howard Hawks

For Hawks, there is only the male and the non-male: in order to be accepted into the male universe, the woman must *become* a man; alternatively she becomes woman-as-phallus (Marilyn Monroe in *Gentlemen Prefer Blondes*). This disturbing quality in Hawks' films relates directly to the presence of woman; she is a traumatic presence which must be negated. Ford's is a very different universe, in which women play a pivotal role: it is around their presence that the tensions between the desire for the wandering existence and the desire for settlement/the idea of the wilderness and the idea of the garden revolve. For Ford woman represents the home, and with it the possibility of culture: she becomes a cipher onto which Ford projects his profoundly ambivalent attitude to the concepts of civilisation and psychological 'wholeness'.

While the depiction of women in Hawks involves a direct confrontation with the problematic (traumatic) presence of Woman, a confrontation which results in his need to repress her, Ford's use of woman as a symbol for civilisation considerably complicates the whole question of the repression of woman in his work and leaves room for more progressive elements to emerge (e.g. *Seven Women* and *Cheyenne Autumn*).

Towards a Counter-Cinema

There is no such thing as unmanipulated writing, filming or broadcasting.

> The question is therefore not whether the media are manipulated, but who manipulates them. A revolutionary plan should not require the manipulators to disappear; on the contrary, it must make everyone a manipulator (Hans Magnus Enzensberger in "Constituents of a Theory of Media," *New Left Review*, no. 64).

Enzensberger suggests the major contradiction operating in the media is that between their present constitution and their revolutionary potential. Quite clearly, a strategic use of the media, and film in particular, is essential for disseminating our ideas. At the moment the possibility of feedback is low, though the potential already exists. In the light of such possibilities, it is particularly important to analyse what the nature of cinema is and what strategic use can be made of it in all its forms: the political film/the commercial entertainment film. Polemics for women's creativity are fine as long as we realize they are polemics. The notion of women's creativity *per se* is as limited as the notion of men's creativity. It is basically an idealist conception which elevates the idea of the 'artist' (involving the pitfall of elitism), and undermines any view of art as a material thing within a cultural context which forms it and is formed by it. All films or works of art are products: products of an existing system of economic relations, in the final analysis. This applies equally to experimental films, political films and commercial entertainment cinema. Film is also an ideological product – the product of bourgeois ideology. The idea that art is universal and thus potentially androgynous is basically an idealist notion: art can only be defined as a discourse within a particular conjuncture – for the purpose of women's cinema, the bourgeois, sexist ideology of male dominated capitalism. It is important to point out that the workings of ideology do not involve a process of deception/intentionality. For Marx, ideology is a reality, it is not a lie. Such a misapprehension can prove extremely misleading; there is no way in which we can eliminate ideology as if by an effort of will. This is extremely important when it comes to discussing women's cinema. The tools and techniques of cinema themselves, as part of reality, are an expression of the prevailing ideology: they are not neutral, as many 'revolutionary' film-makers appear to believe. It is idealist mystification to believe that 'truth' can be captured by the camera or that the conditions of a film's production (e.g. a film made collectively by women) can *of itself* reflect the conditions of its production. This is mere utopianism: new meaning has to *be manufactured* within the text of the film. The camera was developed in order to accurately reproduce reality and safeguard the bourgeois notion of realism which was being replaced in painting. An element of sexism governing the technical development of the camera can also be discerned. In fact, the lightweight camera was developed as early as the 1930s in Nazi Germany for propaganda purposes; the reason why it was not until the 1950s that it assumed common usage remains obscure.

Much of the emerging women's cinema has taken its aesthetics from television and cinema vérité techniques (e.g. *Three Lives, Women Talking*); Shirley Clarke's *Portrait of Jason* has been cited as an important influence. These films largely depict images of women talking to camera about their experiences, with little or no intervention by the film maker. Kate Millett sums up the approach in *Three Lives* by saying, 'I did not want to analyse any more, but to express and film is a very powerful way to express oneself.'

Clearly, if we accept that cinema involves the production of signs, the idea of non-intervention is pure mystification. The sign is always a product. What the camera in fact grasps is the 'natural' world of the dominant ideology. Women's cinema cannot afford such idealism; the 'truth' of our oppression cannot be 'captured' on celluloid with the 'innocence' of the camera: it has to be constructed/manufactured. New meanings have to be created by disrupting the fabric of the male bourgeois cinema within the text of the film. As Peter Wollen points out, 'reality is always adaptive'. Eisenstein's method is instructive here. In his use of fragmentation as a revolutionary strategy, a concept is generated by the clash of two specific images, so that it serves as an abstract concept in the filmic discourse. This idea of fragmentation as an analytical tool is quite different from the use of fragmentation suggested by Barbara Martineau in her essay. She sees fragmentation as the juxtaposition of disparate elements (cf *Lion's Love*) to bring about emotional reverberations, but these reverberations do not provide a means of understanding within them. In the context of women's cinema such a strategy would be totally recuperable by the dominant ideology: indeed, in that it depends on emotionality and mystery, it invites the invasion of ideology. The ultimate logic of this method is automatic writing developed by the surrealists. Romanticism will not provide us with the necessary tools to construct a women's cinema: our objectification cannot be overcome simply by examining it artistically. It can only be challenged by developing the means to interrogate the male, bourgeois cinema. Furthermore, a desire for change can only come about by drawing on fantasy. The danger of developing a cinema of non-intervention is that it promotes a passive subjectivity at the expense of analysis. Any revolutionary strategy must challenge the depiction of reality; it is not enough to discuss the oppression of women within the text of the film; the language of the cinema/the depiction of reality must also be interrogated, so that a break between ideology and text is effected. In this respect, it is instructive to look at films made by women within the Hollywood system which attempted by formal means to bring about a dislocation between sexist ideology and the text of the film; such insights could provide useful guidelines for the emerging women's cinema to draw on.

Dorothy Arzner and Ida Lupino

Dorothy Arzner and Lois Weber were virtually the only women working in Hollywood during the 1920s and 1930s who managed to build up a consistent body of work in the cinema: unfortunately, very little is known of their work, as yet. An analysis of one of Dorothy Arzner's later films, *Dance, Girl, Dance*, made in 1940 gives some idea of her approach to women's cinema within the sexist ideology of Hollywood. A conventional vaudeville story, *Dance, Girl, Dance* centres on the lives of a troupe of dancing girls down on their luck. The main characters, Bubbles and Judy, are representative of the primitive iconographic depiction of women – vamp and straight-girl – described by Panofsky. [Working from this crude stereotyping, Arzner succeeds in generating within the text of the film, an internal criticism of it.] Bubbles manages to land a job, and Judy becomes the stooge in her act, performing ballet for the amusement of the all-male audience. Arzner's critique centres round the notion of woman as spectacle, as performer within the male universe. The central figures appear in a parody form of the performance, representing opposing poles of the myths of femininity – sexuality vs. grace & innocence. The central contradiction articulating their existence as performers for the pleasure of men is one with which most women would identify: [the contradiction between the desire to please and self-expression]. Bubbles needs to please the male, while Judy seeks self-expression as a ballet dancer. As the film progresses, a one-way process of the performance is firmly established, involving the humiliation of Judy as the stooge. Towards the end of the film Arzner brings about her tour de force, cracking open the entire fabric of the film and exposing the workings of ideology in the construction of the stereotype of woman. Judy, in a fit of anger, turns on her audience and tells them *how she sees them*. This return of scrutiny in what within the film is assumed as a one-way process constitutes a direct assault on the audience within the film and the audience of the film, and has the effect of directly challenging the entire notion of woman as spectacle.

Ida Lupino's approach to women's cinema is somewhat different. As an independent producer and director working in Hollywood in the 1950s, Lupino chose to work largely within the melodrama, a genre which, more than any other, has presented a less reified view of women, and as Sirk's work indicates, is adaptable for expressing rather than embodying the idea of the oppression of women. An analysis of *Not Wanted*, Lupino's first feature film gives some idea of the disturbing ambiguity of her films and their relationship to the sexist ideology. Unlike Arzner, Lupino is not concerned with employing purely formal means to obtain her objective; in fact, it is doubtful whether she operates at a conscious level at all in subverting the sexist ideology. The film tells the story of a young girl, Sally Kelton, and is told from her subjective viewpoint and filtered through her imagination. She has an illegitimate child which is eventually adopted; unable to come to terms with losing the child, she snatches one from a pram and ends up in the hands of the authorities. Finally, she finds a substitute for the child in the person of a crippled young man, who, through a process of symbolic castration – in which he is forced to chase her until he can no longer stand, whereupon she takes him up in her arms as he performs child-like gestures, – provides the 'happy ending'. Though Lupino's films in no way explicitly attack or expose the workings of sexist ideology, reverberations within the narrative, produced by the convergence of two irreconcilable strands – Hollywood myths of woman *vs* the female perspective – cause a series of distortions within the very structure of the narrative; the mark of disablement puts the film under the sign of disease and frustration. An example of this process is, for instance, the inverted 'happy ending' of the film.

The intention behind pointing to the interest of Hollywood directors like Dorothy Arzner and Ida Lupino is twofold. In the first place it is a polemical attempt to restore the interest of Hollywood from attacks that have been made on it. Secondly, an analysis of the workings of myth and the possibilities of subverting it in the Hollywood system could prove of use in determining a strategy for the subversion of ideology in general.

Perhaps something should be said about the European art film; undoubtedly, it is more open to the invasion of myth than the Hollywood film. This point becomes quite clear when we scrutinise the work of Riefenstahl, Companeez, Trintignant, Varda and others. The films of Agnes Varda are a particularly good example of an *oeuvre* which celebrates bourgeois myths of women, and with it the apparent innocence of the sign. *Le Bonheur* in particular, almost invites a Barthesian analysis! Varda's portrayal of female fantasy constitutes one of the nearest approximations to the facile day-dreams perpetuated by advertising that probably exists in the cinema. Her films appear totally innocent to the workings of myth; indeed, it is the purpose of myth to fabricate an impression of innocence, in which all becomes 'natural': Varda's concern for nature is a direct expression of this retreat from history: history is transmuted into nature, involving the elimination of all questions, because all appears 'natural'. There is no doubt that Varda's work is reactionary: in her rejection of culture and her placement of women outside history her films mark a retrograde step in woman's cinema.

Conclusion

What kind of strategy, then, is appropriate at this particular point in time? The development of collective work is obviously a major step forward; as a means of acquiring and sharing skills it constitutes a formidable challenge to male privilege in the film industry: as an expression of sisterhood, it suggests a viable alternative to the rigid hierarchical structures of male-dominated cinema and offers real opportunities for a dialogue about the nature of women's cinema within it. At this point in time, a strategy should be developed which embraces both the notion of films as a political tool and film as entertainment. For too long these have been regarded as two opposing poles with little common ground. In order to counter our objectification in the cinema, our collective fantasies must be released: women's cinema must embody the working through of desire: such an objective demands the use of the entertainment film. Ideas derived from the entertainment film, then, should inform the political film, and political ideas should inform the entertainment cinema: a two-way process. Finally, a repressive moralistic assertion that women's cinema *is* collective film-making is misleading and unnecessary: we should seek to operate at all levels: within the male-dominated cinema and outside it. This essay has attempted to demonstrate the interest of women's films made within the system. Voluntarism and utopianism must be avoided if any revolutionary strategy is to emerge. A collective film *of itself* cannot reflect the conditions of its production. What collective methods do provide is the real possibility of examining how cinema works and how we can best interrogate and demystify the workings of ideology: it will be from these insights that a genuinely revolutionary conception of counter-cinema for the women's struggle will come.

14

Refocusing Authorship in Women's Filmmaking

Angela Martin

Angela Martin's essay "Refocusing Authorship in Women's Filmmaking" appeared originally in an anthology of feminist film criticism published in 2003 entitled *Women Filmmakers: Refocusing*. Martin's contribution to the collection examines the masculine biases of classic auteurism, arguing that the position of women directors in the industry is necessarily different from that of men. Auteurism's traditional masculine paradigms restrict women filmmakers to being considered as auteurs in particular ways. Attempting to move beyond the trap of gender binarism, Martin calls for feminist authorship to be defined by a distinctive style that does not necessarily rely on the locatable presence of a female voice.

This chapter has two points of departure. The first is my teaching of film theory and practice; the second is the availability of women's films – specifically within the education context but also within the wider context of distribution and exhibition. It seems to me that we are experiencing two new kinds of omission of women filmmakers:

1. In addition to the many lost films by women from the earliest period of the cinema, we have also lost a disturbing number from the 1970s. For example, when I was putting a festival program strand together on pioneer women documentary filmmakers,[1] I could not get hold of the prints of films by the London Women's Film Group[2] or of Heiny Srour's *The Hour of Liberation* (Lebanon 1974). The filmmakers themselves were not entirely aware that their films were no longer in distribution.[3] Many more recent films are often available only during brief cinema runs, and only a few of these find their way onto video; even fewer will be widely available on video.
2. This loss of important films by women reflects and is reflected in the discipline of film studies, which tends to ignore or omit women's films – not consciously, but because the theory that informs the discipline is still largely only concerned with male filmmakers. This applies to film history, genre studies, authorship, narrative, film language, and so on. Furthermore, while feminist film theory has, rightly, had a great impact on film theory in general, its attention, too, has tended to focus on the work of male filmmakers. As a teacher and as a film worker, I find this extremely worrying and would suggest that we need to look at film theory in general from this point of view.

Angela Martin, "Refocusing Authorship in Women's Cinema," pp. 29–37 from Jacqueline Levitin, Judith Plessis, and Valerie Raoul (eds.), *Women Filmmakers: Refocusing* (Vancouver: University of British Columbia Press, 2003).

But I wish here to address the issue only in two related ways: by looking at the notion of authorship and by suggesting a different angle on women's filmmaking.

Authorship is the main aspect of film theory that directly affects women filmmakers; however, for historical reasons, it actually contributes to the omission of women's films from circulation and from film theory. I want to argue, therefore, that unless we talk about women's films in a different way, we will not be able to address that omission. And although I am not going to talk here about Kathryn Bigelow, her work as a woman filmmaker makes the need for this argument very clear; so I will start and end with references to her.

I originally intended to produce a paper on Bigelow's work and the possibility of talking about a gendered authorship, with particular reference to her film *Point Break*, but I found the proposal of "authorship" increasingly problematic. At the same time, excellent publications have appeared in English on the work of Agnès Varda, Diane Kurys, Marguerite Duras, and Dorothy Arzner;[4] and Christina Lane has published an important article on Bigelow.[5] All these texts point to the uneasy relationship between theoretical notions of authorship and women's filmmaking:

> I will not claim that Arzner's films are unqualified successes from beginning to end; I am far too suspicious of such a "great genius" theory of authorship.[6]

> Within the specific context of French cinema and French culture . . . the concept of the *auteur*, if ostensibly ungendered, remains resolutely masculine.[7]

> It is . . . hard to deny to Varda's work that rather over-used title of *cinéma d'auteur.*[8]

However, as Carrie Tarr points out: "feminist critics and historians have argued the political necessity for defending female authorship as a useful and necessary category."[9] Otherwise the theory of authorship continues its tendency towards a "league table" of "great genius" (read male), and: "female-authored films may be more open to representations of women reworked to feminist or woman-identified ends."[10]

At the same time, several women filmmakers (Kurys and Coline Serreau amongst them)[11] do not identify themselves or their work with a feminist (or even specifically female) project; on the other hand, the theory of authorship has become something of a tangled web, and I want now to look briefly at a few of the signposts along the way of film theory and of film studies as I pursue my argument that "auteurism," as we call it in English has nothing to do with women's filmmaking.[12]

The original suggestion that the filmmaker should be an auteur was a matter of policy, not of theory: it was about the desire for a cinema of self-expression, a generational revolt on the part of the young *Cahiers du cinéma* critics, who were demanding a break with the persistently traditional mainstream French cinema, which they saw as heavy, entrenched, and tied to the wordiness of the theatre-inspired script. They spoke about auteurs because they desperately wanted to claw the creative centre away from the writers of these scripts. Everything, they said, should be geared towards, shaped, and even produced by the "true brilliance"[13] of the director, the film auteur's "self-expression"[14] of "primary emotion."[15] In his attempt "to make a personal work,"[16] the auteur transforms, "as if by magic, a screenplay written by someone else."[17] And they saw the epitome of the *politique* in the work of a number of hitherto little thought of commercial Hollywood directors. One example illustrates the gender-bound nature of their enthusiasm. In his announcement of the arrival of "the age of the *auteurs*," Jacques Rivette names four filmmakers: Nicholas Ray, Richard Brooks, Anthony Mann, and Robert Aldrich, who, if one accepted nothing else about them, he wrote, share the common trait of youth. But of the virtues of youth that they share, violence is the primary one:

> not that easy brutality which constituted the success of a Dmytryk or a Benedek, but a virile anger, which comes from the heart, and lies less in the scenario or the choice of events, than in the tone of the narrative and the very technique of the *mise en scène*. Violence is never an end, but a means of approach . . . to drill an opening: in short, to open the shortest routes. And the frequent resort to a technique which is discontinuous, halting, which refuses the conventions of cutting and continuity, is a form of that "superior madness" which Cocteau speaks about, born out of the need for an immediate expression which accounts for and shares in the primary emotions of the *auteur* . . . trying to make a personal work . . . In short, violence is the external sign of rupture.[18]

Actually, this male-centredness notwithstanding, the demands of the *Cahiers* critics were understandable within their own historical and political context – being part of the first new post-Second World War generation, implicated in the French colonial war against the Algerian struggle for independence, and disillusioned by the state, the Church, and bourgeois culture. But virility is, by definition, masculine,[19] which is easily attached to notions of violence, anger, and "the need for an immediate expression"; and the *Nouvelle Vague*'s call for a personal self-expression is very different from the later feminist call for the personal to be political rather than ego-centric.

The inevitable male-centredness of the *politique des auteurs* was compounded by Andrew Sarris's theory that the source of value was *the director*. At the same time, the British film journal *Movie* published "The talent histogram" in its first issue in June 1962,[20] categorizing directors according to "Great, Brilliant, Very Talented, Talented, Competent or Ambitious, and The Rest." Two women appear in it, in the last two categories – Shirley Clarke was in the longest (American) "Competent or Ambitious" column, while Muriel Box was one of "The [almost as many British] Rest."[21] Victor Perkins summarized the theory and critical practice of auteurism as looking for "the achievement within the single film of values like economy, unity, eloquence, subtlety, depth and *vigour* [on the one hand; and on the other] recurrent themes in a director's films considered as a series . . . themes, viewpoints and methods of sufficient personal significance to carry over from film to film" (emphasis mine).[22]

We have now moved on a long way from this position, but it is apparently still alive and well. Just a cursory keyword computer reference check produced a dozen or so journal articles between 1981 and 1993 that defend the greatness of, for example, Fassbinder, Kazan, John Ford (revisited), Jacques Doillon, Louis Malle, Sirk, and the Marx Brothers but not a single woman filmmaker. However, if we attempted to apply the theory to women filmmakers, as Claire Johnston understandably suggested in 1973,[23] we could then have applied it only to the work of Arzner or Lupino because only those filmmakers had produced a body of work within a single production context. Bigelow would be one of the few current women filmmakers who would be eligible, if one wanted to make the claim.

Later, as auteur analysis, the theory looked to *the text* as the source of a meaning of which the filmmaker himself may not have been aware. This involves

> tracing a structure (not a message) within the work, which can *then post factum* be assigned to an individual, the director . . . [However,] there can be no doubt that the presence of a structure in the text can often be connected with the presence of a director on the set, but the situation in the cinema, where the director's primary task is often one of co-ordination and rationalisation, is very different from that in the other arts, where there is a much more direct relationship between artist and work. It is in this sense that it is possible to speak of a film *auteur* as an *unconscious catalyst*.[24] (my emphasis)

The problem here, as far as women filmmakers are concerned, is that they are not unconscious industry hacks or jobbing directors, churning out one film after another within recognizable commercial cinema genres. Most women filmmakers we would be interested in are thinking filmmakers, usually working within an independent cinema framework, and many have been to film school, even if, like Chantal Akerman, they didn't stay very long. Kathryn Bigelow, for example, attended classes with Milos Forman and Peter Wollen, among others. She was, therefore, engaged in dialogue about film theory almost as soon as she picked up a camera. It seems reasonable to assume, therefore, that when she approaches the making of a film, she does so with knowledge of the issues of representation, ideology, film history, and aesthetics. In other words, she – like Wollen himself – is a very conscious filmmaker.

Between the publication of *Movie*'s "Talent Histogram" and Wollen's distancing the filmmaker's person from his function, Roland Barthes published "The Death of the Author" (1968), which made it clear that meaning was produced by *the reader*: "As soon as a fact is *narrated* . . . the voice loses its origins, the author enters into his own death . . . a text's unity lies not in its origin but in its destination. Yet this destination cannot any longer be personal: the reader . . . is simply that *someone* who holds together in a single field all the traces by which the written text is constituted . . . [and] the birth of the reader must be at the cost of the death of the Author."[25]

One cannot claim a filmmaker as auteur if, effectively, the author is dead. Of course, the debate about authorship – in its proper, unabridged context – has developed into extremely important work on language, signification, and enunciation. But the work of women filmmakers remains of marginal interest to it;[26] and it seems to me that the title of Audre Lorde's text, *The Master's Tools Will Never Dismantle the Master's House*, has a useful resonance here, as does a recent comment I understood Germaine Greer to be making[27] – that the way poetry is lauded is actually as male display and, therefore, there is no point in arguing that any woman poet could be better than Shakespeare because, clearly, she is unlikely to be engaging in that kind of poetry. By the same token, the kind of poetry women do write is not accounted for in the "league tables" of poet-names.

Both film theory and film studies have, thank goodness, acknowledged the work of feminist film theorists; however, largely for the reasons already outlined, they only pay lip service to the presence and contribution of women filmmakers – with the possible exception of those filmmakers who are, as Dudley Andrew puts it, "serious and progressive critics themselves," like Duras, Mulvey with Wollen, and Huillet with Straub.[28] Looking at what film studies uses as course literature, this is abundantly clear. I'll give just a couple of recent examples. In his overview of authorship in the important *Oxford Guide to Film Studies*,[29] Stephen Crofts outlines ten modes. The "author as gendered" mode is the *shortest* section, despite the fact that it begins: "The most influential theoretical discourse affecting film theory in the last two decades, feminism has necessarily impinged [sic] on Authorship."[30]

Arzner alone is mentioned here, and only briefly. Otherwise, the *Oxford Guide* effectively mentions female directors only in its chapters dealing with "otherness" – feminism and film; gay, lesbian, and queer cinema; the avant-garde; and non-American cinemas. Chantal Akerman is the only woman director to be given one of the "special mention" boxes. In *The Oxford History of World Cinema* there appears to be no mention whatever of Lois Weber (nor is there any mention of her in Thompson and Bordwell's *Film History*) and only passing mention of Alice Guy Blaché (within the contexts of Gaumont, her husband, and Louis Feuillade, whom she taught). Yet these important texts form part of the material that informs much of the practice of film studies.

Unfortunately, though for very good reasons, feminist film theory has also paid most attention to male-directed mainstream cinema, often with a view to at least understanding, if not "dismantling[,] the master's house," and to those avant-garde women filmmakers mentioned by Dudley Andrew, who can be said to be working within the same theoretical framework; that is, on questions of "the gaze," representations of the body, desire, subjectivity, and so on. For the most part, this work takes place within (or near) the academy. Meanwhile, women have been working in more and more sections of the industry, no longer just in theory-based (or campaign) filmmaking. The associations representing women in production are now more industry-based and, rightly and inevitably, are about women being recognized by, and getting on in, the industry. As a result, while we used to talk in terms of whether there was a feminist aesthetic or a woman's voice that informed women's filmmaking, such questions are now less productive, and, though necessary and very important at the time, they have, in some ways, become as limiting as the auteur theory. It is not surprising that several women filmmakers who became known as feature directors were reluctant to be tied by such a tight framework. Consequently, from the mid-1980s or so there was a divergence of interests. Kathryn Bigelow, for example, has, on the whole, been on the industry side of the divide, and she has not attracted the volume of theory-informed articles that Sally Potter or Jane Campion have (though, admittedly, this is changing).[31] Within authorship theory, what feminist film criticism/theory has done is talk about *female* or *feminist* authorship. Interestingly, however, Kathryn Bigelow's work seems to me to raise considerable problems for this approach, largely *because* of her mainstream position. But I believe the problem is wider than this and that it emanates from the question of definition.

Strictly speaking, there are two definitions of the word "authorship": one concerns the (legal) ownership of an idea or its mode of expression, the other concerns the act and the occupation of writing. But female or feminist authorship tends to be sought in what can be identifiably linked to the filmmaker (as woman):

Figure 14.1 Kate Winslett and Harvey Keitel embody the dynamics of gender politics in Jane Campion's *Holy Smoke* (Miramax, 1999). Produced by Jan Chapman

- a film's autobiographical reference
- a filmmaker's actual presence in the film
- the evidence of a female voice within the narrative (however located).[32]

But none of these, as factors in a film, guarantees authorship. And if a woman filmmaker's film does not produce evidence of a female voice, this does not preclude her from being the film's author (in either of the strict senses). Bigelow's films, for example, do not show easy evidence of her presence or even of a clear female or feminist voice. How to talk about her films, then, from a feminist authorship point of view?

Bigelow's films are produced within Hollywood's mainstream film *industry* context, with a crew. This, of course, is one of the arguments against the theory of "author-name" authorship, and her work confounds this argument. Obviously she works with other people on her films, but she appears to have managed to work with and for empathetic people (and I don't mean in a cosy sense). Although *Point Break* was not, to begin with, a personally initiated project, she was the director the producers kept returning to when they were setting up the film's production. She herself asked for James Cameron to be brought onto the project. Editor Howard Smith had already worked with her on *Near*

Figure 14.2 Repressed homoeroticism in the action film: Kathryn Bigelow's *Point Break* (Twentieth Century Fox, 1991). Produced by James Cameron

Dark. Bigelow says she rewrote the script, originally written by Peter Illiff (who scripted *Patriot Games*). Also, having been a painter before becoming a filmmaker, she knows, sooner than she knows anything else about the shoot, how she wants a film to look. Don Peterman, the DOP on *Point Break*, is quite categorical when he says that the look his team produced was the look Bigelow wanted. She also works with storyboards, which she has said was particularly important because several second units were involved in the shooting of *Point Break* and it was essential for their different images to cohere with the rest of the material. It would seem ridiculous, therefore, to suggest that she did not have considerable aesthetic and conceptual control of the film. I would certainly argue for a reading of the film that is informed by feminism, but this does not seem to fit the definition of female or feminist authorship summarized above.

Much more helpful, it seems to me, is the sense of a film being produced in a context of dialogue within which the filmmaker, the context, and the reader/spectator all participate and from which they all produce meanings that will at least overlap if not actually agree. We need to find a way of recognizing this kind of conceptual and aesthetic work around the production of a film. We particularly need to do this for women filmmakers, and we need to do it for exactly the same reasons as we need to claim women filmmakers as auteurs or to define and defend notions of female authorship. One useful way forward would be to take the concept Agnès Varda uses for her work: *cinécriture*[33] (which translates, rather less happily, as "filmic writing"):

> A well-written film is also well-filmed, the actors are well chosen, so are the locations. The cutting, the movement, the points-of-view, the rhythm of filming and editing have been felt and considered in the way a writer chooses the depth and meaning of sentences, the type of words, number of adverbs, paragraphs, asides, chapters which advance the story or break its flow, etc. In writing it's called style. In the cinema, style is *cinécriture*.[34]

I see this as a starting point rather than as an ending point because questions of style are also problematic. However, as a starting point, it would allow us to avoid having to go through and be marginalized by the arguments about the authorship theory, or having to find the filmmaker or her female voice in the text in order to give it authorial credence. It also allows us to move away from the legal definition of "authorship" and towards the definition dealing with the practice of writing, which may or may not emerge from a single person but, in terms of film production, will certainly be organized around the director. It also allows us to talk about women auteur filmmakers[35] and to make a different historical link – a link made through filmmakers like Lois Weber, Germaine Dulac, Arzner, and many others who would never be seen as auteurs but who, like a number of male directors, are filmmakers who produced eloquent filmic writing.

Notes

1 Sheffield International Documentary Festival (England) 1995.

2 The LWFG was active between 1972 and 1977, and amongst the films produced by members of the group (which included Claire Johnston) were the very moving *Women of the Rhondda* (1972); a feature-length "political burlesque," *The Amazing Equal Pay Show* (1974); and the campaign documentary with fictional elements, *Whose Choice?* (1976).

3 As the rights on shorts and documentaries came to the end of their term, Metro (formerly The Other Cinema [TOC]) sadly but necessarily moved away from this area, not renewing the rights but, rather, concentrating on feature film distribution. For material on the excellent work of TOC, see Sylvia Harvey, in "The Other Cinema: A History, 1970–77," *Screen* 26, 6 (November/December 1985): 40–57; and *Screen* 27, 2 (March/April 1986): 80–96.

4 Alison Smith, *Agnès Varda* (Manchester: Manchester University Press, 1998); Carrie Tarr, *Diane Kurys* (Manchester: Manchester University Press, 1999); Judith Mayne, *Directed by Dorothy Arzner* (Bloomington and Indianapolis: Indiana University Press, 1994); Leslie Hill, *Marguerite Duras: Apocalyptic Desires* (London: Routledge, 1993).

5 Christina Lane, "From *The Loveless* to *Point Break:* Kathryn Bigelow's Trajectory in Action," *Cinema Journal* 37, 4 (1998): 59–81.

6 Mayne, *Directed by Dorothy Arzner*, 1.

7 Tarr, *Diane Kurys*, 3.

8 Smith, *Agnès Varda*, 17.

9 Tarr, *Diane Kurys*, 4.

10 Ibid., 5.

11 See Brigitte Rollet's book, *Coline Serreau* (Manchester/New York: Manchester University Press: St. Martin's Press, 1998).

12 An excellent reader on the subject is John Caughie's *Theories of Authorship* (London: RKP/BFI, 1981).

13 Eric Rohmer (Maurice Schérer), "Renoir Américain," *Cahiers du Cinéma*, 8 (January 1952): 33–40, extracted and translated in Caughie, *Theories of Authorship*, 38–9. My quotations here all come from extracts chosen by John Caughie (1981) to represent the *Cahiers* position (although obviously not with the slant I am now giving them).

14 Pierre Kast, "Des confitures pour un gendarme," *Cahiers du Cinéma* 2 (January 1951): 40, extracted and translated in Caughie, *Theories of Authorship*, 38.

15 Jacques Rivette, "Notes sur une révolution," *Cahiers du Cinéma* (special issue on American cinema), 54 (Christmas 1955): 12–21, extracted and translated in Caughie, *Theories of Authorship*, 41–2.

16 Ibid.

17 Fereydoun Hoveyda, "La réponse de Nicholas Ray," *Cahiers du Cinéma* 107 (May 1960): 41–6, extracted and translated in Caughie, *Theories of Authorship*, 42–3.

18 Rivette, "Notes sur une révolution," 41.

19 The dictionary definition of "virile" is: relating to, or having, the characteristics of an adult male; strong, forceful, vigorous. It surfaced in the fifteenth century and is probably based on a combination of the Latin words "vir," meaning man, and "vis," meaning strength.

20 The concern of the histogram was actually to show "British cinema's lack of what we would consider as talent."

21 Shirley Clarke had recently made *A Scary Time* (1960) and had possibly not long before completed *The Connection* (1961); Muriel Box had recently made *Too Young to Love* and *The Piper's Tune* (both 1960).

22 V.F. Perkins, "Film Authorship: The Premature Burial," *Cine Action* 21/22 (1990). Edward Buscombe talks about "the notion of the 'divine spark,' which separates off the artist from ordinary mortals, which divides the genius from the journeyman." This idea seems particularly indebted to Romantic artistic theory. See "Ideas of Authorship," in Caughie, *Theories of Authorship*, 24; see also Michel Foucault, "What Is an Author?" in *Language, Counter-Memory, Practice* (Oxford: Basil Blackwell, 1977), 121–38, and in *Screen* 20, 1(1979): 13–29; originally published in *Bulletin de la Société Française de Philosophie* 63, 3 (1969): 73–104. Janet Staiger gives a useful (feminist) critique of this "Romantic auteurism" in "The Politics of Film Canons," in *Multiple Voices in Feminist Film Criticism*, ed. D. Carson, L. Dittmar, and J.R. Welsch (Minneapolis: University of Minnesota Press, 1994), 197–200.

23 Claire Johnston, "Women's Cinema as Counter Cinema," in *Notes on Women's Cinema* (London: Society for Education in Film and Television, 1973), 26–7.

24 Peter Wollen, "Conclusion," in *Signs and Meaning in the Cinema*, 2nd edn. (London: Martin Secker and Warburg, 1972), 168. See also Foucault, "What Is an Author?"

25 Roland Barthes, "The Death of the Author" *Image-Music-Text* (London: Fontana, 1977 [1968]), 20.

26 One can wonder how far the texts mentioned earlier (i.e., those on Arzner, Bigelow, Kurys, Serreau, and Varda) will impinge upon the agenda of the wider debate about authorship.

27 On a BBC Radio discussion program, March 1999.

28 Dudley Andrew, *Concepts in Film Theory* (Oxford: Oxford University Press, 1984), 126.

29 John Hill and Pamela Church Gibson, eds., *The Oxford Guide to Film Studies* (Oxford/New York: Oxford University Press, 1998).

30 Ibid., 320.

31 See, for example, Colleen Keane, "Director as 'Adrenaline Junkie,'" in *Metro* 109 (1997): 22–7; Laura Rascaroli, "Steel in the Gaze: On POV and the Discourse of Vision in Kathryn Bigelow's Cinema," *Screen* 38, 3 (Autumn 1997): 232–46; Lane, "From *The Loveless* to *Point Break*"; Yvonne Tasker, "Bigger Than Life," *Sight and Sound* 9, 5 (May 1999): 12–15; and the forthcoming collection on Bigelow, edited by Deborah Jermyn and Sean Redmond.

32 Extremely important in this context is Kaja Silverman's *The Acoustic Mirror: The Female Voice in Psychoanalysis and Cinema* (Bloomington and Indianapolis: Indiana University Press, 1988), especially the chapter entitled "The Female Authorial Voice." Interestingly, Leslie Hill's book on Duras does not problematize the notion of authorship, and in his chapter entitled "Images of Authorship," he goes right into talking about Duras's work in terms of, for example, authorial persona and performativity, authorial commentary and self-commentary, and authority.

33 See Smith, *Agnès Varda*, 13–15.

34 Varda, "Varda par Agnès," *Cahiers du Cinéma* (1994): 14, translated in Alison Smith, *Agnès Varda*, 14.

35 As Ginette Vincendeau indicated in Hill and Church Gibson, *Oxford Guide*, 444.

15

The Men with the Movie Cameras

Richard Koszarski

Richard Koszarski teaches film history in the Department of English at Rutgers University in New Jersey and is the editor-in-chief of *Film History: An International Journal*. His books include *Fort Lee, The Film Town, Von: The Life and Films of Erich von Stroheim, An Evening's Entertainment: The Age of the Silent Feature Picture* and *The Man You Loved to Hate: Erich von Stroheim and Hollywood.* This article on the importance of cinematographers in expressing the look and the vision of a film originally appeared in the New York magazine *Film Comment* in 1972. Noting the historical marginalization of the cameraman in favor of the director in early Hollywood cinema, Koszarski discusses the eclectic internationalized nature of the Hollywood style of cinematography generally as a context for understanding the distinctive work of specific cinematographers individually and sometimes in their relationship with individual directors.

When applying the spotlight theory of film history, attention is directed from one "golden age" to another, flitting back and forth across Europe, back and forth across the Atlantic, following the cinematic muse as it settles first with one national cinema and then another. This theory is quite serviceable in the writing of cursory film histories, but always raises the problem of specifically delineating each national cinema to which the author seeks to attribute greatness. Those who apply this technique most strictly tend to choose movements that are easy to talk about in terms commonly employed in literary analysis. It is a strong thematic quality which unites the Soviet, German, or post-war Italian schools for these writers, and any utilization of editing, design or camerawork is shuffled uncomfortably to a far corner and discussed as ancillary technique. This is only to be expected, given the state of film historical study and the predilections of many film historians. Occasionally the more daring among them will try to relate the "style" of a particular movement to the "content" of that movement, but seldom will you find any admission that the style *is* the movement, and the way a story is told *is* the story. Our conditioned vocabularies resist defining a movement in terms of juxtaposition or special relationships, and consequently, the only film movements that get generally discussed *as* movements are those who have a strong and unifying thematic core susceptible to analysis in literary fashion.

When film criticism grew into a more artist-centered format, it was still these thematic values that dominated the conversation. Directors, even such obvious visual stylists as Ophuls or Dreyer, were discussed primarily in terms of the story content of their work, certainly a strange approach for criticism of this most modern of art forms. Recently the grip

Richard Koszarski, "The Men with the Movie Cameras," pp. 27–9 from *Film Comment* 8, no. 2 (Summer 1972).

of director-as-auteur criticism has loosened, and fleeting spotlights of attention have been directed to other participants in the filmmaking process. Last year *Film Comment* devoted a whole issue to the work of the screenwriter, certainly a fresh approach in the welter of director-centered criticism that has appeared in the past decade, but predictably devoted to a type of filmmaker intimately bound up with story and narrative elements, and thus susceptible to the standard forms of literary/thematic analysis employed previously.

Written criticism necessarily tends towards what can be verbalized most satisfactorily, and so film criticism has always centered on those elements of this variegated art form which are most manageable in literary terms. But the form demands critics equipped to discuss it not only in the terms of written literature, but with a critical vocabulary conscious of developments in post-war music and art as well, prepared to discuss the *moving picture* in terms of the questions raised by these related disciplines. Only then can we successfully appreciate the work of those whose creative contribution is involved most directly with the more plastic and rhythmic elements of the medium, those who lend form and movement to the structure of the moving image. At this state in film history a monograph on Margaret Booth would be most welcome. Or on the other hand, a study of those who put the images on the film in the first place. It is simply preposterous that there is not a *sentence* on the art of Lee Garmes or Gregg Toland, not any proper critical evaluation. What were these men doing? It is a very hopeful sign that the American Film Institute has been spending more attention lately in compiling oral histories of cinematographers, and that several books have appeared recently with similar information. But these are only tools for scholars and critics, with little value as ends in themselves.

The same might be said for the filmographies listed here: they are only starting points in analysis. They do, however, represent new material not previously collected and absolutely crucial to any understanding of the work of the film artists involved. Even more importantly, they illuminate still another "golden age," which unlike that of Germany or Italy or Great Britain was not one defined so easily by its content as by its style – the Hollywood golden age, the classic period of the American studios, from 1915 up to the Fifties. In looking over these filmographies it becomes clear that here was the key unifying element of the Hollywood style, a visual hallmark which effectively evaded the attentions of most previous historians.

The process of absorption, synthesis and change is what marks Hollywood photography throughout, the idea of building on earlier models, foreign models, contemporary models, taking everything of quality in sight and putting it to use for their own particular ends. This eclecticism was developed into an unmistakeably fluid and dynamic style by Hollywood cameramen over the four or five decades of Hollywood's ascendance, and its roots may be traced back to the very beginnings of American production. When G. W. Bitzer began work at Biograph in 1898 the motion picture had just left the laboratories of its inventors. Lumière, Dickson – Friese-Greene if you insist – had demonstrated just before the turn of the century the success of their mechanical contrivances in catching and reduplicating action in movement. But after perfecting the device they left its development to other hands, and the motion picture passed from inventors and mechanics fascinated by the problem of movement to businessmen and artists enthralled by the fact of movement itself. To Méliès and Porter, to Smith and Selig and Lubin and dozens of other vague figures of this transitional period, the fate of this latest Victorian marvel was entrusted. The manner of their success is still something that awaits the proper Gordon Hendricks treatment, but one factor which unified all of their work was an intense personal contact with all the elements of the filmmaking process.

This was the scene into which Bitzer wandered in 1898. A film was generally conceived, shot, developed and printed by one man – a not infelicitous situation for 50- or 100-foot productions. This is the way Bitzer himself learned filmmaking, and his early work preserved on Library of Congress paper prints casts an interesting light on the nature of his collaboration with Griffith years later. But of all these functions, by far the chief was photography. "Making a moving picture" meant turning the crank; thinking up a story, handling the actors and cutting the material together was just icing on the cake. Soon a primitive division of labor was introduced for the more complicated productions, and specialized film "directors" like Wallace McCutcheon began to restrict themselves to working solely with the stories and actors of the increasingly complicated narrative films. But the mechanical portion of the machine art was left to the cameramen, and when the time came this is what Bitzer and many

Figure 15.1 Billy Bitzer provided the bravura camerawork in *Birth of a Nation* (Epoch Films, 1915). Produced and directed by D.W. Griffith

others chose to specialize in. The responsibility of this position was such that when Griffith arrived in 1908 he found his cameramen were often slow to implement the suggestions and improvements he thought of for his films. They reasoned that if anything went wrong with the film, if an image failed to register, it was the cameraman and not the director who was in trouble. The camera was still the whole show.

But the growth of the modern cinema restructured all of this again. The Hollywood studio tradition grew up around the idea of division of labor, of departmentalization, of a specialist for every aspect of the production – literary, scenic, photographic, or whatever. Screenwriters decided what Hollywood films had to say, and directors how it would be said. But putting the image on film – "making the moving picture" – was still the responsibility of the cameraman. And in the pre-war years this was no mean accomplishment. Lethargic emulsions, sputtering or non-existent lighting, crotchety camera mechanisms and super-slow lenses made great cameramen out of anyone who could succeed in getting a clearly focused image on the film – yet those troublesome days were certainly a fruitful training ground. By 1915 mechanical difficulties had been swept away and expression in terms of light was made possible on a major scale.

Three films of that year, fortunately all extant in fine quality prints, offer good examples: De Mille's *The*

Cheat, shot by Alvin Wyckoff; Dwan's *David Harum*, shot by Hal Rosson; and Griffith's *The Birth of a Nation*, shot by Billy Bitzer. In these three films one can see already formed the basis of the whole tradition of American cinematography: Wyckoff's use of shadows for psychological effect, of superb figure molding, of intricately accomplished trick work, points to the whole romantic-expressionist tradition of Lee Garmes, John Seitz and Bert Glennon. Rosson's warm and documentary-like examination of the countryside (complete with precocious deep focus and tracking movements) prefigures the deceptively uncomplicated styles of George Schneiderman or William Clothier. And Bitzer's bravura camerawork, which can encompass intimate human drama and grandscale panorama in the same shot (as in Sherman's march to the sea), has been carried on by such men as Leon Shamroy and Robert Surtees.

Over the intervening years the continuity of this visual style was fostered by a number of methods which enabled younger cameramen to work under more experienced veterans in a direct way, either as operators, second cameramen, or assistants. Thus, an informal "school" of one particular visual style can be traced in a reasonably clear manner (something which can't be done with directors, for example, whose assistants were usually busy rounding up extras). Many cameramen were under contract to studios for years, and such cross-pollination no doubt resulted in one particular style heavily influencing a wide variety of younger assistants who were also under contract at the time. One can discuss an Ernest Palmer or Arthur Miller or Leon Shamory style at Fox, for example, which would exist outside of any particular trend in studio production. Of course, when such a studio style was definitely promoted, it was the cameraman who carried it along. Warner Brothers films of the Thirties are probably visualized more clearly in terms of Sol Polito, Tony Gaudio and Barney McGill, than through Wellman, LeRoy or even Curtiz. Paramount's glossiest period was the result of Victor Milner and Lee Garmes as much as Lubitsch, Sternberg or Mamoulian. William Daniels, Oliver Marsh and Harry Stradling Sr. went a long way toward producing the MGM look. And Joe Walker was Columbia all by himself.

Once such a studio style had been fixed it seemed to pervade the rafters of the studio itself. George Folsey moved from Paramount (*Applause, The Smiling Lieutenant*) to Metro (*Meet Me in St. Louis, The White Cliffs of Dover*) but his style didn't move with him. Only those cameramen with the strongest personal styles were able to cross studio boundaries with impunity and imprint their own vision on everything. Hal Rosson could make a Metro Fleming (*Red Dust*) look like a Paramount Sternberg (*The Docks of New York*), and Bert Glennon, Joe August or Gregg Toland could do the same thing.

Just as many of the great cameramen were associated most strongly with individual studios, another group was so linked to individual directors that their work together created a fusion of personal styles similar to some of the studio/cameraman associations. Bitzer and Griffith are the chief examples, but John Seitz and Rex Ingram (and later Billy Wilder), Karl Brown and James Cruze, and Robert Burks and Alfred Hitchcock are also notable pairings and, when these associations broke up, the effect on the visual style of both partners was often quite noticeable (Hitchcock's work after Burks' death, for example).

But Hollywood's visual style was not a purely inbred tradition. As with everything else, the studios could appropriate a pictorial style from overseas and make it their own. In the late Twenties and early Thirties a "German look" was highly cultivated, but there was no mistaking *Flesh and the Devil* or *Svengali* as anything but pure Hollywood, no matter how hard they tried. The finest Hollywood cameramen always added to the techniques they adopted from overseas, and to see this most clearly look at *Sunrise* against the context of Murnau's earlier films. The German cameramen had retained their primary interest in engineering; creative photography was concerned with the designing of tracking and dollying equipment. But Struss and Rosher quickly adapted to the moving style called for by Murnau and combined with this their own backgrounds in portrait photography. The visual difference between *Sunrise* and *The Last Laugh* can be seen in the figure molding on the faces of George O'Brien and Janet Gaynor, a lighting sophistication undreamed of in Germany at the time, but well grounded in American camerawork throughout the Twenties. Karl Freund and the other German cameramen who successfully worked in America quickly adapted themselves to these new complexities of shading, and we can trace this change by watching their earliest American work.

The post-World War II period brought the influence of the documentarists and Italian neo-realists, but

Figure 15.2 Charles Rosher and Karl Struss contributed the expressionist cinematography for F.W. Murnau's *Sunrise* (Fox Film Corp., 1927). Produced by William Fox

here again it was digested and made part of the evolving tradition. Look at James Wong Howe's *The Rose Tattoo*, which echoes the grim texture of Magnani's Italian films – an amazing hybrid, but still a most polished piece of Hollywood craftsmanship underneath. And when the studios weren't borrowing stylistic touches from overseas they were often borrowing the cameramen themselves: Freund, Maté, Planer and others came over and brought part of the European tradition with them. Karl Freund made *Murders in the Rue Morgue* a sequel to *Caligari* and *The Golem*. One can see Dreyer's wall-eyed lighting effects behind Rita Hayworth in Rudolph Maté's photography of *Gilda*. As for Franz Planer, his work with Ophuls on both sides of the Atlantic is reflected in the elegance of such diverse work as *Holiday* and *Breakfast at Tiffany's*. The list could go on and on.

In the flow of these influences, as well as their absorption into the general fabric of Hollywood style [. . .] one not only sees the growth of the individual artist, but the historical context that prompted certain developments and his reactions and contributions to them. [. . .] Taken together these form the fabric of Hollywood's visual style with all the individual strands showing through. Combined with the work of directors, writers, designers and others, they form a picture of classic Hollywood as the Florence of the West, bringing together creative ideas and creative talents from all over the world, then blending them into a new and dynamic synthesis.

This fabled mixture held so long as there was a framework to support it all. When that dropped out it meant more than the collapse of the studio method of filmmaking. Without this structure to support growth and change, American cinematography turned from inspired eclecticism to fragmented inspiration. It came full circle again to the days of Billy Bitzer, as today's pioneers roam the streets with portable equipment and Angenieux lenses, starting their own traditions.

16

Notes on a Screenwriter's Theory, 1973

Richard Corliss

At one time the editor of New York's *Film Comment* magazine in the 1970s, Richard Corliss is a longtime writer for *Time* magazine who focuses primarily on movies. His work has appeared in such publications as the *New York Times, Film Quarterly, National Review* and the *Village Voice*. Corliss has helped draw attention to the role of the screenwriter rather than the director in the making of films. This reading, the introductory chapter to Corliss's book *Talking Pictures: Screenwriters in the American Cinema, 1927–1973* (1974), was, as its title implies, inspired by Sarris' 1968 book on Hollywood directors and explicitly acknowledged by the author as his primary influence. Yet Corliss suggests that Sarris has distorted film history by his exclusive focus on directors, and observes that an auteurism truly concerned with visual style would be more concerned with the images directors created in relation to the words in the scripts that screenwriters wrote. Corliss moves on to offer a screenwriter's pantheon and to discuss the writing of a number of Hollywood screenwriters in relation to the different directors with whom they worked.

1. Thesis: The Director as Auteur

I was driving by Otto Preminger's house last night – or is it "a house by Otto Preminger"?

– Burt Kennedy, 1971

It's a full decade now since Andrew Sarris published, in *Film Culture* magazine, his two-part Americanization of the *politique des auteurs*. At the time it could be taken as a thoughtful and provocative challenge to that near-monopoly in serious English-language film criticism, the Social Dialectic. Refreshingly, Sarris examined films as the creations of artists rather than of social forces – whether capitalist, communist, or fascist – and, in doing so, he helped liberate the scrupulous study of American film from the numbing strictures of solemnity. We could finally admit without shame that the best Hollywood movies succeeded not only as delightful entertainments but as art works rivaling those from the culture capitals of Europe.

Sarris wasn't the first American to argue that "the director is the author of a film." Hollywood itself had accepted this policy in the silent days, when directors received billing just below their stars; *The Rise of the American Film* and *The Liveliest Art* devote long chapters to the careers of Hollywood *metteurs-en-scène*; even Bosley Crowther, back in 1940, seconded William

Richard Corliss, "Notes on a Screenwriter's Theory, 1973," pp. xvii–xxviii from *Talking Pictures: Screenwriters in the American Cinema, 1927–1973* (Woodstock, NY: Overlook Press, 1974).

Wyler's assertion that "the final responsibility for a picture's quality rests solely and completely upon the shoulders of the man who directed it." But it was Sarris's call to arms that started the auteur revolution. First the specialized journals, then the mass-market magazines, then *The New York Times, Cue*, and *TV Guide* began crediting directors not only with authorship but with ownership: "Arthur Hiller's *Love Story*." By the time the trend had reached Hollywood, it had become something of a joke. Thus *Play It Again, Sam* – starring Woody Allen, screenplay by Woody Allen, from a play by Woody Allen – is heralded in the screen credits as "A Herbert Ross Film."

Sarris's version of the *politique* was extraordinarily helpful in calling attention to neglected American directors in a fistful of infra dig genres, but it may have done more harm than good in citing the director as the sole author of his film. What could have begun a systematic expansion of American film history – by calling attention to anonymous screenwriters, cinematographers, art directors, and, yes, even actors – bogged down in an endless coronation of the director as benevolent despot, in his enshrinement as solitary artist, with his collaborating craftsmen functioning merely as paint, canvas, bowl of fruit, and patron.

By establishing the director as the Creator of a Work of Art, the auteurists were falling into the same critical traps that had snared the no-less-well-meaning Social Realism crowd some thirty years earlier. The notion persists that a work of art is the product of one man working alone to carve a personal vision out of the marble of his sensibility. Ideally, perhaps, but not invariably – and, in Hollywood, not even generally. Yet this notion, very romantic and very American, is the basis upon which most recent film histories stand. It is so basic that it is taken for granted: in the standard book-length studies of Sternberg and Stevens, Hitchcock and Hawks, the critics' auteur bias is a given that needn't be proven.

A number of critical labels have to be spindled and mutilated before we can begin to appreciate the collaborative complexity of American cinema more fully. *Art vs. entertainment*: a rather precious distinction by now, since any supremely entertaining movie should reveal deeper (or at least broader) levels upon further viewings, and since any work of art cannot help but entertain, if only in the viewer's delight in discovering it. *Solitary art vs. corporate art*: The fact that Chartres, or *Charade*, was the work of a number of individuals contributing their unique talents to a corporate enterprise doesn't necessarily make either work less "artistic" than, say, Van Gogh's "Wildflowers" or Snow's *Wavelength*. It just makes it more difficult for the critic to assign sole authorship, which is more a critical convenience than a value judgment – or should be, anyway.

The creative artist vs. the interpretive artist: Both Stanley Donen and Michael Snow are, shall we say, artists; but Snow is a creative artist and Donen an interpretive artist. Snow is almost literally a film *maker*, collaborating with his film strips and his Movieola in an intimate, incestuous way that has very little to do with the way Donen collaborates with his scriptwriter, actors, and technicians. The traditional view was that the solitary, creative artist produced Art, while the corporate, interpretive craftsman produced Entertainment. It would seem that the auteur theory, which one might have assumed would demolish this old canard, is actually reinforcing it. If Donen is worthy of sustained critical study (and I believe he is), so are, say, Arthur Freed, Gene Kelly, Betty Comden and Adolph Green, Richard Avedon, George Abbott, Cary Grant, Peter Stone, Christopher Challis, and all the other talented men and women whose careers intersected Donen's at mutually felicitous points.

Cinema is not the only medium in which authorship is bestowed upon the director (or, for that matter, the art director – as witness John Simon's recent critical study, *Ingmar Bergman Directs*, which the title page describes, in a type size equal to Mr. Simon's credit, as "a creation of Halcyon Enterprises"!). Determining authorship in the theater can be a complicated business. Is Harold Pinter the "author" of *Old Times*? Most assuredly. And yet the difference between the London and New York productions of the play amounted to more than a subtle shift in tone, or even in effect; it was a difference in *meaning*. As played by Colin Blakely (London), the Deeley character was the audience's very vulnerable identity figure; as played by Robert Shaw (New York), he was a self-deceiving boor. As played by Vivien Merchant (London), the Anna character was menacing, predatory; as played by Rosemary Harris (New York), she was helpful, sympathetic. Same author, same director, same pauses – but different casts and, almost, two different plays.

It's probably fair to consider Tom O'Horgan the prime mover (whether as creator or defiler) of his later theatrical extravaganzas, because he shapes, packages, controls his productions as completely as, say, Ken Russell controls *his* films. In a less mannerist vein, the Broadway career of Elia Kazan – whose collaborations with Tennessee Williams, Arthur Miller, and S. N. Behrman, among others, were both intense and enduring – could be profitably studied for Kazan's personal approach to themes and styles. But could he exercise "directorial authority" as powerfully on Broadway as in Hollywood? In one case at least, *yes*: at his insistence, Williams wrote an entirely new third act for *Cat on a Hot Tin Roof*. To be sure (and to be lamented), one can*not* study Kazan's theater work, because his productions died on closing night, while his playwrights' scripts live on in book form. One reason for directorial supremacy in the cinema may be that, there, the reverse is true: screenplays are rarely published (and barely consulted even then), while the films made from them are available at the flick of a TV channel selector.

William Wyler was absolutely right to hold the director responsible for "a picture's quality" – just as a conductor is responsible for the composer's symphony, or a contractor for the architect's plans. But he must also be responsible *to* something: the screenplay. With it, he can do one of three things: ruin it, shoot it, or improve it. [. . .]. Realizing a screenplay is the director's job; transcending it is his glory. Despite the Writers Guild's immemorial gripes, directing is a fine art, not a lead-pipe cinch (as too many screenwriters have proved when they tried to direct a picture). It's no coincidence that most of the films selected for praise in this book [Corliss 1974] were directed by Hollywood's finest auteurs – no more a coincidence than that these same films were scripted by Hollywood's finest authors.

Andrew Sarris has said that the directors he prefers are those with an unconscious – who, presumably, speak from the soul, and not from the scenario. I think that this statement also suggests why Sarris prefers a director's cinema to a writer's. One restraint on the poetic tendencies of a screenwriter-oriented critic, as opposed to those of an auteurist, is that the screenwriter *makes* words and situations occur, while the director *allows* actions to occur. Thus, the process of creating a screenplay is more formal, less mystical than the image, which is created by the director, photographer, designer, and actors. This inexactness of the visual process gives the auteurist an opportunity to infer reams and realms of metaphysical nuance. Typewriter keys seem to spring to the paper with grandiose generalizations: "a world of . . . ," "the cinema of . . ." And since the director allowed these filmic epiphanies to take place, who's to say he didn't *make* them happen?

This is the notion of the artist as inspired dervish – literally "in-spired." The Muse breathes the spirit into a director, and he exhales this inspiration, filling the sound stage with a magic that affects cast and crew and results in a privileged moment. To the great directors, making their greatest films, this fantasy may apply. One gets the feeling that John Ford creatively controlled every moment of *The Searchers*, from first opening door to last closing door. But the greatness of even so controlled a film as *Psycho* is partly due to Anthony Perkins's performance, which at least extended, and probably transcended, Hitchcock's understanding of Norman Bates's character.

The director *is* right in the middle of things. At the very least, he's on the sound stage while the cinematographer is lighting the set that the art director has designed and, later, while the actors are speaking the lines that the screenwriter wrote. At best, he steers all these factors (story, actors, camera) in the right *direction*, to the extent that many films are indeed dominated by his personality – though not, perhaps, in the way the auteurists mean. The phrase "directorial personality" may make more sense if it's taken quite literally. Anyone who's seen Stanley Donen or Sam Peckinpah or Howard Hawks or Radley Metzger in action knows that the effective director is usually a man with a strong, persuasive personality. He has to combine the talents of salesman (to get a job in the first place), tough guy (to make the technicians respond to his commands), and best friend (to coax a good performance out of a volatile actress). Whether he directs with a riding crop (Stroheim), an icy stare (Sternberg), or some lightweight banter (Cukor), his personality is often crucial to the success of a film. The importance of a director's personal – or even visual – style is not at question here, only the assumption that he creates a style out of thin air instead of adapting it to the equally important styles of the story and performers.

Indeed, if auteur criticism had lived up to its early claim to be truly concerned with visual style, there would be no need for any systematic slighting of the screenwriter. Given a certain text, or pretext, the

Figure 16.1. Howard Hawks directing Humphrey Bogart and Lauren Bacall on the set of *The Big Sleep* (Warner Bros, 1946). Produced by Howard Hawks

director could be said to weave the writer's design into a personal, visual subtext through the use of camera placement and movement, lighting, cutting, direction of actors, etc. Such a *politique* would go far toward elucidating the work of superior *metteurs-en-scène* on the order of Cukor, Donen, Michael Curtiz, Mitchell Leisen, and Don Siegel. But visual style is not the auteurist's major interest. Auteur criticism is essentially theme criticism; and themes – as expressed through plot, characterization, and dialogue – belong primarily to the writer.

2. Antithesis: The Screenwriter as Auteur

> In my opinion, the writer should have the first and last word in filmmaking, the only better alternative being the writer-director, but with the stress on the first word.
>
> – Orson Welles, 1950

The cry "*cherchez l'auteur*" can lead unwary film scholars astray when the auteur happens to be the author – or rather, when the script is the basis of a film's success. As often as not, when a fine film is signed by a middle-rung director, the film's distinctive qualities can be traced to the screenwriter. There's no need to rescue Mitchell Leisen, Garson Kanin, Sam Wood, and William D. Russell from the underworld of neglected directors simply because each was fortunate enough to direct a comedy written, in his best period, by Norman Krasna (*Hands Across the Table*, *Bachelor Mother*, *The Devil and Miss Jones*, and *Dear Ruth*, respectively). The direction of these films *is* usually adroit and sensitive, and the presence of charming comediennes enhances them even further; but the delightfully dominant personality behind the screen is undoubtedly Krasna's.

Krasna's "mistaken-identity" theme, which he milked for more than thirty years, is as unmistakable

Figure 16.2. Apple-pie-in-the-face Americana in *Hail the Conquering Hero* (Paramount, 1944). Produced, written, and directed by Preston Sturges

as an Eric Rohmer plot – but he's hardly the only Hollywood screenwriter with thematic or tonal obsessions. Ben Hecht's penny-ante cynicism, Preston Sturges's apple-pie-in-the-face Americana, Frank Tashlin's breast fixation, Peter Stone's schizophrenia, George Axelrod's impotent Svengalis, Howard Koch's *liebestod* letters, Borden Chase's wagon trains of Western Civilization, Abraham Polonsky's economic determinism, Billy Wilder's creative con men, Samson Raphaelson's aristocratic *bourgeoisie*, Garson Kanin and Ruth Gordon's eccentric marriages, Dudley Nichols' instant redemption, Joseph L. Mankiewicz's endless articulation, Dalton Trumbo's gilt-edged propaganda, Robert Riskin's demogogic populism, Sidney Buchman's democratic republicanism, Jules Furthman's noble adventurers, Charles Lederer's sassy misanthropy, Ring Lardner, Jr.'s brassy misogyny, Terry Southern's practical joking, Erich Segal's ivy-covered sentimentality, Jules Feiffer's cartoon morality plays, David Newman and Robert Benton's likable losers . . . look at the films of these screenwriters half as closely as an auteurist would examine the work of Otto Preminger or Robert Mulligan, and chances are you'll find yourself staring at some dominant theme or style or plot or mood – some strong personal trait of film authorship. After all, film is (as Andrew Sarris has observed) essentially a dramatic medium; and the screenwriters are the medium's dramatists.

It's clear that some method of classification and evaluation is necessary, both to identify and to assess the contribution of that overpaid but unsung *genus* known as the screenwriter. But that is a game that conceals even more pitfalls than does the Sarris Hit Parade of Directors. Once the auteur scholar accepts the myth of the omnipotent director – that nonexistent Hawks or Stevens who writes, produces, photographs, acts in, and edits every film he makes – his game is won. Indeed, even the stanchest adherent of the *politique des collaborateurs* can be fairly sure that the director of record is the man who hollered "Action!" and "Cut!" – though his importance in controlling what went on between those two commands may be disputed. But the size of a screenwriter's contribution to any given film is often more difficult to ascertain.

A writer may be given screen credit for work he didn't do (as with Sidney Buchman on *Holiday*), or be denied credit for work he did do (as with Sidney Buchman on *The Awful Truth*). The latter case is far more common than the former. Garson Kanin co-wrote *The More the Merrier*, but his name didn't appear on-screen because he had already been inducted into the wartime Army. Ben Hecht toiled for seven days rewriting the first nine reels of *Gone With the Wind*, but David O. Selznick wanted Sidney Howard's name to appear alone on the screenplay. Michael Wilson wrote the screenplay for *Friendly Persuasion* and co-scripted *The Bridge on the River Kwai* and *Lawrence of Arabia*, but the Hollywood blacklist kept his name off all three films, and the writing Oscar for *Kwai* was awarded to Pierre Boulle, who had nothing at all to do with the film adapted from his novel.

The American Screen Writers Guild has a ridiculous rule that disallows screenplay credit to any director who has not contributed at least fifty per cent of the dialogue – ridiculous if only because it permits auteur critics to infer that their favorite directors consistently contributed, say, forty-nine percent. (When the Guild discovered that *Bad Company*, a script by the writing team of Benton and Newman, was going to be directed by Benton, it routinely scheduled an arbitration hearing to determine whether director Benton was stealing a credit on poor writer Newman's script!) In Europe, the auteurists tell us, things are more enlightened: there, the director receives screenplay credit whether he wrote anything or not. Certainly Bergman, Fellini, Antonioni, Chabrol, Truffaut (all writers before they were directors) work either as sole authors or as collaborators – and not just as editors – on their screenplays. But reliable sources indicate that *Tout Va Bien*, the new "Godard" film, was written solely by Jean-Pierre Gorin; and Luis Buñuel has admitted in print that he contributed not one word of dialogue to Jean-Claude Carrière's script for *Le Charme Discret de la Bourgeoisie*, although Buñuel is listed ahead of Carrière as an author of the screenplay. Joseph Losey, who never takes screenplay credit, says he works as closely with the screenwriter as he does with the cinematographer, editor, and actors – should he share official credit with these collaborators as well? Losey needn't worry: auteur critics would have him share credit with *nobody*.

In the Golden Age of Hollywood, things were a bit different. A director would be given a script and instructed to start shooting Monday; so much for shaping a personal vision through creative rewriting. But what about the screenwriter who specializes in adaptations? Who's the auteur then? It's true that, in the case of a Donald Ogden Stewart, the problem is more subtle. Few screenwriters can boast a more impressive list of credits than Stewart's. As with George Cukor, the director for whom he produced his finest scripts, Stewart's "filmography is his most eloquent defense." Both Stewart and Cukor, however, had the good luck to be assigned adaptations of some of the wittiest and most actable theater pieces of their time – *Holiday, The Women* (for which Stewart received no screen credit), *The Philadelphia Story*, and *Edward, My Son* – and Stewart's transferrals of these works from stage to screen adhered closely to both the spirit and the letter of the originals.

Stewart's achievement should not be dismissed; many screenwriters failed at the delicate craft he mastered. But, as with directors, one can distinguish several layers of screenwriting authorship: the indifferent work of a mediocre writer, whether it's an original script or an adaptation (which we may call procrustean); the gem-polishing of a gifted adapter like Stewart (protean); and the creation of a superior original script, like Herman J. Mankiewicz's *Citizen Kane* or Abraham Polonsky's *Body and Soul* (promethean). When faced with the career of a Stewart, the critic who has discarded the convenience of the auteur theory must compare Stewart's adaptations with the source works, in hopes of detecting such changes as plot compression or expansion, bowdlerization, addition or deletion of dialogue, and differences in theme and tone. At worst, this research will exhaust and discourage the critic; at best, it will convince him that the creation of a Hollywood movie involves a complex weave of talents, properties, and personalities.

When a screenwriter, like Preston Sturges or George Axelrod, has a distinctive authorial tone, his contributions to films with multiple script credits can usually be discerned. But the hallmark of many fine screenwriters is versatility, not consistency. Subject matter dictates style. Given the Cheshire Cat nature of these writers, how are we to know which part of the *Casablanca* script is the work of the sophisticated but self-effacing Howard Koch, and which part was written by Julius and Philip Epstein? Well, recent archaeological studies have indicated that the Epsteins began to rework the plot of an unproduced play, *Everybody Comes to Rick's* (which has, in sketch form, most of the film's characters, including a Negro named Sam who is told to "Play it, Sam," and plays "As Time Goes By"), but then were called to the War; and that Koch developed these contributions into the final, full-blooded screenplay.

We don't have many of these memoirs, though – screenwriters being a notoriously underinterviewed breed (ever read one with Herman Mankiewicz?) – and since most Hollywood egos are approximately the size of the Graf Zeppelin, the accounts of screenwriters may be taken with the same pillar of salt we keep handy for directors' interviews and actors' autobiographies. Nevertheless, a screenwriter's work should and can be judged by analyzing his entire career, as is done with a director. If a writer has been associated with a number of favorite films, if he has received sole writing credit on some of these films, and if we can decipher a common style in films with different directors and actors, an authorial personality begins to appear. The high polish and understated irony of Koch's other work – from his script for the Mercury Theatre *War of the Worlds*, through his ten-year tenure at Warners, to his late-forties scripts for *Letter from an Unknown Woman* and *No Sad Songs for Me* – and his fulfillment of our three conditions, give credence to this account of the writing of *Casablanca*. In fact, most of the best Hollywood screenwriters were sole authors of a substantial number of scripts.

The paucity of critical and historical literature makes all screenwriters "Subjects for Further Research." The cavalier group headings on the following lists are meant only to emphasize the tentative nature of the classification (as opposed to the groupings of screenwriters in the body of this book, which attempts to categorize without polemicizing). As more films are seen from the writers' point of view, names will be shuffled from one list to another. Ultimately, each of them, and many more, should have an artistic identity clear enough to make such capricious classification unnecessary. Until that enlightened time comes to pass, we must make do with an Acropolis of Screenwriters something like this one – which considers only the writers who are evaluated in [Corliss's *Talking Pictures: Screenwriters in the American Cinema, 1927–1973* (Overlook Press, 1974)].

Parthenon. Borden Chase, Betty Comden and Adolph Green, Ben Hecht, Nunnally Johnson, Garson Kanin (and Ruth Gordon), Howard Koch, Frank S. Nugent, Samson Raphaelson, Preston Sturges, Billy Wilder.

Erechtheion. George Axelrod, Sidney Buchman, Jules Feiffer, Norman Krasna, Ernest Lehman, Herman J. Mankiewicz, David Newman and Robert Benton, Abraham Polonsky, Casey Robinson, Peter Stone.

Propylaea. Charles Brackett, Delmer Daves, Jules Furthman, Buck Henry, Ring Lardner, Jr., Charles Lederer, Joseph L. Mankiewicz, Robert Riskin, Morrie Ryskind, Frank Tashlin.

Outside the Walls. Edwin Justus Mayer, Dudley Nichols, Erich Segal, Terry Southern, Dalton Trumbo.

All of these screenwriters – even those infidels muttering curses outside our Acropolis walls – deserve monographs or books devoted to their Hollywood careers. If the critical winds reverse themselves, and if publishers' generosity to unsalable film books continues, dawn may yet break over a bookshelf stocked with such titles as *The Cinema of Samson Raphaelson* and *The Collected Letters of Howard Koch*. It seemed to me of primary importance, however, to provide a general but detailed introduction to as many screenwriters as possible. [. . .] Within the bounds of available films and the limitations of my own prejudices, I have tried to select representative works of each writer's career, and representative writers from the several genres, periods, and styles of the Hollywood talkie. My aim has been to avoid facile generalizations by confronting specific films, thus not merely pinpointing a writer's themes but discovering how he related his preoccupations to the job at hand.

In the main, the screenwriters who appear in this book [Corliss, 1974] are those who, by adapting their conspicuous talents to the Byzantine demands of the trade, developed the most successful screenwriting techniques. Success usually begat power, and power begat authority. By authority is meant the right to complete your own script without being forced to surrender it to the next fellow on the assembly line, the right to consult with any actor or director who wants changes, and the right to fight for your film through the taffy pull of front-office politics, pressure groups, and publicists. If directors have been pre-eminent in Hollywood since long before the arrival of the auteur theory, it is probably because, among all of Tinseltown's employees, they were the ones with the most power.

3. Synthesis: The Multiple Auteur

> There was the era of the actor, when a film was its star, and we had Mary Pickford, Douglas Fairbanks, Greta Garbo. Then we had the era of the director, and the films of King Vidor, Sternberg, Feyder and Clair. A new era is beginning: that of the author. After all, it's the author who makes a film.
>
> – Jean Renoir, 1939

Despite their own kvetching about functional impotence in the moviemaking process, and despite the criminal negligence of a new breed of critics, screenwriters have done so much in making a film entertaining, moving, even ennobling. But such has been the factory nature of the Hollywood movie that writers can still do *only* so much. A screenwriter is, as often as not, the middleman between the author of the original property and the director – and the man who gets his hands on the flypaper last is the one whose fingerprints will show up first. The writers' movement in the thirties and forties, inextricably bound up with inter-Guild hostilities and jealousies as it was, drew its limited power by sucking as much blood as possible from the *metteur-en-scène* as the Directors Guild would allow. The effect of the auteur theory was to steal back whatever authority (and authorship) the writers had usurped: at best, it was proposed, the writer writes a script but the director makes the film. The two crafts were seen as riding on opposite sides of a seesaw, with the weight of contemporary critical opinion deciding which group was to be left stranded in the air.

Perhaps a synthesis of these presumably antithetical functions is in order. The films that receive the highest praise in this book [Corliss, 1974] are those whose writers and directors – in creative association with the actors and technicians – worked together toward a collaborative vision. You could call *Citizen Kane* either the culmination of Herman Mankiewicz's dreams or the beginning of Orson Welles' nightmares, but it would be silly to ignore either man's contribution. Who is the auteur of *Ninotchka:* Ernst Lubitsch, or the Charles Brackett–Billy Wilder–Walter Reisch team, or Greta Garbo? Obviously, all of them. I've tried in this book [Corliss, 1974] to make a case for the screenwriter without libeling either the director or the actor. Once the contribution of all these crafts – individually and collectively – have been accepted and examined, studies of other vital film collaborators could begin and be meshed into a giant matrix of coordinate talents. One ultimate result of this process of synthesis should be to open the critical shutter a few more stops upon that strange and glorious hybrid: the artistic-entertaining, solitary-corporate, creative-interpretive talking picture.

17

Who Makes the Movies?

Gore Vidal

Gore Vidal is an important American writer and political commentator. His books include the novel *Myra Breckinridge (1968)* and the plays *Visit to a Small Planet (1957)* and *The Best Man (1960)*, all of which were adapted as films. Vidal also is an actor and screenwriter, including scripts for Joseph L. Mankiewicz's adaptation of Tennessee Williams' play *Suddenly, Last Summer* and William Wyler's remake of Lew Wallace's 1880 bestselling novel, *Ben-Hur: A Tale of the Christ.* In this piece about authorship in the movies, originally published in the *New York Review* in 1976, Vidal offers an important contribution to the debate about who is responsible for what in a film by providing an articulate insider's ability to reflect upon his personal experience in the making of one major and in many ways typical Hollywood production. Vidal's observation that screenwriter Paddy Chayevsky was an auteur whose "pencil" was the director is a brilliantly provocative recasting of the director-oriented notion of "le camera-stylo."

Forty-nine years ago last October Al Jolson not only filled with hideous song the sound track of a film called *The Jazz Singer*, he also spoke. With the words "You ain't heard nothin' yet" (surely the most menacing line in the history of world drama), the age of the screen director came to an end and the age of the screenwriter began.

Until 1927, the director was king turning out by the mile his "molds of light" (André Bazin's nice phrase). But once the movies talked, the director as creator became secondary to the writer. Even now, except for an occasional director-writer like Ingmar Bergman,[1] the director tends to be the one interchangeable (if not entirely expendable) element in the making of a film. After all, there are thousands of movie technicians who can do what a director is supposed to do because, in fact, collectively (and sometimes individually) they actually do do his work behind the camera and in the cutter's room. On the other hand, there is no film without a written script.

In the Fifties when I came to MGM as a contract writer and took my place at the Writers' Table in the commissary, the Wise Hack used to tell us newcomers, "The director is the brother-in-law." Apparently the ambitious man became a producer (that's where the power was). The talented man became a writer (that's where the creation was). The pretty man became a star.

Even before Jolson spoke, the director had begun to give way to the producer. Director Lewis Milestone saw the writing on the screen as early as 1923 when "baby producer" Irving Thalberg fired the legendary director Erich von Stroheim from his film *Merry Go Round*. "That," wrote Milestone somberly in *New Theater and Film* (March 1937), "was the beginning of the storm and the end of the reign of the director. . . ."

Gore Vidal, "Who Makes the Movies?" pp. 35–9 from *New York Review of Books* (November 25, 1976). © 1976 by Gore Vidal. Reprinted by permission of the author.

Even as late as 1950 the star Dick Powell assured the film cutter Robert Parrish that "anybody can direct a movie, even I could do it. I'd rather not because it would take too much time. I can make more money acting, selling real estate and playing the market."[2] That was pretty much the way the director was viewed in the Thirties and Forties, the so-called classic age of the talking movie.

Although the essential creator of the classic Hollywood film was the writer, the actual master of the film was the producer, as Scott Fitzgerald recognized when he took as protagonist for his last novel Irving Thalberg. Although Thalberg himself was a lousy movie maker, he was the head of production at MGM; and in those days MGM was a kind of Vatican where the chief of production was Pope, holding in his fists the golden keys of Schenck. The staff producers were the College of Cardinals. The movie stars were holy and valuable objects to be bought, borrowed, stolen. Like icons, they were moved from sound stage to sound stage, studio to studio, film to film, bringing in their wake good fortune and gold.

With certain exceptions (Alfred Hitchcock, for one), the directors were, at worst, brothers-in-law; at best, bright technicians. All in all, they were a cheery, unpretentious lot, and if anyone had told them that they were *auteurs du cinema*, few could have coped with the concept, much less the French. They were technicians; proud commercialites, happy to serve what was optimistically known as The Industry.

This state of affairs lasted until television replaced the movies as America's principal dispenser of mass entertainment. Overnight the producers lost control of what was left of The Industry and, unexpectedly, the icons took charge. Apparently, during all those years when we thought the icons nothing more than beautifully painted images of all our dreams and lusts, they had been not only alive but secretly greedy for power and gold.

"The lunatics are running the asylum," moaned the Wise Hack at the Writers' Table, but soldiered on. Meanwhile, the icons started to produce, direct, even write. For a time, they were able to ignore the fact that with television on the rise, no movie star could outdraw the "$64,000 Question." During this transitional decade, the director was still the brother-in-law. But instead of marrying himself off to a producer, he shacked up, as Jimmy Carter would say, with an icon. For a time each icon had his or her favorite director and The Industry was soon on the rocks.

Then out of France came the dreadful news: all those brothers-in-law of the classic era were really autonomous and original artists. Apparently each had his own style that impressed itself on every frame of any film he worked on. Proof? Since the director was the same person from film to film, each image of his *oeuvre* must then be stamped with his authorship. The argument was circular but no less overwhelming in its implications. Much quoted was Giraudoux's solemn inanity: "There are no works, there are only *auteurs*."

The often wise André Bazin eventually ridiculed this notion in *La Politique des Auteurs*, but the damage was done in the pages of the magazine he founded, *Cahiers du cinéma*, The fact that, regardless of director, every Warner Brothers film during the classic age had a dark look owing to the Brothers' passion for saving money in electricity and set-dressing cut no ice with ambitious critics on the prowl for high art in a field once thought entirely low.

In 1948, Bazin's disciple Alexandre Astruc wrote the challenging "*La Caméra-stylo*." This manifesto advanced the notion that the director is – or should be – the true and solitary creator of a movie, "penning" his film on celluloid. Astruc thought that *caméra-stylo* could

> tackle any subject, any genre. . . . I will even go so far as to say that contemporary ideas and philosophies of life are such that only the cinema can do justice to them. Maurice Nadcau wrote in an article in the newspaper *Combat*: "If Descartes lived today, he would write novels." With all due respect to Nadcau, a Descartes of today would already have shut himself up in his bedroom with a 16 mm camera and some film, and would be writing his philosophy on film: for his *Discours de la Méthode* would today be of such a kind that only the cinema could express it satisfactorily.[3]

With all due respect to Astruc, the cinema has many charming possibilities but it cannot convey complex ideas through words or even, paradoxically, dialogue in the Socratic sense. *Le Genou de Claire* is about as close as we shall ever come to dialectic in a film and though Rohmer's work has its delights, the ghost of Descartes is not very apt to abandon the marshaling of words on a page for the flickering shadows of talking heads. In any case, the Descartes of Astruc's period did not make a film; he wrote the novel *La Nausée*.

But the would-be camera-writers are not interested in philosophy or history or literature. They want only to acquire for the cinema the prestige of ancient forms without having first to crack, as it were, the code. "Let's face it," writes Astruc:

> between the pure cinema of the 1920s and filmed theater, there is plenty of room for a different and individual kind of film-making.
>
> This of course implies that the scriptwriter directs his own scripts; or rather, that the scriptwriter ceases to exist, for in this kind of film-making the distinction between author and director loses all meaning. Direction is no longer a means of illustrating or presenting a scene, but a true act of writing.

It is curious that despite Astruc's fierce will to eliminate the scriptwriter (and perhaps literature itself), he is forced to use terms from the art form he would like to supersede. For him the film director uses a *pen* with which he *writes* in order to become – highest praise – an *author*.

As the French theories made their way across the Atlantic, bemused brothers-in-law found themselves being courted by odd-looking French youths with tape recorders. Details of long-forgotten Westerns were recalled and explicated. Every halting word from the *auteur*'s lips was taken down and reverently examined. The despised brothers-in-law of the Thirties were now Artists. With new-found confidence, directors started inking major pacts to meg superstar thesps whom the meggers could control as hyphenates: that is, as director-producers or even as writer-director-producers. Although the icons continued to be worshipped and over-paid, the truly big deals were now made by directors. To them, also, went the glory. For all practical purposes the producer has either vanished from the scene (the "package" is now put together by a talent [!] agency) or merged with the director. Meanwhile, the screenwriter continues to be the prime creator of the talking film, and though he is generally paid very well and his name is listed right after that of the director in the movie reviews of *Time*, he is entirely in the shadow of the director just as the director was once in the shadow of the producer and the star.

What do directors actually do? What do screenwriters do? This is difficult to explain to those who have never been involved in the making of a film. It is particularly difficult when French theoreticians add to the confusion by devising false hypotheses (studio director as *auteur* in the Thirties) on which to build irrelevant and misleading theories. Actually, if Astruc and Bazin had wanted to be truly perverse (and almost accurate), they would have declared that the cameraman is the *auteur* of any film. They could then have ranked James Wong Howe with Dante, Braque, and Gandhi. Cameramen do tend to have styles in a way that the best writers do but most directors don't – style as opposed to preoccupation. Gregg Toland's camera work is a vivid fact from film to film, linking *Citizen Kane* to Wyler's *The Best Years of Our Lives* in a way that one cannot link *Citizen Kane* to, say, Welles's *Confidential Report*. Certainly the cameraman is usually more important than the director in the day-to-day making of a film as opposed to the preparing of a film. Once the film is shot the editor becomes the principal interpreter of the writer's invention.

Since there are few reliable accounts of the making of any of the classic talking movies, Pauline Kael's book on the making of *Citizen Kane* is a valuable document.[4] In considerable detail she establishes the primacy in that enterprise of the screenwriter Herman Mankiewicz. The story of how Orson Welles saw to it that Mankiewicz became, officially, the noncreator of his own film is grimly fascinating and highly typical of the way so many director-hustlers acquire for themselves the writer's creation. Few directors in this era possess the modesty of Kurosawa, who said, recently, "With a very good script, even a second-class director may make a first-class film. But with a bad script even a first-class director cannot make a really first-class film." The badness of so many of Orson Welles's post-Mankiewicz films ought to be instructive.

A useful if necessarily superficial look at the way movies were written in the classic era can be found in the pages of *Some Time in the Sun*. The author, Mr Tom Dardis, examines the movie careers of five celebrated writers who took jobs as movie-writers. They are Scott Fitzgerald, Aldous Huxley, William Faulkner, Nathanael West, and James Agee.

Mr Dardis's approach to his writers and to the movies is that of a deeply serious and highly concerned lowbrow, a type now heavily tenured in American Academe. He writes of "literate" dialogue, "massive" biographies. Magisterially, he misquotes

Henry James on the subject of gold. More seriously, *he misquotes Joan Crawford*. She did not say to Fitzgerald, "Work hard, Mr. Fitzgerald, work hard!" when he was preparing a film for her. She said "*Write* hard. . . ." There are many small inaccuracies that set on edge the film buff's teeth. For instance, Mr Dardis thinks that the hotel on Sunset Boulevard known, gorgeously, as The Garden of Allah is "now demolished and reduced to the status of a large parking lot. . . ." Well, it is not a parking lot, Hollywood has its own peculiar reverence for the past. The Garden of Allah was replaced by a bank that subtly suggests in glass and metal the mock-Saracen façade of the hotel that once housed Scott Fitzgerald. Mr Dardis also thinks that the hotel was "demolished" during World War II. I stayed there in the late Fifties, right next door to fun-loving, bibulous Errol Flynn.

Errors and starry-eyed vulgarity to one side, Mr Dardis has done a good deal of interesting research on how films were written and made in those days. For one thing, he catches the ambivalence felt by the writers who had descended (but only temporarily) from literature's Parnassus to the swampy marketplace of the movies. There was a tendency to play Lucifer. One was thought to have sold out. "Better to reign in hell than to serve in heaven," was more than once quoted – well, paraphrased – at the Writers' Table. We knew we smelled of sulphur. Needless to say, most of the time it was a lot of fun if the booze didn't get you.

For the Parnassian writer the movies were not just a means of making easy money; even under the worst conditions, movies were genuinely interesting to write. Mr Dardis is at his best when he shows his writers taking seriously their various "assignments." The instinct to do good work is hard to eradicate.

Faulkner was the luckiest (and the most cynical) of Mr Dardis's five. For one thing, he usually worked with Howard Hawks, a director who might actually qualify as an *auteur*. Hawks was himself a writer and he had a strong sense of how to manipulate those clichés that he could handle best. Together Faulkner and Hawks created a pair of satisfying movies, *To Have and Have Not* and *The Big Sleep*. But who did what? Apparently there is not enough remaining evidence (at least available to Mr Dardis) to sort out authorship. Also, Faulkner's public line was pretty much: I'm just a hired hand who does what he's told.

Nunnally Johnson (as quoted by Mr Dardis) found Hawks's professional relationship with Faulkner mysterious. "It may be that he simply wanted his name attached to Faulkner's. Or since Hawks liked to write it was easy to do it with Faulkner, for Bill didn't care much one way or the other. . . ." We shall probably never know just how much Bill cared about any of the scripts he worked on with Hawks. Yet it is interesting to note that Johnson takes it entirely for granted that the director wants – and must get – *all* credit for a film.

Problem for the director: how to get a script without its author? Partial solution: of all writers, the one who does not mind anonymity is the one most apt to appeal to an ambitious director. When the studio producer was king, he used to minimize the writer's role by assigning a dozen writers to a script. No director today has the resources of the old studies. But, he can hire a writer who doesn't "care much one way or the other." He can also put his name on the screen as co-author (standard procedure in Italy and France). Even the noble Jean Renoir played this game when he came to direct *The Southerner*. Faulkner not only wrote the script, he liked the project. The picture's star Zachary Scott has said that the script was entirely Faulkner's. But then other hands were engaged and "the whole problem," according to Mr Dardis, "of who did what was neatly solved by Renoir's giving himself sole credit for the screenplay – the best way possible for an *auteur* director to label his films."

Unlike Faulkner, Scott Fitzgerald cared deeply about movies; he wanted to make a success of movie writing and, all in all, if Mr Dardis is to be believed (and for what it may be worth, his account of Fitzgerald's time in the sun tallies with what one used to hear), he had a far better and more healthy time of it in Hollywood than is generally suspected.

Of a methodical nature, Fitzgerald ran a lot of films at the studio. (Unlike Faulkner, who affected to respond only to Mickey Mouse and Pathé News). Fitzgerald made notes. He also did what an ambitious writer must do if he wants to write the sort of movie he himself might want to see: he made friends with the producers. Rather censoriously, Mr Dardis notes Fitzgerald's "clearly stated intention to work with film producers rather than with film directors, here downgraded to the rank of 'collaborators.' Actually, Fitzgerald seems to have had no use whatsoever for directors as such." But neither did anyone else.

During much of this time Howard Hawks, say, was a low-budget director known for the neatness and efficiency of his work. Not until the French beatified him twenty years later did he appear to anyone as an original artist instead of just another hired technician. It is true that Hawks was allowed to work with writers but then he was at Warner Brothers, a frontier outpost facing upon barbarous Burbank. At MGM, the holy capital, writers and directors did not get much chance to work together. It was the producer who worked with the writer, and Scott Fitzgerald was an MGM writer. Even as late as my own years at MGM (1956–1958), the final script was the writer's creation (under the producer's supervision). The writer even pre-empted the director's most important function by describing each camera shot: Long, Medium, Close, and the director was expected faithfully to follow the writer's score.

One of the most successful directors at MGM during this period was George Cukor. In an essay on "The Director" (1938), Cukor reveals the game as it used to be played. "In most cases," he writes, "the director makes his appearance very early in the life story of a motion picture." I am sure that this was often the case with Cukor but the fact that he thinks it necessary to mention "early" participation is significant.

> There are times when the whole idea for a film may come from [the director], but in a more usual case he makes his entry when he is summoned by a producer and it is suggested that he should be the director of a proposed story.[5]

Not only was this the most usual way but, very often, the director left the producer's presence with the finished script under his arm. Cukor does describe his own experience working with writers but Cukor was something of a star at the studio. Most directors were "summoned" by the producer and told what to do. It is curious, incidentally, how entirely the idea of the working producer has vanished. He is no longer remembered except as the butt of familiar stories: fragile artist treated cruelly by insensitive cigar-smoking producer – or Fitzgerald savaged yet again by Joe Mankiewicz.

Of Mr Dardis's five writers, James Agee is, to say the least, the lightest in literary weight. But he was a passionate film-goer and critic. He was a child of the movies just as Huxley was a child of Meredith and Peacock. Given a different temperament, luck, birthdate, Agee might have been the first American cinema *auteur*: a writer who wrote screenplays in such a way that, like the score of a symphony, they needed nothing more than a conductor's interpretation . . . an interpretation he could have provided himself and perhaps would have provided if he had lived.

Agee's screenplays were remarkably detailed. "All the shots," writes Mr Dardis, "were set down with extreme precision in a way that no other screenwriter had ever set things down before. . . ." This is exaggerated. Most screenwriters of the classic period wrote highly detailed scripts in order to direct the director but, certainly, the examples Mr Dardis gives of Agee's screenplays show them to be remarkably visual. Most of us hear stories. He saw them, too. But I am not so sure that what he saw was the reflection of a living reality in his head. As with many of today's young directors Agee's memory was crowded with memories not of life but of old films. For Agee, rain falling was not a memory of April at Exeter but a scene recalled from Eisenstein. This is particularly noticeable in the adaptation Agee made of Stephen Crane's *The Blue Hotel*, which, Mr Dardis tells us, no "film director has yet taken on, although it has been televised twice, each time with a different director and cast and with the Agee script cut to the bone, being used only as a guidepost to the story." This is nonsense. In 1954, CBS hired me to adapt *The Blue Hotel*. I worked directly from Stephen Crane and did not know that James Agee had ever adapted it until I read *Some Time in the Sun*.

At the mention of any director's name, the Wise Hack at the Writers' Table would bark out a percentage, representing how much, in his estimate, a given director would subtract from the potential 100 percent of the script he was directing. The thought that a director might *add* something worthwhile never crossed the good gray Hack's mind. Certainly he would have found hilarious David Thomson's *A Biographical Dictionary of Film*, whose haphazard pages are studied with tributes to directors.

Mr Thomson has his own pleasantly eccentric pantheon in which writers figure hardly at all. A column is devoted to the dim Micheline Presle but the finest of all screenwriters, Jacques Prévert, is ignored. There

Figure 17.1 MGM's remake of *Ben-Hur*, directed by William Wyler (1959), was the product of several collaborators. Produced by Sam Zimbalist and William Wyler

is a long silly tribute to Arthur Penn; yet there is no biography of Penn's contemporary at NBC television, Paddy Chayefsky, whose films in the Fifties and early Sixties were far more interesting than anything Penn has done. Possibly Chayefsky was excluded because not only did he write his own films, he would then hire a director rather the way one would employ a plumber – or a cameraman. For a time, Chayefsky was the only American *auteur*, and his pencil was the director. Certainly Chayefsky's early career in films perfectly disproves Nicholas Ray's dictum (approvingly quoted by Mr Thomson): "If it were all in the script, why make the film?" If it is not all in the script, there is no film to make.

Twenty years ago at the Writers' Table we all agreed with the Wise Hack that William Wyler subtracted no more than 10 percent from a script. Some of the most attractive and sensible of Bazin's pages are devoted to Wyler's work in the Forties. On the other hand, Mr Thomson does not like him at all (because Wyler lacks those redundant faults that create the illusion of a Style?). Yet whatever was in a script, Wyler rendered faithfully: when he was given a bad script, he would make not only a bad movie, but the script's particular kind of badness would be revealed in a way that could altogether too easily boomerang on the too skillful director. But when the script was good (of its kind, *of its kind!*), *The Letter*, say, or *The Little Foxes*, there was no better interpreter.

At MGM, I worked exclusively with the producer Sam Zimbalist. He was a remarkably good and decent man in a business where such qualities are rare. He was also a producer of the old fashioned sort. This meant that the script was prepared for him and with him. Once the script was ready, the director was summoned; he would then have the chance to say, yes, he would direct the script or, no, he wouldn't. Few changes were made in the script after the director was assigned. But this was not to be the case in Zimbalist's last film.

For several years MGM had been planning a remake of *Ben-Hur*, the studio's most successful silent film. A Contract Writer wrote a script; it was discarded. Then Zimbalist offered me the job. I said no, and went on suspension. During the next year or two S.N. Behrman and Maxwell Anderson, among others, added many yards of portentous dialogue to a script which kept growing and changing. The result was not happy. By 1958 MGM was going bust. Suddenly the remake of *Ben-Hur* seemed like a last chance to regain the mass audience lost to television. Zimbalist again asked me if I would take on the job. I said that if the studio released me from the remainder of my contract, I would go to Rome for two or three months and rewrite the script. The studio agreed. Meanwhile, Wyler had been signed to direct.

On a chilly March day Wyler, Zimbalist, and I took an overnight flight from New York. On the plane Wyler read for the first time the latest of the many scripts. As we drove together into Rome form the airport, Wyler looked gray and rather frightened. "This is awful," he said, indicating the huge script that I had placed between us on the back seat. "I know," I said. "What are we going to do?"

Wyler groaned: "These Romans. . . . Do you know anything about them?" I said, yes, I had done my reading. Wyler stared at me. "Well," he said, "when a Roman sits down and relaxes, what does he unbuckle?"

That spring I rewrote more than half the script (and Wyler studied every "Roman" film ever made). When I was finished with a scene, I would give it to Zimbalist. We would go over it. Then the scene would be passed on to Wyler. Normally, Wyler is slow and deliberately indecisive; but first-century Jerusalem had been built at enormous expense; the first day of shooting was approaching; the studio was nervous. As a result, I did not often hear Wyler's famous cry, as he would hand you back your script, "If I knew what was wrong with it, I'd fix it myself."

The plot of *Ben-Hur* is, basically, absurd and any attempt to make sense of it would destroy the story's awful integrity. But for a film to be watchable the characters must make some kind of psychological sense. We were stuck with the following: the Jew Ben-Hur and the Roman Messala were friends in childhood. Then they were separated. Now the adult Messala returns to Jerusalem; meets Ben-Hur; asks him to help with the Romanization of Judea. Ben-Hur refuses; there is a quarrel; they part and vengeance is sworn. This one scene is the sole motor that must propel a very long story until Jesus Christ suddenly and pointlessly drifts onto the scene, automatically untying some of the cruder knots in the plot, Wyler and I agreed that a single political quarrel would not turn into a lifelong vendetta.

I thought of a solution, which I delivered into Wyler's good ear. "As boys they were lovers. Now Messala wants to continue the affair. Ben-Hur rejects him. Messala is furious. *Chagrin d'amour*, the classic motivation for murder."

Wyler looked at me as if I had gone mad. "But we can't do *that*! I mean this is Ben-Hur! My God. . . ."

"We won't really do it. We just suggest it. I'll write the scenes so that they will make sense to those who are tuned in. Those who aren't will still feel that Messala's rage is somehow emotionally logical."

I don't think Wyler particularly liked my solution but he agreed that "anything is better than what we've got. So let's try it."

I broke the original scene into two parts. Charlton Heston (Ben-Hur) and Stephen Boyd (Messala) read them for us in Zimbalist's office. Wyler knew his actors. He warned me: "Don't ever tell Chuck what it's all about, or he'll fall apart." I suspect that Heston does not know to this day what luridness we managed to contrive around him. But Boyd knew: every time he looked at Ben-Hur it was like a starving man getting a glimpse of dinner through a pane of glass. And so, among the thundering hooves and clichés of the last (to date) *Ben-Hur*, there is something odd and authentic in one unstated relationship.

As agreed, I left in early summer and Christopher Fry wrote the rest of the script. Before the picture ended, Zimbalist died of a heart attack. Later, when it came time to credit the writers of the film, Wyler proposed that Fry be given screen credit. Then Fry insisted that I be given credit with him since I had written the first half of the picture. Wyler was in a quandary. Only Zimbalist (and Fry and myself – two interested parties) knew who had written what, and Zimbalist was dead. The matter was given to the Screenwriters Guild for arbitration and they, mysteriously, awarded the credit to the Contract Writer whose script was separated from ours by at least two other discarded scripts. The film was released in 1959 (not 1959–1960 as my edition of *The Filmgoer's Companion* by Leslie Halliwell states) and saved MGM from financial collapse.

I have recorded in some detail this unimportant business to show the near-impossibility of determining how a movie is actually created. Had *Ben-Hur* been taken seriously by, let us say, those French critics who admire *Johnny Guitar*, then Wyler would have been credited with the unusually subtle relationship between Ben-Hur and Messala. No credit would ever have gone to me because my name was not on the screen, nor would credit have gone to the official scriptwriter because, according to the *auteur* theory, every aspect of a film is the creation of the director.

The twenty-year interregnum when the producer was supreme is now a memory. The ascendancy of the movie stars was brief. The directors have now regained their original primacy; and Milestone's storm is only an echo. Today the marquees of movie houses feature the names of directors and journalists ("*A work of art*," J. Crist); the other collaborators are in fine print.

This situation might be more acceptable if the film directors had become true *auteurs*. But most of them are further than ever away from art – not to mention life. The majority are simply technicians. A few have come from the theater; many began as editors, cameramen, makers of television series, and ominously, of television commercials. In principle, there is nothing wrong with a profound understanding of the technical means by which an image is impressed upon celluloid. But movies are not just molds of light any more than a novel is just inked-over paper. A movie is a response to reality in a certain way and that way must first be found by a writer. Unfortunately, no contemporary film director can bear to be thought a mere interpreter. He must be sole creator. As a result, he is more often than not a plagiarist, telling stories that are not his.

Over the years a number of writers have become directors, but except for such rare figures as Cocteau and Bergman, the writers who have gone in for directing were generally not much better at writing than they proved to be at directing. Even in commercial terms, for every Joe Mankiewicz or Preston Sturges there are a dozen Xs and Ys, not to mention the depressing Z.

Today's films are more than ever artifacts of light. Cars chase one another mindlessly along irrelevant freeways. Violence seems rooted in a notion about what ought to happen next on the screen to help the images move rather than in any human situation anterior to those images. In fact, the human situation has been eliminated not through any intentional philosophic design but because those who have spent too much time with cameras and machines seldom have much apprehension of that living world without whose presence there is no art.

I suspect that the time has now come to take Astruc seriously . . . after first rearranging his thesis. Astruc's *caméra-stylo* requires that "the script writer ceases to exist. . . . The filmmaker/author writes with his camera as a writer writes with his pen." Good. But let us eliminate not the screenwriter but that technician-hunter – the director (a.k.a. *auteur du cinéma*). Not until he has been replaced by those who can use a pen to write from life for the screen is there going to be much of anything worth seeing. Nor does it take a genius of a writer to achieve great effects in film. Compared to the works of his nineteenth-century mentors, the writing of Ingmar Bergman is second-rate. But when he writes straight through the page and onto the screen itself his talent is transformed and the result is often first-rate. (As was very often the work of René Clair.)

As a poet, Jacques Prévert is not in the same literary class as Valtéry, but Prévert's *Les Enfants du paradis* and *Lumière d'été* are extraordinary achievements. They were also disdained by the French theoreticians of the Forties who knew perfectly well that the directors Carné and Grémillon were inferior to their scriptwriter; but since the Theory requires that only a director can create a film, any film that is plainly a writer's work cannot be true cinema. This attitude has given rise to some highly comic critical musings. Recently a movie critic could not figure out why there had been such a dramatic change in the quality of the work of the director Joseph Losey after he moved to England. Was it a difference in the culture? the light? the water? Or could it – and the critic faltered – could it be that perhaps Losey's films changed when he . . . when he – oh, dear – got Harold Pinter to write screenplays for him? The critic promptly dismissed the notion. Mr Thomson prints no biography of Pinter in his *Dictionary*.

I have never much liked the films of Pier Paolo Pasolini but I find most interesting the case with which

Figure 17.2 *Les Enfants du paradis* (1945): A film where the director (Marcel Carné) was clearly inferior to the writer (Jacques Prévert). Produced by Raymond Borderie and Fred Orain

he turned to film after some twenty years as poet and novelist. He could not have been a filmmaker in America because the costs are too high; also, the technician-hustlers are in total charge. But in Italy, during the Fifties, it was possible for an actual *auteur* to use for a pen the camera (having first himself composed rather than stolen the narrative to be illuminated).

Since, the talking movie is closest in form to the novel ("the novel is a narrative that organizes itself in the world, while the cinema is a world that organizes itself into a narrative" – Jean Mitry), it strikes me that the rising literary generation might think of the movies as, peculiarly, their kind of novel, to be created by them in collaboration with technicians but without the interference of The Director, that hustler-plagiarist who has for twenty years dominated and exploited and (occasionally) enhanced an art form still in search of its true authors.

Notes

1 Questions I am advised to anticipate: What about such true *auteurs du cinéma* as Truffaut? Well, *Jules et Jim* was a novel by Henri-Pierre Roché. Did Truffaut adapt the screenplay himself? No, he worked with Jean Gruault. Did Buñuel create *The Exterminating Angel*? No, it was "suggested" by an unpublished play by José Bergamin. Did Buñuel take it from there? No, he had as co-author Luis Alcorisa, So it goes.

2 Robert Parrish, *Growing Up in Hollywood* (Harcourt Brace Jovanovich, 1976).

3 Astruc's essay is reprinted in Peter Graham, ed., *The New Wave* (Doubleday, 1968).

4 *The Citizen Kane Book* (Atlantic Monthly Press, 1971).

5 Cukor's essay is reprinted in Richard Koszarski, ed., *Hollywood Directors 1914–1940* (Oxford University Press, 1976).

18

Script/Performance/Text: Performance Theory and Auteur Theory

Peter Lehman

Peter Lehman is Director of the Interdisciplinary Humanities Program at Arizona State University. He has published widely in film studies and is the author or co-author of many books including *Authorship and Narrative in the Cinema*, *Thinking About Movies* and the edited collection *The Searchers: Essays and Reflections on John Ford's Classic Western*. With *Running Scared: Masculinity and the Representation of the Male Body* Lehman contributed significantly to the understanding of cinema's representation of masculinity. Here, comparing the differences between scripts, screenplays, and performances, Lehman theorizes the nature of performance in the making of films and the relation of such performance to the work of the director and auteurism.

It is not uncommon in newspapers or magazines to find the drama critic contributing an occasional film review or, in fact, serving simultaneously as reviewer for both of those arts. Much more attention has been paid to studying the relationship between literature and film than between theater and film. This is unfortunate for several reasons. Many unstated assumptions which dominate a great deal of American film criticism derive from unexamined feelings about the connection between theater and film, hence the moonlighting drama critics. We speak, for example, about actors' performances and dramatic events in the two forms in almost exactly the same way. Moreover, the failure to critically examine these notions obscures the larger question as to how film relates to performing arts in general.

We generally agree, for example, that theater and music are performing arts. And we generally agree on what that means. If a music critic goes to hear Leonard Bernstein conducting the New York Philharmonic in a "performance" of Beethoven's Fifth Symphony, he/she feels secure in knowing who is responsible for what. What Beethoven did and what Bernstein is doing are taken to be known entities. Praise and blame are easily distributed. If the critic hates the performance, he/she doesn't confuse that with hating the work created by Beethoven. In other words, a clear notion exists of what constitutes the aesthetic text and what constitutes a performance of the text. We know how to attribute critical praise and blame for authorship of the text as well as for performance of the text. We could not do one without the other. Unfortu-

Peter Lehman, "Script/Performance/Text: Performance Theory and Auteur Theory," pp. 197–206 from *Film Reader* 3 (Northwestern University). © 1978 by Peter Lehman. Reprinted by permission of the author.

nately, in film we have not yet learned how to do these things.

A good deal of the problem surrounding film in relation to performance theory derives from the history of the terminology employed. The word "script" was originally used in connection with stage plays. Actors were given scripts, they memorized lines, and under the supervision of a director, a performance was staged. Nor does the common term "screenplay" instead of "script" imply anything different. It merely suggests a play written for the screen as opposed to a play written for the stage. William Froug, a screenwriter himself, in attacking the auteur theory, speaks about the filmmaking process in the same language he would use to speak about a play:

> But the history of American films is drastically opposed to the auteur concept. The director was often brought to the production long after the conceptual work had been done. His job was to interpret the work of the writer, just as the actor's job was to interpret the role, the character, that the writer had conceived.[1]

Similarly, Richard Corliss remarks that a film director is "less a composer than a conductor," that is, the director is less a creator of a work than an interpreter of some previous creation.[2] How much sense does it make to speak of a film director "interpreting" a writer's script as a stage director "interprets" a play script or a musical conductor "interprets" a composer's score? A decisive difference exists between a film director and a theater director or a musical conductor.

Only the most undisciplined, polemical critical milieu could allow terms like these to be bantered about without further investigation. Just such a climate has prevailed in the auteur debates. Of all the participants, Peter Wollen raises the question most directly. He concludes that there are two types of directors: some who merely interpret a pre-existent text and transpose it into cinematic codes and others who overlap that level of manifest performance with a newly created text in the making of the film.[3] This distinction shows some of the confusion of the Corliss and Froug remarks but also points the way towards a solution to the problem: a consideration of performance theory.

At the end of his discussion of the issue, Wollen remarks, "We need to develop much further a theory of performance . . ."[4] Surprisingly, that statement is unqualified in the later edition of Wollen's book which appeared in 1972. Nelson Goodman had already contributed a much more highly developed theory of performance in his 1968 book, *Languages of Art*. Goodman's work helps clarify some of the issues.

Taking up the subject of authenticity and fakery in art, Goodman investigates the difference between autographic and allographic art:

> Let us speak of a work of art as autographic if and only if the distinction between original and forgery of it is significant; or better, if and only if even the most exact duplication of it does not thereby count as genuine . . . Thus painting is autographic, music non-autographic, or allographic.[5]

Goodman then observes:

> One notable difference between painting and music is that the composer's work is done when he has written the score, even though the performances are the end-products, while the painter has to finish the picture (Goodman, pp. 113–14).

This line of inquiry leads Goodman to the conclusion that "an art seems to be allographic just insofar as it is amenable to notation" (Goodman, p. 121).

Only autographic works of art involve forgeries, and a forgery is, in effect, a false claim to a certain history of production. How and by whom the object was produced is crucial. Allographic arts, on the other hand, are emancipated from the history of production as a test of authenticity. This requires a suitable notational system. That notational system must include "All the constitutive properties of the work in question" (Goodman, p. 122). In a score of Beethoven's Fifth Symphony, for example, there can be no relevant question about the history of production of the particular score a musician looks at. It means nothing to argue who made that score or from what other "copy" of the score it was copied. The man Beethoven and the personal history involved in writing the symphony has nothing to do with what other person or machine copies down the score, how they do it, and when they do it. All that matters is that they do it accurately, without making "spelling mistakes" – here meaning, for example, copying a wrong note. Accuracy and fidelity to the characters in the notational system count for everything; who (Beethoven himself or a school child), how (pen or pencil), and when (1900 or 1950) count for nothing.

Not surprisingly, Goodman uses music as an example of an art existing in a nearly pure notational system. The only issue is compliance with the accurate score. The performers have to do exactly what is notated. The only problem arises concerning verbal language written in scores (e.g., allegro):

> Thus the verbal language of tempos is not notational. The tempo words cannot be integral parts of a score insofar as the score serves the function of identifying a work from performance to performance. No departure from the indicated tempo disqualifies a performance as an instance – however wretched – of the work defined by the score. For the tempo specifications cannot be accounted integral parts of the defining score, but are rather auxiliary directions whose observance or nonobservance affects the quality of a performance but not the identity of the work. (Goodman, p. 185)

However much we might disagree with, for example, Leonard Bernstein's nonobservance of a temporal verbal direction in a performance of Beethoven's Fifth Symphony, we nevertheless acknowledge the identity of the work in question.[6] Were he to play wrong notes or alter the metronomic specifications of tempo, we would no longer call it a performance of Beethoven's Fifth Symphony. It is important to bear in mind that some features of a performance may vary considerably from performance to performance. Even in music not all features are part of a notational system, though all the constitutive properties of the work are in a notational system.

What distinguishes a notational system from other languages is a complicated matter. The two major characteristics of scores in notational systems are that they separate performances that belong to the work from those that do not and that, given a notational system, scores can be determined from a performance. In a notational system nothing is a sample of more than one compliance class. This is not the case in discursive language. At best, a good definition determines what objects conform to it, but the definition is not determined by each of its instances. This double movement is essential in notational systems. If I hear a note in a musical performance and am familiar with the notational system, I can mark down the note only one way. Everyone familiar with the system would mark it down the same way. The sounded note is a compliance only of that notational character. If, on the other hand, someone points to their car I can, using discursive language, place it in the class "car," "Volkswagen," "metal objects," "objects on wheels," "white objects," etc., etc. It belongs to all those classes and many more. There is no uniquely determining double movement. Perhaps all of this is best summed up by Goodman's observation that, "The criteria that distinguish notational systems from other languages are in terms of interrelationships among compliance classes . . ." (Goodman, p. 200).

Discursive language, for a final example, cannot determine the constitutive properties of a painting. A description of a certain color of blue and how and where it is applied to the canvas cannot be uniquely determined – no matter how many qualifying terms we use. Likewise, given a painting with blue in it, no one can precisely and uniquely encode that blue in discursive language. Imagine a hundred people with full knowledge of a discursive language describing the exact same painting. Now compare this with people fully acquainted with a notational system working from a performance to a score.

In this framework, a sketch which an artist may do before he/she makes a painting is not a score, rather it is an autographic work. The sketch and the painting are two different works; the painting is in no way an instance of a compliance with the sketch. The constitutive properties of the painting are not notated in the sketch. This does not imply that a painter could not use a sketch while painting a picture.

This brings us to scripts which, in the case of films, like sketches can be used in the creation of an art work whose constitutive properties they do not notate: "A script, unlike a sketch, is a character in a notational scheme and in a language, but unlike a score, is not in a notational system" (Goodman, p. 199). "Script" here includes the work of playwrights and screenwriters. In literary works, Goodman goes on to observe that an actual utterance is in no way more an instance of the work than the written inscription of the text. Reading a novel aloud is not a compliance-class performance. Rather than having a compliance-class, a literary work is the text. Goodman's remarks about drama and his later sole reference to film are of particular importance here:

Figure 18.1 Natalie Wood, John Wayne, and Jeffrey Hunter in John Ford's *The Searchers* (Warner Bros, 1956). Produced by C.V. Whitney

> In the drama, as in music, the work is a compliance-class of performance. The text of the play, however, is a composite of score and script. The dialogue is in a virtually notational system, with utterances as its compliants. This part of the text is a score; and performances complicit with it constitute the work. (Goodman, pp. 210–11)

Stage directions and descriptions of scenery, etc., are features which are not part of the notational system. They are supplementary instructions and in no way constitute the work. It is for this reason that Goodman can make the all-important observation which returns us, once again, to the subject of film:

> The script for a silent film is neither the cinematic work nor a score for it but, though *used* in producing the film, is otherwise as loosely related to the work as is a verbal description of a painting to the painting itself. (Goodman, p. 211. Italics mine)

The corollary to this, of course, is that in a sound film only the spoken dialogue is in a notational system, that is the sole relevant difference between a silent film and a sound film as relates to the script.

The dialogue in a film script is in a notational scheme, but that is not sufficient to qualify it as an aesthetic text. The dialogue in a play script, on the other hand, is a totality unto itself, speaks of what is fundamentally at issue and creates the diegesis and decor. It is, in short, what Metz calls a "continuous verbal tissue."[7] This is, of course, what enables us to read and aesthetically evaluate a Shakespeare play without seeing it performed. This is also what accounts for us being able to attribute creation of the aesthetic work to Shakespeare when we are watching a performance.

This is not to suggest, as perhaps some have done, that there is some clear division between two kinds of language, theatrical on the one hand, cinematic on the other. What I am speaking of here is not kinds of dialogue but rather, the status of dialogue in the aesthetic work. An example from John Ford's *The Searchers* should clarify this crucial point.

Towards the end of the film, Ethan Edwards, instead of killing Debbie, sweeps her up into his arms and says, "Let's go home, Debbie." Like any profilmic event, it could be photographed in any number of ways and then edited into an infinite number of shot sequences as relate to the shots which come before and after it. In terms of any verbal patterns within the line (or in relationship to any others in the film), it is quite unexceptional. No doubt, banal to many. Furthermore, considered solely as a narrative event which any number of directors could handle in any number of ways, the action seems ludicrously sentimental. Indeed, to many it may appear that after five years of trying to find Debbie and kill her, the Hollywood happy ending wins out and Ethan lovingly takes her home.

When viewed as part of the cinematic text, however, it becomes part of an aesthetic text, full of rich and complex connections. Briefly, the previous shot is from within a cave. This refers formally to earlier shots from within a cave and, in fact, an entire scene set in a cave. It also refers to a whole series of doorway and teepee shots which structure the film. The shot where Ethan actually picks up Debbie includes a gesture of lifting her above his head, recalling a similar moment which transpired between them five years earlier in front of a fireplace in the Edwards's home. None of these complex associations are implicit in the profilmic event nor in the dialogue. Yet, exactly what the shots "say" and their aesthetic value result precisely from these elements. Considered abstractly within the film's narrative or merely on the dialogue level (or as a scripted event before filming), the moment collapses into near meaninglessness. Even if the compositional features were described in discursive language (an historical study of Ford's work with varying scriptwriters and his scriptwriters' work with other directors indicates that even the general compositional ideas characterize his work, not theirs), the delicate work of actual creation remains to be done. Even if we are to believe Alfred Hitchcock's extraordinary claims that he knows exactly what his films will look like before he begins shooting, the fact remains that only he can make them look that way, which is why he has to put up with the awful tedium of making movies. Furthermore, it would be a serious mistake to view such compositional features as those in *The Searchers* example as window dressing; they actively shape and structure the moment, give it complex textual references, as well as meaning and aesthetic worth.

The way in which Umberto Eco discusses the relationship between a verbal description and a painting is instructive when applied to the relationship between a script and a film text:

> Suppose that one had to express the following (content) situation: Solomon meets the Queen of Sheba, each leading a procession of ladies and gentlemen dressed in Renaissance style, and bathed in a pure and still morning light that gives bodies the air of mysterious statues, etc., etc. Everyone would recognize in this 'verbal' discourse something vaguely similar to a well-known pictorial 'text' by Piero della Francesca: but the verbal expression does not 'interpret' the pictorial one. At most, the former suggests the latter only because the latter has already been expressed and recorded by our culture. And even in this case only certain of the verbal expressions refer to recognizable content units (Solomon, to meet, Queen of Sheba, etc.), while many others by no means convey the sort of content that one might receive when looking at the painting (it goes without saying that even such an expression as (the sign vehicle) /Solomon/ represents a rather imprecise interpretant of the corresponding image painted by Piero). When the painter begins work, the content (in its nebula-like structure) is neither coded nor divided into precise units. It has to be invented . . . The sign producer has a fairly clear idea of *what* he would like to 'say' but he does not know *how* to say it; and he cannot know *how* to do so until he has discovered *precisely what* to say.[8]

Even given the existence of a film script, the most we can say is that the director may have a fairly clear idea of what he/she would like to say. It is exactly in the area of discovery of how and thus what to "say" that the creative process works. The verbal discourse of the script cannot of course code these units of the aesthetic text.

Murray Krieger, discussing poetry, comes to a remarkably similar conclusion:

> The poet begins with a vague impulse, a vague something he wants to say; but this something need have little relation to what his work will finally say . . . He cannot say precisely what it is, or else his poem would already be written . . . As the poet creates, he discovers what it is he is creating . . . But he may prefer to believe that the poem is merely an embodiment of what seems to him

> to have been a thoroughly lucid original idea. To the extent that he is an artist he will be – happily – mistaken; and if he persists in this belief, it will remain for the critic to show him what he has really done.[9]

In order to understand what it is that the filmmaker "really does," it is necessary to distinguish between the profilmic event and the film text. The camera is commonly viewed as a window upon the events presented in the film, a device that simply records a pre-existent occurrence. The rationale behind the placement of the camera in relation to the image recorded and the cutting from one shot to the next is generally assumed to be determined by the dramatic imperatives inherent in the event.

This assumption about the integrity of the profilmic event reduces the viewer to a spectator of the dramatic performance. Whereas a great deal of recent scholarship has excellently demonstrated how this aspect of Hollywood films operates, it would be a serious mistake to reduce the entire perception of the filmic text to this level.[10] A good director establishes an aesthetic text in which many elements other than profilmic performance determine the work itself. The profilmic event is not equivalent to the text, a viewer is not equivalent to a spectator, and a stage director is not equivalent to a film director.[11]

Peter Wollen's crucial distinction between two types of directors, *metteurs en scène* and *auteurs*, cannot stand up for several reasons. The meaning of a film of a *metteur en scène* cannot exist *a priori* since the meaning of the work cannot be abstracted from the context of that work without altering it and since no aesthetic text exists before the *metteur en scène* makes his/her film; the film must be something other than a "translation" of that meaning into cinematic codes. As I have demonstrated in the first part of this paper, it is insupportable to view any director as being in "command of a performance of a pre-existing text."[12] A symphony orchestra conductor and a stage director have that opportunity, a film director doesn't. In art forms where someone may be seen as being in command of a performance, there has to be a notational system capable of notating the constitutive elements of the work. No such system exists in the cinema.

All films are autographic, and thus in a sense all directors are *auteurs*. This brings up the second serious problem with the *metteur en scène/auteur* distinction: it reveals a confusion of hierarchic levels. If a careful look at performance theory shows that the meaning of a film cannot exist *a priori*, a careful look at single films and their relationship to larger groupings shows that the latter cannot determine the meaning of the former. The organization of a film is different than the organization of a career.

Leonard Meyer introduces the useful term "hierarchic level" to discuss such differing planes of organization, not only in art but also in science and history. Modes of analysis in all these areas contain various hierarchic levels:

> It is, as we have seen, a serious mistake to assume that the principles or "laws" governing the organization of one hierarchic level are necessarily the same as those of some other level. As a rule, the forces creating structure and organization do not remain the same – are not uniform from one level to another . . . There is no logical staircase running from the physics of 10^{28} cm. to the physics of 10^{28} light years . . . Similarly in the theory and analysis of music it is doubtful that the several different hierarchic levels are governed by the same syntactical and grammatical principles of organization.[13]

The concept of jumping from one level to another involves, in the *auteur* theory, the leap from the individual film to the career overview. Meyer further elaborates about these types of organizational levels:

> The world – including the world of music – is not, however, in this sense homogenous; and it is not so precisely because hierarchic differentiation and articulation are non-uniform. Just as the forces governing the way in which chemicals unite to form molecules are different from the forces involved in the organization of molecules into cells, so the ways in which tones combine to form motives are different from the ways in which motives are organized to create larger, more complex musical events.[14]

The auteurists have never properly appreciated this concept. If looking at John Ford's career proves interesting, it is not because it locates the meaning of, say, *The Searchers*. A consideration of this point may lead to some conclusions about performance theory and *auteur* theory.

A sketch can be used in creating a painting and a script can be used in creating a film. In both cases the antecedent stage does not notate the constitutive properties of the work. In many ways the script of a film can be seen as analogous to a verbal description that precedes a poem. Thus, it is not useless, but the author of it cannot be credited with the authorship of the work. The major portion of the creative process is yet to take place.

It is precisely within this zone of creativity between general description and realization, between general idea of what to say and discovery of how, and thus precisely what, to say, that the authorship of the text takes place. The text is neither created before filming nor reconstituted after an entire career. This goes a long way toward explaining what led to the false distinction between *metteurs en scène* and *auteurs* and also toward explaining apparent discrepancies within the work of a single director.

Different directors work differently within that all-important creative zone, and in fact the same director may work differently from film to film.[15] Some directors may never be able to conceive of anything other than viewing the camera as a recording device ruled over by the performance level of action taking place within the profilmic event. Thus, entire Hollywood films are constructed almost solely on principles of cutting on action – reaction – and dialogue. This situation would be very similar to that of the poet whose final poem in fact is just like his/her original idea; neither is much of an artist. At the other extreme are directors who frequently (though seldom always) use the profilmic event as a starting point for creative activity, thus reducing the importance of profilmic performance in the completed film text. What we really have is a continuum, not a magical distinction. And for this reason, the greats are not always that great; they sometimes fail at the creative effort. And the lesser directors sometimes surpass themselves.

If John Ford's *Gideon of Scotland Yard* seems unexceptional by any standards, it merely indicates that, for whatever reason, Ford was unable to work creatively on that occasion. As in all the arts, the movement from general conception to precise discovery is never guaranteed. *Mogambo* is many respects has general conceptual features remarkably similar to those found in Ford's best post-War work: a cross-cultural situation, a strange remote environment, and a journey into an even remoter area. Yet, the film can't begin to compare to Ford's best work from that period. Even more puzzling perhaps than *Gideon of Scotland Yard* where the material seems conceptually far removed from Ford's usual interests, *Mogambo* shows a creative failure of a similar kind.

At times, of course, interference on the set or post-production manipulation of the text account for a failure. And at times, in the midst of threatening circumstances, directors still succeed in creating an interesting aesthetic text. *Auteurs*, I have suggested, don't exist magically as a group, and there is no reason to expect that any director always succeeds in the creative zone, even when there is no production interference.

If we place *Mogambo* in a career context, it may become very interesting. But this tells us something about the hierarchic construct of John Ford's career, and nothing about *Mogambo*. We have not discovered something hidden in *Mogambo* beneath a manifest level of performance. We have made it part of another construct with different principles of organization. In all films by all directors the level of performance is located within the profilmic event, the level of aesthetic achievement (however clichéd or banal) is located at the level of the constructed film text, and the level of auteurism is located at the hierarchic grouping of many films. The three levels are separate and distinct.

A final word may be in order concerning the aesthetic implications of the notion of the filmic text given here. As the theoretical thrust of the argument and the brief example from *The Searchers* should indicate, what distinguishes the good from the bad depends primarily upon complex and structured use of compositional features, organization of screen space, sound, camera movement, etc. As is well known by now, Peter Wollen discussed and evaluated entire directors' careers without attending to these aspects of the constructed film text. Some of his articles never cite a single shot from a specific film yet alone relate it to anything else in the film.[16] But auteurism is not alone in having been plagued by this problem.

On the most basic level, what a film is about cannot even be discussed without first attending to compositional features of the projected filmic text. Many critics rush to discuss important sounding subjects (significant themes, interesting characters. etc.) as if they exist separate from the projected film, as if in some unstated way, the film text is merely a record of a performance of those things. Thus a critic might assert that *The Searchers* is a racist film. Approached in this way, to discuss compositional features and patterns of off-screen space sounds *merely* formal. The point becomes: If the film is racist, why bother to discuss how petty or complex that racism is? Doesn't this detract from the racism?

The very posing of such questions, of course, already assumes that the film is a recording of a performance, that it is little more than window dressing, be it a pretty window we look through or an ugly one. If in fact a film is racist, the only way that *that* racism can be discussed is by speaking about the aesthetic text. For just this reason, so many discussions of such topics as women "in film" or blacks "in film," however well intentioned, are so limited. They don't place a particular woman or a particular black in a particular film. They immediately grab the image of the performer out of it, assuming that the image speaks for itself and that to worry about any possible spatial features, for example, is merely to digress into a formalism that moves away from the important point. In fact, the so-called formalism is the important point. The topics could frequently be better entitled along such lines as "Blacks Out of Film."

Aesthetic texts do not embody something which already exists, they do not say something we already know, they do not translate something which can be said a hundred different ways. They are, rather, self-focusing texts where how something is said uniquely becomes part of what is said.[17] Nor does this fact sever aesthetic texts from life and ban them into the clichéd never-never land of art for art's sake; nor does it trivialize politics and social contexts. On the contrary, by insisting on the particular qualities of the aesthetic text and what it says and it alone says, this approach then returns to us precisely what needs to be politically understood or placed within the social context. The irony we have to understand is that by insisting that aesthetic texts are in some way autonomous, we do not divorce them from life, but rather, make them more valuable. Aesthetic texts tell us things which other kinds of texts cannot tell us, and critics have to attend to those things. If literary critics have learned to slow down what Jonathan Culler calls "the unseemly rush from word to world," film critics have to learn to slow down the rush from the screen to the world.[18] This doesn't make the world or film any less important; it simply does them both justice. In order to achieve this justice, we have to pay much more attention to the projected film text and to precisely understand the place of the script and the profilmic performance within such a text.

Notes

1 William Froug, *The Screenwriter Looks at the Screenwriter* (New York: Delta, 1972), p. ix.

2 Richard Corliss, *The Hollywood Screenwriters* (New York: Avon Books, 1970), p. 10.

3 Peter Wollen, *Signs and Meaning in the Cinema* (Bloomington: Indiana University Press, 1972), p. 78 and pp. 112–13.

4 Wollen, p. 113.

5 Nelson Goodman, *Languages of Art* (Indianapolis: Bobbs-Merrill, 1968), p. 113.

6 A highly qualified position is taken on this point in William Luhr and Peter Lehman, *Authorship and Narrative in the Cinema* (New York: G. P. Putnam's Sons, 1977), pp. 31–2. William Luhr felt strongly that Goodman's point should be modified to include general obeyance with discursive directions; there is leeway but not limitless leeway. I agree with Goodman's position as stated here. If the discursive directions indicate slowing down and Leonard Bernstein speeds up, we may hear a wretched performance but the work being performed is still intact. Nevertheless, this area needs further investigation. As it now stands, playing one wrong note disqualifies the work while the most systematic and outrageous abuse of discursive directions does not threaten the work's integrity. Goodman himself acknowledges this point with the warning that through a series of single note changes Beethoven's Fifth Symphony can become "Three Blind Mice" (Goodman, p. 187).

7 Christian Metz, "On Jean Mitry's *L'Esthétique et Psychologie du Cinéma*, vol. II," trans. by Diana Matias, *Screen*, vol. 14, nos. 1/2 (Spring/Summer 1973), p. 52.

8 Umberto Eco, *A Theory of Semiotics* (Bloomington: Indiana University Press, 1976), p. 188.

9 Murray Krieger, *The New Apologists for Poetry* (Minneapolis: The University of Minnesota Press, 1956), p. 69.

10 See Christian Metz, "The Imaginary Signifier," *Screen*, vol. 16, no. 2 (Summer 1975); Daniel Dayan, "The Tutor-Code of Classical Cinema," *Film Quarterly*, vol. XVIII, no. 1 (Fall 1974); and Nicholas Browne, "The Spectator in the Text," *Film Quarterly*, vol. XXIX, no. 2 (Winter 1975–6).

11 This point about the difference between the spectator and the viewer has been well developed recently by Robert Eberwein,

"Spectator–Viewer," *Wide Angle*, vol. 2, no. 2 (1978) pp. 4–9. The point I wish to stress here is that the viewer can be a conscious evaluator taking into account many more things than a spectator of a dramatic event – even if the camera placement implicates him/her as a spectator of the event.

12 Wollen, p. 112.

13 Leonard Meyer, *Music, The Arts and Ideas* (Chicago: The University of Chicago Press, 1967), p. 258.

14 Meyer, p. 258.

15 It should be added that it need not be the credited director or even a single person who is responsible for the work in the creation of the aesthetic text. Circumstances vary from project to project. The point here is merely to indicate where the creation of aesthetic value takes place, not necessarily who does it. Whoever is responsible for the creation of the aesthetic text, it cannot be someone whose work is completed in a stage antecedent to that text's creation.

16 See for example, the articles Peter Wollen wrote for *The New Left Review* under the pen name of Lee Russell. The articles appear between January–February 1964 and March–April 1966 in Nos. 23, 24, 26, 29, 32, 35, and 36.

17 For discussion of this approach to the nature of aesthetic texts, see Eco, pp. 270–1; Meyer, pp. 210–17; and Roman Jakobson, "Linguistics and Poetics," in *The Structuralists from Marx to Lévi-Strauss* ed. by Richard and Fernande DeGeorge (Garden City: Anchor Books, 1972), pp. 93–6.

18 Jonathan Culler, *Structuralist Poetics* (Ithaca: Cornell University Press, 1975), p. 130.

19

Studio Authorship, Corporate Art

Jerome Christensen

As André Bazin had famously put it in discussing auteurism in relation to the Hollywood studio system, "Auteur yes, but what of?" Although Bazin praised "the genius" of the studio system for its ability to support the work of directors with a vital genre system, considerably more critical work has been done on genres than on studios. In this essay, Jerry Christensen, chair of the Department of English at the University of California at Irvine, continues his examination of the role of the studio in the context of authorship that he explored in an analysis of King Vidor's film adaptation of Ayn Rand's novel *The Fountainhead* (1949) originally published in *Velvet Light Trap* in 2006. Christensen there argues that the individualist capitalism espoused by the movie's narrative accords with the business philosophy of its producing studio, Warner Bros., which thus might be considered the author of the film as much as its director or writer. In this essay Christensen considers more broadly the question of studio authorship in relation to concepts of corporations and Hollywood cinema, challenging the auteurist model of American film history from yet another perspective.

In its 1932 profile of Metro-Goldwyn-Mayer, *Fortune* departs from analysis of the studio's history, structure, and personality to herald the advent of corporate art:

> MGM is neither one man nor a collection of men. It is a corporation. Whenever a motion picture becomes a work of art it is unquestionably due to men. But the moving pictures have been born and bred not of men but of corporations. Corporations have set up the easels, bought the pigments, arranged the views, and hired the potential artists. Until the artists emerge, at least, the corporation is bigger than the sum of its parts. Somehow, although our poets have not yet defined it for us, a corporation lives a life and finds a fate outside the lives and fates of its human constituents.[1]

In other words, the condition for the emergence of cinematic works of art is not individual genius, not technology, not even money, but the corporate organization of the studio. *Fortune* does not promise that Hollywood motion pictures will transport like art or that they will endure like art, but, it affirms, if any do they will count as examples of *corporate* art.

Fortune's corporate art thesis has attracted few adherents in film studies. Richard Maltby's generalization in 1998 still holds true: "There has . . . been a fairly clear division between a practice of textual analysis that has either avoided historical contextualization or engaged in it only minimally, and economic film history that has largely avoided confronting the movies as formal objects."[2] The predominant theoretical approach to American film history descends from

Jerome Christensen, "Studio Authorship." Adapted from "Studio Authorship, Warner Bros and *The Fountainhead*," pp. 17–21 from *The Velvet Light Trap* 57 (Spring 2006).

David Bordwell, Janet Staiger, and Kristen Thompson's landmark 1987 book *The Classical Hollywood Cinema*, which comprehends Hollywood films as industrial commodities. According to *The Classical Hollywood Cinema*, by the mid-1920s feature filmmaking had evolved from the individualistic enterprise of the early silent era into an industrial system organized on quasi-Fordist principles of mass production. Supervised by an inelastic hierarchy of managers, propelled by a rhythm of technological innovation and standardization, characterized by a coherent set of "ideological signifying practices," and driven to maximize profit, the motion picture industry produced, distributed, and exhibited marginally differentiated commodities for mass consumption.[3] *The Classical Hollywood Cinema* does combine extraordinary attention to film form with its equally impressive analysis of the industrial system. Those perspectives, however, work together because "group style" finally matters insofar as it contributes to the construction of a classical narrative, which, in the last instance, has as its function making a profit.[4] Whatever the distinctions between the mode of production in Detroit and Hollywood, it was the mode of production that mattered. Responsive to the market and changing practices, Hollywood product may have been elegantly varied, but individual films had no more meaning than the stylish tailfin on a Chevrolet or the newest hue of a Frigidaire.

Because meaning is incidental to the mode of production, questions of authorship are just not relevant. Form follows function, not intention. What an owner, manager, or worker wants to do or thinks he or she is doing has little bearing on what is finally done. In defending *The Classical Hollywood Cinema*'s functionalism, Dirk Eitzen seconds the view that in Hollywood "there is a clear discrepancy between the motivations for innovation and the actual causes of change. It was the consequences of inventions that determined their 'success,' and consequences, though they were deliberately sought, could very rarely be fully anticipated."[5] Thus although there were competing innovations by Hollywood practitioners, it was the system, not the individual inventors or even their managers, which determined their success: "The innovations that won out were always those that fit best into the established 'modes' of practice and production" (p. 77). For the functionalist any supposed motive, whether individual or corporate, is a secondary effect of the dynamism of an industrial system that is fundamentally a technology for efficient self-reproduction through profit-maximization.

As applied by followers of *The Classical Hollywood Cinema*, the functionalist model normalizes the complex and peculiar business of making motion pictures by amalgamating the Hollywood studios into an industry, "a group of firms producing products that are close substitutes for each other."[6] Those firms may compete strenuously; or, as in the film industry, they might collectively agree to restrain competition in order to maintain a certain level of prices and restrict entry into the industry. Unlike a corporation, an industry is not a person, which is to say that although it may be incidentally personified (as "Hollywood" regularly is in the pages of *The Classical Hollywood Cinema*) and assigned "wants" or "needs," an industry can actually "want" or "decide" only when firms with shared interests formally establish an association or council, appoint representatives, agree on objectives, collaborate on policies, and hire spokesmen. Journalists at *Variety* in the 1930s could learn what the motion picture industry "thought" by consulting individuals charged to speak on its behalf, such as Will Hays, or by surveying an aggregate, such as the studio heads or the members of the Academy of the Motion Picture Arts and Sciences. They could learn nothing about what the industry wanted, needed, or planned by watching motion pictures. An industry perspective does have the considerable benefit of isolating the common denominators that permit cooperation on technical standards, establishment of conventions of representation, recognition of spheres of influence, and the traffic of personnel among the studios. But looking at Hollywood as a generic industry has the considerable disadvantage of erasing the strategies of individual studios, each of which – oligopolistic agreements notwithstanding – had a distinctive corporate intention that informed the meanings its films communicated to their various audiences. The phrase "MGM wanted" or "Warner Bros. decided" is not shorthand for an aggregate of individual opinions; it is the apt recognition of a corporate "person" capable of strategic intentions and tactical maneuvers, a person who has an achieved social reality and is the bearer of constitutional rights. When Jolson sang, Warner Bros. performed. When the Lion roars, MGM speaks.

When corporate theory is invoked in the landmark multi-volume *History of the American Cinema*, it involves a repudiation of the agency of persons – individuals and corporations – in favor of systemic inexorability. Donald Crafton speaks for the consensus when he asserts, "Symptomatic of the newer academic treatment of sound is the rejection of history told as the exploits of business geniuses or of individual stars, like Jolson. We now see these movers and shakers as cogs in the larger system."[7] In the volume devoted to the Hollywood of the 1930s, Tino Balio identifies two phases in the understanding of the motion picture industry as a corporate enterprise: outmoded accounts of Hollywood as under the virtual control of the Wall Street financiers who owned the studios, and "revisionist" accounts that "rest more or less on contemporary critiques of finance capitalism that focus on corporate hegemony. Robert Sklar," Balio says, "summarized the new thinking when he said that it is not so important 'who owns the movie companies but who manages them.'" Like Bordwell, Staiger, and Thompson, Balio cites as his authority on the "new thinking" Alfred D. Chandler's *Visible Hand*, which

> defined the modern business enterprise as having two specific characteristics: "It contains many distinct operating units and is managed by a hierarchy of salaried executives." Motion-picture firms took on the first characteristic during the teens and the twenties when they integrated both horizontally and vertically. As they grew in size, these firms became managerial, which is to say, they rationalized and organized operations into autonomous departments each headed by a professional manager.[8]

The thinking is neither new nor revisionist. Well before Balio consecrated *Visible Hand* as the foundation on which contemporary histories of Hollywood should build, Martin J. Sklar had argued that Chandler's thesis that the increased efficiency of operation naturally selected large scale, well-coordinated corporations for dominance of the economy echoes the apologies made on behalf of the corporate system in the early years of the century by "pro-corporate partisans," who defended the social dislocation attendant on the rapid transition to a new, highly organized system of industrial production and market control as "simply a matter of submission to 'objective' laws of economic evolution."[9] In that light, the film historians who uncritically take Chandler for gospel do not represent the reality of the corporate revolution; rather, they reproduce highly interested corporate self-representations. The understandable desire of these scholars to legitimate Hollywood historiography has led them to subscribe unwisely to the approach that has predominated in business history among those scholars committed to explain how what is had to be.

The work of a new generation of institutional historians has restored contingency to the account of the corporate revolution. William G. Roy has distilled the terms of the "major underlying debate" among contemporary historians and theorists of the modern corporation: those who insist that "the economy operates according to an economic logic based on efficiency" are opposed by those who are convinced that it "operates according to a social logic based on institutional arrangements, including power."[10] Roy's own case histories of the tissue of decisions made by financiers, entrepreneurs, stockbrokers, and legislators at the turn of the twentieth century seek to explain why, for example, James Duke's American Tobacco Company and not the National Tobacco Works rose to dominance in the cigarette industry. The efficiency of the business organization was rarely decisive in such contests. The success of particular corporations in specific industries was contingent on both the mix and mastery of the actors (entrepreneurs, financiers, legislators, judges) involved and the material and political opportunities available for exploitation. By committing to the efficiency thesis, ignoring both corporate intentions and the realization of those intentions in articulate artifacts, overvaluing technological determination, and undervaluing the studios' strategic exercise of behavioral, structural, and symbolic power, functionalist film scholars typically construct a history of unintended but preordained consequences and tell a story that could have gone no other way. To get the story right, we need to learn how corporate enterprises determined what they wanted, to reconstruct what corporate actors did to get what they needed in order to acquire what they wanted, and to pay close attention to the way in which corporate representations helped achieve corporate objectives.

For anyone interested in what motion pictures mean – what arguments they make, what actions they perform – it is as important to know that *The*

Figure 19.1 Mervyn LeRoy's *Gold Diggers of 1933*: A definitive Warner Bros film with musical sequences directed by Busby Berkeley. Produced by Robert Ward and Jack L. Warner

Gold Diggers of 1933 (1933) is a Warner Bros. film as it is that Mervyn LeRoy and Busby Berkeley directed it. What was distinctive about Berkeley's choreography was adequately imitated in MGM's *Dancing Lady*, which was rushed into production in the summer of 1933 to capitalize on the popularity of Warners' *42nd Street* and which, under David O. Selznick's supervision, did its best to mimic Berkeley's spectacular dance numbers. Yet the commitment to studio identity trumps copycatting for dollars. It would have never occurred to MGM (and therefore to Selznick) to mount a musical that features the commutative chorus rather than an inimitable star. In *Gold Diggers* the leading characters – Polly (Ruby Keeler), who sometimes impersonates Carol; Carol (Joan Blondell), who sometimes impersonates Polly; Trixie (Aline MacMahon), and the aptly named Fay Fortune (Ginger Rogers) – emerge from the chorus as a group still bound by friendship and rivalry. In *Dancing Lady*, Janie Barlow, a burlesque dancer avid for "art," gets her start on Broadway as a member of the chorus, but that's merely a plot point on the royal road of Janie's destiny; there is no evidence that she knows anyone else's name or could be mistaken for any of the other dancers. And when Janie emerges as featured performer, she does it alone and is justified by a star quality that has nothing to do with her singing or dancing ability and everything to do with the fact that she is played by Joan Crawford. MGM showed little respect for directors: when Berkeley went to Metro he lost his style and when LeRoy signed on for more money than any other director in the history of the studio he lost all the dynamism that the raggedy, fast-paced environment of Warners had supplied him. MGM did not worry about directors, but it did worry about stars. It faces down the threat of star insurgency in *Singin' in the Rain* (1952) where one star who aspires to dictate to the studio is destroyed (and all stars both in the film and on the lot warned)

Figure 19.2 Edward G. Robinson in Mervyn LeRoy's *Little Caesar* (Warner Bros/First National, 1931): A film that MGM never could have made. Produced by Hal B. Wallis and Darryl F. Zanuck

by the demonstration *on the screen* of how the studio can exploit its formidable apparatus to synthesize the intra- and extra-diegetic and make a new star right before the eyes of the audience *in* the film and the audience *of* the film. That *Morocco* (1930) was made by Paramount may appear to be a fact of less significance than that Josef Von Sternberg directed and that Marlene Dietrich and Gary Cooper starred in the film – but it seems that way only because *Morocco was* made by Paramount. As a later Paramount motion picture, *Sunset Boulevard* (1950), would argue, in Hollywood only at Paramount were the directors and their stars more important than the studio – a hierarchy that was Paramount's brand identity.

To put the case more stringently, numerous Hollywood films could only have been made by the studios that released them. It is inconceivable that MGM could have made *Little Caesar* (1931) even if L.B. Mayer had both Edward G. Robinson and Mervyn LeRoy under contract. *The Gold Diggers of 1933* (1933) and *Bonnie and Clyde* (1967) are definitive Warner Bros. pictures. Cecil B. de Mille's *Ten Commandments* (Paramount, 1956) is about a sacred text in the Judeo-Christian tradition; it *is* a sacred text in the Paramount canon of brandlore, the set of films that ponder the conception, founding, consolidation, and transformation of the Paramount brand, which includes *The Cheat* (1916), *The Covered Wagon* (1925), *The Virginian* (1929), *Love Me Tonight* (1932), *Christmas in July* (1940), *Road to Utopia* (1946), and *Sunset Boulevard* (1950).[11] If, to entertain an impossibility, *The Philadelphia Story* (MGM, 1940) had been made, scene by scene, shot by shot, star by star, by Warners rather than MGM, the film would mean something entirely different from what it does, because *The Philadelphia Story* as we have it is saturated with Metro's corporate intention to justify the ways of Louis B. Mayer, studio head, to Nick Schenck, the boss of Loew's Inc. Like *The Jazz Singer* (1928), *Gabriel Over the White House* (MGM, 1933), *Bullets or Ballots* (Warners, 1934), *Boys Town* (MGM, 1938), *Pinocchio*

(Disney, 1940), *Mrs Miniver* (MGM, 1942), *Twelve O'Clock High* (Fox, 1949), *The Fountainhead* (Warners, 1949), *Singin' in the Rain* (MGM, 1952), *Psycho* (Shamley, 1960), *Jaws* (Universal, 1975), *Invasion of the Body Snatchers* (UA, 1978), *Batman* (Warners, 1989), *You've Got Mail* (Warners, 1998), and *Minority Report* (Dreamworks, 2002), *The Philadelphia Story* is a strong instance of studio authorship.

To show that certain films are in accord with documented or inferred studio interests would be insufficient evidence to validate the thesis of studio authorship, for that test would ultimately appeal to the judgment of the market. To make the case that Hollywood motion pictures mean and that the studio makes that meaning in order to define its interests and to shape its future depends on the persuasiveness of the prior claim that a corporation can intend. And that depends on what one means by intention. To begin to specify the character of corporate intention, it will be useful to lay out an argument advanced by Noel Carroll on behalf of a theory of interpretation that he calls "moderated actual intentionalism." Carroll initially developed his theory in opposition to Beardsley and Wimsatt's postwar statement of "the intentional fallacy," which Carroll broadly renders as the view that "the realm of art and literature . . . is or should be sufficiently different from other domains of human intercourse so that the difference mandates a different form of interpretation, one in which authorial intent is irrelevant."[12] In his subsequent elaboration of the theory Carroll presupposes agreement that texts, which he also calls "artworks," can only be understood as meaningful and, therefore, subject to interpretation if they have been intended by an author. Carroll's presupposition enfolds my argument to a point: no interpretation without meaning; no meaning without intention; no intention without an author. Carroll does not approve of all intentionalists, however. He repudiates "the most extreme form" of intentionalism, which, he says, "maintains that the meaning of an artwork is fully determined by the actual intentions of the artist (or artists) who created it" – a view that leads to what he refers to as "'Humpty-Dumpty-ism': the idea that an author could make a work mean anything simply because he wills it so." In the name of moderation and the service of common sense, Carroll insists that an author's statement of intention must be supported by the language of the text.

Carroll's chief objective, however, is to contest adherents of "hypothetical intentionalism," who claim that "the correct interpretation or meaning of an artwork is constrained not by the actual intentions of authors (compatible with what they wrote), but by the best hypotheses available about what they intended." The hypothetical intentionalist, Carroll reports, goes so far as to reject the actual writer as a privileged informant in favor of information that would have been publicly available to an ideal reader of the text. Jerrold Levinson, Carroll's chief adversary, explains that hypothetical intentionalism:

> acknowledges the special interests and attendant constraints of the practice or activity of literary communication, according to which works – provided they are interpreted with maximal attention to relevant author-specific context . . . are ultimately more important than, and distinct from, the individuals who author them and those individual's inner lives; works of literature thus retain, in the last analysis, a certain autonomy from the mental processes of their creators during composition at least as far as resultant meaning is concerned. It is this small but crucial dimension of distinctness between agent's meaning and work's meaning . . . which is obliterated by actual intentionalism but safe-guarded by the hypothetical variety (Carroll, 2001: 201–2).

Carroll denies that there is a distinction between the literary work and ordinary communication. For Carroll there is no author who is not (or was not) a conversationalist, that is, someone who could personally explain the meaning of his artwork. Therefore, we ought to seek out the intention of an author with the same interpretive skills that we "deploy constantly in our everyday commerce" by asking the author what he intended or consulting documents in which he says what he intended to mean. Carroll accuses hypothetical intentionalism of being "parasitic on the aims of actual intention." Hypotheses about intentions are never in truth hypotheses about some "author-construction, the postulated author," he argues; they are always hypotheses about the author's actual intentions. Levinson asserts that "the core of utterance meaning can be conceived of analytically as our best appropriately informed projection of an author's intended meaning from our positions as intended interpreters."[13] Carroll asks, "why should we stick with the results of the hypothetical intentionalist's interpretation when a true account of an author's actual intention is available?" "Appropriately informed" should always mean best informed; and best informed means that we should not project an author's intended meaning from our position; we should learn the meaning that the author intended from his or her position. The hypothetical intentionalist has no justification for substituting a "warrantable assertion" for "the truth" when the truth is available by consulting "things like notebooks" that enable the interpreter "to identify the relevant authorial intention correctly" (Carroll, 2001: 202–4).

Despite its serious flaws as a defense of "moderated actual intentionalism," Carroll's strict constructionist critique of the hypothesists is serviceable just so far as it applies to literary and other ordinary texts that *do* have an actual individual author, someone with whom we could imagine conversing. Hollywood motion pictures do not. Any claimant of that status can be effectively contested; at the end of the day, the distributive justice of the credit roll is the only authority that matters.[14] Consequently, most interpretive debates within film studies, whether or not they are explicitly informed by intentionalist commitments, have to do with a "theoretical entity" called an "author-construction." Positions on the authorship of studio films tend to cluster antithetically: at one pole are auteurist accounts which stipulate that some actual individual's contribution, whether director, screenwriter, or producer, qualifies her to be credited as auteur despite her limited participation and control; at the other extreme are materialist accounts that render some mode or means of production, some apparatus, or set of industrial conditions as the functional equivalent of the author. There is, however, a third, more comprehensive alternative: a person who is not actual but who, by warrantable assertion, nonetheless qualifies for the status of the intending author: the corporate studio itself.

By "the corporate studio itself," I include those Hollywood production companies that were incorporated (such as Samuel Goldwyn, Inc. and MGM until the end of the 1930s), those that were the production subsidiaries of larger corporations which included distribution and exhibition companies (Twentieth Century-Fox Film Corporation, RKO Radio Pictures, Inc., Paramount Pictures, Inc.), the one that straddled that distinction (Warner Bros.), and production companies that shared the structure, practices, and objectives of the major studios (Universal Pictures, Selznick International, United Artists after 1950). Organizational commitment to the "concept of the corporation" as "a social institution organizing human efforts to a common end" is decisive in determining studio authorship, not strict adherence to any particular organizational form.[15]

By "corporate studio itself" I also intend to exclude the agents of the corporation, its managers, at least as an ideal type. Managers may be employees of the corporation, but they work on behalf of capital.[16] Managers *qua* managers do not think and decide; they coordinate activities and make operational choices regarding the allocation of resources which respond to market dictates and are calculated in terms of their contribution to the control of production cost.[17] The managerial ideal is frictionless functionality. Managers make the charts that represent the abstract, two-dimensional, technically meaningless world in which they imagine that they efficiently communicate. The ideal corporate communication flowing from upper management down the check-listed ranks does not have the status of a text (literary or ordinary) in Carroll's terms; it more closely approximates the status of his idealized author's notebook: a privileged, transparent, operational statement that requires acceptance not construal.[18] Unlike communications between individuals or between authors and readers, the normative inter-office memo does not mean what the author intends it to mean; it means exactly what it says. To inquire of bosses what they meant here and here and here is to challenge their ability to make their intentions clear and, therefore, to perform their job effectively. The subordinate manager who is interested in keeping his own job and has no designs of toppling his superior does not interpret a memo from his boss, but acts on it.

Now it is not necessary to believe in the truth of that account of corporate communication. It is only necessary to acknowledge that managers *as* managers perform as though it is true – just as book reviewers, in Carroll's account, act as though it is true that authors' statements in conversation or notebooks are transparent accounts of their intentions in order that they may do their job of transmitting those intentions to their readers as meaning itself.[19] Most book reviews appear in newspapers for good reason; their appeal to an author's stated views is what we ordinarily call journalism, not criticism: it involves reporting, not interpreting. Insofar as Carroll's "moderated actual intentionalism," like the managerial flow chart or the compliantly self-editing reviewer, is reflexively responsive to the operational authority of a detected fact, it is not a theory of interpretation at all.

Hypothetical intentionalism is not parasitic on actual intentionalism any more than corporations are parasitic on actual humans. To state the studio authorship thesis in its full extension: no interpretation without meaning, no meaning without intention, no intention without an author, *no author without a person, and no person with greater right to or capacity for authorship than a corporate person.* Unlike the conversational model, which requires the interpreter to acquire her meanings from what humans say about texts, the studio authorship thesis funds a theory of how persons make texts as well as how persons should interpret them.

Hypothetical intentionalism is not parasitic on actual intentionalism because, unlike the conversational model, it is a theory of how texts are made as well as how they should be interpreted. A version of hypothetical intentionalism has a place in the history of organizational theory. Chester I. Barnard urged that the authority to make executive decisions, that is, decisions not ordained by the price mechanism, attaches to that not so ideal type of manager within an organization who effectively constructs himself as the ideal reader of the organization by interpreting its actions in light of a common purpose, not in order to report on that discovery but in order to render his orders as the appropriate means to execute that purpose. Barnard's executive dictates memos to employees in order to communicate his wishes; but he has authority over his subordinates insofar as he persuasively refers his wishes to a common purpose. Success or failure is determined by the recipient of that order, who must decide whether or not to accept its authority by making a similar interpretive move: determining whether the order actually harmonizes with the common purpose of the organization. Although Barnard acknowledges that there is a "zone of indifference," where orders are merely processed, his model of vertical communication within an organization requires of a leader the rhetorical skill to negotiate the boundary between indifference and interest, a skill that must be applied in the full consciousness that every order received by a subordinate is, in principle, the occasion for a crisis of authority, the decision to obey or defy, to stay or leave.[20] Put less abstractly, in terms of the manager in a *business* organization, as Peter F. Drucker does, persuasion becomes marketing, or, if you prefer, rhetoric becomes poesis. That is, in light of the *general* purpose of the business enterprise, as Drucker conceives it, the particular task of persuading subordinates to acknowledge executive authority so that they will obey is most effectively imagined as the creation of a customer who wants to buy what the executive has to sell.[21]

Though published in 1938, Barnard's *The Functions of the Executive* achieved its greatest influence during the postwar era, when, largely due to the American experience during World War 2, the big corporation emerged as something more than a special example of the theory of organizational behavior. The title of Drucker's 1946 *Concept of the Corporation* echoes Barnard's both to suggest a continuity and to indicate the shift that he will execute from the study of organizational behavior to analysis of the corporation as "a social institution organizing human efforts to a common end." The difference that the concept of the corporation made can be clearly seen in important studies published by Phillip Selznick (1957) and Kenneth R. Andrews (1971), which respond to two weaknesses of Barnard's approach: 1) its inattention to the condition of institutionality – that is, what makes organizations hang together despite the formal possibility for dissidence and disobedience; 2) a vagueness about the status and role of what Barnard calls "common purpose" in different kinds of organizations, especially corporations.

Selznick supplemented Barnard's account of organizational behavior with an influential definition of the social character of institutions: "In what is perhaps its most significant meaning, 'to institutionalize,'" he wrote, "is to infuse with value beyond the technical requirements of the task at hand . . . Whenever individuals become attached to an organization or a way of doing things as persons rather than as technicians, the result is a prizing of the device for its own sake."[22] Selznick's version of "attachment" recalls the psychological explanation of organizational identification proposed by Thurman Arnold in *The Folklore of Capitalism* 20 years before. There Arnold had argued that "when men are engaged in any continuous cooperative activity, they develop organizations which acquire habits, disciplines, and morale; these give the organizations unity and cause them to develop something which it is convenient to describe as personality or character."[23] That development is no mere phase, for "once the personality of an organization is fixed, it is as difficult to change as the habits of an individual" (Arnold, 1937: 352). And, as Arnold argues, the personality of the individual *is* at stake in the formation of the personality of the organization, for "organizations which are personified in the mind of the public have the effect of making their members unconsciously submerge their own personalities and adopt the personality of the organization while they are acting as a part of it" (Arnold, 1937: 353).

The difference between Arnold's psychological and Selznick's philosophical explanation is substantial. Selznick's Kantian phrasing effaces Arnold's implications of social and individual neurosis by describing a process that involves a change of perspective among technicians who become persons by treating the device of the corporation as if it were a person and not just a mechanism for making products, profit, and persons. No more than Arnold does Selznick restrict his account of the change in the organization to the kind of organization called a corporation, although neither man would likely have been able to frame his particular account of attachment without the precedent of the naturalization of the device of corporate personhood which occurred in the courts and the legislatures and then in the popular mind during the first two decades of the twentieth century, as the corporate form, once a mechanism for accumulating capital, became a person valued for its own sake.[24] The corporation was not only a person but a person of privilege, endowed with the capacity to make new figures, whether internally through "the conversion of the specialized technician needed in the day to day conduct of business into the well-educated personality capable of judgment who is needed for policy making decisions (Drucker, *Concept*: 14)" or externally by turning loyal citizens into loyal customers. *Those* figures are not valued for their own sake but as personifications (e.g., the "organization man," "the suit," "the Pepsi generation") of the corporation whose economic performance and social prominence they enable. For Drucker the "unconscious" plays no part in either conversion. The process is clarified and given some historical context if we replace "technician" with "actor" and "well-educated personality" (with the emphasis on *personality*) with "star" and simply change "loyal customer" into "fan." Like the Wizard of Oz, the Hollywood studio is a person with the capacity to personify – and the process works no matter how much anyone endeavors to demystify it, no matter who bares the device: in *The Wizard of Oz* it is the skeptical Toto who pulls back the curtain to expose the fraud; in *Singin' in the Rain* it is the head of the studio who gives the nod and pitches in to yank the ropes, draw back the curtain, and display the star-construction. Corporate theory came of age in the postwar era when it discovered in the business enterprise as such the conceptual reach, marketing acumen, and organizational tools that had constituted the culturally transformative prowess of the Hollywood studio since the 1910s.

In the preface to the second edition of *Managing for Results* (1986), Drucker credited his 1964 book with being the "first to address itself to what is now called 'business strategy.' "[25] By 1971, however, Kenneth R. Andrews could say that "business strategy," which defines the "choices of product or service and market of an individual business" had become distinguished from "corporate strategy," which applies to "the whole enterprise." Working with that distinction, Andrews revises Barnard's notion of the "common purpose" in light of the objectives of strategic management in the contemporary corporation. As Andrews defines it, "corporate strategy is the pattern of decisions in a company that determines and reveals its objectives, purposes, or goals, and defines the range of business the company is to pursue, the kind of economic and human organization it is or intends to be and the nature of the economic and non-economic contribution it intends to make to its shareholders, employees, customers, and communities."[26] Intention here emerges as a manager deduces from "decisions observed, what the pattern is and what the company's goals and policies are" (Andrews, 1987: 18). Corporate strategy cannot be referred to any empirical individual such as, say, the writer of a mission statement ("What exactly did you mean by saying our mission was 'the general welfare?' ") or the innovator of a product line ("Does this mean that all our shorts have to be baggy?") or the CEO ("What was the *real* reason we merged with AOL, Mr. Levin?"). Because the "essence of the definition of strategy . . . is *pattern*. . . . it is the unity, coherence, and internal consistency of a company's strategic decisions that position the company in its environment and give the firm its identity, its power to mobilize its strength, and its likelihood of success in the marketplace" (Andrews, 1987: 15). Corporate employees become effective executives insofar as they are able to discern a pattern and, discounting the professed intentions of the actual agent of any particular decision, make a decision consistent with the operant intention.

Andrews' corporate executive is an *actor* who interprets a set of decisions as establishing the character of the organization, which he impersonates in order to make a decision that will accomplish corporate objectives and do so as if the corporation, not he, were the author of that strategy. Impersonation is the norm for successful performance in the corporation as, Barry King argues, it is in the theater and motion pictures:

> The actor's intention to portray a specific character in a specific way may seem at first sight, and the case of a leading actor is often so represented, to correspond to authorship conceived as the creative principle of the fixed, delimited text. But the process of character representation through impersonation entails that the actor should strive to obliterate his or her sense of identity in order to become a signifier for the intentionality inscribed in character. Such obliteration returns the project of intentionality to the level of the narrative itself which is usually "authored" reductively in terms of the director's or playwright's "vision," rather than as a meaning emergent from a collective act of representation. The full participation of the actor in the narrative as character thereby depends upon the suppression of the literary conception of the author.[27]

If we substitute "corporation" for "character" and "strategy" for "narrative," we are on firm ground making our conversion. It's when we get to the reduction that things get sticky. There is no question that such reduction occurs in all kinds of corporations: Ken Lay becomes the man with the vision for Enron, Gerald Levin for Time-Warner. Both men were gifted actors who had seized the opportunity to impersonate corporate intention; both cultivated a *reputation* for vision that reduced them to personifications of the company they led: the CEO as star. Eventually that status as personification became an alibi for each man when the strategy pursued by his company ended in disaster.

The template for that corporate device was the career of Irving Thalberg, whose pre-eminence at MGM was owed both to the unparalleled success of the motion pictures the studio produced under his supervision and to his decision *not* to take credit for any of the motion pictures that he produced. That willed anonymity was read by *Fortune* (as it had already been read by Hollywood) as Thalberg's preternaturally effective impersonation of the corporate intention in his work as vice-president of production even as he raised MGM to pre-eminence by attributing authorship to the studio. Of course, *Fortune*'s project was to pull the veil aside and bare the device by which Thalberg lost himself in the part of the studio; but as always at MGM, baring the device does not mean demystification, for although Thalberg is pressed into service as the personification of the studio that is the personification of Hollywood, in certifying Thalberg as the genius he has been called, *Fortune* renders him as the personification of the essential mystification that Hollywood, that corporate art, is and, not incidentally, the magazine makes Thalberg the first star executive in Hollywood and, arguably, in corporate America. *Fortune* never exactly called Thalberg a "star" – it took F. Scott Fitzgerald to do that – but the star-making machinery that would be applied to Alfred P. Sloan of General Motors, Joseph P. Kennedy of the US Maritime Commission, and Benito Mussolini of Italy was fabricated in its first profile of a Hollywood studio.

Neither the corporation nor the executive, MGM or Thalberg, is the actual author of the motion pictures that played in Loew's theaters. *There is no actual author*. And because there is none, the corporate intention cannot possibly be recovered from notebooks or minutes. In objecting to the "fictional" aspect of the implied author in Levinson's model, Carroll complains, "It is difficult to see how this theoretical construct could really explain the features of a text, since this theoretical construct could not have causally influenced the text in any way" (Carroll, 2001: 206). Yet that does not make sense for corporations. Whatever one's point of view on the merits of or limits to corporate personhood, no one has seriously doubted that the theoretical construct called the corporate person has causally influenced work of all kinds. At a more local level, consider a scene in which a writer, balked in the course of composition, asks herself, "what does all this mean?" She may look through her notes and drafts but not to search out a note that says, "I intend this." She is trying to discern a pattern in the decisions that she has made during the process of composition. The "I" that is the subject of her question can only be hypothesized; and if the hypothesis causally influences the making of the artwork, it is because the writer has been able successfully to impersonate the shaping intention of the work.

Let's look at an actual person, R. S. Crane – a theorist from the postwar era of corporate hegemony and an adversary of Beardsley and Wimsatt on the intentionalism front. Crane begins one of his essays with a short reflection on the process of his own writing, which, despite ample preparation, does not proceed with ease unless he is directed by a "synthesizing idea." Crane's account of how this works is worth quotation:

> As a conception my idea may be tight or loose, complex or simple; I call it a shaping cause for the very good reason that, once such a principle has come to me for a particular essay, it generates consequences and problems in the detailed working out of my subject which I cannot well escape so long as I remain committed to writing the essay as I see it ought to be written. It exerts, that is, a kind of impersonal and objective power, which is at once compulsive and suggestive, over everything I attempt to do, until in the end I come out with a composition which, if my execution has been adequate, is quite distinct, as an ordered whole, from anything I myself completely intended or foresaw when I began to write, so that afterwards I sometimes wonder, even when I applaud, how I could ever have come to say what I have said.[28]

We can certainly see the lineaments, if not the visage, of hypothetical intentionalism in this bit of self-illumination. It does some violence to Crane to translate his 1953 account of a person's commitment to an "impersonal and objective power" to a generalization about the corporate studio, but it is the right violence to do. For Crane's "conception" of an impersonal, generative principle or "shaping cause" is what Drucker had in mind when, in 1946, he annunciated pax corporate America by promoting the "concept of the corporation" as "the dynamic element" of American society, the "symbol through which the facts are organized in a social pattern." Drucker might have anticipated that thoughtful people in the 1950s would have "intuitions" like Crane's in a society whose "representative institution" is the corporation, "which sets the standard for the way of life and the mode of living of our citizens; which leads, molds and directs; which determines our perspective on our own society" (Drucker, *Concept*: 6–8). Crane departs from the model of studio authorship by relying on a hit or miss intuition caused by an impersonal power. The impersonal person of the corporation is so organized that conceptions and decisions can be routinely generated by managerial technique.[29] When intuition hits it causes Crane to commit himself to an inescapable compulsion, but making movies cannot wait on intuition. The motion picture studio is so organized that to make movies filmmakers must impersonate a studio intention often unarticulated by any executive at the studio and then (here it goes the theater one better) *act* as if they are lost in the part. The motion picture studio is so organized that it remains the representative corporation in a society where the corporation is the representative institution, for in pursuing its own individual objectives the Hollywood studio equips its customers as no other business does with the tools to thrive if not in an actual corporation then in a society that inescapably labors under the concept of the corporation.

The tasks that follow from the studio authorship thesis are threefold: (1) to discern the pattern of studio productions that define its identity, represent its objectives, and that endeavor to achieve those objectives; (2) to account for how the corporate intention was realized in individual motion pictures within the organizational hierarchy; and (3) to contribute to the debate regarding "The New Hollywood," especially regarding the effects of changes in the entertainment industry since the breakup of the studio system in the 1950s and 1960s on the social character, the system of representation, and the strategic aspirations of Hollywood studios.[30] We should look at movies, study the companies that made them, and ask whether the concept of the studio developed in the classical era and "the concept of the corporation" formulated by Drucker and others in the postwar era are still compatible and, if so, whether they are still pertinent in the globalized digital economy of the twenty-first century. A useful hypothesis might be that insofar as corporations increasingly understand their objectives in terms of a marketing paradigm and as long as that marketing paradigm depends on a traffic in identities (which make persons who become actors by becoming customers), the concept of the studio will remain vital to the success of corporate art.

Notes

1 *Fortune* (6 December 1932); in *The American Film Industry*, ed. Tino Balio (Madison: University of Wisconsin Press, 1976), p. 263.

2 Richard Maltby, "'Nobody Knows Everything': Post-Classical Historiographies and Consolidated Entertainment," in Steve Neale and Murray Smith (eds.), *Contemporary Hollywood Cinema* (London: Routledge, 1998), pp. 25–6.

3 David Bordwell, Janet Staiger, and Kristin Thompson, *The Classical Hollywood Cinema: Film Style and Mode of Production to 1960* (New York: Columbia University Press, 1985).

4 Elizabeth Cowie, "Storytelling: Classical Hollywood Cinema and Classical Narrative," *Contemporary Hollywood Cinema*, p. 180.

5 Dirk Eitzen, "Evolution, Functionalism, and the Study of the American Cinema," *Velvet Light Trap*, no. 28 (Fall 1991), p. 76.

6 M.E. Porter, *Competitive Strategy* (New York: Free Press, 1980), p. 5. Quoted in Arnold Windeler, "Project Networks and Changing Industry Practices – Collaborative Content Production in the German Television Industry," *Organization Studies* (November 2001), n.p.

7 Donald Crafton, *The Talkie: American Cinema's Transition to Sound, 1926–1931*; Vol. 4 of *History of the American Cinema* (Berkeley: University of California Press, 1997), p. 5.

8 Tino Balio, *The Grand Design: Hollywood as a Modern Business Enterprise, 1930–1939*; vol. 5 of *History of the American Cinema* (Berkeley: University of California Press, 1993), pp. 25–6.

9 Martin J. Sklar, *The Corporate Reconstruction of American Capitalism, 1890–1916* (Cambridge: Cambridge University Press, 1988), p. 12.

10 William Roy, *Socializing Capital: The Rise of the Large Industrial Corporation in America* (Princeton NJ: Princeton University Press, 1997), p. 6. See also Charles Perrow, *Organizing America: Wealth, Power, and the Origins of Corporate Capitalism* (Princeton: Princeton University Press, 2002).

11 See Jared Gardner, "Covered Wagons and Decalogues: Paramount's Myths of Origins," *Yale Journal of Criticism* 13, no. 2 (Fall 2000), pp. 361–89; Paul Grainge, "Branding Hollywood: Studio Logos and the Aesthetics of Memory and Hype," *Screen* 45, no.4 (Winter 2004), pp. 354–60.

12 Noel Carroll, "Art, Intention, and Conversation," *Beyond Aesthetics: Philosophical Essays* (Cambridge: Cambridge University Press, 2001), pp. 157–8. Tellingly, Carroll gets "The Intentional Fallacy" wrong. A better, though still inadequate, statement of the purpose of the essay would be that "the realm of poetry is or should be segregated from personal expression so that the poem can be objectively evaluated."

13 Jerrold Levinson, *The Pleasures of Aesthetics: Philosophical Essays* (Ithaca: Cornell University Press, 1996), p. 178.

14 Carroll invokes as evidence for his argument a moment at the end of the motion picture *Stand By Me* (1986), where it is difficult to tell whether a computer has been turned off accidentally or deliberately. Starkly different interpretations of the conclusion follow from each option. Carroll suspects that "most viewers would be loath to commend the producers of *Stand By Me* if it turned out they just didn't know what they were doing. But if we discovered, perhaps by asking them, that they did make the relevant scene with the exorcism interpretation in mind, the modest actual intentionalist would be happy . . ." (Carroll, 2001: 210). Carroll does not clarify who the "producers of *Stand By Me*" are, those who are given screen credit as producers, according to Hollywood convention, or those who actually had a hand in the artistic production of the film. And if he would prefer the latter, would he be happy with a few producers, say, the director and maybe the screenwriter, or might he not feel compelled to poll all the producers, of the film: the assistant director responsible for monitoring activity on the set or all prop men who might have had occasion to touch the computer? If there is problem enough in identifying the actual producers of the film, deciding on a protocol to adjudicate different claims for responsibility would be seriously complicated. Would the producers be asked in a group or separately? Could we really expect any producer to confess to an accident? Would unanimous agreement be necessary or only agreement by a majority? Carroll's example actually shows that whatever one thinks of the merit of moderate actual intentionalism as an interpretive protocol for novels and poems, it cannot be applied to motion pictures with anything approaching the confidence his theory requires.

15 Peter F. Drucker, *Concept of the Corporation* (New York: John Day, 1946), p. 12.

16 Janet Staiger approvingly quotes this definition of managers proposed by Antony Cutler, Barry Hindess, Paul Hirst, and Athar Hussain: "managers are economic agents employed to exercise the capacity of direction of behalf of a capital" [sic], *Classical Hollywood Cinema,* p. 93. The definition is notable for its substitution of "capital" for "stockholders."

17 The best studio representation (or caricature) of the ideal type of the modern manager is the character of Loren Shaw (Fredric March), the bean-counting Machiavelli who is the comptroller of the Tredway Corporation in MGM's *Executive Suite* (1954).

18 A view of the memorandum in the large-scale business organization proposed by JoAnne Yates, "The Emergence of the

Memo as a Managerial Genre," *Management Communication Quarterly* 2 (May 1989), pp. 485–510. John Guillory discusses Yates's thesis in the context of modernity's suspicion of the motive of persuasion in "The Memo and Modernity," in *Critical Inquiry* 31 (Autumn 2004), pp. 114–22.

19 For an account based on intensive fieldwork of the way information actually moves up and down the corporate hierarchy and the way authority is personalized in corporate bureaucracies, see Robert Jackall, *Moral Mazes: The World of Corporate Managers* (New York: Oxford University Press, 1988), pp. 17–40.

20 Chester I. Barnard, *The Functions of the Executive* (1938; rpt., Cambridge: Harvard University Press, 1968), pp. 165–84. For a later, influential examination of the reasons some employees (and customers) stay and some go, see Albert O. Hirschman, *Exit, Voice, and Loyalty: Responses to Decline in Firms, Organizations, and States* (Cambridge, MA: Harvard University Press, 1970).

21 Peter F. Drucker, *The Practice of Management* (1954; rpt., New York: Harper Business, 1993), p. 37.

22 Quoted in Henry Mintzberg and James Brian Quinn, *The Strategy Process: Concepts, Contexts, Cases* (Englewood Cliffs, NJ: Prentice Hall, 1991), p. 39.

23 Thurman Arnold, *The Folklore of Capitalism* (New Haven: Yale University Press, 1937), p. 350.

24 See Roland Marchand's formidable *Creating the Corporate Soul: The Rise of Public Relations and Corporate Imagery in American Business* (Berkeley: University of California Press, 1998). The legal literature on corporate personhood is immense, and a review of its development is beyond the scope of this chapter. A good, brief summary of the theories of corporate personhood appears in the note "Constitutional Rights of the Corporate Person," *Yale Law School Journal* 91, no. 8 (July, 1982), pp. 1641–58, which divides the dominant theories into three categories: (1) the fiction theory, which takes the position that the corporation "exists as a person only because it is recognized by the law, and it is granted standing in the court only because it has been brought into being by the state"; (2) the contract theory, which regards the corporation "as a product of contractual agreement"; and (3) realism, which asserts that "the law does not create its own subjects . . .; rather, it is forced to recognize the extra-legal existence of certain 'persons' – some natural, others not" (pp. 1645–9). This paper shares the twin foci that the note suggests: "first, the notion that a corporation, like all complex organizations, should be understood not as an object, but as a set of role relations, and, second, the observation that in any particular relation, the corporation, unlike a natural person, must be represented by an agent" (p. 1652). It should be added that as a matter of practice that view can only be maintained in full recognition that the other theories, especially realism, have long held and continue to hold sway in the courts, business literature, and the public imagination.

25 Peter R. Drucker, *Managing for Results* (1964; rpt., New York: Harper and Row, 1986), vii.

26 Kenneth R. Andrews, *The Concept of Corporate Strategy* (1971; 3rd edn., Homewood IL: Irwin, 1987), p. 13.

27 Barry King, "Articulating Stardom," *Screen* 26, no. 5 (September-October, 1985), p. 31.

28 R.S. Crane, "Towards a More Adequate Criticism of Poetic Structure," in *The Languages of Criticism and the Structure of Poetry* (Toronto: Toronto University Press, 1953), pp. 141–2.

29 With space, the illustration drawn from Crane could be complemented by a more self-conscious example of corporate theory from 1953: Dowling Productions' remarkable *Donovan's Brain*. That picture radically departs from its source, Robert Siodmak's novel, and earlier adaptations to explore with unprecedented incisiveness the thematics of the corporate takeover, represented as a scientist's ability to communicate with and be directed by the brain of a rapacious corporate executive, which has been extracted from the dying man's body. *Donovan's Brain* anticipates less the polyvalent *Invasion of the Body Snatchers*, directed by Don Siegel in 1956 for Walter Wanger Productions than the aggressively anti-corporate allegory of *The Invasion of the Body Snatchers* of 1978, directed by Philip Kaufman in spite of United Artists and its parent, the Transamerica Corporation.

30 For examples, see the numerous superb essays on the New Hollywood collected in Steve Neale and Murray Smith (eds.), *Contemporary Hollywood Cinema* (London: Routledge, 1998) and Jon Lewis (ed.), *The New American Cinema* (Durham: Duke University Press, 1998).

20

The Producer as Auteur

Matthew Bernstein

Matthew Bernstein is Chair of the Department of Film Studies at Emory University in Atlanta, GA. A film historian, he has approached Hollywood history from a number of critical perspectives, including genre, authorship, studio, censorship, race, reception, and ideology. Bernstein's book *Walter Wanger, Hollywood Professional* is a significant study of a producer and the producer-function within Hollywood, and an important corrective to the general view of producers merely as crass money-men. In this essay, Bernstein considers the role of the producer in both the classic studio system and in contemporary Hollywood and discusses the collaborative authorship of a number of important producers.

Can a film producer be an auteur? On its face, the question seems preposterous. After all, a central axiom of the auteur "theory" in its original form was that great directors made great films by overcoming the Hollywood classical studio system's impersonal machinery of filmmaking for the masses. Andrew Sarris famously wrote that "the auteur theory values the personality of a director precisely because of the barriers to its expression" and that the auteur "would not be worth bothering with if he were not capable now and then of a sublimity of expression almost miraculously extracted from his money-oriented environment."[1]

If any one individual could be said to embody that impersonality, those barriers, that money-oriented environment, it was the film producer. If any one person could be accused of insisting that a film's storyline, characterization, and plot development be generic, it was the producer. If anyone demanded that principal photography be completed on time and under budget, no matter how exhilarating or gracious the long take could be, it was the producer. If a studio denied the director the right of final cut, it was the producer who wrestled the film out of the director's hands.

On this view, the producer represented the economic, profit-seeking basis of the studio system, its fundamental rationale. Screenwriter extraordinaire Ben Hecht remarked late in his career that "The producer is sort of a bank guard. He's there to protect the bankroll. His objective is to see that nothing is put on the screen that people are going to dislike. This means practically 99 per cent of literature, thinking, probings of all problems."[2] To quote Tom Wilkinson's character of Hugh Fennyman in *Shakespeare in Love*, the producer is "the money." The producer could not possibly have any artistry or vision to express. Producers are managers, supervisors; they are all about the bottom line.

Certainly, a cursory look at Hollywood history supports this view. The film producer arose when American filmmaking made the transition from short films to more expensive and elaborate features. Following the model of Thomas Ince in the mid-teens, studio producers devised a system to keep track of a

Matthew Bernstein, "The Producer as Auteur." New contribution.

film's progress – in terms of schedule and budget – during production. The film producer in the studio era was a middle manager, an administrator.[3] By the 1920s, Hollywood was full of stories in which studio executives or producers took films from directors before the films were complete. Irving Thalberg grabbed Erich von Stroheim's films at Universal (*Foolish Wives*, 1922, and *Merry-Go-Round*, 1923), and at MGM (*Greed*, 1924), and cut them down dramatically. MGM destroyed Buster Keaton's career when he moved there from his own independent company during the transition to sound by imposing strict screenwriting policies and procedures on a gag-based artist. David O. Selznick fired George Cukor after a few weeks of shooting began on *Gone with the Wind* (1939), and replaced him with Victor Fleming. Selznick peppered Alfred Hitchcock with so many production memos in the early 1940s that Hitchcock quipped 20 years later that he was still reading one of them. The RKO powers that be mangled Orson Welles's *The Magnificent Ambersons* (1942) and Hollywood in general, destroyed his career.[4] Darryl F. Zanuck, the head of production at Twentieth Century Fox, told master director Jean Renoir that his work so far on *Swamp Water* (1941) had "too much background," too many dolly shots, too many camera angles and too much improvising on the set; Zanuck concluded, "I am behind you and I am going to see you through on the picture – but, by the same token, I expect you to play ball my way."[5]

Whether it was playing ball or (as Orson Welles had it) playing with a train set, the producer had the final say. Joel Siegel, writing the most in-depth study of the making of RKO producer Val Lewton's horror films eleven years after Sarris's "Notes on the Auteur Theory in 1962," expresses this point of view perfectly:

> Although something of an over-simplification . . . the art went out of Hollywood when producers began to appear. The producer, in charge of the film's economics and logistics, was usually a money-man, pure and simple, an overseer of the artists who took his orders from the bankers. . . . It is generally nonsensical to speak of producers as creators when, in all but a few cases, they were the enemies of creation.[6]

Sarris wrote that "Ideally the strongest personality should be the director, and it is when the director dominates the film that the cinema comes closest to reflecting the personality of a single artist."[7] The problem was that producers were the strongest personalities on any project and their energies were directed to the bottom line.

From this perspective, the only producer-auteurs who could possibly exist were the screenwriters and directors who added the producer's hat to their portfolio, such as Frank Capra, William Wyler, and George Stevens in the mid-1940s; Alfred Hitchcock in the late 1940s after his contract with David O. Selznick expired; and Billy Wilder in the 1950s. Or the producer-auteur may take the form of an actor with a producing company; while this phenomenon began in the 1940s as a dodge for punishing income tax rates, it also gave many actors great freedom after being under studio contracts for seven years and longer (James Cagney, Kirk Douglas, Burt Lancaster, and many more). Whatever their past careers, such creative talents became their own producers precisely to overcome the obstacles to personal expression which producers represented as representatives of the studio system. However, the existence of these screenwriter-director-star-producers, and their fine work, sidesteps the question of whether a producer could be an auteur.

The answer to the question is "rarely." An individual producer on certain films could be an auteur, because he (and it was usually a he) provided a strong personal vision that informed the film's conception, scripting, direction and editing. It is fair to say that the classic monster film *King Kong* (1933), so central to American twentieth-century popular culture and the public's imaginary, was producer and co-director Merian C. Cooper's brainchild. Cooper had something of a lifelong obsession with gorillas and was a war veteran and world traveler. He had previously co-directed with Ernest Schoedsack a number of feature documentaries inspired by *Nanook of the North* (1922), including *Grass* (1925) and *Chang* (1927). He had been an associate producer and executive assistant to David O. Selznick at RKO before he became head of production after Selznick left for MGM. While Cooper developed the idea for *King Kong* before assuming that post, his authority enabled him to follow through on the project. After supervising the script, Cooper collaborated on the direction again with Schoedsack to create this autobiographical tale of a movie director who seeks adventure (as Cooper had) in remote parts of the world (as Cooper and Schoedsack had) in the form of capturing a giant ape. As Cooper's case shows, production executives functioned on occasion as auteurs, and at times made extremely personal works. Certainly, there is a strong connection between the Cooper-Schoedsack documentaries, *King Kong* and their other exotic adventure films, such as *The Most Dangerous Game* (1932).[8] In the strictest sense, this barely makes Cooper an auteur at all – since one major principle of the auteur theory as Andrew Sarris expressed it was the ability of the critic to discern a skill, a personal style and a core of interior meaning in a body of work. Moreover, Cooper the producer-co-director of *King Kong* could also be classified as another multi-hyphenate producer. Being a studio head enabled Cooper to ensure that the film was made, but does not account for the possible connections among the films he co-directed. David O. Selznick, Cooper's predecessor at RKO, is most famous for his independent productions, especially the blockbuster *Gone with the Wind*. Selznick chose to work as an independent so he could lavish his attention on each film he produced, something not possible at the major studios, which in the 1930s cranked out many, many films each year. As an independent, Selznick was completely in charge of the films he produced. "Selznick's idea of collaboration," Rudy Behlmer has stated, "was to hire first-rate talent, extract certain attributes from that talent, and mold them to suit his vision."[9]

Selznick believed in supervising every detail of production or substituting his own writing and visualization ideas for those of the directors he hired. On *Gone with the Wind*, he launched an infamous talent search for the actress to play Scarlett O'Hara, a brilliant publicity stunt. He centrally contributed to the many, many script drafts for the film secured from different writers, rewriting their efforts as he saw fit. He fired George Cukor and hired Victor Fleming weeks into shooting. He closely supervised the editing and post-production of the film. He was intimately involved in planning the film's marketing via distributor MGM and even had directions for projectionists for the film's showing. Selznick went so far as to crystallize a new type of creative Hollywood technician, the Production Designer, to account for William Cameron Menzies' contributions to the look of the Civil War epic.[10] Certainly, Selznick struggled with other directors on certain projects (most notably and productively Alfred Hitchcock on *Rebecca*, 1940), and he has been accused of meddling in director's work (and in fact being a frustrated screenwriter-director). Still, *Gone with the Wind* was the film he wanted to create. We can find continuities in the thematics of Selznick's films – what Thomas Schatz calls a fondness for "sentimental dramas with forceful heroines, relatively heavy themes, and lavish production values," which Selznick shared with director George Cukor, as seen in such films as *A Bill of Divorcement* (1932), *What Price Hollywood?* (1932), and *Little Women* (1933).[11] But since Selznick so constantly adapted works of literature, he might be comparable to the tradition of quality directors whom Truffaut denounced in his original formulation of *la politique des auteurs*. In addition, in spite of being an early champion of Technicolor, Selznick did not have an appreciably distinctive visual style, apart from his films' high production values, evident again in *Duel in the Sun* (1946), another Technicolor epic Selznick fussed over. His films reserve major stylistic flourishes for moments of great drama, such as the celebrated crane shot rising on the war-wounded lying in downtown Atlanta. Moreover, while most historians have been content to claim *Gone with the Wind* as Selznick's creation, Michael Sragow's forthcoming biography of Victor Fleming, who shot the majority of the footage of the nearly four-hour film, makes the case for Fleming's important contributions to the film in terms of sensibility and visual style.

Merian C. Cooper and David O. Selznick demonstrate how close a producer could come to being considered an auteur for single projects within the classical studio system, whether employed by a major studio or running his own production company. Val Lewton, a protégé of Selznick's, provides the best example of the producer as auteur within the terms of the original auteur theory. Lewton's low-budget horror series for RKO in the first half of the 1940s – including *Cat People* (1942), *I Walked with a Zombie* and *The Leopard Man* (both 1943), *The Curse of the Cat People* (1944), *The Body Snatcher* (1945), and *Bedlam* (1946) – were realized with three different directors (Mark Robson, Jacques Tourner, and Robert Wise) and multiple screenwriters. Lewton famously was restricted to budgets of $150,000, and he had to

Figure 20.1 *Cat People* (1942), directed by Jacques Tourneur, was one of producer-auteur Val Lewton's low-budget horror films made for RKO

work with film titles that studio heads had market-tested, regardless of the film's storyline. By all accounts, Lewton had an unusual amount of freedom to make the first film, *Cat People*, according to his taste, in part because his unit was to turn out such low-budget genre films that no member of the RKO studio brass would pay much attention to his productions.[12] That film's success only affirmed Lewton's right to autonomy within the studio.

Lewton, who had written several novels before entering the film industry, often created original storylines and was heavily involved in script revisions. In fact, he usually drafted the final shooting script. Lewton's staff have recounted how Lewton rewrote scripts but used a pseudonym to avoid the appearance of a conflict of interest (that he would rewrite others' work to gain that credit only, rather than in the interests of creating the best possible film). When forced to take a credit late during his sojourn at RKO, he used a favorite nom de plume, Carlos Keith. In fact, Lewton referred to himself as a "writer-producer." Lewton biographer and critic Joel Siegel writes: "It would be grossly unfair to conclude that Lewton's writers did not make important contributions to his films, but a look at the subsequent credits of those writers will show that none ever managed to match the quality of the work he did for Lewton."[13]

But insofar as auteur-ship relies on a discernible pattern of meaning and style, Lewton's films fit the bill. Critically, the Lewton horror films have been praised for what Siegel describes as "their attention to detail, their unusually literate screenplays, their skilful, suggestive use of shadow and sound."[14] The Lewton films represented an innovative form of horror that relied less on on-screen monsters such as Universal's Frankenstein and Dracula and more on evoking the psychological fears of the characters, who were in turn more roundly conceived than typical horror victims like the stereotypical little girl who befriends the monster in *Frankenstein* (1931). At their best, the Lewton horror films created a sense of dread that was heightened not only by character development but also by low-key lighting and off-screen threats signaled only by sound effects, such as the footsteps at night as Alice (Jane Randolph) walks through Central Park in *Cat People.*

The same could be said for Walt Disney, who led a struggling independent production company from the 1920s through the 1950s. Disney himself stopped actively animating films after 1928's *Steamboat Willie*, but as the head of his own small company, he was closely involved in creative decisions on his films, and closely supervised the work on film storylines and character designs. Clearly, the classic Disney films had extraordinary techniques, a discernible and clear visual style, and a core of interior meanings that remain associated with the company to this day.

Cooper, Selznick, Lewton, and Disney may have been exceptional among studio producers, but their examples demonstrate that some major studio producers under certain conditions could be seen as auteurs in the studio era – in Lewton and Disney's case imposing a world view and a distinctive style across a series of films comparable to that of Howard Hawks, Alfred Hitchcock, or John Ford. But such producers were exceedingly rare in classical era Hollywood.

Rethinking the Producer as Auteur

Another way of thinking about the question of whether or not producers can be auteurs is to reframe the question. In the 1980s, several Hollywood historians complicated Sarris's conception of the auteur as an artistic visionary who produces art in a commercial system. In some ways, this could be compared to the move from auteurism in its original highly romantic formulation to auteur-structuralism, a means of decentering the individual artist in critical and historical thinking.[15] Robert Carringer concluded from his comprehensive study *The Making of "Citizen Kane"* that collaboration better defines Hollywood artistry than auteur-ship. As Carringer writes in the preface to his book, "By *collaborative process* I mean the sharing of the creative functions by the director with others. A collaborator, in the most general sense of the term, is anyone who makes a distinguishable contribution to a film . . ."[16] Having surveyed Welles's pre-*Kane*, unrealized project *Heart of Darkness* and his succeeding film *The Magnificent Ambersons*, Carringer was ready to draw some additional conclusions. Where Orson Welles had commented to Carringer that "Collaborators make contributions, but only a director can make a film. He is the one element in the formula that cannot be sacrificed," Carringer added a "corollary" in his volume's very last sentences:

> The quality of a film is partly a measure of the quality of its collaborative talents. On *Citizen Kane*, Welles was fortunate to have collaborators ideally suited to his temperament and working methods and capable of performing at his level of ambition. From the evidence of *Heart of Darkness* and *The Magnificent Ambersons* and the rest of Welles's career, I am willing to go further: had it not been for this particular combination, we might not have *Citizen Kane* at all.[17]

The notion of collaboration provides a different way of thinking about the producer's role in Hollywood. While the work of Cooper, Selznick, and Lewton remains undiminished, the concept of collaboration enables us to think about the ways producers contribute to filmmaking in less traditionally creative terms.

Carringer's study also told us a great deal about the systematic nature of classic era studio production via the author's exploration of how RKO's art department worked, and how scripts were customarily developed at the studio. (Carringer duly noted early in this volume that "it should be stated unequivocally for the historical record that without Schaefer's gamble and continued trust in his own instincts on Welles, *Citizen Kane* would never have been possible.")[18] Yet *Citizen Kane* was hardly the typical film for illustrating the workings of the classic era studio system, particularly since Welles was given considerable creative freedom at the studio. Janet Staiger's study of the division of labor in Hollywood provides a more far-reaching look at how, on a regular basis, producers, stars, directors, screenwriters, and all technicians worked in Hollywood's heyday, from 1917 to 1960.[19] She and other scholars have helped us understand what producers actually do, which might also help us think about how producers could be constructive forces in the making of a film.

Most notably, Thomas Schatz built upon Staiger's study of Hollywood's division of labor to accord classical era studio production executives and producers a creativity that was unthinkable in Sarris's formulation. Examining the workings of MGM, Universal, Warner

Bros., and David O. Selznick, Schatz calls these men "the most misunderstood and undervalued figures in American film history."[20] While Carringer focused on collaboration in the strictly creative aspects of *Citizen Kane*, Schatz's influential argument is that Hollywood's studio era flourished when a balance of forces (commercial and artistic) and skills (those of the above and below the line talents) were put to work on particular film projects in a system that balanced competing pressures. Responding to Carringer's notion of "collaboration," Schatz wrote that: "studio filmmaking was less a process of collaboration than of negotiation and struggle – occasionally approaching armed conflict," a system that worked beautifully when no one force or pressure overpowered another.[21] In deploying their authority at the studio, production executives and producers could ensure that the system worked, helping screenwriters, directors, and stars realize their most powerful and popular screen creations. In this view, the producer could of course interfere with an auteur's work, but actually functioned to facilitate it.

Like Carringer, Schatz argues that auteur theory is wrong to emphasize particular individuals in the creation of outstanding films: "isolating the producer or anyone else as artist or visionary gets us nowhere." Instead, Schatz argues,

> The quality and artistry of all these films were the product not simply of individual human expression, but of a melding of institutional forces. In each case the "style" of a writer, director, star – or even a cinematographer, art director, or costume designer – fused with the studio's production operations and management structure, its resources and talent pool, its narrative traditions and market strategy. And ultimately any individual's style was no more than an inflection on an established studio style.[22]

While traditional auteurists dismiss Schatz's formulation, it is undeniably useful in any effort to understand who producers were and what they did. The studio production heads, often holding the title Vice President in charge of production, included the likes of Irving Thalberg through 1932 at MGM, and Darryl F. Zanuck at Warner Bros. through 1933, then at Twentieth Century Fox from 1935 until the mid-1950s. These men were solely responsible for the company's entire filmmaking slate – choosing properties, casts, talents, and technicians within the budget handed them by the New York office. Zanuck entered the film industry as a gag man and then screenwriter for Warner Bros.' *Rin Tin Tin* movies in the 1920s. As he rose through the ranks, he became closely involved in all aspects of the filmmaking process at Warner Bros. in the early 1930s, helping that studio formulate its house style of fast-paced, urban, low-budget realism, as evidenced in such films as *I am a Fugitive from a Chain Gang*, *The Public Enemy*, and *Little Caesar* (all 1931), as well as the early Busby Berkeley musicals. His successor, Hal Wallis, likewise provided key supervision to the studio's major films, such as *The Adventures of Robin Hood* (1938). Wallis famously contributed Humphrey Bogart's final line to Claude Rains in *Casablanca* (1942), "Louis, I think this is the beginning of a beautiful friendship," helping to seal the closure on a film whose ending had been in doubt during production.

Zanuck's involvement in supervising filmmaking at Twentieth Century Fox was as close as a studio executive could come to auteur status without actually doing so. He held extensive script conferences, often dictating changes in plot and characterization and inserting possible dialogue which he felt would make the film more effective. He insisted on quick-moving action, and if need be, he would personally recut the films. In fact, screenwriter-producer Nunnally Johnson once called Zanuck "the greatest editor of movies, the greatest editor of scripts" in Hollywood, and praised his absolute insistence on getting a script set first.[23] Zanuck's personal involvement ensured that the studio followed production policy that distinguished it from the other filmmaking companies: a program of unabashed Americana, creating historical comedies, musicals and dramas tinged with nostalgia – *Coney Island* (1943), *Alexander's Ragtime Band*, and *In Old Chicago* (both 1938). While Zanuck had made a major contribution to the creation of Warner Bros.' early 1930s gritty style and hard-hitting social problem and gangster films, at his own studio Zanuck only occasionally ventured into controversial or topical films which he nurtured while a production executive at Warner Bros. in the early 1930s – and these only during and after World War 2 with such films as *Wilson* (1944), *Gentlemen's Agreement* (1947), *Pinky* (1949), and *No Way Out* (1950). Much as Irving Thalberg is celebrated for establishing MGM's high gloss, high quality production values from the 1920s through the early 1930s, we can say that Zanuck's creativity informed an entire studio's output. Zanuck fans can debate with director John Ford's admirers how much Ford's Fox films owe to Zanuck, but Zanuck is one of the few creative production executives in Hollywood's classical era about whom one could even ask such a question.[24] Still, no one would claim that Zanuck was an auteur.

In the 1930s, production executives (Zanuck to a limited extent) delegated authority to unit producers who reported to and took advice from the major executive producer, if one still functioned centrally. This ensured that a particular film could synthesize a studio star, a favored genre, and a directorial sensibility under the aegis of a studio's house style. At MGM, college-educated Al Lewin (spoofed in the James Cagney studio satire *Boy Meets Girl* (Warner Bros., 1938) supervised the high-class stage adaptations (sometimes of Noel Coward plays, and starring Alfred Lunt and Lynn Fontaine). Harry Rapf specialized in Joan Crawford melodramas. Eddie Mannix was adept at producing action films or films set in exotic locales, such as *Trader Horn* (1931) or *Red Dust* (1932). Hunt Stromberg supervised the *The Thin Man* series. Greta Garbo preferred working with director Clarence Brown and cinematographer William Daniels, as well as screenwriter and friend Salka Viertel; after Thalberg returned to MGM to work as a producer rather than a production executive, she demanded that he produce all her films.[25]

It is *these* producers-associate producers-supervisors who are the typical villains in Sarris's and Siegel's classic auteurist scenario. They could carry directives from the production head to the screenwriting conference or the set, and were most likely, in the 1930s and 1940s, to interfere with a project.

Yet producers could also make important contributions to a film's realization. Walter Wanger was in the late 1930s a prestigious, semi-independent producer prone to letting filmmakers develop their projects their way. He produced Ford's *Stagecoach* (1939), but he openly admitted that all he did was provide financing and a distribution deal, and that the film was a John Ford Production.[26] Yet, fifteen years later, while working at low budget Allied Artists in the 1950s after serving a short prison term, Wanger insisted on realistic detail in the depiction of prison conditions and routine during script development on *Riot in Cell Block 11* (1954). The film, which Don Siegel directed in a compelling, straightforward, postwar realistic style, marked an innovation in the prison film genre on many counts – the lack of a romantic interest, a multifaceted presentation of the issues and concerns which inmates and prison administrators contended with, and the absence of a happy ending. Wanger's involvement here, and in the later *I Want to Live!* (1958), were atypical of his usual filmmaking methods. Indeed, the decision to spend the last forty minutes of *I Want to Live!* watching the preparations for Barbara Graham's (Susan Hayward) execution in the gas chamber – without question the most powerful part of the film and the core of its anti-capital punishment statement – was made by the director Robert Wise while doing research on the film. So was the decision to use Johnny Mandel's jazz music for the film's score. Neither were part of Wanger's original conception, but he encouraged Wise to pursue these ideas. Still, the impact of Wanger's contributions to these two 1950s films is undeniable. Wise himself would later characterize the film as Wanger's "baby."[27] On a more costly scale, Wanger had fought to produce a big budget version of *Cleopatra* for years. Yet when Joseph L. Mankiewicz took over the troubled production of *Cleopatra* in early 1961, Wanger was perfectly happy to have Mankiewicz create "an entirely new, modern, psychiatrically rooted concept of the film."[28] Perhaps at that point, he had no choice.

As such examples illustrate, understanding the division of labor in Hollywood helps to clarify why producers were – with the rarest of exceptions – not auteurs in Hollywood's classical studio era. Whether they were studio producers at the major studios or worked within their own "independent production" companies, Hollywood's approach to filmmaking militated against it. The producer as auteur was clearly an exception.

The Producer as Auteur Today

Beginning in the late 1960s, Hollywood recognized the value of the auteur as a marketing brand. While the studios maintained the same division of labor as in the classical period, the director, whose creativity was constantly suppressed, was now given considerable

Figure 20.2 Walter Wanger with cinematographer Russell Harlan on location at San Quentin during production of Don Siegel's *Riot in Cell Block 11* (Allied Artists, 1954). Produced by Walter Wanger. Photo courtesy Wisconsin Center for Film and Theater Research

creative freedom as the classical era studio system crumbled.

Now the auteur as such was defined not by overcoming barriers to personal expression, but by the nature of that expression – a situation that obtains even today. For example, the Coen Brothers' sense of postmodern irony, Martin Scorsese's exploration of desperate masculinity and violence, Wes Anderson's insight into the childlike innocence of beleaguered male protagonists, and Christopher Guest's improvised mockumentaries – all are readily sold to filmgoers and understood to be the creations of the director or director-producer teams. Directors are no longer under the heel of the producer. The director, in the strictest sense, no longer needs a producer to make films, though there are cases in which a director might have benefited from a producer's restraining hand (as with Michael Cimino's 1980 *Heaven's Gate*). In fact, today, the auteur director – such as Steven Spielberg, Clint Eastwood, Martin Scorsese, and Warren Beatty – often serves as his or her own producer or co-producer.

Indeed, the most prominent Hollywood producers working today, with rare exceptions, are partnered – and collaborate – with major directors whose work they facilitate. Brian Grazer produces films apart from director Ron Howard, but his most memorable and successful films so far, such as *Apollo 13* (1995) and *A Beautiful Mind* (2001), were directed by Howard. Tom Cruise produces his films with Paula Wagner; and they have just recently agreed to run a former major company, UA-MGM. James Schamus produces films for and with Ang Lee. Unlike Grazer or Wagner, Schamus often scripts Ang Lee's films, as in the case of *The Ice Storm* (1997) and *Crouching Tiger, Hidden Dragon* (2000). This makes Schamus a creative producer-screenwriter, but it does not make him an auteur.

The best known American film producer today who is not partnered with a major director or star is Jerry Bruckheimer. One keynote of his output has been the action-packed buddy/rival films, from *Beverly Hills Cop* (1984) through *Top Gun* (1986), *Armageddon* (1998) to *Bad Boys* (2001). Industry observers have noted his diversification into historical dramas such as *Pearl Harbor* (2001) and comic adventures such as the *Pirates of the Caribbean* franchise since 2003 (not to mention the television series *CSI*). Bruckheimer has been celebrated for defending his own decisions against studio objections, such as the casting of Johnny Depp in the first *Pirates* film. He is known for hiring stylish directors such as Tony Scott and Michael Bay to make his films visually arresting. Even if we acknowledge that he is the most successful producer working today, Jerry Bruckheimer cannot be considered an auteur in any sense of the word. But like the most accomplished of his predecessors in the classical era, he, and other producers, can help to facilitate the contemporary auteurs' work. Perhaps the most fruitful way to think about producers and their relation to creative work is as a brand name, much as today's auteur-directors are marketed to the moviegoing public. The Bruckheimer brand denotes the action film or action-packed adventure, typically featuring two heroes who work together or compete against each other. This generalization holds even as Bruckheimer now produces other kinds of films. The producer as brand name – rather than the creative artist who generates an admirable body of films – could apply equally as well to the outstanding classical studio era producers like Selznick or Goldwyn, Disney or Wanger. This places producers at some remove from the kind of artistic creativity the auteur concept was meant to identify. But that is as it should be.

Notes

1 Andrew Sarris, "Toward A Theory of Film History," in *The American Cinema: Directors and Directions, 1929–1968* (New York: E. P. Dutton City, 1968), pp. 31, 37.

2 Ben Hecht Interview, Columbia University Oral History Project, Popular Arts Collection, Butler Library, New York: E. P. Dutton City, quoted in Matthew Bernstein, *Walter Wanger, Hollywood Independent* (1994; rpt., Minneapolis: University of Minnesota Press, 2000), p. 394.

3 See Janet Staiger's discussion in David Bordwell, Janet Staiger and Kristin Thompson, *The Classical Hollywood Cinema: Film Style and Mode of Production, 1917–1960* (New York: Columbia University Press, 1985), pp. 85–95, 320–37.

4 Andrew Sarris pointed out that D.W. Griffith, von Stroheim, Buster Keaton, Josef von Sternberg, and Welles were all victims of the studio system (p. 21).

5 Zanuck's memo to Jean Renoir appears in Rudy Behlmer, ed., *Memo from Darryl F. Zanuck: The Golden Years at Twentieth Century Fox* (New York: Grove Press, 1993), pp. 51, 54.

6 Joel E. Siegel, *Val Lewton: The Reality of Terror* (New York: Viking Press, 1973), pp. 21–3.

7 Sarris, p. 24.

8 See Mark Cotta Vaz, *Living Dangerously: The Adventures of Merian C. Cooper, Creator of "King Kong"* (New York: Villard, 2005), for an account of Cooper's career.

9 Behlmer, p. xv.

10 See David Alan Vertrees, *Selznick's Vision: Gone with the Wind and Hollywood Filmmaking* (Austin: University of Texas Press, 1997), for a sustained discussion of Selznick's multifaceted work on the film.

11 Thomas Schatz, *The Genius of the System: Hollywood Filmmaking in the Studio Era* (1988; rpt., New York: Henry Holt, 1996), p. 130. For additional accounts of Selznick's career, see Behlmer, Vertrees, and David Thomson, *Showman: The Life of David O. Selznick* (New York: Knopf, 1992).

12 See Paul Kerr, "Out of What Past? Notes on the B Film Noir," in Paul Kerr, ed., *The Hollywood Film Industry* (London: BFI, 1986), pp. 220–44. A thorough account of Lewton's creative working methods and contribution to his films appears in Siegel.

13 Siegel, pp. 23–6.

14 Siegel, p. 23.

15 I am referring of course to the work of Peter Wollen and the introduction of auteur-structuralism in his *Signs and Meanings in the Cinema* (Bloomington: Indiana University Press, 1973), and the various developments and refinements in the auteur theory since then.

16 Robert Carringer, *The Making of "Citizen Kane"* (Berkeley: University of California Press, 1985; revised edn., 1996), p. x.

17 Carringer, p. 134.

18 Carringer, p. 3.

19 See Staiger's discussion of the various modes of production in Hollywood in *The Classic Hollywood Cinema*, pp. 85–95, 320–37.

20 Thomas Schatz, *The Genius of the System*, p. 8.

21 Schatz, p. 12.

22 Schatz, p. 6.

23 Nunally Johnson, Columbia University Oral History Project; quoted in Bernstein, *Walter Wanger, Hollywood Independent*, p. 396.

24 The case for Zanuck as auteur production executive is made in George Custen's *Twentieth Century's Fox: Darryl F. Zanuck and the Culture of Hollywood* (New York: Basic Books, 1997).

For a sampling of Zanuck's correspondence, see Behlmer's edited selection in *Memo from Darryl F. Zanuck*. There is also Mel Gussow's *Don't Say Yes Until I Finish Talking: A Biography of Darryl F. Zanuck* (1971; rpt. New York: Pocket Books, 1983).

25 Schatz, pp. 159–75.

26 On Wanger and *Stagecoach*, see Bernstein, pp. 146–50.

27 For more on Wanger's contributions to *Riot in Cell Block 11* and *I Want to Live!* see Bernstein, pp. 281–301, 317–39. Interestingly, Sarris, pp. 30–1, suggested that producers were more likely to interfere with a storyline than a visual style, so that screenwriters were "more victimized" than directors, but the producers were the bad guys. But this was also, or perhaps primarily, a function of the producer's role in script development.

28 Wanger quoted in Bernstein, p. 359.

21

Authorship, Design, and Execution

Bruce Kawin

Bruce Kawin taught literature and film in the Department of English at the University of Colorado at Boulder. The author of *Telling It Again and Again: Repetition in Literature and Film, Faulkner and Film* and *Mindscreen: Bergman, Godard, and First-Person Film,* his work has focused on considering the differences of narration in the two forms. This discussion of auteurism is from the section of Kawin's book *How Movies Work* (1987) entitled "The Film Artist and the Movie Business." The section is comprised of chapters devoted to the different phases of the production process, beginning with a chapter addressing questions of authorship, from which this reading is taken. Kawin echoes earlier authors who have argued that auteurism neglects the collaborative nature of the filmmaking process, but in addition to discussing important examples of collaboration in cinema Kawin introduces the idea of collaboration as a system of human interaction.

Applauding the Conductor

Imagine that you are at a concert performance of Mozart's Fortieth Symphony. The last movement has just ended, and the audience is applauding the conductor. Not only did the conductor not write the music, he or she has not even played an instrument. Yet it is the conductor whose interpretation of the material is being praised. Next the conductor shakes hands with the concertmaster, and another round of applause ensues. Although the concertmaster's violin was not featured in an extensive solo, this violinist is a representative of the entire orchestra, and now the audience is rewarding them for having played well.

There are at least three artistic entities involved here: the composer, the conductor, and the orchestra. In film terms the composer is often the writer, the conductor is often the director, and the orchestra is a vast array of professionals, from actors to lab technicians. The parallel to the concert hall is the sound stage or location where the movie is shot and the theater where it is exhibited. Behind both operations is a sophisticated financial network that must remain solvent if further concerts or films are to be presented. As a link between the producers and the paying audience, advertisers have let the public know when and where the performance will take place, and they have emphasized those artists whose creative accomplishments are well known and whose personal styles are likely to attract an enthusiastic crowd.

Mozart's Fortieth Symphony existed as a complete textual entity when Mozart finished composing it. Any performance of that composition is itself an artistic event with its own unity and integrity, yet it is still *a* performance of an autonomous text. In a film the situation is markedly different, because the performance *is* the text.

Dashiell Hammett wrote *The Maltese Falcon*, and the novel is still available in its original form for anyone who chooses to read it. It became the basis of three films: Roy Del Ruth's *The Maltese Falcon* (1931), William Dieterle's *Satan Met a Lady* (1936), and John Huston's *The Maltese Falcon* (1941). All four of these are autonomous texts, distinct works of art. In the Huston version, Sam Spade is inseparable from the way Humphrey Bogart incarnated and enacted him, even if we can sort out the differences between Spade and Bogart when we step back from the film. Huston wrote the screenplay and directed the movie, so that the final product became his as much as Hammett's. Yet Huston did not "play an instrument."

The resolution to this quandary is to realize that the instrument that a conductor plays is, in fact, the orchestra. The orchestra members depend on the conductor to keep time and to let them know when and with what emphasis to play. The conductor organizes the performance, and it is therefore up to her or him how the composition will be realized. As the designer of an independent work, the director may have claims to authorship – but such claims are not at all automatic, and film authorship is rarely sole.

The Auteur Theory

Sole authorship is a matter of conceiving, designing, executing, and owning a work. Hammett planned *The Maltese Falcon*, wrote it, and had the sole right to sell it to a publisher. In the majority of films, design, realization, and ownership are necessarily split among many people and companies, and "authorship" becomes problematic.

Recall the moment when Queen Christina removes her crown. The physical movement was executed by Greta Garbo. The position of the camera, with its background view of a crown that cannot be removed, was chosen by the director, Rouben Mamoulian, and by the cinematographer, William Daniels. The action was designed in the first place by a team of screenwriters, based loosely on a historical event. The editor juxtaposed that shot with others that would enhance its impact. And the director, of course, coached Garbo on how to act the scene. But could Mamoulian have *told* Garbo every nuance of that gesture? Who took off that crown? Who should get credit for the brilliant, slow tenderness of Garbo's motions and the exquisite complexity of her face, in that light, at that moment? Who is the author of the total effect, of this scene, of this movie?

In this example there is no sole author. But there may have been a conductor – an artist with ultimate responsibility for approving the work of others – and it may well have been Mamoulian. The director is usually involved – or at least has a say – in all the major creative decisions from development through post-production, notably script approval, casting, production and costume design, the details of performance, and editing. That puts him or her in a position to unify the project and coach the team. But in the absence of reliable information about who did what while a picture was being made, there is little or no justification for assuming that the director has, in fact, performed this unifying function, let alone originated the themes, tropes, and gestures that have proved most distinctive and valuable in the finished work. It is difficult to make sense of the whole body of cinema, or even of any individual movie, until some critical method, informed by a careful understanding of real filmmaking practices, makes it possible to give credit where credit is due. Critical interpretations, especially of creative intentions and decisions, can be more reliable and sophisticated when one knows who the author is; otherwise, intentions are ascribed to a generalized vacuum.

First proposed by François Truffaut in the 1950s and further developed by Andrew Sarris in the 1960s, the *auteur theory* set out to provide just such a critical tool. It begins by acknowledging (or perhaps simply gives lip service to the idea) that film is a collaborative art, then goes on to argue that when a film reveals a thematic and stylistic coherence, that coherence can usually be attributed to the guiding vision of a single artist who was expressing his or her personal convictions and tastes. In order to have such power, the artist must almost invariably have been the director, though it is even better if the director has also written the

Figure 21.1 Greta Garbo wearing her crown in Rouben Mamoulian's *Queen Christina* (MGM, 1933). Produced by Walter Wanger

screenplay. To distinguish this artist from a sole author, he or she is referred to as an "auteur" (French for "author," but used in English to connote this more ambiguous position of control).

The problem with the auteur theory is that it may allow the critic to ignore creative collaboration and leap straight to the director. The special merit of the auteur theory is that it is *capable* of acknowledging the collaborative structure of the cinematic enterprise *and* the evidence of patterns of coherence that have the integrity of authorship. These may be stylistic patterns, characteristic approaches to recurring subject matter, or attitudes and strategies that have developed in the course of a career. Hitchcock's work, for example, is characterized by recurring content – notably the problematic relations between guilt and innocence – and a visual style that no one has been able to imitate with authority. This observation does not imply that an artist always says the same thing in the same way; rather, it allows for development and maturation within a structure whose consistency is that of the artist.

In the role of director, then, which touches nearly every aspect of the filmmaking process and may let an artist dominate a work without actually taking center stage, the auteurists found a site for these patterns of coherence. It is quite plain to them that Renoir films are Renoir films, that von Steinberg films could not have been made by Lumet, and that Welles was the auteur of *Citizen Kane*. This makes it simple to talk about a movie as a direct expression of one person's creative intentions. But auteurism has often been applied carelessly. It is by no means true that every film has an auteur. There are auteurs who are not directors, and directors who are not auteurs. Many auteurists have not taken the trouble to check these matters out, nor have they even begun to applaud the concertmaster.

Auteurism has had critical implications that are far-reaching and sometimes off-target. It appears, for one thing, to have been the only academic debate ever to affect the film industry. In its later critical manifestations it has become a cult of personal style, so that a director is considered interesting – or an author at all – only when he or she has exhibited a consistent style and a matrix of recurring interests. Directors in whose work such patterns cannot be discerned have often been dismissed by critics as "hacks." The industry itself has become "director-conscious," while many non-directors have become auti-auteurists. Under the influence of auteurism, many fledgling film artists have gathered that directing is the only important job and that they have to make *their* mark. But there is more to good directing than self-expression, and there are distinctly creative aspects to other film jobs. The public view now appears to be simply that films are made and signed by directors.

Critically, the conventional test of an auteur is that a pattern emerges when all of his or her pictures are viewed together or are considered in relation to each other. But the real value of auteurism – once it is extended beyond directors and as it may be critically applied to a single picture – is that it offers a reasonable explanation for a fact about cinema: that an often personal coherence *can* emerge from a collaborative project.

Even when a film does have an auteur – a Bergman or a Hitchcock, for example – the critical methodology is sometimes applied irresponsibly. Many auteurists want to find a single author and let it go at that. Although they may understand that actress Bibi Andersson and cinematographer Sven Nykvist are independent beings, they prefer to analyze every image and instant of *Persona* as if it proceeded directly from Ingmar Bergman's consciousness. Bergman himself has always been generous in acknowledging the contributions of the group he has worked with and would never endorse such a critical position.

Collaborative Decision-Making

Not every film has a single director, let alone a single guiding consciousness. Both Stanley Donen and Gene Kelly directed *Singin' in the Rain*, and Arthur Freed produced it. Director Vittorio de Sica and writer Cesare Zavattini were lifelong collaborators, from *Shoeshine* (1946) and *The Bicycle Thief* through *A Brief Vacation* (1973). Resnais directed *Marienbad*, Alain Robbe-Grillet wrote it, and the two men disagreed about what happens in the story. The finished film reflects this authorial ambivalence and presents the lovers as having met before (Resnais's interpretation) and as never having met before (Robbe-Grillet's interpretation). This doubleness is responsible for much of *Marienbad*'s characteristic tone and style, and it would not be adequate to identify it simply as Resnais's movie. It has as many significant connections with Robbe-Grillet's novels as it has with Resnais's other movies.

Although one can identify most of Spielberg's movies as his, the Indiana Jones films are clearly the result of his collaboration with Lucas. As their producer, Lucas is the auteur of the *Star Wars* series, and his control of those pictures was so personal and exacting that *The Empire Strikes Back* (1980) and *Return of the Jedi* (1983), which he did not direct, are nearly indistinguishable from *Star Wars*, which he did direct. Yet the Indiana Jones films are not the same as the *Star Wars* films, and *Raiders* in particular shares many important characteristics with both Spielberg's *Jaws* (1975) and Lucas's *American Graffiti* (1973). Once you know the pictures, all of these distinctions are obvious, yet a conventional auteurist would approach *Raiders* as a Spielberg film and might dismiss *Jedi* from serious consideration if it did not bear the stamp of Richard Marquand's directorial personality. It is only

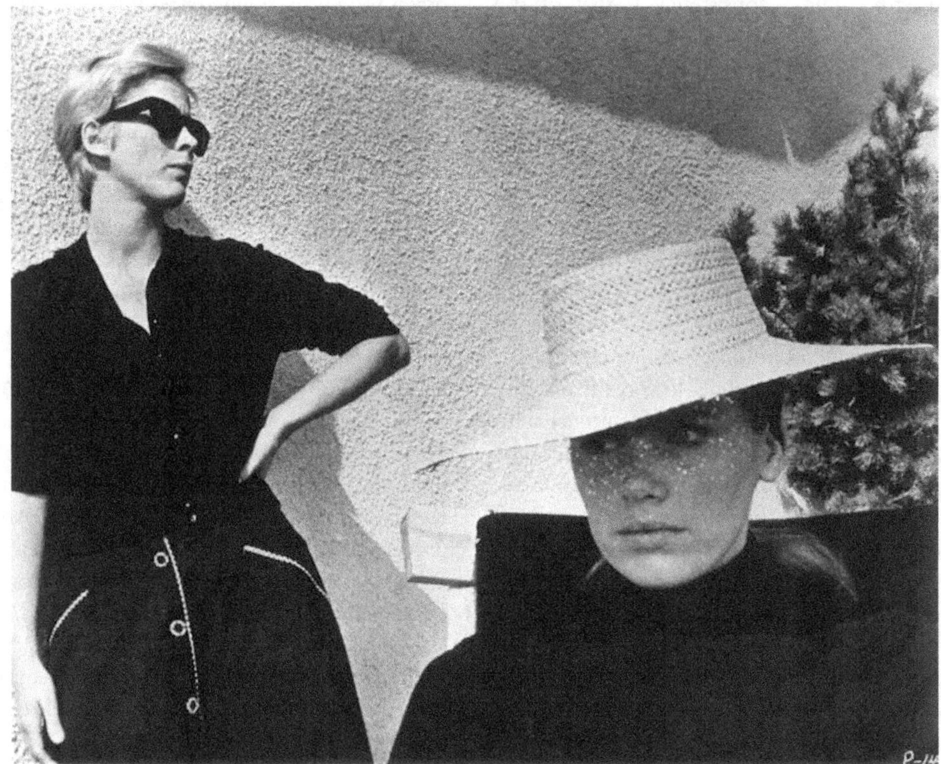

Figure 21.2 *Persona* (Svensk Filmindustri, 1966), a personal film written, produced, and directed by Ingmar Bergman that nonetheless reveals the contributions of the actresses (Bibi Andersson and Liv Ullman) and cinematographer (Sven Nykvist)

recently that writers, producers, and actors have begun to be considered possible auteurs, even though it should long have been obvious that there is such a thing as a Horton Foote film, a Walt Disney film, and a Marx Brothers film. But even to settle on such sites of coherence can be to sidestep the realities of development and production.

Let us take up some examples of creative collaboration, both fruitful and unfortunate. In 1943 director Henry Hathaway was developing a story idea about the Unknown Soldier. He kept evaluating suggestions from his colleagues and rejecting them. Finally one writer said, in simple exasperation, "You'll never be satisfied until the Unknown Soldier is Jesus Christ!" Hathaway replied, "Hey, that's a good idea!" This was the key juxtaposition for which Hathaway had unknowingly been searching, and his colleague's quip precipitated the insight. Hathaway and writer William Bacher then drew up a new story idea, and William Faulkner was assigned to develop it into a treatment (an extended story outline from which a screenplay can be further developed). Faulkner warmed up to the idea and turned in a 51-page treatment, but the picture (to have been entitled *Who?*) was never made. Faulkner went on to expand the idea into a novel called *A Fable* (1954), and he gave credit to Hathaway and Bacher on the dedication page.

Eugène Lourié worked as the art director on Jean Renoir's *Grand Illusion* (1937). When he and Renoir were scouting locations for that film, they decided to use the mountain castle of Haut-Koenigsburg, which had been built by Kaiser Wilhelm. Lourié, according to his own account in *American Film* (Jan./Feb. 1985), "noticed a small pot of geraniums on the windowsill of the janitor's lodging. I was impressed by this little speck of color amid the gray stone surroundings. I

Figure 21.3 The geranium metaphor in *Grand Illusion* (1936) was the result of collaboration between director Jean Renoir and art director Eugène Lourié. Produced by Albert Pinkovitch and Frank Rollmer

asked Jean if he would not object to my placing a geranium in Stroheim's room. 'By all means, put it there,' he said, 'I could use it.' This little flower became a highly poetic symbol. Stroheim's cutting this flower became the emotional final touch during the scene showing the death of the Fresnay character." It is clear from this example that the art director did not get the entire idea, did not anticipate how Renoir would ultimately use the geranium in *Grand Illusion*, but it is also clear that there would have been no geranium in the film had Lourié not noticed one on location and intuited that it somehow belonged in the design of the picture. Although Renoir justifiably took credit as the principal author of *Grand Illusion*, he also referred to Lourié as his "accomplice."

Sometimes, however, too many cooks can in fact spoil the broth. Hitchcock's *Suspicion* (1941) was based on a brilliant mystery novel by Francis Iles, *Before the Fact*. The novel is about a woman who discovers that she has married a murderer. When she realizes that he intends to kill her, too, she lets him do it. The scene in which the husband, Johnny, brings his wife a glass of poisoned milk and realizes that she knows what he is doing, yet acquiesces to her demand – "Give it me, Johnny" – is deeply affecting. In what seemed to be perfect casting decisions, Cary Grant and Joan Fontaine were signed to play the leads. But then the RKO studio heads decided that no star of Grant's importance could be cast in the role of a murderer. It became necessary to devise an incredible ending in which the wife is revealed as having misunderstood her husband's good intentions. This happily-ever-after resolution is a classic example of "the Hollywood treatment," and the equivocal terms in which it more-or-less succeeds have nothing to do with the novel.

To see how input from various sources can affect a finished product, even one of classic status, consider the production history of *The Cabinet of Dr Caligari* (a story vividly recounted by Siegfried Kracauer in his study *From Caligari to Hitler*). The writers, Carl Mayer and Hans Janowitz, developed a story about an insane doctor (Caligari) who forces a somnambulist (Cesare) to commit a series of murders. When the doctor is eventually exposed by the vigilant hero and committed to his own asylum, what Janowitz and Mayer hoped to show was that insane authority can be challenged and even overthrown, that its insanity can be revealed. They saw Caligari – whom each of them drew from a particularly threatening figure in his own past – as a symbol of the criminally deranged, militaristic, authoritarian system and Cesare as a youth turned into a killing machine, like a conscripted soldier.

Producer Erich Pommer bought the script and determined to make, if not an avant-garde feature, then at least an arty movie capable of attracting international attention. He hired Fritz Lang to direct.

Lang suggested that framing sequences be added: one, at the start of the film, to establish that the story (that is, Janowitz and Mayer's script) is being narrated by the central character (Franz or Francis), and one, at the end of the film, to reveal that Francis is insane. In the script and in the body of the movie, Francis is a friend of one of Cesare's victims and is the one who tracks Caligari to his lair, but in the closing scenes he is shown to be an inmate of the asylum run by the benevolent and insightful doctor whom, in his delusion, he calls Caligari. Perhaps Lang conceived this purely as a dramatic twist, and perhaps Pommer appreciated its show business value, but the fact is that their adding the closing frame drastically altered the meaning of the story and sent the writers into a rage. What the revised version preached was submission and self-doubt. Doctor Caligari knows what is good for you.

Lang did not, however, direct the picture; he was reassigned to *Spiders* (1919). Pommer hired Robert Wiene, who did direct it. Wiene agreed with Lang about the value of the framing sequences and the reversal of the story's original intentions. So now it was set: rather than a film of rebellion, *Caligari* was to be a film of repression, of the fear and the denial (and, in fact, the *rescripting*) of rebellion.

It was either Pommer or Janowitz who first conceived of *Caligari* as a film with stylized, painted sets. Janowitz suggested that the designer be Alfred Kubin, but the actual choice of designer was made by Wiene, and he chose Hermann Warm. It was Warm who wrote that "Films must be drawings brought to life," and he and Walter Röhrig and Walter Reimann, all of whom were Expressionist artists, created the sets and the costumes. Without Pommer's approval, however, there is no way that *Caligari* would have become an Expressionist film, and it makes relatively little difference whether Janowitz or Wiene suggested it to him. Under Pommer's guidance, or as a result of the emerging logic of the revisions, the Expressionist style became problematic in the same terms as the framing sequences, and *Caligari* became neither a film of rebellion nor a film of repression but a paradox and a "dream play." As it stands, it might well be compared to a dream whose terms and whose repressed, eruptive meanings have been changed and distorted.

Expressionist distortion was not inconsistent with the meaning and dramatic project of the original script, and Janowitz clearly had no objection to it. In the context of the script alone, the Expressionist distortions would have portrayed and critiqued the state of the culture, or of the German "soul" if you will, shortly after World War I. They would have enhanced the dramatization of the madness of the world that must answer to insane tyranny.

But with the framing sequences added, of course, all these distortions signify is that Francis is crazy. That implies that the world is fine. The action of the closing frame implies that it is not the authority figure but the insightful postromantic rebel who is psychologically disturbed. So far, then, the official message of *Caligari* is almost exactly the opposite of what the writers intended it to be, as the result of suggestions made by Lang and Wiene and approved by Pommer. Creative distortion has become delusion.

Then Wiene made a mistake – or perhaps, in this context, a Freudian slip. He failed to instruct the designers to restore *normal* sets, makeup, and costumes for the closing frame. (The opening frame is relatively neutral.) If the world when it is not being narrated by Francis looks much the same as when it *is*, then all of the Expressionist distortions cannot simply be written off as expressions of the narrator's madness. The Expressionism of the final scenes leaks over from the main story, erupts out of it, and is ultimately both subversive and paradoxical. A hint of what might be called the writer's perspective survives, then, and not only the closing frame but also the entire film appears divided against itself. Thanks to all of these internal contradictions (the impossible closing landscape; the different interpretations of the story held by the writers, Lang and Wiene, and Pommer; the praise of conformity and submission and the impulse to revolt etc.), *Caligari* actually *does* portray the ambivalence of Germany between the wars, torn between the desire to discover and submit to an authoritarian father figure and the impulse to revolt; it says both things at once. *Caligari* also plays out perfectly the often contradictory message systems of dreaming, and that is one of the reasons, among many, that it became the paradigm of the horror film rather than a unique political melodrama.

None of its makers foresaw how *Caligari* would turn out, and at the very least, it had several authors. The true, or ur-*Caligari* was conceived by Janowitz and Mayer. Wiene directed the film (often very poorly), selected Warm and approved the terms of the design, and is usually credited as the film's auteur. But if anyone had overall creative approval at every stage of production, it was Pommer, the producer. And the addition of the framing sequences, which was as important a development as the decision to use Expressionist sets, was Lang's idea. We are not even speaking here of the definitive, brilliant contributions made by the actors who played Caligari (Werner Krauss) and Cesare (Conrad Veidt), who were cast, as it happens, by Pommer.

Although it may seem rather tangled, the production history of *Caligari* is just as representative as the story of the geranium in *Grand Illusion*. Well after the writer surrenders the script, people are always getting bright ideas, and sometimes the ideas actually enhance what the writer has envisioned. Even a Renoir needs help, and even a script as coherent as that for *Caligari* may be worked over by many people who "improve" it to the point of incoherence. As complex as it is to establish how a collaborative venture may be guided, and to what ends, it is a worthwhile critical effort. And to be comprehensive, that effort must take into account the business context within which feature films are made.

Most of the arts, at some point, touch the world of commerce. If you want to write a novel for your own amusement and satisfaction, that is up to you. But if you want someone to publish it, you will have to deal with business people and listen to many suggestions for improving the work or making it more marketable. In the case of a feature film, where you will have to convince someone to put up at least a million dollars before you can even begin to shoot the picture, the business component is extremely significant.

This is a matter of aesthetics as well as of sheer power. In the first place, the ideas contributed by agents, story editors, producers, and marketing specialists can turn out to be valuable. In the second place, the filmmaker is answerable to an unpleasant reality: filmmaking is one of the only arts that an accomplished artist can be kicked out of. Without the trust of the studios and banks, the artist may simply not be allowed to work. That is what happened to Griffith, Stroheim, and Welles: they were denied the expensive tools they needed to realize their designs. Even a solo filmmaker like Brakhage must scrape together the money to make his films, To ignore this practical context is to introduce the danger of reading a movie in *completely* aesthetic terms and losing sight of the complexities of design and execution – of reading *Suspicion*, for example, as if Hitchcock had had his own reasons for changing the story, or *Caligari* as Wiene's masterpiece.

Collaboration as a System

Many people make creative decisions in the course of a filmmaking project, and several people – at various levels of authority – approve or reject them. The student and the critic must, then, resolve two apparently contradictory facts: (1) that filmmaking is a collaboration, and (2) that some films do reveal the workings of a particular stylistic imagination, one that tends to recur in other films made by the same artist(s).

The auteurists have resolved these contradictions by arguing that the director imposes his or her vision on the entire crew, bucks the system, and heroically conveys a personal statement through the oppressive mechanism of a dense industry. That might be thought of as the model of the conductor and the orchestra, except that the conductor is also being given credit for the equivalent of writing and playing the music. There is something plainly wrong about giving a director credit for the insights and the structural imagination of a writer, especially if the director has worked from a completed script. And even if one views the essence of cinema as lying in the treatment and the mounting of the material – the discourse rather than the story – all that is done by still other professionals who have their own special interests and skills.

Nevertheless, it is simply true that there are styles associated with certain individual filmmakers. There is a "Hitchcock camera" whether or not the cinematographer was Robert Burks. There is a "Toland camera" whether the director was Ford, Wyler, or Welles. There are worlds that can accurately be described as Chaplin's or Keaton's or Lloyd's.

A partial explanation is that a director (and by the same token, a producer) is often given his or her choice of projects. Out of the many available scripts in development at a studio, or sent to the director by agents, the one that the director picks – probably because he or she finds it interesting – is often the one that gets produced. A recognized director also selects his or her major collaborators, knowing their previous work. Part of the "Huston" flavor of a John Huston film can be explained by Huston's having selected only those properties that struck him as "his kind of material," whereas the ones he rejected might wait around to be picked up by other filmmakers who were interested in other things. By the same logic, the look of the image can be read as the one that he hired that particular cinematographer to achieve. In these terms, one can discover Huston's personal tastes – and business acumen – by studying and comparing the properties he agreed or fought to direct. All that is easier if you also know which ones he did *not* want or agree to direct, but it is still possible to find evidence of the connecting thread of Huston through "his" films.

But are they his films? Let me propose that they are "Huston" films. The name is in quotes to suggest that they do have a recognizable and developing style, that that style is reliably associated with all of the films directed by Huston, and that all of them were produced as collaborations. Like Mamoulian in the "crown" example, Huston could not have dictated every significant aspect of all these films. If my argument is correct, solution to this paradox rests in the intuitive dynamics of collaboration.

Cinematographer Robby Müller has said that he and director Wim Wenders rarely discussed how a scene should be shot but often seemed to share the same ideas. One explanation is that Wenders chose Müller as his cameraman because he liked the way Müller had worked on other projects. But that would not explain the nature of the understanding between them, nor the differences in Müller's work for other directors.

Over and over, in the course of researching this book, I encountered cinematographers who said that although they had their own sense of style and craft, they studied the director and any of his or her previous films in order to discover the director's characteristic approach and to "give the director what he wants." I heard the same thing film editors, sound mixers, research librarians, assistant directors, and actors. The director is acknowledged as the person who is in a position to have a finger in every pie, at least up to the first edited version of the picture. But it is the position, not really the person, that is at so crucial a place in the filmmaking system. The director has the opportunity to live up to that position.

It is not that the director issues instructions to everybody in sight and they then carry them out; rather, every creative member of the filmmaking team comes to *share* a vision of how the film ought to be, a vision that they may well identify with the desires of the director. They each do their part, and the parts are coherent because they were each fashioned in relation to an ideal of the whole. The rays come to a point of focus, and whether that point is a shared construct of "what the director wants" or the director as a person, it is most crucially the ideal toward which the filmmakers are working and, with luck, the shape of the finished product.

What the group of artists does, in other words, is to agree to work together in a certain style and toward a particular goal. When they are working with Huston, that goal is a "Huston" film. They associate this style with "giving the director what he wants," but that does not mean that the director has or even could have told them all how to do that. What it does mean is that style in a collaborative enterprise is not just the *result* but often the *evidence* of a group effort. The more coherent the style, the better must have been the working understanding among the members of the team.

There are still cases where stylistic coherence reflects the comprehensive and specific instructions of a single person. There are others in which the group ideal has been stimulated not by the director but by the inherent logic of the script, the story to be told – or by the studio, which wants to put out a certain kind of product. But in general, and in the majority of cases, the rich coherence of a movie can be ascribed to the shared vision of its makers.

If that redefined auteur method leaves us examining the politics of Capra, the conflict of guilt and desire in Hitchcock, or the social vision of Ford, there will be no problem – as long as we do not forget that none of those individuals can be given absolute credit for and title to the films they guided to completion. Directors, too, are parts of the system, and if they generate an abstraction that proves to inspire and unify the activities of their many collaborators, that is an intriguing explanation of how the parts of the cinematic system – people, arts, and shots – might be drawn together into a coherent whole.

Further Reading

Bordwell, David. "The Art Cinema as a Mode of Film Practice." *Film Criticism* 4, no. 1 (Fall 1979), pp. 56–64.

Bordwell, David, Staiger, Janet, and Thompson, Kristin. *The Classical Hollywood Cinema: Film Style and Mode of Production to 1960.* New York: Columbia University Press/London: Routledge & Kegan Paul, 1985.

Brown, Nick (ed.). *Cahiers du Cinéma: The 1970s.* Cambridge, MA: Harvard University Press, 1990.

Caughie, John (ed.). *Authorship in the Cinema: A Reader.* London and Boston: Routledge & Kegan Paul, 1981.

Cook, Pam, King, Noel, and Miller, Toby, "Authorship," in Pam Cook and Mieke Bernink (eds.), *The Cinema Book,* 2nd edn. London: British Film Institute, 1999, pp. 235–319.

Crofts, Stephen. "Authorship and Hollywood," in John Hill and Pamela Church Gibson (eds.), *American Cinema and Hollywood: Critical Approaches.* New York: Oxford University Press, 2000, pp. 310–24.

Fisher, Lucy. *Shot/Countershot: Film Tradition and Women's Cinema.* Princeton: Princeton University Press, 1989.

Foucault, Michel. "What is an Author?" in Donald F. Bouchard (ed.), *Language, Counter-Memory, Practice,* trans. Donald F. Bouchard and Sherry Simon, Ithaca, NY: Cornell University Press, 1977, pp. 118–38.

McCarthy, Todd, and Charles (eds.). *Kings of the Bs: Working within the Hollywood System.* New York: E.P. Dutton, 1975.

Saxton, Christine. "The Cultural Voice as Collective Voice." *Cinema Journal* 26, no. 1 (Fall 1986), pp. 19–30.

Schatz, Thomas. *The Genius of the System: Hollywood Filmmaking in the Studio Era.* New York: Pantheon, 1988.

Society for Education in Film and Television. *Screen Reader 1.* London: Society for Education in Film and Television, 1977.

Tasker, Yvonne (ed.). *Fifty Contemporary Filmmakers.* London and New York: Routledge, 2002.

Wood, Robin. *Hollywood from Vietnam to Reaganand Beyond.* New York: Columbia University Press, 2003.

Part III

Close Readings

22

Hitchcock's Imagery and Art

Maurice Yacowar

A Canadian film critic and former Dean of Fine Arts at the University of Calgary and the Emily Carr School of Art in Vancouver, Yacowar's books include *A Method in Madness: The Comic Art of Mel Brooks*, *Loser Take All: The Comic Art of Woody Allen*, and *Tennessee Williams and Film*. The essay here is taken from another of Yacowar's auteurist studies, *Hitchcock's British Films* (1977), devoted to an analysis of the films made by Alfred Hitchcock in his native Britain before moving to Hollywood at the invitation of David O. Selznick. Like Claude Chabrol and Eric Rohmer's book on Hitchcock, the first book of auteur criticism 20 years earlier, Yacowar looks at each film in chronological order; but where Chabrol and Rohmer emphasize a spiritual reading, Yacowar is more concerned with the social and psychological dimensions of Hitchcock's work. Here, in his book's conclusion, Yacowar offers a persuasive auteurist analysis of Hitchcock's personal vision as he connects the themes and stylistic elements of the director's British films to his more well-known American movies.

Of the twenty-three feature films that Hitchcock directed in his first fifteen years, none is without some interest and some lively personal character. Hitchcock was Hitchcock from the outset – perceptive, progressive, playful, in his mischievous machinations against the simple securities of his audience, yet profound in the implications of his ironic stance. The early films show the same thematic concerns for which his later work is known, and the same expertise.

As in his later work, Hitchcock often parallelled characters of ostensible innocence and guilt, to dramatize the thin line that separates man from his pretensions to purity. Thus we have Patsy Brand contrasted to Jill Cheyne in *The Pleasure Garden*, the romantic policeman contrasted to The Lodger, and the two men of *The Manxman*. In *Easy Virtue, Rich and Strange, The Skin Game*, and *Jamaica Inn*, figures of simple innocence are inadvertently seduced into criminal complicity. These foreshadow the drama of Bruno and Guy in *Strangers on a Train*.

Often the Hitchcock innocent is drawn into evil by boredom, which functions as the image of moral lassitude. Thus we have the passionless marriages of *The Pleasure Garden, The Manxman*, and *Sabotage*; the premature marriages in *The Ring, Easy Virtue*, and *The Skin Game*; and the boredom which prompts the girl to flirt with the artist in *Blackmail*. Hitchcock realizes how dull morality is and how exciting sin is. His delight is to make his moral points through exciting fictions, reminding his audiences of the difficulties and pain of the moral life – albeit in his delightful way. These marriages foreshadow the cold, antiromantic situations that are developed in *Notorious, North by Northwest*, and *Topaz*.

Maurice Yacowar, "Hitchcock's Imagery and Art," pp. 256–69 from *Hitchcock's British Films* (Hamden, CT: Archon Books [Shoestring Press], 1977).

Because innocence and guilt are so radically intertwined, a Hitchcock hero never enjoys a simple success, The innocent will die along with the guilty: the native girl in *The Pleasure Garden*, the pirate in *Rich and Strange*, Stevie Verloc in *Sabotage*, as later the children and Annie will in *The Birds*, and Marion Crane will *after* she has resolved to surrender to police in *Psycho*. For man's laws fail in the allocation of justice.

In *Rope*, Jan asks playfully of a friend's description of her: "Did he do me justice?" Rupert replies sharply: "Do you deserve justice?" From the lovers of *The Pleasure Garden* through the murders of *Family Plot*, Hitchcock's heroes are of at best a dappled virtue, and his villains of civilized elegance. Indeed, his villains are often extremely sympathetic people, as Verloc is, or Fane of *Murder*! Even the nasty Levet in *The Pleasure Garden* is allowed a death of charming civility.

Hitchcock's justice is tricky, poetic rather than legal. For his world is full of uncertainty. *Shadow of a Doubt* may seem to have a happy ending, but the killer is eulogized by the small town, and an innocent man was fed to an airplane propeller by mistake. Similarly in *Blackmail*, the murderers go free while a small-time blackmailer is killed in their stead. Even the happy endings, then, refuse the confidence of a secure order. No simple justice, no simple psychology, can be sustained in Hitchcock's world of quicksand insecurity. So almost all Hitchcock's films end on an uncertain image, from the new lovers in *The Pleasure Garden* to the mass of abiding doom at the end of *The Birds*. And in *Frenzy*, Blaney establishes his innocence by performing the crime for which he was wrongly sentenced; no matter that the woman he attacks in Rusk's bed is already dead.

Hitchcock often uses the X-image to express his sense of man as a complex of innocence and evil. Thus in *The Pleasure Garden* we found the two women forming an X to suggest their equivalence in their lover's mind; the husband moves to kill his wife in order to complete the X, in response to his murdered mistress's imagined demands. In *Blackmail* a similar editing completes an X between the corpse's hand and the policeman's, where the plot develops the illegality of the police's activities and the criminal parodies justice. The X imagery is developed most fully, of course, in *Strangers on a Train*.

Perhaps Hitchcock presents two different concepts of man's makeup. First, opposite tendencies may unite to form a single, composite whole, as the ladies do in *The Pleasure Garden* and as the strangers on a train do. Here the X would represent the unity of opposite motions and values in human nature. Similarly, in *I Confess* an X variant, the cross, unites Father Logan and killer Keller in a criminal sacrament that costs them Alma (the soul in its earthly existence). But in the second image of human nature, opposite wholes are paralleled. Charlie and Uncle Charlie in *Shadow of a Doubt* are parallel opposites, albeit with such similarities as name, selfishness, vanity, and telepathic connection. They are not a unity. The good Charlie may have some flaws and the evil Uncle Charlie some elegant pretense to justice in his effect, but the characters are clearly separable and they diverge by the impulse of their respective wills. So too in *Psycho*, Norman Bates pretends to be an X with his mother, but she is innocent, misrepresented even after she was murdered by her spoiled, jealous son. Norman and his mother are antitheses who only intersect in Norman's malevolent rationalizing. The bantering and bickering lovers in Hitchcock's romances (*Champagne*, *Mr and Mrs Smith*) and in his thrillers (*The 39 Steps*, *Saboteur* and on through *Marnie*) are spirited strokes who discover themselves to be fulfilled as Xs.

The other quintessential Hitchcock image is the staircase. Again the early films show ample use of this device for which his later work is known. Whether upwards or down, Hitchcock's stairs take his characters and his audience to the fears, dangers, and rewards of self-discovery. The most common staircase shot is downward through a seeming spiral, which leaves the impression of stairs within stairs. One finds this shot from *The Lodger* through *Vertigo*. As an emblem it recalls Peer Gynt's onion, concentric layerings around a void, with the addition of the danger that height always means in Hitchcock.

The occasional round staircase, as in *The Pleasure Garden* and *The Secret Agent*, also suggests a plunge through layers of one's self. There are even three staircases in *Waltzes from Vienna*: The rickety ladder down which Schani's rival carries the heroine in the opening fire scene; its parallel, the ladder the girl climbs at the end to save Schani from the duel and to reclaim him romantically; and the palatial staircase down which the Count rolls his valet in a piano rift, an image of their difference in privilege and station. In *Juno and the Paycock* the stairs provide a single straight and dark

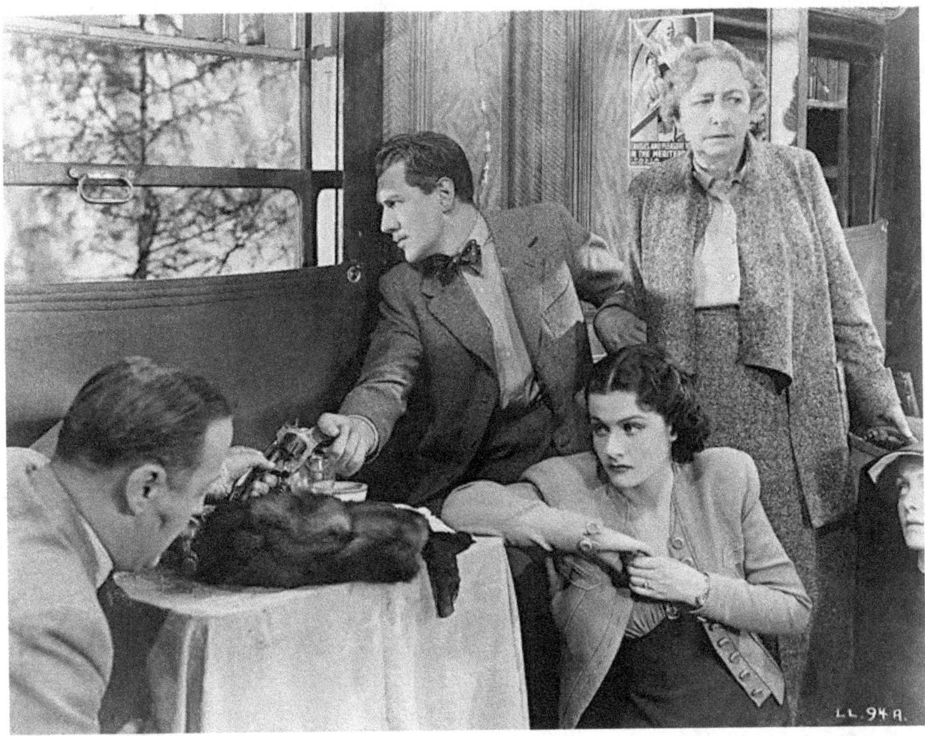

Figure 22.1 The individual's private life is shattered in Alfred Hitchcock's *The Lady Vanishes* (Gaumont British, 1938). Produced by Edward Black

descent from the family warmth to the cold public funeral and to their dispossession.

In *Shadow of a Doubt* Charlie's home has two parallel staircases, the clean public front and the dangerous, steep, private back, the latter which Uncle Charles uses to escape and to threaten Charlie. The two-staired house works as an image of the human psyche and as an image of a societal ideal, both of which project a front that is more attractive and safer than their hidden natures.

Stairs compel movement and with it, fear, as in Constance's ascent to Murchison's office in *Spellbound*, and Bates's in *Psycho*. The camera (the maker) has a liberty over space and stairs that the character has not. Hence the open, expressionistic staircase in *The Lodger* and the brittle one in *No. 17*. Hitchcock's stairs image both man's composition and the rigors and fears of his rise or plunge to awareness. The danger that always lurks around the stairs is the anxiety that undercuts all confidence (in the Hitchcock vision), all sense of secure footing, and that provides both the central metaphor and title for *Downhill* and for *Vertigo*. The source of the latter was a novel titled *Between Two Deaths*, but "Vertigo" conveys Hitchcock's primary interest: man's uncertainty in stepping between two moments of living.

Hitchcock's art is based on the dramatic appeal of the insecure. In the first place, his characters are typically secure people whose footing is swept out from under them. Thus Patsy loses her independence in *The Pleasure Garden* and the hero loses his whole world in *Downhill*. Sanders loses his station in *The Ring* and the fisherman his bliss, friend, and wife in *The Manxman*. Love provides only a false sense of security in *The Pleasure Garden*, *The Farmer's Wife*, *The Manxman*, and *Champagne*, where the reconciled lovers begin to quarrel anew over their marriage arrangements. And in *Mr and Mrs Smith* a marriage suddenly ceases to exist.

Nor is there security in the social contract. The processes of justice go awry in *Easy Virtue*, *Blackmail*, *Juno and the Paycock*, *Murder!* And in the thriller series from *The Man Who Knew Too Much* through *The Lady*

Vanishes the individual's private life is shattered by the social processes that are supposedly functioning to protect him. Hence Hitchcock's frequent twist where the hero is threatened by the police as much as by the enemy: *The Lodger, Blackmail, The 39 Steps, North by Northwest, Psycho, Frenzy*. Virtue and Hitchcock's justice are endangered by the merely human law. Joe in *The Lodger* eventually subordinates his romantic interest to his public duty. But not until *Frenzy* will we have a Hitchcock policeman whose arrival at the truth is based upon his sense of the criminal potential within himself.[1] For the others, the police are sheep (*The 39 Steps*) or careless shots (*Strangers on a Train*). In *The Trouble with Harry*, the springy villagers have but a single fear – discovery by the sheriff's deputy, a cold Puritan named Calvin whose resurrections are confined to antique autos.

Hitchcock usually presents his theme of man's limited freedom in society as a conflict between love and duty. The tension is between love and friendship (a personal duty) in *Downhill, The Manxman,* and *The Farmer's Wife*. In the policeman drama the hero must choose between what his job requires and what his heart (and the lady) deserve: *The Lodger, Blackmail, Young and Innocent, Sabotage, Stage Fright, The Paradine Case*. The spy thrillers adjust the love versus duty debate to the tensions of the cold war, where the hero must choose between his personal love and his international duty: *Foreign Correspondent, Notorious, North by Northwest, Torn Curtain, Topaz*. Another form of this debate is the conflict between privacy and public involvement. Although the fullest presentation of this theme is in *Rear Window*, it is fully developed in both versions of *The Man Who Knew Too Much*, *The Secret Agent, Sabotage*, and *The Lady Vanishes*. Possibly its earliest statement, however, is in the scene of the switchboard operator in *Easy Virtue*.

But if love and citizenship are two areas in which Hitchcock afflicts his characters with insecurity, the most dramatic is the family relationship. Richard Roud relates the motif of parental tyranny to the espionage plots:

> Even his domestic dramas involve a kind of espionage in the sense that his characters, having discovered frightening realities buried beneath the surface, are obliged to turn spy themselves in order to discover the whole truth. Often it has something to do with the past, the past that comes back to confound the present, to compromise the future.[2]

Thus we find so many tyrannical parents in Hitchcock's work, as we have noted in our discussion of *Downhill*. Cruel fathers spring readily to mind: *Downhill, Champagne, The Manxman, Waltzes from Vienna*. Then there are the treacherous father surrogates in *Sabotage, The Lady Vanishes*, and *Jamaica Inn* (particularly after Hitchcock's revision of the villain in the latter). Even where the parent figures are not oppressive or negative, the parent must be abandoned at least temporarily, as in *Young and Innocent*. The family is presented as a fragile, sometimes false and always vulnerable, unit in all Hitchcock's thrillers of the late thirties. In *Psycho* we have a pervasive feeling of parental oppression, by Marion Crane's mother, Sam's father, and the happiness-buying Texas daddy; but in the main thrust of the film, it is the sick son that projects his guilt and inhibitions upon his parental image. The parent is blamed for the child's violent weakness.

In this respect one of the key Hitchcock's films is his comedy, *The Trouble with Harry*. A little boy discovers a man dead in the forest; it's his stepfather, unknown to the boy. The dead Harry Warp harmonizes the entire community as each member assumes guilt for his death and they all combine to conceal him. In one shot the corpse is so arranged that his feet and legs seem to complete the body of the little boy (Jerry Mather), whom we see from the waist up. Later we see the Captain (Edmund Gwenn) dozing in his rocker; we see all but the Captain's feet, but on the wall behind him we see the shadows of the corpse's feet. These two shots prove Roud's point. The dead complete and shape the living, but the living can make their own use of the dead.

Thus we have the fatal "haunting" of Levet in *The Pleasure Garden*, the heroine's haunting by her past in *Easy Virtue* and in *Blackmail*, and the community's haunting by the past in *Juno and the Paycock* and *The Skin Game*. The individual can succumb to the pressure of his past – or blame it for his own weakness. But the haunting can work as a regeneration, as it does in *The Trouble with Harry*. In *The Farmer's Wife*, too, the dead wife's message provides a new lease on life for her husband, as the lovers' exile will in *The Manxman*. As Roger Thornhill emerges chastened and solidified by his false death in *North by Northwest*,

Richard Hannay assumes a responsibility from the death of the strange woman at the start of *The 39 Steps*; so do Ashenden and his lady from Caypor's death in *Secret Agent*. Even in *Waltzes from Vienna*, Schani descends through the hell of the pastry cook, abandoned suitor, duelling rake, and disowned son, to emerge an Orphic hero. Hitchcock's hero can prove himself by surviving the tribulations that befall him (or that he claims to inherit).

Even more than the insecurity of his characters, though, Hitchcock exploits the insecurity of his audience. Hence his penchant for subjective shooting angles. His early films abound with attempts to depict the character's mind through what he sees. Hence, too, Hitchcock's penchant for expressionistic devices. The camera and printing tricks of *The Lodger*, the hallucinations of *The Pleasure Garden, Downhill*, and *The Ring*, the swoop in *Young and Innocent*, all serve as nonrealistic rhetoric to dramatize the character's state of mind. Hitchcock used images of the concrete to express the reality of the imagination. As Tom Ryall points out, "the openings from *The Lodger* (1926), *The Manxman* (1928), and *Blackmail* (1929) could be documentaries of the newspaper industry, the fishing industry and the police force respectively."[3] So too Hitchcock's delirium sequences document the hot currents of the character's mind. Durgnat's distinction between Hitchcock's "piercing realism" and his "vibrant irrealism" is a merely formal distinction, for Hitchcock's basic interest has always been in how our perceptions reshape our world. His realism constantly shades off into the expressionistic imagery and extravagant technical devices by which he conveys the realism of the emotional state. So his aquarium explosion of Piccadilly Circus in *Sabotage* ranks with the best documentary poetics of Vertov.

Hitchcock continually violates his viewer's expectations. Thus we have the romantic deflations in *The Pleasure Garden, Champagne*, and the surprise of Drew's innocence in *The Lodger*. Where the genre requires a fight, Hitchcock will provide a comic fight, as in *Downhill, No. 17, Waltzes from Vienna*, and *The Lady Vanishes*, for there is no room in Hitchcock's world of vertiginous insecurities for the conventional fight, which makes its protagonists appear efficient.

And from time to time Hitchcock allows his comic spirit, the vision of an anarchic principle at the heart of the universe, to run free. So we get the chaotic consequences of the courtships in *The Farmer's Wife*, the fumbling villains of *The Man Who Knew Too Much*, and old Ben in *No. 17*. Of course, these comedies of chaos are only lighter versions of Hitchcock's essential vision that man's civilization is underpinned by chaos, as we have it in *The Pleasure Garden, Downhill, The Manxman, Champagne, Rich and Strange, Murder!, The 39 Steps*, and *Sabotage*. In his later work, Marion Crane must die *because* she is played by the star, Janet Leigh. For Hitchcock's films are a relentless assault upon the viewer's security, as well as his moral assumptions.

The English films also prove that from the outset Hitchcock's technical innovations were close to the thematic center of the work. The experimental devices of *The Lodger* and *Blackmail* served those film's basic themes, the preoccupation of the former with the misleading power of the perception, and of the latter with the obscurities and difficulties of communication. Then, too, the scenes with off-camera orchestras in *Juno* and *Murder!* were the pivotal points in the psychological development of the narratives. This observation serves as well when we approach Hitchcock's later work.

For example, his massive orchestration of birds for *The Birds*, a staggering technical challenge, is an assertion of the power of the human enterprise in the face of the film's assault upon man's pre-Copernican arrogance. The technical challenge in *Lifeboat* is analogous to its political theme, the fatal isolation of the Allies and their need for a selfless unity. The continuous shooting of *Rope*, which Hitchcock calls his "abandonment of pure cinema"[4] because it eschewed his normal dependence upon dramatic editing, grows out of both the title image – something continuous that will tie one up – and the main theme of the film – the continuity of word into deed; a murderous human reality is spun out of a musing that was considered safely theoretical. The restricted isolation of the camera in *Rear Window* relates to that film's central concern: the distinction between respecting one's brother's privacy and meeting his needs for a keeper. What Durgnat calls Hitchcock's "calmly hermetic aesthetic satisfaction"[5] might be better considered as his passionate synthesis of idea, irony, and technique. In his achievement of the emotional idea and the intellectual image he meets the aim of that other great film editor, Eisenstein. By so brilliantly uniting idea, image, and emotion, Hitchcock has come to make our

Figure 22.2 *The Man Who Knew Too Much* (Gaumont British, 1934): The villain (Peter Lorre) as the anarchic heart of the universe. Produced by Michael Balcon

nightmares for us with a clarity and thrust no other film maker has commanded.

Hitchcock's ironic detachment also explains those moments in his work where we see the seams of his craft, where his technical work may seem to be rough. One lesson which the British films should teach us is that Hitchcock always knows what he is doing. His plots are carefully crafted. For example, he has Drexler rehearse the orchestra of Strauss Sr. so that their surprise performance of Schani's new waltz will not seem implausible. And where Hitchcock's technical work seems shoddy what we really have is not a craftsman nodding but an artist extending his resources. Where Hitchcock's craft seems loose, we usually find his technique subserving his content, his literal realism shading off into vibrant metaphor.

To put it another way, it is safe to assume that what seems to be a Hitchcock error is likely our failure to work out what he is doing. In *The Lady Vanishes*, for instance, the palpably false opening shot and the unreal proportions of the departing train are typical of how Hitchcock extends his realism into expressionism – only to be charged with poor technique. This liberty came from the German cinema. Thus Fritz Lang inserts a jarring interlude of false scenery into a key moment of *Rancho Notorious*.

William Johnson describes Hitchcock's "failure" in *Marnie*:

> It so happens that there are certain departments in which Hitchcock has a patently blind eye. These include the phony backdrops that grate like TV commercials (especially in color), the bits of rapid montage that do not quite fit together, and the two-shots that are held so long that they almost ossify.[6]

The false backdrops in *Marnie* are a concise image of the heroine's predicament: she lives in dislocation from her surroundings and from her own past. The false backgrounds provide a physical expression of the disjunction in her mind. Thus the first false back projection scene is her first scene aboard Florio, when she is

Figure 22.3 Structure is theme in Alfred Hitchcock's *Psycho* (Paramount, 1960). Produced by Hitchcock and Alma Reville

enjoying an artificial respite from her alienation. A loud, rhetorical swell in the music coheres with the rhetoric of the false background. The second is the scene at her mother's home, where the ships' dock is flat and false behind the tenement. The painted ships loom larger than life and paler, imaging the phantom sailor unacknowledged from her past. The false register of both backgrounds move the shots from setting to active symbol. A false front stands behind the Rutland building, a building stripped of its back, or, a foreground unsupported by an integrated backing, as Marnie is. Mark varies this motif by giving Marnie a $42,000 ring instead of a family heirloom; he wants her to "have something that never belonged to anyone before." The line jocularly refers to her thefts, poignantly recalls her childhood, without a bed of her own, and provides another instance of an object without a past, a foreground without an integrated background.[7]

Similarly in *Torn Curtain* the palpable falseness of the garden path up which Newman leads Andrews (Hud leads Mary Poppins) undercuts the noble pretense of the hero's ambitious venture. And what Samuels finds to be the "contentless virtuosity" of *North by Northwest*[8] is the heart of the film: the film's central theme/effect is that total dislocation which the complacent hero and the typically injudicious cinema audience share. As the title tells us, the film deliberately pursues a fantastical course.

It is similarly wrong to consider Hitchcock a craftsman first and only secondarily, accidentally, as it were, an artist. From his first feature on, even through that period of self-conscious "respectable" adaptation, Hitchcock's films had something to say, sometimes an obvious message (*Easy Virtue, Lifeboat*) but more often an integrated theme (*Pleasure Garden, Downhill*). Only because form is content can Hitchcock say "I am interested not so much in the stories I tell as in the means of telling them."[9] Structure is theme in *Psycho, Vertigo, The Trouble with Harry*, but also as early as *The Pleasure Garden, Downhill*, and *The Ring*.

The early films are also notable for their ambitious conception. Though working in an unacknowledged medium, Hitchcock showed himself a serious artist even then. For Hitchcock, popular film is art. His art is the manipulation of the audience's emotions and fantasy through a variety of felt dangers and thrills, to send his viewers out at the end, calm of mind, all smugness spent, ready to brave the hairline moralities of real life. In his early films Hitchcock also dealt with the responsibilities of the artist. The dance-floor meat markets of *The Pleasure Garden*, *Downhill*, and *Champagne*, and the squared circle of *The Ring*, are fairly tawdry arenas of human enterprise. But even in those settings it is possible for an individual to achieve art, to fulfill his own creative and expressive impulses and to establish a community with an audience.

The laughing clown in *Blackmail* provides the neatest statement Hitchcock makes about art. Coherent with the fertility of silent montage, the portrait gains new meaning from each juxtaposition, each context, yet it maintains the same detached, ironic stance regardless of its changing set. When all about are noisy, loud, ambiguous, Hitchcock's mute jester remains silent. Yet the portrait is eloquent in its accusatory stare, its lively eye, its shameless traditional garb. Beyond the inflections of that painting in the story itself, Hitchcock devotes himself to a career of critical irony that will be independent of changes in mode and in medium. The jester retains his acrid independence even when stored in the vaults of the most conventional (the police station; the commercial bastions of light, diversionary cinema).

From *Murder!* we can infer why Hitchcock was never to stray into the esoterica of Bergman, late Godard, or even the Penn of *Mickey One*. For *Murder!* is the drama of an artist who takes his artistic skills and interests into the prosaic business of real life. In *Murder!* some fulfill themselves through art (the theater folk), some conceal themselves in their art (the transvestite trapeze artist), but the noblest and most gifted turn their art to the service of humanity (Sir John), to the discovery of truth and self-knowledge and the saving of lives – from prison and from boredom. The West End artist-aristocrat brings his style and sensitivity to the service of the hurly-burly world.

For Hitchcock life is a matter of drawing art and reality together. In *Stage Fright*, Eve Gill comes from a separated family, a realistic but theatrical father and a whimsical but prosaic mother. Eve's salvation lies in ordinary Smith, a policeman who plays the piano, and in her own abilities at acting and setting scenes. The clues point to the guilt of the Marlene Dietrich figure, but as her song warns us, she is too lazy to be either criminal or moral. The real villain is the Richard Todd character. He is unable to distinguish pretense (art) from reality, so he kills for Dietrich and is ultimately prepared to kill Eve to prove his own insanity. As befits his unharmonized dichotomy, he is chopped in half by the safety curtain on the theater stage.

For Hitchcock, art is to come from life (*Waltzes from Vienna*). But often life emulates art, as in the film parodies in *Sabotage*, *Saboteur* and *North by Northwest*. Art at its best will cultivate, free, and invigorate the human spirit, both the emotion and the will, as the cartoon does for Sylvia in *Sabotage*. Sometimes art will deliver a narrow truth, as Mr Memory does, or deliver one from bondage, as the child is freed by song and by shot in the two versions of *The Man Who Knew Too Much*. But its deeper function is to free the emotions. So Hitchcock often sets up a theatrical situation to expedite a character's physical escape: *The Pleasure Garden*, *Downhill*, *The Ring*, the fashion show in *The Lodger*, the auction in *The Skin Game*, Roger Thornhill's auction in *North by Northwest*, the ballet in *Torn Curtain*. In *Vertigo* even more fully than in *Murder!* and *Stage Fright*, Hitchcock explores the corollary danger: losing one's self in the act of performance. Hence the penultimate image in *Psycho*: Norman Bates dissolves into the skull; the hidden reality overwhelms the muted, visible reality; the role overtakes the self. But like the Todd figure in *Stage Fright*, Norman Bates lost the sense of where life and art were to be distinguished. Upon this distinction and interplay Hitchcock thrives for fifty years of splendid film making.

Hitchcock's genius lies in his synthesis of mind, eye, and heart in the dynamic film experience. Some critics prefer the craft of the American period over the English, or the profundity of the later American films over the earlier diversions. William Pechter prefers Hitchcock's detailed realism of the English thrillers, and bemoans his loss of contact with his audience in the American period. But even in 1931 C.A. Lejeune was to complain of Hitchcock's lack of "the warm humanity of a director like Griffith" and "Pabst's psychological insight":

> His figures are photographic records of synthetic men, not men of flesh-and-blood translated into the medium of the motion picture . . . The fault with Hitchcock's unreality lies in the fact that he has been essentially a director of realistic films; his subjects have been intimate, detailed and individual. He has dealt with one man, not with men . . .[10]

Pechter harkens back to the golden age of the thrillers and Lejeune cavils before them, but both find Hitchcock naturalistically unsatisfying. Nor could anyone accuse the golden thrillers of realism!

Surely the realism of Hitchcock ranges from the physical settings of *The Lodger* to the imaginative inner worlds of *Downhill* and *The Ring*, and between those poles throughout his later career. Always he is a poet and always he is engaged with the moral and perceptual nature of man. The early films are full of emotionally charged scenes, it is true: the praying scene, the fevered kiss, the final killing, in *The Pleasure Garden*; or the private reconciliation of old Strauss in *Waltzes from Vienna*. But there is a well of feeling in Lydia's scenes with the coffee cups in *The Birds* too. The films of Alfred Hitchcock are rich enough, varied enough, yet of a spiritual piece, to make their total enjoyment preferable to any arbitrary choice of preferences. One can watch Hitchcock's British films in order to come to a better understanding of the American ones. But also because they are so good in themselves, so moving, so thoughtful and so much fun.

Notes

1 See Leland Poague, "The Detective in *Frenzy*," *Journal of Popular Film*, Winter, 1973, pp. 47–59.

2 Richard Roud, "In Broad Daylight," *Film Comment*, July–August, 1974, p. 36.

3 Tom Ryall, "Durgnat on Hitchcock," *Screen*, Summer, 1975, p. 123.

Hitchcock told Leslie Perkoff: "I would like to make documentary films, because here you have states of action or movement which can easily be treated by photography and cutting. But a cataclysm in any film, for example, is akin to documentary material. It begins with the camera and goes directly to the cutting room." This is in "The Censor and Sydney Street," *World Film News*, March, 1938, p. 4. Hitchcock here yearns for the fantastical opportunities provided by documentary! He exploited them most obviously in the plot-line and settings of *Rich and Strange*, and in the opening scenes of *Champagne*, *Blackmail*, *The Manxman*, *The Wrong Man*, etc.

4 Peter Bogdanovich, *The Cinema of Alfred Hitchcock* (New York: Museum of Modern Art Film Library, 1963), p. 28.

5 Raymond Durgnat, *The Strange Case of Alfred Hitchcock* (Cambridge, MA: MIT Press, 1974).

6 William Johnson, "*Marnie*," *Film Quarterly*, XVIII, i, pp. 38–42.

7 David Thomson provides a more general interpretation of the device in *Movie Man*, London: Secker and Warburg, 1971, p. 72.

8 Charles Thomas Samuels, "Hitchcock," in *Encountering Directors* (New York: Capricorn/Putnam, 1972), p. 301.

Of course, Hitchcock is famous for the painstaking attention he gives his work before going on the set. See the following articles from *American Cinematographer* as evidence: Hilda Black, "The Photography is Important to Hitchcock: *I Confess*," December, 1952, pp. 524–5, 546–7, 549; Frederick Foster, "Hitchcock Didn't Want it Arty," February, 1957, pp. 84–5, 112–14; Charles Loring, "Filming *Torn Curtain* by Reflected Light," October, 1966, pp. 680–3, 706–7; Herb Lightman, "Hitchcock Talks About Lights, Camera, Action," May, 1967, pp. 332–5, 350–1.

Hitchcock's famous preplanning and subsequent appearance of casualness about the actual shooting may have contributed to the ready disdain for his technical "sloppiness." It certainly alienated André Bazin (see his "Hitchcock vs. Hitchcock," in *Cahiers du Cinema in English*, no. 2, pp. 51–60).

9 Bazin, ibid., p. 55.

10 William Pechter, *Twenty-four Times a Second* (New York, 1971) pp. 175–94. C.A. Lejeune, *Cinema* (London, 1931), pp. 11–12.

23

John Ford's *Young Mr Lincoln*

Editors of *Cahiers du Cinéma*

This essay has been considered a critical milestone since it was first published in *Cahiers du Cinéma* (no. 223) in 1970. By the end of the 1960s *Cahiers* had become a more politically oriented magazine than before. In a previous issue published in 1969, two members of the new editorial board, Jean Comolli and Jean-Louis Narboni, sought to categorize Hollywood films in terms of their relation to ideology. Although their approach helped shape the discussion of directors such as Douglas Sirk, their categories minimized the importance of the director in film analysis. Comolli and Narboni's category "(e)," films that reveal an ideological tension that threaten to crack apart their coherence, have attracted the most critical attention. In this essay, excerpted here, *Cahier*'s editors offer an exhaustively detailed analysis of *Young Mr Lincoln* (1939) by favorite auteur John Ford wherein the director becomes merely one code at play in a series of others, including political, industrial, ideological, and historical forces, that determine the film's meaning. Some of the detailed scene-by-scene textual discussion has been deleted here for reasons of length.

Lincoln is not the product of popular revolution: the banal game of universal suffrage, ignorant of the great historical tasks that must be achieved, has raised him to the top, him, a plebeian, a self-made man who rose from being a stone breaker to being the Senator for Illinois, a man lacking intellectual brilliance, without any greatness of character, with no exceptional value, because he is an average, well-meaning man.

(*Friedrich Engels and Karl Marx,* Die Press, *12-10-1862*)

At one point in our interview, Mr Ford was talking about a cut sequence from Young Mr Lincoln*: and he described Lincoln as a shabby figure, riding into town on a mule, stopping to gaze at a theatre poster. 'This poor ape,' he said, 'wishing he had enough money to see Hamlet'. Reading over the edited version of the interview it was one of the few things Ford asked me to change; he said he didn't much like 'the idea of calling Mr Lincoln a poor ape'.*

(*Peter Bogdanovich,* John Ford, *Studio Vista, London, 1967*)

Young Mr Lincoln: American film by John Ford. *Script:* Lamar Trotti. *Photography:* Bert Glennon. *Music:* Alfred Newman. *Art director:* Richard Day, Mark Lee Kirk. *Set decorations:* Thomas Little. *Editor:* Walter Thompson. *Costume:* Royer. *Sound assistant:* Robert Parrish. *Cast:* Henry Forda (Abraham Lincoln), Alice Brady (Abigail Clay), Arleen Wheelan (Hannah Clay), Marjorie Weaver (Mary Todd), Eddie Collins (Efe Turner), Pauline Moore (Ann Rutledge), Ward Bond (J. Palmer Cass), Richard Cromwell (Matt Clay), Donald Meek (John Felder), Judith Dickens (Carrie Sue), Eddie Quillan (Adam Clay), Spencer Charters (Judge Herbert A. Bell), Milburn Stone (Stephen A. Douglas), Cliff Clark (Sheriff Billings), Robert Lowery (juror), Charles Tannen (Ninian Edwards), Francis Ford (Sam Boone), Fred Kohler, Jr. (Scrub White), Kay Linaker (Mrs Edwards), Russel Simpson

Editors of *Cahiers du Cinéma*, "John Ford's *Young Mr Lincoln*" (excerpt), from *Cahiers du Cinéma* 223 (1970). Reprinted in *Screen* 13, no. 3 (1972).

(Woolridge), Charles Halton (Hawthorne), Clarence Wilson (Dr Mason), Edwin Maxwell (John T. Stuart), Robert Humans (Mr Clay), Jack Kelly (Matt Clay boy), Dickie Jones (Adam Clay boy), Harry Tyler (barber), Louis Mason (clerk), Jack Pennick (Big Buck), Steven Randall (juror), Paul Burns, Frank Orth, George Chandler, Dave Morris, Dorothy Vaughan, Virginia Brissac, Elizabeth Jones. *Producer:* Kenneth Macgowan. *Executive producer:* Darryl F. Zanuck. *Production:* Cosmopolitan/Twentieth Century Fox, 1939. *Distribution:* Associated Cinemas. Length: 101 mn.

1.

This text inaugurates a series of studies the need for which was indicated in the editorial of issue No. 218. We must now specify the objects and method of this work, and the origin of its necessity which has hitherto been merely affirmed.

1. Object: a certain number of 'classic' films, which today are *readable* (and therefore, anticipating our definition of method we will designate this work as one of reading) insofar as we can distinguish the historicity of their inscription:[1] the relation of these films to the codes (social, cultural . . .) for which they are a site of intersection, and to other films, themselves held in an intertextual space; therefore, the relation of these films to the ideology which they convey, a particular 'phase' which they represent, and to the events (present, past, historical, mythical, fictional) which they aimed to represent.

For convenience we will retain the term 'classic' (though obviously in the course of these studies we will have to examine, and perhaps even challenge it, in order finally to construct its theory). The term is convenient in that it roughly designates a cinema which has been described as based on analogical representation and linear narrative ('transparence' and 'presence') and is therefore apparently completely held within the 'system' which subtends and unifies these concepts. It has obviously been possible to consider the Hollywood cinema as a model of such 'classicism' insofar as its reception has been totally dictated by this system – and limited to a kind of non-reading of the films assured by their apparent non-writing, which was seen as the very essence of their mastery.

2. Our work will therefore be a *reading* in the sense of a *rescanning* of these films. That is, to define it negatively first: (a) it will not be (yet another) commentary. The function of the commentary is to distill an ideally constituted sense presented as the object's ultimate meaning (which however remains elusive indefinitely, given the infinite possibilities of talking about film): a wandering and prolific pseudo-reading which misses the reality of the inscription, and substitutes for it a discourse consisting of a simple ideological delineation of what appear(s) to be the main statement(s) of the film at a given moment.

(b) Nor will it be a new *interpretation*, i.e. the translation of what is supposed to be already in the film into a critical system (meta-language) where the interpreter has the kind of absolute knowledge of the exegetist blind to the (historical) ideological determination of his practice and his object-pretext, when he is not a hermeneute à la Viridiana slotting things into a pre-ordained structure.

(c) Nor will this be a dissection of an object conceived of as a closed structure, the cataloguing of progressively smaller and more 'discrete' units: in other words, an inventory of the elements which ignores their predestination for the film maker's writing project and, having added a portion of intelligibility to the initial object, claims to deconstruct, then reconstruct that object, without taking any account of the dynamic of the inscription. Not, therefore, a mechanistic structural reading.

(d) Nor finally will it be a demystification in the sense where it is enough to re-locate the film within its historical determinations, 'reveal' its assumptions, declare its problematic and its aesthetic prejudices and criticise its statement in the name of a mechanically applied materialist knowledge, in order to see it collapse and feel no more needs to be said. This amounts to throwing the baby out with the bathwater without getting wet. To be more precise, it would be disposing of the film in a moralist way, with an argument which separates the 'good' from the 'bad', and evading any effective reading of it. (An effective reading can only be such by returning on its own deciphering operation and by integrating its functioning into the text it produces, which is something quite different from brandishing a method – even if it is marxist-leninist – and leaving it at that.)

It is worth recalling that the external and mechanistic application of possibly even rigorously constructed concepts has always tried to pass for the exercise of a theoretical practice: and – though this has long been established – that an artistic product cannot be linked to its socio-historical context according to a linear, expressive, direct causality (unless one falls into a reductionist historical determinism), but that it has a complex, mediated and *decentred* relationship with this context, which has to be rigorously specified (which is why it is simplistic to discard 'classic' Hollywood cinema on the pretext that since it is part of the capitalist system it can only reflect it). Walter Benjamin has insisted strongly on the necessity to consider literary work (but similarly any art product) not as a reflection of the relations of production, but as having a place *within* these relations (obviously he was talking of progressive works, past, present, and to come: but a materialist reading of art products which appear to lack any intentional critical dimension concerning capitalist relations of production must do the same thing. We will return later at greater length to this basic notion of 'the author as producer'). In this respect we must once again quote Macherey's theses on literary production (in particular those concerning the Leninist corrections to Trotsky and Plekhanov's simplistic positions on Tolstoy) and Badiou's concerning the autonomy of the aesthetic process and the complex relation historical truth/ideologies/author (as place and not as 'internalisation')/work.

And that, given this, denouncing ideological assumptions and ideological production, and designating them as falsification and error, has never sufficed to ensure that those who operated the critique themselves produced truth. Nor what's more has it sufficed to bring out the truth about the very things they are opposing. It is therefore absurd to demand that a film account for what it doesn't say about the positions and the knowledge which form the basis from which it is being questioned; and it is too easy (but of what use?) to 'deconstruct' it in the name of this same knowledge (in this case, the science of historical materialism which has to be practised as an active method and not used as a guarantee). Lest we be accused of dishonesty, let us make it clear that the points made in paragraph (d) refer to the most extreme positions within *Cinethique*.

3. At this point we seem to have come up against a contradiction: we are not content to demand that a film justify itself vis à vis its context, and at the same time we refuse to look for 'depth', to go from the 'literal meaning' to some 'secret meaning'; we are not content with what it says (what it intends to say). This is only an apparent contradiction. What will be attempted here through a re-scansion of these films in a process of active reading, is to make them say what they have to say *within* what they leave unsaid, to reveal their constituent lacks; these are neither faults in the work (since these films, as Jean-Pierre Oudart has clearly demonstrated – see the preceding issue – are the work of extremely skilled film makers) nor a deception on the part of the author (for why should he practise deception?); they are *structuring absences*, always displaced – an overdetermination which is the only possible basis from which these discourses could be realised, the unsaid included in the said and necessary to its constitution. In short, to use Althusser's expression – 'the internal shadows of exclusion'.

The films we will be studying do not need filling out, they do not demand a teleological reading, nor do we require them to account for their *external* shadows (except purely and simply to dismiss them); all that is involved is traversing their statement to locate what sets it in place, to double their writing with an active reading to reveal what is already there, but silent (cf the notion of *palimpsest* in Barthes and Daney), to make them say not only 'what this says, but what it doesn't say because it doesn't want to say it' (J. A. Miller, and we would add: what, while intending to leave unsaid, it is nevertheless obliged to say).

4. What is the use of such a work? We would be obliged if the reader didn't envisage this as a 'Hollywood revisited'. Anyone so tempted is advised to give up the reading with the very next paragraph. To the rest we say: that the structuring absences mentioned above and the establishment of an ersatz which this dictates have some connection with the sexual *other scene*, and that 'other scene' which is politics; that the double repression – politics and eroticism – which our reading will bring out (a repression which cannot be indicated once and for all and left at that but rather has to be written into the constantly renewed process of its repression) allows the answer to be deduced; and this is an answer whose very question would not have been possible without the two discourses of overdetermination, the Marxist and the Freudian. This is why we will not choose films for their value as 'external

masterpieces' but rather because the negatory force of their writing provides enough *scope* for a reading – because they can be re-written.

2. Hollywood in 1938–9

One of the consequences of the 1929 economic crisis was that the major banking groups (Morgan, Rockefeller, DuPont, Hearst, General Motors, etc.) strengthened their grip on the Hollywood firms which were having problems (weakened by the talkies' 'new patents war').

As early as 1935, the five Major Companies (Paramount, Warner, MGM, Fox, RKO) and the three Minor (Universal, Columbia, United Artists) were totally controlled by bankers and financiers, often directly linked to one company or another. Big Business's grip on Hollywood had already translated itself (aside from economic management and the ideological orientation of the American Cinema) into the regrouping of the eight companies in the MPPA (Motion Pictures Producers Association) and the creation of a central system of self-censorship (the Hays code – the American bank is known to be puritanical: the major shareholder of the Metropolitan in New York, Morgan, exercised a real censorship on its programmes).

It was precisely in 1935 that, under the aegis of the Chase National Bank, William Fox's Fox (founded in 1914) merged with Darryl F. Zanuck's 20th Century Productions, to form 20th Century Fox, where Zanuck became vice-president and took control.

During the same period, and mainly in 1937–38 the American cinemas suffered from a very serious drop in box-office receipts (this is first attributed to the consequences of the recession, then, with the situation getting worse, to lack of regeneration of Hollywood's stock of stars); the bank's boards, very worried, ordered a *maximum reduction in costs of production*. This national marketing crisis (in a field in which Hollywood films previously covered their entire costs, foreign sales being mainly a source of profits) was made even worse by the reduced income from foreign sales; this was due to the political situation in Europe, the gradual closure of the German and Italian markets to American films, and the currency blockade set up by these two countries.

3. The USA in 1938–9

In 1932, in the middle of the economic crisis, the Democrat Roosevelt became President, succeeding the Republican Hoover whose policies, both economic (favourable to the trusts, deflationist) and social (leaving local groups and charitable organisations to deal with unemployment: cf *Mr Deeds Goes to Town*, Capra) had been incapable of avoiding the crisis and also of suppressing its effects. Roosevelt's policies were the opposite; federal intervention in the whole country's economic and social life, States as private powers (New Deal); establishment of federal intervention and public works agencies, impinging on the rights and areas previously reserved to State legislature and private companies; a controlled economy, social budget etc.): so many measures which encountered violent opposition from the Republicans and Big Business. In 1935 they succeeded: the Supreme Court declares Roosevelt's federal economic intervention agencies to be unconstitutional (because they interfere with the rights of the States). But Roosevelt's second victory in 1936 smashed these manoeuvres, and the Supreme Court, threatened with reform, ended up by recognising the New Deal's social policies and (among others) the right to unionise.

At the level of the structures of American society, the crisis and its remedies have caused the strengthening of the federal State and increased its control over the individual States and the Trust's policies: by its 'conditional subsidies', its nationwide economic programmes, its social regulations, the federal government took control of vast areas which had previously depended only on the authority of the States and on the interests of free enterprise. In 1937, 'the dualist' interpretation of the 10th amendment of the Constitution – which forbade any federal intervention in the economic and social policies of the States (their private domain) – was abrogated by the Supreme Court from its judgments. This strengthening of federal power at all levels had the effect of *increasing the President's power*.

But, as early as 1937, a new economic crisis emerged: economic activity dropped by 37% compared to 1929, the number of unemployed was again over 10 million in 1938, and despite the refloating of major public works, stayed at 9 million in 1939 (cf *The Grapes of Wrath*). The war (arms industries becoming predominant in the economy) was to help end the new crisis by allowing full employment . . .

Federal centralism, isolationism, economic reorganisation (including Hollywood), strengthening of the Democrat–Republican opposition, new threats of internal and international crisis, crisis and restrictions in Hollywood itself; such is the fairly gloomy context of the *Young Mr Lincoln* (1939) undertaking.

It is no doubt difficult, but necessary to attempt to estimate the total and respective importance of these factors to the project and the ideological 'message' of the film. In Hollywood, more than anywhere else the cinema is not 'innocent'. Creditor of the capitalist system, subject to its constraints, its crises, its contradictions, the American cinema, the main instrument of the ideological super-structure, is heavily determined at every level of its existence. As a product of the capitalist system and of its ideology, its role is in turn to reproduce the one and thereby to help the survival of the other. Each film, however, is inserted into this circuit according to its specificity, and there has been no analysis if one is content to say that each Hollywood film confirms and spreads the ideology of American capitalism: it is the precise articulations (rarely the same from one film to the next) of the film and of the ideology which must be studied (see 1).

4. Fox and Zanuck

20th Century Fox (which produced *Young Mr Lincoln*), because of its links with Big Business, also supports the Republican Party. From its inception the Republican Party has been the party of the 'Great Families'. Associated with (and an instrument of) industrial development, it rapidly became the 'party of Big Business' and follows its social and economic directives: protectionism to assist industry, anti-unionist struggle, moral reaction and racism (directed against immigrants and Blacks – whom the party had fleetingly championed in Lincoln's time: but it is common knowledge that this was due once again to economic reasons and to pressures from religious groups, groups which fifty years later were to lead a campaign against everything that is 'unamerican'.

In power from 1928 to 1932 with Hoover as president, the Republican Party is financed by some of Hollywood's masters (Rockefeller, Dupont de Nemours, General Motors, etc.). At the elections in 1928 87% of the people listed in *Who's Who in America* supported Hoover. He has put the underwriters of Capital at key posts in the administration: the Secretary to the Treasury is none other than Mellon, the richest man in the world (take an example of his policies: he brings down the income tax ceiling from 65% in 1919 to 50% in 1921, and 26% in 1929).

Forced by Roosevelt to make a number of concessions, American Big Business goes to war against the New Deal as soon as the immediate effects of the depression decrease (for example, the private electricity companies withdraw their advertising – which, in the USA is equivalent to a death sentence – from the newspapers which support Roosevelt and his Tennessee Valley Authority) and they do everything in their power to win the 1940 election.

All this allows us to assume that in 1938–9, Fox, managed by the (also) Republican Zanuck, participated in its own way in the Republican offensive by producing a film on the legendary character Lincoln. Of all the Republican Presidents, he is not only the most famous, but on the whole the only one capable of attracting mass support, because of his humble origins, his simplicity, his righteousness, his historical role, and the legendary aspects of his career and his death.

This choice is, no doubt, all the less fortuitous on the part of Fox (which – through Zanuck and the contracted producer Kenneth Macgowan – is as usual responsible for taking the initiative in the project, and not Ford) that during the preceding season, the Democrat Sherwood's play 'Abe Lincoln in Illinois' had been a great success on Broadway. With very likely the simultaneous concern to anticipate the adaptations planned in Hollywood of Sherwood's play (John Cromwell's film with Raymond Massey came out the same year and, unlike Ford's, was very successful), and to reverse the impact of the play and of Lincoln's myth in favour of the Republicans, Zanuck immediately put *Young Mr Lincoln* into production – it would, however, be wrong to exaggerate the film's political determinism which cannot, under any circumstances, be seen, in contrast, for example, to Zanuck's personal productions, *The Grapes of Wrath*, or *Wilson*, as promoting the company's line.

Figure 23.1 Fordian Americana with Will Rogers in *Judge Priest* (Fox Film, 1934). Produced by Sol Wurtzel

Producer Kenneth Macgowan's past is that of a famous theatre man. Along with Robert Edmond Jones and Eugene O'Neill, he has been manager of the Provincetown Playhouse; they had had a considerable influence on American theatre. A friend of Ford's, whom he met at RKO during the period of the *The Informer*, he moved over to Fox in 1935 (there he produced *Four Men and a Prayer* among others) and became the man responsible for historical biographies which constitute the core of the company's productions.

Young Mr Lincoln is far from being one of Fox's most important productions in 1939, but this film was shot in particularly favourable conditions; it is one of the few cases in which the original undertaking was least distorted, at least at the production stage: of thirty films produced by Macgowan in the eight years he spent at Fox (1935–43) this is one of the only two which were written by only one scriptwriter (Lamar Trotti) (the other being *The Return of Frank James*, written by S. M. Hellman). Another thing to remark on: these two scripts were written in close collaboration with the directors, who were, therefore, involved at a very early stage instead of being chosen at the last minute, as is the custom, even at Fox (the 'directors studio'). Ford even says of the script: 'We wrote it together' (with L. Trotti), a rare if not exceptional statement coming from him.

Lamar Trotti had already written two comedies on old America for Ford (of the species known as 'Americana'), *Judge Priest* and *Steamboat Round the Bend*, before specialising in historical films with Fox (such as *Drums Along the Mohawk*, directed by Ford after *Young Mr Lincoln*).

The background to a whole section of the script is the obsession with lynching and legality which is so strong in the thirties' cinema, because of the increase in expeditive justice (lynching), the consequences of gangsterism, the rebirth of terrorist organizations such as the KKK (cf Lang's *Fury*, Mervyn LeRoy's *They*

Won't Forget, Archie Mayo's *Black Legion*). Trotti, a southerner (he was born in Atlanta and had been a crime reporter before editing a local Hearst paper), combined one of Lincoln's most famous anecdotes with a memory from his youth. 'When Trotti was a reporter in Georgia he had covered the trial of two young men accused of murder at which their mother, the only witness, would not tell which son had committed the crime. Both were hanged' (Robert G. Dickson, 'Kenneth Macgowan' in *Films in Review*, October 1963). In Lincoln's story, a witness stated having seen, in the moonlight, an acquaintance of Lincoln's (Duff Armstrong) participate in a murder. Using an almanac as evidence, Lincoln argued that the night was too dark for the witness to have seen anything and thus obtained Armstrong's acquittal with this plea.

5. Ford and Lincoln

Ford had already spent the greater part of his career with Fox: he made thirty-eight movies between 1920 and 1935! Since Zanuck's take-over, he had made four movies in two years, the first in 1936, *The Prisoner of Shark Island* ('I haven't killed Lincoln'). Thus it was to one of the company's older and more trustworthy directors that the project was entrusted. The same year, again with Zanuck, Ford shot *Drums Along the Mohawk* (whose ideological orientation is glaringly obvious: the struggle of the pioneers, side by side with Washington and the Whigs against the English in alliance with the Indians) and in 1940 *The Grapes of Wrath* which paints a very gloomy portrait of the America of 1938–39. Despite the fact that he calls himself a-political we know that Ford in any case greatly admires Lincoln as a historical figure and as a person: Ford, too, claims humble peasant origins – but this closeness with Lincoln as a man is, however, moderated by the fact that Ford is also, if not primarily, Irish and Catholic.

In 1924 already, in *The Iron Horse*, Lincoln appears as favouring the construction of the intercontinental railway (industry and unification); at the beginning of *The Prisoner of Shark Island* we see Lincoln requesting 'Dixie' from an orchestra after the Civil War (this is the tune which he 'already' plays in *Young Mr Lincoln*): symbolically, the emphasis is put on Lincoln's unifying, nonvindictive side and his deep southern sympathies by means of the hymn of the Confederation; in *Sergeant Rutledge* (1960) he is evoked by the Blacks as their Saviour; the anti-slavery aspect; in *How the West Was Won* (1962) the strategist is presented; finally in *Cheyenne Autumn* (1964), a cornered politician turns to a portrait of Lincoln, presented as the model for the resolution of any crisis.

Each of these films thus concentrates on a particular aspect either of Lincoln's synthetic personality or of his complex historical role; he thus appears to be a sort of universal referent which can be activated in all situations. As long as Lincoln appears in Ford's fiction as a myth, a figure of reference, a symbol of America, his intervention is natural, apparently in complete harmony with Ford's morality and ideology; the situation is different in a film like *Young Mr Lincoln* where he becomes the protagonist of the fiction. We will see that he can only be inscribed as a Fordian character at the expense of a number of distortions and reciprocal assaults (by him on the course of fiction and by fiction on his historical truth).

6. Ideological Undertaking

What is the subject of *Young Mr Lincoln*? Ostensibly and textually it is 'Lincoln's youth' (on the classic cultural model – 'Apprenticeship and Travels'). In fact – through the expedient of a simple chronicle of events presented (through the presence and actualisation effect specific to classic cinema) as if they were taking place for the first time under our eyes, it is the *reformulation* of the historical figure of Lincoln on the level of the myth and the eternal.

This ideological project may appear to be clear and simple – of the edifying and apologetic type. Of course, if one considers its statements alone, extracting it as a *separable ideological statement* disconnected from the complex network of determinations through which it is realized and inscribed – through which it possibly even criticises itself – then it is easy to operate an illusory deconstruction of the film through a reading of the demystificatory type (see 1). Our work, on the contrary, will consist in activating this network in its complexity, where philosophical assumptions (idealism, theologism), political determinations (republicanism, capitalism) and the relatively autonomous aesthetic process (characters, cinematic *signifiers*, narrative mode) specific to Ford's writing, intervene simultaneously. If our work, which will necessarily be held to the linear sequentiality of the discourse, should isolate the orders of determination interlocking in the film, it will always be in the perspective of their relations: it therefore demands a recurrent reading, on all levels.

7. Methodology

Young Mr Lincoln, like the vast majority of Hollywood films, follows linear and chronological narrative, in which events appear to follow each other according to a certain 'natural' sequence and logic. Thus two options were open to us: either, in discussing each of the determining moments, to simultaneously refer to all the scenes involved; or to present each scene in its fictional chronological *order* and discuss the different determining moments, emphasising in each case what we believe to be the main determinant (the key signification), and indicating the secondary determinants, which may in turn become the main determinant in other scenes. The first method thus sets up the film as the object of a reading (a text) and then supposedly takes up the totality of its overdetermination networks simultaneously, *without taking account of the repressive operation* which, in each scene, determines the realisation of a key signification; while the second method *based itself on the key signification of each scene*, in order to understand the scriptural operation (overdetermination and repression) which has set it up.

The first method has the drawback of turning the film into a text which is *readable a priori*; the second has the advantage of making the reading itself participate in the *film's process of becoming-a-text*, and of authorising such a reading only by what authorises it in each successive moment of the film. We have therefore chosen the latter method. The fact that the course of our reading will be modelled on the 'cutting' of the film into sequences is absolutely intentional, but the work will involve breaking down the closures of the individual scenes by setting them in action with each other and *in* each other.

8. The Poem

After the credits (and in the same graphic style: i.e. engraved in marble) there is a poem which consists of a number of questions which 'if she were to come back on earth', Lincoln's mother would ask, concerning the destiny of her son.

(a) Let us simply observe for the moment that the figure of the mother is inscribed from the start, and that it is an absent Mother, already dead, a symbolic figure who will only later make her full impact.

(b) The enumeration of questions on the other hand programmes the development of the film by designating Lincoln's problematic as being that of a choice: the interrogative form of this poem, like a matrix, generates the binary system (the necessity to choose between two careers, two pies, two plaintiffs, two defendants, etc.) according to which the fiction is organised [. . .].

(c) In fact, the main function of the poem, which pretends that the questions posed therein haven't yet been answered (whereas they are only the simulation of questions since they presume the spectator's knowledge of Lincoln's *historical character*), is to set up the dualist nature of film and to initiate the process of a double reading. By inviting the spectator to ask himself 'questions' to which he already has the answers, the poem induces him to look at history – something which, for him, has already happened – as if it were 'still to happen'. Similarly by on the one hand playing on a fictional structure of the 'chronicle' type ('natural' juxtaposition and succession of events, as if they were not dictated by any determinism or directed towards a necessary end), and on the other hand by contriving, in the scenes where a crucial choice must be made by the character, a margin of *feigned indecisiveness* (as if the game had not already been played, Lincoln had not entered history, and as if he was taking every one of his decisions on the spot, in the present), the film thus effects a *naturalisation* of the Lincolnian myth (which already exists as such in the mind of the spectator).

The retroactive action of the spectator's knowledge of the myth on the chronicle of events, and the naturalist rewriting of the myth in the divisions of this chronicle thus impose a reading in the future perfect. 'What is realised in my story is not the past definite of what once was since it is no more, nor the perfect of what has been in what I am, but the future perfect of what I will have been for what I am in the process of becoming' (Lacan).

A classic *ideological* operation manifests itself here, normally, through questions asked after the event whose answer, which has already been given, is the very condition for the existence of the question.

9. The Electoral Speech

First scene. A politician dressed in townclothes (John T. Stuart, later to become Lincoln's associate in Springfield) addresses a few farmers. He denounces the corrupt politicians who are in power and Andrew Jackson, President of the USA; he then introduces the local candidate whom he is sponsoring: young Lincoln. The first shot, in which we see Lincoln, shows him sitting on a barrel leaning backwards, in shirtsleeves, wearing heavy boots (one recognises the classic casualness of Ford's hero, who has returned and/or is above everything). In the next shot, addressing the audience of farmers, Lincoln in a friendly tone (but not without a hint of nervousness) declares: 'My politics are short and sweet like your ladies' dances; I am in favour of a National Bank and for everybody's participation in wealth.' His first words are 'You all know who I am, plain Abraham Lincoln' – this is meant not only for the spectators in the film, who are anyway absent from the screen, but also to involve the spectator of the movie, brought into the cinematic space; thus this treatment in the future perfect is immediately confirmed (see 8).

This programme is that of the Whig party, at that time in opposition. It is in essence the programme or nascent American capitalism: protectionism to favour national industrial production, National Bank to favour the circulation of capital in all the states. The first point traditionally has a place in the programme of the Republican Party (it is thus easily recognisable to the spectator of 1939); the second calls to mind a point in history: while in power before 1830, the Whigs had created a National Bank (helping, industrial development in the North) whose powers Jackson, who succeeded them, attempted to weaken: the defence of this bank was thus one of the demands of the Whigs, who later became Republicans.

(a) The specifically *political* notations which introduce the film, have the obvious function of presenting Lincoln as the candidate (that is, in the future perfect, the President, the champion) of the Republicans.

(b) But the scorn which is immediately shown towards the 'corrupt politicians' and the strength in the constrast of Lincoln's programme which is simple as 'a dance', have the effect of introducing him (and the Republicans in his wake) as the opposition and the remedy to such 'politics'. Furthermore we will see later that it is not only his opponents' politics which are 'corrupt', but all politics, condemned in the name of morality (the figure of Lincoln will be contrasted, with that of his opponent Douglas, with that of the prosecutor, as the defender of Justice versus the politicians, the Uncompromising versus the manipulators).

This disparagement of politics carries and confirms the *idealist* project of the film (see 4 and 6): moral virtues are worth more than political guile, the Spirit more than the Word (cf 4, 6, 8). (Likewise, politics appears again, later, as the object of discussion among drunks – quarrel between J.P. Cass and his acolyte – or of socialite conversation: carriage scene between Mary Todd and Douglas).

But what is most significant here is that the points of the electoral programme are *the only indications* of a *positive relation* between Lincoln and politics, all others being negative (separating Lincoln from the mass of 'politicians').

(c) We may be surprised that a film on Lincoln's youth could thus empty out the truly political dimension from the career of the future President. This massive omission is too useful to the film's ideological purpose to be fortuitous. By playing once again on the spectator's knowledge of Lincoln's political and historical role it is possible to establish the idea that these were founded on and validated by a Morality superior to all politics (and could thus be neglected in favour of their Cause) and that Lincoln always draws his prestige and his strength from an intimate relationship with Law, from a (natural and/or divine) knowledge of Good and Evil. Lincoln *starts* with politics but soon rises to the moral level, divine right, which for an idealist discourse – originates and valorises all politics. Indeed, the first scene of the film already shows Lincoln as a political candidate without providing any information either on what may have brought him to this stage: *concealment of origins* (both his personal – family – origins and those of his political knowledge, however basic: that is 'his education') which establishes the mythical nature of the character; or on the results of this electoral campaign (we know that he was defeated, and that the Republicans' failure resulted in the shelving of the National Bank, among other things): as if they were in fact of no importance in the light or the already evident significance of fate and the myth. Lincoln's character makes all politics appear trivial.

But this very *repression* of politics, on which the ideological undertaking of the film is based, is itself a *direct result* of political assumptions (the eternal false idealist debate between morality and politics: Descartes versus Machiavelli) and at the level of its reception by the spectator, this repression is not without consequences of an equally political nature. We know that the ideology of American Capitalism (and the Republican Party which traditionally represents it) is to assert its divine right, to conceptualise it in terms of permanence, naturalism and even biology (cf Benjamin Franklin's famous formula: 'Remember that money has genital potency and fecundity') and to extol it as a universal Good and Power. The enterprise consisting of the concealment of politics (of social relations in America, of Lincoln's career) under the idealist mask of Morality has the effect of regilding the cause of Capital with the gold of myth, by manifesting the 'spirituality' in which American Capitalism believes it finds its origins and sees its eternal justification. The seeds of Lincoln's future were already sown in his youth – the future of America (its eternal values) is already written into Lincoln's moral virtues, which include the Republican Party and Capitalism.

(d) Finally, with the total suppression of Lincoln's political dimension, his main historico-political characteristic disappears from the scene of the film: i.e. his struggle against the Slaver States. Indeed, neither in the initial political sequence, nor in the rest of the film is this dominant characteristic of his history, of his legend even, indicated, whereas it is mainly to it that Lincoln owes his being inscribed into American history more than any other President (Republican or otherwise).

Strangely enough, only one allusion is made to slavery (this exception has the value of a signal): Lincoln explains to the defendants' family that he had to leave his native state since 'with all the slaves coming in, white folks just had a hard time making a living'. The fact that this comment emphasises the economic aspects of the problem at the expense of its moral and humanitarian aspects would appear to contradict the points outlined above (primacy of morality over politics) if Lincoln had not spoken these words in a scene [. . .] where he puts himself in the imaginary role of the son of the poor farmer family. He recalls his own origins as a poor white who, like everyone else, suffered from unemployment. The accent is thus put on the economic problem, i.e. the problem of the whites, not the blacks.

The *not-said* here, this exclusion from the scene of the film of Lincoln's most notable political dimension, can also not be fortuitous (the 'omission' would be enormous!), it too must have *political significance.*

On the one hand, it was indeed necessary to present Lincoln as the unifier, the harmoniser, and not the divider of America (this is why he likes playing 'Dixie': he is a Southerner). On the other hand, we know that the Republican Party, abolitionist by economic opportunism, after the Civil War rapidly reappeared as more or less racist and segregationist. (Already, Lincoln was in favour of a progressive emancipation of the blacks, which would only slowly give them equal rights with the whites). He never concealed the restrictions he asked for concerning the integration of blacks. Considering the political impact that the film could have in the context described above (see 3, 4) it would have been in bad taste on both these accounts to insist on Lincoln's liberating role.

This feature is thus silenced, excluded from the hero's youth, as if it had not appeared until later, when all the legendary figure's other features are given by the film as present from the outset and are given value by this predestination.

The shelving of this dimension (the Civil War) which is directly responsible for the Lincolnian Legend thus allows a political use of this legend and at the same time by castrating Lincoln of his historico-political dimension, reinforces the idealisation of the myth.

But the exclusion of this dominant sign from Lincoln's politics is also possible because *all the others* are rapidly pushed out (except for the brief positive and negative notations mentioned above which in any case are in play as *indicators* – of the general repression of politics – and of stamping of the Republican cause by the seal of the Myth) and because this fact places the film immediately on the purely ideological plane (Lincoln's a-historical dimension, his symbolic value).

Thus what *projects the political meaning* of the film is not a directly political discourse: it is *a moralising discourse.* History, almost totally reduced to the time scale of the myth with neither past nor future can thus at best only survive in the film in the form of a *specific repetition:* on the teleological model of history as a continuous and linear development of a pre-existing *seed,* of the future contained in the past (anticipation, predestination). Everything is there, all the features and characters of the historical scene are in their place (Mary Todd who will become Lincoln's wife, Douglas whom he will beat at the presidential elections, etc, right up to Lincoln's death: in a scene which Fox cut, before the film was first released, one could see Lincoln stop in front of a theatre presenting Hamlet and facing one of the (Booth family) troupe of actors – his future murderer), the problematic of deciding [. . .] and of unifying is already posed . . . The only missing thing is the main historical feature, this being the one on which the myth was first constructed.

But such repression is possible (acceptable by the spectator) only inasmuch as the film plays on what is *already known* about Lincoln treating it as if it were a factor of *non-recognition* and at the limit, a not-known (at least, something that nobody wants to know any more, which for having been known is all the more easily forgotten): it is the already constituted force of the myth which allows not only its reproduction, but also its reorientation. It is the universal knowledge of Lincoln's fate which allows, while restating it, the omission of parts of it. For the problem here is not to build a myth, but to negotiate its realisation and even more to rid it of its historical roots in order to liberate its universal and eternal meaning. 'Told', Lincoln's youth is in fact *rewritten* by what has to filter through the Lincolnian myth. The film establishes not only Lincoln's total predestination (teleological axis) but also that *only that to which he has been shown to be predestined* deserves immortality (theological axis). A double operation of addition and subtraction at the end of which the historical axis, having been abolished and mythified, returns cleansed of all impurities and thus recuperable to the service not just of Morality but of the morality re-asserted by capitalist ideology. Morality not only rejects politics and surpasses history, it also rewrites them.

10. The Book

Lincoln's electoral speech seems to open up a fiction: electoral campaign, elections . . . A problem is presented, which we have the right to expect to see solved, but which in fact will not be solved. To use the Barthesian formula, we have the elements of a hermeneutic chain: enigma (will he or won't he be elected?) and non-resolution. This chain is abandoned by the use of an abrupt fictional displacement: the arrival of the family of farmers. Lincoln is called away to help them. This family comprises the father, the mother and two twelve year old boys. They want to buy some material from Lincoln thus informing us of his occupation: he is a shopkeeper. But the family has no money: Lincoln offers them credit, and confronted by the mother's embarassment, argues that he himself has acquired his shop on credit, The situation is resolved by the use of barter: the family owns a barrel full of old books (left behind by the grandfather). Delighted at the mere mention of a book (legendary thirst for reading) Lincoln respectfully takes one out of the barrel: as *if by chance,* it is Blackstone's 'Commentaries'. He dusts the book, opens it, reads, realises that it is about Law (he says: 'Law') and is delighted that the book is in good condition (the Law is indestructible).

(a) It's a *family* [. . .] of pioneers who are *passing through* that gives Lincoln the opportunity of coming in contact with Law: emphasis on the luck-predestination connection as well as on the fact that *even without knowing it* it is the humble who transmit Law (religiously kept by the family as a legacy from the ancestor). On the other hand we have here a classic Fordian fictional feature (apart from the family as a displaced centre): meeting and exchange between two groups whose paths need not have crossed (a new fictional sequence is born from this very meeting; it is first presented as a suspension and simple digressive delay of the main narrative axis, later it constitutes itself as being central, until another sequence arises, functioning in the same mode, Ford's total fiction existing finally only as an articulation of successive digressions).

(b) Lincoln makes a brief but precise speech in praise of credit: 'I give you credit' – 'I don't like credit' (says the farmer-woman incarnating the dignity of the poor) – 'I myself bought my shop on credit': when one is aware of the role played by the extension of credit in the 1929 crisis, this kind of publicity slogan uttered by an American hero (who later, with ever increasing emphasis will be the Righteous man) tends to appear as a form of exorcism: without credit, the development of capital is impossible; in a period of recession (1935–40) when unemployment is high and wages have gone down, the maintenance of the level of consumption is the only thing which allows industry to carry on,

(c) The fact that Law is acquired by barter introduces a circuit of debt and repayments which is to run through the film (see 23).

(d) The principle function of this sequence is to introduce a number of constituent elements of the symbolic scene from which the film is to proceed, by *varying* and activating it (in this sense it is the true expository scene of the fiction, the first scene becoming pretextual and possibly even *extra-textual*): The Book and the Law, the Family and the Son, exchange and debt, predestination . . . This *setting up* of the fictional matrix means *putting aside* the first sequence (political speech): a simple digression, first believed to be temporary, but then seen to be in fact the first step in the operation of the repression of politics by morality which will continue through the whole film (see 9).

[. . .]

24. Work of the Film

With the fiction reaching saturation point here, what culminates in the final sequence is nothing other than the effects of meaning, re-scanned by our reading through the film as a whole, taken to their extreme. That is: the unexpected results (which are also contrary in relation to the ideological project) produced by the inscription – rather than flat illustration – of this project within a cinematic texture and its treatment by a writing which, in order to carry through the project successfully, maximising its value *and only that* (it's obvious that Ford takes practically no distance in relation to the figure and the ideology of Lincoln) is led to: such distortions (the setting up of a system of deception); such omissions (all those scenes, necessary in the logic of the crime thriller but whose presence could have lessened the miraculous dimension of Lincoln's omnipotence: the confrontation with the accused, the least one could expect of a lawyer); such accentuations (the dramatisation of the final scenes); such scriptural violence (be it for the repression of violence – the lynching, the trial); such a systemisation of determination and election (throughout a film which at the same time wants to play on a certain suspense and free choice without which the fiction could neither develop nor capture interest); in short to such a *work* that today simply delimiting its operation and the series of means it puts into action allows us to see the price at which such a film could be made, the effort and detours demanded to carry the project through.

And which Jean-Pierre Oudart in the following conclusion, the point of departure of our study, cannot but repeat.

25. Violence and Law

I. A discourse on the Law produced in a society which can only represent it as the statement and practice of a moralist prohibition of all violence, Ford's film could only reassert all the idealist representations which have been given it. Thus it is not very difficult to extract from it an ideological statement which seems to valorise in all innocence the ascetic rigour of its agent, making it into the unalterable value which circulates throughout the film from scene to scene; it is also easy to observe that this cliché, presented as such in the film and systematically accentuated, is not there merely to ensure the acceptability of the Fordian inscription. Without this cliché which provides the fiction with a kind of metonymic continuity (the same constantly re-asserted figure) – whose necessity is moreover overdetermined, it's function being more than simply setting up a

Figure 23.2 The lawyer and future president (Henry Fonda) defends the family and the Law in John Ford's *Young Mr Lincoln* (Twentieth Century Fox, 1939). Produced by Darryl F. Zanuck

character whose 'idealism' can most conveniently be signified by the external signs of the very puritan sense of election – the film would appear, in fact does appear in spite of it, to be a text of disquieting unintelligibility; through its constant disconnections, it places us in a forced position for the reading and in fact its comprehension demands:

(1) That one first take no account of this at once insistent and fixed statement;
(2) That one listens carefully to what is stated in the succession of so obviously 'Fordian' scenes which support this statement, and in the relations between the figures, all more or less part of the Fordian fiction, which constitute these scenes;
(3) That one tries to determine how all these are involved; i.e. to discover what the operation by which Ford inscribes this character into his fiction consists of, insofar as, despite appearances, it is not superimposed on Ford's 'world', does not traverse it like a foreign body, but finds through this inscription into his fiction a designated place as representative of his Law; for the film maker promotes the character to the role to which his (legendary) historical referent destines him only at the price of his subjection to the (Fordian) fictional logic. This determined his entry there in advance insofar as his role was already written and his place already set out in Ford's fiction. The work of Ford's écriture only becomes apparent in this film through the problem involved in producing the character in this role, in that he took a place which was already occupied.

II. It is the character of the mother that incarnates the idealised figure of Ideal Law in Ford's fiction. Moreover, it is often, as in *Young Mr Lincoln*, the widowed mother, guardian of the deceased father's law. It is for her that the men (the regiment) sacrifice the cause of their desire, and under her presidency that the Fordian celebration takes place; this in fact consists in a simulacrum of sexual relations from which all effective desire is banned. But it is in the constantly renewed relationship of this group with another (the Indians), in the dualism of Ford's universe that the inscription of the structural imperative of Law which dictates the deferment of desire and imposes exchange and alliance is realised, in violence, guided by the mediating action of the hero (often a bastard) who is placed at its intersection.

III. In *Young Mr Lincoln* one of the results of using a single character for both roles is that he will have both their functions, which will inevitably create, by their interference and their incompatibility (insofar as one secures the taboo on the violence of desire, the other is agent of its inscription), disturbances, actions which oppose the order of Ford's world, and it is remarkable that each comical effect always shows them up (there is no film in which laughter is so precisely a sign of a constant disorder of the universe). The compression of their functions will in fact be used only on the one level of the castration of the character (signified at the ideological level by its puritan cliché, and at the same time written, in the unconscious of the text, as the effect of the fictional logic on the structural determination of the character) and of his castrating action, in a fiction ruled by Ideal Law alone since the dualism of Ford's world is abandoned in favour of the mass-individual opposition. (In fact the political conflict intervenes only as a secondary determination of the fiction and literally only acts backstage). In fact, we see that:

(1). The character's calling originates in his renouncing the pleasures of love; it is strengthened because he resists its attraction: Lincoln becomes so well integrated in the fiction and so vigilant against the violences and plots which take place there only because he refuses to give in to the advances constantly made to him by women, affected by a charm which is due only to the prestige of his castration.

(2). This extreme postponement of the hero's desire soon becomes meaningful since it permits him to become the restorer of Ideal Law, whose order has been perturbed by a crime which the Mother has not been able to prevent but which she will attempt to stifle.

This shows that:

(1). The puritan cliché which Ford emphasises has the very precise function of promoting the character to his role as mediator, insofar as the pleasure which he rejects allows him to thwart any attempt at sexual and political corruption; it thus simultaneously guarantees the credibility of the figure of Lincoln and the position of the character as the figure of Ideal Law in Ford's fiction. At the obvious price of installing him within a castration, whose comical aspects Ford uses sufficiently to indicate how indifferent he is to producing an edifying figure, and how much more attentive he is to the disturbing results of its presence in the fiction: for example in the dance scene in which his character perturbs the harmony, where the agent of Law behaves like a kill-joy, thus making visible what the harmony of the Fordian celebration would conceal.

(2). The fact that the character literally takes the place of the Mother, i.e. takes on simultaneously her ideal position and her function (since he assumes responsibility for her children, and promises to feed them well in the new home which the prison becomes) gives rise to a curious transformation of the figure, as this repetition of roles is effected under the sign of a secret which the Mother must (believes she does) keep to try to prevent any violence – even, inconceivably, that of the Ideal Law which she incarnates – against her children; and by thus incubating the crime she projects her role into a quasi erotic (almost Hitchcockian) dimension never presented as such by Ford, since usually the fiction protects her from any relationship with the crime (since it is part of her function to be ignorant of violence). This is comically reintroduced in the final scene of the trial, when the real proof (an almanac on a sheet of which should have been written the letter of love which Lincoln was planning to write for her, only to lull her attention and extract confessions from her) is pulled out of Lincoln's hat; it was necessary for the re-establishment of Law that by the end of the trial a signifier (the proof of the crime) be produced whose very occultation renders it erotic; and that it must necessarily be produced by the figure of Law to fit into the fictional logic since it is from this ideal Law that originated the cancellation of the criminal act in the fiction, the statement of the taboo on violence (on pleasure), the position of the Mother as the figure of forbidden violence (pleasure), the possession of the phallus by this figure (as a signifier of this pleasure) and the production of the proof of the crime as if it were a phallic signifier obviously proceeding from the same statement. In such fictions this usually means, either that the weapon, the trace of the crime, acts like a letter which Law must decipher, since its very proscription has written it, or that the confession be produced by the criminal as a return of the repressed in an erotic form. The two results are here compressed, Law producing the proof of the crime (the writing which reveals the murderer) as if it were a phallic object which Ford's comedy presents like the rabbit pulled out of the conjuror's hat; the improbable levity with which Ford brings the trial to its close really can only be read as a masking effect which conceals to the end the 'human' context, thus allowing the logic of the inscription to produce this gag as its ultimate effect, a final consequence of Lincoln's re-enactment of the Mother's role, a fantastic return of the mask.

IV. The fact that the overdetermination of this inscription of the Lincoln figure, as agent of the Law, in Ford's fiction by all the idealised representations of Law and its effects produced by the bourgeoisie, far from having been erased by Ford, has been declared by his writing and emphasised by his comedy, shows what a strange ideological balancing act the film-maker has insisted on performing, and what strange scriptural incongruities he has insisted on exploiting; to the extent that by the fictional constraints he gave himself, by giving up the usual bisection of his fiction and the sometimes truly epic inscription of Law thereby articulated (which recalls Eistenstein in *The General Line*) he could only produce the Law as a pure prohibition of violence, whose result is only a permanent indictment of the castrating effects of its discourse. Indeed to what is the action of his character reduced if not hitting his opponents at their weakest point – weaknesses which Ford always perversely presents as being capable of provoking a deadly laughter? So that the sole but extreme violence of the film consists of verbal repression of violence which, in certain scenes (the unsuccessful lynching) is indicated as really being a death sentence, a mortal interdict which has no equivalent except maybe in Lang and which shows the distance Ford, or rather his writing, keeps between himself and the idealist propositions which he uses.

V. For, with a kind of absolute indifference to the reception given to his stylistic effects, the film-maker ends by practising stubbornly a scriptural perversion which is implied by the fact that, paradoxically, in a film meant to be the Apology of the Word, the last word is always given to the iconic signifier, entrusted by Ford with the production of the determining effects of meaning. And as in this film what is to be signified is always either the (erotic, social, ideological) separation of the hero relative to his surroundings, or the immeasurable distance between him and his actions, or the absence of any common denominator between the results he obtains and the means he uses, and those obtained by his opponents (insofar as he holds the privilege of the castrating speech), Ford succeeds, by the economy of means which he uses to that effect – his style forbidding him the use of effects of implicit valorisation of the character which he could have drawn from an 'interiorised' writing – in simultaneously producing the same signifier in completely different statements: (for example in the moonlight scene, where the moonlight on the river indicates at the same time the attempted seduction, the past idyll, and the hero's 'idealist' vocation); or even in renewing the same effect of meaning in totally different contexts (the same spatial disconnections of the character used in the dance scene and the murder scene). So that the intention of always making sense, of closing the door to any implicit effect of meaning, of constantly re-asserting these same meanings, in fact results – since to produce them the film-maker always actualises the same signifiers, sets up the same stylistic effects – in constantly undermining them, turning them into parodies of themselves. (With Ford parody always proceeds from a denunciation of the writing by its own effects.) The film's ideological project thus finds itself led astray by the worst means it could have been given to realise itself (Ford's style, the inflexible logic of his fiction) mainly to the benefit of a properly scriptural projection (obtained not by the valorisation after the event of previously constituted effects of meaning, but proceeding directly from the inscription, produced anew and resolved in each scene, of the character in Ford's fiction) of the effects of the repression of violence: a violence whose repression, written thus turns into exorcism, and gives to its signifiers, in the murder and the lynching scenes, a fantastic contrast which contributes considerably to the subversion of the deceptively calm surface of the text.

Note

1. This usage of inscription (*l'inscription*) refers to work done by Jacques Derrida on the concept of *écriture* in *Theorie d'ensemble* (Collection Tel Quel, 1968) which will be taken up in a future issue of *Screen*. *Cahiers'* point here is that all individual texts are part of and inscribe themselves into one historically determined 'text' (*l'histoire textuelle*) within which they are produced; a reading of the individual text therefore requires examining both its dynamic relationship with this general text and the relationship between the general text and specific historical events.

24

Towards an Analysis of the Sirkian System

Paul Willemen

Despite being dismissed as sentimental trash by Pauline Kael, Douglas Sirk's films have been long embraced by critics and filmmakers such as Rainer Werner Fassbinder and Todd Haynes, who have admired Sirk's ability to work within the studio system making commercially successful movies that are at once characteristic entertainments of their era and devastating social critiques. British critic Paul Willemen, who has published books on Indian cinema and Israeli director Amos Gitai and co-edited *Questions of Third Cinema* and other volumes on film and cultural studies, was involved in several of the auteurist studies produced by the Edinburgh Film Festival, including those devoted to Douglas Sirk and Frank Tashlin. In this essay Willemen discusses the formal elements of Sirk's style, particularly as they relate to irony and a Brechtian notion of distanciation, and how these stylistic choices allow Sirk to make his complex melodramas during a conservative era in the United States.

Since the *Screen* issue of Summer 1971, a great deal has been written on Sirk's work: the interview book *Sirk on Sirk*[1] by Jon Halliday was published and a book of essays compiled by the Edinburgh Film Festival and edited by Jon Halliday and Laura Mulvey, *Douglas Sirk*,[2] was published recently. In addition, the magazine *Monogram* devoted a special issue to the melodrama with special emphasis on Sirk's work and *Positif* reviewed the *Screen* issue, adding new material, some of which was translated into English and included in the Edinburgh book. In conjunction with the book, the Edinburgh Film Festival mounted an extensive retrospective of Sirk's work which was subsequently taken over en-bloc by the National Film Theatre. Douglas Sirk himself spent a great deal of time and energy answering questions and helping critics and students in the arduous but rewarding task they had set themselves: to try and understand how a Sirk film works.

As Jon Halliday points out in *Douglas Sirk* (p. 60), Sirk has been praised either for his stylistic qualities or else for being a master of the weepie. With the exception of the two articles by Halliday and J-L Bourget, the essays in *Douglas Sirk* reflect these two apparently irreconcilable approaches. Sirk is either praised for making extraordinary films in spite of the exigencies of the weepie as a genre, or else it is the weepie-genre itself which is validated, and Sirk is brought forward as its most accomplished practitioner. Indeed it is these genuine contradictions within the

Paul Willemen, "Towards an Analysis of the Sirkian System," pp. 128–34 from *Screen* 13, no. 4 (Winter 1972/1973).

work of Douglas Sirk which to some extent invite both approaches.

In order to understand this contradiction and to assess the function of such contradictions in the Sirkian system, one must again turn to Sirk's theatrical experience in Germany in the twenties. In 1929 Sirk staged Brecht's *Threepenny Opera* with immense success, As left-wing intellectuals in the German theatrical world, both artists reacted against expressionism, although it is quite clear that both were equally influenced by the movement. Brecht's early plays bear witness to this, as do some of Sirk's Hollywood films; *The Tarnished Angels* in particular. In fact, Sirk makes a direct allusion to expressionist ideas in the phantasmagoria speech in *Captain Lightfoot.* Although it is not clear whether Brecht approved of Sirk's production of the *Threepenny Opera* (*Sirk on Sirk*, p. 23), during his career in Hollywood Sirk made frequent use of techniques Brecht had pioneered in the play and achieved very similar results. In his study *Lecture De Brecht*[3] Bernard Dort describes Brecht's pre-epic technique as that of the 'boomerang image'. Brecht presented the theatre public with the image of life that it wanted to see on the stage, but in order to denounce the unreality of such an image, to denounce its ideological character (p. 189). Brecht himself explained that the *Threepenny Opera* attacks bourgeois conceptions not only by choosing them as a content, by the mere fact of presenting them on the stage, but also by the manner of presentation itself. The play shows a way of life which the spectator wishes to see portrayed in the theatre. At the same time, however, he is forced to confront aspects of this life with which he would rather not be confronted: he not only sees his wishes fulfilled, but he sees them criticised and is thus forced to perceive himself as object, rather than subject. Bernard Dort continues:

> The picturesque robbers of the *Threepenny Opera* are not bandits: they are robbers only as the bourgeoisie dreams them. In the final analysis we realized that they are in fact members of the bourgeoisie. Or, more precisely, it is through the disguise of the robbers that the spectators will come to recognise themselves as being bourgeois. A subtly engineered set of displacements and discontinuities facilitates such a self-recognition. In this way Brecht has attempted to sabotage the notion of the theatre as a mirror (for our fantasies). . . . Brecht puts on the stage what seems to be the image of the kind of exotic society that the spectator wants to see. In fact what the spectator discovers in the very unreality of such an image, is himself. The mirror of the stage does not reflect the world of the audience any more, but the ideological disguises of the audience itself. Suddenly, at that point, the mirror refers us back to our own reality. It bounces the images of the spectacle back to us – like a boomerang. (pp. 190–1)

Sirk's films operate in a similar way. It has been shown how Sirk takes distance from the spectacle he presents, but that there is no distance between the audience and the film (*Douglas Sirk*, p. 23). In fact, Sirk mercilessly implicates the audience by the use of techniques deliberately designed to involve the spectator emotionally (*Sirk on Sirk*, p. 70). In contradistinction to social-comment-melodramas such as *A Tree Grows In Brooklyn, Gentleman's Agreement* (both by Elia Kazan), *Peyton Place* (by Mark Robson), *No Down Payment* (by Martin Ritt) etc., Sirk's films short circuit the so-called channel of communication between director and audience. Instead of inscribing the director's personal view or message into the film and thus by extension denying that any 'personal' statement must to a very large extent be dictated by both the society and the industry within which the director works, Sirk inscribes his distance from the spectacle into the film. In this way, the diegesis ceases to appear transparent: it becomes the point beyond which the spectator cannot go. It is this sense of an absence behind the diegesis, so to speak, which Fred Camper (*Douglas Sirk*, p. 79ff) quite mistakenly describes as a two-dimensionality within Sirk's films.

Sirk's films could be described as the opposite of a distorting mirror: the world the audience wants to see (an exotic world of crime, wealth, corruption, passion, etc.) is a distorted projection of the audience's own fantasies to which Sirk applies a correcting device, mirroring these very distortions. This conjunction of, or rather contradiction between distantiation and implication, between fascination and its critique, allows Sirk to thematise[4] a great many contradictions inherent in the society in which he worked and the world he depicted. It equally gives us the means to read Sirk's own contradictory position within that society and vis-à-vis that world.

Jon Halliday has indicated (*Douglas Sirk*, p. 59ff) and has been supported on this point by Sirk himself

Figure 24.1 *Written on the Wind* (Universal-International, 1956): Douglas Sirk's melodramas are the opposite of a distorting mirror. Produced by Albert Zugsmith

(*Sirk on Sirk*, p. 89) that the society depicted in most of the films is characterised by a smugness and complacency masking decay and disintegration from within, just beneath the surface. Sirk also indicates his own contradictory position within the society in which he found himself (*Sirk on Sirk*, p. 86). He was attempting to make critique of a society which: (a) provided him with the money and the tools to make his films, but (b) would not be offended to the extent that it would withdraw its support in the form of box-office receipts. These primary contradictions generated further, secondary contradictions in Sirk's work:

1. Although the films were products of, for and about Eisenhower-America, they were misunderstood at that time. Sirk explained this in terms of the American audience's failure to recognise irony (*Sirk on Sirk*, p. 73) and the lack of a genuine film culture based on a theory of aesthetics (*Sirk on Sirk*, p. 72).
2. Now that these films are beginning to be understood, even in English-speaking countries, American society has undergone a process of social change and now produces quite different films. This change contributes to some extent to the contemporary critic's tendency to misread Sirk's films: critics tend to judge Sirk's presentation of Eisenhower-America by the standards of contemporary critiques of ideology, thus committing the mistake of neglecting the true relevance and meaning of the films at the time they were produced. One of the major contributions of Jon Halliday's writing on Sirk is precisely that he situates Sirk's films in their own historical context, a fact the critic has to grasp before he can comment on the relevance of Sirk's films in our own historical context. Within the films themselves, these

externally determined contradictions are mirrored in a wide variety of ways, often differing from film to film:

- Displacements and discontinuities in plot construction: 'The supporting part in the picture is your hidden leading man' (*Sirk on Sirk*, p. 98). Examples of this can be found in *Sign of the Pagan, Written on the Wind, Thunder on the Hill,* etc. A creative use of discontinuity can be seen in Sirk's comments on his happy-endings: 'It makes the crowd happy. To the few it makes the aporia more transparent' (*Sirk on Sirk*, p. 132).
- Contradictions in characterisation: '(Taza is) a symbolic in-between man: he is an Indian, but there has seeped into the character this element of civilisation' (*Sirk on Sirk*, p. 82). Also Kyle Hadley's invitation to Lucy (in *Written on the Wind*) to come and 'meet an entirely different character' which manifests itself only when he's 'up in the blue' but is present in the background throughout the film. In fact, all Sirk's best films contain such split-characters.
- Ironic use of camera-positioning and framing: in *The Tarnished Angels*, the identification with the solid character, Burke Devlin, is undermined by the camera which shoots him in low angles, so that he appears to hover over the Shumanns as a bird of prey. As we 'see' through Devlin's eyes, this is a classic example of the camera-style achieving a boomerang-image. In *All that Heaven Allows*, such irony is achieved in the first scenes within the close-knit Scott family by framing Cary Scott in such a way that she always remains separated from her two children. In this context, Tim Hunter's comments on *Summer Storm* (*Douglas Sirk*, pp. 31 sq) and Mike Prokosh's essay on *Imitation of Life* (*Douglas Sirk*, pp. 89ff) abound with examples of such inner contradictions.
- Formal negations of ideological notions inherent in the script: *Magnificent Obsession* contains many such elements of parody: the 'true source of spiritual life' is compared to electricity supplying the current for a non-descript sort of table-lamp; the camera movement revealing the god-like purveyor of worldly wisdom benignly nodding to Bob Merrick when the latter is about to perform a tricky operation. Other examples of such elements of parody and of the ironic use of cliché are given in the essay *Distantiation and Douglas Sirk* (*Douglas Sirk*, pp. 23ff).
- Irony in the function of camera-movement: Sirk's camera, as a rule, remains at some distance from the actors. The space in the diegesis, although rigorously circumscribed, is vast and solidly established. Long-shots and mid-shots predominate. The camera, however, is almost continuously in motion. This mobility of the camera is designed to implicate the viewer on an emotional level (*Sirk on Sirk*, p. 43), while the distance from the characters suggests detachment.

This last type of contradiction, that between mobility (i.e. insecurity, emotional involvement) and distance (i.e. detachment, solidly establishing a locus for the diegesis) refers to a dialectic which is perhaps the most dynamic aspect of the Sirkian system, because it underpins the very notion of the Sirkian spectacle: people put themselves on show in order to protect themselves. Mirrors are nearly always there, in the background, to remind them of the fact that they live in a world where privacy is virtually non-existent. The characters are aware of being under scrutiny, so their best protection is to try and take command of the situation by determining their own appearance, if necessary even by deliberately putting on an act. However, the persona developed in this way functions as a trap: it is the persona, the pretence which comes to dominate, causing conflicts against which there is no further defence. Thus the persona in fact is shown to reveal them in a far more naked and vulnerable way. At the same time, the audience is presented with what it would like to see – such as people suffering the extremes of anxiety, titillating sexual image – while the criticism of such voyeurism is inscribed in the film itself, We are not just looking into a world which is unaware of our watchful presence (the mirrors amongst other things convey this lack of privacy within the film), nor are the characters in the diegesis mere puppets in the hands of the

Great-Manipulator-Behind-The-Scenes. We watch them, they are aware of being watched and perform accordingly, attempting to protect themselves by controlling what they allow us – and their fellow characters – to see. The effect is that the audience sees nothing more than the distortions and constraints which it forced upon the spectacle in the first place. In other words, the audience's ideology is unmasked and is made to rebound back upon itself. Awareness of its own reality is forced upon it, against its wishes. This dialectic also finds its representation within the film: although the characters are aware of being under scrutiny (a form of surveillance manifested as pressures to conform to standards of behaviour imposed on them by their environment), they refuse to recognise the mirror-image of themselves, or better still, they refuse to look into the mirror. This is amply illustrated by Gary Scott's fear of the TV-set in *All that Heaven Allows*. Blindness can be another such refusal to see, as in *Magnificent Obsession*. Helen Phillips has lost her sense of security (security being a husband whose life depended on the immediate availability of a resuscitator!) and refuses to see the man who wants to restore that security. A Sirk film sets out to do for the audience what the TV-set does for Cary Scott or surgery for Helen Phillips. This dialectic between self-protection and exhibitionism, sensationalism and puritanism is particularly relevant for the whole of the Hollywood cinema, even today (see Charles Barr's analysis of Sam Peckinpah's rape-scene in *Straw Dogs*, in *Screen*, vol 13 n 2, 1972).

Only now, after Jon Halliday's interview book and the preliminary explorations published in the Edinburgh Film Festival's book of essays, has the ground been cleared for a more accurate and comprehensive study of the work of Douglas Sirk. Such a study would have to examine in some detail this extremely complex web of contradictions, the interaction of which forms the Sirkian system.

Both the views of Sirk as a Marxist critic of Eisenhower-America or of Sirk as the greatest exponent of the bourgeois weepie are equally misguided. In fact, Sirk's position in the history of the American cinema closely parallels Tolstoy's position in the history of Soviet literature. Lenin considered Tolstoy to be a unique and extremely valuable artist because he dramatised and presented the contradictions within Russian society at the turn of the century, a time when Tsarism wasn't strong enough to prevent a revolution while the revolution did not yet have enough strength to defeat Tsarism. Sirk performed a similar function in the American cinema in the fifties: he depicted a society which appeared to be strong and healthy, but which in fact was exhausted and torn apart by collective neuroses.

In this context, it becomes possible to understand and explain the enormous success of many of Sirk's best films at the time of their release, and the subsequent neglect and/or rejection of his work by the 'intelligentsia for many years. The reason for this is analogous to the reason why Brecht's *Threepenny Opera* was, and still is, such a huge public success. As Bernard Dort points out, the technique of the boomerang-image carries with it some ominous pitfalls. Either the sophistication of the process is ignored, thus allowing the bourgeois audience to operate a recovery-manoeuvre: the audience indeed recognises its own image as bourgeois, but enhanced with the exotic prestige of robbers (or corrupt millionaires, actresses or stunt fliers). Or alternatively, if the audience is more knowledgeable about aesthetic processes, they have to reject such a representation, as their ideology does not allow them to recognise themselves in that mirror-image. Hence the rejection or wilful misreading (by turning it into camp) of Sirk's films by the reviewers and nostalgia-freaks.

In spite of these pitfalls, the fact remains that, taking into account the historical and economic context within which he worked, Sirk developed the most refined and complex possible system to convey his critique under the circumstances. Even if they did not allow him to make this critique as explicit as he might have wanted to (except perhaps in films such as *Written on the Wind* and *The Tarnished Angels*), the Sirkian system at least manifested and thematised the contradictions within that society in a way which, throughout American film history, has perhaps only been equalled by Ernst Lubitsch.

Notes

1 Jon Halliday, *Sirk on Sirk*, Cinema One Series. Secker & Warburg, London 1971.

2 Jon Halliday and Laura Mulvey (eds.), *Douglas Sirk*. Edinburgh Film Festival, Edinburgh 1972.

3 Bernard Dort, *Lecture De Brecht*, Eds du Seuil, Paris, 1960.

4 This term is used in the sense of transforming the conditions of production into a theme through a process of internalisation. American capitalism can be internalised into a theme by a systematic refusal to use, or alternatively by a systematic use of, extremely expensive camera movements, such as crane-shots or tracking-shots.

My Name is Joseph H. Lewis

Paul Kerr

This article, which appeared in the journal *Screen* in 1983, looks at the question of authorship in the case of a Hollywood director whose career for the most part consisted of B genre films. Apart from a few cult favorites, notably the films noir *Gun Crazy* (aka *Deadly is the Female*, 1949) and *The Big Combo* (1955), Lewis' films are mostly efficient formula movies that have attracted virtually no critical attention. He had no defining relationship with a specific studio or genre, and Kerr is less interested in identifying the personal vision of Lewis as an auteur than in examining how a director who had to work within not only the studio system but also the meager means of B film production managed to use those very constraints to distinguish his films from other similar movies. If there is no consistent core of thematic and stylistic motifs in Lewis' films, it is because their textual qualities were determined by the changing economic conditions of B film production.

Despite the recent publication of John Caughie's excellent anthology, *Theories of Authorship*,[1] auteurism has been conspicuously absent from the agenda of *Screen*[2] in particular and film studies in general of late. But auteurism refuses to go away. It crops up in Festival retrospectives, in the programming of repertory cinemas, as the organising principle behind cinema seasons on television, in educational syllabuses and among the assumptions of articles in *Screen* itself. Indeed there remains, as Caughie argues, a reluctant sense in which while it is assumed that authorship (in both its traditional humanist 'exception to the Hollywood rule' and its post-structuralist 'subject's construction of and by a reading' guises) is an inadequate critical concept, it is difficult – if not altogether impossible – to entirely dispense with it. Caughie's anthology itself collects much of the best writing on the relation between texts and authors but is quick to acknowledge the relative absence of work on the relation between authors and contexts. Understandably dubious of the liberal extensions of auteurism to embrace non-directorial personnel and similarly sceptical about the contextualising work done on Hollywood genres and Hollywood as industry,[3] Caughie admits that his book

> has very little to say on the place of the author within institutions (industrial, cultural, academic), or on the way in which the author is constructed by and for commerce. Partly this reflects a dissatisfaction with most of what has been written, which has tended to remain within the romantic concept of the artist, with its concentration on questions of artistic freedom and industrial interference, and with its continual desire to identify the true author out of the complex of creative personnel. At the same time, questions of the author's relation to institutional and commercial contexts are increasingly being recognized as crucial . . .[4]

Paul Kerr, "My Name is Joseph H. Lewis," pp. 48–67 from *Screen* 24, nos. 4–5 (July/October 1983).

This article attempts to sketch out – if not yet to fill in – some of the gaps discussed by Caughie concerning the place of the author within those institutions.

The title of this piece has both a playful and a polemical purpose. Playful because it marries the title of Joseph H. Lewis' first major success, *My Name is Julia Ross*, with an echo of the first clause of John Ford's famous statement 'My name is John Ford. I make Westerns.' Unlike Ford, Lewis – in spite or perhaps because of the cult status of some few of his films – is not familiar enough to assume such an easy equivalence with a directorial oeuvre, let alone to conjure up a conventional genre, nor can his name even be relied upon to guarantee recognition among readers of specialist journals like *Screen*. And this, to risk repeating myself, is important. There is no obvious genre that Lewis can claim to have made his own – as Ford could modestly associate himself with the Western, Lewis began and ended his career with Westerns, but in between was a decade or more in which he made none at all and it is that decade, in which he essayed the musical, the comedy, the war film and the crime thriller, with which I am primarily concerned here, and in which Lewis made his name as a director. Indeed, if it can be said that Lewis made any categorisable and consistent type of film at all in those years then the critical consensus can suggest only two coherent candidates for such continuity. First, that they are all 'Lewis' films, a formulation which simply elides the problem by transforming the auteur canon itself into a virtual genre; and second, that they are all 'B' films destined for the bottom half of Hollywood's double bills.

There is, however, a third and rather more contentious case to be made for Lewis: indeed, a number of critics have already argued that the bulk of his 1945–55 output falls into the category now known as *film noir*. This may, of course, be no more than a symptom of the very real difficulty auteurists have experienced attempting to define and describe these films. Nevertheless, their eccentricities, their excessiveness, their expressiveness as texts of and for their time, combined with their centrality in, their representativeness of a particular professional strategy at a specific moment and mode of the American cinema's, and indeed the American film industry's, development is what interest me now.

This article grew out of a paper I presented at the 1980 Edinburgh Film Festival which included a pretty comprehensive retrospective of Lewis' films. That retropective itself says a great deal about Lewis' standing in 1980 though the conclusions reached by the various contributors to the event all share the conviction that Lewis is and was something of an unsuitable case for the Edinburgh treatment. It is also significant that the Edinburgh Retrospective, unlike many of its predecessors, did not transfer to the National Film Theatre in London or inspire a tie-in publication. On the other hand, this article itself is a part of the expanding Lewis bibliography. The draft presented in Edinburgh was itself derived from an earlier article published in *Screen Education*[5] and this case study of Lewis, however schematic, presents an opportunity for amending the more obvious weaknesses and filling in some of the more gaping omissions of that previous piece. What it does not attempt is textual analysis – not because this is not considered crucial in relocating authors in institutions, but because there are several very useful examples of such analyses already available.[6]

What follows can be divided into three relatively distinct parts: first, a claim for the surprisingly continuous results of, but historically and institutionally extremely diverse reasons for, expending energy in familiarising exhibitors, audiences and critics with Lewis' name; second, a sketch of the landmarks in the industrial terrain in which Lewis operated and a discussion of the ways in which 'he' achieved some of the 'effects' for which he has since been celebrated; and third, a survey of the history of attempts to construct Lewis as an author within the critical and academic institutions.

In 1942 the United States government reached a temporary settlement with the major studios in the so-called Paramount Case and, for the 'big five' vertically integrated majors at least, the twin practices of block booking and blind selling were either effectively curtailed or banned outright.[7] For the first time all their products had to be sold to exhibitors individually and this included 'B' films which were even, occasionally, now subject to press previews and trade shows. Relatively rapidly B films were encouraged to become increasingly competitive, compulsorily and compulsively different, distinctive. What had previously, perhaps, been a rather static aesthetic and occupational hierarchy between Bs and As became suddenly more flexible. No longer could a company like Columbia guarantee outlets for its films in blocks – it had to sell them singly and it could consequently no longer rely on its own 'trade name' to attract exhibitors or assure quality. Rather paradoxically perhaps, one of the avenues this opened up among the 'ambitious Bs' involved the contravention of current formulas and standard stylistic practices (too often referred to as the Classic Hollywood style), as indulgence in excess, individuality, idiosyncrasy, virtuosity as if for its own sake. Within these differences, however, residues of Hollywood's cinematic standardisation remained. First, of course, the constraints within which such 'experiments' took place were real and tight; secondly, the conventions against which such reactions were expressed remained relatively common among a large number of different film-makers wishing to 'make a name for themselves'; and thirdly, in order for a director like Lewis to differentiate his work from that of his contemporaries he would be obliged to standardise his own style wherever possible, for purposes of recognition – and reward.

Today, the naming of such directors as Fuller, Karlson, Mann, Ray, Siodmak, Tourneur, Ulmer and so on continues for rather different reasons. At the level of British distribution and exhibition there remains a need to 'authorise' Hollywood directorial retrospective repertory screenings as Art in order to attract art-cinema audiences otherwise antipathetic to American cinema; film critics, meanwhile, require authors to 'credit' for the films they review in columns still dominated by the methods of literary criticism. And at a more academic level, the fashion for *film noir* in particular and for Hollywood's post-war years in general which has characterised the 1970s and early '80s can be understood as nostalgia for a certain style, specifically a style which contravened not only the supposed 'standard practices' of the time but also the theoretical accounts of more generalised Hollywood practices articulated in *Screen* and elsewhere. More cynically, it adds another 'individual' name to the 'traditional' pantheon of teachable 'talents'. Finally, the presence of television, historically, has not only had an arguable effect on the development of *film noir* but also – it is often alleged – complied readily and in an almost parodic manner with some at least of the rules of that realism which *film noir* has been hailed as having broken.

Attempting to locate the author, Lewis, in the place and time of Hollywood in the late forties and early fifties is far from simple. In 1974 Edward Buscombe, writing an article for another of Edinburgh's Hollywood director retrospectives – this time on Raoul Walsh – sought, by sketching out the 'house style' of Warner Brothers, where Walsh worked continuously for some years, and relating it, albeit tentatively, to that studio's industrial structure, to 'call into question the simple notion of Walsh as an auteur who dictated the style and contents of his pictures.[8] Instead, Buscombe argued that

> working for a studio with as distinctive a policy and style as Warners imposed a number of constraints on any director. Yet these constraints should not be thought of as merely negative in their operation. Working for the studio meant simply that the possibilities for good work lay in certain directions rather than in others.[9]

In attempting to adapt Buscombe's approach to a specific period in the cinematic career of Joseph H. Lewis, a number of problems rapidly appear. First of all, Lewis – unlike Walsh (or, for that matter, Ford) – was never exclusively involved with a single studio for more than four or five consecutive years. From the first film he directed, in 1937 to the last, in 1958, Lewis worked at Grand National (1937), then Universal (1937–8), then Columbia (1940), then Monogram (1940–1), then PRC (1941), then Universal again (1942), back to PRC (1944), then PKO (1945), Columbia again (1945–9), then for the King Brothers (distributed by United Artists, 1950), then MGM (1950), then for United States Pictures (distributed by Warner Brothers, 1951), then back to MGM (1952–5), then for Security-Theodora Productions (distributed by Allied Artists, 1955), then for Scott-Brown (distributing through Columbia, 1955–6), and finally two films for Collier Young Associates and Seltzer Films (both of which were distributed by United Artists, 1957–8). Whether this almost incessant mobility is more characteristic of the Bs than of more prestigious productions or whether it is more specific to Lewis is difficult to determine. The number of companies that Lewis worked for, however, together with the fact that the peak period of his career coincides with the decline (and divorce) of the vertically integrated studio system (as the presence of so many independents towards the end of the Lewis list bears out) suggests that a director/studio study is inappropriate here. Furthermore, as an unprestigious director Lewis' career is relatively undocumented. In order to overcome some at least of these problems I restrict my attention here to an industrially defined (sub-)enre, the B *film noir*, an area in which, it has been argued, a large proportion of Lewis' 1945–55 output can comfortably be situated; this focus allows me to draw in some detail on my *Screen Education* article.

There I associated the development of the B *film noir* with what I called 'a negotiated resistance to the realist aesthetic on the one hand and an accommodation to restricted expenditure on the other',[10] a formula which should become clearer in the following paragraphs. Very schematically, the argument boils down to the conviction that *film noir*, far from being reducible to a specific socio-political atmosphere, aesthetic ancestry or a set of émigré authorial signatures, actually related to the particular conditions of its production, distribution and exhibition. Indeed, I suggested that *film noir* combined an economically determined 'low budget' mode with an ideologically determined 'anti-realist' mode. What I did not discuss in that article, and what I would like to briefly draw attention to here, are what Althusserians would describe as the political determinants of the genre.

Very briefly. I would suggest that the B *film noir* is an ambitious B, a B bidding for critical and/or commercial prestige. The Supreme Court rulings against blind selling and block booking encouraged and indeed obliged the B companies (and the B units within the majors, though perhaps here the pressures were somewhat diluted and delayed) to inject an element of expressive individuality into their products. At the same time the shift to independent production (partly accelerated by tax incentives) and the rise of the Directors Guild professionalised the directors, reaffirming the rhetoric of individuation, creativity and differentiation. The Directors Guild, founded in 1936, succeeded in drawing up an agreement with the studios in 1939 recognising the creative function of the director, ensuring salary minimums and safeguarding contracts.

Low key lighting – a characteristic as common to *film noir* as it was rare in other contemporary genres and almost entirely absent from the thrillers of the previous decade – functioned simultaneously to conceal the meagre production values of the B *film noir* while itself constituting a striking style. This propensity away from realist denotation toward 'expressionist' connotation was also a consequence of (and could cash in on) the constraints of the Production Code. Furthermore, the 'hybrid' quality of the *film noir* was perhaps, at least in part, attributable to increasing studio insecurities about marketing their B product (covering all their generic options, as it were, in each and every film). The experience of directors like Lewis in companies as different as MGM and PRC and genres as distinct as spy films, horror films, musical westerns, screwball comedies and war films – experiences denied many contemporary directors who worked only at the prestige end of the industry – may also have contributed to the curiously cross-generic quality of the B *film noir*. Similarly, if low key lighting styles, for example, were more economic than their high key alternatives they were also dramatically and distinctively different from them, from the A films that tended to employ them and from the new technologies of Technicolor, television and deep focus, all of which necessitated high key.

By the end of the 1950s the studio system, the double bill, black and white cinematography, the Production Code, the very status of cinema as the most popular – and profitable – art were all being eroded. In their place, a shift was already taking place to independent production, to single feature programmes, colour cinematography, wide and small screens and an audience classification system. The period of this transition, the period in which the equation between black and white on the one hand and realism on the other was at its most fragile is that of the B *film noir*, the period in which Joseph H. Lewis made his name.

Between 1945 and 1955 Lewis directed twelve films; of these, one is a light comedy, one is a swashbuckler and another a (noirish) war film. The other nine are *The Falcon in San Francisco* (1945), *My Name is Julia Ross* (1945), *So Dark the Night* (1946), *The Undercover Man* (1949), *Gun Crazy (1950)*, *A Lady Without Passport* (1950), *Desperate Search* (1952), *Cry of the Hunted (1953)* and *The Big Combo* (1955). The latter was his last black and white film and his last *film noir*. Lewis' career in cinema continued with four Technicolor Westerns; he then turned to television where he continued to direct episodes of Western series into the 1960s.

Before looking in any detail at the production of any of Lewis' B *films noirs* (all of which had running times under 90 minutes and almost all of which were made on the conventionally derisory schedules and budgets of the second feature), it is worth making a

Figure 25.1 *The Big Combo* (Allied Artists, 1955) was Joseph H. Lewis' last film in black and white and his last *film noir*. Produced by Sidney Harmon

few observations about his earlier career. Lewis had worked as a director for almost ten years by this time at the smaller B companies and in the B units of the 'little three' majors. Consequently he was already identified (as many B directors were) with specific series of second features, in Lewis' case the Bob Baker/Fuzzy Knight singing Westerns and the Bowery Boys films. *The Falcon in San Francisco* was also one of a series of RKO Falcon films but Lewis' employment there seems to have been on a strictly one-off contract. Perhaps the ever-fluid administration at RKO meant that for a director to exercise any consistent or coherent 'creativity' there s/he needed a strong producer/production unit behind which to shelter (viz. Val Lewton). From RKO Lewis turned to Columbia where he was to make the film that was to bring him critical and even commercial success for the first time. At Columbia, the production unit structure seems to have exercised considerably less importance than at RKO; at Columbia, the crucial factor seems to have been the favour of Harry Cohn.

Lewis worked at Columbia from 1945–9, his most prolonged period with any company. His first film there was *My Name is Julia Ross*, a project he claims to have chosen for himself and for which he was allocated a twelve-day shooting schedule and a 125,000 dollar budget – limits which Lewis apparently exceeded by four or five days and 50,000 dollars respectively.[11] Having gone considerably over both budget and schedule without severe reprimand Lewis even managed to secure a sneak preview for the finished film (which ran only 65 minutes) – an apparently almost unprecedented event for a B film but presumably a part of Columbia's new 'ambitious B' strategy. According to Lewis the film grossed four or five million dollars; certainly Lewis' future with Columbia was guaranteed and positive reviews by the likes of James Agee together with a New York Critics Award cannot have damaged the film's chances.

The little three companies (Columbia, Universal and United Artists – so-called to distinguish them from the theatre-owning big five: Paramount, Twentieth

Century Fox, MGM, Warner Brothers and RKO) had refused to sign the 1940 Consent Decree eliminating blind selling and block booking among the majors. Compliance with the Decree obliged the majors to introduce trade shows for all their films and to opt for a maximum of five films per sales package. With their theatre chains regularly hungry for new product the majors understandably opted for the continuation of the mass production system which they had already operated for more than a decade. The minors, on the other hand, decided to slim down, producing fewer, better films. The little three's refusal to endorse the Decree did not prevent the other majors from transforming the industry. Paramount, RKO and Fox reduced their selling blocks to five; MGM went to blocks of ten, Warners and UA used unit sales while Columbia and Universal stayed with full season blocks. But the Big Five's transformed strategy inevitably influenced even the least flexible companies: selling by studio brand name became increasingly untenable, even for companies like Columbia which still sold films in large blocks; and B competition and consequent differentiation intensified. Thus, Columbia's ambitious risk with *My Name is Julia Ross* was reprised elsewhere, especially in the B *film noir*. At Universal, Siodmak's *The Killers* began as a B; at Fox Preminger's *Laura* had similar low-budget origins and was destined for the bottom half of the bill; and at Warner Brothers Huston's *The Maltese Falcon* was also allegedly conceived and cast as a second feature. Lewis describes in *Positif* how Columbia could not stretch to a budget for extras on *Julia Ross* (each of whom would have cost fifteen dollars a day) but forced him to create an 'English' atmosphere through imaginative assembly of stock footage, studio streets and sets, fog, fountains and back projection. James Agee, in the *Nation*, wrote 'The film is well planned, mostly well played, well directed and in a somewhat boomhappy way, well photographed – all around, a likeable, unpretentious, generally successful attempt to turn good trash into decently artful entertainment.'[12]

At the success of *Julia Ross* Columbia encouraged Lewis to direct another 'crime melodrama' (a phrase that recurs throughout the trade press reviews of Lewis' *films noirs*, as well as those of other directors). Based on an inexpensive *Readers' Digest* story, the script of *So Dark the Night* necessitated twenty days shooting and a French town set but Lewis' B budget – probably no more than for *Julia Ross* – could not meet the twenty dollars a day that Fox demanded in rent for theirs. Lewis has described in some detail how he and his art director and sketch artist walked round the Columbia back lot looking for a possible, passable location:

> We walked around that back lot which was over in the valley, I'll bet you six times, and I kept coming back to one spot. One spot. And that one spot – there was a town – they had made a war film and they bombed the hell out of it, and half a church was left. And the buildings were just demolished. And I was inspired by that steeple, that church steeple. And we walked around into a field . . . Now this is just a field – no sets, nothing – and way in the background is that steeple. And I looked at the art director and I said 'if you took a bulldozer and you made a winding road here, and a dirt road that led past that steeple; and you took a thatched roof in the foreground, just a roof and a side of a building, and over here further back in perspective so you have it, you know, one in the foreground, one in the background, to cover up all the burned-out buildings and everything, and you had another flat there, and down this sliding road I saw a little donkey cart or some French villager came or an automobile came, would I give the impression of a French village?' And the art director leapt for joy, and by the time I had finished, the sketch artist had drawn a French village for me with two flats in the foreground and out of a field we made a dirt road. That's the French village. . . .
>
> When the girl is found dead, the little French guy comes running up to her mother and there's a long dialogue scene where he tells her mother the girl is dead and she screams and cries and all that. And I got on the set and I rehearsed it and I said oh, no, no, no, impossible. How can I supply dialogue to meet this kind of situation? And so, I threw out all the dialogue . . . I put the camera outside of the house and way in the background was a big window that was cut up into about sixteen different little panes and there you saw the mother busy polishing some silverware or something. And through the scene as taken from outside the farmhouse, in runs this little Frenchman, but in extreme long shot, and he runs through the house and he disappears behind a wall and then reveals himself in front of this window. They're two tiny figures . . . in an extreme long shot and you can't hear. He's talking of course, but you can't hear it. We're shooting it, you know, without sound. And the only noise, shattering noise, that you hear when she drops that silver platter or whatever it was, and that's all you see. . . .[13]

The point of reprinting these anecdotes here is not to salute the 'imagination' of the director and his production team but rather to acknowledge the complex ways in which the much commented-on 'Bressonian' spareness of Lewis' settings and yet the fluid 'Ophulsian' manner of his shooting style both originate precisely in the industrial constraints under which the film was made. Once again Cohn and the Columbia hierarchy were happy with the result and, by way of promotion, 'miscast' Lewis to direct the musical sequences in the far more prestigious and hugely successful Larry Parks vehicle *The Jolson Story*. This was followed by two further, equally uncharacteristic projects: a second Parks vehicle, *The Swordsman*, and an unsuccessful Cary Grant style comedy about a man reincarnated as a horse, *The Return of October*. Finally, Lewis was allowed to return to the path he had begun to carve out with *Julia Ross*, and directed his third crime melodrama for Columbia, *The Undercover Man*. Here again, in spite of the film's B status, Lewis was allowed unusual licence, including the luxury of a three camera set-up (quite a conventional A film technique but, because of its expense, almost unheard of among Bs), and even rehearsal time for an improvisatory dialogue scene. (Once again, censorship pressures prevented a straightforward, denotative narrative of the Capone case on which the script was based; instead, Capone's identity behind the 'big fellow' could only be connoted by careful recreation of Capone's familiar hat.) *Time* magazine commented 'Director Joseph H. Lewis has turned out a neat little job. It is more entertaining than most of the better-advertised movies it will get paired with on double feature bills . . . It just goes to show that thoughtful direction and handsome camera work can lift a mediocre movie a long way above its humble origins.'[14]

In respect of my general remarks about the industrial imperatives of *film noir* it is perhaps pertinent here to mention that it was in 1945, Lewis' first year at Columbia, that that company was finally formally charged with conspiracy to infringe the Anti-Trust laws; indeed, the very same issue of the *Motion Picture Herald* (November 17, 1945) which reviewed *Julia Ross* also carried an article about the Anti-Trust suit and the probable outcome and consequences of the then imminent decision on block booking. Similarly, the same issue of the *MPH* (September 4, 1946) in which *So Dark the Night* was reviewed included news of Columbia's response to those charges and that decision. It is also worth noting that it was in 1945 that Columbia first employed Technicolor as well as the cheaper Cinecolor process. In 1949, following the Anti-Trust case conclusion, which finally outlawed the film industry's vertical integration and instructed the majors to divest themselves of their theatrical holdings, Columbia decided to discontinue the last of its B series (including crime thriller series like *Boston Blackie* and *Crime Doctor*) and concentrate its efforts on the ambitious B and modest A end of the industry; the same year it was the first of the majors to launch its own television subsidiary, Screen Gems. Much could be said about the determining role of Columbia studios as a structuring 'author' of Lewis' films there in the early 1940s; similarly, it is clearly worth considering the contribution of contract cameraman Burnett Guffey who was cinematographer on *Julia Ross, So Dark the Night* and *The Undercover Man*. Suffice it to say here, though, that such considerations cannot displace Lewis entirely from the films that carry his credit as director.

Lewis followed *Undercover Man* by leaving Columbia (for unknown reasons) and working for the King Brothers, an independent and slightly suspect production outfit distributing through United Artists. According to Lewis, the King Brothers were extremely generous and non-interfering and his budget and schedule were consequently increased from their Columbia levels. The King Brothers had apparently made their money installing slot machines and were anxious to legitimate themselves by going Hollywood. Based on MacKinlay Kantor's *Saturday Evening Post* story, *Gun Crazy* cost about 450,000 dollars and took 30 days to shoot, even employing a new portable sound system for the famous two mile location tracking shot. Contemporary critics and film-makers apparently besieged Lewis with queries about the mysterious multiple back projection technique the sequence seemed to have demanded: they could not believe that it was actually shot from the back of a car driven down a street on location in a single take. But Lewis had learned to experiment with exceptionally long takes and unconventional location tracking shots much earlier in his career, with, for example, the celebrated ten minute, single-take court room sequence in *The Silent Witness* and the polo pony-mounted cameraman in *The Spy Ring* (1938). United Artists, who had arranged to distribute *Gun Crazy*,

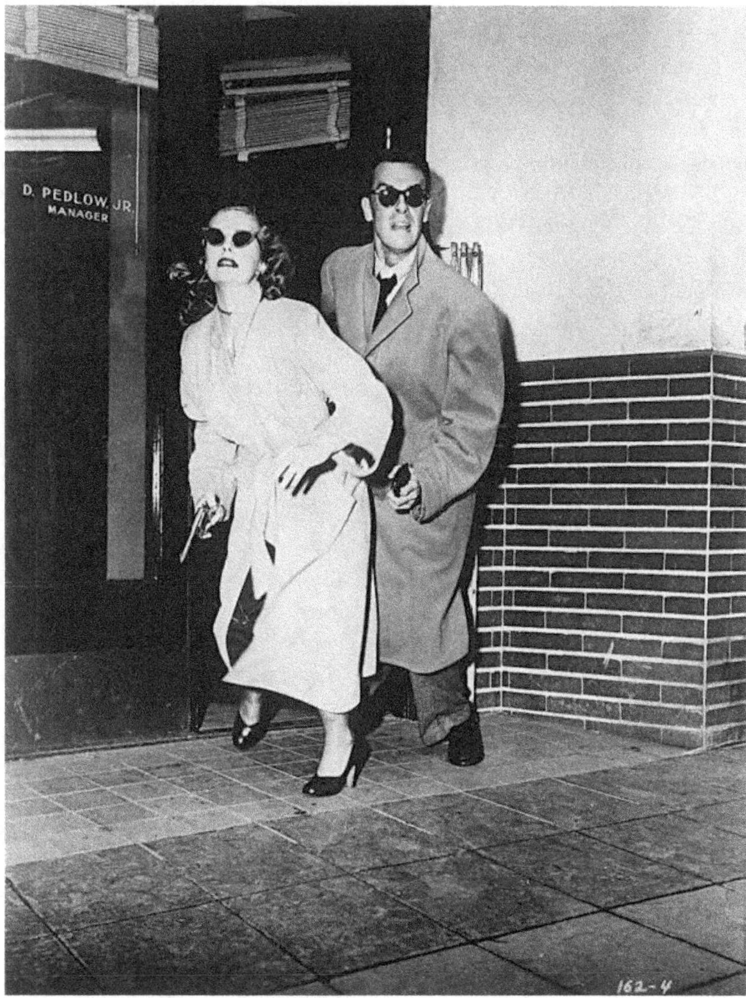

Figure 25.2 Peggy Cummins and John Dall as the outlaw couple in Lewis' *Gun Crazy* (King Bros/United Artists, 1949). Produced by Frank King and Maurice King

offered the King Brothers a sum of money to take the latter's names off the film but they refused. Perhaps as a result of – or in retribution for – this conflict UA were reluctant to push the film and it was eventually launched twice, once under an alternative title, *Deadly Is the Female*. UA had been named, along with the rest of the majors, in the 1948 Anti-Trust decision and, despite its own lack of theatres, had to adapt to meet the needs of a changing market. An administrative reshuffle in 1950 had led to a new regime and a new distribution strategy: under Krim and Benjamin the new policy involved the active pursuit of quality Bs or what were considered bargain basement As.

From the King Brothers, Lewis went to the other end of the prestige spectrum, MGM, to direct a film entitled *A Lady without Passport*. On this occasion, instead of being expected to create an atmospheric set out of virtually nothing – as at Columbia – Lewis was able to exploit MGM's extensive backlot and existing sets from previous features. The main bordertown set in *A Lady without Passport*, in fact, is a revised version of the Verona Square set on MGM's lot 2, which had been built for *Romeo and Juliet* in 1936. *A Lady without Passport* was one of the first of MGM's quasi-documentary crime cycle of second features, fictionalising the *Crime Does Not Pay* format (a 1935–48 MGM series) but expanding the two-reeler length. (Lewis complains in *Positif* that the presence of Hedy Lamarr in the cast unnecessarily glamourised the project.) In 1948, the year of the Anti-Trust decision, Dore Schary had been appointed as head of MGM's B productions and immediately set about supervising the transformation of the studio's formulaic series, serials and spin-off properties into fewer, better Bs, Bs which would simultaneously 'express' and 'exploit' topical issues like, in this case, the plight of illegal immigrants. Lewis left MGM after *A Lady without Passport* and made a war film for Warner Brothers, *Retreat, Hell!* but returned in 1952 to make *Desperate Search* and *Cry of the Hunted* (1953). It was not until 1955, however, towards the end of the *film noir* period, that Lewis was to direct his last and most fully blown work in the genre. *The Big Combo* was distributed by Allied Artists and that company's president at that time, Steve Broidy, has described the 'nervous A' (as ambitious Bs and modest As were sometimes known) as an important strategy in Monogram's 'premeditated attempt to upgrade our status in the industry', an attempt to achieve 'a percentage deal, as opposed to the flat rental'[15] fee for the second features and the new co-features it was providing for exhibition:

> One of the big things that kept us from making as much progress as we deserved to make, at a time when we were making a fairly good run of product, was the fact that the exhibitor, in those days, bought pictures based on the precedent he had paid for product ... That's what led to the creation of Allied Artists. It was the same company, same personnel, same everything, but we created a totally different image by calling it Allied Artists.[16]

Thus, in 1953, Monogram changed its name. Only one of Lewis' films was ever distributed by the company but as an example of the new strategy it is as good as any other – a gangster film for 'adults', full of 'sock, shock and brutality' (*Hollywood Reporter*, February 10, 1955), 'grim, sordid, sexy and candid ... likely to satisfy most adults ... but in no sense a film for children' (*Motion Picture Herald*, February 19, 1955). Describing the torture scene, *Variety* was rather less generous, commenting that 'The moronic fringe of sadists will enjoy this and all the little kiddies will be sick to their stomachs' (February 16, 1955). *The Big Combo* is undoubtedly the blackest of Lewis' *films noirs*; the cinematographer was John Alton and, in *Cahiers du Cinéma*, the reviewer restricted his comments entirely to Alton's contribution. But it is, in fact, a very understated film – Robert Mundy, for instance, has remarked on the subjectively shot and recorded machine-gun sequence and the sexuality of the Jean Wallace character, both of which pushed at the Production Code but, by virtue of their very subtlety, escaped the censor's scissors.[17]

At the time, however, (as well as ever since) most critics focused on a comparison between Lewis' *Big Combo* and Lang's 1953 film *The Big Heat*, generally asserting the former's indebtedness and alleged inferiority to the latter. (A similar comparison has haunted almost every article about *Gun Crazy*, which is traditionally measured up against Ray's *They Live by Night*, Lang's *You Only Live Once* and Penn's *Bonnie and Clyde*.) Essentially, Lewis is accused of plagiarism at the level of both plot, style and even title, but the accusation is extremely uninformed. Firstly because the American film industry and the American cinema both depended – as did genre cinema in general and *film noir* in particular – on repetitions, conventions and familiar formulas. Thus the plot of *The Big Combo* (1955), scripted by Phillip Yordan, was indeed based to some extent at least on the success of *The Big Heat*. And *The Big Heat* (1953) was scripted by Sydney Boehm, produced by Columbia and starred Glenn Ford. Four years earlier, in 1949, Columbia had produced another film with a very similar plot-line, also scripted by Sydney Boehm and also starring Glenn Ford. The film was called *Undercover Man* and it was directed by Joseph H. Lewis.

The point of this anecdote is not to prove Lewis somehow more original than Lang, but simply to illustrate how self-perpetuatingly the hierarchies of value within film culture (and all its institutions) function. *Undercover Man* was a B film, for all its ambitions. It was well enough received and did reasonably enough at the box office but Lewis, unlike Lang, was never a name to put up in lights; he was not a German émigré, veteran of UFA expressionism, but a contract director, verteran of PRC. Most importantly, he was a B not an A director. Consequently, *Undercover Man* was not sold with the same sort of energy or expectations as accompanied *The Big Heat*. It received less press coverage, fewer prints were struck, its theatrical run was brief. All these factors put severe constraints on the possibilities for retrospectives and re-viewings (and, thus, for rejigging the pantheon). In Britain and America – though this is perhaps less true of France – the criteria employed for the selection and preservation of films in the National Archives and equivalent bodies bore (and still bears) a direct relation to their respective critical and/or commercial success. If a film is considered to be critically prestigious enough it will be acquired and preserved, budgetary constraints permitting; if, on the other hand, the film is a big box-office success and/or a big budget production then it is likely that among the large number of prints produced one will eventually find its way into the archives, often via donation. But a film like *Undercover Man* and, by extension, not only all of Lewis' work but B films in general, fits neither of these categories; it remains forever outside the self-perpetuating system of profitability and prestige which is so scrupulously guarded and guaranteed by the allocation of production finance and facilities, by Academy Awards, and so on. In the event, the print of *Undercover Man* destined for Edinburgh almost fell apart under the strain of projection.

Which brings me to the role of the cultural, academic and critical institutions in the history of attempted 'authorisations' of Lewis. Tim Pulleine, in the *Monthly Film Bulletin*,[18] has usefully traced some of the English language perspectives on Lewis and while what follows is certainly no more comprehensive than Pulleine's account it does cover a longer period and a wider area. Paul Willemen, in his Edinburgh article on Lewis,[19] relates the apparent retrospective interest in Lewis to what he describes as 'the phenomenon of cinephilia' which he associates with the 'residues of surrealism in post-war French culture'.[20] Richard Thompson, in his piece in *Cinema*, sees *Gun Crazy* as a precursor of the *nouvelle vague* and elsewhere the film has been estimated as an influence on Godard in general and *A Bout de Souffle* in particular.[21] Avoiding such problematic but provocative notions, however, Willemen is undoubtedly right to point to the French and specifically the surrealists as being (among) the first serious critics to acknowledge Lewis. Ado Kyrou's *Le Surréalisme au Cinéma* (1953) describes *Gun Crazy* as 'an admirable film, which alone of all cinema clearly marks the road which leads from l'amour fou to la revolte folle'.[22] Two years later, the publication of Borde and Chaumeton's *Panorama du Film Noir Américain* (1955), the first booklength study of the genre, also saluted that film as deserving 'a place by itself' as 'a nearly unclassifiable work . . . a kind of Golden Age of American film noir . . .'.[23]

In the United States it seems that Andrew Sarris was one of the first to take Lewis seriously (perhaps through the critic's connections with the American *Cahiers*); in his book, *American Cinema*, Sarris slots Lewis into a section entitled 'expressive esoterica' alongside the likes of Budd Boetticher, Phil Karlson, Don Siegel, Robert Siodmak, Jacques Tourneur and Edward G. Ulmer. Sarris saluted Lewis' 'somber personality . . . revealed consistently through a complex visual style' but today Lewis remains one of the only directors so relegated to have resisted promotion.[24] In 1962 Sarris had issued a challenge in the pages *of Film Culture*, warning Lewis' admirers that 'in this direction lies madness'[25] – a warning that the writer was to withdraw the following year, but which has somehow stayed alive through the terms of appraisal Lewis' critics have employed ever since, from Sarris' 'expressive esoterica' to Willemen's 'cinephilia'. In 1971, the American magazine *Cinema* (then edited by Paul Schrader) devoted eleven pages to Lewis, comprising three articles, an interview[26] and a filmography. If Lewis proved less than forthcoming about his 'personality' there is some material about the production of a number of his films. More interesting, however, are the articles on Lewis by Schrader himself, by Thompson and by Robert Mundy. Schrader regards *Gun Crazy* as quite simply 'one of the best American films ever made'[27] but is unable to offer any explanation for the alleged excellence of the film, in the light of what he clearly considers the relative mediocrity of most of the rest of Lewis' work; indeed, he found his enthusiasm for the quality of the director decreasing in direct proportion to the quantity of his films viewed. Predictably, Schrader compares *The Big Combo* negatively to Lang's *The Big Heat* and adds that Lewis' only other strong film, *Undercover Man*, pales beside Mann's *T Men*. Mundy is more generous, though his conclusion that 'Lewis' work presents a problem of classification . . . To look at his work in genres is of little . . . use'[28] is ultimately unhelpful. Richard Thompson's rather longer consideration is less cautious, arguing that, the early work apart,

> Lewis found his metier, if not his personal vision, in the new popularity of the film noir. From *Julia Ross* on, all his successful films were either outright films noirs (*Gun Crazy, Undercover Man, Big Combo, Lady without Passport*) or contained maudit elements (*Desperate Search, So Dark the Night, Cry of the Hunted, A Lawless Street, Halliday Brand, Terror in a Texas Town*). Upon these films – of varying quality, but none without interest – Lewis' reputation rests. Though it seems difficult to claim for Lewis a consistently black vision, his visual style contained several elements conducive to the genre: a taste for Bazinian depth of focus; and for its temporal twin the long take; for camera movement (relativity) rather than alternating static cuts (isolated specificity); for cinematographers with dramatic, concrete styles, often harshly black and white; for naturalistic location shooting, or failing that, for modestly scaled back-lot work stressing character/environment interfaces rather than explicit spectacle.[29]

Lewis didn't rate an entry in the 1972 *International Encyclopaedia of Film* but in 1974 Tom Flinn's article 'The Big Heat and The Big Combo' appeared in *Velvet Light Trap*'s special issue on the 1950s, and was entirely devoted to a textual and 'political' comparison between the two oft-compared films.[30] The same year, the first lengthy appreciation of Lewis, retaining Sarris' 'insanity clause' appeared, 'Joseph H. Lewis: Tourist in the Asylum'.[31] In 1975 a second interview with Lewis, this time by another American critic, Gerald Peary, appeared in the French magazine *Positif*;[32] as if to outdo *Cinema, Positif* provided seventeen pages for several critics to consider Lewis but once again, the interview elicited little more than the few already familiar anecdotes, some additional production details, while the articles reprised the assertions about Lewis' alleged affinity for *film noir.*

In 1980 Lewis' status for 'cinephiliacs' rose further still. The BFI's *Monthly Film Bulletin* ran retrospective reviews of *The Falcon in San Francisco, Gun Crazy, A Lady without Passport, That Gang of Mine, Undercover Man, The Big Combo, The Halliday Brand, Retreat, Hell!,* and *Terror in a Texas Town* and devoted its back cover to Tim Pulleine's essay on the director.[33] These efforts comprised part of the preparations for the Edinburgh Film Festival Retrospective for which the first draft of this article was written and to which Paul Willemen, Paul Taylor and Richard Combs also contributed.[34] Unlike previous retrospectives at Edinburgh, however, there was no tie-in publication from either the Festival itself, the BFI or *Screen*. Nor was the retrospective taken up later in London at the National Film Theatre – though a small season was mounted at a repertory cinema, Riverside Studios, some weeks before the festival.[35] More important in the British promotion of Lewis in the early eighties were the reviews run in the London listings magazine, *Time Out*. The magazine then exercised a virtual monopoly on the audiences of the more adventurous repertory/independent exhibitors in the capital and the reviews duly alerted large (new?) audiences to the films. The two films that received caption reviews were, perhaps predictably, *Gun Crazy* and *The Big Combo*, though, rather less conventionally, it was *The Big Combo* which first attracted exhibitor and consequently reviewer attention in this case. It's worth printing the two reviews in full:

> Everything you always loved about American 'film noir' in one sensational movie: Joseph Lewis' *The Big Combo* (Electric, from Sunday). Police lieutenant Cornel Wilde searches neurotically for evidence to pin on mobster Richard Conte – because he nurses a pathetic crush on his victim's moll Jean Wallace. Along the way, through the night and fog, he clutches at fragmentary clues (a name, a photo), goes to bed with a stripper and lovingly helps her on with her shoes, and suffers torture – by hearing aid. Sent to get him are two thugs (Lee Van Cleef and Earl Holliman), who share not only guns but also beds; their relationship provides the movie with its most tender moment. The pace is brutal, the tone is harsh, the dialogue is cruel. Almost certainly the greatest movie ever made, as heady as amyl nitrate and as compulsive as stamping on insects. (Tony Rayns)[36]

> From its opening moments, it's clear that *Gun Crazy* (Independents: Electric) is a B-picture classic. Directed by Joseph H. Lewis – whose later noir thriller, *The Big Combo*, was also recently rediscovered by the Electric – it features an amiable but gun-crazy hero who abandons Hometown USA to elope with the (lady) sharpshooter from a travelling circus. Deep in mutual obsession, they run out of money, patience, and time; then take to armed robbery and the road that leads (inevitably) to death. Flatly passionate, never vampish, Peggy Cummins turns in a staggering performance which threatens, singlehanded, to overthrow the cultural and sexual certainties of middle American life. Even, at the very end, this last romantic couple refuse to pay the price of their rebellion: hunted down in a misty, echoing swamp,

> their tormented faces express only pain and fear, never a trace of guilt or regret. Compulsive genre cinema, wearing its low budget and Freudian motifs with almost equal disdain; it simply knocks spots off senile imitations like *Bonnie and Clyde.* (Chris Auty)[37]

Also in 1980 the American Telluride Film Festival mounted an impressive *film noir* retrospective, which featured the attendance of Lewis himself, who was interviewed at length by Paul Schrader.

Paul Willemen's paper for Edinburgh is the latest piece on Lewis I have been able to trace – though I should repeat that my aim here is not an exhaustive bibliography but rather a schematic scrutiny of that bibliography as part of the case study of attempted 'authorisations'. And Willemen's article neatly opens up (and yet rather peremptorily also simultaneously closes off) that debate, noting that

> Many avowed auteurists in France, the US and Britain have attempted to claim him as an author. All have failed. Not because it would be impossible to construct a thematic coherence covering a substantial proportion of his work, but because the films appear to resist such efforts, locating their pleasure elsewhere, on a more disturbing though fascinating level.[38]

But is it indeed possible to construct such a coherence? Mundy proposes some potential significance in the recurrence of swamp scenes, the predilection for long takes, tracking shots and depth of focus, and a thematic concern for memory and its loss.[39] Thompson underlines Lewis' liaison with *film noir* and further notes that 'Lewis seems instinctively to cast his films in the form of hunter-hunted chases' but concludes that 'no consistent style of mise-en-scène is apparent, no Lewis look or Lewis POV or Lewis conceptual slant that can be spotted from film to film,'[40] Meisel reiterates the hunter-hunted motif and adds another recurrent item of Lewisiana in 'the inseparability of individual identity from social action'. He notes an irreconcilable collision between 'the noir determinism of his style' and 'his brief for family ties as the root of moral responsibility'. Meisel goes on to unpack this assertion a little, describing how Lewis' apparent penchant for 'characters (who) express themselves exclusively through their actions' makes for what he calls 'good visceral cinema'.[41] The former emphasis, on family ties, is repeated by Pulleine; the latter is reprised in Tom Milne's remarks on Godard's debts to Lewis.[42]

More generally, however, all the critics surveyed seem to agree: that Lewis' films are often stronger in parts than as wholes, as is Lewis' *oeuvre* itself; that the B *film noir* provides a useful way into understanding Lewis, if only so as to distinguish his films that fall outside its parameters; that his stylistic 'signature', however difficult to determine, did preempt some of the attributed innovations of the *nouvelle vague* and yet at the same time functioned as a symptom of and a valediction for a certain sort of American cinema. Finally, there seems to be a critical consensus that Lewis was unwilling and/or unable to 'impose' his personality on his films, but that

> Picking through Lewis' diverse filmography, it is quite easy to find evidence of a director with a strong personality – and just as much evidence of one who never really found a subject. Lewis might almost embody the kind of caricatured figure that an auteurist critic would hold up as the epitome of the cult of the director: stylistic authority operating in a vacuum.[43]

Lewis clearly poses a problem for auteurism – as for genre criticism – acknowledged by almost all who have written seriously about his work (with the possible exception of Paul Willemen). But such problems do little to deter the desperate search of anachronistic auteurists, the cry of the hunters. Trying to identify a coherent, consistent 'thematic core' in the Lewis *oeuvre*, of course, begs the too rarely raised question of just what constitutes such an *oeuvre*, such a core. This article has attempted to argue that neither are static but rather that both are conjunctural and are continuously being reconstructed. Nevertheless, it is interesting to note that the film which 'made Lewis' name', in the industry, at least, *My Name is Julia Ross,* should have made the memorisation of a name, an identity, so central to its plot and, indeed, its title. Apparently Lewis chose this project for himself – in fact it seems to have been the first occasion on which he was able to select a script rather than simply being himself selected to direct one. And Lewis himself changed the title from the script's *Woman in Red. So Dark the Night* retains the identity/memory thematic (and was also a project selected by Lewis himself). While it may be dubious at best to make much more of this than ironic coincidence, it is worth adding that several of Lewis' films carry this idea, from the undercover identities of the detectives in *A Lady without*

Passport and *Undercover Man* to the uncovered identities of the mysterious Alicia in *The Big Combo* and the fleeing Bart named by the press in *Gun Crazy*. More intriguingly, perhaps, two more films express the urgency of names and naming in their very titles, *A Lady without Passport* and *The Halliday Brand*.

It's tempting to reject Willemen's remarks about Lewis' films – 'the scripts are unchallenging, the acting stereotyped and haphazard, the ideologies unfailingly reactionary' – as no more than impassioned polemic against auteurist excesses. But the films are worth defending against such charges; not because of any disservice such remarks may do to Lewis or his films but because of their disservice to film history and film studies. Certainly several of the scripts as well as the actors Lewis worked with were imperfect; equally certainly, however, the scripts for *My Names is Julia Ross, A Lady without Passport, The Undercover Man, Gun Crazy, The Big Combo* and *The Halliday Brand* were actually excellent as were many of the performances in Lewis' films and, as a number of critics have suggested, it was Lewis who failed to match them. More seriously, Willemen's allegation that Lewis' films embraced unfailingly reactionary ideologies, its impact as polemic apart, risks returning film studies to the prestigious theatrical values of pre-auteurist days, long before the publication of Comolli and Narboni's influential essay, 'Cinema/Ideology/Criticism'.[44] Of all Lewis' work in the period, only *Retreat, Hell!* seems to have had an indisputably propagandist project; and in Hollywood, as elsewhere, it is essential to be wary of intentions. Labelling the entire Lewis *oeuvre* as reactionary seems at best impulsive and at worst critically reactionary itself. Indeed, Willemen could be accused of echoing the Korean War utterance (of General Smith) which gave Lewis' film its name: 'Retreat, Hell! We're just attacking in a different direction.' The 'different direction' in which Willemen is in danger of advancing film theory is toward Adorno and (High) Cultural pessimism and away from the kind of acknowledgement of the films' historical context, their institutional place that this article has been urging as a necessary precondition of any analysis – let alone evaluation – of cinema, from levels of writing or acting to ideology.

For Willemen, however, the present status and historical locus of Lewis' work is simply to be regretted:

> When cinephilia disappears, Lewis' films will cease to have any function, their specificity will vanish along with the spectator's inability to acknowledge a desire for cinema, the asocial, politically irresponsible joy of looking.[45]

It is hard to take this kind of combination of cultural pessimism and radical puritanism seriously as polemic, let alone as prophecy. But if Lewis' films have had a 'political' role in the last three decades, then that has been their function as hiccups, indigestible exceptions to theories about the general applicability of certain propositions about Hollywood as industry and as cinema, about genre, about the classic realist text, about authorship itself, about the impossibility of attributing essential 'ideologies' to texts outside of their institutional site and historical moment; about specifically the history of Hollywood's modes of production and their relation to modes of representation/signification. That mode of production actively prohibited and delimited the possibilities of individual authorship. But the moment and specific site of such productions as Lewis' between 1945 and 1960 also importantly coincides with another political determinant on Hollywood, that of the HUAC hearings and the consequent blacklist. The blacklist made all too literal the cliché about the authorless anonymity of the average Hollywood film. After the first HUAC hearing (in 1947) and particularly after the first trials (in 1951) a number of film-makers were forced to work anonymously either for the Bs or for the new independents. Victor Navasky's *Naming Names*, a study of the blacklist era, comments:

> Independent filmmakers . . . were by definition antagonistic to studio values. Some were independents because they were incapable of functioning other than on the margin (and on the cheap). And it seems fitting that one of these, the King brothers, should have made it a regular practice to employ blacklisted personnel under pseudonyms – not as a protest against repression but as a calculated risk, a shrewd economy, getting top talent for minimal money. It was the King brothers who hired Dalton Trumbo.[46]

Trumbo's first script for the Kings was apparently *Gun Crazy*. Lewis admits that the MacKinlay Kantor script was far too long; he does not, however, admit that the crediting of Millard Kaufman as co-screenwriter was simply a 'front' for the 'unemployable', blacklisted Trumbo.[47] Lewis had collaborated with people on the liberal left at Columbia in the late forties. In 1958 he was to be associated even more strongly with blacklistees. The script for his last film, *Terror in a Texas Town*, is attributed on the films credits to Ben L Perry. Lewis notes in his interview with Bogdanovich that Ned Young, a blacklisted writer who also appears in the film, contributed to the script uncredited. So, according to Navasky, did another eminent blacklistee, John Howard Lawson.[48] In this light, the film's gunfight between (HUAC friendly witness) Sterling Hayden and (the blacklisted) Young takes on new charges.

To paraphrase Buscombe's formulation about Walsh and Warners, it has been the ambition of this piece to call into question the predictable – if problematic – promotion of Lewis to the auteur pantheon; to recognise that working in an industrially defined sub-genre with as distinctive a strategy and style as the B *film noir* imposed a number of constraints on 'creativity' but to insist that such constraints should not be seen as merely negative in their operation. Working in the area of the B *film noir* meant simply that the opportunities for commercial and critical success lay in certain (industrial, generic) directions rather than in others. Sheila Johnston, in an article on the production context of the New German Cinema, has argued

> Not just that some highly individualistic West German films in the sixties and seventies seem to invite an auteurist reading, but that the conditions for an Autor cinema were deliberately cultivated (in conjunction with certain industrial, political and cultural developments) rather than accidentally propitious.[49]

Were Johnston's observations about German art cinema extended to Hollywood, they would go some way to meeting Caughie's suggested relation of 'the author ... to institutional and commercial contexts'. Indeed, I would like to suggest, by way of a conclusion, that the late forties and early fifties in Hollywood, particularly in the competitive realm of the ambitious B/nervous A picture, provided similarly decisive developments, developments which at least partially encouraged the authorial hallmarking and, indeed, the directorial 'expressiveness' of people like Lewis. Countless critics have remarked on the richness of *film noir*, the number of familiar and unfamiliar filmmakers who excelled themselves in the genre. Perhaps that genre, though never named as such at the time, was an accidentally propitious arena in which the process of 'authorisation' could be played out and institutionally inscribed. In the 1970s and '80s, on the other hand, *film noir* in general and the B *film noir* in particular have indeed been deliberately recultivated around a number of names – names like Karlson, Fuller, Siodmak, Mann, Tourneur and Ulmer. Among them that of Joseph H. Lewis has functioned to literally re-authorise and consequently categorise a number of B *films noirs* in this period just as, in the '40s and '50s, that subgenre itself could be said to have helped to authorise Lewis.

Notes

1 John Caughie (ed.) *Theories of Authorship*, London, British Film Institute and Routledge & Kegan Paul, 1981. See also Stephen Jenkins (ed.) *Fritz Lang: The Image and the Look*, London, British Film Institute, 1981. Jenkins conceives of 'Lang' neither biographically nor structurally, since the former assumes a romantic artist behind every aspect of 'his' work, while the latter 'implies that such a structure exists as something to be grasped.' Instead, Jenkins addresses 'Lang' as a 'space where a multiplicity of discourses intersect, an unstable, shifting configuration of discourses produced by the interaction of a specific group of films (Lang's filmography) with particular, historically and socially locatable ways of reading/viewing those films', p. 7.

2 See, however, Steve Neale's article 'Authors and Genres' in *Screen* vol. 23 no. 2, pp. 84–9.

3 Caughie, op. cit., p. 14.

4 Ibid., p. 2.

5 Paul Kerr, 'Out Of What Past? Notes on the B Film Noir', *Screen Education* nos. 32/33, Autumn/Winter 1979/80, pp. 45–65.

6 A number of such textual analyses are referred to in the footnotes to this article. See below.

7 See Janet Staiger's overview of the shift to independent production *Screen*, vol. 24 nos. 4–5.

8 Edward Buscombe, 'Walsh and Warner Brothers' in Phil Hardy (ed.) *Raoul Walsh*, Edinburgh Film Festival, 1974. See also Steve Jenkins' article 'Edgar G. Ulmer and PRC: A Detour down Poverty Row', in *Monthly Film Bulletin* July 1982, vol. 49 no. 582, p. 152.

9 Buscombe op. cit., p. 60. That such 'constraints' and 'directions' could be much more than simply stylistic is central to Buscombe's argument. While Lewis' career at Columbia is too brief to benefit from the kind of studio/director study devoted

to Walsh and Warners, it is worth noting that elsewhere Buscombe has published an article on Columbia itself, 'Notes on Columbia Pictures Corporation 1926–41', *Screen*, Autumn 1975, vol. 16 no. 3, pp. 65–82. In this article Buscombe addressed the question of Columbia's studio style and political affiliations, asking whether or not that company's relative independence from Wall Street finance freed its film-makers politically. Buscombe's conclusion is negative, but he does point out that precisely half of the Hollywood Ten were employed at Columbia in the 1930s. Among the radicals/black-listees that Lewis worked with at the studio were Larry Parks (who starred in *The Jolson Story* and *The Swordsman*), Sydney Buchman (who was an uncredited contributor to the script of *The Jolson Story*), Robert Rossen (who produced *Undercover Man*) and Nedrick Young (who appeared in *The Swordsman* and who worked with Lewis on and off throughout his career after they had both left Columbia).

10 Kerr, op. cit., p. 45.

11 These and other figures in this article derive from Peter Bogdanovich's interview with Lewis in *Cinema* Fall 1971, vol. 7 no. 1, and from Gerald Peary's interview in *Positif* July/August 1975, nos. 171–2. They have not been verified against the extensive Lewis material held by the Chicago Institute of Art.

12 Quoted in Doug McClelland, *The Golden Age of B Movies*, Bonanza Books, 1978, p. 146.

13 Lewis interviewed by Bogdanovich, op. cit., p. 48.

14 Quoted in McClelland, op. cit., p. 186.

15 Interview with Broidy in Charles Flynn and Todd McCarthy (eds.) *Kings of the Bs*, E. P. Dutton, 1975, p. 271.

16 Ibid., p. 272.

17 See Robert Mundy's untitled article in *Cinema* Fall 1971, vol. 7 no. 1.

18 Tim Pulleine, 'Undercover Director or: The Name is Joseph H. Lewis' in *Monthly Film Bulletin* March 1980, vol. 47 no. 554, p. 60.

19 Paul Willemen's paper is reprinted, with a new afterword, under the heading 'Edinburgh – Debate', *Framework* no. 19, pp. 48–50.

20 Ibid., p. 49.

21 Richard Thompson's untitled article on Lewis appeared in *Cinema* Fall 1971, vol. 7 no. 1, with articles by Schrader and Mundy and an interview by Peter Bogdanovich (op. cit.). Tom Milne has also referred to an alleged influence on Godard in his review of *Gun Crazy* in *Monthly Film Bulletin* March 1980, vol. 47 no. 554, p. 57.

22 Quoted by Thompson, op. cit., p. 46.

23 Quoted by Thompson, ibid.

24 Andrew Sarris, *The American Cinema*, New York, Dutton, 1968, pp. 132–3.

25 Andrew Sarris, 'The High Forties Revisited', *Film Culture* no. 24, Spring 1962, p. 66.

26 The interview makes a useful comparison with Bogdanovich's previously published 'interview books', *Fritz Lang in America*, Movie Paperbacks, Studio Vista, 1967 and *John Ford*, Movie Paperbacks, Studio Vista, 1968.

27 Schrader in *Cinema*, op. cit., p. 43.

28 Mundy in *Cinema*, ibid., p. 45.

29 Thompson in *Cinema*, ibid., p. 46.

30 '*The Big Heat* and *The Big Combo* – Rogue Cops & Mink-Coated Girls' in *The Velvet Light Trap* no. 11, pp. 23–8.

31 Myron Meisel, 'Joseph H. Lewis: Tourist in the Asylum', in Charles Flynn and Todd McCarthy (eds.), *Kings of the Bs*, op. cit.

32 *Positif*, op. cit., pp. 39–55.

33 Pulleine, op. cit.

34 Paul Willemen's and Richard Combs' contributions were printed in the 1980 *Edinburgh Film Festival* brochure. Paul Taylor has written on Lewis in *Time Out*, May 2–8, 1980, p. 51 and p. 53.

35 See Paul Taylor's remarks, op. cit.

36 *Time Out*, March 2–8, 1979, p. 43.

37 *Time Out*, September 21–27, 1979, p. 49.

38 Willemen in *Framework*, op. cit., p. 49.

39 *Cinema*, op. cit.

40 Ibid.

41 Meisel, op. cit.

42 Milne, op. cit.

43 Richard Combs' review of *Undercover Man* appeared in *Monthly Film Bulletin*, op. cit., p. 58.

44 Reprinted in *Screen Reader 1*, SEFT, London, 1977. I am referring here to Comolli and Narboni's notorious category 'e'.

45 Willemen, *Framework*, op. cit., p. 50.

46 Victor S. Navasky, *Naming Names*, Penguin, 1981, p. 155.

47 'Ghostwriting – Unraveling the Enigma of Movie Authorship' by Michael Sragow, *Film Comment* March/April 1983, vol. 19 no. 2, p. 9.

48 Navasky op. cit., p. 345.

49 Sheila Johnston, 'The Author as Pubic Institution', *Screen Education* nos. 32/33 Autumn/Winter 1979/80, p. 68.

26

Authorship as a Commodity: The Art Cinema and *The Cabinet of Dr Caligari*

Michael Budd

In this essay Michael Budd, a professor of film studies at Florida Atlantic University in Boca Raton, examines the complex authorship of the classic German Expressionist film, *The Cabinet of Dr Caligari* (1920). It builds on discussions by David Bordwell and Steve Neale of art cinema as an institution, with a distinct infrastructure (specialized cinemas, festivals, journals) and stylistic conventions, a central one of which is its foregrounding of the author's presence through stylistic traits that disrupt the norm of standard narrative cinema. In Bordwell's account, art cinema is "a distinct mode of film practice" featuring looser narrative structure, ambiguity, and noticeable stylistic gestures that function like authorial signatures. Art cinema addresses the viewer as a knowledgeable spectator who will recognize the characteristic stylistic touches of directors from their other films. In the case of *The Cabinet of Dr Caligari*, not only is its production history unclear and fraught with changes involving director Robert Wiene, producer Erich Pommer, and screenwriters Hans Janowitz and Carl Mayer, but Budd's analysis of the film contextualizes its marketability within the context of art cinema, where authorship has legal status and concrete economic exchange value.

A Footnote to Film History

By the early 1940s, the principal makers of *The Cabinet of Dr Caligari* (1919), like many other German writers and artists, had fled Hitler's regime. Director Robert Wiene had died in France in 1938 after having claimed ownership of the film and having sold the rights to Rex Films of Paris in 1934. Carl Mayer had emigrated to London where he wrote scripts until his death in 1944. Hans Janowitz, the Czech poet who co-authored the screenplay with Mayer, was living in New Jersey. Erich Pommer, who produced the film while head of Decla-Bioscop and later became head of production at UFA, Germany's largest studio, was with Mayflower Productions in England and later with the Producers Corporation of America in Hollywood.

In 1944 Janowitz and Pommer, through their lawyers, began elaborate negotiations over the legal rights to the famous film, which each of them wanted to remake in Hollywood.[1] These legal maneuverings, which apparently never reached the courtroom, were

Michael Budd, "Authorship as a Commodity: The Art Cinema and *The Cabinet of Dr Caligari*," pp. 12–19 from *Wide Angle* 6, no. 1 (1984).

complicated not only by multiple claims on the film, but also by the problem of silent versus sound rights and the imposition of Nazi law in Germany, which was not recognized in the United States. English language versions of the original film were being held by the Custodian of Alien Property. At one point in January 1945, Janowitz, who already had written an extensive treatment for a remake, was offered a minimum guarantee of $16,000 against 5% royalties for his rights to the original plus a script to be written by him for a production to be directed by Fritz Lang.[2] Later, when the satisfaction of all claims to the original seemed impossible, Janowitz wrote a script for a sequel, entitled *Caligari II*, and offered his property, both *Caligari I* and *II*, to a Hollywood producer for $30,000.[3] None of these negotiations resulted in the production of a film, although the preliminary clearing of legal rights probably contributed to the use of the title (and little else) in a 1962 production by 20th Century Fox.

The Art Cinema

If all this talk of Hollywood remakes and legal rights sounds a bit bizarre in its relation to that hoary classic shown in film history courses and dutifully extolled in textbooks, then the reader has begun to grasp the argument to be made in this paper. For *The Cabinet of Dr Caligari* is an early example of art cinema, a mode of cinematic discourse which differentiates itself in limited modernist directions from the dominant mode of classical narrative, but which nevertheless is produced and consumed largely *within* the commodity relations of advanced capitalist societies. As delineated by David Bordwell and Steve Neale with somewhat different emphases, the art cinema is not just a type of film, but a set of institutions, an alternative apparatus within the commercial cinema: cultural patronage, "enlightened" producers or state subsidies for production, festivals and prizes, art theaters, publicity, reviews, criticism and "theory" in books and magazines for consumption.[4] Implicated also is the small academic industry of courses and textbooks in film, which often functions to recruit new consumers and help direct recuperative reading strategies. Central to these reading strategies is the discourse of authorship, which sees the art cinema's characteristic partial or intermittent foregrounding of style in relation to narrative – its limited deviation from the norm – as motivated by the personal vision of its author, usually the director. This was particularly true during the period of art cinema's institutional consolidation in the fifties and sixties, when European and Japanese national cinemas carved out a niche in the American market with auteurs like Fellini, Antonioni, Bergman, Truffaut, Resnais, Kurosawa, et al., promoted by art theaters, state subsidies, international festivals and "serious" criticism oriented toward an aesthetics of personal expression. The heterogeneity of art cinema, the force even of its limited modernist transgressions, is contained in a co-optation distinctive to advanced capitalism: "the name of the author can function as a 'brand name,' a means of labeling and selling a film."[5] There is no document of individualism which is not at the same time a document of conformity.

The beginnings of the art cinema go back at least to the late teens, to the consolidation of the hegemony, in both economic and signifying practices, of the dominant classical narrative discourse in relation to which the art cinema differentiated its product. A full examination of the history of art cinema is beyond the scope of this essay, but we can gain certain insights into its operation by examining two specific processes: first, how *The Cabinet of Dr Caligari* acquired the exchange value which was the subject of negotiations in our historical footnote, and second, the contribution of both legal authorship as private property and the actual relations of production among employees and bosses to the generation of that exchange value. Moreover, since *Caligari* as art cinema exists on the fringes of the commercial cinema, it may help define the limits and boundaries of the latter mode, and in particular, to argue and explore rather than to assert the process so often identified with commercial cinema – commodification. The concept of the commodity form offers a way of understanding the whole production/consumption process and a means of demystifying the relation between dominant and oppositional modes.

The Commodity

> Objects of utility become commodities only because they are the products of the labour of private individuals who work independently of each other. . . .

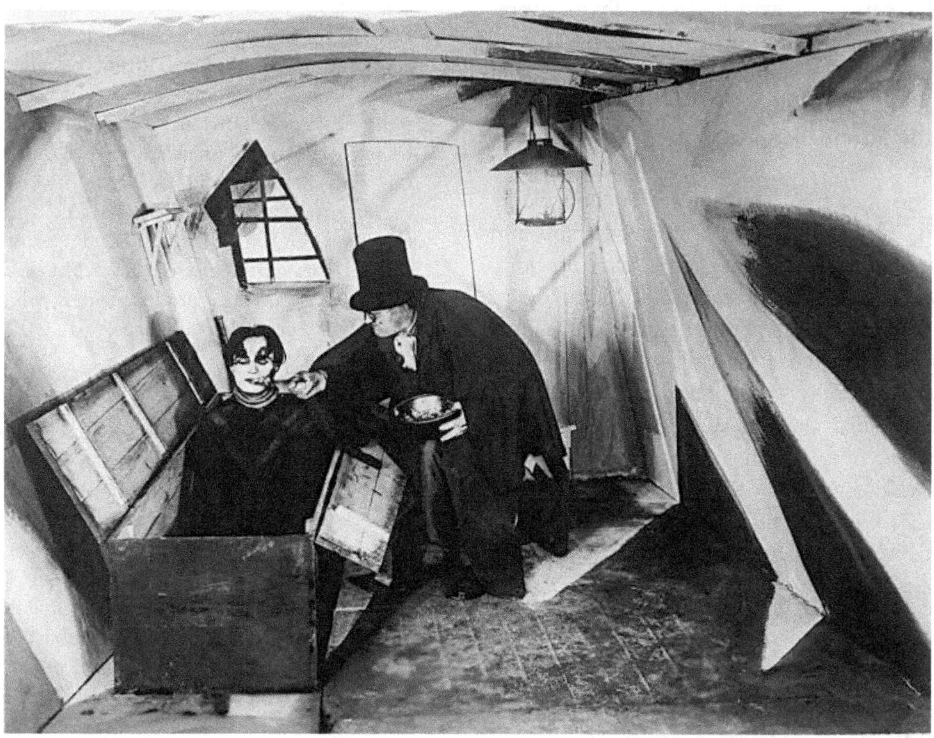

Figure 26.1 Robert Wiene's *The Cabinet of Dr Caligari* (Decla-Film, 1920): An early example of authorship understood within the Romantic category of art cinema. Produced by Erich Pommer

> It is only by being exchanged that the products of labour acquire a socially uniform objectivity as values, which is distinct from their sensuously varied objectivity as articles of utility. This division of the product of labour into a useful thing and a thing possessing value appears in practice only when exchange has already acquired a sufficient extension and importance to allow useful things to be produced for the purpose of being exchanged, so that their character as values has already to be taken into consideration during production.[6]

The historical process described in this last sentence by Marx is a reciprocal one: the growing importance of exchange value in relation to use value gradually transforms the latter so that the human needs satisfied by the product are increasingly defined by the market, by the exchange value of the commodity. The pervasive influence of exchange value on use value within the consumption-dominated phase of advanced capitalism applies to both consumers and producers; advertising and publicity help define use value for consumers, while a different kind of rationalization segments the "creative contributions" of producers into categories based on marketability. As the commodity-form becomes increasingly dominant, even "artists" who work closely together in making a film, who seem to be collaborating in a work of genuine cultural innovation, end up with separate ("congealed" is Marx's word) contributions as "private individuals who work independently of each other."

In art cinema, the privacy of one of those individuals is fetishized, and an imaginary unity, the "personal vision," is projected onto the social process of production and consumption. Partly through the qualities given to the film in production, and partly through the reading strategies promoted by international film culture, which generally accept authorship uncritically, art cinema mystifies its own division of labor, separating (alienating) manual labor from intellectual labor and assigning exchange value to the latter. Differentiating its product largely by reference to a unique and private artistic personality which supposedly motivates its difference from the dominant mode, art cinema denies the social dimension in art's human uses and in its own production, thus helping transform those uses and that artistic personality into exchangeable commodities.

Perhaps the most trenchant analysis of commodification in the film industry, in both production and consumption, is contained in Bertolt Brecht's long essay, "The Threepenny Opera Trial, A Sociological Experiment."[7] In 1929 Brecht and Kurt Weill signed a contract with Nero-Film for a film version of their very popular *Threepenny Opera*. The contract specified that they controlled the scenario and music; when Brecht's outline was rejected by Nero-Film, they sued.[8] The trial, in October 1930, attracted much of Berlin's literary elite and high society. Brecht argued that "he was in no way defending his copyright, his literary property, but . . . *the property of the spectator*."[9] Brecht lost and the film was scripted by Béla Balázs and directed by Pabst in 1931.

In his commentary on the *Threepenny Opera* trial, Brecht develops Marx's argument about the growing hegemony of exchange value into an analysis of how, in the capitalist film industry, all relations of production are dominated by the marketplace: the film's character as commodity must be taken into account during production, so the demand for an abstract equivalence of isolated elements of the work (setting, plot, happy ending, characters, title, author's name and author's reputation are some of Brecht's examples) comes increasingly to shape the production process itself.

> "A film must be the work of a collective." This conception is progressive. . . . In contrast to an individual, a collective cannot work without a fixed point of direction, and evening conferences are no such fixed point. Had the collective some determined pedagogical design, it could immediately build an organic body. It is the essence of capitalism . . . that everything "one-of-a-kind" and "exceptional" can only come forth from an individual, while collectives can only bring forth mediocre dime-a-dozen works. What have we got for a collective these days in film? The collective puts itself together from the financier, the salesman (the public-relations man), the director, the technicians, and the writers. A director is necessary because the financier will have nothing to do with Art; the salesman, because the director must be corrupted; the technicians not because the apparatus is complicated (it is unbelievably primitive), but because the director has not the most primitive notion of technical things; and the writers, finally, because the audience itself is too lazy to learn to write. Who wouldn't wish right off that his individual part in the production would be unrecognizable? At no moment during the work on the *Threepenny* film did the parties involved, including those carrying out the lawsuit, have coinciding interpretations of the subject matter, the intent of the film, its audience, its apparatus, etc. The fact of the matter is that a collective can only produce works which can build collectives out of the "audience."
>
> . . . In order for an art work, which according to bourgeois ideology is the expression of one individual, to reach the market it must be submitted to a completely determined operation, which cleaves it up into its parts; the parts enter the marketplace in particular ways. . . . The author's work can be broken up, in that its subject matter can be invested with another form or its form invested with another . . . subject matter. Further, with respect to form, it is possible for the linguistic form and the scenic form to appear without the other. The plot of the subject matter can be played out by other characters; these characters can be placed in another plot, and so on. This dismantling of the art work appears to follow the laws of the marketplace in the same way as automobiles, which have become non-utilitarian, which one can no longer drive, and which one now dissects into their tiny idiosyncrasies (type of metal, leather upholstery, headlights, etc.) and then buys. We are seeing the unavoidable and therefore to-be-sanctioned decay of the individualistic art work. It can no longer attain the marketplace as a unity; the stressful nature of its contradiction-filled unity must soon shatter it into pieces. . . . For all that, the work thus constituted appears as a unity on the marketplace.[10]

Caligari as Art Cinema as Commodity

Art cinema, then, according to this line of reasoning, must differentiate its product by producing a distinctive commodity fetish – a particularly prestigious, cultured and individualistic one, we might even say. Certainly this is present from the fifties on, with the continuity and economic stability of art cinema constructed around two discourses of international film culture: first, authorship, and second, the "adult" and explicit "representation of sexuality."[11] Yet before World War II and the proliferation of state subsidies to national art cinemas, the mode had only the most intermittent and uneven existence. Its exhibition centered around the ciné-clubs in Paris which began to appear in the early Twenties. Those clubs served as the basis for an avant-garde film movement; the London Film Society and The Film Society at the New Gallery Cinema on Regent Street; and the Film Associates, The Film Guild and other "little Cinemas" in New York.[12] But production depended either on short-lived movements at the fringes of the commercial industry, like German Expressionism, or fell entirely outside the industry itself, as with such fully modernist works as *Un Chien Andalou* and *Entr'Acte*.[13]

Clearly, the art cinema had its beginnings in the first alternative, even radical institutions to challenge the hegemony of the dominant mode. In part this must be because the romantic discourse of authorship, which removes a text from its economic and social context and places it in an ideal realm of personal expression, remains within the subculture of *cognoscenti* until the culture industry takes it up as a marketing strategy. There is little evidence that *Caligari* was read or promoted as an author's film at least until Siegfried Kracauer adopted the screenwriters' reading in his book, *From Caligari to Hitler* – and even then its ostensible author was not its director. *Caligari*'s exhibition spans the possibilities of the art cinema in the pre-World War II period: it played initially in large commercial theaters, in Berlin, Paris, London and New York, then apparently became a kind of early standard for the ciné-clubs and film societies in the same cities.[14] Yet in both these situations, critical discourse seems to have centered around the film's techniques: in the ciné-clubs these were extolled as revolutionary or attacked as derivative and theatrical, while the publicity apparatus of the culture industry could only flail away ineffectively about the film's novelty.

Caligari did not succeed as a commodity even though its origins were hidden, its context commodified, even the text itself altered.[15] The point is not just that a cultural product can be commodified in one conjucture and not in another, but also that the history of *Caligari* as a text marks an early point in the development of art cinema, when deviation from the norm as novelty is seen as the only promotable reading strategy, and *Caligari*'s novelty is inadequately consumable. The film's Expressionist settings, costumes and acting can be attributed to the expressive subjectivity of a character *within* the film, but not yet to an author; it is still too weird to produce that imaginary unity off the assembly line to which Brecht refers. Interestingly, ads in the New York trade papers in 1921 for *Caligari* stressing its novelty are juxtaposed with ads for D.W. Griffith's *Dream Street* selling a rudimentary version of authorship – dignified portraits of Griffith, lists of earlier films "under his personal direction," biographical information.[16] One would have thought that the transgressions of *Caligari* would require the recuperations of an authorial reading much more than those of *Dream Street*. On the other hand, advertising characteristically tries to produce difference exactly where there is none, since a real difference between products, an authentic choice presented to the buyer, minimizes its influence. Perhaps the culture industry has its own forces and relations of production, and only a Marxist theory of uneven development will help here.

Caligari's status both as art cinema and as commodity centers around the place of Expressionism within it, exactly because that place is a carefully limited one which can function, in certain conjunctures, as the separable and exchangeable part of a commodity. I have argued elsewhere that this film is profoundly contradictory in its form, "grafting a visual style from [modernist] painting and theatrical set design onto a conventional narrative form, ignoring the modernist experiments in Expressionist literature, poetry, and drama."[17] In other words, precisely the quality which made the film avant-garde also made it accessible to the commodity culture; precisely the aspect which made the film unique became that which linked the detail of the work to the system of the culture industry as a whole. To explain this contradiction it must be traced, following Brecht, backwards from consumption to production, to understand the product which presented itself to Janowitz and Pommer in 1944 as exchange value. For Brecht it was not so much the division of labor which commodified but the lack of collective aim, of genuine collaboration.

Here one can see how the double function of *Caligari*'s limited Expressionism originated in the divergent aims of its makers. For the employees, the designers Warm Rohrig and Reimann, the aim was to unify setting and narrative, while for the producer, Pommer, the aim was to differentiate his product – just enough but not too much – in order to open new international markets.[18] (Of course the designers probably had mercantile interests as well, and Pommer was not without artistic sensitivities – on both sides, contradictions within contradictions.) During his negotiations with Janowitz in 1944, Pommer argued in a letter to his lawyer that the "value" of the original *Caligari* was

> not so much in the basical (sic) story but in the revolutionary way the picture was produced. . . . It was the suggestions of the two art directors, Herlth and Rohrig (sic) who proposed the style and treatment which then made the film world famous. All these values are positively vested in UFA's silent rights. . . .[19]

Brecht believed that commodification was making individual authors and unified works of art anachronistic, but Pommer's argument symptomatically revealed the beginnings of a use which the commercial film industries found for authors.[20] Because exchange value was as stake, Pommer wanted to elevate the art directors from the status of employees paid by wages to that of authors with immaterial rights. Authorship as creativity (use) is recognized only in terms of authorship as property (exchange); an author, then, is someone who can by his or her work directly produce exchange value.[21] A price can be put on that quality which differentiates *Caligari* from those films made only for a price.

The commodity form, then, is not just an aspect of the work itself but a social relation of isolation, divergent interests, even mutual antagonism for most of the humans who produce and consume. In the case of *Caligari*, the war of all against all which starts at the beginning of the production process is not revealed until decades later, when the film's use value has been defined across the new space of an emergent art cinema, between the commodity and the avant-garde. But the commodification of art cinema is always uneven and incomplete; if consumability is based on a tension, largely invisible to viewers, between standardization and novelty,[22] then this tension is out of balance in the art cinema before World War II, preventing the smooth rationalization of audience needs and industrial practices. Brecht began his essay on the *Threepenny Opera* trial with the admonition, "In contradictions lie our hopes!" In the contradictions of *Caligari* and the art cinema lie their use values for a genuinely critical theory.

Notes

1 Letter from Fowler Legg to Julius B. Salter, May 8, 1946. This and other private correspondence regarding *Caligari* cited below are held in the Deutsche Kinemathek, West Berlin. My thanks to the staff of the Kinemathek, especially Mr. Gero Gandert.
2 Telegram from Hans Janowitz, New York, to Paul Rotha, London, Jan. 19, 1945.
3 Letter from Julius B. Salter to Ernest Matray, Aug. 31, 1945.
4 David Bordwell, "The Art Cinema as a Mode of Film Practice," *Film Criticism* 4, no. 1 (Fall 1979), 56–64; Steve Neale, "Art Cinema as Institution," *Screen* 22, no. 1 (1981), 11–39.
5 Neale, p. 36.
6 Karl Marx, *Capital*, vol. 1, tr. Ben Fowkes (New York: Vintage Books, 1977), 165, 166.
7 Bertolt Brecht, "Der Dreigroschenprozess, Ein Soziologisches Experiment," in *Schriften Zur Literatur und Kunst I* 1920–1932 (Suhrkamp Verlag, 1967), 143–234. Also in Bertolt Brecht, *Gesammelte Werke in 20 Banden*, vol. 18 (Frankfurt-m-Main, 1967), 139–209. Translated into French in Bertolt Brecht, *Sur le Cinéma* (Paris: L'Arche, 1970), 148–242. A valuable commentary in English is Ben Brewster, "Brecht and The Film Industry" and "Discussion," *Screen* 16, no. 4 (Winter 1975/6), 16–33.
8 Bertolt Brecht, "Collective Presentation (Editors' Notes)," *Screen* 15, no. 2, (Summer 1974), 47.
9 Lotte Eisner, "Appendix: The Dreigroschenoper Lawsuit," in *The Haunted Screen*, tr. Roger Greaves (Berkeley: University of California Press, 1973), 344–5.
10 Brecht, "Der Dreigroschenprozess," 185–6, 195–6, 197. Translation by Richard Garrett.
11 Bordwell, 57; Neale, 30–3.
12 Standish D. Lawder, *The Cubist Cinema* (New York: New York University Press, 1975), 184–5.
13 Neale, 33.
14 Michael Budd, "*The Cabinet of Dr Caligari*: Conditions of Reception," *Ciné-Tracts* 3, no. 4 (Winter 1981), 41–9.
15 Budd, passim.
16 *Moving Picture World* and *Motion Picture News*, various issues in April and May, 1921.
17 Budd, 48.
18 George A. Huaco, *The Sociology of Film Art* (New York: Basic Books, 1965), 35–6.
19 Letter from Erich Pommer to Paul Kohner, Aug. 3, 1944.
20 Brewster, 22–3.
21 Sue Clayton and Jonathan Curling, "On Authorship," *Screen* 20, no. 1 (Spring 1979), 48.
22 Janet Staiger, "Mass Produced Photoplays: Economic and Signifying Practices in the First Years of Hollywood," *Wide Angle* 4, no. 3 (1980), 19–24.

27

The Place of Women in the Cinema of Raoul Walsh

Pam Cook and Claire Johnston

Along with Claire Johnston, whose work is represented earlier in this collection, Pam Cook was a pioneering voice in British feminist film criticism in the 1970s. Cook is the co-editor of *The Cinema Book*, a comprehensive overview of film theory, criticism, and history, among other volumes, and she has served as associate editor for *Sight and Sound* magazine. In this essay on Hollywood director Raoul Walsh, the authors examine the work of a Hollywood stalwart director whose career spanned the studio era with over 100 films to his credit. Choosing an auteur whom Sarris includes in his accomplished second rank ("The Far Side of Paradise") and whom he describes as a "virile" director whose masculine characters periodically succumb to "feminine" emotion, Cook and Johnston offer an analysis of some of his films in terms of how they treat women characters. More interested in "Raoul Walsh" than in Raoul Walsh, they trace the trajectory of women in his films as objects of exchange in a masculine discourse. If Walsh, in these terms, is an auteur, it is less because he expresses a personal vision in his films than that an ideologically determined meaning (in this case, the inevitable contradictions of a patriarchal capitalist social order) can be found in them.

Presentation

The following analysis of the place of women in some of Raoul Walsh's films relies on concepts borrowed from the psychoanalyst Jacques Lacan, whose work constitutes a radical re-reading of Freud. The basis of that reading is the insight that Freud thought his theory of the unconscious in terms of a conceptual apparatus which he forged in the face of pre-Saussurian linguistics, anticipating the discoveries of modern linguistics. Lacan therefore proceeds to a re-reading of Freud's theory in the light of concepts produced by and for structural linguistics. This obviously involves the rejection of the vast bulk of post-Freudian psychoanalysis. Now that it has become clear that Freud conceived the unconscious as being structured like a language, any decipherment of the discourse of the unconscious must abandon all the unfortunately widespread misconceptions regarding the reading – i.e., selection – of "symptoms" and of the kind of sexual "symbolism" propagated by Jung.

J. Lacan distinguishes the *Symbolic* from the *Imaginary* and the *Real*. The Imaginary relationship with the other occurs in a dual situation which is primarily narcissistic. Aggressiveness and identification with the image of the

Pam Cook and Claire Johnston, "The Place of Women in the Cinema of Raoul Walsh," pp. 93–109 from Phil Hardy (ed.), *Raoul Walsh* (Edinburgh: Edinburgh Film Festival, 1974).

> other predominate at this stage. The *Symbolic* element is one that intervenes to break up an Imaginary relationship from which there is no way out. The child meets the "third element" upon birth; he enters a world ordered by a culture, law, and language, and is enveloped in that Symbolic order. Finally, Lacan distinguishes the *Other*, the locus from which the code emanates, from the Imaginary *other*. (M. Mannoni, *The Child, his 'Illness' and the Others*, London, 1970, p. 23n.)

The Other, as the locus of the Law (e.g., the law of the prohibition of incest), as the Word (i.e., the signifier as unit of the code) is the "Name-of-the-Father" around which the Symbolic order is constructed. The child, or indeed, any human being, as a subject of desire is constituted from the place of the Other: his "I" is a signifier in someone else's discourse and he has to find out how and where "I" fits into the social universe he discovers.

It has often been argued that there are a number of films directed by Raoul Walsh which appear to present women as strong and independent characters. The authors of the following essay take issue with this type of reading and attempt to demonstrate that women (e.g., Mamie Stover) in fact function as a signifier in a circuit of exchange where the values exchanged have been fixed by/in a patriarchal culture. Although Lévi-Strauss pointed out that real women, as producers of signs, could never be reduced to the status of mere tokens of exchange, i.e., to mere signs, the authors argue that, in films, the use of images of women and the way their "I" is constituted in Walshian texts play a subtle game of duplicity: in the tradition of classic cinema and nineteenth-century realism, the characters are presented as "autonomous individuals"; but the construction of the discourse contradicts this convention by reducing these "real" women to images and tokens functioning in a circuit of signs the values of which have been determined by and for men. In this way, the authors are attempting to help lay the foundations of a feminist film criticism as well as producing an analysis of a number of films directed by Walsh.

Between 1956 and 1957 Raoul Walsh made three films which centre around the social, cultural and sexual definition of women. At first sight, the role of woman within these films appears a "positive" one; they display a great independence of spirit, and contrast sharply with the apparent "weakness" of the male protagonists. The first film in this cycle depicts a woman occupying the central function in the narrative; the Jane Russell vehicle, *The Revolt of Mamie Stover*, tells the story of a bar-room hostess's attempts to buck the system and acquire wealth and social status within patriarchy. *The King and Four Queens*, made the same year, depicts five women who hide out in a burnt-out ghost town to guard hidden gold. *Band of Angels*, made the following year, tells the story of a Southern heiress who suddenly finds herself sold into slavery at the time of the American Civil War. Walsh prefigured the problematic of the independent woman before this period, most notably in a series of films he made in the 1940s, some of which starred the actress Ida Lupino, who later became one of the few women film-makers to work in Hollywood: *They Drive by Night*, *High Sierra* and *The Man I Love*. However, undoubtedly the most useful films for providing a reference point for this cycle are *Manpower* (1941) and *The Bowery* (1933); in these films, Walsh celebrates the ethic of the all-male group, and outlines the role which women are designated to play within it. Walsh depicts the male hero as being trapped and pinned down by some hidden event in his past. In order to become the Subject of Desire he must test the Law through transgression. To gain self-knowledge and to give meaning to memories of the past, he is impelled towards the primal scene and to the acceptance of a symbolic castration, For the male hero the female protagonist becomes an agent within the text of the film whereby his hidden secret can be brought to light, for it is in woman that his "lack" is located. She represents at one and the same time the distant memory of maternal plenitude and the fetishized object of his phantasy of castration – a phallic replacement and thus a threat. In *Manpower* Walsh depicts an all-male universe verging on infantilism – the camaraderie of the fire-fighters from the "Ministry of Power and Light". Sexual relationships and female sexuality are repressed within the film, and Marlene Dietrich is depicted as only having an existence within the discourse of men: she is "spoken", she does not speak. As an object of exchange between men, a sign oscillating between the images of prostitute and mother-figure, she represents the means by which men express their relationships with each other, the means through which they come to understand themselves and each other. *The Bowery* presents a

Figure 27.1 Marlene Dietrich in *Manpower* (Warner Bros, 1941): Raoul Walsh's films explore the problem of the independent woman. Produced by Hal B. Wallis

similar all-male society, this time based totally on internal all-male rivalry; within this highly ritualised system the women ("the skirts") assume the function of symbols of this rivalry. Whatever the "positive" attributes assigned to them through characterisation, woman as sign remains a function, a token of exchange in this patriarchal order. Paul Willemen in his article on *Pursued* describes the role of the female protagonist Theresa Wright/Thorley as the "specular image" of the male protagonist Robert Mitchum/Jeb: she is the place where he deposits his words in a desire to "know" himself through her.

In her book *Psychoanalysis and Feminism* Juliet Mitchell, citing Lévi-Strauss, characterizes a system where women are objects for exchange as essentially a communications system.

> The act of exchange holds a society together: the rules of kinship (like those of language to which they are near-allied) are the society. Whatever the nature of the society – patriarchal, matrilineal, patrilineal, etc. – it is always men who exchange women. Women thus become the equivalent of a sign which is being communicated.

In Walsh's oeuvre, woman is not only a sign in a system of exchange, but an empty sign. (The major exception in this respect is Mamie Stover, who seeks to transform her status as object for exchange precisely by compounding a highly articulated, fetishized image for herself.) The male protagonist's castration fears, his search for self-knowledge all converge on woman: it is in her that he is finally faced with the recognition of "lack". Woman is therefore the locus of emptiness: she is a sign which is defined negatively: something that is missing which must be located so that the narcissistic aim of the male protagonist can be achieved. The narrative structure of *Band of Angels* is particularly interesting in the light of this model. The first half of the story is concerned with events in Manty/Yvonne de Carlo's life which reduce her from the position of a lady to that of a slave to be auctioned in the slave market. Almost exactly half way through the story – at the "centre" of the film – Clark Gable appears and takes possession of her: from that moment the unfolding of his "dark secret" takes precedence. It becomes clear that Manty/Yvonne de Carlo's story was merely a device to bring into play the background (the slave trade, crumbling Southern capitalism) against which the "real" drama is to take place. Manty/Yvonne de Carlo is created in Clark Gable's image: half black and half white, she signifies the lost secret which must be found in order to resolve the relationship between Clark Gable and Sidney Poitier – the "naturalisation" of the slave trade.

One of the most interesting aspects of this *mise-en-scène* of exchange in which woman as sign is located is the way Walsh relates it directly and explicitly to the circulation of money within the text of the film. Marx states that under capitalism the exchange value of commodities is their inherent monetary property and that in turn money achieves a social existence quite apart from all commodities and their natural mode of existence. The circulation of money and its abstraction as a sign in a system of exchange serves as a mirror image for woman as sign in a system of exchange. However, in Walsh's universe, women do not have access to the circulation of money: Mamie Stover's attempt to gain access to it takes place at a time of national emergency, the bombing of Pearl Harbor, when all the men are away fighting – it is described as "theft". As a system, the circulation of money embodies phallic power and the right of possession; it is a system by which women are controlled. In *Band of Angels* Manty/Yvonne de Carlo is reduced to a chattel and exchanged for money on the slave market; she is exchanged for money because of her father's "dark secret" and because of his debt. In *The King and Four Queens* the women guard the gold but they cannot gain access to it directly. Its phallic power lies hidden in the grave of a dead husband, surrounded by sterility and devastation. Clark Gable gains access to it by asserting his right of possession by means of tossing a gold coin in the air and shooting a bullet through the middle of it, a trick which the absent males of the family all knew: the mark of the right of possession. The ticket system in *The Revolt of Mamie Stover* takes the analogy between money and women one stage further: men buy tickets at "The Bungalow" and at the same time they buy an image of woman. It is the symbolic expression of the right men have to control women within their imaginary system. This link between money and phallic power assumes its most striking image in Walsh's oeuvre when Jane Russell/Mamie, having accumulated considerable savings as a bar hostess in Pearl Harbor, declares her love for Richard Egan/Jimmy by asking him if she can place these savings in his safety deposit box at the bank: "there's nothing closer between friends than money". Recognising the significance of such a proposition, he refuses.

The Revolt of Mamie Stover is the only one of these films in which the female protagonist represents the central organising principle of the text. As the adventuress *par excellence* she is impelled to test and transgress the Law in the same way that all Walsh's heroes do: she would seem to function at first sight in a similar way to her male counterpart, the adventurer, within the narrative structure. But as the film reveals, her relationship to the Law is radically different. Her drive is not to test and transgress the Law as a means towards understanding a hidden secret within her past, but to transgress the forms of representation governing the classic cinema itself, which imprison her forever within an image. As the credits of the film appear on the screen, Jane Russell looks into the camera with defiance, before turning her back on America and walking off to a new life in Pearl Harbor. This look, itself a transgression of one of the classic rules of cinematography (i.e., "don't look into the camera") serves as a reference point for what is to follow. Asserting herself as the subject rather than the object of desire, this look

Figure 27.2 Jane Russell (r.) with Agnes Moorhead in Raoul Walsh's *The Revolt of Mamie Stover* (Twentieth Century Fox, 1956). Produced by Buddy Adler

into the camera represents a reaching out beyond the diegetic space of the film and the myths of representation which entrap her. The central contradiction of her situation is that she can only attempt to assert herself as subject through the exploitation of a fetishised image of woman to be exchanged within the circulation of money; her independence and her desire for social and economic status all hinge on this objectification. The forms of representation generated by the classic cinema – the myths of woman as pin-up, vamp, "Mississippi Cinderella" – are the only means by which she can achieve the objective of becoming the subject rather than the object of desire. The futility of this enterprise is highlighted at the end of the film when she returns once more to America in a similar sequence of shots; this time she no longer looks towards the camera, but remains trapped within the diegetic space which the film has allotted to her.

The film opens with a long-shot of a neon-lit city at night. Red letters appear on the screen telling us the time and place: SAN FRANCISCO 1941. *The Revolt of Mamie Stover* was made in 1956 – the story is therefore set within the living memory/history of the spectator. This title is the first indication that the film will reactivate the memory of an anxiogeflic situation: the traumatic moment of the attack on Pearl Harbor and the entry of the United States into the Second World War. Simultaneously, on the sound band, sleazy night-club music swells up (clip-joints, predatory prostitution, female sexuality exchanged for money at a time when the country, its male population and its financial resources are about to be put at risk). A police car (one of the many representations of the Law in the film), its siren wailing insistently over the music (a further indication of imminent danger) drives fast onto a dock-side where a ship is waiting. As it draws up alongside the ship, a female figure carrying a coat and a small suitcase gets out of the car and appears to turn back to look at the city from which she has obviously been expelled in a hurry. Jane Russell then looks straight into the camera (see above).

Up to this point the text has been multiply coded to signify danger/threat. The threat is closely associated with sexuality – besides the music, the red letters on the screen indicate red for danger and red for sex. Paul Willemen has pointed out that the "look" in *Pursued* is a threatening object: the *Cahiers du Cinéma* analysis of *Young Mr Lincoln* also delineates Henry Fonda/Lincoln's "castrating stare" as having the same threatening significance. Besides this threatening "look," Jane Russell has other dangerous connotations: qualities of aggression, of preying on the male to attain her own ends. Her "look" – repeated many times during the film, directed towards men, and explicitly described at one point as "come hither" – doubly marks her as signifier of threat. In the absence of the male, the female might "take his place": at the moment of Jane Russell's "look" at the camera, the spectator is directly confronted with the image of that threat. The fact that this image has been expelled from a previous situation is also important: Jane Russell actually represents the repudiated idea: she *is* that idea. Thus the threat is simultaneously recognised and recuperated: the female cannot "take the place" of the male; she can only be "in his place" – his mirror image – the "you" which is the "I" in another place.

This moment of dual fascination between the spectator and Jane Russell is broken by the intervention of a third organising principle representing the narrative, as the titles in red letters "Jane Russell Richard Egan" appear over the female figure. The title has the effect of immediately distancing the spectator: it reminds him of the symbolic role of the narrative by locating Jane Russell as an imaginary figure. In psychoanalytic terms the concept "imaginary" is more complex than the word would immediately seem to imply. It is a concept central to the Lacanian formulation of the "mirror stage" in which the "other" is apprehended as the "other which is me", i.e., my mirror image. In the imaginary relationship the other is seen in terms of resemblance to oneself. As an imaginary figure in the text of the film Jane Russell's "masculine" attributes are emphasised: square jaw, broad shoulders, narrow hips, swinging, almost swashbuckling walk – "phallic" attributes which are echoed and re-echoed in the text; for example, in her aggressive language – she tells a wolf-whistling soldier to "go mend your rifle, soldier"; when Richard Egan/Jimmy fights Michael Pate/Atkins at the Country Club she shouts "give him one for me, Jimmy". The girls at "The Bungalow" hail her as "Abe Lincoln Stover". Jane Russell/Mamie is the imaginary *counterpart* of the absent spectator and the absent subject of the text: the mirror image they have mutually constructed and in whom both images converge and overlap.

Again, borrowing from Lacan, the function of the "Symbolic" is to intervene in the imaginary situation and to integrate the subject into the Symbolic Order (which is ultimately the Law, the Name of the Father). The narrative of *The Revolt of Mamie Stover*, in that it presents a particular model of the world historically, culturally and ideologically overdetermined, could be said to perform a symbolic function for the absent spectator. The anxiety-generating displacement Jane Russell/Mamie appears to threaten the narrative at certain points. For example, after having promised to marry Richard Egan/Jimmy, give up her job at "The Bungalow" and become "exclusively his", and having taken his ring in a symbolic exchange which is "almost like the real thing" and "makes it legal", Jane Russell/Mamie leaves her man at the army camp and returns to "The Bungalow" to resign. However, she is persuaded by Agnes Moorhead/Bertha Parchman to continue working there, now that Michael Pate/Atkins has gone (been expelled), for a bigger share of the profits and more power. Richard Egan/Jimmy is absent, so he won't know. His absence is important: it recalls another sequence earlier in the narrative which shows in a quick succession of shots Richard Egan/Jimmy and the army away at war while Jane Russell/Mamie is at the same moment buying up all the available property on the island, becoming "Sto-Mame Company Incorporated" with Uncle Sam as her biggest tenant. Jane Russell/Mamie makes her biggest strides in the absence of men: she threatens to take over the power of exchange. By promising to marry and give it all up, she is reintegrated into an order where she no longer represents that threat. Richard Egan/Jimmy can be seen as the representative of the absent spectator and absent subject of the discourse in this structure: they are mutual constructors of the text – he is a writer who is constantly trying to write Jane Russell/Mamie's story for her. When Jane Russell/Mamie goes back to work at "The Bungalow" she in effect negates his image of her in favour of an image which suggests destruction and purging – "Flaming Mamie" – and becomes again a threatening displacement, reproduced and enlarged 7 foot high. When Richard Egan/Jimmy is confronted with this threatening image at the army camp, when a soldier shows him a photograph of her, a bomb drops and he is wounded. In the face of this renewed threat he returns to "The Bungalow" and in his final speech to Jane Russell/Mamie repudiates her as his imaginary counterpart; the narcissistic fascination with her is ended; he realises he can no longer control her image.

The symbolic level of the narrative in maintaining its order in the face of a threat is reasserted in the final sequence where the policeman at the dockside re-echoes Richard Egan/Jimmy's words of rejection: "Nothing's changed: Mamie. You aren't welcome here". Jane Russell/Mamie replies that she is going home to Leesburg, Mississippi (this is what Richard Egan/Jimmy was always telling her she must do). When the policeman remarks that she does not seem to have done too well, she replies: "If I told you I had made a fortune and given it all away, would you believe me?" When he says "No", she replies "I thought so". This exchange contains a final assertion that the protagonist cannot write her own story: she is a signifier, an object of exchange in a play of desire between the absent subject and object of the discourse. She remains "spoken": she does not speak. The final rhetorical question seals her defeat.

On the plane of the image, the symbolic order is maintained by an incessant production, within the text, of images for and of Jane Russell/Mamie from which she is unable to escape, and with which she complies through a *mise-en-scène* of exchange. In order to become the subject of desire, she is compelled to be the object of desire, and the images she "chooses" remain locked within the myths of representation governed by patriarchy. This *mise-en-scène* of exchange is initiated by her expulsion by the police at the dockside – the image of predatory whore is established. This image is elaborated during the next scene when the ship's steward tells Richard Egan/Jimmy about her reputation as sexual predator ("she ain't no lady"). Mamie interrupts the conversation, and realising that Richard Egan/Jimmy as a scriptwriter in Hollywood is interested in her, she suggests he should write and buy her story – the hard-luck story of a "Mississippi Cinderella". Growing emotional involvement with him leads her to reject the idea of being "written" in favour of "writing" her own story, and to seek out an image more consistent with the wealthy "hilltop" milieu of which Richard Egan/Jimmy is part, epitomised by Jimmy's girlfriend ("Miss Hilltop"). Jane Russell/Mamie asks Richard Egan/Jimmy to "dress her up and teach her how to behave"; he refuses. Their relationship from then on is characterised as one of transgression: they "dance without tickets" at the country club, away from the "four don'ts" of "The Bungalow". For her image as a performer and hostess at "The Bungalow" Jane Russell/Mamie has dyed her hair red and has assumed the name of "Flaming Mamie" ("Mamie's not beer or whisky, she's champagne only"). The image of "Flaming Mamie" is at one and the same time an assertion and a negation of female sexuality; sexually arousing ("Fellas who try to resist should hire a psychiatrist" intones the song) but at the same time the locus of sexual taboo ("Keep the eyes on the hands" she says in another number – they tell the story). It is at "The Bungalow" that the ticket system formalises this *mise-en-scène* of exchange; men literally buy an image for a predetermined period of time. (It is this concept of exchange of images which Jane Russell/Mamie finally discards when she throws the ticket away as she leaves the boat at the end of the film.) Reduced once again to the image of common prostitute when they go dancing at the country club and having decided to stay at "The Bungalow" in spite of Richard Egan/Jimmy, she finally assumes the iconography of the pin-up, with the "come hither" look; an image emptied of all personality or individuality; an image based on the effects of pure gesture. This image was prefigured in an extraordinary sequence at the beach when Jane Russell/Mamie jumps up from the sand where she has been sitting with Richard Egan/Jimmy in order to take a swim. As she does so, she turns back to look at him and her image becomes frozen into the vacant grin of a bathing suit advertisement. Talking about money, Jane Russell/Mamie describes herself at one point as a "have not"; this recurrent imbrication of images, the telling of story within a story which the film generates through a *mise-en-scène* of exchange, serves to repress the idea of female sexuality and to encase Jane Russell/Mamie within the symbolic order, the Law of the Father.

Walsh criticism to date has been dominated by the notion of "personality"; like the American adventurer *par excellence* he so often depicts, Walsh, as one of the oldest pioneers, has come to be regarded as of the essence of what is called "classic" Hollywood cinema – a cinema characterised traditionally by its linearity, its transparency: in short, the effect of "non-writing". Andrew Sarris has even gone so far as to say of him: "only the most virile director can effectively project a feminine vulnerability in his characters". This notion of authorship has been criticised by Stephen Heath in the following terms: "the function of the author (the effect of the idea of authorship) is a function of unity; the use of the notion of the author involves the organisation of the film . . . and in so doing, it avoids – this is indeed its function – the thinking of the articulation of the film text in relation to ideology." A view of Walsh as the originating consciousness of the Walsh oeuvre is, therefore, an ideological concept. To attribute such qualities as "virility" to Walsh is to foreclose the recognition of Walsh as subject within ideology. This feminist reading of the Walsh oeuvre rejects any approach which would attempt to delineate the role of women in terms of the influence of ideology or sociology, as such an approach is merely a strategy to supplement auteur analysis. We have attempted to provide a reading of the Walsh oeuvre which takes as its starting point Walsh as a subject within ideology and, ultimately, the laws of the human order. What concerns us specifically is the delineation of the ideology of patriarchy – by which we mean the Law of the Father – within the text of the film. As Lévi-Strauss has indicated: "The emergence of symbolic thought must have required that women, like works, should be things that were exchanged." The tasks for feminist criticism must therefore consist of a process of de-naturalisation: a questioning of the unity of the text; of seeing it as a contradictory interplay of different codes; of tracing its "structuring absences" and its relationship to the universal problem of symbolic castration. It is in this sense that a feminist strategy for the cinema must be understood. Only when such work has been done can a foundation for a feminist counter-cinema be established. Woman as signifier of woman under patriarchy is totally absent in most image-producing systems, but particularly in Hollywood where image-making and the fetishistic position of the spectator are highly developed. This is indeed why a study of "woman" within the Hollywood system is of great interest. A study of woman within Walsh's oeuvre, in particular, reveals "woman" as the locus of a dilemma for the patriarchal human order, as a locus of contradictions. *Cahiers du Cinéma* in an editorial described such texts in the following terms: "an internal criticism is taking place which cracks the film apart at the seams. If one reads the film obliquely, looking for symptoms, if one looks beyond its apparent coherence one can see that it is riddled with cracks; it is splitting under an internal tension which is simply not there in an ideologically innocuous film. The ideology thus becomes subordinate to the text. It no longer has an independent existence; it is presented by the film." The function of "woman" in Walsh as the locus of "lack", as an empty sign to be filled, the absent centre of a phallocentric universe marks the first step towards the de-naturalisation of woman in the Hollywood cinema. In a frenzied imbrication of images (*The Revolt of Mamie Stover*) the Phallus is restored; but in this distanciation the first notes of the "swan-song of the immortal nature of patriarchal culture" (cf. Juliet Mitchell) can be heard.

28

Female Authorship Reconsidered (The Case of Dorothy Arzner)

Judith Mayne

An American feminist critic, Judith Mayne teaches in the Department of French and Italian at Ohio State University in Columbus. Mayne is the author of several books including *Cinema and Spectatorship, Framed: Lesbians, Feminists and Media Culture*, as well as studies of Dorothy Arzner and French director Claire Denis. This essay, taken from her book *The Woman at the Keyhole: Feminism and Women's Cinema* (1990), begins by considering how the question of female authorship has been understood in film studies, and then proceeds to consider the films of Dorothy Arzner, one of the very few women directors to work in Hollywood during the studio era. Mayne explores the possibility of female authorship in the case of Arzner, who has been a favorite filmmaker for feminist critics. While she does not claim that Arzner is an auteur in the strict sense of a consistent and identifiable style, Mayne argues that her films nevertheless are consistently concerned with the limitations of and challenges to patriarchal definitions of femininity.

[. . .]

In this chapter, I will examine how female authorship has been theorized in feminist film studies, and I will focus in particular on the example of Dorothy Arzner, one of the few women to have been successful as a director in Hollywood in a career that spanned from the late 1920s to the early 1940s. Arzner was one of the early "rediscoveries" of feminist film theory, and she and her work remain to this day the most important case study of female authorship in the cinema. While the most significant work on Arzner's career was done in feminist film studies of the early to mid-1970s, I will suggest that important dimensions of her status as a female author have yet to be explored.

In contemporary feminist literary criticism, inquiries into the nature of female authorship have been shaped by responses to two somewhat obvious assumptions: first, that no matter how tenuous, fractured, or complicated, there is a connection between the writer's gender, her personhood, and her texts; and second, that there exists a female tradition in literature, whether defined in terms of models of mutual influence, shared themes, or common distances from the dominant culture. A wide range of critical practice is held within these assumptions. But insofar as a self-evident category of womanhood may be implicit in the female author defined as the source of a text and as a moment in a female-specific tradition, these seemingly obvious

Judith Mayne, "Female Authorship Reconsidered (The Case of Dorothy Arzner)," pp. 89–105, 110–15 from ch. 5 of *The Woman at the Keyhole: Feminism and Women's Cinema* (Bloomington and Indianapolis: Indiana University Press, 1990).

assumptions evoke what has become in contemporary theory a dreaded epithet: essentialism.

A decade or so ago, a friend of mine remarked sarcastically upon the prevalence of "oedipus detectors" at a Modern Language Association meeting, that is, critics eager to sniff out any remnants of oedipal scenarios in work that was ostensibly "progressive," "feminist," or "postoedipal." Contemporary feminist criticism – and feminist film studies in particular – is marked by a similar presence of "essentialist detectors." For virtually any mention of "real women" (especially insofar as authors are concerned) tends to inspire a by-now-familiar recitation of the "dangers" of essentialism – an affirmation of the difference between men and women as given, and an attendant belief in the positive value of female identity which, repressed by patriarchy, will be given its true voice by feminism. While there is obviously much to be said about the risks of essentialism, the contemporary practice of essentialism detection has avoided the complex relationship between "woman" and "women," usually by bracketing the category of "women" altogether.

Even though discussions of the works of women filmmakers have been central to the development of feminist film studies, theoretical discussions of female authorship in the cinema have been surprisingly sparse. While virtually all feminist critics would agree that the works of Germaine Dulac, Maya Deren, and Dorothy Arzner (to name the most frequently invoked "historical figures") are important, there has been considerable reluctance to use any of them as privileged examples to theorize female authorship in the cinema, unless, that is, such theorizing affirms the difficulty of women's relationship to the cinematic apparatus. This reluctance reflects the current association of "theory" with "antiessentialism." In the realm of feminist literary theory and criticism, however, antiessentialism has not had quite the same widespread effects of negation. In the works of critics such as Margaret Homans and Nancy K. Miller, for instance, female authorship is analyzed not in terms of simple categories of agency and authority, but rather in terms of complex textual and cultural processes which dramatize and foreground women's relationships to language, plot, and the institutions of literature.[1] My point is not that feminist film critics have the proverbial "much to learn" from feminist literary critics, but rather that the paradigm of female authorship in literature may provide a useful point of departure to examine the status of female authorship in the cinema.

For such a point of departure, I turn to two anecdotes, one "literary" and one "theoretical," both of which stage an encounter between women's writing and the cinema in similar ways. My first anecdote, the more "literary" one, concerns two contemporary novels by women concerned with the vicissitudes of female writing. In both novels, cinema becomes a persuasive metaphor for the difficult and sometimes impenetrable obstacles that confront the woman writer. Doris Lessing's novel *The Golden Notebook* explores the relations between female identity and artistic production, and a formulation of that relation is represented through the cinema. Woman is the viewer, man the projectionist, and the whole viewing process a form of control and domination. Writer Anna Wulf describes her vision of events from her own past as films shown to her by an invisible male projectionist. The films represent what Anna calls the "burden of recreating order out of the chaos that my life has become." Yet Anna is horrified by this vision of cinematic order:

> They were all, so I saw now, conventionally, well-made films, as if they had been done in a studio; then I saw the titles: these films, which were everything I hated most, had been directed by me. The projectionist kept running these films very fast, and then pausing on the credits, and I could hear his jeering laugh at *Directed by Anna Wulf*. Then he would run another few scenes, every scene glossy with untruth, false and stupid.[2]

Lessing's cinematic metaphor is informed by a relationship between viewer and image, and between projectionist and screen, that is profoundly patriarchal in the sense that separation, hierarchy, and power are here synonymous with sexual division. The conventionality and gloss of untruth of the films are complicit with Anna Wulf's alienation from her name that appears on them. If, for Lessing, the conditions of film viewing suggest patriarchal domination, then the most immediate terms of that metaphor are the simultaneous evocation and denial of female authorship. Cinema embodies distance from the self – or at least, distance from the *female* self, a distance produced by the mockery of female authorship in the titles of the film. As evoked in *The Golden Notebook* within the context of the female narrator's relationship to language and to experience, cinema functions as a particularly and peculiarly negative inflection of the female authorial signature.

In her novel *The Quest for Christa T.,* Christa Wolf evokes the cinema as a form of illusory presence, as a fantasy control of the past. The female narrator of *The Quest for Christa T.* describes her search for Christa, as well as for the very possibility of memory: "I even name her name, and now I'm quite certain of her. But all the time I know that it's a film of shadows being run off the reel, a film that was once projected in the real light of cities, landscapes, living rooms."[3] Film may create images of the past, but the images are contained by a reified memory. The cinema thus suggests a past that has been categorized, hierarchized, and neatly tucked away.[4] Like Lessing's Anna Wulf, the narrator of *The Quest of Christa T.* searches for the connections between female identity and language. While less explicit in its patriarchal configuration, Wolf's metaphor nonetheless posits cinema as resistant to the process of active searching generally, and female self-expression specifically. The female narrator in *The Quest for Christa T.* is engaged, in Wolf's words, in a search for "the secret of the third person, who is there without being tangible and who, when circumstances favor her, can bring down more reality upon herself than the first person: I." As in *The Golden Notebook,* cinema obstructs the writing of female self-representation, thus embodying what Wolf calls "the difficulty of saying 'I.' "[5]

If we are to take Lessing's and Wolf's metaphoric representations of the cinema at their word, then the difficulty of saying "I" for the woman filmmaker is far greater than for the woman writer. Feminist interrogations of the cinema have supported Lessing's and Wolf's metaphors, for the narrative and visual staging of cinematic desire relies, as most theoretical accounts would have it, on the massive disavowal of sexual difference and the subsequent alignment of cinematic representation with male-centered scenarios. To be sure, one could argue – with more than a touch of defensiveness – that such metaphoric renderings of the cinema suggest the strategic importance of the works of women filmmakers. For if the cinema is symptomatic of alienation (Lessing) and reification (Wolf), then the attempts by women directors to redefine, appropriate, or otherwise reinvent the cinema are crucial demonstrations that the boundaries of that supremely patriarchal form are more permeable, more open to feminist and female influence, than these film-inspired metaphors would suggest. At the same time, it could be argued that the works of women filmmakers offer reformulations of cinematic identification and desire, reformulations that posit cinematic metaphors quite different from those in the passages from Lessing and Wolf cited above. In other words, the "difficulty of saying 'I' " does not necessarily mean that female authorship is impossible in the cinema, but rather that it functions differently than in literature.

If Lessing's and Wolf's formulations reflect the spirit of much feminist writing about film, suggesting that the cinema is peculiarly and forcefully resistant to the female creator, yet another obstacle to the theorizing of female authorship in the cinema emerges when the literary comparison is pursued in another direction. My second, more properly "theoretical" anecdote of the relationship between female authorship in its literary and cinematic forms is drawn from the introduction to *Revision,* a collection of essays on feminist film theory and criticism. The editors of the volume note that feminist film critics have "reason to be envious" of those feminist critics working in literature who "were able to turn to a comparatively substantial canon of works by women writers." Unlike literature, the cinema has no such evidence of a female-authored cinema to which feminist critics might logically turn to begin to elaborate the components of women's cinema or of a feminist film aesthetic. "For where in the classic cinema," the editors ask, "do we encounter anything like an 'autonomous tradition,' with 'distinctive features' and 'lines of influence'? And if, with some difficult, we can conceive of Lois Weber and Dorothy Arzner as the Jane Austen and George Eliot of Hollywood, to whom do they trace their own influence?"[6]

While feminist literary critics have their own disagreements about the validity of the concept of a "female tradition" (autonomous or not) or a female "canon" (substantial or not), it is true that feminist film critics simply do not have the body of evidence to suggest how and in what ways female-authored cinema would be substantially different from cinema directed and created by men. The absence of this body of evidence notwithstanding, however, it seems to me that the reluctance of many feminist critics to speak, as feminist literary critics do, of a "female tradition" in cinema had to do with a number of other factors, ranging from theoretical frameworks in which any discussions of "personhood" are suspect, to the peculiar status of authorship in the cinema. Particularly insofar as the classical Hollywood cinema is concerned, the conventional equation of authorship with the role of the film director can repress or negate the significant ways in which female signatures *do* appear on film. For instance, consideration of the role of the often-forgotten, often-female screenwriter might suggest more of a female imprint on the film text; and the role of the actress does not always conform to common feminist wisdom about the controlling male gaze located in the persona of the male director – witness Bette Davis as a case in point.[7]

The reluctance to speak of a "female tradition" has perhaps been most influenced, however, by the fear of essentialism – the fear, that is, that any discussion of "female texts" presumes the uniqueness and autonomy of female representation, thus validating rather than challenging the dualism of patriarchal hierarchy. However, the act of discarding the concept of female authorship and of an attendant female tradition in the cinema as necessarily compromised by essentialist definitions of woman can be equally dualistic, in assuming that the only models of connection and influence are unquestionably essentialist ones. Sometimes it is assumed that any discussion of authorship is a throwback to the era of biographical criticism, to the text as transparent and simple reflection of the author's life. While the limitations of such an approach are obvious, purely textual models of cinematic representation have their own limitations insofar as the narrative strategies of many contemporary women's films are concerned, for these strategies frequently involve an inscription of authorship in literal terms, with the director herself a performer in her film.

Any discussion of female authorship in the cinema must take into account the curious history of definitions of cinematic authorship in general.[8] It was not really until the 1950s that "auteurism" became a fixture of film theory and criticism. The French term did not connote then, as French terms have in the past two decades of film studies, a particularly complex entity. For *auteurism* refers to the view that the film director is the single force responsible for the final film, and that throughout the films of a given *auteur* a body of themes and preoccupations will be discernible.[9] The obviousness of these claims is complicated, rather, by the fact that the object of inquiry for auteurist critics was primarily the Hollywood cinema. To speak of a "Hitchcock" or a "John Ford" or a "Nicholas Ray" film as opposed to an "MGM" or a "John Wayne" film was, if not a necessarily radical enterprise, then at least a historically significant one, in that a shift was marked in the very ways in which one speaks of film. For the corporate industrial model of film production was being challenged by a liberal humanist one, and "Hitchcock" does not carry quite the same capitalist, industrial, or corporate baggage as "MGM."

Despite the opposition between the industry and the creative individual from which auteurism emerges, however, the terms do not differ all that much in their patriarchal connotations; "MGM" and "Hitchcock" may be patriarchal in different ways, but they share a common ground. The cinematic *auteur* was identified as a transcendental figure resistant to the leveling forces of the Hollywood industry; to use Roland Barthes's words, the *auteur* theory in cinema reinstated the "formidable paternity" of the individual creator threatened by the institutions of mass culture of which the cinema is a paradigmatic and even privileged example.[10] Thus it does not require too much imagination to see Alexandre Astruc's famous equation of the camera with a writer's pen, in his phrase "caméro-stylo," as informed by the same kind of metaphorical equivalence between pen and penis that has defined both the Western literary tradition (symptomatically) and feminist literary history (critically).[11] The phallic denominator can be read several ways, most obviously as a denial of the possibility of any female agency. Conversely, it can be argued that the privileging of female authorship risks appropriating, for women, an extremely patriarchal notion of cinematic creation. At stake, then, is whether the adjective *female* in female authorship inflects the noun *authorship* in a way significant enough to challenge or displace its patriarchal and proprietary implications.

Whether authorship constitutes a patriarchal and/or phallocentric notion in its own right raises the specter of the "Franco-American Disconnection" (to use Domna Stanton's phrase) that has been the source of much critical debate, or confusion, depending upon your point of view, in contemporary feminist theory.[12]

The position usually described as "American" – and therefore empirical and historical – would claim female authorship as basic to the goals of a feminist appropriation of (cinematic) culture, and the position described as "French" – theoretical and deconstructive – would find "authorship" and "appropriation" equally complicitous in their mimicry of patriarchal definitions of self, expression, and representation.[13] Although it is a commonly held assumption that contemporary film studies, especially as they developed in England, are virtually synonymous with "French theory," the fate of auteurism, particularly in relationship to feminist film theory, has not followed such an easily charted or one-directional path. In a famous 1973 essay, for example, Claire Johnston argued against the dismissal of the *auteur* theory. While acknowledging that "some developments of the *auteur* theory have led to a tendency to deify the personality of the (male) director," Johnston argues nonetheless for the importance of auteurism for feminism. She notes that "the development of the *auteur* theory marked an important intervention in film criticism: its polemics challenged the entrenched view of Hollywood as monolithic, and stripped of its normative aspects the classification of films by director has proved an extremely productive way of ordering our experience of the cinema."[14]

Johnston's argument recalls Peter Wollen's writings on *auteur* theory, where the cinematic *auteur* is defined less as a creative individual and more as a figure whose imprint on a film is measured by the repetition of sets of oppositions and the network of preoccupations, including unconscious ones.[15] Her analysis needs to be seen in the context of a certain moment in feminist criticism, when notions of "good roles" for women (and therefore "positive" versus "negative" images) had much critical currency. Johnston turns that critical currency on its head in a comparison of Howard Hawks and John Ford. She argues that the apparently more "positive" and "liberated" heroines of Hawks's films are pure functions of male desire. For John Ford, women function in more ambivalent ways. Whereas in Hawks's films woman is "a traumatic presence which must be negated," in Ford's films woman "becomes a cipher onto which Ford projects his profoundly ambivalent attitude to the concepts of civilisation and psychological 'wholeness.' "[16] Defined as a narrative and visual system associated with a given director, Johnston's auteurism allows for a kind of analysis which goes beyond the categories of "good" and "bad" (images of roles) and into the far more productive critical territory of symptom and contradiction.

While Johnston's analysis seems to stress equally the importance of auteurism and of "symptomatic readings," her work is read today far more in the context of the latter. As with Peter Wollen's work on authorship, one senses that perhaps the auteurist part is a backdrop upon which more significant critical and theoretical assumptions are projected – those of structuralism and semiotics in the case of Wollen, and those of Althusserian-based critical readings in the case of Johnston. The kind of analysis for which Johnston argues – analysis of the position of "woman" within the narrative and visual structures of the cinema – has by and large been pursued without much direct consideration of the *auteur* theory, or for *auteurs*.[17] Despite the importance of auteurism in staking out what Johnston would call progressive claims for film criticism, the analysis of the kinds of structures to which Johnston alludes in the films of Hawks or Ford has been pursued within the framework of textual and ideological analyses of that ubiquitous entity, the classical Hollywood cinema, rather than within the scope of authorship.

By and large, the preferred mode of textual analysis, given its particular attention to unconscious resonances within narrative and visual structures, has had little room for an exploration of auteurism. One notable exception is Raymond Bellour's analyses of Hitchcock's role as "enunciator" in his films, which nonetheless define authorship in explicity literal and narrow textual terms – i.e., the fact that Hitchcock's famous cameo appearances in his films occur at crucial moments of the exposition and/or resolution of cinematic desire.[18] More frequently in contemporary film studies, one speaks of a "Hawks" film or a "Ford" film in the same way one would speak of a "horror" film or a "film noir" – as a convenient categorization of films with similar preoccupations and similar stylistic and narrative features. Such a demystification of authorship might well be more progressive than Johnston's defense of authorship. Conversely, authorship itself may have assumed a symptomatic status, in which case it has not been demystified so much as concealed within and displaced onto other concerns, evoking a process similar to what Nancy K.

Miller has observed in the field of literary studies, where the concept of authorship has been not so much revised as it has been repressed "in favor of the (new) monolith of anonymous textuality."[19]

In film theory and criticism of the last decade, auteurism is rarely invoked, and when it is, it is more as a curiosity, as a historical development surely influential, but even more surely surpassed. In this context, Kaja Silverman has suggested that a curious slippage occurs in feminist discussions of the avant-garde works of women filmmakers, for the concept of authorship – largely bracketed in textual analysis – reappears, but in an extratextual way.

> The author often emerges . . . as a largely untheorized category, placed definitively "outside" the text, and assumed to be the punctual source of its sounds and images. A certain nostalgia for an unproblematic agency permeates much of the writing to which I refer. There is no sense in which the feminist author, like her phallic counterpart, might be constructed in and through discourse – that she might be inseparable from the desire that circulates within her texts, investing itself not only in their formal articulation, but in recurring diegetic elements.[20]

Silverman recommends a theorization of female authorship that would account for a diversity of authorial inscriptions, ranging from thematic preoccupations, to the designation of a character or group of characters as a stand-in for the author, to the various enunciative strategies (sonoric as well as visual) whereby the film *auteur*'s presence is marked (whether explicitly or implicitly), to the "fantasmatic scene" that structures an author's work.[21]

The concept of female authorship in the cinema may well have a currency similar to categories of genre or of style. But can female authorship be so easily assimilated to the existing taxonomy of the cinema? Present categories of authorship are undoubtedly much more useful in analyzing the configurations of "woman" on screen than in coming to terms with the ways in which women directors inflect cinematic practice in new and challenging ways. The analysis of female authorship in the cinema raises somewhat different questions than does the analysis of male authorship, not only for the obvious reason that women have not had the same relationship to the institutions of the cinema as men have, but also because the articulation of female authorship threatens to upset the erasure of "women" which is central to the articulation of "woman" in the cinema. Virtually all feminist critics who argue in defense of female authorship as a useful and necessary category assume the political necessity for doing so. Hence, Kaja Silverman urges that the gendered positions of libidinal desire within the text be read "in relation to the biological gender of the biographical author, since it is clearly not the same thing, socially or politically, for a woman to speak with a female voice as it is for a man to do so, and vice versa."[22] The notion of female authorship is not simply a useful political strategy; it is crucial to the reinvention of the cinema that has been undertaken by women filmmakers and feminist spectators.

One of the most productive ironies of feminist theory may be that, if "woman" and "women" do *not* coincide (to borrow Teresa de Lauretis's formulation), they also connect in tenuous and often complex ways. It is customary in much feminist film theory to read "subject" to "object" as "male" is to "female." But a more productive exploration of female authorship insofar as "woman" and "women" are concerned may result when subject-object relationships are considered within and among women. Visions of "woman" that appear on screen may be largely the projections of patriarchal fantasies, and the "women" who make films and who see them may have problematic relations at best with those visions. While it is tempting to use de Lauretis's distinction as an opposition between traditional cinematic representations of "woman" and those "women" filmmakers who challenge and reinvent them, the gap, the noncoincidence, is better defined by exploring the tensions within both "woman" and "women."[23]

One such strategy has been directed toward the "reading against the grain" of traditional cinematic representations of women, demonstrating how they can be read in ways that contradict or otherwise problematize their function within male-centered discourse.[24] Surprisingly little comparable attention has been paid, however, to the function and position of the woman director. Central to a theorizing of female authorship in the cinema is an expanded definition of texuality attentive to the complex network of intersections, distances, and resistances of "woman" to "women." The challenge of female authorship in the cinema for feminist theory is in the demonstration of *how* the divisions, overlaps, and distances between "woman" and "women" connect with the contradictory status of cinema as the embodiment of both omnipotent control and individual fantasy.

The feminist rediscovery of Dorothy Arzner in the 1970s remains the most important attempt to theorize female authorship in the cinema. Arzner may not be feminist film theory's answer to George Eliot, but her career as a woman director in Hollywood with a significant body of work (and in whose work – true to the most rudimentary definitions of film authorship – a number of preoccupations reappear) has posed issues most central to a feminist theory of female cinematic authorship. As one of the very small handful of women directors who were successful in Hollywood, particularly during the studio years, Arzner has served as an important example of a woman director working within the Hollywood system who managed, in however limited ways, to make films that disturb the conventions of Hollywood narrative.

The significance of this argument, advanced primarily by Claire Johnston and Pam Cook, in which Arzner is defined as a director "critical" of the Hollywood cinema, needs to be seen in the context of the development of the notion of the film *auteur*. Arzner was very definitely *not* one of the directors for whom auteurist claims were made in the heyday of auteurist criticism. For despite the core themes and preoccupations visible across her work, Arzner does not satisfy any of the specific requirements of cinematic authorship as they were advanced on either side of the Atlantic – there is little of the flourish of mise-en-scène that auteurists attributed to other directors, for instance, and the preoccupations visible from film to film that might identify a particular signature do not reflect the life-and-death, civilization-versus-the-wilderness struggles that tended to define the range of more "properly" auteurist themes.[25]

Given the extent to which feminist analysis of the cinema has relied on the distinction between dominant and alternative film, the claims that can be made for an alternative vision that exists within and alongside the dominant cinema will be crucial in gauging the specific ways in which women directors engage with "women's cinema" as divided between representations that perpetuate patriarchal definitions of femininity, and representations that challenge them and offer other modes of identification and pleasure. One can read in responses to Arzner's work reflections of larger assumptions concerning the Hollywood cinema. At one extreme is Andrew Britton's assessment of Arzner, in his study of Katharine Hepburn, as the *auteur* of *Christopher Strong* (1933), the film in which Hepburn appears as an aviatrix who falls in love with an older, married man.

That *Christopher Strong* functions as a "critique of the effect of patriarchal heterosexual relations on relations between women" suggests that the classical cinema lends itself quite readily to heterogeneity and conflicting ideological allegiances, whether the "critique" is the effect of the woman director or the female star.[26] At the opposite extreme, Jacquelyn Suter's analysis of *Christopher Strong* evolves from the assumption that whatever "female discourse" there is in the film is subsumed and neutralized by the patriarchal discourse on monogamy.[27] If the classical cinema described by Britton seems remarkably open to effects of subversion and criticism, the classical cinema described by Suter is just as remarkably closed to any meanings but patriarchal ones, and one is left to assume that female authorship is either a simple affirmation of agency, or virtually an impossibility as far as Hollywood cinema is concerned.

In contrast, Claire Johnston's analyses of Arzner are reminiscent of Roland Barthes's description of Balzac as representative of a "limited plurality" within classical discourse.[28] For Johnston suggests that the strategies of her films open up limited criticisms of the Hollywood cinema. Johnston's claims for female authorship in Arzner's films rely on notions of defamiliarization and dislocation, and more precisely on the assumption popularized within film studies, primarily by Jean-Louis Comolli and Jean Narboni, that there exists within the classical Hollywood cinema a category of films in which realist conventions are criticized from within, generating a kind of internal critique. Claims for this "progressive" text have been made from a variety of vantage points, virtually all of them concerned with ideological value – with, that is, the possibility of a Hollywood film that critiques the very values that are ostensibly promoted, from the literal dark underside of bourgeois ideology "exposed" in *Young Mr Lincoln* to the impossibility of familial ties for women in *Mildred Pierce*.[29] For Johnston, female desire is the *auteurist* preoccupation that generates a critique of patriarchal ideology in Arzner's films.

Initially, Johnston's analysis of Arzner appears to rely on a definition of the classical cinema that allows for more heterogeneity and more articulation of contradiction than is the case in those analyses that posit a rigid distinction between the classical cinema and its alternatives. However, Arzner's films can be identified as "progressive" only in relationship to a norm that allows for no divergences from purely classical filmmaking. More problematical within the present context, there is nothing in this kind of analysis to suggest what these marks of dislocation and critique have to do with distinctly *female* authorship. Many "woman's films" are motivated by the representation of female desire, and feminist critics have shown how these films might also be read as driven by such an internal – if often unconscious – critique.[30] It is not clear, in other words, to what extent the fact of female authorship gives a particular or distinct inflection to the representation of female desire.

The "political" reasons for insisting on the relevance of the author's gender are not adequate in and of themselves, for they can easily harden into an idealized abstraction, and the name "Dorothy Arzner" would thus become just one more signature to add to the pantheon of (male) directors who critique the conventions of Hollywood cinema from within. While the importance of Arzner's signature in extratextual terms is undeniable, stressing that importance should not be a substitute for an examination of the textual ramifications of female authorship. Yet Johnston's approach to those textual ramifications in Arzner's work seems torn between female authorship understood ("politically") as agency and self-representation, on the one hand, and as a negative inflection of the norms of classical cinema, on the other.[31] This ambivalence – which could be read in terms of the conflicting claims of the so-called American and French positions – is not particularly productive, for the agency thus affirmed dissolves into negation and the impossibility of a female position, evoking Julia Kristéva's extremely limited hypothesis that "women's practice can only be negative, in opposition to that which exists, to say that 'this is not it' and 'it is not yet.'"[32]

Noting that structural coherence in Arzner's films comes from the discourse of the woman, Johnston relies on the notion of defamiliarization, derived from the Russian formalists' *priem ostranenie*, the "device of making strange," to assess the effects of the woman's discourse on patriarchal meaning: "the work of the woman's discourse renders the narrative strange, subverting and dislocating it at the level of meaning."[33] Johnston discusses in this context what has become the single most famous scene from any of Arzner's films, when Judy (Maureen O'Hara), who has played ballet stooge to the vaudeville performer Bubbles (Lucille Ball) in *Dance, Girl, Dance* (1940), confronts her audience and tells them how *she* sees *them*. This is, Johnston argues, the only real break between dominant discourse and the discourse of the woman in Arzner's work, and it is a break that is quickly recuperated within the film, for the audience applauds Judy, and she and Bubbles are quickly dispatched to center stage, where they engage in a catfight, to the delight of the audience. The moment in *Dance, Girl, Dance* when Judy faces her audience is a privileged moment in feminist film theory and criticism, foregrounding as it does the sexual hierarchy of the gaze, with female agency defined as the return of the look, thus "citing" the objectification of woman.[34]

The celebrity accorded this particular scene in Arzner's film needs to be evaluated in the context of feminist film theory in the mid-1970s. Confronted with the persuasive psychoanalytically based theoretical model according to which women either did not or could not exist on screen, the discovery of Arzner, and especially of Judy's "return of the gaze," offered some glimmer of historical hope as to the possibility of a female intervention in the cinema. To be sure, the scope of the intervention is limited, for as Johnston herself stresses, Judy's radical act is quickly recuperated within the film when the audience gets up to cheer her on, and she and Bubbles begin to fight on stage. But the need to revise Johnston's model of authorship is most apparent in this reading of recuperation, for it is informed by the assumption that such a "break" can be only a brief eruption, and can occur in classical cinema only if it is then immediately contained within the laws of male spectatorial desire.

Only one kind of look (Judy's return of the look to her audience) and one kind of spectacle (where men are the agents of the look and women its objects) have received attention in *Dance, Girl, Dance*. In other words, the disruptive force of female desire central to Arzner's work exists primarily within the symmetry

Figure 28.1 A double site of female objectification and bonding: Bubbles (Lucille Ball) and Judy (Maureen O'Hara) in Dorothy Arzner's *Dance, Girl, Dance* (RKO, 1940). Produced by Erich Pommer and Harry E. Edington

of masculinity and femininity.[35] However, I would suggest that female authorship acquires its most significant contours in Arzner's work through relations between and among women. The female gaze is defined early on in the film as central to the aspirations of women as they are shaped within a community of women. Madame Basilova, the older woman who is in charge of the dancing troupe of which Judy and Bubbles are a part, is seen gazing through the rails of a stairway as Judy practices her ballet, and the gaze of Judy herself is isolated as she looks longingly at a rehearsal of the ballet company which she wishes to join. Even Judy's famous scolding of the audience is identified primarily as a communication, not between a female performer and a male audience (the audience is not, in any case, exclusively male) but between the performer and the female member of the audience (secretary to Steven Adams, the man who will eventually become Judy's love interest) who stands up to applaud her.[36] And the catfight that erupts between Judy and Bubbles on stage is less a recuperative move – i.e., transforming the potential threat of Judy's confrontation into an even more tantalizing spectacle – than the claiming by the two women of the stage as an extension of their conflicted friendship, rather than as the alienated site of performance.

To be sure, the men – promoters as well as onlookers – eagerly consume the spectacle of Judy and Bubbles in a catfight. But I see this response less as a sign of pure recuperation by the male-centered system of looks and spectacles, and more as the dramatization of the tension between performance and self-expression which the film attempts to resolve. Although Johnston is more concerned with the devices that give Arzner's films "structural coherence," it is tempting to conclude from her analysis that Judy functions as a metaphoric rendering of the woman filmmaker herself, thus establishing something of a homology between Arzner's position vis-à-vis the classical Hollywood cinema and Judy's position on stage.[37] The stage is, in other words, *both* the site of the objectification of the female body *and* the site for the theatricalizing of female friendship. This "both/and" – the stage (and, by metaphoric implication, the cinema itself) is an arena simultaneously of patriarchal exploitation and of female self-representation – stands in contrast to the more limited view of Arzner's films in Johnston's work, where more of a "neither/nor" logic is operative – neither patriarchal discourse nor the "discourse of the woman" allows women a vantage point from which to speak, represent, or imagine themselves.

Reading Arzner's films in terms of the "both/and" suggests an irony more far-reaching than that described by Johnston. Johnston's reading of Arzner is suggestive of Shoshana Felman's definition of irony as "dragging authority as such into a scene which it cannot master, of which it is *not aware* and which, for that very reason, is the scene of its own self-destruction . . ."[38] The irony in *Dance, Girl, Dance*, however, does not just demonstrate how the patriarchal discourse of the cinema excludes women, but rather how the cinema functions in two radically different ways, both of which are "true," as it were, and totally incompatible. I am borrowing here from Donna Haraway's definition of irony: "Irony is about contradictions that do not resolve into larger wholes, even dialectically, about the tension of holding incompatible things together because both or all are necessary and true."[39] This insistence on two equally compelling and incompatible truths constitutes a form of irony far more complex than Johnston's analysis of defamiliarization.

Johnston's notion of Arzner's irony assumes a patriarchal form of representation which may have its gaps and its weak links, but which remains dominant in every sense of the word. For Johnston, Arzner's irony can be only the irony of negativity, of puncturing holes in patriarchal assumptions. Such a view of irony has less to do, I would argue, with the limitations of Arzner's career (e.g., as a woman director working within the inevitable limitations of the Hollywood system) than with the limitations of the film theory from which it grows. If the cinema is understood as a one-dimensional system of male subjects and female objects, then it is not difficult to understand how the irony in Arzner's films is limited, or at least would be *read* as limited. While rigid hierarchies of sexual difference are indeed characteristic of dominant cinema, they are not absolute, and Arzner's films represent other kinds of cinematic pleasure and desire.

An assessment of Arzner's importance within the framework of female authorship needs to account not only for how Arzner problematizes the pleasures of the cinematic institution as we understand it – e.g., in terms of the voyeurism and fetishism reenacted through the power of the male gaze and the objectification of the female body – but also for how, in her films, those pleasures are identified in ways that are not reducible to the theoretical clichés of the omnipotence of the male gaze. The irony of *Dance, Girl, Dance* emerges from the conflicting demands of performance and self-expression, which are linked in their turn to heterosexual romance and female friendship. Female friendship acquires a resistant function in the way that it exerts a pressure against the supposed "natural" laws of heterosexual romance. Relations between women and communities of women have a privileged status in Arzner's films. To be sure, Arzner's films offer plots – particularly insofar as resolutions are concerned – that are compatible with the romantic expectations of the classical Hollywood cinema; communities of women may be central, but boy still meets girl.

Claire Johnston claims that the conclusion of *Dance, Girl, Dance*, where Judy is embraced by Steven Adams, destined for a fusion of professional mentoring and romance, is marked by Judy's defeat. This strikes me more as wishful feminist thinking than as a convincing reading of the film's conclusion, which "works" within the conventions of Hollywood romance. Noting Judy's final comment as she is in Steven's arms – "when I think how simple things could have been, I just have to laugh" – Johnston says that "this irony marks her defeat and final engulfment, but at the same time it is the final mark of subversion of the discourse of the male."[40] If the "discourse of the male" is subverted in *Dance, Girl, Dance*, it has less to do with the resolution of the film and more to do with the process of heterosexual initiation which the film has traced. Judy's attractions to men are shaped by substitutions for women and female rivalry – Steven Adams is a professional mentor to substitute for Basilova, and Jimmie Harris is an infantile man who is desirable mainly because Bubbles wants him too.[41] Therefore, the heterosexual romance provides the conclusion of the film, but only after it has been mediated by relationships between women.

A controversial area in feminist theory and criticism has been the connection between lesbianism and female friendship in those fictional worlds which, like Arzner's, take communities of women as their inspiration. Barbara Smith's suggestion that the relationship between Nel and Sula in Toni Morrison's novel *Sula* can be read in lesbian terms has been provocative to say the least, particularly given Toni Morrison's own assertion that "there is no homosexuality in *Sula*."[42] But the case of Arzner is somewhat different. What is known about Arzner implies that she herself was a lesbian.[43] But this assertion raises as many questions as it presumably answers, concerning both the responsibility of a critic vis-à-vis an individual who was presumably in the closet, and the compulsion to define lesbianism as something in need of proof.[44] Bonnie Zimmerman has suggested that "if a text lends itself to a lesbian reading, then no amount of biographical 'proof' ought to be necessary to establish it as a lesbian text."[45] The point is well taken, but in Arzner's case another "text" mediates the relationship between director, her films, and their reception. For Arzner's films are virtually no longer read independently of her persona – an issue to which I will return momentarily. Nonetheless, if relationships between and among women account for much more narrative and visual momentum than do the relations between men and women in Arzner's work, then one begins to wonder about the perspective that informs these preoccupations.

For all of the attention that has been given to Arzner's work, one striking aspect of her persona – and of her films – has been largely ignored. Although the photographs of Arzner that have accompanied feminist analyses of her work depict a woman who favored a look and a style connoting lesbian identity, discussions of her work always stop short of any recognition that sexual identity might have something to do with how her films function, particularly concerning the "discourse of the woman" and female communities, or that the contours of female authorship in her films might be defined in lesbian terms. This marginalization is all the more notable, given how *visible* Arzner has been as an image in feminist film theory. With the possible exception of Maya Deren, Arzner is more frequently represented visually than any other woman director central to contemporary feminist discussions of film. And unlike Deren, who appeared extensively in her own films, Arzner does not have the reputation of being a particularly self-promoting, visible, or "out" (in several senses of the term) woman director.

Sarah Halprin has suggested that the reason for this omission is, in part, the suspicion of any kind of biographical information in analysis of female authorship:

> most discussions of Dorothy Arzner's films, especially those by the English school, carefully avoid any mention of Arzner's appearance in relation to some of the images in her films. Lengthy analyses of *Dance, Girl, Dance* ignore the fact that while the "main" characters, Judy and Bubbles, are recurrently placed as immature within the context of the film, there are two "minor" characters who both dress and look remarkably similar to Arzner herself (i.e., tailored, "mannish," in the manner of Radclyffe Hall and other famous lesbians of the time) and are placed as mature, single, independent women who are crucial to the career of young Judy and who are clearly seen as oppressed by social stereotyping, of which they are contemptuous. Such a reading provides a whole new way of relating to the film and to other Arzner films, encouraging a discussion of lesbian stereotypes, relations between lesbians and heterosexual women as presented in various films and as perceived by any specific contemporary audience.[46]

Indeed, one of the most critical aspects of Arzner's work is the way in which heterosexuality is assumed equivocally, without necessarily violating many of the conventions of the Hollywood film.

In his book on gay sexuality and film, Vito Russo quotes another Hollywood director on Arzner: "an obviously lesbian director like Dorothy Arzner got away with her lifestyle because she was officially closeted and because 'it made her one of the boys.'"[47] An interview with Arzner by Karyn Kay and Gerald Peary gives some evidence of her status as "one of the boys," at least insofar as identification is concerned, for in discussing both *Christopher Strong* and *Craig's Wife*, Arzner insists that her sympathies lie with the male characters.[48] However, one has only to look at the photographs of Arzner that have accompanied essays about her work in recent years to see that this is not a director so easily assimilated to the boys' club of Hollywood. Arzner preferred masculine attire, in the manner, as Halprin says, of Radclyffe Hall.

Figure 28.2 Studio portrait of Dorothy Arzner

Two dominant tropes shape the photographic mise-en-scène of the Arzner persona. She is portrayed against the backdrop of the large-scale apparatus of the Hollywood cinema, or she is shown with other women, usually actresses, most of whom are most emphatically "feminine," creating a striking contrast indeed.

[. . .]

The photographs of Arzner are interesting not only in the biographical terms suggested by Sarah Halprin, but also in textual terms. For one of the most distinctive ways in which Arzner's authorial presence is felt in her films is in the emphasis placed on communities of women, to be sure, but also in the erotic charge identified within those communities. If heterosexual initiation is central to Arzner's films, it is precisely in its function as rite of passage (rather than natural destiny) that a marginal presence is felt – an authorial presence that is lesbian, as well as female. Consider, for instance, *Christopher Strong*. Katharine Hepburn first appears in the film as a prize-winning object in a scavenger hunt, for she can claim that she is over twenty-one and has never had a love affair. Christopher Strong, the man with whom she will eventually become involved, is the male version of this prize-winning object, for he has been married for more than five years and has always been faithful to his wife. As Cynthia Darrington, Hepburn dresses in decidedly unfeminine clothing and walks with a swagger that is masculine, or athletic, depending upon your point of view. Hepburn's jodhpurs and boots may well be, as Beverle Houston puts it, "that upper-class costume for a woman performing men's activities."[49] But this is also clothing that strongly denotes lesbian identity, and which (to stress again Sarah Halprin's point) is evocative of the way Arzner herself, and other lesbians of the time, dressed.

Cynthia's "virginity" becomes a euphemistic catch-all for a variety of margins in which she is situated, both as a woman devoted to her career and as a woman without a sexual identity. The film traces the acquisition of heterosexual identity, with some peculiar representations of femininity along the way, including Hepburn dressed as a moth. I am not arguing that *Christopher Strong,* like the dream which says one thing but ostensibly "really" means its mirror opposite, can be decoded as a coherent "lesbian film," or that the real subject of the film is the tension between gay and straight identities. The critical attitude toward heterosexuality takes the form of inflections, of bits and pieces of tone and gesture and emphasis, as a result of which the conventions of heterosexual behavior become loosened up, shaken free of some of their identifications with the patriarchal status quo.

Most important, perhaps, the acquisition of heterosexuality becomes the downfall of Cynthia Darrington. Suter has described *Christopher Strong* in terms of how the feminine discourse, represented by the various female characters in the film, is submerged by patriarchal discourse, the central term of which is monogamy. The proof offered for such a claim is, as is often the case in textual analysis, convincing on one level but quite tentative on another, for it is a proof which begins from and ends with the assumption of a patriarchal master code. Even the "feminine discourse" described by Suter is nothing but a pale reflection of that master code, with nonmonogamy its most radical expression. The possibility that "feminine discourse" in *Christopher Strong* might exceed heterosexual boundaries is not taken into account.[50] As should be obvious by now, I am arguing that it is precisely in its ironic inflection of heterosexual norms, whether by the mirroring gesture that suggests a reflection of Arzner herself or by the definition of the female community as resistant to, rather than complicitous with, heterosexual relations, that Arzner's signature is written on her films.

These two components central to female authorship in Arzner's work – female communities and the mirroring of Arzner herself – are not identical. The one, stressing the importance of female communities and friendship among women, may function as a pressure exerted against the rituals of heterosexual initiation, but is not necessarily opposed to them. This foregrounding of relationships among women disturbs the fit between female friendship and heterosexual romance, but the fit is still there, the compatibility with the conventions of the classical Hollywood cinema is still possible. The representation of lesbian codes, as in the mirroring of Arzner's – and other lesbians' – dress, constitutes the second strategy, which is more marginal and not integrated into narrative flow. These two authorial inscriptions – the emphasis on female communities, the citing of marginal lesbian gestures – are not situated on a "continuum," that model of continuity from female friendship to explicit lesbianism so favored in much contemporary lesbian-feminist writing.[51] Rather, these two strategies exist in tension with each other, constituting yet another level of irony in Arzner's work. Female communities are compatible with the classical Hollywood narrative; the lesbian gesture occupies no such position of compatibility, it does not mesh easily with narrative continuity in Arzner's film.

Thus, in *Dance, Girl, Dance,* Arzner accentuates not only the woman's desire as embodied in Judy and her relationships with other women, but also secondary female figures who never really become central, but who do not evaporate into the margins, either – such as the secretary (who leads the applause during Judy's "return of the gaze" number) and Basilova (the dance teacher and director of the troupe). That these figures do not simply "disappear" suggests even more strongly their impossible relationship to the Hollywood plot, a relationship that *is* possible insofar as Judy is concerned. In *Craig's Wife,* however, there is more of an immediate relationship between marginality and female communities, although in this case, the marginality has less of a lesbian inflection, both dress- and gesturewise. Julia Lesage has noted that in *Craig's Wife,* Arzner rereads George Kelley's play, the source of the film, so that the secondary women characters are treated much more fully than in the play.[52]

Craig's Wife – preoccupied with heterosexual demise rather than initiation – shows us a woman so obsessively concerned with her house that nothing else is of interest to her. Harriet Craig (Rosalind Russell) married as "a way towards emancipation. . . . I married to be independent." If marriage is a business contract, then Harriet Craig's capital is her house. Indeed, Harriet's sense of economy is pursued with a vengeance. And the men in the film are the victims, explicit or not, of her obsession. It is Harriet's husband who married for love, not money, and in a subplot of the film, a friend of Walter Craig is so obsessed by his wife's unfaithfulness that he kills her and then himself.

At the conclusion of the film, virtually everyone has cleared out of Harriet's house. Her niece has left with her fiancé, her servants have either quit or been fired, and Walter has finally packed up and left in disgust. Harriet seems pathetically neurotic and alone. The widow next door (Billie Burke) brings Harriet some roses. In Kelley's play, Harriet has become a mirror image of her neighbor, for both are portrayed as women alone, to be pitied. But in Arzner's film, the neighbor represents Harriet's one last chance for connection with another human being. Thus the figure who in Kelley's play is a pale echo of Harriet, becomes in the film the suggestion of another identity and of the possibility of a female community. The resolution of Arzner's *Craig's Wife* has little to do with the loss of a husband, and more to do with situating Harriet Craig's fantasy come horribly true alongside the possibility of connection with another woman. And while Billie Burke is hardly evocative of lesbianism (as Basilova is in *Dance, Girl, Dance*), she and Rosalind Russell make for a play of contrasts visually similar to those visible in photographs of Arzner with more "feminine" women.[53]

To be sure, Arzner's authorship extends to an ironic perspective on patriarchal institutions in general, and in this sense her films do not require or assume a lesbian audience, as if this was or is likely to happen within the institutions of the Hollywood cinema. At the same time that the irony of Arzner's films appeals to a wide range of female experiences, and is thus readable across a wide spectrum, ranging from lesbian to heterosexual and from female to feminist, the marks of female authorship in her work do not constitute a universal category of female authorship in the cinema. The female signature in Arzner's work is marked by that irony of equally compelling and incompatible discourses to which I have referred, and the lesbian inflection articulates the division between female communities which do function within a heterosexual universe, and the eruptions of lesbian marginality which do not. This lesbian irony taps differing and competing views of lesbianism within contemporary feminist and lesbian theory. Lesbianism has been defined as the most intense form of female and feminist bonding, on the one hand; and as distinctly opposed to heterosexuality (whether practiced by women or men), on the other. In Arzner' s own time, these competing definitions were read as the conflict between a desexualized nineteenth-century ideal of romantic friendship among women, and the "mannish lesbian" (exemplified by Radclyffe Hall), defined by herself and her critics as a sexual being.[54] Arzner's continued "visibility" suggests not only that the tension is far from being resolved, but also that debates about lesbian identity inform, even (and especially!) in unconscious ways, the thinking of feminists who do not identify as lesbians.

I see, then, several points to draw from the example of Dorothy Arzner as far as female authorship in the cinema is concerned. The preoccupations with female communities and heterosexual initiation are visible and readable only if we are attentive to how the cinema, traditionally and historically, has offered pleasures other than those that have received the most sustained critical and theoretical attention in recent years. Female authorship finds an inadequate metaphor in the female gaze as it returns the ostensibly central and overriding force of the male gaze. Other forms of the female gaze – such as the exchange of looks between and among women – open up other possibilities for cinematic meaning and pleasure and identification. In addition, a female signature can take other forms besides the gaze – costume and gesture, and the strategies of reading "marginality" in the case of Arzner. Textually, the most pervasive sign of female authorship in Arzner's film is irony, and that irony is most appropriately described as the confrontation between two equally compelling, and incompatible discourses. [. . .]

Notes

1 See Margaret Homans, *Bearing the Word: Language and Female Experience in Nineteenth-Century Women's Writing* (Chicago: University of Chicago Press, 1986); and Nancy K. Miller, *Subject to Change: Reading Feminist Writing* (New York: Columbia University Press, 1988).

2 Doris Lessing, *The Golden Notebook* (1962; rpt. New York: Simon and Schuster, 1973), p. 619.

3 Christa Wolf, *The Quest for Christa T.* (1968; English trans. Christopher Middleton, New York: Delta, 1970), p. 4.

4 In her essay on the relation between feminism and Christa Wolf's work, Myra Love analyzes the status of film as an image "used to evoke the connections among domination, manipulation and experiential impoverishment." See "Christa Wolf and Feminism," *New German Critique* 16 (Winter 1979), 36.

5 Wolf, *The Quest for Christa T.*, p. 170.

6 Mary Ann Doane, Patricia Mellencamp, and Linda Williams, "Feminist Film Criticism: An Introduction," in Doane, Mellencamp, and Williams, eds., *Revision: Essays in Feminist Film Criticism* (Frederick, Md.: The American Film Institute/University Publications of America, 1984), p. 7. The editors are responding to a definition of feminist literary criticism by Elizabeth Abel, as the exploration of "distinctive features of female texts" and "lines of influence connecting women in a fertile and partially autonomous tradition." Abel's comments are drawn from "Editor's Introduction," *Critical Inquiry* 8, no. 2 (Winter 1981), 173.

7 Maria LaPlace argues for Bette Davis's significance as a creative force in her own right. See "Producing and Consuming the Woman's Film: Discursive Struggle in *Now, Voyager*," in Christine Gledhill, ed., *Home Is Where the Heart Is: Studies in Melodrama and the Woman's Film* (London: British Film Institute, 1987), pp. 138–66.

8 An excellent survey of the most significant texts on cinematic authorship is John Caughie, ed., *Theories of Authorship* (London: Routledge and Kegan Paul, 1981).

9 A useful survey and analysis of the different meanings that have been attached to the term *auteurism* can be found in Peter Wollen, *Signs and Meaning in the Cinema* (Bloomington: Indiana University Press, 1969), chapter 2.

10 Roland Barthes, *The Pleasure of the Text* (New York: Hill and Wang, 1975), trans. Richard Miller, p. 27.

11 Alexandre Astruc, "The Birth of a New Avant-Garde: *La caméra-stylo*," in Peter Graham, ed., *The New Wave* (London: Secker and Warburg, 1968), pp. 17–23. Susan Gubar and Sandra Gilbert begin their analysis of women writers with a query into the equivalence between pen and penis; see *The Madwoman in the Attic* (New Haven: Yale University Press, 1979), p. 3.

12 See Domna Stanton, "Language and Revolution: The Franco-American Disconnection," in Hester Eisenstein and Alice Jardine, eds., *The Future of Difference* (1980; rpt. New Brunswick, NJ: Rutgers University Press, 1985), pp. 73–87.

13 For particularly lucid expositions of these two positions, as well as the problems involved in defining the positions as opposing in the first place, see Peggy Kamuf, "Replacing Feminist Criticism," and Nancy Miller, "The Text's Heroine: A Feminist Critic and Her Fictions," *Diacritics* 12, no. 2 (Summer 1982), 42–53.

14 Claire Johnston, "Women's Cinema as Counter-cinema," in Claire Johnston, ed., *Notes on Women's Cinema* (1973; rpt. London: British Film Institute, 1975), p. 26.

15 See Wollen, *Signs and Meaning in the Cinema,* chapter 2.

16 Johnston, "Women's Cinema as Counter-cinema," p. 27. A comparison between Hawks and Ford as *auteurs* is also central in Wollen's discussion of auteurism *(Signs and Meaning in the Cinema,* chapter 2).

17 One notable exception is Tania Modleski's study of women and female spectatorship in the films of Alfred Hitchcock, although it is in no way a conventional "auteurist" study. See *The Women Who Knew Too Much* (New York: Methuen, 1988).

18 See Raymond Bellour, "Hitchcock the Enunciator," *camera obscura,* no. 2 (Fall 1977), 66–91.

19 Nancy K. Miller, "Changing the Subject: Authorship, Writing, and the Reader," in Teresa de Lauretis, ed., *Feminist Studies/Critical Studies* (Bloomington: Indiana University Press, 1986), p. 104.

20 Kaja Silverman, *The Acoustic Mirror: The Female Voice in Psychoanalysis and Cinema* (Bloomington: Indiana University Press, 1988), p. 209.

21 Ibid., pp. 212–17.

22 Ibid., p. 217.

23 This is suggested by de Lauretis herself: "the differences among women may be better understood as differences within women." See "Feminist Studies/Critical Studies: Issues, Terms, and Contexts," in de Lauretis, *Feminist Studies/Critical Studies,* p. 14.

24 Kaja Silverman refers to such a process as the "re-authoring" of a traditional text in feminist terms. See *The Acoustic Mirror,* p. 211.

25 For an insightful discussion of the ideology of auteurist critics in France, see John Hess, "La Politique des auteurs: Part One: World View as Aesthetic," *Jump Cut,* no. 1 (1974), 19–22; and "La Politique des auteurs: Part Two: Truffaut's Manifesto," *Jump Cut,* no. 2 (1974), 20–2.

26 Andrew Britton, *Katharine Hepburn: The Thirties and After* (Newcastle upon Tyne: Tyneside Cinema, 1984), p. 74.

27 Jacquelyn Suter, "Feminine Discourse in *Christopher Strong*," *Camera Obscura,* no. 3–4 (Summer 1979), 135–50.

28 Roland Barthes, *S/Z* (New York: Hill and Wang, 1974), trans. Richard Miller, p. 8.

29 See the editors of *Cahiers du cinéma*'s collective text, "John Ford's *Young Mr Lincoln*," *Screen* 13 (Autumn 1972), 5–44; on *Mildred Pierce,* see Joyce Nelson, "*Mildred Pierce* Reconsidered," *Film Reader,* no. 2 (1977), 65–70; Pam Cook, "Duplicity in *Mildred Pierce*," in E. Ann Kaplan, ed., *Women in Film Noir* (London: British Film Institute, 1978), pp. 68–82; Janet Walker, "Feminist Critical Practice; Female Discourse in *Mildred Pierce*," *Film Reader,* no. 5 (1982), 164–72; Judith

Mayne, *Private Novels, Public Films* (Athens: University of Georgia Press, 1988), pp. 142–54; and Linda Williams, "Feminist Film Theory: *Mildred Pierce* and the Second World War," in Deidre Pribram, ed., *Female Spectators: Looking at Film and Television* (London and New York: Verso, 1988), pp. 12–30.

30 One of the best examples of this kind of analysis is Lea Jacobs, "*Now, Voyager:* Some Problems of Enunciation and Sexual Difference," *Camera Obscura,* no. 7 (1981), 89–109.

31 I am not arguing here, as Janet Bergstrom has done in her criticism of Johnston, that the problem is the ultimate recuperability of all forms of difference by the apparatus of the Hollywood cinema. Referring specifically to the work of Stephen Heath, and more generally to textual analyses by critics such as Raymond Bellour and Thierry Kuntzel, Bergstrom criticizes Johnston's proto-feminist claims for elements which, she says, fit quite readily into classical narrative cinema. Bergstrom speaks of the "seemingly unlimited capacity for classical narrative film to create gaps, fissures, ruptures, generated most of all by its difficulty in containing sexual difference, only to recover them ultimately and to efface the memory, or at least the paths, of this heterogeneity. It is just this rupturing activity that is said to be characteristic of the classical text, and which, moreover, is thought to be the condition of a large part of its pleasure." While I would agree with Bergstrom that Johnston makes somewhat extravagant claims for elements which may well be incorporated into the overall narrative and visual momentum of the individual film, the view of the Hollywood cinema put forth by those critics to whose work she points approvingly is no less monolithic in the articulation of oedipal scenarios and male heterosexual desire. And needless to say, if heterogeneity is effaced, then there is no room in which to speak of female authorship. See Janet Bergstrom, "Rereading the Work of Claire Johnston," *camera obscura,* no. 3–4 (1979), 27.

32 "Interview – 1974: Julia Kristéva and Psychanalyse et politique," trans. Claire Pajaczkowska, *m/f,* no. 5–6 (1981), 166.

33 Claire Johnston, "Dorothy Arzner: Critical Strategies," in Claire Johnston, ed., *The Work of Dorothy Arzner: Towards a Feminist Cinema* (London: British Film Institute, 1975), p. 6.

34 Lucy Fischer reads *Dance, Girl, Dance* in terms of this "resistance to fetishism." See *Shot/Countershot* (Princeton: Princeton University Press, 1989), pp. 148–54.

35 Karyn Kay and Gerald Peary's reading of the film, however, focuses much more centrally on women's friendships and the rites of initiation. See "Dorothy Arzner's *Dance, Girl, Dance,*" in Karyn Kay and Gerald Peary, eds., *Women and the Cinema: A Critical Anthology* (New York: Dutton, 1977), pp. 9–25.

36 Barbara Koenig Quart stresses the relationship between Judy and the secretary in her reading of the scene. See *Women Directors: The Emergence of a New Cinema* (New York and Westport, CT: Praeger, 1988), p. 25.

37 Barbara Quart (ibid.) suggests a connection between Arzner's career and the show-business world depicted in *Dance, Girl, Dance:* "Arzner is clearly ambivalent about the vital, glamorous vulgarity of Bubbles, the Lucille Ball showgirl – but the scorn for Hollywood implicit in the film, and for the need to be a flesh peddler to survive there, is doubtless something Arzner herself felt in no small part, in this next to last of her films, close to her retirement."

38 Shoshana Felman, "To Open the Question," *Yale French Studies,* no. 55–56 (1980), 8.

39 Donna Haraway, "A Manifesto for Cyborgs: Science, Technology, and Socialist Feminism in the 1980s," *Socialist Review,* no. 80 (1985), 65.

40 Johnston, "Dorothy Arzner: Critical Strategies," p. 7.

41 The relationships of desire between women in Arzner's films are developed at length in my book-length study of Arzner (*Directed by Dorothy Arzner,* Bloomington: Indiana University Press 1994). For an analysis of the secondary roles men play in Arzner's films, see Melissa Sue Kort, "'Spectacular Spinelessness': The Men in Dorothy Arzner's Films," in Janet Todd, ed., *Men by Women, Women and Literature* (New Series), vol. 2 (1982), pp. 189–205.

42 Barbara Smith, "Toward a Black Feminist Criticism," *Conditions,* no. 2 (October 1977), 25–44; Interview with Toni Morrison in Claudia Tate, ed., *Black Women Writers at Work* (New York: Continuum, 1983), p. 118.

43 See, for example, Vito Russo, *The Celluloid Closet: Homosexuality in the Movies* (New York: Harper and Row, 1981), p. 50.

44 Sharon O'Brien addresses these questions in her study of Willa Cather. Noting that the definition of "lesbianism" and "lesbian writer" has been important in recent feminist criticism, O'Brien says, "For good reason, genital sexual experience with women has been the least-used criterion. As several critics have observed, to adopt such a definition requires the unearthing of 'proof' we do not think necessary in defining writers as heterosexual – proof, moreover, that is usually unav-ailable. . . . " See *Willa Cather: The Emerging Voice* (New York and Oxford: Oxford University Press, 1987), p. 127.

45 Bonnie Zimmerman, "What Has Never Been: An Overview of Lesbian Feminist Criticism," *Feminist Studies* 7, no. 3 (Fall 1981), 457.

46 Sarah Halprin, "Writing in the Margins (Review of E. Ann Kaplan, *Women and Film: Both Sides of the Camera*)," *Jump Cut,* no. 29 (1984), 32.

47 Russo, *The Celluloid Closet,* p. 50.

48 Karyn Kay and Gerald Peary, "Interview with Dorothy Arzner," in Johnston, *The Work of Dorothy Arzner,* pp. 25–6.

49 Beverle Houston, "Missing in Action: Notes on Dorothy Arzner," *Wide Angle* 6, no. 3 (1984), 27.

50 See Suter, "Feminine Discourse in *Christopher Strong.*"

51 The phrase "lesbian continuum" comes from Adrienne Rich, "Compulsory Heterosexuality and Lesbian Existence," *Signs* 5, no. 4 (Summer 1980), 631–60.

52 Julia Lesage, "The Hegemonic Female Fantasy in *An Unmarried Woman* and *Craig's Wife,*" *Film Reader,* no. 5 (1982), 91. In Karyn Kay and Gerald Peary's interview, Arzner states

that Kelley was angry at the changes in emphasis that were made.

53 Melissa Sue Kort also discusses Arzner's reading of the Kelley play, noting that the "shift from play to film changes Harriet from villain to victim." See her discussion of the film in "'Spectacular Spinelessness,'" pp. 196–200.

54 See Esther Newton, "The Mythic Mannish Lesbian: Radclyffe Hall and the New Woman," *Signs* 9, no. 4 (Summer 1984), 557–75. See also Lillian Faderman, *Surpassing the Love of Men: Romantic Friendship and Love between Women from the Renaissance to the Present* (New York: William Morrow and Co., 1981), esp. parts II and III.

29

Man's Favorite Sport?: The Action Films of Kathryn Bigelow

Barry Keith Grant

A professor of film studies at Brock University in Ontario, Canada, Barry Keith Grant has published widely in the area of popular cinema and film genre. His books include *Film Genre Reader*, *The Dread of Difference: Gender and the Horror Film*, *John Ford's Stagecoach*, *Film Genre: From Iconography to Ideology*, and *Voyages of Discovery: The Cinema of Frederick Wiseman*, in which he considers film authorship in the context of documentary filmmaking practices. In this essay, originally published in Yvonne Tasker's 2004 anthology on *Action and Adventure Cinema*, Grant brings a feminist perspective to an analysis of the action films of Kathryn Bigelow within their various generic traditions. He shows how Bigelow's work questions the values and assumptions of masculinity, particularly the central importance of violence, that typically provide pleasure in such genre films even as it offers those very pleasures.

Introduction

With only a few features to her credit – *The Loveless* (1983, co-directed with Monty Montgomery), *Near Dark* (1987), *Blue Steel* (1990), *Point Break* (1991), and *Strange Days* (1995)[1] – writer/director Kathryn Bigelow succeeded in establishing herself as the only female filmmaker specializing in action films who, at least to this point, can claim the status of auteur. Bigelow's films employ, in the words of Anna Powell, 'stunning and expressionistic visuals, rapid narrative pacing, thrilling and visceral scenes of eroticized violence and physical action',[2] providing all the expected pleasures of action films. Yet at the same time they also work within the various genres that fall within the category of action cinema – cop films, buddy and road movies, westerns and horror films – to question their traditional and shared ideological assumptions about gender and violence.

Some critics have hesitated to call Bigelow an auteur because of her personal and professional association with James Cameron, the creator of such muscular action movies as *Terminator* (1984) and *Terminator 2: Judgment Day* (1991) who also produced *Point Break* and wrote and produced *Strange Days*. Certainly her biological status as a woman has entered into the discourse surrounding Bigelow, with critics and reviewers often referring not only to her gender

Barry Keith Grant, "Man's Favorite Sport?: The Action Films of Kathryn Bigelow," pp. 371–84 from Yvonne Tasker (ed.), *Action and Adventure Cinema* (London and New York: Routledge, 2004).

but also to her physical attractiveness – hardly the kind of discourse that generally surrounds male directors.[3] Yet close analysis of her films reveal a remarkable consistency of style and theme that, as with most canonical male auteurs, works in relation to the parameters of genre.

The action film is perfectly suited to Bigelow's themes. The representation of violence is of course central to the genre, and as Steve Neale notes, the ideology of masculinity which it traditionally has worked so hard to inscribe centers on 'notions and attitudes to do with aggression, power, and control'.[4] Bigelow's first film, the short *Set-Up* (1978), which shows two men fighting in an alley while on the soundtrack two theorists interpret the violence, is in a sense a paradigm for her features to follow. All explore the nature of masculinity and its relation to violence, especially within the context of spectatorship, largely by playing on the look of the viewer as conditioned by the generic expectations and conventions of traditional action films. The 'false' beginnings of both *Blue Steel* and *Near Dark*, which are tests of perception for Bigelow's protagonists as well as for the viewer, are only the most obvious instances of the importance of looking and the look in her films.

Critics have duly noted the thematic and stylistic importance of vision in Bigelow's films – her 'cinema is essentially a discourse on vision', writes one[5] – a theme that likely has its roots in her days as a films studies student at Columbia University in New York City, at a time when the influence of feminist gaze theory was at its height. Much as Sirk and Fassbinder had approached the genre of melodrama or 'the woman's film', providing their pleasures while critiquing the ideology that underpinned them ('bending', in Sirk's phrase), so Bigelow works within the action film. Her music video for the pop band New Order's 'Touched by the Hand of God is indicative of her approach: just as in the video she incongruously films the new wave band with the iconography of costume and the conventions of performance associated with heavy metal, thus foregrounding and questioning their masculine coding, so Bigelow's films mobilize a range of the genres traditionally regarded as 'male' precisely to interrogate that term specifically, as well as the politics and pleasures of gendered representations in genre films more generally. Gavin Smith is thus absolutely correct in describing her work as 'metacinema of the first rank'.[6]

Men with Guns

While action in film has been popular ever since the Lumières' train entered the Ciotat Station, the action film as a recognizable genre for the definition and display of male power and prowess was clearly established with the rousing swashbucklers of Douglas Fairbanks (*The Mark of Zorro*, 1920; *The Black Pirate*, 1922) and Errol Flynn (*Captain Blood*, 1935; *The Adventures of Robin Hood*, 1940). The depth of the genre's masculine perspective is painfully clear in a movie like *True Lies* (1994, written and directed, ironically, by Bigelow's former husband, James Cameron). At one point in the narrative Jamie Lee Curtis is forced to succumb to the humiliating process of visual objectification in a scene that exceeds any narrative requirement (thinking she must do so to save her husband's life, she is made to enter a hotel room and strip for the pleasure of an unknown male spectator sitting in the shadows). The apparent joke is on her, since she does not realize (but we do) that the mysterious man is in fact her husband, whom she does not know is a spy. The husband is played by Arnold Schwarzenegger – 'an anthropomorphised phallus, a phallus with muscles', in the apt words of Barbara Creed[7] – the actor who more than any other embodies the action film in the 1980s and 1990s and who, in this scene, explicitly functions as the ego ideal of the male viewer.

It is stating the obvious to say that successful action stars often rely on anatomy rather than acting. Male action stars such as Schwarzenegger, Sylvester Stallone, Jean-Claude Van Damme, Steven Seagal, Chuck Norris, and Bruce Willis offer impressively muscular bodies for visual display and as the site of ordeals they must undergo in order to triumph at narrative's end. Critics such as Yvonne Tasker and Susan Jeffords have discussed the contemporary action film's exaggerated masculinity as an expression of patriarchal ideology, the reassertion of male power and privilege during and after the Reagan administration and in an era of eroding hegemony.[8] It is no accident that the hyperbolically masculine action film gained popularity roughly at the same time that other genres, traditionally regarded as 'male', were beginning to be opened up to revisionist readings.

Into the 1980s, genres and genre movies remained almost exclusively the cultural property of a white male consciousness, the centre from which and difference regarding race, gender, and sexuality was defined and marginalized. In all the action genres, it was white men who had to get the job done, whether driving the cattle, solving the crime, capturing the spies, or defeating the aliens. Movies such as *Westward the Women* (1951), in which a wagon train of women successfully make the cross-country trek to California, were only the exceptions that proved the rule. In every type of action film, women and visible minorities assumed subsidiary and stereotyped roles, serving as hindrances, helpers, or rewards for the white male's doing. With the ghettoized exceptions of musicals and melodramas – at one time referred to in the industry as 'women's films' – most genre movies addressed an assumed viewer who was, like almost all of the film-makers who made them, white, male, and heterosexual. But by the next decade many contemporary genre movies sought to grapple with and redress the implications of traditional generic representations of race and gender, often deliberately acknowledging and giving voice to those previously marginalized by mainstream cinema, including women, blacks and gays.

The film that more than any other provided the impetus for this new generic transformation was, undoubtedly, *Thelma and Louise*. One of the most popular movies in North America in 1991, *Thelma and Louise* is a generic hybrid of the western, the buddy film, and the road movie – three of those genres traditionally regarded as male – and the outlaw couple movie, the protagonists of which had always romantically involved heterosexual couples. *Thelma and Louise* reversed Hollywood's conventional definition of woman's place as the domestic sphere and reimagined the buddy movie as female adventure. The acts of rebellion on the part of the two women, like blowing up the tanker truck of a driver who makes obscene gestures at them, come to seem nothing less than imaginative acts of retribution for all women, transcending their personal plight. As Peter Chumo observes, 'what Bonnie and Clyde do for Depression evils, Thelma and Louise do for the evil of sexual violence . . .'[9]

In the film's controversial ending, Thelma and Louise drive over the edge of the Grand Canyon rather than capitulate to the police. The last image is a freeze frame of the car in midair, just beyond the apogee of its arching flight, followed by a fade to white. This ending is, of course, a direct reference to one of the most famous of buddy movies, *Butch Cassidy and the Sundance Kid* (1969), and it sparked considerable debate regarding *Thelma and Louise*'s political value. Did it signify suicidal defeatism or triumphant transcendence? This debate in itself was significant for, as Rebecca Bell-Metereau noted:

> Critics did not concern themselves with the outcome of *Butch Cassidy and the Sundance Kid* [or] *Easy Rider*, because a male death in the conclusion is sacrificial, symbolic, and Christ-like. A female death at the end of the story rarely receives such a heroic interpretation, from feminists or nonfeminists.[10]

The contentious but popular reception of *Thelma and Louise*'s ending suggests how novel the film was at the time.

Regardless of how one reads the film's ending, the fact that it was the subject of such heated debate suggests both the complexities of gendered representations in popular cinema generally and the difficulty of finding a place for women in the action film specifically. Many recent genre films are content merely to borrow *Thelma and Louise*'s gender 'gimmick', simply plugging others into roles traditionally reserved for white men. But in reversing conventional representations, they are prone to fall into the trap of repeating the same objectionable values. The question of whether female action heroes such as Sigourney Weaver's Ripley in *Alien* (1979) and its sequels or Linda Hamilton's Sarah Connor in *Terminator 2: Judgment Day* are progressive representations of women or merely contain them within a masculine sensibility has been a matter of considerable debate. It is just here that Bigelow's films constitute a site of generic intervention, for while they often reverse generic expectation (the female cop in *Blue Steel*, for example, or the black female bodyguard and feminized male protagonist in *Strange Days*), they also employ a variety of stylistic means to question the gendered values that animate action film genres.

Figure 29.1 Kathryn Bigelow's *The Loveless* (Atlantic Films/Pioneer Releasing, 1982) displays the bikers in Brechtian tableau. Produced by A. Kitman Ho and Grafton Nunes

The Children of Eisenhower and Coca-Cola

The Loveless, Bigelow's first feature film, remains her most avant-garde or experimental. Set in the 1950s, the film is a generic amalgam of mainstream biker movies of the period, particularly *The Wild One* (1954), and the celebration of gay iconography in Kenneth Anger's experimental film *Scorpio Rising* (1963). As such, *The Loveless* might more accurately be described as an anti-action film because of its stylized compositions and deliberately slow pace – especially curious given the kinetic potential of a movie about guys on motorcycles. The main character, Vance (Willem Dafoe), accurately describes the film's style when he tells the other bikers: 'We're going nowhere . . . fast.'

The minimal plot involves a group of bikers (all men, with the notable exception of the bleach-blonde Debbie Sportster) who converge on a small Southern town on their way to the drag races at Daytona, waiting while one of them does some necessary repairs to his motorcycle. Their presence catalyzes the townspeople, who respond to them either with desire or fear, these extreme and polar reactions coming together in a violent climax featuring a shoot-out in a roadside bar and the suicide of a local girl. The bikers function like the monstrous other of the horror film (in fact, there are a number of correspondences between them and the vampire clan in the later *Near Dark*), a graphic representation of the return of the repressed. And like the more sympathetic monsters of some progressive horror films, they are less evil than merely different in their bohemian lifestyle.

The Loveless works toward its violent climax not so much as a necessary dramatic resolution, but more because, like Michel and Patricia in Jean-Luc Godard's *A bout de souffle* (1959), the characters are trapped within the constraints of genre. A tragic outcome seems inevitable, a given, the kind of ending we expect when free-spirited bikers confront rednecks in movies like *Easy Rider* (1969). But the specific form this violent climax takes in *The Loveless*, turning in on the town and making the townspeople the victims, is a more subtle political critique. Appropriately, *The Loveless* contains many references to Godard's work –

most obviously in the shots of Vance driving in the open convertible with Telena (Marin Kanter), the local jailbait. The sense of buoyant freedom as they drive, the way Kanter turns her head away from the camera, and her short, boyish haircut, all deliberately echo Jean Seberg in *A bout de souffle*. *The Loveless*'s bold colour palette, use of deliberately choreographed tracking shots (a central element of what Brian Henderson calls Godard's 'non-bourgeois camera style'),[11] and vivid deployment of consumer iconography (the brilliant red Coke machine in the filling station) all invoke Godard's distinctive style of political filmmaking.

The actors are often filmed doing nothing, even being completely motionless, in Brechtian tableaux. Vance tellingly says in the opening scene, when the woman with the flat tyre asks him what he does for a living, 'not a whole lot'. These shots are frequently held longer than the time required for narrative comprehension, encouraging us to examine their studied composition. As a result, the characters – male and female – become objects of aesthetic contemplation for the spectator. The images are often composed so that the actors are decentred in the frame, emphasizing the iconographical import of gesture (smoking a cigarette, drinking a Coke) or costume (motorcycle jacket, boots). In the roadside diner – Bigelow's equivalent to the Parisian cafe for Godard – when they wonder where one of their group is, Debbie comments that he must be outside 'fine-tuning his sideburns'. The film's first image is of Vance laconically combing his hair before heading out on the highway. Bigelow thus subverts the traditionally masculine gaze of the camera, fetishizing, as in Anger's more experimental work, the accoutrements of the biker subculture. The languorous shots of the bikers ultimately reveal them as poised, posed, performing, so that any sense of a monolithic or essential masculinity is called into question. This subversion is literalized in the climax, and the violence precipitated, when Telena's abusive and belligerent father discovers one of the bikers wearing women's undergarments beneath his leather in, significantly, the bar's men's room.

Terror in a Texas Town

Bigelow's second feature, *Near Dark*, is a generic hybrid of the western and the vampire film in the venerable tradition of such unassuming genre fare as *Curse of the Undead* (1959), *Billy the Kid vs Dracula* (1965) and *Jesse James Meets Frankenstein's Daughter* (1966), but with considerably more serious ambitions. As Christina Lane points out, both genres 'have traditionally been used to work through ambivalent feelings toward nature and civilization, and both usually tell stories in which threatening natural forces are purged for the sake of society'.[12] Both genres are structured by binary oppositions that at root reflect the ongoing tension between individual desire and social responsibility – civilization and its discontents, in Freud's terms – in the western, as a topographical mapping onto the frontier and in the horror film, as a psycho-social projection.[13] *Near Dark* mixes elements of both genres, revealing their common conventional gendered assumptions.

A midwestern farm boy, Caleb (Adrian Pasdar), seemingly falls in love at first sight with an attractive female vampire named Mae (Jenny Wright) after a romantic evening together. Mae bites Caleb, who turns almost immediately into a vampire and is snatched away by the vampire clan, a terrible family reminiscent of those in horror movies like *The Texas Chainsaw Massacre* (1974) or *The Hills Have Eyes* (1977) or westerns like *My Darling Clementine* (1946) or *Wagon Master* (1950). But Caleb, like the classic western hero, refuses to kill except in self-defence, allowing Mae to do it instead and then drinking her blood. In a final showdown at high midnight on main street, Caleb, now cured by a blood transfusion performed by his father, destroys the vampire clan, literally earning his spurs.

In the denouement, Caleb administers the same cure to Mae, who in the film's final shot can now step into the sunlit promise of domesticity, the place typically reserved for women in the western – see, for example, *High Noon* (1952) or *Shane* (1953) – and a gaping absence in Caleb's family, given the unexplained absence of a mother. (This absence, unmentioned by the characters, is addressed by the film in the scene of the three family members having dinner, the fourth chair at the table noticeably empty.) This ending recalls that of numerous horror films, particularly Tod Browning's *Dracula* (1931), which concludes with the romantic couple ascending a long flight of stairs in the vampire's dark crypt to the security of sunny daylight and church bells on the soundtrack.

Near Dark's narrative closure thus seems emphatically to restore patriarchal gender politics, as do both the classic horror film, when the monster is destroyed and civilization made safe, and the western, when the bad men or Indians are defeated and the frontier tamed for settler families. But given the rest of the film, this ending rings hollow, like the apparently happy ending of Sirk's *All that Heaven Allows* (1955) in which the heroine, seeking to define herself as a desiring subject, can be reunited with her lover only when she is summarily forced into the position of nurturer after he is seriously injured while hunting. In both cases the apparent happy ending fulfils generic convention but lacks thematic conviction.

Bigelow suggests that the happy ending of *Near Dark* is intended to be read as similarly perfunctory and ironic, given the sexual meanings of vampirism both within generic tradition and in *Near Dark* specifically. The sexual basis of the vampires' allure is shown when, during a typical night of feeding, we see Severen (Bill Paxton) use his charm as a hitchhiker to attract two women who pick him up in their truck hoping for a good time. The attractive Mae, a seemingly archetypical bluejean baby, arouses such strong desire in Caleb that it threatens to destroy his traditional family by luring him away from home and the daytime world. Further, this desire threatens to erupt and destroy bourgeois stability at any moment, as we see when Mae comes back, a literal return of the repressed, after Caleb is cured of his vampirism. Unhesitatingly, Caleb rushes to hug Mae, noticeably exposing his neck to her as they embrace. Like the popular song, the film asks, 'How are you gonna keep 'em down on the farm after they've seen Paree?' – a question that directly acknowledges the necessity of repression for maintaining traditional social values. Like Bohemian Paris, Mae represents the siren song of desire, so in the course of the narrative she must be literally defanged and thrust into the glaring sunlight of normalcy. Now saved by her man, no longer feminized, she will likely take her place in that empty chair, adopting the kind of maternal role Caleb had tried to impose on her when they were vampires and he fed from her blood like a helpless, hungry infant suckling at its mother's breast.

The film consistently contrasts Caleb's normal, good family with the undead, evil family of the vampires. The vampires are capable of terrible violence, as we see several times in the film and especially in its memorable set piece, their decimation of a roadhouse and its occupants. This violence is tinged with eroticism throughout, and it intoxicates even as it repels, a perfect expression of Susan Sontag's description of the appeal of monster movies as 'the aesthetics of destruction, with the peculiar beauties to be found in wreaking havoc, making a mess'.[14] During the massacre, Caleb, like the spectator, watches mesmerized, even finding himself participating against his will when he sends a tough-looking biker flying through the air with one punch ('Did I do that?' he asks with bemusement). Christopher Sharrett complains that the vampire clan is 'wholly repugnant and destructive', so that, in contrast to the kinds of horror films Robin Wood calls progressive, there is no sympathy generated toward them.[15] He views the vampires as unproblematically other, but I would suggest that *Near Dark* does indeed problematize the relation of the normal and monstrous once we accept the seductive and violent pleasures the film offers. Their inherent appeal is underscored by the fact that the monstrous patriarch Jesse (Lance Henrickson) is associated with American history (he claims to have fought for the Confederacy), and that the clan travel across middle America, the centre of what poet Allen Ginsberg called the 'heart of the Vortex' out of which American violence emanates.[16] Despite the film's apparent rigid contrast between the daytime world of the farm family and the night-time world of the vampire clan, we are implicated in the latter, all of us near dark.

Sleeping with the Enemy

Blue Steel is a stylish police thriller that exploits to the fullest the action film's conventional association of the gun with the phallus, exploring the representation of the gun as a totem of masculine power. From the opening credit sequence in which the camera penetrates the interior of a Smith and Wesson handgun, *Blue Steel* (according to one critic, the term is American slang for an erection)[17] explores the genre's iconographical fetishization of the pistol. By making possession and control of the gun a contest between a police*woman* and a male criminal, the film foregrounds the metaphorical and gendered implications of one of the primary icons of the action film.

The plot involves a rookie female cop, Megan Turner (Jamie Lee Curtis), whose gender troubles all the men in the film once she dons her uniform. Intervening in a supermarket robbery, Turner shoots and kills the hold-up man, while one of the cowering bystanders in the store, Eugene Hunt (Ron Silver), secretly pockets the thief's handgun. As the film progresses, Eugene becomes increasingly psychotic, obsessed with the image of Turner wielding her weapon and usurping phallic power. In the final violent confrontation, Turner manages to kill the seemingly unstoppable Eugene.

Some have read the film as empowering for women. Megan is like the hero of a rape revenge film, an example of Carol Clover's 'final girl'. In this sense, the casting of Curtis, protagonist of the prototypical slasher film *Halloween* (1978), is particularly resonant.[18] After all, it is Megan who defeats Eugene in battle, not her superior, the suitably named Detective Nick Mann (Clancy Brown), who is 'disarmed' when Megan handcuffs him to their car door during her penultimate confrontation with Eugene. Nevertheless, *Blue Steel* suggests that the triumph of Megan and the femininity she represents can only be limited because of the entrenched power of patriarchy since the film contextualizes the male world of Eugene as a monstrous extension of normative masculinity.

Employing a standard motif of the horror film, Eugene is doubled with Megan's abusive father (Philip Bosco), emphasizing a continuity between apparently masculine norms and the horribly psychotic. Also, like Patrick Bateman in Brett Easton Ellis's controversial novel *American Psycho* (1991), published the year after the release of the film, Eugene is a stockbroker, his position of economic privilege apparently allowing him the power to commit horrible criminal acts, including murder, with impunity. Both works link their central male character's craziness to capitalism, competition, masculine identity, and violence. Eugene hears voices in his head and so expresses a desire for quietude – an understandable wish given his profession: on two occasions we see him screaming and wildly gesticulating in a sea of commodity traders, all male, on the floor of the stock exchange. (It is in this same space that Eugene first fantasizes shooting the gun he has picked up at the supermarket.) When Mann asks Megan why she became a cop, she ambiguously replies, 'Him', which, as Tasker notes, may refer to her abusive father specifically or more generally to 'the man', to men, to the many potential Eugenes.[19]

The film employs other conventions of the horror film, particularly the werewolf film. Eugene is hirsute, with a dark beard, and associated with the night; at one point we see him digging for his gun like an animal under the full moon in New York's Central Park (Eugene's last name, remember, is 'Hunt'). These associations of masculinity with violence and animality appear throughout Bigelow's films: hothead biker Davis (Robert Gordon) in *The Loveless* literally barks at his friends and yelps wildly as he fires his gun in the violent climax in the bar, while in *Near Dark*, when Caleb thinks he has killed Severen by running over him with a diesel truck, another icon of phallic power, he similarly howls with satisfaction.

Violence is associated with male animality in Bigelow's films because violence is seen as an inherently masculine quality. *Blue Steel* demonstrates this idea visually, in its painterly images combined with careful foley work that emphasize the physical and sensual qualities of the gun. Frequently the film emphasizes the texture and tactility of guns – the way hands caressingly grip them, how they slide across a table or are provocatively unbuttoned from a holster – as well as the sounds they make. Viewers are seduced, within the context of the action film, by the power of the phallus, like the men in the film in their more extreme ways.

Megan's desire to be a cop thus becomes a desire to enter into the phallic domain, literalized in her struggle with Eugene over possession of the gun. Her uniform is a sign of transgression as Megan encroaches on a traditionally male world, an idea made clear at the beginning of the film in the montage of Megan suiting up for graduation. Individual shots fetishize parts of her uniform reminiscent of the shots of the bikers' costumes in *The Loveless*. The character's gender is initially indeterminate, but then, as she buttons her shirt, we glimpse her lace bra underneath. Viewers are likely taken aback for a moment, 'disarmed' like the several men in the film when they see her in uniform the first time or learn what her job is. Megan's wearing of a traditionally male uniform also suggests the extent to which, apart from the masculine propensity toward violence, gender is a constructed performance, dependent upon the semiotics of style for meaning.

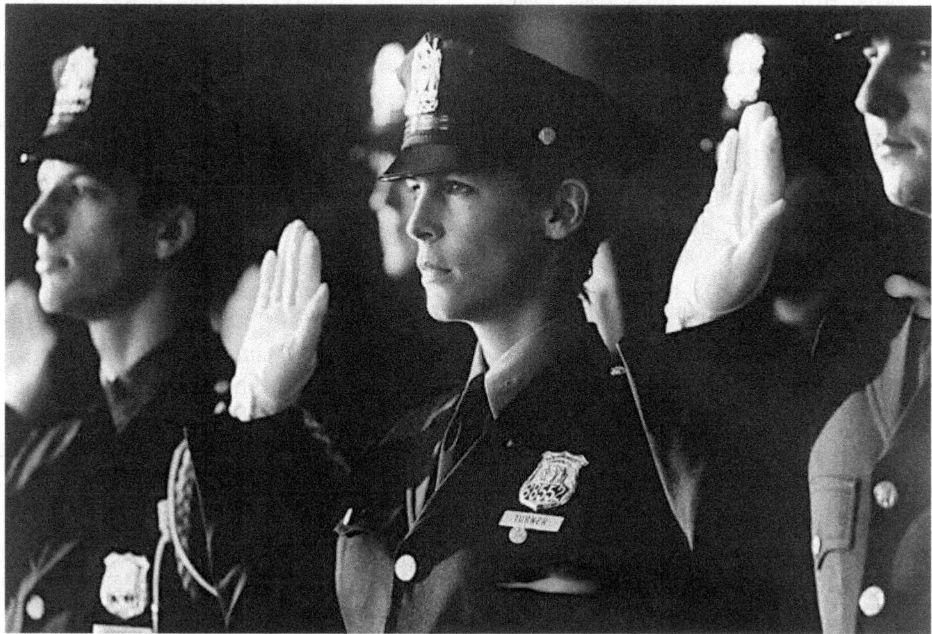

Figure 29.2 In Bigelow's *Blue Steel* (MGM, 1990), Megan Turner (Jamie Lee Curtis) attempts to enter the phallic domain. Produced by Lawrence Kasanoff

Imitation of Life

If *The Loveless* deconstructs the action, *Point Break* is a thoroughly successful reconstruction. As the story unfolds, viewers are treated to some terrific action sequences, the most memorable of which is an extended chase, effectively photographed through alleys, houses, and backyards with a modified Steadicam that adeptly places us squarely within the action. (Bigelow would use the same strategy more trenchantly in the opening of *Strange Days*.) A combination of buddy and caper movie, it nevertheless has the same objective of subverting the power of masculinist generic myth by challenging our sense of the conventions of 'realism' characteristic of classic Hollywood cinema. In Sirkian fashion, Bigelow treats the action excessively in *Point Break*, pushing the macho mysticism into overblown spectacle. As Tyler (Lori Petty) – the lone woman in the film's hypermasculine world of skydiving, surfing, and bankrobbing – disgustedly opines at one point while the men are busy bonding on a beach, 'There's too much testosterone here for me'.

The film's plot concerns a band of bank robbers who commit heists because they are devoted surfers who need to maintain their cash flow as they travel around the world in search of the perfect wave. The gang is known as the Ex-Presidents because they wear masks of former US presidents while committing their robberies. The case is being investigated by a pair of FBI agents, seasoned Angelo Pappas (Gary Busey) and hotshot rookie Johnny Utah (Keanu Reeves). Undercover, Utah infiltrates the gang and experiences a conflict between his duty as agent of the law and the spiritual bond he has developed with the gang's leader Bodhi (Patrick Swayze).

The film, it is true, offers some direct (and humorous) social criticism with its band of presidential bank robbers – particularly when 'Nixon' jumps up on a counter to declare 'I am not a crook!' and when Bodhi, wearing his Reagan mask, waves a gas pump in the air and ignites a filling station into a flaming fireball.[20] But for the most part *Point Break* is more sly in its subversion of the masculine myths of action cinema, frequently reminding us that it is only a movie, a generic construction. The male characters are clearly types rather than rounded individuals. Keanu Reeves' typically flat performance style ironically works well here, emphasizing Johnny Utah's lack of psychological depth. His name is itself something of a mythic amalgam, at once evoking the American West and the western, as well as legendary athleticism in the masculine world of football (Utah was a college football star; his name recalls that of both Johnny Unitas and Joe Montana, two legendary quarterbacks), and the fact that he is a fictional character in the tradition of *Johnny Guitar* (1954) and *Johnny Handsome* (1989).[21]

If action movies exhibit a masculine homosocial hysteria mapped onto the excessive display of the male body,[22] then *Point Break* is a paradigmatic action movie. The male characters are on constant display, even to the point that the gang are identified by the tan lines on their buttocks when they 'moon' for the security cameras at one of the banks they rob. The film emphasizes Swayze's body and long blonde tresses, and pushes its representation of the surfer gang's macho comraderie to the point of parody. This excessive treatment comes to a head, as it were, in the climax when Utah jumps out of an airplane without a parachute in a determined attempt to catch Bodhi, who had jumped moments before with the last one. The sequence of Utah's windy free-fall toward Bodhi and clasping of him in midair becomes a hysterical visualization of the repressed homoerotic subtext of the buddy movie. The two men embrace as they grapple, their windswept faces together in intimate close-up as they tussle for either the gun or the pullcord ('Pull it, pull it,' Bodhi cries). And as we see in the subjective zoom shot of the ground rapidly coming nearer, for both men it is an experience in which the earth has moved. The sequence ends with them rolling on the ground, the parachute flapping gently to the ground in post-coital calm.

Back to the Future

Strange Days is set just slightly in the future of the film's release, in Los Angeles on the day before New Year's Eve, 1999. Lenny (Ralph Fiennes), a black market dealer in 'clips', an outlawed form of total cinema produced by a new technology that taps directly into the cerebral cortex for both recording and playback, must learn to abandon the simulated memories of his former girlfriend (Juliette Lewis), however realistic, and embrace a new life in the real world with Mace (Angela Bassett). Through this meta-cinematic metaphor, violent action and eroticism are critiqued as voyeuristic, sadistic, and decidedly masculine. It is not surprising that Bigelow has called *Strange Days* her most personal film.[23]

The film begins by positioning us as viewers of one of these clips, although it is only in retrospect that we realize this, since no exposition precedes it. On the soundtrack we hear someone say 'Boot it', and the image seems to form as pixels, but the meaning of this is unclear. Once the clip boots, there is no apparent difference, such as a frame within a frame or disparity in image resolution, to mark these images as a film within the film rather than as images within the world of the film. For all intents and purposes, what we are seeing *is* the film – and by extension, any action film. We are thrust immediately into the viewing dynamic, our identification fully mobilized, despite the fact that as yet we do not know who 'we' are. Like clip users within the world of the film, we are fooled by the reality status of the sequence.

As in *Point Break*, we are immersed in the action, a part of it, featuring Bigelow's tour-de-force use of the subjective camera. In what seems like one lengthy, technically breathtaking shot (there are actually a couple of disguised cuts) on a par with the opening shot of Welles's *Touch of Evil* (1958) or Altman's *The Player* (1992), the viewer is put into the perspective of one of the participants. 'We' drive up to an Asian restaurant with a group of robbers, sitting in the back seat; commit robbery, intimidating staff and patrons in the process; frantically flee from the arriving police in a confusing shootout; attempt to escape across a series of rooftops, police in hot pursuit; and finally, plunge to 'our' death in the street below when we fail to make the leap from one rooftop to another. In this opening sequence we know only that we are male, as indicated by the dialogue, and by the hands we see from 'our' physical point of view, à la *Lady in the Lake* (1946). But the individual man here is in fact irrelevant – we are, the film immediately suggests, *masculinity itself*. The apparent long take maintains a consistent point of view and thus heightens our sense of presence throughout the action, the appeal of which is marked as racist and sexist since the victims of our abuse are 'fucking chinks' and 'bitches', as our invisible surrogate calls them.

This astonishing opening sequence exposes the subjective camera common to such genres as action and slasher movies as nothing less than a tool of naked male aggression. Many of the violent action sequences that follow in *Strange Days* involve the victimization of women with the SQUID apparatus, in the infamous manner of Mark Lewis (Karl Bohm) in Michael Powell's *Peeping Tom* (1960). It is no coincidence that (with the exception of Mace's one reluctant SQUID trip for Lenny's sake) the only users we see in the film are male. (The extent to which women are involved in the production or consumption of SQUID clips may be read as an indication of their moral corruption, as in the case of Faith.) Thus the subsequent scenes of violent action in the film cannot be viewed with the same kind of 'innocent' pleasure we may have brought to the opening sequence, for we have been made aware of the gendered dynamics involved in such pleasure.

But strangely – or perhaps not strangely, since this is, after all, a Hollywood movie – *Strange Days* builds to a climax that denies what has come previously, that seems to recuperate its own ideological critique. In the climax, Lenny, along with his friend, a female bodyguard (Angela Bassett), try to give to the police commissioner a clip that has recorded the truth about the killing of a popular militant black rock star by two racist white cops. The two policemen confront the woman during the wild celebration on the eve of the millennium and begin to assault her with their nightsticks. The scene obviously invokes the infamous tape of the Rodney King beating, which also occurred in Los Angeles; but in the movie, unlike the real world, the crowd of onlookers responds by actively banding together to fight this act of racial oppression. Finally, the honest white male commissioner, brandishing the evidence in his raised hand, parts the suddenly compliant crowd like the archetypal patriarch Moses parting the Red Sea and calls for the arrest of the two rogue cops. Power, ultimately, is retained in the (literal) hands of the white male, who now supersedes the once-capable and independent black woman.

Conclusion

Robin Wood has angrily dismissed *Strange Days* as 'a tease and a cheat' because of the emphatic way it compromises its own premises.[24] But this response may be somewhat ungenerous, for it is no more an ideological cheat than the majority of mainstream American movies are. Perhaps it seems more disappointing because of how radical its initial premise is. Wood more accurately might have called *Strange Days*, in his own terms, 'an incoherent text'. Such texts, for Wood, are fractured or fragmentary, but have a 'consciously motivated incoherence [that] becomes a structuring principle, resulting in works that reveal themselves as perfectly coherent once one has mastered their rules'.[25] Bigelow herself has described *Strange Days* as 'at war with itself'.[26] From this perspective, the film's ideological contradictions speak quite eloquently of the tensions inherent in the situation of a woman making action movies about the traditionally male genre of action movies. Indeed, this position seems as fraught with difficulties as Megan Turner seeking phallic power in the male world of the police force, only with the penetrating, affective power of the motion picture camera instead of a gun. *Strange Days* does collapse at the end – an ending, significantly, that Bigelow stretches out for almost twenty minutes rather than elides – but this collapse serves to emphasize the limited place and power of women in mainstream cinema, whether in front of the camera or behind it.

In a sense, Bigelow's embrace of the action genre's pleasures while simultaneously critiquing them demonstrates a mastery of the master's own language. Although excess is more often associated with melodrama and the musical, it is certainly an important quality of the action film as well. The excess in Bigelow's action films serves as self-reflexive commentary on the genre and the masculine culture it celebrates, much as the excess in Douglas Sirk's melodramas commented on the ideology of the genre in which he was working and the cultural contexts of Eisenhower America. Although Sirk was working within the constraints of the studio system while Bigelow has made her films in the postclassical context of the new Hollywood, the analogy is apt, for both directors exist within the contexts of popular cinema, which is so thoroughly structured at every level by generic principles.

In the introduction to their pioneering anthology, *Screening the Male*, Steven Cohan and Ina Rae Hark note that:

> film theory has for the most part confidently equated the masculinity of the male subject with activity, voyeurism, sadism, fetishism, and story, and the femininity of the female subject with passivity, exhibitionism, masochism, narcissism, and spectacle. In this scheme of homologous differences the power, stability, and wholeness of masculine subjectivity at the expense of femininity seem all too axiomatic and thus, universal and uncontestable.[27]

Kathryn Bigelow uses the action film to address fundamental issues of genre, gender and spectatorship, and to negotiate a place for women both in front of and behind the camera within traditionally masculine discourses. While many recent action movies have tended to reinscribe traditional patriarchal values,[28] Bigelow's work includes a remarkable series of films that have resisted the genre's conservative thrust. Like the new genre films of the 1970s that John Cawelti described as 'set[ting] the elements of a conventional popular genre in an altered context, thereby making us perceive these traditional forms and images in a new way',[29] Bigelow's action films are generic interventions that invite and encourage speculation about the nature of popular cinema.

Notes

1 *The Weight of Water* (2000), a melodrama featuring Sean Penn and Elizabeth Hurley weaving together two narratives a century apart, has received rather limited release. Le Studio Canal+, the French company that produced the film, has not yet released it on video. *K19: The Widowmaker* (2002), a Cold War thriller, has Bigelow returning to the masculine terrain of the action genre as it is often emphatically depicted in submarine films.

2 Anna Powell, 'Blood on the Borders – *Near Dark* and *Blue Steel*', *Screen*, 35: 2, Summer 1994, p. 136.

3 Christina Lane discusses some of these comments in *Feminist Hollywood: From Born in Flames to Point Break*, Detroit: Wayne State University Press, 2000, pp. 103–4.

4 Steve Neale 'Masculinity as Spectacle', *Screen*, 24: 6, November/December 1983, p. 5.

5 Laura Rascaroli 'Steel in the Gaze: On POV and the Discourse of Vision in Kathryn Bigelow's Cinema', *Screen*, 38: 3, Autumn 1997, p. 232.

6 'Momentum and Design: Kathryn Bigelow Interviewed by Gavin Smith', *Film Comment*, 31: 5, September/October 1995, p. 46.

7 Barbara Creed 'From Here to Modernity: Feminism and Postmodernism', *Screen*, 28: 2, Spring 1987, p. 65.

8 Yvonne Tasker *Spectacular Bodies: Gender, Genre and the Action Cinema*, London and New York: Routledge, 1993; Susan Jeffords *Hardbodies: Hollywood Masculinity in the Reagan Era*, New Brunswick, NJ: Rutgers University Press, 1994.

9 Peter N. Chumo II, 'At the Generic Crossroads with *Thelma and Louise*', *Post Script*, 13: 2, Winter/Spring 1994, p. 5.

10 Rebecca Bell-Metereau *Hollywood Androgyny*, 2nd edition, New York: Columbia University Press, 1993, p. 248.

11 Brian Henderson 'Towards a Non-Bourgeois Camera Style', *Film Quarterly*, 24: 2, Winter 1970–1, pp. 2–14.

12 Lane *Feminist Hollywood*, p. 110.

13 See, for example, Jim Kitses *Horizons West*, London: British Film Institute, 1969/Bloomington: Indiana University Press, 1970, chapter 1; and Robin Wood 'An Introduction to the American Horror Film' in Robin Wood and Richard Lippe (eds) *American Nightmare: Essays on the Horror Film*, Toronto: Festival of Festivals, 1979, especially pp. 8–11.

14 Susan Sontag 'The Imagination of Disaster', in *Against Interpretation and Other Essays*, New York: Delta, 1966, p. 213.

15 Christopher Sharrett 'The Horror Film in Neoconservative Culture', in Barry Keith Grant (ed.) *The Dread of Difference: Gender and the Horror Film*, Austin: University of Texas Press, 1996, pp. 259–61. For Robin Wood's distinction between 'progressive' and 'reactionary' horror films, see Wood 'Introduction to the American Horror Film'.

16 Allen Ginsberg 'Wichita Vortex Sutra', *Planet News*, San Francisco: City Lights, 1968.

17 Powell 'Blood on the Borders', p. 145.

18 Powell 'Blood on the Borders', p. 147. See also Carol Clover *Men, Women and Chainsaws: Gender in the Modern Horror Film*, Princeton, NJ: Princeton University Press, 1992.

19 Tasker *Spectacular Bodies*, p. 147.

20 Kathleen Murphy describes the scene as 'berserker campaign iconography promising good times, a tiger in every tank'. 'Black Arts', *Film Comment*, 31: 5, September/October 1995, p. 53.

21 Interestingly, Reeves would later star in an even more apt role as *Johnny Mnemonic* (1995).

22 See Cynthia J. Fuchs 'The Buddy Politic', in Steven Cohan and Ina Rae Hark (eds) *Screening the Male: Exploring Masculinities in Hollywood Cinema*, London and New York: Routledge, 1993, pp. 194–210.

23 'Momentum and Design', p. 48.

24 Robin Wood 'The Spectres Emerge in Daylight', *CineAction*, 43, 1997, p. 7.

25 Robin Wood *Hollywood from Vietnam to Reagan*, New York: Columbia University Press, 1986, p. 46.
26 'Momentum and Design', p. 49.
27 Cohan and Hark *Screening the Male*, p. 2.
28 Karen Schneider 'With Violence if Necessary: Rearticulating the Family in the Contemporary Action-Thriller', *Journal of Popular Film and Television*, 27: 1, Spring 1999, pp. 2–11.
29 John Cawelti '*Chinatown* and Generic Transformation in Recent American Films' in Barry Keith Grant (ed.) *Film Genre Reader II*, Austin: University of Texas Press, 1995, p. 191.

Authorship and New Queer Cinema: The Case of Todd Haynes

Michael DeAngelis

Michael DeAngelis, an associate professor of cinema and cultural studies at DePaul University's School for New Learning in Chicago, is the author of *Gay Fandom and Crossover Stardom: James Dean, Mel Gibson, and Keanu Reeves*. This essay appeared originally in the anthology *New Queer Cinema: A Critical Reader*, published in 2004, and is here expanded to include discussion of *Far From Heaven* (2002), which appeared subsequent to its writing and which has been Haynes' biggest commercial success to date. DeAngelis identifies Haynes' style as expressing a uniquely queer perspective in focusing on ambiguities and fantasies in his films that serve to destabilize normative definitions of sexuality and other aspects of socially constructed identity.

In her seminal 1992 article, B. Ruby Rich describes the shared characteristics of the evolving "New Queer Cinema" in terms of a "Homo Pomo" style involving "appropriation and pastiche, irony, as well as a reworking of history with social constructionism very much in mind," and an associated break from the identity politics of an earlier era.[1] By the time of a follow-up piece in 2000, however, Rich reflects upon the decade-old New Queer Cinema as a product of a specific historical and now lost moment – a cinema that has since devolved into "just another niche market, another product line pitched at one particular type of discerning consumer."[2] As Rich intimates, the directions of New Queer Cinema are shaped by the ways in which a subculture constructs and imagines its own history – relations of past, present, and future certainly, but also, and more specifically, relations of remembering and forgetting. Many gay and lesbian filmmakers in the early 1990s confronted historical dynamics by attempting to "rework" them; disconnected from their cinematic antecedents as well as formative social and political movements, recent films which qualify as New Queer Cinema appear to disavow historical relations altogether. Certainly, New Queer Cinema has changed partly because, from the perception of mainstream, popular film industries, things "queer" have attained a renewed popularity and qualified public acceptance. If the "product line" to which Rich refers comprises those films identified as "queer" solely on the basis of themes and characterizations, the "niche

Michael DeAngelis, "Authorship and New Queer Cinema: The Case of Todd Haynes." Revised version of "The Characteristics of New Queer Filmmaking: Case Study – Todd Haynes," pp. 42–51 from Michele Aaron (ed.), *New Queer Cinema: A Critical Reader* (New Brunswick, NJ: Rutgers University Press, 2004).

market" is certainly prominent and well established through the subgenre of queer coming-of-age and "coming out" narratives. Alongside these more conventional narratives the experiments of filmmakers such as Gregg Araki continue to maintain a closer relation to the more dynamic "PoMo" style that originally inspired Rich to classify New Queer Cinema as a movement in the first place.

And then there's Todd Haynes, the director who became notorious even before the New Queer Cinema was ever labeled as such, with his now-suppressed version of the Karen Carpenter story enacted by Barbie dolls (*Superstar*, 1987), and the subsequent National Endowment for the Humanities funding controversy surrounding his first full-length feature, *Poison*, in 1990. At first glance, Haynes might appear to be firmly grounded in the PoMo/social constructionist tradition, with a body of films that renounces the realist aesthetic while highlighting pastiche, irony, and the blending of seemingly discordant genres, as well as his open rejection of the notion of an "essential gay sensibility."[3] Especially (though not exclusively) in some of his post-*Poison* films, however, Haynes has developed narrative strategies that steer New Queer Cinema towards a version of social constructionism that strives to express something integral to a uniquely queer perspective on human experience. In a 1993 interview with Justin Wyatt, Haynes explains that:

> I have a lot of frustration with the insistence on content when people are talking about homosexuality. People define gay cinema solely by content: if there are gay characters in it, it's a gay film. It fits into the gay sensibility, we got it, it's gay. It's such a failure of the imagination, let alone the ability to look beyond content. I think that's really simplistic. Heterosexuality to me is a structure as much as it is a content. It is an imposed structure that goes along with the patriarchal, dominant structure that constrains and defines society. If homosexuality is the opposite or the counter-sexual activity to that, then what kind of a structure would it be?[4]

What would it be? Vehemently rejecting any notion of essence in identity, Haynes' discoveries in the exploration of this question comprise his unique contributions to the New Queer Cinema. Using a variety of cinematic forms, Haynes "queers" heterosexual, mainstream narrative cinema by making whatever might be familiar or normal about it strange, and in the process hypothesizing alternatives that disrupt its integrity and ideological cohesiveness. He accomplishes this by arranging an intricate juxtaposition and dialectic of "realities" and restructuring the spatial and temporal relations that order them. What emerges from this dialectic is the imagination of new times and spaces that exist apart from, and in opposition to, dominant, patriarchal culture.

The resonances of Haynes' dialectic extend, however, far beyond this ideological intervention, ultimately engaging in a dynamic historical confrontation that extends Rich's original prescription for an oppositional New Queer Cinema. This confrontation situates gay culture within a set of historical relations that includes the social, personal, and psychological, and that also emphasizes gay culture's political responsibilities of remembering its own past, as well as the associated implications of forgetting and disavowing. The vehicle of this dialectic "imagining" is fantasy, and Haynes engages his central protagonists in fantasy scenarios that succeed in both momentarily stabilizing time and ultimately re-ordering relationships between past, present, and future. The result of Haynes' use of fantasy and his interrogation of history is a politically engaged version of New Queer Cinema whose power and momentum stem from relationships of identification and desire, the dynamics of which implicate protagonists and viewers alike. Through a close examination of formal and representational matters affecting the historical relationship between past and present "realities" in three films steeped in networks of history and heavily invested in the workings of fantasy – the short video narrative *Dottie Gets Spanked* (1993) and two of his features, *Velvet Goldmine* (1998) and *Far From Heaven* (2002) – I will illuminate the workings of Haynes' queer aesthetic as well as the sexual and political confrontations that it enables.

Although it is anything but didactic, the 27-minute *Dottie Gets Spanked* could readily serve as a textbook illustration of the workings of identification in Freudian psychoanalysis; indeed, the first of its two fantasy sequences is conspicuously interrupted with the intertitle "A Child Is Being Beaten" referencing the case study of the same name that Freud himself used to describe identification within the fantasy network.[5] The film begins by revealing the daily, suburban, early 1960s life of eight-year-old Stevie (Evan Bonifant) as sharply divided between two realities. The first to be introduced is his close relationship with Dottie Frank (Julie Halston), the protagonist of a *Lucy Show*-like sitcom who inspires Stevie to produce vibrant artistic sketches as he sits silent and transfixed before the television screen; as a contest winner later in the film, Stevie earns the honor of visiting the set of the show, meeting the actress who inspires him, and witnessing the rehearsal of an episode. The second reality comprises Stevie's not-so-inspiring, wholly isolated, routinized, extra-Dottie existence, made bearable only by a doting mother (Harriet Harris) who intervenes when her husband (Robert Pall), glued to the TV screen watching a football game, rudely dismisses Stevie's fandom. Stevie's life outside the home extends the domestic tensions, as he yearns to participate in his female schoolmates' heated conversations about Dottie, instead earning only their ridicule since, like Stevie's father, they find his devotion to the screen star a pursuit unsuitable for a male ("My sister says you're a feminine," a younger girl jeers).

This second daily reality positions Stevie as a rather helpless subject, at the mercy of divisive gender politics that monitor his identity within and outside the home. His relationship with the Dottie character initially seems to provide momentary release from social restrictions, as well as a creative outlet in which to interpret experience on his own terms, especially through the illustrated narrative that Stevie prepares as a gift for Dottie in anticipation of their meeting. Soon enough, however, his drawings belie this "escapist" function when the TV taping that Stevie witnesses begins to replay the gender relations that surround the young boy in his everyday life: as punishment for a lie told to her husband (Adam Arkin), Dottie is forced to endure a carefully staged, brutal spanking which Stevie struggles furiously to recapture in a vivid color drawing.

The inseparability of the two realities is driven home by Stevie's two dream-nightmares, both of which center upon beating and the exercise of power. In waking life, Stevie maintains the role of observer and acted-upon subject at home and with Dottie Frank, but the polymorphously perverse nightmares compel the boy to move among a number of positions in relationships of identification. In the first dream, Stevie initially assumes the role of a ruthless king who humiliates Dottie in the same ways that her husband does on the TV show. The scene then shifts to a male adult beating a male child who appears to be Stevie (the lighting conditions and camera distance obscure the child's identity). The beaten child is transformed into a young girl who exists in Stevie's daily reality as a schoolmate who ignores him, and who undergoes frequent spankings at her father's hand. With this transformation, Stevie switches to the role of observer, cheering on her beating as he looks on smiling. Occurring after Stevie's visit to the Dottie set, the second nightmare finds King Stevie himself punished for the murder of a woman, and sentenced to be beaten by "the strongest man in the kingdom"; with a forceful hand raised to inflict the punishment, the aggressor's face becomes a mustachioed Dottie's. As the final beating is carried out, the scene juxtaposes all of the positions and participants from the first nightmare, to which confusion is added the beating of another son by his father – a beating that Stevie and the schoolgirls witnessed earlier that day in the playground. With the frenzy of this accelerated and out-of-control spanking, a startled Stevie soon awakens in a panic, meticulously folds up his latest drawing of Dottie, secures the artwork in Reynolds Wrap, and buries it under a rock in his backyard.

Do Stevie's fantasies constitute an unconscious attempt to liberate himself from oppressive social restrictions, or are they instead a symptom of something inherently "wrong" with the young boy? Psychoanalytic frameworks provide a useful starting point here. While Freud asserts that dreams and fantasies constitute a desire for the fulfillment of a wish, Elizabeth Cowie explains that representation in fantasy is altered and transformed by defensive mechanisms.[6] Freud's essay "A Child Is Being Beaten" concerns a fantasy of the child's attempt to seduce his own father, and the child's movement among various positions of identification is less an act of liberation than a result of repressive processes that guard the child from bringing the wish to the surface.

This fantasy is also a primal fantasy, an investigation requiring a movement backward in time to help the boy in his search for answers about his own origin as a subject in the world. According to Freudian logic, Stevie's nightmare fantasies constitute an investigation of the past – in this case, a psychic past – that informs the way he lives each moment of his life in the present. Thinking about the protagonist's conflict as an (ultimately, and perhaps necessarily, failed) attempt to negotiate the boundaries between "then" and "now" brings us closer to an understanding of Haynes' narrative strategies in the structuring of queer sexual desire. Working from concepts originally theorized by Laplanche and Pontalis, Cowie explains that fantasy "involves . . . not the achievement of desired objects, but the arranging of, a setting out of, desire; a veritable *mise-en-scène* of desire."[7] Stevie's own story comprises a series of settings and scenes, from those staged on the set of a television show, to those played out in his uneasy dreams. His burial of the product of his emotions and fantasies once and for all demonstrates a rather naïve belief that these scenes could ever remain separate in the first place, and an equally naïve (as it could only be, for a young boy) conviction that the scenes could be ordered such that fantasies would ever become the exclusive realm of the "past." The uneasy juxtaposition of past and present enacted by both Stevie's story and the film itself comments upon the inescapability of desire (the inevitable return of the repressed) and the inability to do anything else but to continue to repress it, in a culture that offers its subjects no other options. Considering how fantasy is kept alive throughout most of *Dottie Gets Spanked*, the final burial quite self-consciously plays like a conclusion imposed upon the narrative by the demands of the normative version of sexuality circulated at the time the story takes place. Or is it Stevie who gets the last laugh, his formal burial of the artwork only a means of keeping desire "safe" for some unrevealed future moment?

A "gay" film less in its overt representation of homosexuality than in what its narrative both actively and self-consciously represses, *Dottie Gets Spanked* speaks of a desire that is not, or not yet, accessible to its central protagonist. It articulates a structure of repression imposed upon its subject because of his own youth and the constraints of a society that demands that deviant youngsters grow out of their bad habits and assimilate with heterosexual normalcy. Whether or not Stevie will achieve this desired result is never revealed, but for journalist Arthur Stuart (Christian Bale), the central protagonist of *Velvet Goldmine*, the matter of assimilation is self-admittedly a given as the narrative begins in present-day 1984 New York. After his superiors at the *Herald* commission Arthur to investigate what happened to Brian Slade (Jonathan Rhys-Meyers), a 1970s glam rocker who faked his own assassination in a failed publicity ploy, Arthur reflects in voiceover narrative that "suddenly I was being paid to remember all the things that money, future, and the serious life made so certain I'd forget." *Velvet Goldmine* continues and responds to Stevie's final act in *Dottie Gets Spanked*, extending Haynes' queer version of everyday life by articulating the ultimate effects of any attempt at "burying the past" of fantasy and desire. As a narrative much more overtly concerned with the workings of both the personal/psychic and social/political history, *Velvet Goldmine* also situates the past as a field of resistance that induces an inevitable confrontation with present realities, providing an opportunity for Haynes to "queer" the present by reconstituting the notion of "reality" itself through multiple juxtapositions of histories remembered, forgotten, and repressed.

The film announces its temporal confrontation of repression in the first words of its voiceover narrative, juxtaposed against a visual field of twinkling stars: "Histories, like ancient ruins, are the fictions of empires, while everything forgotten hangs in dark dreams of the past, ever threatening to return." Initiating a historical trace spanning over 130 years, the artifact that survives the ruins of time is a jewel pinned to the blanket of the newborn and abandoned Oscar Wilde, who is discovered on the doorstep of a family in the 1850s on a dark, Dublin street. Over the course of the narrative, the jewel is recovered from a gutter in the 1950s by the soon-to-be glam rocker Jack Fairy (Osheen Jones) after he is beaten by schoolmates, stolen by Brian Slade 20 years later after the men's New Year's Eve sexual encounter, and offered to Brian's lover Kurt Wilde (Ewan McGregor) as a gift, before it is ultimately coughed up from Arthur Stuart's throat during his final meeting with Kurt in a tavern, at which time Kurt reveals the legend of the jewel's origin. Against the progression of this historical narrative of the survival of a form of sexual rebellion and resistance are counterposed active processes of disavowal, forgetting, and "burial," by both investigative subject and object. The reasons motivating the feigned, onstage assassination of Brian (and his adopted onstage persona, Maxwell Demon) are never explained, though the narrative does suggest connections between the act and Brian and Kurt's recent breakup. It also offers an indirect comparison to the fate of Dorian Gray (quoted and referenced in the first part of the film),

Figure 30.1 Arthur Stuart (Christian Bale) and glam rock friends in Todd Haynes's *Velvet Goldmine* (Miramax, 1998). Produced by Christine Vachon. Photo courtesy Photofest

who elected an aging self-portrait over an aging body; in *Velvet Goldmine*, however, the "deceased" rock star himself ages into the portrait of the more famous yet less glamorous persona of another musical performer, Tommy Stone, who has effectively disguised the identity and sexual ambiguity of his former incarnation as Brian/Maxwell until Arthur discovers the secret.

While Haynes does not assign clear motives and cause/effect relationships in human experience, Arthur's own conflict with the past is more fully elaborated than Brian's, because of the narrative's investment in Arthur as the film's primary perspective and central protagonist.[8] The investigation of another's disappearance sets the stage for Arthur's self-examination, initially occurring not out of his innate desire to know, but specifically because he has been professionally commissioned to do so. Arthur is the ideal vehicle for the type of remembering that this search requires: even before he is given his press assignment – and before the narrative has situated the 1970s as "the past" – the film reveals scenes of his teenage days as a glam fan, running through the streets of Manchester with his friends, one of whom accidentally bumps into Jack Fairy (played as an adult by Micko Westmoreland). Arthur is also "present" at the concert where Brian is "assassinated," and an eyewitness to a later interaction between Brian's by-then ex-wife Mandy (Toni Colette) and Kurt Wilde after a "Death of Glitter" concert.

Unlike Brian, who has summarily excluded his 1970s' glam-rocker incarnation, Arthur acknowledges the source of his conflict between past and present, and between remembering and forgetting, quite early in the film. After receiving his investigative charge, he admits in voiceover that "clearly, there was something, something from the past, spooking me back. I didn't realize at the time that it was you." Instead of providing any sort of explanation, however, his admission sets forth a deeper temporal paradox. Although the narrative never specifically identifies the "you," Arthur appears to be referring to Kurt Wilde, foreshadowing the interview with Kurt in the tavern at the end of the film – a meeting intercut with scenes of the two men before, during, and after a sexual encounter on a rooftop in the "past" of the 1970s. The voiceover of the early scene is thus presented at a double remove from the incident(s) to which it refers, from the perspective of the most recent version of Arthur, reflecting back to the start of his journalistic search, to incidents occurring some ten years earlier.

The voiceover also establishes a plot trajectory that is both motivated and undermined by repressive processes. According to Haynes, the film "had to be about a lost time from the start, about something repressed – and great fears had risen up around whatever this was, which had changed completely and buried it. That's why for Arthur it's an ambivalent search back."[9] His ambivalence clearly does not stem from any perfect or idealized present moment in Arthur's life that memories of the past might disrupt; the search engages him in a subjectively rendered revision of experience in space and time, such that the familiar present is rendered queer and strange. Arthur's version of the 1984 New York that he inhabits is rather gruesome, sterile, and alienating: sunless exteriors; cold, dark and colorless spaces stripped of ornament; crowds of workers with blank and worn-out expressions; muffled voices over loudspeakers announcing the clichéd platform of an unseen President Reynolds, who urges citizens to join the "Committee to Prosper." Arthur is depicted in work settings where he remains apart from his co-workers; more often, he is entirely alone, the narrative providing neither an indication of social ties or connections, nor any domestic spaces or situations that are not related to his work.

In sharp contrast, the spaces of Arthur's memories of the 1970s in the streets and clubs of Manchester are immersed in light, color, ambient movement, and the crisp and seductive sounds of glam rock music, signaling the sexual awakenings of a past that is more real to him than the present. The pleasant memories are, however, those confined to Arthur's life outside of the domestic sphere, within which he is depicted as alienated from his parents on the rare occasions when they happen to inhabit the same space. At home, Arthur finds respite only when he retires to his room filled with posters of rock stars, perusing album covers and music magazines with the same devoted attention that Stevie invests in Dottie. In fact, the similarities between the "fans" of the two films are most prominent when the males inhabit the only tentatively private spaces of their respective bedrooms. As Stevie draws his latest sketch of the spanking he witnessed on the TV set, his father enters the room unannounced, insisting that an embarrassed Stevie show him the portrait. Arthur's confrontation with his parents is more traumatic: as the teenager masturbates over a newspaper picture of Brian and Kurt kissing, both of his parents barge into his room, his father decrying the boy's actions as disgraceful while Arthur retreats in shame from their view.

The colors, sounds, and rhythms of the glam rock scene that Arthur later embraces (at first through his fandom and subsequently by sexual encounters with two rock performers) are thus chronologically situated between two more uninviting realities – the bleakness of the journalist's life in the present, and the memories of his equally constraining upbringing decades earlier. Accordingly, for Arthur, the glam scene signals a most uneasy intersection of time trajectories, initiating both a willing movement forward and a reluctant movement backward. If the planned death of Brian/Maxwell becomes the impetus for investigating what appears to be the much more gradual and less conspicuous death of Arthur's past life, the identity of the "you" that spooks Arthur back is not only Kurt Wilde, but also a "self" that demands to be reclaimed – a self once but no longer elated by its own identifications and desires. No wonder, then, that Arthur is so bitter when his ultimate revelation of Brian's new "Tommy Stone" incarnation is almost stifled by what appears to be an elaborate political hush maneuver, and a premature curtailment of his commissioned investigation; his conviction to "out" Brian as Tommy has become the result of a rigorous struggle with his own demons.

If the glam rock past is the setting upon which repressive operations converge in the story of *Velvet Goldmine*, the workings of identification and desire in fantasy effect a parallel convergence in the space of queer desire, at the level of the film's structure. Through the contrast between the visual splendor of the glam rock scenes and the starkness of both present and childhood realities, the film appears to offer no "present" at all except for its immersion in the continuous present of fantasy. While Stevie's nightmare fantasies in *Dottie Gets Spanked* ultimately signal a most frightening relinquishing of control of his own repressive operations – as well as his own compulsion to bury his desires – the fantasies of *Velvet Goldmine* are structured as scenes of a much more carefully orchestrated and idealized desire, rendered so that it can be remembered as perfect, unchangeable, and insusceptible to the workings of time.

As *Dottie Gets Spanked* illustrates, fantasy scenarios carry and rework the residues of daily realities that the fantasy subject has experienced, and the stagings and scenes of any individual fantasy clearly require a subject who imagines and who orchestrates. Part of the queer pleasure that *Velvet Goldmine* offers is in the plethora of fantasy perspectives that the film intermingles in scenes of identification and desire. As does its structural model *Citizen Kane* (1941), *Velvet Goldmine* "hands off" its narration to other characters as the film progresses: both Brian's first agent, Cecil (Michael Feast), and Mandy Slade assume the role of central storyteller at different points in the film. Unlike its predecessor, however, the investigator in Haynes' film is also a witness to several of the scenes narrated by these other storytellers (even, at some points, encountering the narrators themselves), resulting in an instability and fluidity in the act of remembering, even though the extended flashback to the 1970s is rendered chronologically. In the same way that this investigative journalist motivates the progression of the narrative from the time that his present-day character is introduced, Arthur Stuart also functions as the orchestrator of fantasy – what induces pleasure in the film emerges from his own memories of past events that situate him as an emerging queer subject steeped in his own identifications and desires, even when these memories are triggered by the narration of others. Arthur's function within the narrative and fantasy of the film parallels the "lesson" from Oscar Wilde that Arthur's schoolteacher directly addresses to Arthur in an early scene:

> There were times when it appeared to Dorian Gray that the whole of history was merely a record of his own life – not as he had lived it in acts and circumstance, but as his imagination had created it for him, as it had been in his brain, and in his passions. He felt that he'd known them all, those strange, terrible figures that had passed along the stage of life, and made sin so marvelous and evil, so full of subtlety. It seemed that in some mysterious way, their lives had been his own.

Echoing and reiterating the responsibilities of resuscitating history that B. Ruby Rich identifies as integral to the vitality of a New Queer Cinema, the "lesson" that Arthur is about to learn through his investigation is that the history of an era that the journalist is commissioned to investigate objectively is also his own history, and one which cannot be relegated to the past – precisely the lesson that Stevie is denied the opportunity to learn in *Dottie Gets Spanked*. The fact that fantasy provides the vehicle by which the past is made "real" to the investigative subject helps us to come to terms with the ways in which the fantasy scene – real and imagined – becomes the only setting of reality for Arthur.

"The genealogy of desire is always a history of the subject's identifications," Leo Bersani proposes, and the untroubled move from identification to desire is inherent in the fantasy scenarios that Arthur constructs and orchestrates, evidencing his self-constitution as a queer subject in these very "real" scenes of his own historical past.[10] This movement is apparent in Arthur's masturbation scene, part of an elaborately orchestrated segment that begins with press photographers capturing a kiss between Brian and Kurt – a kiss then reproduced in the pages of a newspaper that Arthur peruses in his bedroom. Brian and Kurt's onstage performance of Brian Eno's "Baby's on Fire" provides the musical orchestration, as extreme closeups of Arthur are intercut with shots of the two stage performers enacting a slow, graceful, and balletic seduction scene – one which eventually finds Brian on his knees, licking the strings of Kurt's electric guitar in erotic frenzy. As tongue touches wire, the scene shifts to Arthur turning the newspaper pages to witness a photo of the encounter. The music bridges to a third scene, of an orgy taking place after the night's performance, as Kurt and Brian reciprocate beckoning glances before they surreptitiously retreat to a private room. Before Arthur can bring himself to a climax, the fantasy scenario is disrupted, and the music is softened as his parents barge into the room. "Stand up!" the father exclaims, but as the terrified and ashamed Arthur rises to view his image in a mirror, the scene shifts to Brian himself standing up in the orgy room, moving away to meet Kurt. This vivid remembering of the imaginations of fantasy is at the same time both firmly grounded in space and time (a specific room, a specific moment in Arthur's past), and entirely liberated from spatial or temporal groundings: the three separate spaces intercut in the sequence build upon and extend one another, with Brian continuing movements initiated by Arthur, and the "real" space of both the kiss and the musical fellatio magically transported via print media to the fantasy space that Arthur imagines at home. The musical continuity that unites the three spaces also effects a sense of simultaneous action and "continuous present," emphasized by the slow pace of action and movement in each of the spaces.[11]

Here and elsewhere, however, the fantasies of the film – whether comprising past memories or wholly imagined scenes – are enacted as "settings" for the playing out of desire rather than scenes in which desire itself yields to climax or ultimate fulfillment. The emphasis upon settings adds to the feeling that fantasy suspends time in the film. From the frozen images of Brian constructed for media circulation, to the stagings of musical numbers with either real or implied audiences, to the more private stagings of sexual attractions now lost or past, the film presents desire as an intersection of knowing glances. An immanent possibility of queer desire is always in the process of being fulfilled. "Come closer," a voice on a rooftop beckons, "Don't be frightened." As Arthur ultimately yields to the signals sent by Kurt, this man "who ended my life . . . in waves," the scene plays out as a ballet of gradually approaching bodies, a hand caressing the flesh of another, all magically lit by a shooting star and spaceship above, as the camera slowly retreats from the connected couple, a snowy shower of stars obscuring them from view.

The erotic charge of these hypnotically orchestrated scenarios appears to have been lost on several of the film's critics. "Haynes doesn't want to show us the dirty parts, that ecstasy, excess, and eroticism have no place in his portrayals of gay sexuality,'" Christopher Kelly suggests, adding that "the emotions and experiences [the film] relates are hardly ones that connect to real gay people."[12] Craig Seligman argues that in the second half of the film the love scenes aren't charged, and the characters are underdeveloped: "The sex feels like a gay artist's statement: obligatory and earnest."[13] Such criticisms, however, arise from the presumption that eroticism is limited to those artworks that engage a realist aesthetic – a presumption that Todd Haynes' reliance upon fantasy networks challenges at every juncture, just as extensively in his intricate reworking of melodrama in *Far From Heaven*. Indeed, if one confines oneself to matters of erotic representation and thematic emphasis, it might initially seem implausible to describe *Far From Heaven* as a "queer" film at all, given that its diegetic perspective is that of a white, heterosexual woman, and its representational treatment of homosexuality is limited to a few sequences, none of which is particularly sexually graphic. As is the case with *Dottie Gets Spanked* and *Velvet Goldmine*, however, *Far From Heaven* "queers" by rendering the familiar uncomfortable and strange, through intricate and subversive cinematic processes of historical disjuncture.

If the look of *Far From Heaven* harbors familiar and recognizable groundings, it is because its reference points are situated in the Technicolor-saturated cinematic past of Douglas Sirk's social and domestic melodramas of the 1950s – a past already heavily mediated and stylized, and one which signals to contemporary audiences a pronounced spatial and temporal distance. It is the look of a genre that was even in its heyday continually at odds with the conventions of the realist aesthetic and considered critically suspect for that very reason, even while it enjoyed heightened popularity with mainstream American audiences of the 1950s. However extensively Haynes borrows from Sirk, Haynes' intent in *Far From Heaven* is not a literal re-creation of the Sirkean world of his film's most obvious reference point, *All That Heaven Allows* (1955), but instead a positioning of these two seemingly similar past worlds in an intricate historical dynamic, one in which the temporal remove effected by the film's genre and style facilitates a critical distance by which to assess past and present. Sirk's film focuses primarily upon class inequities ensuing from the growing attraction of wealthy widow Cary Scott (Jane Wyman) to her gardener Ron Kirby (Rock Hudson), whose Walden-inspired naturalist values are at odds with the country-club conventions and studied affluence of Cary's close circle of "friends" who, along with the widow's two over-indulged teenage children, harshly judge her decision to abandon their world for Ron's as selfish and misguided. Haynes' update of Sirk's melodrama certainly does to a great extent retain and recreate the formal and stylistic attributes of its referent, including the panoramic crane shots of the sleepy New England town that open both narratives, and his use of saturated color motifs and accentuating musical crescendos throughout the film often outdo Sirk's. Still, whatever might seem familiar

Figure 30.2 In *Far From Heaven* (Focus Features, 2002) Haynes updates Douglas Sirk's melodramas to address issues of race and sexuality. Produced by Jody Patton and Christine Vachon

through this extended take on the generic, melodramatic past through *All That Heaven Allows* is strategically disrupted by changes and substitutions which result in a quite different set of social and political conflicts in Haynes' "version" of the story: rather than widowed, Cathy Whitaker (Julianne Moore) is here married to successful sales executive Frank (Dennis Quaid), who is struggling with the "problem" of his homosexual tendencies; and the gardener in Haynes' film, Raymond Deagan (Dennis Haysbert), is African-American.

In addition to integrating the class issues of *All That Heaven Allows* with matters of sexuality and race, the result of these substitutions is a narrative that retains the visual, formal, and stylistic semblance of an "authentic" Sirkean melodrama while conspicuously deviating from Sirk's model in terms of theme, and perhaps more significantly, of representation. If the paradox of this displacement renders the film susceptible to criticism on the basis of a seeming disloyalty to its cinematic antecedents, its infusion of undeniable historically authentic realities of racial and sexual stereotyping and oppression into a narrative set in the affluent suburbs of America in the late 1950s looks and seems far fetched only to the extent that the representation of these issues sometimes registers as not "belonging" here generically.[14] Certainly, one need look only as far as Sirk's slightly later film *Imitation of Life* (1959) to verify that melodrama – and perhaps especially Sirkean melodrama – is well equipped to dramatize historically pertinent issues of racial injustice effectively, but Haynes pushes the limits of generic representational "accuracy" by taking on the greater white, heteronormative enterprise in positioning his open-minded and deeply empathetic heroine between African-American heterosexual and white homosexual objects of affection.

Through such positioning, Haynes enables his narrative to explore and extend structures of repression which already figured prominently in *Dottie Gets Spanked* and *Velvet Goldmine*. In fact, the stylistic codes that he uses to represent homosexuality in *Far From Heaven* already configure such representation as a spatio-temporal impossibility, as something that must inevitably be censored as a condition of its representability. The sequence in which Frank's homosexual tendencies are first revealed offers a cogent example. After witnessing two men furtively and silently signaling one another to meet in a movie theater balcony, Frank follows a homosexual couple out of the theater at a safe distance through the dark streets of downtown Hartford, his focus so intent that he fails to acknowledge the beggar asking for his money or the female prostitute soliciting his affection. Largely obscured and visible only as a deep-blue lit, shadow-casting silhouette tracking the two men as they proceed into a barren alley, canted angles signal the protagonist's almost unknowing surrender to "deviant" desire. The camera then tracks Frank from the front as he emerges into the dark, green-lit space of a male homosexual lounge, startled by an older man at the door who asks him for identification. The sequence concludes with Frank drinking a scotch at the bar as he becomes trapped within an intricate network of glances – some unreturned, others very cautiously acknowledged and reciprocated – until the scene ends in a fade-out as one of the men moves towards Frank's position at the bar. The strictures of the Production Code Administration would certainly have guaranteed that an approved film of the late 1950s would find no place – except on the cutting room floor – for such representations as those included in this sequence, so that the inclusion of such a scene in Haynes' twenty-first-century narrative references an implausible narrative past while simultaneously serving as a striking and historically accurate reminder of a very real and convincingly portrayed representation of "deviant" sexuality from the perspectives of that same past historical moment. The sequence's narrative strategy is further accentuated by its canted angles, obscure lighting schemes, and perhaps especially its ultimate fade to black, highlighting a "forbidden-ness" consonant with dominant 1950s perspectives on homosexuality, even as it also posits the anachronism of such perspectives from the seemingly more enlightened position of the contemporary viewer.[15]

This representation/repression dynamic plays out in the larger narrative scheme of *Far From Heaven* as an extended conflict – and also a conflation – of then and now, one which always interrogates the comforting notion of the present as a time that no longer accommodates such outdated repressive tendencies as those represented here. The struggle also manifests itself in spatial terms through the interplay of seeing and being seen, and ultimately of conspicuity and obscurity, delimiting the very narrow range of acts and discourses authorized at this historical moment as part of "normal" social relations. Accordingly, the "queering" enterprise of *Far From Heaven* relies just as extensively upon the hyper-representation of heterosexuality as the (un)representability of homosexuality. In contrast with the diegetic field spreading across much of Hollywood cinema in the 1950s, which managed to sustain heterosexual identity hegemonically as a default by obscuring the representation of alternative identities as a matter of policy, the presence of homosexual representation in *Far From Heaven* enables a contesting of heteronormative relations by drawing attention to heterosexuality as a social construct.

Haynes emphasizes the conspicuity of this constructedness through the act of isolating the heterosexual "moment" and thereby submitting it to critical scrutiny. The morning after the Whitakers' plans to attend a social function are interrupted by Frank's arrest on a charge of public "loitering," the couple exchange a dispassionate kiss as Frank prepares to leave the house for work. At the very brief instant of this kiss they are illuminated, and wholly startled, by a blinding flash bulb and the loud click of a camera shutter. A team from the *Hartford Weekly Gazette* has already set the stage for an in-depth interview with Cathy, she and her husband having earned the title of "Mr and Mrs Magnatech," the name of the technology corporation where Frank works, and their image is reproduced in product and corporation advertisement sketches captured in gilded frames on the walls of their living room (one reads, "Mr and Mrs Magnatech choose nothing but the best for their home"). Here and elsewhere, *Far From Heaven* emphasizes through role playing the strain of sustaining the image of this ideal relationship between men and women that American culture posited as both desirable and without imaginable alternative – a strain which Cathy soon begins to note when these same society pages begin to describe her as "a woman as devoted to her family as she is kind to negroes," a description that elicits nervous giggles among her woman friends. That such hyper-visibility is rendered appropriate only when it highlights the socially normative is clarified in the art exhibit sequence, which finds Cathy and the gardener Raymond so deeply engaged in conversation about the redemptive possibilities of abstract expressionism that they remain oblivious to the shocked stares of the high society patrons in the gallery – oblivious, that is, until the giggles become audible. It is this same visibility that ultimately results in Raymond and Cathy's undoing when they are spotted together by a gossip outside a restaurant in the "wrong" part of Hartford.

Highlighting the insidious ways in which acceptable social relationships are constructed hegemonically in the world of this film, the hyper-visibility of unattainable heterosexual norms is often contrasted with the normative and highly conspicuous invisibility of the "other." At the upscale cocktail party that Cathy has planned for the Whitakers' home, after one of the guests mentions a contemporaneous act of social resistance in the Civil Rights Movement, another guest assures his listeners that such incidents could never happen in Hartford because "there are no negroes in Hartford," as the camera cuts to an African-American waiter holding a tray of appetizers. Such normative social mechanisms are shown to be so efficient that even those individuals who are marginalized by them eventually succumb to their logic. After Raymond's daughter is attacked by prejudiced white teenage boys and his own African-American community begins to judge him for his attraction to Cathy Whitaker, he decides that he must no longer sustain his relationship with her. More insidiously and disturbingly, Frank finds opportunity at least momentarily to remove himself from his status of "other" by chastising Cathy for her relationship with Raymond on the basis of the humiliation that Frank has just endured from Magnatech colleagues, who learned about Cathy's alleged transgression earlier that day.

Beyond this intricate network of repression, however, lies an unyielding attentiveness to the possibility of a set of human relations that are no longer assessed on the basis of how strictly they conform to stated or implicit norms, and in *Far From Heaven* this possibility is advanced, momentarily and hypothetically, by the fantasy of this impossible relationship between an African-American man who is all too accustomed to his social function as conspicuous absence, and a white woman brave enough to experiment with "what it feels like to be the only one in a room – colored or whatever." That this fantasy may not be sustained under such repressive social conditions is certainly central to its function in the realm of melodrama, a realm in which the resonances of the "if only" ultimately throw into relief the presumptions of the realist aesthetic. Just as Brian Slade loses himself in the masquerade of Tommy Stone, and Stevie buries his final sketch of Dottie in the ground of his backyard, the fantasy of transcendence in *Far From Heaven* ultimately yields to the realities of separations and divisions, yet this ultimate yielding never renders the fantasy less than remarkably powerful in the possibilities that it articulates.

Attesting to this possibility is the fact that Frank does eventually find a way beyond the social structures that he has found to be oppressive – or, at least, the film lets its audience imagine such a path as the final shots of Frank show him with the man who seduced him at the Miami resort. That this ultimate homosexual "togetherness" still feels quite tentative and precarious in the world of *Far From Heaven* attests once more to the filmmaker's resistance of easy solutions which he perceives to be just as complex now as they were in the late 1950s. And the fact that Haynes' films are not overtly graphic in their representation of homosexual acts, and that he always frames such representations in the context of repressive operations that struggle to disrupt heteronormative human relations, does not make him any less integral a contributor to this cinema's vitality; in fact, he has demonstrated a keen ability to move beyond such matters as gay sexual representation and content, enabling Haynes to hypothesize the structure of queer desire more dynamically. Haynes' method fuses sexuality and politics, through the articulation of fantasy scenarios that arrange confrontations between past and present at the levels of the personal, sexual, and social. In the process, he politicizes the human tendency to forget, as well as the inability of the sexual subject to release himself from the history of his own identifications and desires. The lessons he offers are vital not only to individual queer subjects struggling to engage the dynamics of their own sexual histories, but also to the history of a New Queer Cinema that, as B. Ruby Rich has intimated, has lost touch with its historical antecedents in a troublesome case of short-term memory.

Notes

1 B. Ruby Rich, "New Queer Cinema," *Sight and Sound*, 2, no. 5 (September 1992), p. 32.
2 B. Ruby Rich, "Queer and Present Danger", *Sight and Sound* 10, no. 3 (March 2000), p. 24.
3 Justin Wyatt, "Cinematic/Sexual Transgression: An Interview with Todd Haynes," *Film Quarterly* 46, no. 3 (Spring 1993), p. 7.
4 Wyatt, "Cinematic/Sexual Transgression", p. 8.
5 Sigmund Freud, "A Child Is Being Beaten: A Contribution to the Study of the Origins of the Perversions," in *The Complete Psychological Works of Sigmund Freud*, trans. James Strachey (London: The Hogarth Press, 1955), vol. 17. For a discussion of the definition of identification and its relation to object choice, see Sigmund Freud, "Group Psychology and the Analysis of the Ego," in *The Complete Psychological Works of Sigmund Freud*, trans. James Strachey (London: The Hogarth Press, 1955), vol. 18, p. 106.
6 See the chapter "Fantasia" in Elizabeth Cowie, *Representing the Woman* (Minneapolis: University of Minnesota Press, 1997), pp. 123–65.
7 Cowie, *Representing the Woman*, p. 133.
8 In an insightful discussion of causality in Haynes's film *Safe* (1995), Roddey Reid suggests that "the film queers and goes against the grain of what could be called 'a politics of epistemology and visibility,'" in that the film resists any clear explanation of the origins of its central protagonist's environmentally related illness. See "UnSafe at Any Distance: Todd Haynes' Visual Culture of Health and Risk," *Film Quarterly* 51, no. 3 (Spring 1998), pp. 32–44.
9 Nick James, "American Voyeur," *Sight and Sound* 8, no. 9 (September 1998), p. 8.
10 Leo Bersani, *Homos* (Cambridge, MA: Harvard University Press, 1995), p. 63.
11 In "Fantasia," Elizabeth Cowie explains, "The pleasure [in fantasy] is in how to *bring about* the consummation, is in the happening and continuing to happen; is how it will come about, and not in the moment of *having happened*, when it will fall back into loss, the past" (emphasis in the original). See *Representing the Woman*, p. 133.
12 Christopher Kelly, "The Unbearable Lightness of Gay Movies," *Film Comment* 35, no. 2 (March-April 1999), p. 20.
13 Craig Seligman, "All That Glitters," *Artforum International* 37, no. 2 (October 1998), p. 104.
14 This temporal disjunct between representational systems leads James Harvey to describe *Far From Heaven*'s strategy as a "condescension towards the past," leaving the audience with the feeling that "you're seeing a movie in quotes." See "Made in Heaven: How is it that Todd Haynes's Warmest Film is Inspired by Douglas Sirk's Coldest?," *Film Comment* 29, no. 2 (March–April 2003), pp. 52–5.
15 Mary Ann Doane describes the temporal scheme of the film as "doubly accessible, as a naïve yet excessive discourse about a particular historical moment suffused with tensions drawn from the present, and as an extended quotation of *All That Heaven Allows*" (p. 5). See "Pathos and Pathology: The Cinema of Todd Haynes," *camera obscura* 57, no. 19 (2004), pp. 1–21.

31

Twoness and the Film Style of Oscar Micheaux

J. Ronald Green

A professor in the Department of History of Art at Ohio State University in Columbus, Green is the author of two books on pioneering black American filmmaker Oscar Micheaux, *With a Crooked Stick: The Films of Oscar Micheaux* and *Straight Lick: The Cinema of Oscar Micheaux*. In this reading, originally Chapter 3 of *Straight Lick* (2000), Green opens up auteurism to a consideration of race by using black author W.E.B. Dubois' idea of "twoness" as a central feature of the African-American experience to illuminate the stylistic tensions within Micheaux's films and in relation to the hegemonic model of Hollywood cinema. Green shows how these tensions are central to Micheaux's representations of black American life, and questions assumptions based on judging black films against Hollywood paradigms.

The implied nemesis of African-American uplift has always been racism. One of the force fields through which Oscar Micheaux, who wrote, produced, and directed more than 40 films from the 1920s through the 1940s, had to negotiate a path toward his goal of middle-class status was that characterized by the polarized extremes of African-ness and American-ness. W.E.B. DuBois presented the now-familiar, paradigmatic notion of "twoness" in the first few pages of *The Souls of Black Folk*:

> It is a peculiar sensation, this double-consciousness, this sense of always looking at one's soul by the tape of a world that looks on in amused contempt and pity. One ever feels his twoness, – an American, a Negro; two souls, two thoughts, two unreconciled strivings; two warring ideals in one dark body, whose dogged strength alone keeps it from being torn asunder.[1]

African-Americans, that is, individually have faced the simultaneous possibilities of two identities whose relations to each other are bipolar and strained, creating a dilemma that each African-American individual must somehow resolve. The horns of the dilemma are to be found, one, in the dominant white culture that cannot be ignored and that has itself tended to demand and at the same time to reject the assimilation of people of color; and, two, in the ethnic black culture of the African-American community. The concept of twoness has recognized a resistance by blacks to their assimilation by white culture, a will to retain a black ethnic identity. Whereas assimilation seemed necessary for survival by blacks in America, it also threatened black self-esteem and the integrity of their African identity.

Thomas Cripps has identified a debilitating dilemma for African-American film that he has associated with

J. Ronald Green, "Twoness and the Film Style of Oscar Micheaux". Chapter 3 from Straight hick: The Cinema of Oscar Micheaux (Bloomington and London: Indiana University Press, 2000).

DuBois's concept of twoness. Cripps's book *Slow Fade to Black* was the ground-breaking work on the history of race movies, early films made by blacks for black audiences.[2] Cripps's monumental effort, under difficult research conditions, to locate and interpret the primary and secondary source materials of black cinema – alongside the prior pioneering efforts by Donald Bogle and Daniel J. Leab[3] – adumbrates an ethnic cinema that was previously invisible. Cripps's thesis is founded on the historical myth of the American melting pot and the phenomenon of assimilation, addressing black cinema as a problem of non-assimilation.

Cripps has proposed that the future of black cinema, and of black criticism and spectatorship, lies properly with assimilation and thus Hollywood. Though he attempts in *Slow Fade to Black* to find works of artistic value created by the "black underground" outside Hollywood, which included Micheaux and the Colored Players, Cripps nevertheless concludes that no black producer was sufficiently capitalized to produce good films (Cripps revised this opinion in his next book, *Black Film as Genre*). Cripps also concludes that Hollywood was sufficiently capitalized to co-opt any successful idea produced by black producers of race movies – hence, the double meaning of Cripps's title, "slow fade to black" – the slow fade-*out* of the *independent* black producer (the "blackout" of blackness) and the slow fade-*in* of the *Hollywood* black producer (the slowness of the emergence of assimilated blackness).

The *Slow Fade* thesis, however, undervalues the loss represented by the fade-out of the independent race movie, blaming that loss on the inadequacies of independent films. *Slow Fade* also overvalues the gain, both realized and potential, in the African-American fade-in to mainstream film.

After posing the dilemma of twoness, and after considerable detailed criticism of particular films and filmmakers, including Micheaux, Cripps indeed ends his study by celebrating reforms in Hollywood as the best hope for black cinema. Of the written agreement reached by "delegates of the National Association for the Advancement of Colored People and the heads of several Hollywood studios" who "met and codified some social changes and procedures" in 1942, Cripps says: "The studios agreed to abandon pejorative racial roles, to place Negroes in positions as extras they could reasonably be expected to occupy in society, and to begin the slow task of integrating blacks into the ranks of studio technicians."[4] Cripps capped the initial statement of his thesis by observing that "the 1942 agreement accomplished far more than allowing a few blacks to appear in roles that were not overtly racist. It changed the whole tune and nature of Hollywood's response to the Afro-American's role in film and, by extension, in American life as well."[5] The optimism of this denouement seems inappropriate, however, since the agreement of 1942 addressed only the problem of assimilation; only, that is, one horn of the dilemma. The assimilation of blacks might have been expected to ethnicize Hollywood to some extent, but there was little historical evidence on Hollywood screens – in relation to black or any other ethnic groups – that the expectation was realized. The recent successes of black cinema on Hollywood screens are the result of Spike Lee's successful assault on Hollywood as an *independent* – he forced his way in by making money on the outside first. Any success derived from the agreement of 1942 to integrate blacks into the Hollywood culture industry would appear to be a gain primarily for assimilation, for one side of the twoness dilemma but not for the other. While it is the case today that more positive black characters appear on American film and television screens, their African-American characteristics are very often either virtually erased (Bill Cosby) or caricatured (Eddie Murphy). And when African-American characteristics are delivered in a fully rounded fashion, as in *Frank's Place* (1987), Charles Burnett's *To Sleep with Anger* (1990), and Julie Dash's *Daughters of the Dust* (1991), they are often poorly handled by the industry. Still, Cripps is certainly right in emphasizing that Hollywood should be held responsible for its extreme and peculiar misrepresentation of blacks. Nevertheless, even though the efforts of DuBois and the NAACP that resulted in the 1942 agreements were necessary and laudable, they were not and are not sufficient. In response to an earlier published version of this chapter, Cripps has pointed to facts and figures that are signs of progress in black representation in Hollywood; Jesse Rhines has recently argued, however, that similar facts and figures represent a society still racked by fundamental racial, gender, and class injustices and imbalances, thus indicating a continuing need for independent film.[6]

The predictable effects of the 1942 agreements are analogous to the effects of the 1947 decision to sign Jackie Robinson to the roster of the Brooklyn Dodgers that opened major league baseball to the assimilation of black players. As Nelson George points out in *The Death of Rhythm & Blues*, that was "a major event in the integration of America" and "now lies at the heart of this nation's popular culture." He also points out, however, that:

> Unfortunately, not too many people cared that it meant the end of Negro baseball and the demise of a "naturally integrated" black institution. Ask an older black man about it and you'll be told sagely, "That is the price you have to pay for entry into the game. Look at the number of black players who dominate Major League Baseball, making millions and becoming role models for the nation." Yet if, following the advice of Bob Woodward and Carl Bernstein's Deep Throat, we follow the money, we see that this trade-off, while on the surface great for blacks, was in reality an economic steal for baseball's owners.

George was drawing on the analogy of black baseball to support his thesis that black music had been co-opted by the white owners of larger institutions, but the same analogy applies even more faithfully to the co-optation of black film talent by the 1942 agreements between the NAACP and Hollywood film companies. Hollywood, like baseball, had been lobbied hard by blacks to open up, whereas black musicians did not have to lobby the music industry to have their talents co-opted (and they were co-opted in a more underhanded way). As George makes clear, the sort of institutional co-optation that unifies the three historical examples of this triple analogy has consequences in two related dimensions – representational imagination and economic class:

> Since Robinson's debut, blacks have done the same thing in Major League Baseball that they have done in popular music: entertain, make large salaries, and generate money for businesses that funnel precious little of it back into black communities. They feed the dream machine that tells black youths that entertaining – on a stage or a ball field [or a movie screen] – is the surest way to leap racial barriers. But without access to power, blacks lost more than they gained economically from integrating Major League Baseball.[7]

Perhaps Micheaux's greatest contribution, the one that all critics have recognized, is his establishment and successful operation of a black film institution over an extended period, a going concern analogous to pre-integration black baseball. And no matter what one thinks of Micheaux's actual films, what is not debatable is that they could not have been made any other way – certainly not through any arrangements approximating the NAACP-studio agreements of 1942. Micheaux's institutional accomplishment – his ability to turn out film after film addressing directly the needs of an all-black audience – has not been replicated since, though it is more than half a century after the 1942 agreements.[8]

A Knowledge Worth Having

The issue of twoness is important for understanding Micheaux, race movies, and Cripps's thesis about them. As DuBois noted, twoness is not an enviable state and the value of the knowledge of twoness in no way *justifies* the color line. The knowledge, however, may still be valuable and its probable value justifies not only the study of Micheaux but the place of race movies in any canon that claims to represent American cinema, or a cinema of American society. bell hooks makes a related point in discussing whiteness in the black imagination, and Carol Clover makes an analogous point about gender ambiguity in spectators of modern horror films.[9] A canon of such a cinema would need to include representation of the dialectical aspects of American hegemony, including not only Hollywood's role in that hegemony but the effect of Hollywood hegemony on African-American identity. Robert Stam considers this sort of twoness or what he calls "relational vision" as an advantageous aspect of a Bakhtinian approach to ethnic studies:

> A Bakhtinian approach thinks "from the margins," seeing Native Americans, African Americans and Hispanics, for example, not as interest groups to be added on to a preexisting pluralism, but rather as being at the very core of the American experience from the beginning, each offering an invaluable "dialogical angle" on the national experience. . . . A Bakhtinian approach recognizes *an epistemological advantage on the part of those who are oppressed and therefore bicultural.* The oppressed, because they are obliged by circumstances and the imperatives of survival to know both the dominant and the marginal culture, are *ideally placed* to deconstruct the mystifications of the dominant group [emphasis added].[10]

Cripps has, in *Slow Fade to Black*, resolved the dilemma of twoness solely by reference to Hollywood, thus opting for assimilation. There is no evidence so far, however, that Hollywood can handle controversial differences of identity as significant as the color line, economic class, patriarchal sexism, or sexual taboo. Robin Wood's and Carol Clover's studies of sexuality and gender ambiguity and repression in the horror film might seem to suggest that Hollywood can and does deal in a healthy way with difference and denial; but, in fact, their theses ultimately reveal that Hollywood's treatments of gender "bending" leave the prevailing gender relations intact, and that independent, inexpensive, non-Hollywood films treat repressed material more directly.[11] Hollywood has certainly not taken the lead in broaching, much less celebrating, significant differences in society. That sort of leadership in cinema must come from undercapitalized and unassimilated independent and alternative cinemas such as race movies, documentary, and the avant garde. Cripps's answer to the dilemma – to turn away from "underground" films – seems, therefore, inadequate.[12]

If Cripps could, in *Slow Fade to Black* (and again in *Making Movies Black*), write off independent race movies by saying that black-produced cinema acquiesced in segregation, placed white cupidity off limits as a theme, rehashed the stereotypes for which Hollywood had been blamed, set black against black, and imitated white movies, it is because he has accepted the rhetoric and aesthetics of assimilation in Hollywood.[13] The term "aesthetic" refers to the standards of beauty or sensual pleasure displayed or implied by the discourse as evidenced in its style in relation to its rhetoric. For example, if the "good guys" are virtually always white and tall and are photographed from below so that they look even taller and more dominant, and if they are also associated with "beautiful" photography, then the association of these choices of style with the rhetoric of "goodness" of the good guys implies a standard of beauty that is associated positively not only with tallness (and dominance), but also with whiteness itself. "Beauty" and whiteness, by always appearing together, imply each other. Stylistic choices in the production of films are made, consciously or unconsciously, in the context of such mutually inflecting rhetorical and aesthetic fields; those fields may be complex or simple, but they are always operative. All of Cripps's specific criticisms of independent race movies (listed above) are answerable. For example, it is not fair to say that black-produced cinema "acquiesced" in segregation when the necessity to avoid topics of integration was imposed by white censorship, and when black audiences were themselves divided on the benefits of integration – one could be "for" separation without being "acquiescent" to segregation. Race movies did not "place white cupidity off-limits"; white cupidity was placed off-limits by white boards of censorship. Micheaux fought such censor boards for years and still managed to treat white oppression both directly and indirectly in films such as *Within Our Gates* (1920), *Symbol of the Unconquered* (1920), *The Girl from Chicago* (1932), *Birthright* (1938), and others. Some race movies may have "rehashed" Hollywood stereotypes of blacks, but some did not; and some race movies, such as Micheaux's, developed a complex critique of those stereotypes. If race movies sometimes "set black against black," then those movies reflected the reality of all-black-cast narratives as well as the realities of the larger black community, which like any community was unanimous on virtually no issue. If some race movies "imitated white movies," they did so only to a greater or lesser degree. White movies were the only movies that existed; to the extent that there was a community standard of cinema it was a white standard. Even those filmmakers working against that standard had to work with a legacy that was both unavoidable and basically – because historically – white. To reject on the basis of white imitation all non-Hollywood cinemas that used or referred to some aspects of the Hollywood contributions to film style would be to ignore the issue of hegemony and to misunderstand some basic processes of culture such as those discussed by Harold Bloom in *The Anxiety of Influence*.[14]

Twoness and Style

No existing Micheaux film looks much like a well-made Hollywood film, and Cripps's initial intolerance in *Slow Fade to Black* of the deviation in Micheaux's films from Hollywood style still in the 1970s, 1980s, and even 1990s represents a generally negative or uncertain attitude about Micheaux's accomplishment.

Cripps has described the pervasive, typical mistakes in Micheaux's style, and has shown that Micheaux's

Figure 31.1 White oppression is addressed in *Within Our Gates* (Micheaux Film Corp., 1920), produced and directed by Oscar Micheaux

production company was aware of them but unable to correct them because of the prohibitive expense of higher shooting ratios, retakes, master shots, and professional editing. The apparatus of Cripps's own critical assessment, however, ignores the contradiction inherent in twoness. At the beginning of his discussion of Micheaux, Cripps has described the central dilemma for Micheaux (and black-produced race movies) as the "temptation to make mirror images of white movies [in which case] . . . success itself might be a false god for Negroes."[15] Throughout the discussions on Micheaux, Cripps uses the term "mirror images" to signify this dilemma.

One Horn of a Dilemma

The no-win, mirror-image dilemma in race movies and in Micheaux's work remains unresolved in Cripps's treatment. Instead of holding up this dilemma as a structural contradiction (black success at imitating white movies comprises failure; success equals failure) that illuminates the struggles of black filmmakers and critics, Cripps has alternated in his loyalties toward each pole of the dilemma. It remains difficult to discuss Micheaux or the phenomenon of race movies at all until something is said about the possible cinematic outcomes of the dilemma of twoness.

Cripps's critical stance urges assimilation rather than confrontation of the dilemma of black production, a dilemma in which assimilation was half the problem. He regrets the lost opportunity for successful black movie making in Hollywood without positing what that success might mean and how it might accommodate the dilemma of twoness previously introduced. Furthermore, in his argument Cripps castigated criticisms of Matthews and Ottley in the black press that seem now to have suggested the most responsible approach to the dilemma:

> Roi Ottley, a major figure among black newspapermen, called forth even less precise objections and settled for a rhetorical broad racial boosterism:

> *The Green Pastures* will[,] no doubt, receive magnificent and glowing accounts in the Negro press . . . and unhappily so for the Negro public. . . . Negro newspapers on the whole have a false sense of values. . . . They seem to work from the premise that anytime a Negro appears in a play or picture which the whites have produced it should be applauded regardless of its merits. . . . This department goes on record as feeling that Oscar Micheaux, with his inferior equipment, would have produced a better picture.[16]

Ottley (here) and Matthews (elsewhere) insisted that no matter what the technical and stylistic problems, the only future for the production of black culture was through black people, and the only future for black films was through black filmmakers. What heretofore had been seen as technical problems and mistakes in the production values of race movies might then be seen instead as elements of style and texture, as for example the "rough" carving is now understood in the sculpture of Elijah Pierce, or the rough acting, dubbing, and general directing of many of Rainer Werner Fassbinder's films is understood as integral to their artistic success:

> No doubt [Fassbinder] was temperamentally incapable of working in any other way than he did, but this is to say that he was incapable of making anything but flawed films. . . . The advantage of setting a furious pace was that no-one could get bored, and everyone was under tension, especially the actors. The disadvantage was that there would be a good deal of botching in every phase of making the film, from scripting to post-synchronising.[17]

The criteria for "successes" and for failures would then have to be derived from a culture of twoness – from the culture of the maker (whether rural or urban, working- or middle-class, gay or straight), not from the apartheid and assimilationist Hollywood industry.

Judging the Films

It is not necessary to assume that the conventions of Hollywood cinema constitute the only valid basis for narrative cinema. What would a "good" black cinema look like, then, if it did not imitate classical white cinema? Actually, though scholars such as Pearl Bowser, Mark Reid, bell hooks, Ed Guerrero, Jessie Rhines, and Clyde Taylor have provided answers to this question, it should not be necessary to delineate qualities of good black cinema; students of world cinema are familiar with many styles of narrative cinema other than those of the classic Hollywood film. Many of those films have successfully reached supportive audiences, both mass and non-mass audiences such as those who responded to Melvin Van Peebles' *Sweet Sweetback's Baadasssss Song* (1971). *Sweetback* made money as a black-produced independent film, but the movement it spawned, called "blaxploitation," consisted primarily of Hollywood-produced films. Such co-optation suggests that the problem for black independent producers lies not with their films or their audiences, but lies in the machinery of distribution and exhibition, an issue that Roy Armes emphasizes in his book on Third World cinema.[18] Black independent filmmakers can and do make movies in all sorts of ways, just as black musicians, ministers, painters, sculptors, and writers have created different kinds of improvisational music, oral jeremiad, visual art, and narratives, all of which could be understood by their own audiences and which were later celebrated by Euro-centric audiences as well. The contribution of these forms to art, pleasure, and understanding has often been the greater for their ethnic authenticity and has come to be seen as diminished by any forced concessions to classicism.

Since Micheaux did not necessarily assume Hollywood standards, his films may be based on assumed or invented syntagmatics unknown in the film industry. White cinema is important to Micheaux's work, both positively and negatively, but it is not determinant. Micheaux's style and production values were appropriate to his circumstances and can be considered artistically limiting only in the way that the super-refined style and the high production values of *Gone with the Wind* (1939) are artistically limiting in their own way.

The Issue of Assimilation

Micheaux's treatment of racial or ethnic issues has received as much disapprobation as his stylistic artistry. When Cripps concluded that "race movies tended to acquiesce in segregation, place white cupidity off-limits as a theme, rehash many stereotypes . . . , set black against black, and imitate white movies,"[19] he characterized these attributes as failures, at least in Micheaux's films. As bell hooks has pointed out, however, Micheaux's films *interrogated* those issues, among many others.[20] Hollywood movies themselves certainly could not have been relied on to deal with those issues or most of the other issues Micheaux explored; it is equally improbable that Hollywood's content and style could ever reflect such sensitivity to twoness and contradiction as do Micheaux's content and style.

According to Neal Gabler's thesis in *An Empire of Their Own*, Hollywood was constructed almost entirely by immigrants who wanted desperately to assimilate to the characteristics of the founding groups of Europe and New England. Hollywood created an empire of illusion that would do just that – turn immigrants into the image of the power elite, the "New England-Wall Street-Middle West money" – American through the ideals and aesthetics of Hollywood movies.[21] The fact that immigrant Jews created the "White Anglo-Saxon Protestant" cinema *par excellence* may seem to contradict any thesis about the importance of ethnically produced cinemas. It proves, however, very little in itself. It suggests the tendency of a group in power – such as white Anglo-Saxon Protestants in America – to be imitated and flattered; it suggests the power of such a dominant group to attract services from ambitious sub-dominant groups – such as immigrant Jews; and it exemplifies a solid basis for the fears of those critics who point out that even African-American cinema often seeks to look white. Nevertheless, the construction of an assimilationist Hollywood style by immigrant Jews disproves nothing about the value of cultural diversity and the need to encourage it.

Assimilation has had a strong economic impetus, owing to the radical fragmentation of the American labor and consumer markets during the development of mass production. The factories and urban centers were attracting new ethnic groups all the time, including southern blacks who were in the midst of their greatest migration northward. D.W. Griffith and Micheaux were getting into filmmaking at about this time (c. 1908–18). Hollywood, itself seeking a dependable mass market for its films, began trying to assimilate the new urban diversity. In order to cover over the (substantive) near-impossibility of such a job, Hollywood developed a (formal) style of gloss, illusionism, and closure that gave the appearance of a common system of values for all Americans, an appearance of unity that undoubtedly played a part in forming a broad exclusionism intolerant of difference and twoness.

Micheaux's style is sometimes better understood as a retaining of earlier film traits from before the advent of glossy illusionism than as a failed imitation of white assimilationist movies. His style is more closely related to the glossing of a *text* (such as African-American life) than the glossing *over* of a rough surface (such as value differences among whites). A non-assimilative style that glosses a living struggle with twoness – a twoness that, as DuBois said, threatens the dark body with "being torn asunder" – can itself, as a style, be expected to reflect the turmoil of that struggle.

The Case of *The Girl from Chicago*

The Girl from Chicago (1932) serves well as an example of Micheaux's non-assimilative "crooked-stick" style partly because it is not one of his better films from the point of view of conventional Hollywood style. Since it is an extreme case, any diminishment of disdain for it, or any overlooked values that can be claimed for it, might strengthen the case for Micheaux's overall accomplishment. In *The Girl from Chicago*, Mary Austin is a middle-aged southern black woman who runs a boarding house in the small town of Batesburg, Mississippi (reminiscent of the Patesville of *The Conjure Woman*, 1899, by one of Micheaux's favorite black writers, Charles Chesnutt), and wishes to send her sister north to seek her fortune as a singer; Austin's boarding-house savings are all set aside for that purpose. When Norma Shepard, the female lead in the film, arrives in town to take up her position as a new teacher, she stays at Austin's boarding house. The boarding house is the setting for most of the action in the first half of the film, since it also temporarily houses the male lead, Alonzo White, who eventually captures the villain there, thereby saving Norma.

The first five minutes of the film are composed of some 30 short- and medium-length shots – averaging about 10 seconds each with one take of about 60 seconds – of disturbing content (peonage and potential rape) and of disturbing style (flagrantly discontinuous

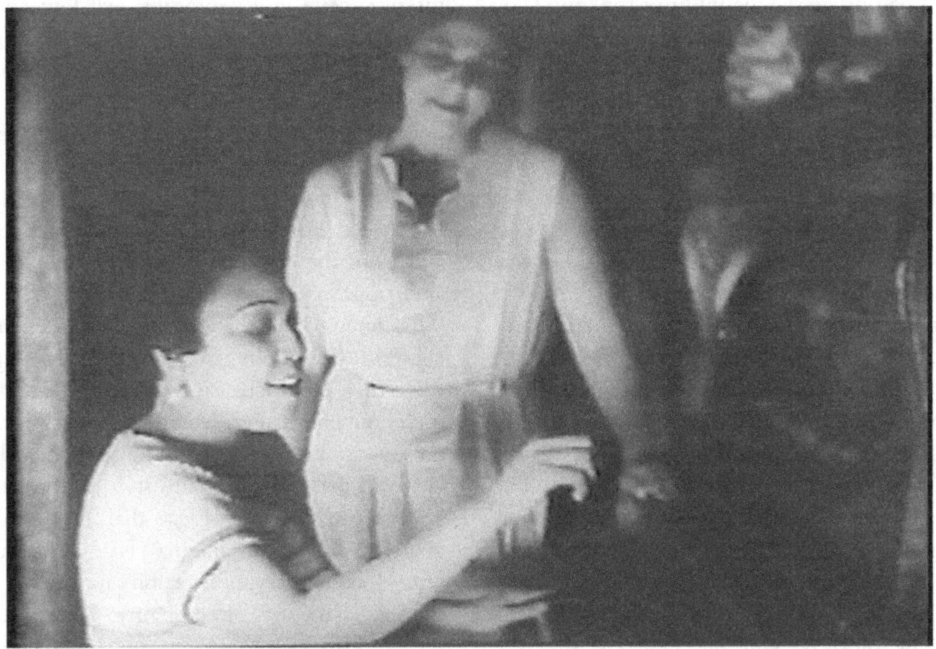

Figure 31.2 *The Girl from Chicago* (Micheaux Film Corp., 1932) is an example of Micheaux's "crooked stick" style. Produced by Oscar Micheaux

matching, expressionistic shooting, some awkward blocking and acting and some practically comic, but also illusion-shattering audio glitches). Then there occurs a "sequence shot" (an entire sequence of "shots" in a single take, with no edits – a "long take") of over three minutes in which Mary Austin, in medium shot, stands beside her sister who, seated in the foreground at the piano, performs an entire song. The transition to this shot (the long take) is accented by a strong piano tone that is struck a fraction of a beat after the cut that begins the long take. Thus, the viewer springs, via syncopation, into this sequence-shot scene out of a previous scene that has been peculiarly and disturbingly fragmented by editing. Mary Austin's sister then sings "Blue Lagoon" in an impressive, but imperfect, light-operatic voice. Partly because the recording quality is poor, the voice seems to break up occasionally, and the humble, upright piano sounds tinny. The weak, single-point lighting and the hard, live acoustics seem consistent with the low production values and discontinuities in editing and with the amateurish, declamatory style of acting of the previous scene. The effect produced is bound to be excruciating or inappropriately comic to anyone used only to Hollywood production qualities.

Yet for a viewer sympathetic to the economic status of the characters (characters for whom the viewer is meant to care, and for whom there is no narrative reason not to care) this shot sequence appears realistic and is appealing. There is both hope and pathos in the desires of the two sisters, emotions that are articulated in the "grain" of the untrained but beautiful voice, and in the "grain of the apparatus" through which that voice is presented. The "grain" of Micheaux's style is analogous in some ways to the grain of Panzera's voice, and the polished and perfect style of Hollywood is analogous to Fischer-Dieskau's voice, as characterized in Roland Barthes' famous essay, "The Grain of the Voice."[22]

There is integrity in the unity of time, place, and action that sets this song apart as a vignette for special appreciation and as a stylistic haven from the surrounding "confusion." The title ("Blue Lagoon") and theme of the song reinforce the stylistic effect of haven. The hopes and fears in this scene are stylistically represented in the contrasts: the confusion of the previous editing versus the unity of the long take; the roughness of the audio recording and of the untrained voice versus the smoothness of the vocal talent and the self-confidence of the singer. These stylistic representations, whether conscious or not, are appropriate.

Even though there is pathos as well as hope, the scene is not pathetic. Pathos does not dominate, since Micheaux's audience would have been aware that some black singers much like Mary Austin's sister (as well as writers, dancers, musicians, and composers) were "making it" in Chicago and Harlem at the time. Jazz, blues, jazz dance, and the Harlem Renaissance were common knowledge in 1932. In the second half of *The Girl from Chicago*, most of the primary and secondary characters, in fact, move to Harlem. The line "Home to Harlem!" uttered by Alonzo in celebration of the move from Batesburg to Harlem is a reference to the famous novel of that title by one of the leading lights of the Harlem renaissance, Claude McKay. Many of those who succeeded during the renaissance period were not "New Negroes" or eastern-educated "dickty"-style ("high-toned") artists, and many of those who were at least partly dickty were also loyal to their humble origins in the South, as was Zora Neale Hurston, for example. Mary Austin's sister's song of the blue lagoon is more dickty, certainly, than Bessie Smith's or Billie Holiday's songs, but not more dickty than some of Marion Anderson's or Ethel Waters'; and the very successes of people like Smith, Holiday, Anderson, and Waters would have lent credibility to the Austin family's hopes. Micheaux's scene represents the hopes and fears of the migration realistically, which Hollywood had never done.

There are several possible objections to this scene. It is possible to object that the sister's voice is not a good one, that it breaks in places – but so did the voices of Louis Armstrong and Bob Dylan, although their styles were more ironic. Armstrong and Dylan were not always ironic, but to the extent that they were, it was part of what made them great. Mary Austin's sister, however, is not meant to represent greatness – she represents hope and pathos, and she may turn out to be unfortunate enough to learn irony too.

It is possible to object that the shot is too dark. But the darkness of the shooting in *The Girl from Chicago* serves its aesthetic purpose in representing an interior scene in a depression-era, lower-middle-class house of American Victorian or southern gothic origins, a house that would typically be dark, compartmentalized in small rooms, and run down. Its lighting loosely resembles the lighting in certain paintings by Micheaux's contemporaries, Thomas Hart Benton, Grant Wood, Edward Hopper, and Charles Burchfield. For Micheaux to have lit this scene strongly and from the classical three points would have given an inappropriately glossy effect. Had Micheaux had the money to shoot "correctly," the scene might have changed stylistically from realistically oppressive to reassuring, mediocre, conventional *realism*. In avoiding such conventionality, Micheaux's work is a significant but overlooked precursor to Italian neo-realism, which changed the course of film style in the late 1940s.

It is possible to object that Micheaux's shot is grainy. Yet shots in cinéma verité and direct cinema, semi-documentary, neo-realism, new wave, and underground styles are often grainy. All those styles are accepted (though they were not originally) as mature, purposeful and effective. They became accepted stylistically as appropriate to the circumstances of their production and to their representational systems, once those systems were understood. The grain in Micheaux's shot reflects lower-middle-class tawdriness and material thinness, approximating the economic status of the (diegetic) boarding house and of the (real-life) film's producer. Micheaux's interiors are reminiscent of the Farm Security Administration (FSA) photographs of the southern poor (those of tenant farmers, for example, by photographers Walker Evans and Russell Lee). The content represented in Micheaux is lower middle class instead of "dirt" poor – Mary Austin's boarding house is plain and run down, but not dirty and falling apart like the FSA tenant farm houses. The style of Micheaux's shots is closer to the production style and aesthetics of his subjects than Evans's and Lee's style is to the style and aesthetics of their subjects, and thus Micheaux's subjects are less set off, embossed, or foregrounded by the style of their representation. Micheaux's dark, grainy shots look like the faded, halftone newspaper and magazine art that decorates the sharecroppers' houses in Evans' and Lee's photographs. Evans and Lee reproduced those sharecroppers' interiors, but they represented those often messy, poverty-stricken interiors through the *artists'* styles of photography, which were often elegant and well-produced. Micheaux as a producer, however, was much closer to the economic status and the messy style of his lower-class subjects, or to the respectable (rather than refined) values of his middle-class ideals, than Evans and Agee were to the status and styles of their subjects.

It is possible to object that the piano in this sequence shot is tinny and out of tune and is presented as such without irony, thus becoming ludicrous – yet the piano in one of Benny Carter's jazz groups, "Benny Carter and His Swing Quintet," is tinny and out of tune and is not used ironically. The instruments in Carter's "Waltzing the Blues" and "Jingle Bells" sound, in relation to earlier jazz, like the "original instruments" movement of Gustav Leonhardt and Nikolaus Harnoncourt in classical music today. A review of one of the major recording projects of the original-instruments movement points to some criticism of that movement that is reminiscent of the criticism of race music and race movies' amateurism and inexpensive production values:

> even sympathetic scholars could find the Leonhardt-Harnoncourt approach disconcerting, what with its clipped non-legato articulations, its rhythmic alterations and dislocations, its easily satirized dynamic bulges, its brusquely punctuated recitatives, its flippant tempos, not to mention the tiny forces, the green and sickly-sounding boy soprano soloists, above all the recalcitrant, sometimes ill-tuned "original instruments."
>
> Some were downright indignant at the loss of traditional scale and weight. The venerable musicologist Paul Henry Lang blasted the "frail performances with inadequate ensembles."

In defense of the original-instruments movement, the same review says:

> Mr. Harnoncourt's style has taken on attributes that "performance practice" alone could never have vouchsafed. They can only have come from those "contemptible" Lutheran texts and their unaccommodating polemic. His increasingly hortatory and unbeautiful way of performing Bach reached a peak about halfway through the series, and the intervening decade has done nothing to lessen its power to shock – or disgust. If you seek contact with the essential Bach at full hideous strength, Mr. Harnoncourt's performances remain the only place to go.[23]

Analogously, if you seek contact with the essential African America at full "hideous" (unwhitewashed) strength, Benny Carter's style of jazz and Micheaux's style of race movies are "the only place to go."

There is no doubt about Benny Carter's ability to produce more polished music, since he has spent much of his career writing music and arrangements for very smooth orchestras, Hollywood films, and mainstream television programs and commercials. His choice of tinny original instruments for some of his recording sessions was consciously judged by him to be aesthetically legitimate and it resulted in some of his most engaging work. Micheaux's performers and instruments were also legitimate, in spite of the fact that Micheaux's choices may have been less intentionally aesthetic because they were more severely bound by economic and cultural constraints. In that sense, his films are comparable in style to the painting and sculpture of the great "outsider" or "self-taught" artists of his era, such as Grandma Moses (1860–1961), William Edmundson (c. 1870–1951), Horace Pippin (1888–1946), Elijah Pierce (1892–1984), William Hawkins (1895–1990), Sister Gertrude Morgan (1900–80), Nellie Mae Rowe (1900–82), and numerous others.[24] The question of whether Micheaux had the talent of a Benny Carter or an Elijah Pierce remains open, but is not relevant to this point of style. The evaluation of Micheaux's accomplishment has hardly begun, and fundamental valuative criteria remain obscure.

After Mary Austin's sister's song ends, the sequence shot continues with Austin congratulating her sister on the perfection of her performance and lamenting the lack of financial resources that prevent Mary from sending her sister to Chicago to pursue a career. Austin strikes her open hand with her fist and says, "If I only had a few more boarders, I could soon send you." Mary Austin's references to her own lack of financial resources can be understood to express the anguish of any "producer" or manager of talent – such as Mary Austin is in relation to her sister, or such as Micheaux himself is as a film producer. Micheaux's production values and style in this shot can be read as part of a representation of the desire for financial means; that is, Micheaux has presented Mary Austin as having a production problem similar to his own, and thus the production values and style of the film become themselves a contributing theme in the narrative. The question of Micheaux's rough style becomes itself a theme treated by the film, as does the struggle with twoness, inherent in the style of all race movies, but absent from the style of the Hollywood films produced for black audiences.

The themes of production financing and representations of the struggle with twoness in this film might be pursued along avenues such as the following: (1) There are several more set-piece singing sequences in the film, two of them in the boarding house in the first half of the film, the others in nightclubs in Harlem in the second half. Each such sequence set in the boarding house is presented in a style different from the preceding one. Those three sequences might be understood as a progression in which the stylistic changes and the narrative meanings constitute a development of underlying themes of the struggle with twoness and with uplift. In these three sequences, the style becomes progressively more upscale but also more fragmented. The intercutting becomes very confusing, the matching of the eyeline vectors of glances becomes complex and unorthodox.

(2) The direct glance is used with poignancy at several points of the narrative. When Alonzo and Norma declare their feelings for each other and conspire to keep their relationship secret, they look at the camera. When they discuss Liza Hatfield's lover of the second half of the film, the numbers-racket magnate, Gomez, during the 'rupture' in Liza's song (this scene is discussed below), they refer to him as furtive. While emphasizing the term "furtive," they speak directly to the camera. These direct glances may be seen as a representation of direct speech, of integrity and good faith, through a simple, pseudo-theatrical address to the audience. They can also be seen as part of a style that is less illusionistic and glossy than that of Hollywood, that does not stitch the implied viewer into the narrative through "furtive" continuity editing. Even if these glances toward the camera or "audience" are unconscious or unwilled by the filmmaker, even if they are "mistakes," they have a consistency of pattern that constitutes a breach of illusionism, an improvisation that tend to advance Micheaux's themes and represent his enunciative directness. They represent an attitude toward making film and an address toward film audiences that is fundamentally different from the classical, an attitude that is not so much anti-illusionistic as a-illusionistic.

(3) The whole production, so to speak, moves to Harlem in the middle of the movie. This might be considered a serious flaw in the film, because the displacement to the North seems to hack the narrative in two, and the Harlem story becomes a seemingly gratuitous second beginning for all the characters. Some story lines are tied off completely, while others are taken up again later. The extreme and messy break is not gratuitous, however, but is integral in ways related to both the theme of twoness and the theme of production financing. John Russell Taylor argues in a similar way in defense of the unity of Satyajit Ray's film, *Aparajito* (*The Unvanquished*, 1957), whose title, interestingly enough, recalls Micheaux's first novel, *The Conquest*, and whose narrated struggles resemble those of Micheaux's characters and his "crooked-stick" style:

> Even many sympathetic critics feel that [*Aparajito*] is broken-backed and lacking in unity . . . and that at best it makes formal sense only as a hinge between the two flanking films [of the Apu trilogy]. I cannot agree with this . . . What gives unity to it, despite *its apparent break in the middle*, when Apu and his mother return from Benares to the country . . . is the continuing theme of Apu's relations with Sarbojaya, and the tug between education and new experience on one hand and traditional ways of life on the other.[25] (emphasis added)

In the case of *The Girl from Chicago* the break in the middle represents the great migration itself, which broke apart black families and societies forever. That migration continued during the Depression (when *The Girl from Chicago* was made) when thousands of ambitious African Americans moved from the agrarian, rural, poorly capitalized South to the industrial, urban, well-capitalized North. Like Ray's rural people, Micheaux's southerners went to northern cities to get jobs. In the terms of the claims of this study about Micheaux's discourse on production values, such migrations can be seen as related to production. The job-seeking was literally an act of personal and household financing; and the seeking of fortunes by artists and entrepreneurs were searches for production opportunities and corporate financing. Mary Austin and her sister, as well as Alonzo and Norma, are among the characters in *The Girl from Chicago* who go north to "refinance" their personal and productive lives.

(4) There are several production numbers in the second half of the film, the most important of which features the girl from Chicago herself, Liza Hatfield, as the lead chanteuse of a jazz band. Liza Hatfield represents the "wrong" approach to the twoness problem and to production values and style, in comparison with the "right" approach represented by the earlier, more amateurish "production number" in the boarding house (discussed above). Narrative anticipation builds around Liza's production number as the film's male lead, Alonzo White, in conversation with Norma, calls Liza exotic and strange, partly because Liza is reputed to be returning from a successful career in Paris and is of unknown African-American origin. Liza's production number is temporally interrupted by a cutaway from the lead-in music to another long discussion of her by Alonzo and Norma at their nightclub table. The cutaway is the kind of time-extending, non-continuity edit found in the naïve style of early films such as Edwin S. Porter's *The Life of an American Fireman* (1903) and in Sergei Eisenstein's (non-naïve) avant-garde style of the 1920s. When Alonzo's and Norma's discussion ends and we return to the production number, the music continues from the same point we left it, the timeline of the production number having been suspended. The scene then continues from there as a long take without further interruption. The song, "Love is a Rhapsody," is intended to be seductive and polished. Although the production number recalls Mary Austin's sister's performance in some ways – it is a long take of a female vocal performance – Liza's number is carefully distinguished from Mary's sister's. Since Liza turns out to be the central, and eponymous, problem in the film, her relation to explicitly high production values – those of Paris and of the Radium Club where she sings in Harlem, higher production values by far than those of the good characters in the boarding house – suggests a definite attitude toward the issues of production financing for African Americans struggling with twoness and uplift. The glossier production number, though it is enjoyed by the protagonist, Alonzo, and is meant for the enjoyment of Micheaux's film audience, is nevertheless located explicitly in a realm of villainy, furtiveness, and seduction.

Conclusion

Micheaux surely did not intend all the rougher aspects of his style explicitly in the ways suggested above, but his style is nonetheless appropriate to and worthy of his situation and his themes and issues. That in itself indicates that his accomplishment may have been greater than has been recognized. Micheaux's style has served important themes, such as the financing of African-American culture, and has provided a complex but worthy approach to the dilemma of twoness. Micheaux has represented the hope for, but also the dangers of, assimilation. He has compared the hopes of one *amateur* singer and the accomplishments of one *professional* singer, and has incorporated ideas about the production and stylistic values of each. The relatively high financing and stylistic values are associated with Liza Hatfield, a virtual prostitute; the lower production values are associated with the hopes of a character with undeveloped talent, but with personal integrity. Micheaux associated his own underdeveloped style and personal integrity with *both* these modes, as a hope, and a fear. He might have liked to have been able to assimilate himself into "high" aspects of the American culture, but he represented such assimilation as dangerous, as well as attractive, for African Americans. The idea of a *dangerous attraction* is a dilemma. It is but one reflection of the struggle with twoness in African-American uplift, a struggle embodied in a style "whose dogged strength alone keeps it from being torn asunder."[26]

Notes

1 W.E.B. DuBois, *The Souls of Black Folk*, in *Three Negro Classics* (New York: Avon, 1965), pp. 214–15.

2 Thomas Cripps, *Slow Fade to Black* (New York: Oxford University Press, 1977).

3 Donald Bogle, *Toms, Coons, Mulattoes, Mammies & Bucks* (New York: Viking, 1973); Daniel J. Leab, *From Sambo to Superspade: The Black Experience in Motion Pictures* (Boston: Houghton Mifflin, 1975).

4 Cripps, *Slow Fade*, p. 3.

5 Cripps, *Slow Fade*, p. 7.

6 Cripps, "Oscar Micheaux: The Story Continues," in Diawara, *Black American Cinema*, pp. 74–5; Jesse Algernon Rhines, *Black*

Film/White Money (New Brunswick, NJ: 1996), pp. 83, 86, and passim.

7 Nelson George, *The Death of Rhythm & Blues* (New York: Pantheon, 1988), pp. 57, 58.

8 As this manuscript was nearing completion, Robert L. Johnson, the chairman and founder of Black Entertainment Television announced a plan "to start a venture to make low-budget films with black stars, financed and produced by African-Americans and aimed largely at the black urban market" (see Geraldine Fabrikant, "BET to Establish a Film Unit Aimed at Black Urban Market," The New York *Times*, July 10, 1998).

9 bell hooks, "Representations of Whiteness in the Black Imagination," in her *Black Looks*; Carol J. Clover, *Men, Women, and Chainsaws: Gender in the Modern Horror Film* (Princeton, NJ: Princeton University Press, 1992).

10 Robert Stam, "Bakhtin, Polyphony, and Ethnic/Racial Representation," in Lester D. Friedman (ed.), *Unspeakable Images: Ethnicity and the American Cinema* (Urbana: University of Illinois Press, 1991), pp. 259–60.

11 Clover, *Chainsaws*; Robin Wood, *Hollywood from Vietnam to Reagan* (New York: Columbia University Press, 1986).

12 This argument is addressed to *Slow Fade*. Cripps revised his assessment of independent film in his ensuing book, *Black Film as Genre*, which recognizes special values in some of those "failed" underground black films. Cripps, however, substantially returns to the argument of *Slow Fade* in his most recent book, *Making Movies Black*. See J. Ronald Green, "The Reemergence of Oscar Micheaux: A Timeline and Bibliographic Essay," in Pearl Bowser, Jane Gaines, and Charles Musser (eds.), *Oscar Micheaux and His Circle: African-American Filmmaking and Race Cinema of the Silent Era* (Bloomington, IN: Indiana University Press, 2001), pp. 211–27, for further discussion of *Black Film as Genre*.

13 The term "rhetoric" refers to the tendency of dominant discourses (such as Hollywood's) or oppositional discourses (such as race movies in relation to Hollywood) to construct arguments, either directly or indirectly. For example, if the "good guys" in Hollywood movies are virtually always white and the "bad guys" include whites but also people of color, then the rhetoric of the discourse of Hollywood movies can be seen as "pro-white." In distinguishing rhetoric from "natural fact" or "reality," it is assumed that in reality not all people of color are "bad" and that some people of color are "good," so the choice not to include those aspects of reality in a discourse becomes rhetorical, whether intentionally so or not. If, in Hollywood cinema, the traits of "rightness" or "competence" are reserved overwhelmingly for male characters while the traits of being wrong or incompetent (or merely supportive) are reserved for women, then the rhetoric of the discourse of Hollywood movies can be deemed "patriarchal."

14 Harold Bloom, *The Anxiety of Influence* (New York: Oxford University Press, 1973).

15 Cripps, *Slow Fade*, p. 172.

16 Cripps, *Slow Fade*, pp. 260–1.

17 Ronald Hayman, *Fassbinder: Film Maker* (New York: Simon and Schuster, 1984), p. 138.

18 Roy Armes, *Third World Film Making and the West* (Berkeley: University of California Press, 1987).

19 Cripps, *Slow Fade*, p. 6.

20 bell hooks, "Micheaux: Celebrating Blackness," *Black American Literature Forum* 25, no. 2 (Summer 1991), pp. 351–60.

21 Neal Gabler, *An Empire of Their Own: How the Jews Invented Hollywood* (New York: Crown Publishers, 1988), p. 5.

22 In Roland Barthes, *Image-Music-Text*, ed. and trans. Stephen Heath (New York: Hill and Wang, 1977).

23 Richard Taruskin, "Facing Up, Finally, To Bach's Dark Vision," *New York Times*, Jan. 27, 1991, pp. H25, H28."

24 See Museum of American Folk Art, *Self-Taught Artists of the 20th Century: An American Anthology* (San Francisco: Chronicle Books, 1998).

25 John Russell Taylor, in Richard Roud (ed.), *Cinema: A Critical Dictionary* (New York: Viking, 1980), vol. 2, p. 817.

26 DuBois, *Souls*, p. 215.

32

Spike's Joint

S. Craig Watkins

S. Craig Watkins teaches in the Department of Radio-Television-Film at the University of Texas at Austin. His publications include the book *Hip Hop Matters: Politics, Pop Culture and the Struggle for the Soul of a Movement.* This reading is excerpted from the chapter on Spike Lee in his book *Representing Hip Hop Culture and the Production of Black Cinema* (1980). With the Success of *Do the Right Thing* (1989) and several subsequent films, Lee has been instrumental in opening up the film industry to greater participation by people of color. Here watkins explores how Lee's films seek to regain control of the representation of African-Americans in popular cinema. Not unlike Green's approach to Micheaux in the previous reading, Watkins locates Lee's authorial style in its differences from the hegemonic, white style of classic Hollywood cinema.

Stylizing the Cinematic Apparatus

Check the technique.

Eric B and Rakim[1]

Spike Lee's varying approaches to filmmaking and the techniques that he employs are especially stylized. Like most filmmakers, Lee struggles to create a signature style that differentiates his films from others. In the course of his commercial filmmaking career, he has incorporated an array of filmmaking repertoires, demonstrating in the process a tendency to resist rigid adoption of the classical forms of popular film production and narration. Lee's stylization of the apparatus constitutes a form of authorial expressivity. This distinctive approach to directing cinema occasionally intrudes upon the filmmaking process by interrupting, violating, and subverting some of the norms and conventional modes of representation that dominate the aesthetic organization of classical film. Moreover, as I discuss below, the more expressive forms of authorship create a very different film-viewing experience for spectators.

The classical Hollywood cinema is the most influential model of filmmaking practice in the world. This particular mode defines the characteristics and aesthetic codes that normalize the art of filmmaking in American cinema. In truth, the narrative structure, camera work, and editing in the cinema have adhered to essentially the same rules throughout the history of modern American filmmaking. The classical model refers to a pattern of representational norms that have evolved over time, shifting now and then in relation to technological, organizational, and social changes but nevertheless retaining many of its core features.[2]

In a rather informative essay, Peter Wollen outlines the central characteristics of classical cinema and what he posits as its antithesis, countercinema.[3] The values and techniques of the latter, according to Wollen,

S. Craig Watkins, "Spike's Joint" (excerpt), pp. 159–66 from ch. 5 of *Representing Hip Hop Culture and the Production of Black Cinema* (Chicago and London: University of Chicago Press, 1998).

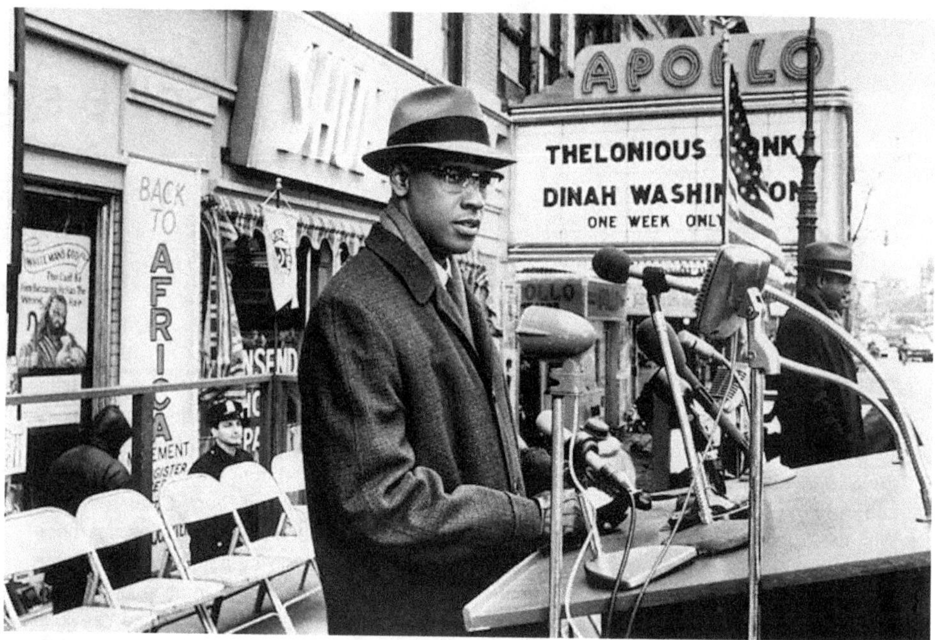

Figure 32.1 Spike Lee's *Malcolm X* (Warner Bros, 1992): Self-conscious authorship within conventional narrative form. Produced by Marvin Worth and Spike Lee

oppose the orthodoxy of the former. A close examination of Lee's filmmaking style suggests that he strategically incorporates some of the elements defined by Wollen as part of the countercinema filmmaking practice. What are some of the ways in which Lee resists the norms and values that typically govern the production of the classical paradigm? First, it is important to note, however, that, like most filmmakers who make feature-length films for theatrical distribution, Lee functions mostly *within* the norms that regulate the production of popular film. For instance, his portrayal of Malcolm X adhered to many of the basic rules and conventions that structure the Hollywood biographical picture. But it is equally important to note that the filmmaker has also combined experimental and nonconventional methods of cinematic authorship in some of his most memorable work.

The classical cinema paradigm privileges the notion of transparency over foregrounding. Whereas the logic of transparency attempts to obscure the constructedness of the fictional world represented on-screen, foregrounding, conversely, attempts to make the construction of the film world more explicit. Most movies produced by the Hollywood machine are governed by the notion of realism, a transparent approach to filmmaking. Discussing the realism style in American popular film culture, film scholar Louis Giannetti writes: "[W]e rarely notice the style in a realistic movie; the artist tends to be self-effacing. Such filmmakers are more concerned with *what's* being shown rather than how it is manipulated. The camera is used conservatively. It's essentially a recording mechanism that reproduces the surface of tangible objects with as little commentary as possible. . . . The realistic cinema specializes in art that conceals art."[4]

To be sure, Lee's cinematic politics have never invested firmly in the notion that he was presenting spectators a nonpartisan, objective view of the world. In fact, his intentions have been, in part, to stake out a particular set of claims on the nature of race relations, and the post-industrial experiences of blacks especially, and manipulate the technology of film production to articulate those claims. Part of carving out this space has also meant developing a style of filmmaking that has been as striking and imaginative as his goal of both gaining and maintaining access to the resources of the major culture industries. Lee's politicization of popular film entertainment, then, has been especially strategic and intentionally provocative. In many of his films, for example, he has often refused to comply with the idea of transparency, preferring instead to practise a method of filmmaking that foregrounds his own authorial presence and distinctively marks his filmmaking signature. Giannetti discusses this manner of filmmaking as formalism and writes: "The formalist cinema is largely a director's cinema: Authorial intrusions are common. There is a high degree of manipulation in the narrative materials, and the visual presentation is stylized. The story is exploited as vehicle for the filmmaker's personal obsessions. . . . This style of cinema deals with ideas – political, religious, philosophical. . . . Its texture is densely symbolic."[5]

On the one side, the features of realism are less noticeable; the filmmaker strives to disguise the constructedness of the story-world presented on screen. On the other, the director strives to unveil the transparency of filmmaking. Still, the idea of realism dominates the production of popular film and television. Considering that classical cinema is at best moderately self-conscious, Lee's approach to filmmaking is determinedly self-conscious, often acknowledging his stylized use of the cinematic apparatus. While some view Lee's filmmaking techniques as gratuitous or self-serving, they nevertheless represent a form of authorial action, a form of agency that contests the intensely regulated forms of cinematic authorship that customarily obscure the fact that all forms of media are a socially constructed, manipulative view of the world.

Take, for example, Lee's use of characters directly addressing the spectator – a consistent narrative motif throughout his early work. This type of address is seldom used in classical cinema, mainly because it interrupts the flow of film events that take place on-screen. In addition, full frontality in cinema ruptures traditional story-space boundaries that generally position the spectator more fully as a voyeur. In the case of classical cinema, characters only address other characters *in* the film. In *Do the Right Thing*, Lee jump-cuts to a sequence that features the character direct-address device. In the sequence, the camera cuts to five different characters who utter racial epitaphs. The sequence is both a playful and serious experimental technique that disorients the normal film-viewing process: jump cuts are deliberately abrupt editing transitions that disrupt the continuity of narrative time and space. Direct character address also establishes a more personalized experience of film viewership by repositioning the spectator as a more active participant in the film-viewing process. As a result of this technique, characters speak directly to spectators.

Furthermore, the narrative structure that defines much of Lee's filmography is antithetical to the norms of classical cinema. The dominant narrative structure usually constructs a single story-plot that contains, according to Wollen, "a unitary homogenous world." In this system, the organization of narrative adheres to a basic formula: the introduction of a harmonious setting; the insertion of a conflict that disrupts the equilibrium; the climactic clash, which generally places the protagonist in some sort of contest; and finally, the restoration of a harmonious world. The narrative structure in the typical Spike Lee Joint, however, privileges multiple story-plots over the single-story-plot formula. In other words, the filmmaker generally deploys the film-within-a-film device, which fractures the primary story-plot. Consequently, his film narratives tend to develop acute fissures. So instead of constructing a single homogenous world, Lee opts for creating a filmic world in which a polyphony of issues, conflicts, and enigmas seem to proliferate unabashedly.

Perhaps Lee's most decisive break from the classical style of filmmaking is the manner in which his film narratives tend to close. Because the classical paradigm generally privileges the notion of a single story-plot, the primacy of this style lends itself to easy resolution and narrative closure. Discussing narrative closure in classical cinema, Bordwell writes:

> [W]e can see it as the crowning of the structure, the logical conclusion of the string of events, the final effect of the initial cause. This view has some validity, not only in the light of tight constructions that we frequently encounter in Hollywood films but also given the precepts of Hollywood screenwriting. Rulebooks tirelessly bemoan the pressures for a happy ending and emphasize the need for a logical wrap-up. . . . Thus an extrinsic norm, the need to resolve the plot in a way that provides "poetic justice," becomes a structural constant.[6]

The happy-ending cliché is arguably the most dominant narrative motif in Hollywood film. Indeed, one of the most taken-for-granted belief systems in Hollywood is the notion that, in order for a film to be a box-office success, the narrative must be compact,

Figure 32.2 *Do the Right Thing* (Universal, 1989): Individual actions cannot solve complex social issues. Written, produced, and directed by Spike Lee

simple, and easily resolved. Moreover, industry insiders strongly believe in making uplifting, "feel-good" movies, which generally translates into a neat resolution of narrative conflict. But the tendency to resolve conflict reaffirms dominant ideological values like individualism and patriarchy and further suggests that heroic, often male, deeds are the solution to social problems.[7]

Yet narrative closure in the Spike Lee Joint is intentionally resisted. Rather than asserting a harmonized world at the end of his films, Lee repeatedly subverts this industry rule by choosing to end many of his film narratives on the curvature of several question marks. This strategy leaves the film/text open-ended and subject to multiple interpretations. At the same time, though, this strategy can also generate discomfort for filmgoers accustomed to narrative closure. Take, for example, the following conclusion of a test screening survey from Lee's second feature film, *School Daze*: "[T]he majority of audience members felt negatively about the ending, finding it confusing, too abrupt and unresolved. Similarly, some audience members (both blacks and whites) complained that the story and the message were confusing."[8] The results of the survey suggest that when moviegoers are exposed to open-ended film narratives, it violates their perception of what constitutes coherence and clarity, thus making the film-viewing experience unpleasant in some instances.

An excellent example of this open-ended structure is, of course, the intensely debated *Do the Right Thing*. The film ends abruptly and declines to resolve the multiple enigmas that motivate conflict and action in the story-plot. In fact, one of the main charges leveled against the film was that Lee raised many issues regarding the volatility of racism but failed to propose any solutions. This critique is, of course, inspired by a set of spectatorial norms accustomed to narrative resolution. The conclusion of *Do the Right Thing* does in fact leave the spectator pondering several questions – for example: What happens to Sal and his pizzeria? Did Mookie "do the right thing" by initiating the destruction of the pizzeria? Did Raheem's death justify burning and looting Sal's property? Is black rage against white property a legitimate expression of political resistance? Whose political philosophy was right, Martin Luther King Jr.'s or Malcolm X's? Paraphrasing Wollen, it can certainly be said that – with its endless counterposition of characters, conflicts, and issues – *Do the Right Thing* can best be understood as an arena, a meeting place in which different discourses encounter each other and struggle for supremacy. The film, according to conventional wisdom, is unfinished and therefore open to a seemingly inexhaustible number of different spins and interpretations. But to the extent that narrative aperture intentionally invites the production of meaning, it also encourages dialogue. Spectators are forced to create their own ending(s) and therefore ponder the many questions the film deliberately refuses to answer. Finally, narrative aperture correctly suggests that complex social issues are *structural* and not *personal*; hence, heroic acts by individuals cannot resolve them. It makes the crucial point that happy endings only exist in the imaginary fantasyscapes of Hollywood.

Lee's recombination of both conventional and more expressive forms of cinematic authorship is indicative of what some film scholars argue is the emergence of a "New Hollywood." The New Hollywood rests, in part, upon technological innovations that facilitate a more definitive break from the dominant conventions and approaches to narrative in the cinema by creating new possibilities in the areas of sound mixing, camera movement, and photography, for example. The New Hollywood is greatly influenced by the European art cinema, which typically employs, according to Bordwell, Staiger, and Thompson, "a looser, more tenuous linkage of events than we find in the classical film."[9] The art cinema generally creates multidimensional characters rather than one-dimensional characters whose traits tend to be overwhelmingly "good" or "bad." Further, Bordwell, Staiger, and Thompson maintain that, whereas characters in the classical cinema have clearly defined traits and characteristics (i.e., heroes and villains), characters in the art cinema lack clear definition and objectives. This new style in Hollywood is generally associated with a generation of film school graduates who have enjoyed tremendous success in the commercial arena employing more expressive forms of cinematic authorship – Martin Scorsese, Francis Ford Coppola, and Robert Altman, to name a few.[10]

Rather than supplant the classical style, art cinema has been assimilated into the dominant paradigm. While participants in the New Hollywood can be described as stylists, they tend to work within the paradigmatic structure of the classical model. Bordwell, Staiger, and Thompson remind us that, despite the achievements of the new stylists, the classical premise of time and space remains powerfully in force, with only subtle alterations. Moreover, the emergence of celebrity directors reinvigorates theatrical film-going, which, in turn, strengthens the popular movie industry and, ironically, the classical paradigm. Lee's stylization of the apparatus, then, appears to be part of a broader, albeit subtle, trend in the commercial filmmaking industry. The filmmaker's own carefully crafted image as an icon of black popular culture, in fact, stimulated interest in other black American-directed films that are more committed to the dominant conventions of film production. So despite Lee's neo-black nationalist image, the stylistic choices that mark his unconventional filmmaking techniques are rooted in the trends and values of European art cinema.[11] Lee's approach to commercial filmmaking is as much a by-product of the genre hybridization of the classical, art, and exploitation styles of filmmaking as it is a decisive shift in the logic of black cultural production or any particular form of black resistance.

Lee's breakthrough success was made possible by several interrelated factors. First, the production, distribution, and consumption of popular media products have changed dramatically during the latter decades of the twentieth century. Technology not only accelerates the production and distribution of products; improvements in technology also make access to communications media resources slightly more democratic than in previous periods. Thus, new players have been able to occupy small niches in the industrial image-making landscape. And while new communication technologies and the information economy do not threaten the hegemony of capitalism or the global spread of corporate influence, they have, albeit inadvertently, created space for the mobilization of new cultural practices and movements that creatively contest social and political domination.

In many ways, the renewal of black filmmaking was made possible by the innovations and growing popularity of the hip hop movement. Hip hop redefined the presence and vitality of black youth culture in the popular cultural landscape. More important, it forged new territories and spaces for African Americans to assert greater control over the shaping and reshaping of the popular culture scene. Consequently, young African American filmmakers who have harnessed the creative energy and spirit of hip hop to their own cinematic imaginations have gained limited access to the corridors and resources of commercial cinema. Spike Lee, to be sure, has responded in an innovative fashion to the changing cultural landscape. He understood that, in order to become a formidable player on the field of popular culture, it was necessary to align himself with some of the more popular movements and sensibilities of the youth scene. Lee's strategic use of hip hop culture certainly enlivened his filmmaking career. But while he has been careful to incorporate some of the expressive elements of hip hop, he has not limited his cultural politics to the sensibilities of the youth movement. The filmmaker, as I have discussed above, has politicized the sphere of popular film production in ways that also move beyond the priorities and preoccupations of hip hop.

Finally, because Lee was responding to rather than creating changes in the popular culture landscape that facilitated his arrival on the cultural stage, his imprint on the production of black cinema, while obviously important, must not be viewed as dominant. In reality, the scope of black cinema broadened far beyond its most distinguished icon in ways that not even he could contain, direct, or anticipate. By the early 1990s, the most dominant characteristics of black commercial cinema were not associated with the neo-black nationalist racial politics and expressive techniques that defined the typical Spike Lee Joint but rather with the popular rhythms of gangsta rap and the proliferation of ghetto imagery in American culture.

Notes

1 This quote is from a popular rap album produced and performed by Eric B and Rakim (1989).

2 Bordwell, D., Staiger, J. and Thompson, K. (1985, *The Classic Hollywood Cinema: Film Style and Mode of Production to 1960*, New York: Columbia University Press), examine the evolution and transformations of the classical style of Hollywood filmmaking. The classical Hollywood cinema has become the dominant model throughout the entire filmmaking world.

3 For a description of countercinema, see Wollen, P. (1986) "Godard and Counter-Cinema: *Vent d'Est*," in P. Rosen (ed.), *Narrative, Apparatus, Ideology: A Film Theory Reader*, New York: Columbia University Press, pp. 120–9.

4 Giannetti, L. (1990) *Understanding Movies*, Englewood Cliffs, NJ: Prentice-Hall, p. 3.

5 Ibid., p. 6.

6 Bordwell, D. (1986) "Classical Hollywood Cinema: Narrational Principles and Procedures," in P. Rosen (ed.), *Narrative, Apparatus, Ideology: A Film Theory Reader*, New York: Columbia University Press, p. 21.

7 For a discussion of how television in particular has employed this technique with a high degree of frequency, see Gitlin, T. (1982) "Prime-Time Ideology: The Hegemonic Process in Television Entertainment," in H. Newcomb (ed.), *Television: The Critical View*, 3rd edn., New York: Oxford University Press, pp. 426–54.

8 Lee, S. (1988) *Uplift the Race: The Construction of* School Daze, New York: Simon & Schuster, p. 178.

9 For a more complete treatment of how the newly introduced filmmaking technologies and techniques have been incorporated into the classical Hollywood cinema, see the final two chapters in Bordwell et al. (1985, pp. 365–85).

10 For a discussion of their respective contributions to film, see, for example: Lourdeax, L. (1990) *Italian and Irish Filmmakers in America: Ford, Capra, Coppola, and Scorsese*, Philadelphia: Temple University Press; Keyssar, H. (1991) *Robert Altman's America*, New York: Oxford University Press, 1991; Stern, L. (1995) *The Scorsese Connection*, Bloomington: Indiana University Press; and Lewis, J. (1995) *Whom God Wishes to Destroy: Francis Coppola and the New Hollywood*, Durham, NC: Duke University Press.

11 For a discussion of Lee's neo-black nationalist politics see Dyson, M.E. (1993) *Reflecting Black: African American Cultural Criticism*, Minneapolis: University of Minnesota Press. Elsewhere Todd Boyd (1997, *Am I Black Enough for You?: Popular Culture from the 'Hood and Beyond*, Bloomington, Indiana University Press), argues that Lee's politics are grounded in a new black aesthetic that is inflected by bourgeois sensibilities and intentions.

Further Reading

Bowser, Pearl. *Oscar Micheaux and His Circle: African-American Film-making and Race Cinema of the Silent Era*. Bloomington and London: Indiana University Press, 2001.

Donalson, Melvin. *Black Directors in Hollywood*. Austin: University of Texas Press, 2003.

Doty, Alexander. *Flaming the Classics: Queering the Film Canon*. London and New York: Routledge, 2000.

Dyer, Richard. *Heavenly Bodies: Film Stars and Society*. London: Macmillan Education, 1987.

Gallagher, Tag. *John Ford: The Man and His Films*. Berkeley and London: University of California Press, 1986.

Gerstner, David A. and Staiger, Janet (eds.). *Authorship and Film*. New York and London: Routledge, 2003.

Grant, Barry Keith. *Voyages of Discovery: The Cinema of Frederick Wiseman*. Urbana and Chicago: University of Illinois Press, 1992.

Halliday, John (ed.). *Sirk on Sirk: Conversations with Jon Halliday*. London: Faber and Faber, 1997.

Johnston, Claire. *The Work of Dorothy Arzner: Toward a Feminist Cinema*. London: British Film Institute, 1972.

Klinger, Barbara. *Melodrama and Meaning: History. Culture and the Films of Douglas Sirk*. Bloomington and London: Indiana University Press, 1994.

Modleski, Tania. *The Women Who Knew Too Much: Hitchcock and Feminist Film Theory*. New York: Methuen, 1988.

Rothman, William. *Hitchcock: The Murderous Gaze*. Cambridge, MA and London: Harvard University Press, 1982.

Wexman, Virginia Wright (ed.). *Film and Authorship*. New Brunswick, NJ and London: Rutgers University Press, 2003.

Wood, Robin. *Hitchcock's Films Revisited*. New York: Columbia University Press, 1989.

CPSIA information can be obtained
at www.ICGtesting.com
Printed in the USA
BVHW012257131020
590954BV00005B/37